THE WILL
OF ZEUS

STRINGFELLOW BARR

THE WILL
OF ZEUS

A HISTORY OF GREECE
FROM THE ORIGINS OF
HELLENIC CULTURE TO THE
DEATH OF ALEXANDER

BARNES
&NOBLE
BOOKS
NEW YORK

For permission to quote from copyright material, thanks are due:

to the Harvard University Press for passages from the various Loeb Classical Library volumes listed on p. 455 and in the Notes, pp. 457-77; reprinted by permission of the publishers and The Loeb Classical Library.

to the University of Chicago Press for passages from *The Complete Greek Tragedies*, edited by David Grene and Richmond Lattimore, 4 vols. (Chicago, 1959), as follows: from Vol. I, Aeschylus, *Oresteia, The Persians, Prometheus Bound*, © 1953, 1956, 1942, by The University of Chicago; from vol. III, Euripides, *The Trojan Women, Heracles*, © 1956 by The University of Chicago.

to the University of Michigan Press for passages from Xenophon's *Anabasis: The March Up Country*, translated by W. H. D. Rouse (Ann Arbor, Mich., 1958).

to Basil Blackwell, Publisher, for passages from Kathleen Freeman's *Ancilla to the Pre-Socratic Philosophers* (Oxford, 1948); reprinted by permission of Sir Basil Blackwell.

The chapter-page decorations are reproduced by courtesy of Ginn & Company, from drawings of Greek coins which appeared in *A History of Greece for Colleges and High Schools*, by Philip Van Ness Myers.

This edition published by Barnes & Noble, Inc.,
by arrangement with HarperCollins, Publishers.

1994 Barnes & Noble Books

ISBN 1-56619-555-1

Printed and bound in the United States of America

M 9 8 7 6 5 4 3 2 1

To Scott Buchanan
who led me to Hellas again

PREFACE

THIS book tries to tell what the ancient Greeks said and did and what seemed to them important. It was never this book's primary purpose to compile the known events of Hellenic history; I have therefore omitted much. I have tried, wherever possible, to let the Greeks tell the tale themselves, and I hope that my effort to let them speak will excuse the unusual length and frequency of my quotations. I have not justified my narrative by pointing out the contributions ancient Greece made to our civilization, because I judge Greek culture to have been so important in its own right as to need no such justification. On the other hand, neither I nor my readers can forget, when we encounter the Greeks, whatever insights we may have gained by living through the glories and miseries of the twentieth century, its destructive wars, its bloody revolutions. We cannot forget the hopes and fears these cataclysms have engendered in our hearts or the questions they have engendered in our minds. It was partly by the light of these questions that I have written this book. I have tried to avoid moralizing, opining, and assigning rewards and punishments. When it has seemed necessary to discuss controversial points, I have used notes in the back of the book for that purpose. The number affixed to each note occurs twice and only twice in this volume: once in the section devoted to notes, pages 457-77, and once in the text itself at the point to which the note applies.

vii

The gap between history and legend, between the truth of courtroom testimony and the truth of a poem was smaller in ancient Greece, even for the better historians, than it is for professional historians today. This has led me to risk annoying the reader with phrases like "according to later tradition" whenever I have felt that the poetic truth of legend had begun to replace the truth of testimony.

I have risked another annoyance, the annoyance of recapitulation, either explicit or by allusion. I have assumed that a reader who may have forgotten his Greek history may not easily recall a character or event mentioned many pages earlier, especially if his reading of this book should have to be an interrupted reading. I hope the reader who does not need such reminders will forgive me.

Nobody to my knowledge has ever reduced to consistency the spelling of Greek names. The names Plato, Solon, and Meno all end in Greek with the same two letters. But in English we never say Platon, never say Solo, and we write Meno for the man in Plato's dialogue of that name and frequently write the same man's name as Menon in the *Anabasis* of Xenophon—not Xenopho! When Greek names ending in ōn were transliterated into Roman letters by authors who wrote in Latin, the last letter was dropped, at least in the nominative case, and the name passed into English in that form. Other such names bypassed Latin, or are now made to bypass it by authors who write in English, whereupon such familiar spellings as Alcibiades and Cyrus become Alkibiades and Kyros. But unless Sappho's Lesbos is to become Lesbus and holy Delos is to become Delus, why should Phoenician interests in Cyprus become Phoinikian interests in Kypros? In general, I have kept the Latin spellings where these were familiar in English and have transliterated other names straight from Greek. But I am under no illusion that I have solved a persistent problem.

Even common nouns can offer a problem. When we took over the word hybris from Greek, we followed the regular rules for transliteration from Greek letters to our own Roman letters, but now writers on Greek tragedy show signs of preferring to write hubris, presumably because, while the Greek letter upsilon could be transliterated into a Latin *y* without changing its sound, that sound changes abruptly when the *y* reaches English, and to this our modern writers object. I shall join them in writing the word as hubris on the day I can draw a chemical mixture of hudrogen and oxugen from the hudrant. In the present volume, I have pedantically stuck to hybris.

In presenting quotations, I was confronted with the thorny problem of choosing a translation. Other things being equal, I have chosen the translations in the Loeb Classics, thereby furnishing the reader who wishes to check further with both a reputable Greek text and an English translation facing it in one readily available edition. At other times my strong preference for some other translation prevailed. And occasionally I have made my own translation, where the Greek yielded a meaning important for my story but not fully captured in the translations at hand.

Many of the events in Greek history, especially in the earlier period, cannot be dated precisely, and I have reluctantly fallen back on such phrases as "about 432," or "c. 432" in the Chronological Summary. Finally, since all the events in this volume occurred before the Christian era, there seemed no point in placing B.C. after any date.

The work on this book extended, with interruptions, over a period of twenty-six years, and was sustained by the generous help of many persons and several institutions. In 1935 a grant from the Institute for Research in the Social Sciences, in the University of Virginia, permitted me to start on a longer road than I then foresaw as necessary. In 1957 the Old Dominion Foundation made a grant to Rutgers University which provided me with a research associate for three years. In addition the Foundation and Rutgers jointly financed a year's leave of absence from teaching in order that I might the sooner finish my journey. During the past three years Dr. William Dix, Librarian of Firestone Library, Princeton University, and members of his staff hospitably supplied my research associate and me with facilities rarely duplicated in this country. In 1957 Professor R. P. Blackmur of Princeton University invited me to conduct a Christian Gauss Seminar on the problems I confronted, and I owe the members of that Seminar thanks for their friendly attacks and suggestions.

I am grateful for patient criticism from Baldwin Barr, Scott Buchanan, Francis Fergusson, R. W. B. Lewis, and Dennis O'Brien, and for assistance far beyond the call of duty from Stewart Richardson, my editor at Lippincott. None of them can be held responsible for my failures, since I did not always follow their advice. Finally, the assistance of Cary T. Peebles, my research associate, over the past three years has often amounted to collaboration, and without her advice, criticism, and unremitting labor this book would not exist. The other persons who helped me are too numerous to mention here, but I must speak of the many students I have taught since 1924 who looked at Hellenic history with fresh eyes and who raised good questions.

STRINGFELLOW BARR

CONTENTS

Preface .... PAGE vii

Maps .... *following* PAGE xiv

1. THE WORLD OF ACHILLES AND ODYSSEUS 3
2. A RACE OF IRON 27
3. THE LAWGIVERS, LYCURGUS AND SOLON 48
4. FOR NONE SAVE ONLY ZEUS IS FREE 73
5. THE SCHOOL OF HELLAS 121
6. THE AGONY OF HELLAS 166
7. THE PHILOSOPHER KING 233
8. THE POLIS IN FLIGHT AND THE THIRTEENTH GOD ... 299
9. FROM THE VOYAGE OF PLATO TO THE EMPIRE OF ARISTOTLE 352
10. ALEXANDER'S WORLD POLIS 393
    Chronological Summary 443
    Bibliographical Note 453
    Notes 457
    Index 479

MAPS

MAPS

Drawn by Guy Fleming

THE MINOAN-MYCENAEAN WORLD

THE AGE OF GREEK COLONIZATION

EUROPEAN BATTLES OF THE PERSIAN WARS

THE LEAGUE OF DELOS AND THE SPARTAN ALLIANCE

THE ANABASIS OF XENOPHON

ALEXANDER'S EMPIRE

MAINLAND GREECE AND GREECE-IN-ASIA

WESTERN GREECE

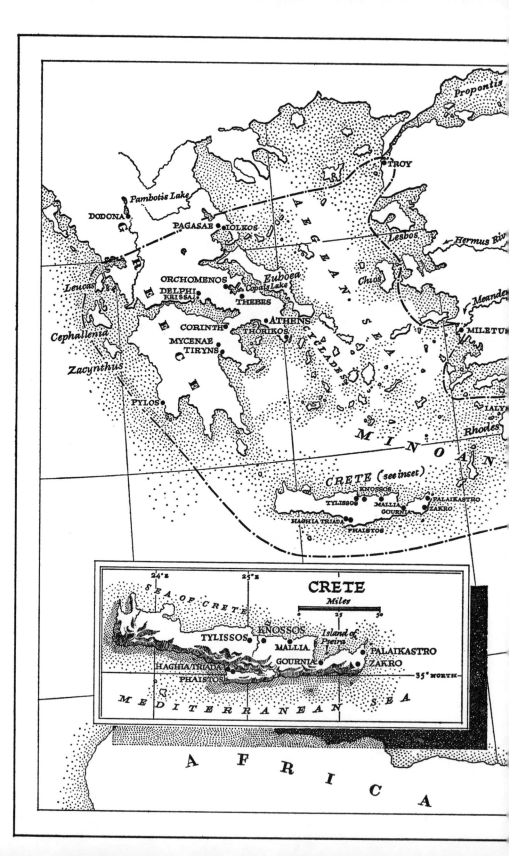

Propontis

TROY

DODONA
Pambotis Lake

PAGASAE
IOLKOS

Lesbos

Hermus Riv.

Leucas

ORCHOMENOS
Euboea
DELPHI
KRISSA
Copais Lake

THEBES

Chios

Meander

Cephallenia

CORINTH
ATHENS
THORIKOS

Zacynthus

MYCENAE
TIRYNS

MILETUS

PYLOS

IALY

Rhodes

M I N O A N

CRETE (see inset)

KNOSSOS
TYLISSOS
MALLIA
GOURNIA
PALAIKASTRO
ZAKRO

HAGHIA TRIADA
PHAISTOS

CRETE

Miles

24° E
25° E

SEA OF CRETE

TYLISSOS
KNOSSOS
Island of
Pseira

MALLIA
PALAIKASTRO
ZAKRO

HAGHIA TRIADA
GOURNIA

PHAISTOS
35° NORTH

M E D I T E R R A N E A N   S E A

A F R I C A

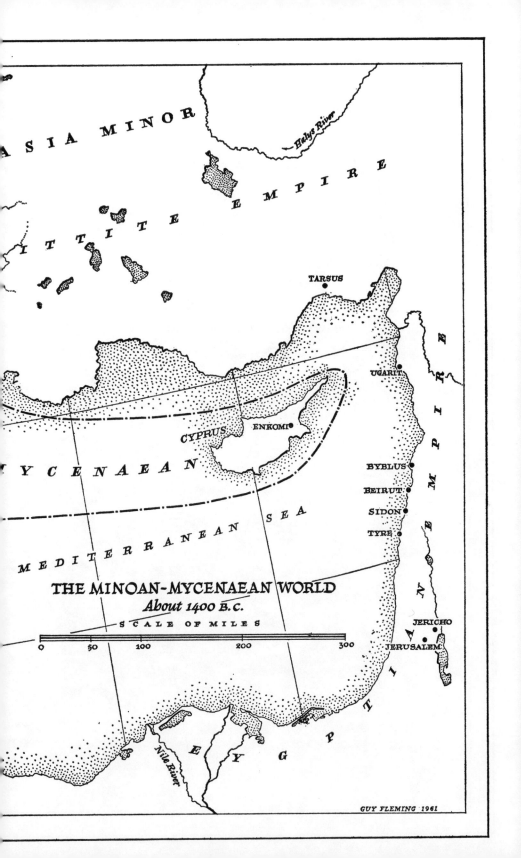

ASIA MINOR

Halys River

HITTITE EMPIRE

TARSUS

UGARIT

CYPRUS   ENKOMI

MYCENAEAN

BYBLUS

BEIRUT

SIDON

TYRE

MEDITERRANEAN SEA

E
M
P
I
R
E

THE MINOAN-MYCENAEAN WORLD
About 1400 B.C.
SCALE OF MILES

0   50   100   200   300

E   G   Y   P   T   I   A   N

Nile River

JERICHO

JERUSALEM

GUY FLEMING 1961

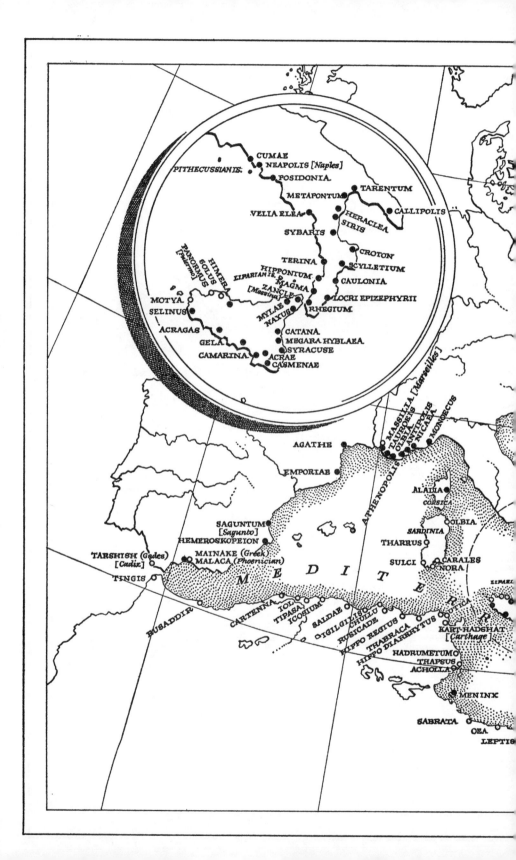

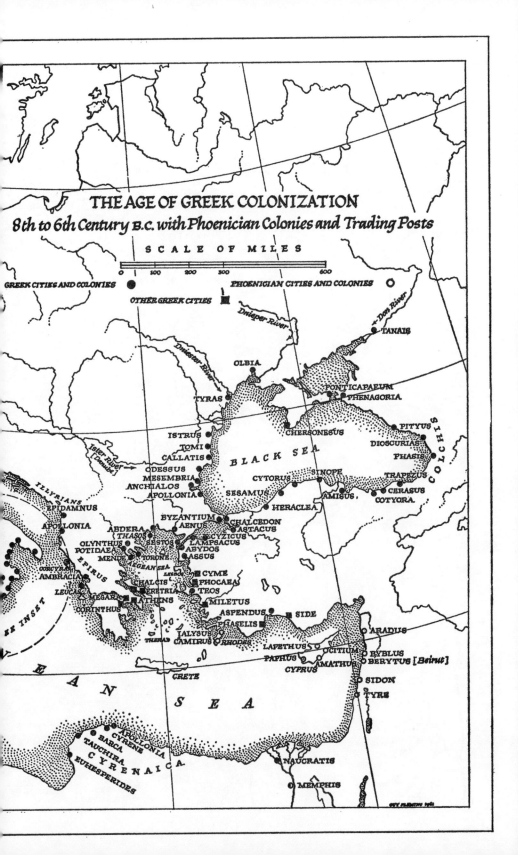

THE AGE OF GREEK COLONIZATION
8th to 6th Century B.C. with Phoenician Colonies and Trading Posts

SCALE OF MILES

0   100   200   300   600

GREEK CITIES AND COLONIES ●   PHOENICIAN CITIES AND COLONIES ○

OTHER GREEK CITIES ■

Dnieper River

Don River

TANAIS

OLBIA

PONTICAPAEUM
PHENAGORIA

TYRAS

PITYUS

CHERSONESUS

DIOSCURIAS

COLCHIS

ISTRUS
TOMI
CALLATIS

PHASIS

BLACK SEA

Ister River
[Danube]

ODESSUS
MESEMBRIA
ANCHIALOS
APOLLONIA

CYTORUS   SINOPE

TRAPEZUS
CERASUS
COTYORA

SESAMUS

AMISUS

HERACLEA

ILLYRIANS
EPIDAMNUS

BYZANTIUM
AENUS   CHALCEDON
ASTACUS

APOLLONIA

ABDERA
THASOS
OLYNTHUS   SESTOS
POTIDAEA   LAMPSACUS
MENDE   TORONE   ABYDOS
ASSUS

CYZICUS

CORCYRA
AMBRACIA
EPIRUS

LESBOS
AEGEAN SEA

CYME

LEUCAS
MEGARA
CORINTHUS

CHALCIS   PHOCAEA
ERETRIA   TEOS
ATHENS

MILETUS

ASPENDUS   SIDE

PHASELIS

ARADUS

IALYSUS
THERA   CAMIRUS   RHODES

LAPETHUS   OCITIUM   BYBLUS
PAPHUS   AMATHUS   BERYTUS [*Beirut*]
CYPRUS

INSET

CRETE

SIDON
TYRE

A N   S E A

APOLLONIA
CYRENE
BARCA
TAUCHIRA
C Y R E N A I C A
EUHESPERIDES

NAUCRATIS

MEMPHIS

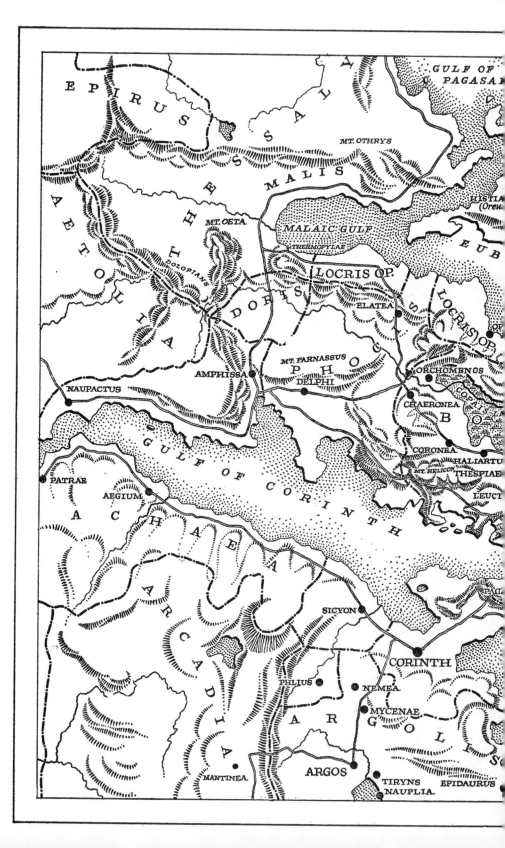

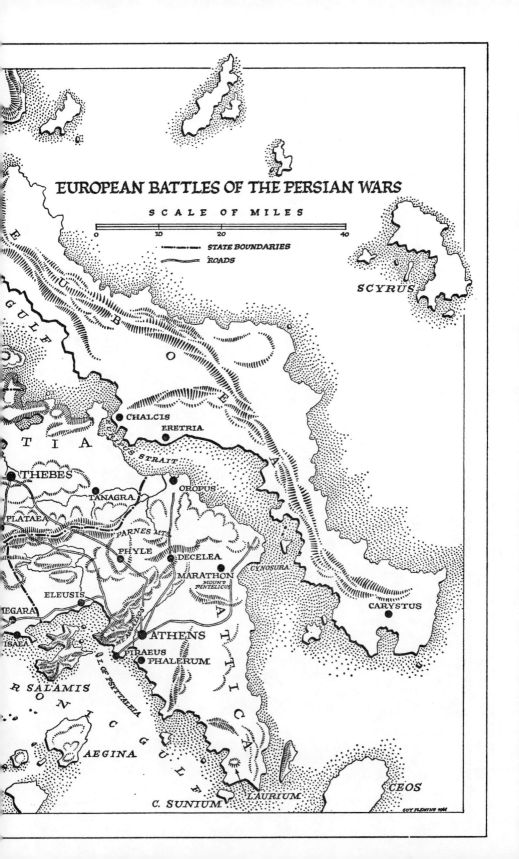

EUROPEAN BATTLES OF THE PERSIAN WARS

SCALE OF MILES

0   10   20   40

— · — STATE BOUNDARIES
═══ ROADS

SCYRUS

E U B O E A

CHALCIS
ERETRIA

EURIPUS STRAIT

THEBES

TANAGRA   OROPUS

PLATAEA

PARNES MT.

PHYLE   DECELEA

MARATHON
MOUNT PENTELICUS   CYNOSURA

ELEUSIS

MEGARA   CARYSTUS

ISAEA   ATHENS

PIRAEUS
PHALERUM

I. OF PSYTTALEIA

SALAMIS

AEGINA

GULF

ATTICA

CEOS

C. SUNIUM   LAURIUM

T I A

GULF

SARONIC GULF

GUY FLEMING 1966

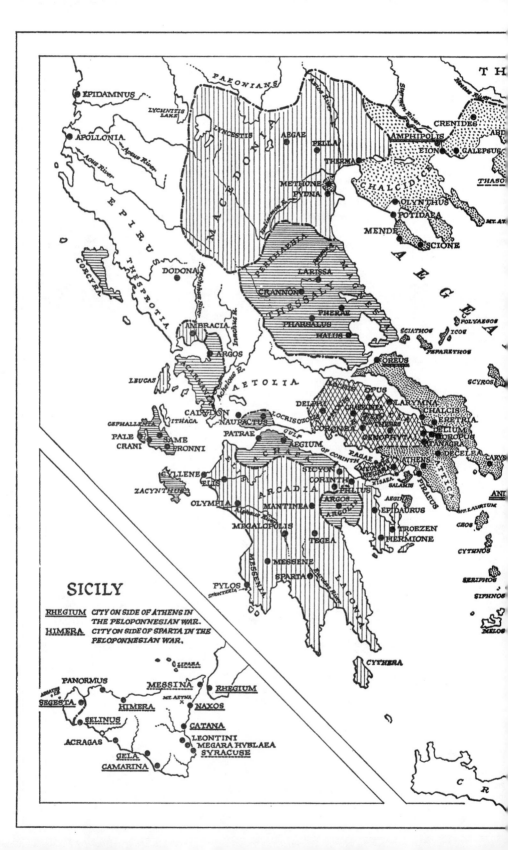

PAEONIANS

EPIDAMNUS

LYCHNITIS LAKE

APOLLONIA

LYNCESTIS
AEGAE
PELLA
THERMA

THRACE

CRENIDES

AMPHIPOLIS
EION
GALEPSUS
ABD

MACEDONIA

THASO

METHONE
PYDNA

CHALCIDICE

OLYNTHUS
POTIDAEA

MT. AT.

MENDE
SCIONE

AEGEA

EPIRUS

CORCYRA

THESPROTIA

DODONA

PERRHAEBIA

MACE

LARISSA

CRANNON

THESSALY

PHERAE

PHARSALUS
HALUS

SCIATHOS
POLYAEGOS
ICOS

PEPARETHOS

SCYROS

AMBRACIA

ARGOS

LEUCAS

AETOLIA

CALYDON

NAUPACTUS

LOCRISOZOL

DELPHI
OPUS

CHAERONEA
CORONEA
THEBES

BOEOTIA

OREUS

LARYMNA
CHALCIS
ERETRIA
DELIUM
OROPUS
TANAGRA

CEPHALLENIA
ITHACA

PALE
CRANI
SAME
PRONNI

PATRAE

ACHAE

AEGIUM

GULF
OF CORINTH

PAGAE

ATTICA

ATHENS
PIRAEUS

DECELEA
CARYS

CYLLENE

ZACYNTHUS

ELIS

OLYMPIA

ARCADIA

MANTINEA

MEGALOPOLIS

MESSENIA

MESSENE

PYLOS
SPHACTERIA

SICYON
CORINTH
PHLIUS
ARGOS
ARGOL

TEGEA

SPARTA

LACONIA

SALAMIS

AEGINA

EPIDAURUS

TROEZEN
HERMIONE

CEOS

CYTHNOS

SERIPHOS

SIPHNOS

MELOS

CYTHERA

SICYLY

<u>RHEGIUM</u> CITY ON SIDE OF ATHENS IN
         THE PELOPONNESIAN WAR.

<u>HIMERA</u> CITY ON SIDE OF SPARTA IN THE
         PELOPONNESIAN WAR.

LIPARA

PANORMUS

SEGESTA

MESSINA

RHEGIUM

MT. AETNA

NAXOS

HIMERA

SELINUS

CATANA

ACRAGAS

LEONTINI
MEGARA HYBLAEA
SYRACUSE

GELA

CAMARINA

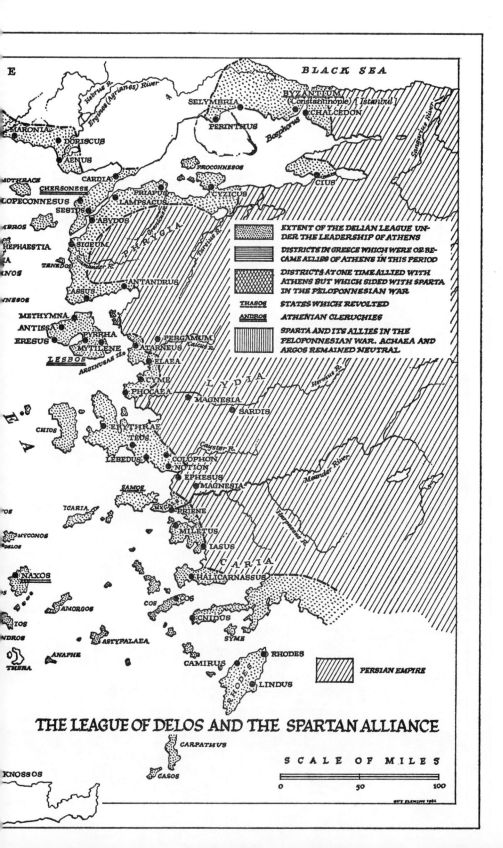

THE LEAGUE OF DELOS AND THE SPARTAN ALLIANCE

EXTENT OF THE DELIAN LEAGUE UNDER THE LEADERSHIP OF ATHENS

DISTRICTS IN GREECE WHICH WERE OR BECAME ALLIES OF ATHENS IN THIS PERIOD

DISTRICTS AT ONE TIME ALLIED WITH ATHENS BUT WHICH SIDED WITH SPARTA IN THE PELOPONNESIAN WAR

THASOS STATES WHICH REVOLTED

ANDROS ATHENIAN CLERUCHIES

SPARTA AND ITS ALLIES IN THE PELOPONNESIAN WAR. ACHAEA AND ARGOS REMAINED NEUTRAL

PERSIAN EMPIRE

SCALE OF MILES
0   50   100

GUY FLEMING 1961

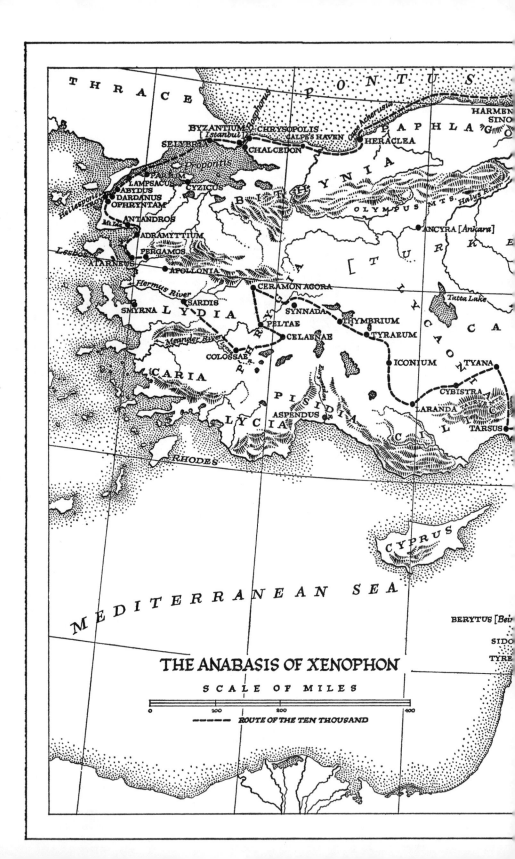

THE ANABASIS OF XENOPHON

SCALE OF MILES

0   100   200   400

------ ROUTE OF THE TEN THOUSAND

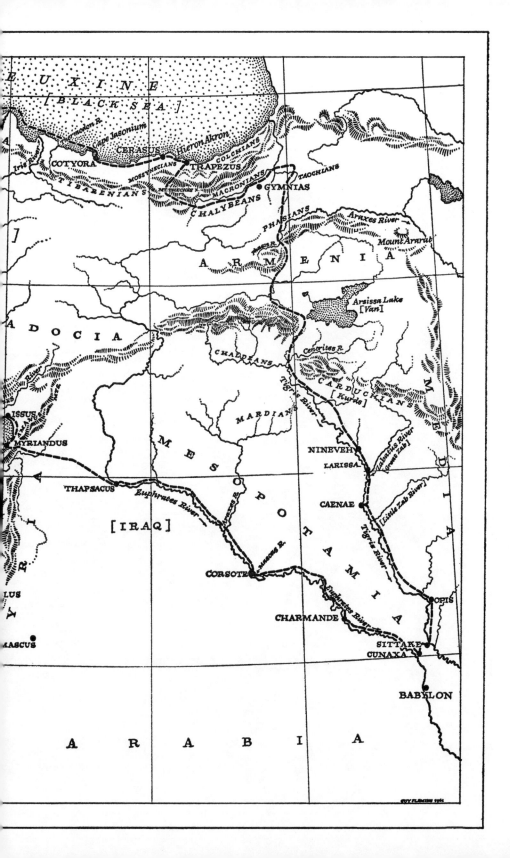

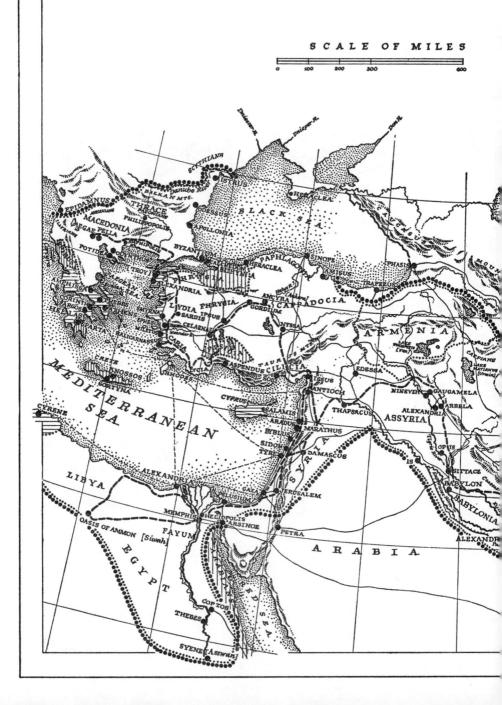

ALEXANDER'S EMPIRE

SCALE OF MILES

0   100   200   300   600

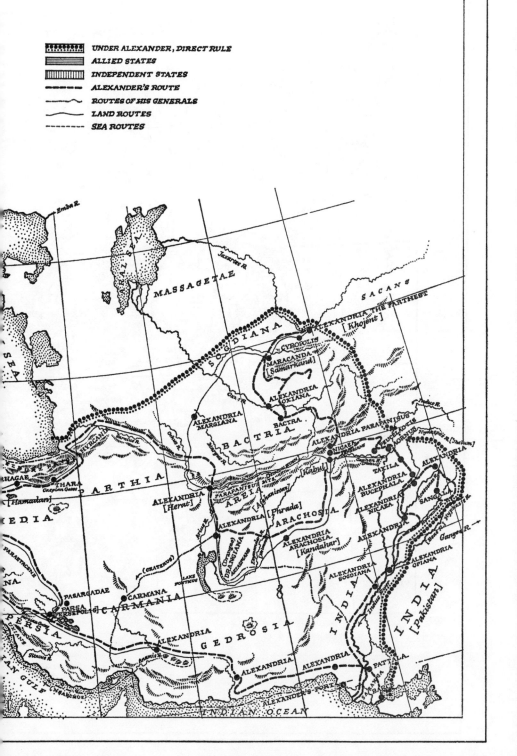

UNDER ALEXANDER, DIRECT RULE
ALLIED STATES
INDEPENDENT STATES
ALEXANDER'S ROUTE
ROUTES OF HIS GENERALS
LAND ROUTES
SEA ROUTES

INTERSTATE BORDERS   ‐ ‐ ‐ ‐

ROADS

GREEK NAME   BYZANTIUM

LATER CLASSICAL NAME   (Constantinople)

MODERN NAME   [Istanbul]

GUY FLEMING 1961

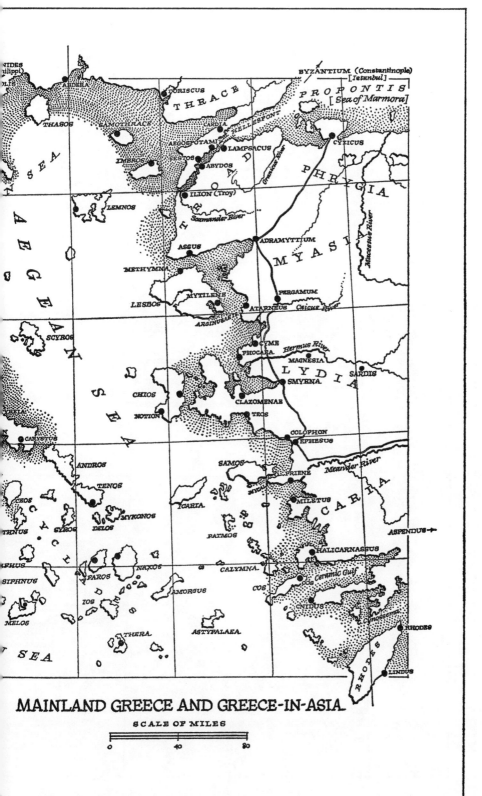

MAINLAND GREECE AND GREECE-IN-ASIA

SCALE OF MILES

0   40   80

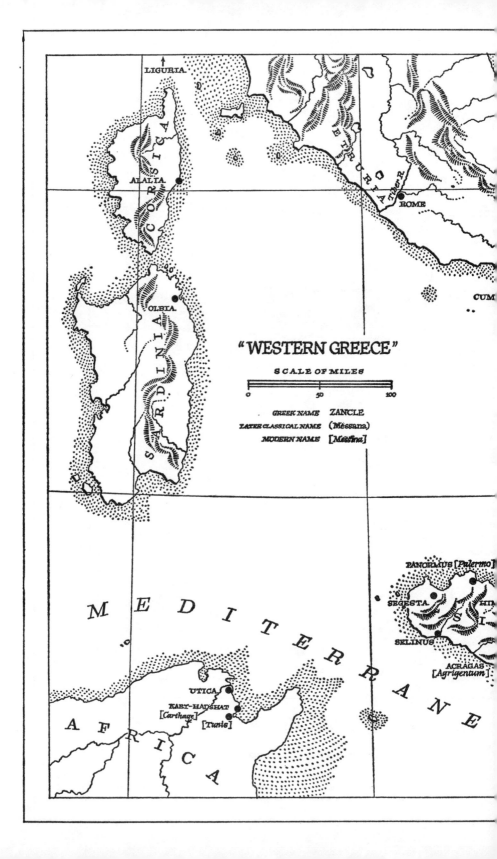

LIGURIA.

C O R S I C A

ALALIA.

OLBIA.

S A R D I N I A

ETRURIA

Tiber R.

ROME

CUM

"WESTERN GREECE"

SCALE OF MILES

0   50   100

GREEK NAME   ZANCLE
LATER CLASSICAL NAME   (Méssana)
MODERN NAME   [Messina]

M E D I T E R R A N E

A F R I C A

UTICA

KART-HADSHAT
[Carthage]

[Tunis]

PANORMUS [Palermo]

SEGESTA

S I

HIM

SELINUS

ACRAGAS
[Agrigentum]

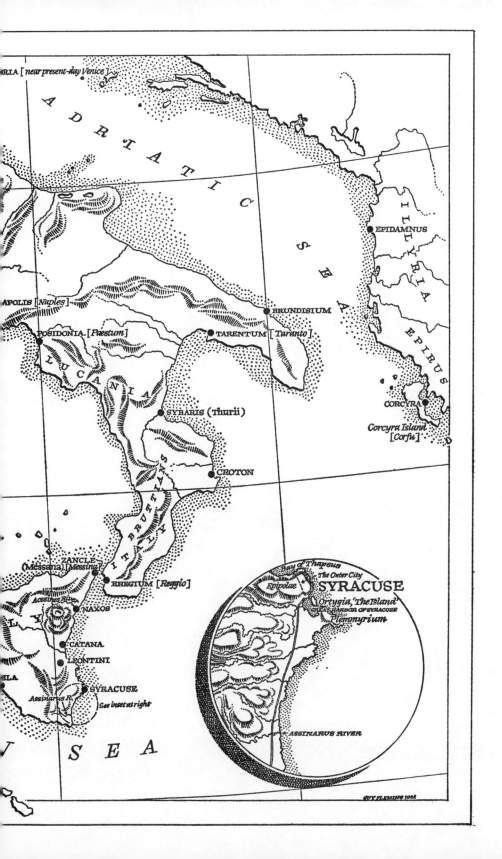

ARIA [near present-day Venice]

A D R I A T I C   S E A

ILLYRIA

EPIDAMNUS

EPIRUS

APOLIS [Naples]

BRUNDISIUM

POSIDONIA [Paestum]

TARENTUM [Taranto]

L U C A N I A

CORCYRA

Corcyra Island [Corfu]

SYBARIS (Thurii)

CROTON

B R U T T I I L Y

ZANCLE (Messana) [Messina]

RHEGIUM [Reggio]

Acesines River

NAXOS

CATANA

LEONTINI

ELA

SYRACUSE

Assinarus R.

See inset at right

I T A L Y

SEA

Bay of Thapsus

The Outer City

Epipolae

SYRACUSE

Ortygia, 'The Island'

GREAT HARBOR OF SYRACUSE

Plemmyrium

ASSINARUS RIVER

GUY FLEMING 1962

And thus the will of Zeus was being brought to fulfilment.

—THE ILIAD, I, 5
Murray translation

The absence of romance in my history will, I fear, detract somewhat from its interest; but if it be judged useful by those inquirers who desire an exact knowledge of the past as an aid to the interpretation of the future, which in the course of human things must resemble if it does not reflect it, I shall be content.

—Thucydides, I, 22
Crawley translation

1

THE WORLD OF ACHILLES
AND ODYSSEUS

SOME eight centuries before Christ a world was born,
the Hellenic world. It emerges to view from the obscure shadows of a
Dark Age. It learns to live in freedom under law; to imagine and create
a magnificent art, a magnificent literature of tragedy, comedy, history, philosophy, mathematics, science. It tries to keep open the paths that lead
from things to ideas and back again to things. It develops a wider commerce both in things and in ideas. It grows rich and waxes fat and im-
poses its will. It tries to base, on force, on military empire, and on domestic
slavery, a wider freedom and a wider law. It fails, and itself passes under
the yoke of a conqueror. It dares less, and asks less of life; it grows weary
and skeptical; and at last it submits to the sword and governance of Rome.
It becomes part of a Roman Empire that absorbs, dilutes, and extends
Hellenic culture. Within its womb a new community is born, the Chris-

3

tian community. Its own gods die or withdraw from men. In the East
the shell of Empire protects a new, Byzantine culture; and in the West,
shell and all collapse, and civilization disintegrates into a new Dark Age.
This book will try to tell the story of the Hellenic world from its first
emergence to the death of Alexander the Great half a millennium later,
when the Hellenic world passes into its Hellenistic phase.

Hellenic culture was born not only out of the meager soil of Greece
and the island-studded Aegean Sea, but also out of myth—out of myths
that dealt with gods and men and with commerce between them, out of
myths put in the mouths of minstrels by a Muse, the goddess daughter of
Zeus, father of gods and men alike. And of all the myths that engendered
that culture out of soil and sea, two were by all odds the most powerful: the
myth of Achilles' wrath, which Homer sang in his epic poem, the *Iliad*,
and the myth of Odysseus' questing voyage, which the same poet[1] sang in
his epic, the *Odyssey*. Both myths were acts: they were verbs, not nouns or
adjectives. In the world of Achilles he and his fellow Achaeans acted in
battle, and their Trojan opponents acted also. Even the gods participated
in the confused struggle on the plains of Troy, some on one side, some on
the other: in this myth, the *Iliad*, even the gods acted. This thrust and
energy perhaps accounted for the fact that Hellenic culture, which did not
wholly create either *Iliad* or *Odyssey*, was nevertheless in large part created
by them. He who reads them today knows that Achilles has at last been
slain and that his soul has gone down to the House of Hades; he knows
that Odysseus has lost all his ships and all his comrades and has stooped
alone to kiss the soil of his native Ithaca. And yet the reader knows, too,
in a different way, that Achilles still fights beneath the walls of Troy and
that Odysseus' black ship, if not his fleet of ships, still skims the wine-dark
sea, seeking whatever Odysseus meant by Home. Are these two illusions,
or poetic insights, of the reader due to the same driving energy that the
Muse put in Homer and that Homer put in his two myths?

4

Neither of these epic myths is history; or they are history so transmuted into poetry that the historian has had to re-transmute them, so far as he could, before he could trust them. Some of the events they record did indeed happen, even in the historian's sense, in the early twelfth century. The Homer who composed the *Iliad* may have lived in the ninth century, and it can be argued that the Homer who composed the *Odyssey* probably lived in the eighth. Since both poems may well have contained minstrel lays composed long before that, the worlds they picture may really correspond in large part with what the historian means by reality. But which parts? From the historian's point of view, both epics contain contradictions and anachronisms. The historian Herodotus in the fifth century and the historian Thucydides in the fourth would each have qualms about the historic value of the poetic legends. But the poets who were to write the great Attic tragedies—Aeschylus, Sophocles, Euripides—would turn to these legends and to others like them, confident that their audiences would recognize the doings of their ancestors. It was indeed through these legends that the fifth-century Greek could continue to belong both to his ancestors and to his gods. Peering back through the long childhood images of the eleventh, tenth, and ninth centuries, peering back through the murk of a Dark Age, these worlds of Achilles and Odysseus were the chief things he remembered. Moreover, modern archaeological research has confirmed a surprising proportion of these transmuted memories. The world of Achilles is therefore fully worth entering.

The immediate world of Achilles is the plain of Troy. It lies between that walled hill city and the mouth of the Hellespont, where the Achaean host have beached the swift, black ships that brought them from Greece and the Aegean Isles, and where they have built themselves huts behind a moat and palisade. They are commanded by Agamemnon, king of Mycenae; and their several contingents are commanded by lesser chieftain-kings. Their most celebrated fighter is Achilles, who has brought a force from a little kingdom in southern Thessaly. These Achaeans are ancestors of the Hellenes, the classical Greeks of history.

It is the tenth year of the siege of Troy. The Achaeans' attack was provoked by Alexander, or Paris, son of Priam, the aged king of Troy. Paris, while a guest of Agamemnon's brother Menelaus, chieftain-king of Sparta, abducted Menelaus' wife, the beautiful Helen. Agamemnon, most powerful of Achaean monarchs, therefore led his fellow kings in a kind of crusade

5

to rescue Helen, to avenge the dishonor Paris had done Menelaus, and to sack and despoil wealthy Troy. To avenge insult, to seize wealth, and to win glory and immortal fame among men, Achilles has spent these years on the plain of Troy, fighting the Trojans and their allies and pillaging the countryside for cattle and women.

Now in the tenth year of this crusade, the god Apollo has sent a pestilence to slaughter the Achaean besiegers. Apollo has acted because one of his priests has prayed him to do so; and his priest has prayed him because Agamemnon holds captive a daughter of the priest, has made her his concubine, and has refused a rich ransom for her.

With the Achaeans perishing from plague, Achilles calls a general assembly, which he has a right to do, and proposes to Agamemnon, general leader of the host, that they consult some soothsayer as to why Apollo, sender of plagues, is angry with the Achaeans. At once an Achaean soothsayer stands up and announces that he can answer that question if Achilles will swear to protect him against one whom all the Achaeans obey, which can only mean Agamemnon. Achilles immediately promises. Whereupon the soothsayer declares that Apollo will not cease to slay them until Agamemnon's concubine has been returned to her father and without ransom.

Agamemnon stands angrily, abuses the soothsayer, declares publicly that he loves this girl more than his wife and queen at home, yet that, rather than see the folk perish, he will return her. But she is his meed of honor, and he demands that she be replaced with some other prize. Instantly Achilles speaks and accuses Agamemnon of wanting more than his share of the booty. Agamemnon threatens to seize a meed of honor from some other king, maybe from Achilles himself, but orders his own concubine returned. The crusade that crossed the sea to right a wrong and avenge the theft of a woman is torn with strife on another point of honor and over another woman, Achilles' captive, Briseis of the fair cheeks. Agamemnon announces next that he will take Briseis, Achilles' meed of honor, so Achilles may know how far greater Agamemnon is than Achilles. Achilles draws his sword. But the goddess Athena comes, makes herself visible to Achilles alone, forbids him to slay Agamemnon, yet permits him to revile the leader. Achilles thereupon swears a mighty, public oath to withdraw his forces from the struggle to their ships until the war shall turn against them, until all the Achaeans shall long for his help, and until Agamemnon

6

shall tear his heart within him for anger that he did in no wise honor the best of the Achaeans. But Achilles declines to defend Briseis by force. Agamemnon has her brought to his hut, and Achilles and his forces temporarily withdraw from the Trojan War.

If this clash had been a mere conflict between two petty clan chieftains about women they had seized for booty; if, indeed, a boastful barbarian pirate had actually sulked in his tent, deserted the ranks, and left his comrades to die, all because his vanity was wounded, one of the world's great poems could not have emerged from the quarrel and no amount of poetic language could have made it emerge. But in terms of Achilles' world, what is at stake is honor and the praise and prizes honor rightly demands if this world is to have meaning. Captive women can be enjoyed physically, but that is not the central point. The point is that meeds of honor for which heroes freely and gladly choose to risk their lives cannot be lightly yielded. They are the outward and visible signs of things that are neither outward nor visible, things that govern the actions of warriors like Achilles. None of his peers considers him a sulky boy or a vain braggart, nor does any of the gods who take sides in the war. Achilles, man of action, is not only quick to seize his sword; he is quick to state his case in the assembly, and he is quick to pray. He does, indeed, speak most often in contest, in order to persuade or threaten, in order to have his way, to work his will. He does, indeed, pray most often to persuade the gods to help him do what he has already decided to do. But he also obeys the gods, as he expects lesser men to obey him. The gods are more powerful than he is and therefore clearly merit his obedience.

In battle other warriors, friend and foe alike, find Achilles ferocious, like a beast of prey. But the epithet Homer frequently uses with his name, as with the names of many other warriors, is "godlike." He and the heroes around him are like gods and also like beasts. Physically, they are made in the image of the gods to whom they pray. It is true that the gods are taller, stronger, swifter, fairer, wiser, and happier. Their meed of honor is unquestionably greater than Achilles' meed or even Agamemnon's, precisely because their excellence is greater. In being jealous of his honor, Achilles is strongly confirming his right to the epithet, godlike. The gods are jealous of men who try to usurp their rights and functions. They are also jealous of each other in cases of overlapping jurisdiction and in cases that violate the hierarchical order on Mount Olympus.

7

The Homeric warrior-kings do not, when they feast, eat ambrosia. They slaughter the cattle they have seized, cut them up, put the pieces on spits, roast, and eat them; but they do not eat until they have burned the thigh-bones, wrapped in rich fat, in sacrifice to the gods. Unlike the gods, these warriors drink no nectar. They drink wine at their feasts, but only after they have poured a little on the ground in libation to the gods. In short they share their feasts with the gods, although these are only earthly feasts and never the nectar and ambrosia served on Olympus. A number of the gods take part in the Trojan War; they advise the combatants; they conceal or whisk away warriors who are in mortal danger; they even fight physically in the melee. More than that, they wound each other and are wounded by men. It is true that where the human warrior bleeds blood, the divine warrior bleeds a liquid called ichor. But, like men, the gods suffer pain and fear, hate and love and grief.

Like men, the gods marry. Like men, they commit adultery, especially Zeus, the father of gods and men. They marry and commit adultery with each other; they occasionally marry human beings; and they often commit adultery with human beings. Generally, it is a god who loves a woman; but sometimes, too, a goddess loves a man. The offspring is almost always human, practically never a god. Achilles himself is the son of a goddess, the sea nymph Thetis, and he is not the only warrior present who can boast of a divine parent. Nearly all of the Achaean heroes trace their ancestry to a god, often to Zeus himself.

It is in this context that Achilles withdraws to his hut and awaits the slaughter of his Achaean comrades to teach the leader of the host a proper respect for him. It is in the context of a war that rages in heaven as well as on earth, "and thus the will of Zeus was being brought to fulfilment."[2] The world in which Achilles moves is therefore penetrated and guided by another world, a divine world, and one which even the godlike Achilles cannot enter. There is a kind of community that includes all gods and all men; yet, between gods and men there is a great gulf fixed. Men are mortal, and the gods are not. In the world of Achilles perhaps the commonest designation of the gods is "the Immortals." Gods are not outside time: they have beginnings but no endings. Most of them were born of divine mothers, but they will never die. They do not even suffer grievous old age, as men must if they outlive youth and strength. Moreover, when Achilles' hour comes, not even his divine mother can gain him entrance into the heaven of Mount Olympus. His soul will descend, wraithlike, to the House of Hades, not, indeed, to torment, but to a kind of half-life devoid of all Achilles loves. Achilles must frequently risk his life in battle because that is the way his world is organized for godlike rulers of men; but he enters battle, knowing he stakes his all. His all, and yet not quite all: Achilles himself will be obliterated; but, until that moment, he may hope to act in such a way that he will leave immortal fame behind him, that men will make songs about him, and that the songs will not die. He himself must die, in youth and glory or in any case after grievous old age and perhaps with no glory; but, if he defends his honor manfully now, it is precisely his honor that will survive, that will be immortal like a god.

It is therefore the enduring thing about Achilles that has withdrawn him and his forces from the war and has made him nurse his wrath in his hut. That part of himself that cannot hope to endure—his youth and beauty and strength and the inestimable joy of living and acting on this earth— these he stands ready to stake again, instantly, once his honor is again free of the taint that Agamemnon has placed upon it.

The *Iliad* reports Achilles' action in and on his world. Almost at the beginning of the poem, he quarrels with Agamemnon and withdraws his forces from the war. The poem has almost sung itself out when he resumes his role in battle. Meanwhile, the fortunes of war swing uncertainly back and forth, and most of the poem narrates what other men than Achilles did on the plain beneath the walls of Troy. Where now is the man of action? Indeed, where now is the hero of the poem?

But Achilles is acting during these weary days as surely as Zeus, who, unlike a number of the Olympic gods, never fights in person on the plain. Achilles' will, like the will of Zeus, is being fulfilled. As Achilles predicted, the Achaeans are driven back to the wall they have built around their beached ships. Agamemnon swallows his pride, admits that he has played the fool, and sends friends of Achilles to his hut to offer apologies; to offer to return Achilles' meed of honor, the woman Achilles loves; and to offer gifts of reconciliation. Achilles is courteous to his friends but grimly declines Agamemnon's offers. Finally, the Trojans begin to fire the ships and thereby to cut the Achaeans off from escape.

Then Patroclus, Achilles' most loved friend and companion in arms, begs Achilles' armor from him that he may join his hard-pressed friends and terrify the Trojans. Achilles consents, and his beloved Patroclus is killed

9

in battle by the Trojans' leading champion, Hector, who, like Paris, is a son of King Priam. Achilles' wild grief for the young Patroclus turns his wrath against Hector, reconciles his tense will with the will of his leader, Agamemnon, and leads him back into battle. Once more it is not only his honor that acts; it is his body, clothed in fresh armor fashioned by a god at the request of Achilles' goddess mother. He goes forth to battle again, knowing that he will shortly die—though his death does not occur in this particular poem. He slays Hector, drags his corpse behind his war chariot past the walls of the city to shame him even in death, and returns to his camp to bury Patroclus, his beloved.

This time Achilles' wrath is not merely redirected; it is purged by his overwhelming grief. And when the aged King Priam ventures secretly from Troy to ransom the torn body of his son—which the gods have miraculously healed after each desecration—Achilles joins his grief to Priam's and together they weep. The body is returned, and the poem ends with the funeral games in Troy, to speed the spirit of Hector to the House of Hades. The theme of the epic, announced in the initial invocation of the Muse, was the wrath of Achilles; and the wrath has worked itself out to the end, to grief and a kind of understanding, an understanding of his friend's death and of his own death to come. A war that has been fought by the will of Zeus between gods as well as between men is also about to work itself out, and its end reaffirms death, the end to which all men come, even godlike men who hold it less important to stay alive than to live their kind of life. What remains is a song about these men, a song that has not died as they had to die, and especially a song about Achilles.

Homer reports that the wall and trench with which the Achaean host had defended their beached ships remained intact so long as Hector lived and Achilles' wrath endured and Troy remained unsacked. But it had been built against the will of the gods. So, when all the bravest of the Trojans had died and the Achaeans had gone back in their ships to their dear native land, then Posidon, god of the sea, took counsel with Apollo and caused all the rivers that flowed down from Mount Ida to sweep against the wall for nine days. And Zeus rained continually. And Posidon's sea waves pounded, there by the river banks where "many shields of bull's-hide and many helms fell in the dust, and the race of men half-divine." Posidon swept away the foundations of beams and stones that the Achaeans had laid with toil, and made all smooth along the strong stream of the

Hellespont, and again covered the great beach with sand, when he had swept away the wall.[3]

So much else has been covered too by sand. Who were the Achaeans? Where did this semi-divine race come from? Our meager evidence, most of it based on archaeological diggings, will as yet yield no history of this folk which can command the agreement of modern scholars. Some two thousand years before Christ, war bands of Achaeans found their way into Greece, and such inroads continued for centuries. These Achaeans were a pastoral people who may have come from the shores of the Caspian or from the nearer Danube basin. They took over the Thessalian plains and, by 1700, they had seized the whole of Greece. They were a warrior class and a minority; and, although their conquered subjects, known as Pelasgians, accepted the language of the intruder, the conqueror in turn was partially assimilated to the local customs.

The land they had entered was a beautiful land but in some ways mysterious. Like the Balkan highlands they had just passed through, it was mountainous. Indeed, four-fifths of it was covered by mountains, which reached heights of only three to five thousand feet in the Attic peninsula but elsewhere included peaks like Parnassus, over eight thousand, and cloud-capped Olympus, nearly ten. Most of the valleys that contained good pasture or arable land were small. The higher mountains were forested with oak and maple, with yew and cypress, with silver fir, pine, and other conifers. Lower down, glades were numerous and shrubs like smilax and ivy flourished. In general, forests were less dense, less towering, less dark than some of those through which the invaders had passed in their long trek toward Greece. Hunting was good. There were the lion, leopard, lynx, panther, bear, wild boar, roe, together with small game like hare, partridge, thrush, quail, and lark.[4] The rare plains could support horse breeding, and even on the mountain slopes there was forage sufficient for cattle. The winters brought rain, but they were rendered mild by a thing the invaders were least familiar with, an omnipresent sea. No point in Greece was more than sixty miles from the Mediterranean, and most of the places in which the war bands settled were far nearer than that. They had left the large lakes behind them in their trek, and they had left the large rivers. Greek rivers were mostly too small to navigate, even if the invader had known how. They usually carried too much sediment to furnish good drinking water. Moreover, Greece was limestone country, full of subterranean cavities, and the rivers had a disconcerting way of disappearing underground. By the same token, it was a land of fresh and delicious springs. The summers were hot, in proportion as one went inland from the sea and its cooling breezes, and were so dry that the glorious profusion of spring flowers was succeeded by dust and dry earth. But it was an invigorating climate, even in summer: it would not enervate the Northern warriors.

The small valleys furnished agricultural oases where spelt and even wheat would grow, and the omnipresent sea offered other nutritious food that these landsmen and herdsmen had not learned to eat: sardines, anchovies, tunny, octopus, squid, oysters. The sea was strange and the Achaeans lacked even a name for it. They called it "the salty" or "the flat" or "the road,"[5] until they adopted from the natives the un-Achaean word, *thalassa*, which would become the regular Greek word for sea. Everywhere this sea and their newly conquered land interpenetrated. The drowned river valleys of a long-subsided coastline formed bays and gulfs and little sheltering harbors that the newcomers did not know how to use. The mountain chains ran out into the Aegean to form peninsulas, turned often into a last, sharp rock cliff, plunged beneath the mysterious sea, and then reared as occasional peaks in a long line of mountain-islands. Standing on such a final cliff, the invader warrior could look off to stepping stones that beckoned man eastward across the Aegean to the coast of Asia Minor. At no point in the Aegean could a sailor get more than forty miles from land, and this in a climate that was generally sunny and in an air that was generally crystal clear.

Having the means of producing bread and meat, the Achaean invader brought with him the sheep that produced his wool and the women's knowledge of spinning and weaving. So food and clothing were his. And for shelter he had good clay in the valleys from which to make sun-dried brick, and, in many places, excellent, soft, and easily worked stone for more pretentious dwellings or for temples. In short, he had found a fairly good home. With his bronze long-sword and his bull's-hide shield he could hope to hold it. There were numerous deposits of copper to make more swords, if he could but find the tin to turn his copper into bronze.

At about the time that the Achaeans entered Pelasgian Greece and carved out little kingdoms for themselves, an advanced civilization was already flourishing on the island of Crete to the southeast. Crete lay strategically between Egypt, the Cyclades, Mainland Greece, and Asia Minor, and during the third millennium B.C. she had become an important commercial center. Before the period 2000-1700, when the Achaeans were conquering Pelasgian Greece, Crete had gained naval control of the Aegean, built large palaces for her kings, developed a fine pottery for export, and a hieroglyphic writing in which to do business. Her goods now penetrated not only Egypt, which already possessed an ancient culture, but also Cyrenaica on the coast of present-day Libya, and Mainland Greece. In Greece, her wares reached as far as central Phocis, perhaps by way of Corinth, which had long traded with the Cyclades. Corinth, in turn, lay on one of the rare roads of Greece, a road that connected Cephissus in Attica with Tiryns in the Argolid, in the eastern Peloponnese. Tiryns, like Corinth, had long traded with the nearby islands of the Cyclades, and now dealt with Crete.

About 1700, when the Achaeans had completed their conquest of Greece, the great royal palaces in Crete, at Knossos, Mallia, and Tylissos, were all sacked[6] and burned, perhaps by rebellious Cretans, perhaps by the Achaeans of Greece. But a new dynasty built a palace at Phaestos and a splendid new one at Knossos, and Crete flourished again. In fact, the art forms she now created excelled her earlier work. She reduced her hieroglyphic writing to a more convenient linear script. Political power seems to have become centralized at Knossos, where the new palace covered some five acres and contained not merely a throne room and royal living quarters, but administrative offices with archives and inventories. Royal factories turned out exquisite pottery, sculpture, and marquetry. Delicate frescoes recorded a luxurious court life. The thalassocracy, or sea power, of this later Crete was fully restored in the Aegean, and Cretan colonies appeared in Miletus on the coast of Asia Minor and on the island of Rhodes. Probably, during the sixteenth and early fifteenth centuries, Crete was the middleman for commerce between wealthy Egypt and the whole Aegean area.

This was the great age of Minoan civilization, an elegant, gracious, and sophisticated culture that not only exchanged commodities with the Achaean Greeks but powerfully influenced their minds and their taste. The Argolid took over the cultivation of the vine and the olive, those crops that would centuries later make Greece's fortune. Palaces rose at Mycenae and Tiryns, in which Achaean ladies imitated the dress and ornaments of Crete. The interior walls of these palaces were covered with Cretan paintings, probably by painters imported from Crete. But there were important differences. The paintings and other locally produced art work compared unfavorably with the great works of Crete. The subjects the artist chose, or that were chosen for him by his half-civilized Achaean patrons, did not express the gay, lovely, tranquil, dancing Cretan world, but tended especially to war and the chase. For although this Argolid was now, if not a political colony of Crete, at least its cultural colony, yet it possessed limited powers of assimilating the elegance of metropolitan Crete.

A thousand years later, the Athenian historian Thucydides would assert that Minos, ruler of Crete, sent his sons as lieutenants, or vice-regents, to his foreign possessions. But the Greeks retained only faint memories of Minos and his empire. They told of a king and great lawgiver of Crete; of Theseus of Athens and the annual tribute ancient Athens had been compelled to send to Minos, a tribute of seven youths and seven maidens; of how Minos' daughter, the princess Ariadne, fell in love with Theseus and helped him slay the Minotaur, half man and half bull, in the tortuous labyrinth. The modern world has now excavated the vast and labyrinthine palace of Knossos and has uncovered the frescoes in which courtiers gaze down while athletes, both men and women, engage in graceful acrobatic feats on the backs of formidable bulls. But so far as history is concerned, the bull and Minos got somehow mixed up in the Achaean legends, as indeed they really are mixed in the name of the monster, Minotaur. Historians now suspect that for many years every king of Crete was a Minos, as every king of Egypt was a Pharaoh. So the historian calls this civilization, which created one of the great arts of all human history, Minoan; or, because of its sea power and its control of the Aegean, simply Aegean. If the present work of decoding its writing fares well, perhaps we shall some day know the secret history of a great civilization, a civilization which radiated art forms into Achaean Greece.

Meanwhile, we possess archaeological evidence that the Mycenaean culture which those radiations helped create existed in varying degrees not only at Mycenae and the nearby hill fortress of Tiryns but, between 1600 and 1400, at such places as Krissa, Delphi, Aegina, Chalcis in Euboea, Thebes, Orchomenos, Thorikos, Iolkos, Pagasae, Athens and the whole of

Attica and finally in distant Thessaly itself. In Boeotia attempts were made to drain Lake Copaïs. In the little Mycenaean kingdoms, the Achaean governing class was learning the art of seafaring, was trying its hand at piracy, and discovering the advantages of peaceful barter with the Cretans. Later, they may have outflanked the Cretans and traded directly with Egypt. About 1400, Knossos, Gournia, Pseira, Zakro, and Palaikastro in Crete met destruction, and Egyptian documents ceased to mention the Keftiu, the men of Crete. The Mycenaeans, with their mixed heritage of Achaean conqueror from the north, of Pelasgian vanquished in Greece, and of civilized Cretan overlord, seem to have conquered Crete itself. Minoan art declined, and what remained of Minoan culture was what her once subject peoples had been able to assimilate and adapt. The center of gravity of the Aegean world had apparently shifted to the Argolid, the land of Mycenae and Tiryns.

Perhaps for a modern, the essential symbol of the shift is the contrast between the spacious and luxurious palace at Knossos, where the queen, at least, possessed plumbing and even a water-closet, and the heavy hill-fortress palaces of Tiryns and Mycenae, where dwelt the Achaean warrior-kings. Where the palace at Knossos had enjoyed the flat roof of so much Mediterranean architecture, the palaces of these half-barbarian imitators of Knossos were crowned with the gabled roofs that recalled the snowy northlands from which the chieftain-kings' ancestors had come, on their long march into sunny southern Greece. And where braziers sufficed to heat the palace of Knossos, the fortress-palace of the Argolid was built around a Great Hall, in the center of which was a fireplace. Above it was a roofed-over aperture to allow the smoke to escape.

At both Tiryns and Mycenae immense new fortifications were built, for the age of a lawgiver, armed with decisive sea power, gave way now to an age of political decentralization. And yet it was also an age of expansion. The Achaeans took over Rhodes, and founded cities, and traded from there with mighty Egypt. They took over Cyprus, penetrated Asia Minor and Egypt itself. They went into Sicily. But they never built a centralized political empire. They seized widely separated sites and set up petty kingdoms. They carried on the arts they had learned from Minoan culture, but these arts declined. Art forms degenerated. As one would expect, techniques in weapon-making remained high. Except in Crete, writing practically disappeared.

It was marauding Achaeans like these who attacked Troy and built the wall and ditch that Posidon and Apollo would destroy. Only a few decades later other destruction came to Greece. Down through Epirus came men with iron weapons, the Dorians, and threw Achaean Greece into great confusion. Many of its inhabitants fled into Attica, whose meager soil could hardly attract the new and fierce invaders. From Attica refugees passed on across the islands of the Aegean to Asia Minor. The Dorians, like the Achaeans, spoke a Greek tongue. But where the Achaeans appropriated Pelasgian Greece, came to terms with it, and together with their subjects adopted a coarsened variant of Minoan culture, the Dorians proved more ruthless than the Achaeans and less assimilative. Their war bands seized parts of central Greece, most of the Peloponnese, and passed on to Melos, Rhodes, and, later, Doris, the southern portion of the Aegean coast of Asia Minor. Mycenaean culture could not recover from this onslaught, and Mainland Greece entered her Dark Age, an age of military and political confusion, of oral tradition in which the art of writing disappeared, of subsistence agriculture on the land, frequently carried on by serf labor, and of piracy rather than trade by sea.

Achilles' wrath against Agamemnon, his grief over the death of Patroclus, his slaying of Hector, the grief he shared with Priam, and the understanding born of grief all happened in the last year of the siege of Troy. When the minstrels sang the *Iliad*, the song made clear that Achilles would not survive the city's fall.

But Odysseus, the hero of the *Odyssey*, having survived the war, spent ten years in wandering about the Mediterranean in quest of his home. Both men acted. Both men were warrior-kings who fought at Troy. Both men sought immortal fame. Both men enlisted the aid of the immortal gods. But even in the *Iliad*, Odysseus is "wise Odysseus"; the epithet "wise" is never once affixed to Achilles' glorious name. He is godlike Achilles, but not godlike in wisdom. And though Achilles was forced by catastrophe to a kind of understanding at last, Odysseus from the start deliberately and continuously sought to understand. He sought to know. He longed to know the unfamiliar, mysterious, and terrible reaches of the cruel sea. He longed to see strange cities and converse with strange men. It is true he was trying to get home, that he was king of Ithaca and that therefore home was Ithaca; but his restless mind kept diverting him. He loved Ithaca, but he kept looking for a home which Ithaca could but reflect. He loved his queen, Penelope, yet he lay with a goddess, the nymph Calypso, who was even more beautiful, and immortal as well. Achilles' world was war, its glory and horror, the lust of battle, the pride of victory, the thrill of the nearness of death, the fear that unloosened the knees of men, and the song the minstrel would one day sing. Odysseus' world was the unknown sea, exploration, discovery, search, learning. The ordeals he underwent were the ordeals of a learner, and the goddess who guided his voyage was the goddess of wisdom, Athena.

Zeus once told Ares, god of war, to his face that he was the most hated of all the gods on Olympus. Yet Ares was an immortal god. The Achaean chieftain-kings who fought at Troy for ten long years often execrated war, as soldiers will, but war intoxicated them too. For another ten long years the sea waged unequal combat with Odysseus, who wanted to find his home; but Posidon, the god of the sea, was Zeus's own brother and almost the equal of Zeus in honor. And like countless other sailors Odysseus both hated the sea and loved it. The sea was salt and barren and unharvested —though the Greek would one day learn to harvest it—and Odysseus yearned to die, in his longing to see his native land or only to see the smoke that curled up from its dwellings.[7] There were times, as in his rescue from the sea on the shores of Phaeacia, when he could sink down in the reeds of a river to kiss the earth, the giver of grain.[8] And yet this barren sea that gave no grain beckoned him; bore him to strange places where he could learn the world beyond beloved Ithaca; in short, taught him. Taught him, and therefore changed him: when at last he reached the shores of Ithaca itself, he knew it not after his long absence, for about him the goddess of wisdom herself had shed a mist. Under her guidance Odysseus entered his kingdom. But he entered it disguised as a beggar, and therefore saw an Ithaca he had never before seen.

And because he came as a beggar, no man knew him. Only his hound, Argos, who lay neglected at his door, knew him. But Argos was old and, though he wagged his tail, he lacked the strength to rise and greet his master, and "the fate of black death seized him straightway when he had seen Odysseus in the twentieth year."[9] Even when his childhood nurse, Euryclea, had recognized him by a scar, his wife Penelope could not recognize him, either disguised as a beggar, or bathed and suitably dressed and transfigured by Athena. But since Penelope too knew guile, she put him to trial by leading him to suppose that the bridal bed he had long ago built for himself and her had been moved; and, speaking in anger, he showed that he knew the bed. Then her knees were loosened where she sat, and her heart melted, for she knew her husband. So was Odysseus recognized in three ways, by dog, by nurse, and by wife.

Though Odysseus returned to his kingdom as a beggar, he never ceased to be an Achaean warrior-chieftain, capable of indignant wrath. He was as ruthless as Achilles when the hour had come to slay the suitors in his own Great Hall and to punish their insolence. Had not his grandfather chosen a name for him, when he was but a baby, that suggested "Child of Wrath"[10]? But he knew the limitations of wrath, too; and Achilles could scarcely have said, as Odysseus did to his host, the king of Phaeacia, "for we are quick to anger, we tribes of men upon the earth."[11] It was Odysseus, too, when still disguised as a wandering beggar, who said to his queen, Penelope: "I am a man of many sorrows."[12]

He could experience wrath, and he also desired glory. When the Cyclops, Polyphemus, the one-eyed cannibal giant, had shut up in his cave both Odysseus and his comrades and had begun to devour those comrades, Odysseus by his own statement devised evil in the deep of his heart, "if in any way I might take vengeance on him, and Athene grant me glory."[13] When he had blinded the Cyclops and his ships were slipping silently out to sea from the shore where the blind giant raged, Odysseus endangered his own life and the lives of all his comrades by a triumphant boast worthy of Achilles himself. He called back to shore exultantly:

Cyclops, if any one of mortal men shall ask thee about the shameful blinding of thine eye, say that Odysseus, the sacker of cities, blinded it, even the son of Laertes, whose home is in Ithaca.[14]

It was then that the blinded Cyclops successfully prayed to his father, the sea god Posidon, to delay Odysseus' return to Ithaca.

But throughout most of his voyage Odysseus was busy less with either vengeance or glory than with solutions to hard and dangerous problems and with learning; and it was a Phaeacian challenger to athletic contests, not the Odysseus he challenged, who made the very Achaean assertion that "there is no greater glory for a man so long as he lives than that which he achieves by his own hands and his feet."[15] Odysseus' greatest glory was achieved by seeking and learning.

18

It was the ship and the oar that symbolized Odysseus, not the sword or the shield nor yet the bow that he nevertheless knew so well how to wield. It was the ship and the oar that brought the Achaeans to Troy to win glory with the sword; they would one day take them homeward; and they were the warriors' last resource if all should be lost and the host should be forced to escape destruction. But in the *Iliad* the ships were mostly beached. In the *Odyssey* it was a swift, black ship that took Odysseus through so many of his ordeals, and the even more marvelous ship of the Phaeacians that at last laid the sleeping Odysseus on the Ithacan shore. Achilles stayed at Troy; he slew Hector to avenge Patroclus and to be remembered as the fairest, bravest, and deadliest warrior of the host. Odysseus of many wiles dared sail and see, passed through many ordeals, and reached a home that was more than the Ithaca he had left twenty long years before.

His adventures took him even beneath the depths of the earth to the House of Hades, where he found the wraiths of Achaean warriors still discussing honor and glory and fame, while thronging about the wraith of Achilles. And Agamemnon's ghost spoke to the ghost of Achilles:

> Fortunate son of Peleus, godlike Achilles, that wast slain in the land of Troy far from Argos, and about thee others fell, the best of the sons of the Trojans and Achaeans, fighting for thy body; and thou in the whirl of dust didst lie mighty in thy mightiness, forgetful of thy horsemanship. . . . Thus for seventeen days alike by night and day did we bewail thee, immortal gods and mortal men . . . Thus not even in death didst thou lose thy name, but ever shalt thou have fair renown among all men, Achilles[16]

—whereas Agamemnon had survived the war and had reached home, only to be murdered ingloriously by an adulterous wife and her paramour. His son Orestes had indeed avenged him; and Athena would urge the son of Odysseus to be valiant like Orestes "that many an one of men yet to be born may praise thee."[17] The spirit of Amphimedon sympathized with Agamemnon's feeling that he had lost his full glory by not falling when Achilles fell, and praised Odysseus' wife for knowing how to wait:

> therefore the fame of her virtue shall never perish, but the immortals shall make among men on earth a pleasant song in honor of constant Penelope.[18]

When Odysseus had reached home, had reconnoitered a difficult political situation, and had finally slain the suitors, the father of the first suitor whom Odysseus had slain urged vengeance in public assembly:

> For a shame is this even for men that are yet to be born to hear of, if we shall not take vengeance on the slayers of our sons and our brothers.[19]

Neither Odysseus nor the men and women of Odysseus' world were immune from this primal call to glory, a glory that would reach men yet to be born. And yet Odysseus in his hollow, black ship, sailing under the protection of the goddess of wisdom, faced his ordeals for another reason.

Though he valued the immortality of fame as Odysseus, sacker of cities, even the son of Laërtes, whose home was in Ithaca, he accepted grievous old age and even grievous death. According to a statement[20] of Athena to Odysseus' son, Telemachus, death is common to all, and the gods themselves could not ward it off from a man they loved when fate decreed his hour had come. Was that why Odysseus' paramour for seven years, the goddess Calypso, who held him on her wooded isle, could not persuade Odysseus to let her make him both immortal and ageless? Did he doubt her power to make him the gift of immortality and to spare him the trials that yet stood between himself and home? Or did he fear that immortality with Calypso would deprive him of the self-knowledge and self-fulfillment implicit in his search for his own proper home? He already knew that the hero, Heracles, took his joy in the feast among the immortal gods and dwelt on Mount Olympus as the son and son-in-law of Zeus himself. But he had also met the phantom of Heracles in the House of Hades. He had slept with Circe, whose magic wand turned men to swine, even though they retained the minds of men, and he had rescued his companions from that swinishness. But neither the immortality of the gods on the one hand nor the brutishness of animals on the other could ensnare him: he steered between them as surely as he steered between Scylla and Charybdis.

He remained, throughout, the wise Odysseus; Odysseus of many wiles; Odysseus, the wise and crafty-minded; Odysseus, the peer of the gods in counsel; neither immortal like the gods, nor yet sunk in animality; and the goddess who guided him homeward against the vengeance of the wrathful Posidon's treacherous sea was Athena, goddess of wisdom. It was this same Athena who assured his son that Odysseus "will contrive a way to return, for he is a man of many devices."[21] But she never ceased to supplement his unusual wisdom with her own divine wisdom. Part of his own wisdom, indeed, consisted in scrupulously following hers. His reward was to see many cities and to learn the minds of many men. As for the immortality of fame, there were more ways to win fame than by muscle and brawn and the long-sword of gleaming bronze and the willingness to die. Could a bronze sword, backed with muscle, outwit the treacherous sea? Human intelligence was better and more godlike than brute force. That was why Odysseus could boast to his gentle host, the king of the Phaeacians: "I am Odysseus, son of Laertes, who am known among men for all manner of wiles, and my fame reaches unto heaven."[22] Fame was a perquisite of wisdom, even among the immortal gods, perhaps especially among the immortal gods.

True, the wisdom Odysseus displayed was primarily a practical wisdom, a shrewdness, a cunning. But the gods favored that, too; or certainly some of them did. Old Autolycus, the maternal grandfather of Odysseus, who had chosen to name him Man of Wrath, had, according to Homer, "excelled all men in thievery,"[23] thanks to the god Hermes, who understood the art well. It was this shrewdness, this cunning, that enabled Odysseus to escape the countless dangers of a Mediterranean world filled with magic, like the wand and potions of Circe and like Hermes' herb to counteract those potions: "Moly, the gods call it."[24] It was the wisdom, too, of his wife, Penelope, and the wisdom of his son, Telemachus, guided by Athena, that laid the groundwork for Odysseus' return and triumph. Athena had endowed Penelope not only with that most valuable of women's skills in Homeric society, a knowledge of fair handiwork, but also "an understanding heart, and wiles."[25] She knew how to weave a web that would serve as shroud for Odysseus' aging father; but she also knew how to unravel it at night and delay its completion and therefore how to postpone her choice of suitors in case her true lord might yet return.

Although Odysseus left eleven of his twelve ships safely behind, he insisted on taking his own ship and its crew to the land of the Cyclopes. He wanted to learn who these Cyclopes were, whether they were cruel, and wild, and unjust, or whether they loved strangers and feared the gods in their thoughts.[26] And even after it became clear that he and his crew were in danger, even after his comrades had besought him to leave, he waited at Polyphemus' cave "to the end that I might see the man himself, and whether he would give me gifts of entertainment."[27] When he was forced to pass the man-devouring, sweetly singing Sirens, he took Circe's advice. He stopped the ears of his crew against that overpowering song, but he had them lash him to the mast with ears unstopped, that with delight he might listen to the voice of the two Sirens.[28] And he was richly rewarded, for the Sirens, according at least to their own boast, "know all things that come to pass upon the fruitful earth."[29] Odysseus wanted to know all too, not merely for immediate practical reasons, but because it is the nature of man to desire knowledge. His voyage had the practical aim of getting himself and his comrades back to the Ithaca they had left behind them twenty long years before. But Odysseus converted a return trip into an exploration; into a kind of education; into an intellectual, not a merely physical, adventure.

The cost of standing in battle, shield to shield, beside Achilles was high; but so was the cost of exploration in Odysseus' ship. There were those men whom the Cyclops had devoured in his blood-spattered cave. There were those others who had, at least temporarily, been turned by Circe into swine. There were the ghastly narrows between Scylla and Charybdis, and these must be followed through. Odysseus knew in advance that, rowed they never so swiftly, the six-headed monster Scylla would yet have time to seize six of his crew. Yet, if the men were warned of this, they might stop rowing at the crucial moment and huddle together in the hold, and then there would be more than six men lost. So he approached the strait, with that special kind of heavyheartedness that the leader is often forced to bear alone. When the monster struck, the six victims "cried aloud, calling upon me by name for that last time in anguish of heart."[30] While she devoured them, they stretched out their hands toward him in their awful death struggle, and, "Most piteous did mine eyes behold that thing of all that I bore while I explored the paths of the sea."[31] The passage between Scylla and Charybdis was, of course, inevitable; but the blood-smeared cave of the Cyclops was not. And when, later, one of Odysseus' followers called him "reckless Odysseus" and recalled that it was "through this man's folly"[32] that those men too had perished, Odysseus must have learned, or learned again, what the restless mind of the thinker could cost those he loved, and could cost the thinker, too.

Part of his wisdom lay in his love of law and justice, and part in his obedience to the gods. For he was a civilized man, and the cannibalism in Polyphemus' cave led him to a more general inference: that the Cyclopes were savages, an overweening and lawless folk, who did not even practice agriculture.

> Neither assemblies for counsel have they, nor appointed laws, but they dwell on the peaks of lofty mountains in hollow caves, and each one is lawgiver to his children and his wives, and they reck nothing of one another.[88]

Polyphemus, despite the fact that he was own son to Posidon, boasted frankly that they recked nothing of Zeus nor of the blessed gods, "since verily we are better far than they."[34] Whereas Zeus himself spoke to Athena of "godlike Odysseus, who is beyond all mortals in wisdom, and beyond all has paid sacrifice to the immortal gods."[35]

Alone at last, on a beach in his beloved Ithaca, yet not recognizing his country through the protective mist Athena had shed about him, he saw a young man approach who told him where he was. Crafty Odysseus began to pose as a newcomer from Crete and began to spin a yarn about how he had reached Ithaca. Athena—for the young man was indeed flashing-eyed Athena in disguise—was so delighted by the imaginative zest of his deception that she smiled and stroked Odysseus' cheek and told him who she was. She then touched him with a wand that transformed him into an aged beggar, ordered him to return to his home without telling anyone who he actually was, and took counsel with him how he might dispose of the importunate wooers who had now for three years lorded it in his halls. But his lies about Crete also led her to say: "Bold man, crafty in counsel, insatiate in deceit, not even in thine own land, it seems, wast thou to cease from guile and deceitful tales."[36] She found him also "soft of speech, keen of wit, and prudent."[37] She declared that he was best of all men in counsel and in speech and claimed that she herself among all the gods was "famed for wisdom and craft."[38] She gave him interesting instructions: he was to make trial of his wife and the others in his kingdom before disclosing his identity; and meanwhile, he was to "endure thy many griefs, and submit to the violence of men."[39] Was this, perhaps, the price that every man must pay who would know and understand, and not merely conquer with the sword? In any case, Athena's admonition led the returned king to take on himself the person of a helpless beggar and to gain for the first time in his life the knowledge of his kingdom that only a beggar could gain.

Achilles had frequently prayed, to get the gods to help him work his unexamined will. But Odysseus knew what Achilles did not: that, since the gods understood more than men, it was possible to get from them a more godlike kind of aid: they could help a man not only to slay his enemies; not only to outwit them; but to understand and to know. It was this that made his odyssey a wise man's pilgrimage and a learning of the human condition. Wisdom brought him a sense of proportion that Achilles lacked, and so this seaman's yarn was suffused with a humor which the *Iliad*, with all its power and majesty, conspicuously lacked.

In the world of Achilles human courage, even the lionlike courage of Achilles himself, was not adequate to the human problem. Something, wisdom could do: it was crafty Odysseus' ruse of the wooden horse, filled with Achaean warriors, that at last brought Troy low. But the sack of Troy brought to Odysseus himself a second ten years of trial and made him a man of many sorrows. For in his world human wisdom, even his many devices, were not adequate to the human predicament either. At Troy Odysseus shared the fame of wisdom with ancient Nestor, king of Pylos; and it was later, at Pylos, that Nestor's own son informed a visiting stranger that all men had need of the gods.[40] Ironically, it was to a goddess, Athena, disguised as the friend and guide of Odysseus' son, now come to Pylos to seek news of his still-missing hero-father, that the information was given. Ironically, that information was given at a sacrifice offered to Posidon, the sea god, who had just spent ten years delaying what Athena had labored to bring about, the return of Odysseus to Ithaca.

Nestor's son merely voiced what every wise man knew: that all men had need of the gods. But this still left difficulties. Beyond the hundred and one daily rituals that kept this terrible need fresh in men's minds, there still were difficulties, even for those wise enough, as Odysseus himself was clearly wise enough, to know that there were things they did not know. Not even the gods knew everything, or they could not have deceived each other. That they knew more than men and that they appeared to men and advised them, seemed certain. But it was troubling that, in those direct encounters of the divine and human, the god was almost always disguised, usually as some human friend of the human party to the encounter. At the conclusion of such an encounter, the god might turn into

24

a sea eagle or some other bird and fly off: Athena repeatedly withdrew in this fashion from the human world of Odysseus. Human witness was uncertain: Athena appeared to Odysseus in the hut of his swineherd, Eumaeus; but Telemachus was there and "did not see her before him, or notice her; for in no wise do the gods appear in manifest presence to all."[41] Yet Telemachus was not blind to gods, as witness the fact that a moment later, when Athena had beckoned Odysseus from the hut, had touched him with a golden wand, and had transfigured him, "his dear son marveled, and, seized with fear, turned his eyes aside, lest it should be a god."[42] And Odysseus reassured him:

> Be sure I am no god; why dost thou liken me to the immortals? Nay,
> I am thy father, for whose sake thou dost with groaning endure many
> griefs and submittest to the violence of men.[43]

But Telemachus, who had "not noticed" Athena, reasoned that only a god could transform himself from an aged beggar into this handsome, kingly man. This sort of transfiguration of man by god happened repeatedly, both in Odysseus' world and in that of Achilles.

A god could put courage in an Achilles or wisdom in an Odysseus. Did not Athena herself "put strength and courage"[44] in Telemachus's heart when he dreaded going among the unfriendly wooers of his mother, to the extent even of making him a "godlike man"[45]? But in urging the voyage to Pylos, she promised that she, or some god, would put wisdom in his mind. Telemachus shrank from encountering Nestor, renowned for his wise words, since he himself was "as yet all unversed in subtle speech."[46] Her answer told something of the relation of gods and men: "Telemachus, somewhat thou of thyself devise in thy breast, and somewhat heaven [daimōn] too will prompt thee."[47] If Telemachus sounded childishly timid, yet in his world men were keenly aware of the mysterious work of what Homer repeatedly called "wingèd words," those symbols that conveyed invisible thoughts from the mysterious recesses of one human mind to the mysterious recesses of another.

Often the gods communicated to men by dreams. But could a dream be trusted? Penelope told Odysseus, her still-disguised husband, that her absent lord had appeared to her in a dream and had foretold his return. But when Odysseus urged her to accept the dream as true, she replied sadly: "Stranger, dreams are baffling and unclear of meaning, and in no wise do they find fulfilment in all things for men."[48] Some dreams were true and some were false, and how could Penelope tell which class her dream belonged to? As a matter of fact, although Penelope presumably did not know it, Zeus had sent a dream to Agamemnon at Troy precisely in order to deceive him into fighting and losing.

Wingèd words, dreams, and gods disguised as men were heard or seen by some bystanders and not by others. Could the human mind be sure of any of them, in its doomed effort to understand its world? Yet some wingèd words seemed to fly straight, from mind to mind; Penelope herself admitted that some dreams came true; and some men had been certain they encountered a god. Should words, then, "remain unwingèd"[49]—that is, should men keep silence? And cease to search their dreams for meaning? And believe the god they were sure they saw was probably but a man? After all, Odysseus, who spoke wingèd words, and urged belief in a dream, and walked and talked with gods—even Odysseus admitted that "Nothing feebler does earth nurture than man, of all things that on earth are breathing and moving."[50] For just this reason he made use of prayer, of signs and tokens, and of words. After the events in the *Odyssey* had all occurred, and Odysseus had understood his kingdom in a new way, and his wife, and his son, did he obey the injunction Tiresias gave him beneath the earth in the House of Hades? Did he reaffirm his belief in the invisible world of the gods that penetrated his own? Did he reaffirm his faith in the power of things to serve as symbols, in the power of his world to have meaning, even to be transfigured?

Tiresias ordered him, when the suitors had been slain, to take a shapely oar and strike inland until he came to men who had never heard of the sea, or of ships, or of the oars that serve ships as wings. And this should be a sign to him: when a wayfarer should mistake the oar on Odysseus' shoulder for a fan with which to winnow grain, then Odysseus should erect the oar in the earth and sacrifice to the god of the sea, Posidon. Later, after a long and prosperous life, death would come to Odysseus—from the sea. Tiresias, of course, was a prophet, with more faith in symbols than most men dared to hold.

2

A RACE OF IRON

THE tales of Achilles' ruinous wrath and of Odysseus' restless quest were not only mighty poems for bards to sing at the feasts of
chieftain-kings and their nobles. They were the collected memories of a
people who had gone to earth beneath the onslaught of the Dorian tribes—
the Mycenaean people, who had achieved a coarsened version of the elegant
life of ancient Crete, of its Minoan sea power, its Minoan law and order.
The *Iliad* and the *Odyssey* and the lesser epics of the Homeric Cycle,
like the legends of Theseus, king of Athens; of Perseus, who reigned in
Tiryns, who slew the Gorgon Medusa, and who founded Mycenae itself;
of King Minos of Crete and his wife's monstrous son, the Minotaur, shut
up in the Labyrinth to feed on human victims; of Oedipus, prince of
Corinth, who in ignorance slew his father and married his mother and
ruled Thebes; of Jason and his Argonauts, who sailed to the Black Sea
in search of the Golden Fleece, and of Medea, the barbarian queen Jason
brought back from his voyage; all these oral legends served the early Greeks
as history. But it was a history that had been half forgotten and that had

been transmuted into poetry, so that the history of many centuries of Minoan culture, of Mycenaean power, of Achaean and Dorian invaders from the north, of the struggle between the invaders' Olympic gods and the local gods of the settled population the invaders overran, of the great Achaean crusade to Troy, and of the political disintegration and military disorder that followed the coming of the Dorians—this history became scrambled, jumbled, like the geological strata of the Grecian land itself, folded by volcanic action, eroded by later rivers, partly drowned in the sea, with only a peak emerging here and there as an island. Invader and invaded had alike gone to earth, to seek their food from the meager soil of Greece, in little isolated communities huddled for protection around the hill fortress of some king. The knowledge of writing disappeared, and where the past lived on, it had to live in song and the spoken word. Art languished, and the scenes of war and the chase that graced the walls and drinking cups of long-buried Mycenaean lords gave way now, in the tenth century, to the primitive geometrical designs on pot and vase and amphora, designs that were painted in some strongly local style, since a pot would rarely sell now far from the home of the man who had made it and painted it. In parts of Greece, clear into the seventh century, this geometric art would endure.

Even the physical remains of Mycenaean palaces were no longer understood: the massive stone walls of the royal fortresses at Tiryns and Mycenae, and the roads that led from those ruined fortresses northward to Corinth, paved with stone and supplied with necessary bridges, now seemed beyond the power of mortal men to build. They had been built, men thought, by the Cyclopes.[51] Growing their own food, making their own clothing, building their own houses, these huddled farmers understood little of commerce, either between their own communities or with the outside world.

But the outside world was beginning to seek them out. With the breakup of Minoan power the ships of Phoenicia began to nose their way among the islands of the Aegean and along the cliffs and into the innumerable bays of Mainland Greece. The Phoenicians were a Semitic people with a trading tradition. The Greeks called them *Phoinikes*, Red Men, perhaps because their skins were swarthier than Greek skins, perhaps because one of their most successful commodities was crimson-to-purple cloth, dyed with the juice of the murex, a shellfish that flourished off the Phoenician coast and that the Phoenician traders were now finding also among the islands of the Aegean. For a while the men of Sidon dominated this trade. By the twelfth century, Sidon's colony, Tyre, rivaled the mother city; and between the tenth and eighth centuries Tyre was the chief port of the entire Mediterranean and Tyrian purple became a commercial term. The Tyrians not only traded; they colonized. They founded Utica on the North African coast, and Palermo in Sicily. Besides Tyre and Sidon, Phoenician trading centers developed at Beirut; at nearby Byblus; and, in distant Spain, where the Phoenicians went in search of metals, they founded Tarshish on the Atlantic coast itself, at the site of modern Cadiz. Beyond such distant trading posts they went for tin, either to the Scilly Isles off Cornwall, or to northwest Spain. Precisely where the tin lay was a jealously guarded secret. For although iron was now gradually replacing bronze in the making of agricultural tools, the processes for hardening it were still poorly developed, and most weapons of war continued to be made of bronze.[52] Bronze could not be made without both copper and tin; and, whereas there were numerous deposits of copper in the eastern Mediterranean, tin was still scarce and highly valued.

The Phoenicians were not empire-builders; they were shrewd businessmen. Few of their trading posts, therefore, ever developed into powerful cities. The most brilliant exception was Kart-hadshat, or New City, which the Tyrians founded at least as early as the eighth century a few miles from the site of modern Tunis. Kart-hadshat, which others would some day call Carthage, possessed fine harborage at a point commanding the main sea passage that connected the eastern Mediterranean and the western. It proved a strategic strong point; and for food it could draw on plentiful and rich wheatlands.

But in general, Phoenicians clung to the coastlines and devoted themselves to trade, and their homeland could not ward off powerful military empires like the Assyrian or the Chaldean. Sennacherib of Assyria conquered Phoenicia in 701; and though it was freed from the Assyrian yoke by the fall of Nineveh in 612, it was gobbled up again, this time in 574 by the Chaldean emperor, Nebuchadnezzar. But even before Nineveh fell, the Red Men's dazzled customers in Greece had learned to rove the sea and were taking over the sea lanes. In the eighth century the Phoenicians still dominated the western Mediterranean; but by about 600 the Greeks of Phocaea in Ionia had founded or taken over Marseilles, which they called Massilia, and could tap the Rhone River route for both tin and amber.

In the early days of their trade with the Greeks, the Phoenicians must have thought of that trade as in large part trinkets for barbarians. For unlike the Greeks, or at least the Mainland Greeks, the Phoenicians were in touch with ancient, powerful, and luxurious civilizations. One of the few return cargoes they could make real profit from was the slaves they bought or kidnaped on their Aegean run. In return, the Greeks got more than trinkets. The tin and other products the Red Men brought had to come from somewhere, and eventually the Greeks took to the sea to find the source. Although the Phoenician art objects tended to be merely copies of the art of other peoples, the Phoenicians were middlemen for better things than they made, and the wares they brought led Greek potters from their primitive geometric ornamentation of pots to a style that more and more represented the objects the artist saw about him.[53] More important, perhaps, was another art the Greeks acquired from the Phoenicians, the art of writing. The Greeks took over the Phoenician alphabet and adapted it to the various dialects of their own tongue. Not even the now dimly remembered Minoans had possessed a true alphabet. Minoan writing had represented syllables, rather than simple sounds. The Greek alphabets had been constructed around the ninth century, in Ionia.[54] Perhaps Homer[55] wrote down the *Iliad* when he composed it, whether or not he wove into it lays that antedated writing. In any case, when the Ionians of Asia Minor and the peoples of Mainland Greece began to take over the Aegean from the Phoenician traders, their early ventures into trade were buttressed by the power to write.

The Aegean Sea furnished a unique school for mariners,[56] a school no other part of the Mediterranean was so well equipped to provide. True, in winter there could be terrible storms, but the Greek sailor did not commonly try to use the Aegean in winter. Even in summer the Aegean was subject to dangerous squalls; yet a ship could often avoid these if it kept close to land, and this the Greek sailor habitually did. Lacking a compass, he depended heavily on landmarks. He soon learned that the stars could guide him—but not on a cloudy night. He lacked the art of tacking against the wind, but his ship was small enough to row; and in a calm he could always fall back on oars. His ship was also too small for the storage of much food or for a convenient place to cook it: normally, therefore, he beached his ship by night and cooked his morning and evening meals ashore. Since for long he carried no anchor, his ideal port was a sheltered beach. Around the middle of the seventh century he developed a wooden anchor, weighted with a lump of metal or a stone; and in the early sixth century metal anchors came into use. With a good anchor, a ship could take refuge from foul weather in a deep-water harbor, even when the harbor lacked a beach.

By the seventh century, if a craft happened to be a warship, it would most likely be a penteconter, a fifty-oared ship with twenty-five men rowing on each side, with two sweeps in the rear to serve as rudders, and with a very small deck at each end. Or it might be a sort of longboat with a long deck and with two tiers of oars, a bireme. In either case, the basic source of a warship's power was human muscle: a warship must be able to count on its power even in a calm, and sails could be at best an auxiliary source, useful only when the wind was right. The penteconter was basically the same kind of swift, black ship that took Achilles to the land of Troy and that bore Odysseus home to Ithaca. The bireme was an improvement, because it packed more motive power into a given length. However, if a Greek sailed a merchantman, she would have been a roundish tub, whose shipwright had sacrificed speed to gain more space for cargo.

All in all, what with the storms and the pirates, life at sea was thoroughly dangerous. The Aegean was indeed a school; it was also a graveyard. But the profits of merchant adventurers in a Greece just learning to exchange commodities were very heavy. On all sides, the blue Aegean beckoned, to danger and to wealth.

Transportation by land could not compete with the sea lanes. Those roads which the one-eyed giants had built remained almost the only roads in Greece. The Greeks did eventually build several short paved roads, with artificially incised ruts for the cartwheels: such were the sacred roads that led from Athens to nearby Eleusis, from Sparta to Amyclae, from Elis to Olympia. But most roads in Greece were mere tracks for pedestrians or pack animals. Even had there been vehicular roads, the designers of harness had proven considerably less skillful than the designers of ships, with the curious result that draft animals could not compete with the oar. Oxen were too slow, so the Greek attempted to make ox harness serve for an ass or a mule. The attempt failed. A draft animal which should have pulled, had he been pulling with his shoulders instead of his throat, fifteen times the load a man could pull actually in this badly designed harness

31

drew only some four times as much, and the mule could already carry that much as a pack animal. Finally the Greek never developed a good enough horseshoe to increase the animal's traction: the carter used removable horseshoes of metal, leather, or even straw. If the sea lanes had invited less urgently, would the Greek merchant have invented a better harness and a better shoe for his draft animals? Would he have built paved roads too, despite the mountainous terrain? Perhaps, but the sea invited him, and the Greek merchant followed where it led.

The Aegean Sea served as a school, not only to Mainland Greece, but to those Greeks, whether they spoke Aeolian Greek or even Ionian or Dorian, who had crossed that sea from the Greek peninsula and colonized the west coast of Asia Minor. In fact, by the close of the Greek Dark Ages, the Aegean Sea rather than European Greece was the geographical center of Hellas. Hellas was clustered around it rather than merely lying west of it.

Nobody knew exactly when the Ionian Greeks had settled in their home, but the pressure of the Dorian invasion had a good deal to do with their original crossing from Europe. The ancient Minoan Empire had never gained much foothold there, since the coast of Asia Minor was then dominated by the powerful kingdom of the Hittites in the mountainous hinterland. But, when pressure from Assyria weakened the Hittites' hold on their Aegean coastline, it was opened to settlement from Mainland Greece. There was no organized Greek invasion: the Greeks came in small parties and included men of Achaean stock as well as of pre-Achaean. In Ionia they found fertile bottom land to cultivate and neighbors able to transmit to them through trade the ideas and crafts developed by the great Near Eastern empires. Of all the Greeks in Asia, the Ionians especially took to the sea. And they early produced an impressive literature. According to later Greek tradition, Homer himself was an Ionian. Following the epics that were composed by him or ascribed to him, there was an outburst, in the eighth and seventh centuries, of lyric poetry that extended from the funeral dirge to martial or festive or patriotic themes.

It was in these two centuries, moreover, that the Greeks on both sides of the Aegean further developed their most characteristic political form, the small city-state, the *polis*. Originally, the polis was the hill fortress of the chieftain-king. Later the word included the cluster of houses that huddled at the foot of that hill, and the hill itself became the *acropolis* or "high city." Eventually the polis included acropolis, huddled houses, and in addition all the agricultural territory surrounding them. It was under the leadership of the chieftain-king that the settled war band formed this city-state, in which the king and his council of nobles ruled and announced their decisions to the assembly of all free males. The nobles, from being the roving warriors who followed the king in raids, tended to form a stable landed aristocracy, ready to defend their little polis, though ready also to make forays, to steal women and cattle. Or, in the good months of July and August, a noble might fit out a ship and turn pirate, or trader, or both.

Since the noble had seized the best land in the city-state, he alone was well enough off to wear proper bronze armor and, above all, to keep a horse. It was the Assyrians, not the Greeks, who had introduced cavalry in the ninth century, but by the eighth the Greek noble's proudest title was Horseman, or Knight. Actually, the Greek, like the Assyrian horseman, was not a true cavalryman: he used the horse, which he rode bareback,[57] to give him mobility between battles; he did not fight on horseback. These Knights, then, were actually mounted infantry. Yet their mounts did give them speed in pursuit. As for the war chariot the Achaeans had used at Troy, that had disappeared, even though the terms that described its two occupants, the fighter and the driver, long survived in an honorific sense, and even though the chariot was still used for an athletic event, the highly honored chariot race. Finally, except in a few localities like the plains of Thessaly, the roughness of Greek terrain severely limited the usefulness of cavalry in war.

The noble defended the polis with his life, and more and more he assumed the right to govern what he defended. During the eighth and seventh centuries, king after king lost all, or a portion, of his powers to his nobles. Monarchy gave way to the aristocratic republic in one polis after another, although kingship usually survived as an elective office, with very limited powers. Custom had always given the council the right to discuss and advise. Now this same council gained the right to vote and decide and, through officials of its own choice, to execute. Law was still unwritten, customary law, which the gods revealed; but they revealed it only to the noble, and only the noble could judge cases by the light of this revealed knowledge. The noble was one of the *Aristoi*—the Best People, who had inherited the right to rule from ancestors who were also the Best People and who, indeed, were occasionally immortal gods. But he must share the rule with other nobles and needed, therefore, not only to wield a sword in battle but to wield words in council.

As for the peasants, the noble despised them. Living in his town house in the polis, where he could keep an eye on politics, he watched the peasants plod in from the country, toil-stained, half-clad. In battle these same peasants formed an undisciplined rabble of under-armed, under-armored men. The noble called them Sheepskin-wearers or Club-bearers, as at Sicyon; or Dustyfeet, as at Epidaurus; or Half-clad, as at Argos; or merely the Poor, the *Penestai*, as in Thessaly, where they were actual serfs, bound to the soil. Just as the noble frequently believed that he himself, in descent at least, was partly a god, the Dustyfoot must have struck him as being partly a brute, certainly unfit to share in the mysterious art of statecraft and hardly fit to share in defending the state in battle.

But just as Achilles could stand up in the Achaean assembly before Troy, take the herald's wand that gave him the right to speak, and call Agamemnon, leader of the host, dog-faced,[58] so Thersites also, the Dustyfoot from the ranks, railed publicly at Agamemnon. True, Odysseus beat him for his impudence, but according to Odysseus it was not the first time Thersites had railed. Now, four centuries later, even the noble who chose to dwell in town, at least part of the year, away from his land can hardly have had the impersonal relationship to those who served him that money would some day bring to the rich. These early nobles were rooted in the soil, like the peasants who worked for them. They ate better food, wore better clothes, and lived in better houses than Dustyfoot; but by later standards, the material gap cannot have been great. It was the spiritual gap that counted.

The noble retained an image of himself that was like the image of Achilles in the poem the noble had heard sung when men feasted in the great hall. He imposed his will, like the powerful gods themselves. Early in the seventh century Archilochus of Paros would state the ideal in a poem:

> In the spear is my kneaded bread, in the spear my Ismarian wine,
> when I drink I recline on the spear.[59]

Even the most land-bound noble retained the conqueror's predatory pride and felt he had the right to seize what he desired.

He felt also a mystical interest in the blood tie. He was passionately bound to his kindred: to those who lived about him, to his ancestors who had already lived out their lives and perished, to his unborn descendants. In the early days of the Greek polis, family pride and family vendetta were towering obstacles to law and justice. There was wergild, or blood money, for murder done; compurgation, in which the relatives and friends of an accused man assembled and swore to his innocence; ordeal by fire; and, even in war, a kind of Truce of God[60] for religious festivals. The ghost of a murdered man drove his kinsmen to avenge his death, and later, to prosecute his murderer in court. The polis still left such prosecution to the slain man's natural defenders, those who shared his blood, some of which had been spilled. This blood tie was so strong that the descendants of a man who had committed an impious act could be polluted by that act. But when the propinquity of the polis had begun to tell—of this polis, this little island of growing order in a sea of disorder—then murder could pollute the entire community, and the polis would take steps to cleanse itself by punishing the offender.

Next to ruling and fighting, the noble loved athletic contests; poetry, especially the *Iliad* and the *Odyssey*; and music. Like Achilles, he sought imperishable honor. Perhaps the best material symbol of that immaterial prize was the materially worthless wreath of laurel that a man could win at Olympia. There the great festivals and competitions were held as early as 776, and by the sixth century the Olympics were drawing Greek competitors from all over the Mediterranean area to Olympia and competitions like the Olympics were taking place regularly at Delphi, at Isthmus, at Nemea. In those places, too, honor could be won by the Best People, people less anxious to live than to live well, people not afraid of death by battle but hopeful that men would make a song about them. At the Sacred Games they sought to excell and to have their excellence recognized.

But the nobles did more than convert monarchies into aristocratic re-publics, more than rule those republics and defend them with their blood. For it was during their rule that the republics of Mainland Greece and Asia Minor alike planted colonies, westward as far as Sagunto on the Mediterranean coast of Spain; eastward as far as Phasis on the eastern coast of the Black Sea; northward as far as Olbia, not far east of the

modern city of Odessa; and southward as far as the coasts of modern
Tunisia and Libya. Acting at home in the image of Achilles, the nobles
led or sent forth explorers and colonists in the image of Odysseus, men
who took to the sea to enrich themselves by trade, like the Phoenicians
whom they supplanted in the Aegean, and, like them, to practice piracy.
Like them, they bought or captured slaves. But, hunting for things to
trade, they also found land to till.

Out to those lands, especially to the rich lands of southern Italy and of
eastern Sicily while the Phoenicians held the western part of the island
and kept the Strait of Gibraltar closed, streamed the Greek colonists. Most
often, though not always, it was by fighting rather than by negotiation that
they secured their new land; and when they had secured it, they promptly
established an independent city-state, a polis, like the little city-states at
home. As a rule they were not sent out by governments. The colonists
went as groups of individuals, seeking their fortune where land was more
plentiful than at home. But they went with the blessing of the aristocratic
republic at home, and they carried their religious beliefs and customs with
them. They even carried sacred fire from the altar of the mother-city, the
metro-polis. Usually, their memories bound them to the polis from which
they came. But sometimes more than one polis contributed colonists to a
given venture.

Their newly founded cities served purposes which the colonists had not
had in mind. They supplied markets for industries, notably pottery, at
home. And the time came when they could send back badly needed wheat
to feed their metropolis. By adding the rich wheatlands of southern Italy,
Sicily, North Africa, and what are now southern Russia and the Turkish
shores of the Sea of Marmora to the total means of production of the
Greek peoples, the colonies permitted eventually a division of labor that
was economically desirable. The home-country had never had enough
wheatlands; or, at least, not under the land system that prevailed. The
poor, the misfits, the restless, the ambitious, the merely adventurous now
dreamed of new lands where they could carve out new lives for themselves.
Their departure relieved the tension between rich and poor and the pressure for reform, and many a noble was glad to see the malcontents depart.

By an apparent paradox, when wheat and metals began to flow back
from the colonies, the little city-states that colonists had gone out from
grew more populous than before the emigration. They were supported by

36

trade with the colonies, by manufactures for colonial markets, by a more specialized and more suitable agriculture at home, especially an agriculture that developed the vine and the olive on terraced slopes where neither wheat nor barley could ever have yielded profit. The bulk of the pottery that went out to the colonies consisted of huge amphorae that carried wine or olive oil. Wine was drunk everywhere in the Greek Mediterranean, although it was habitually mixed with water. To drink wine straight was to resemble the barbarian Thracians north of the Aegean. Olive oil found a multitude of uses. It took the place of the butter of Northern peoples: the Greeks flavored food with it, and cooked with it, too. It supplied the little clay lamps of Greece with illuminating oil. It was what the Greek athlete rubbed down with when he wished to cleanse his body. Or the unpressed fruit was eaten for food. In short, the olive was basic to Greek life; and it was a curious fact that when Greece sent out its colonists in all directions and to great distances, there were few Greek settlements where the olive could not be grown. Both the Mediterranean and the Black Sea tempered and softened the climate of the lands that bordered them: the sea protected the North African coast from the blast of summer heat that afflicted the hinterland, and it protected the Greek in southern Russia or on the French coast from the blast of winter cold that would kill an olive tree a few miles inland. The colonization of the eighth and seventh centuries merely won for the Greek farmer the natural limits of the arts he knew. Yet all the distant lands he settled in he organized politically in small, independent city-states; and everywhere these city-states wrangled and warred with each other, sometimes for the possession of land, the life-giver, but more and more for trade.

Despite these wars between the new colonies, the founding of new cities did much to create unity among Greeks everywhere. By their language, by their customs, by their gods, Hellenes everywhere found themselves set apart from the 'barbarians' and therefore more conscious of their own unity. The fact that many colonies had been founded by emigrants from more than one city-state in Mainland Greece and Greece-in-Asia tended toward the same sense of unity. Even in Mainland Greece, the aristocrats' sense of blood had always made for marriages between noble families in different city-states. Especially in Calabria, the toe of the Italian boot, which comprised the whole of what the Greek colonists termed "Italy," this common sense of being Hellenes developed strongly. And it was in

37

southern Italy that the Greek colonies grew so numerous and so rich that the Hellenes would later call it Great Hellas.[61]

Where Greek colonists went to found some new polis, whether on the shores of the western Mediterranean or on those of the Black Sea, Minoan Crete and later the Mycenaean states had often got there first, centuries before. Whatever else the tale of Odysseus recorded, it also remembered sea routes that were later closed. For the Sicilian towns with which the Mycenaeans had traded had by the ninth century moved inland, to escape the piracy which was the sea's version of the Dark Ages. Essentially, then, the aristocratic republics of the ninth and eighth centuries were opening up a New World. In it they discovered fewer one-eyed giants, and six-headed monsters, and Sirens, and nymphs like Calypso, and magicians like Circe than the long-dead Odysseus had encountered, but they did discover Great Hellas, a land of broader fields and greater wealth. In a sense, like so many colonists, they discovered what Odysseus had restlessly sought: home. For they found at least the good earth often lying idle, land that would have already opened to another's plow in the city-states from which they had just sailed.

By the middle of the sixth century the Hellenes had founded their little city-states rather thickly on the shores of the Dardanelles, which they called the Hellespont. They had penetrated the Black Sea, which they called the Pontus, or open sea, or sometimes the Euxine, or Hospitable Sea—a title they may have given it to propitiate it, since they found rough sailing there. They scattered colonies on the western coast of the Black Sea, and a few on its other coasts. They had already settled the shores of the Propontis, which was the vestibule to the Pontus proper, the Black Sea. They had founded many colonies on the coasts of Sicily, except in the extreme west, and many in southern Italy, from Cumae, near the present site of Naples, to Tarentum, on the heel of the boot. They held both sides of the strategic strait between Italy and Sicily: Messina, which they called Messana, on one side; Reggio di Calabria, which they called Rhegium, on the other. Similarly, at the southern mouth of the Bosphorus, the Ox-ford, which connects the Black Sea with the Propontis, Chalcedon grew up on the eastern shore, and, on the western, the strategic city of Byzantium, which would not for many centuries be called Constantinople. A few colonies were planted on the coast of Epirus and even of Illyria, as far north as modern Albania. On the French coast of the Mediterranean six colonies sprang up, beginning at Marseilles, the Greek Massilia, and stretching westward. There were three on the northern part of Spain's east coast; three on the coast of what is now Libya; five on the south coast of Asia Minor and in Cyprus. There were even two 'treaty ports' in Egypt itself. In short, colonists created a string of Hellenic cities, whose citizens could be found scattered along the shores of the Mediterranean, and the Black Sea too, like frogs about a pond.[62]

Some of these new and distant Greek city-states remained relatively unimportant except for the grain or fish or timber or other things they could furnish in exchange for oil or wine or woolen cloth, but Western Greece evolved a characteristic colonial life of its own. That life was somehow larger and easier than in Mainland Greece, if only because there was more land. Where cities grew rich, as Sybaris did at a strategic spot on the westernmost shore of the present Gulf of Taranto, there developed a degree of luxury that made the Sybarite a byword in Mainland Greece. The Western Greeks loved athletic competition as much as their cousins in the old country, and regularly sent contestants to the Olympics and the other great religious games. They would never equal the final achievements of Mainland Greece in literature or philosophy or the plastic arts; and they would tend to import their art from home. But they would turn early toward medicine, engineering, and the practical art of rhetoric that fitted one for a political career. All that, however, would be in the future.

The geographical expansion of Mainland Greece and Greece-in-Asia involved three economic stages. In the first, merchant adventurers were scouting for metals and selling petty luxuries to the natives, the barbarians, in the fashion of the Phoenicians, whom they were crowding out of many markets. This was why, according to tradition, the first Greek colony on Italian soil was planted not on the nearest and richest Italian land but at Cumae, north of Naples, where there was trade in metals with the Etruscans farther north; and this was why Cumae remained the northernmost outpost of Hellas in Italy. Later, Neapolis, New City, now Naples, was founded farther south, as so many other cities were, farther southward still, and much nearer the mother-cities at home. For the merchant-adventurer stage of colonization was giving way to the stage of permanent settlements by land-hungry settlers, even where those settlers kept at least one eye on trade. It was only in a third stage that Mainland Greece and Greece-in-Asia effected a division of labor between themselves and the colonies they had sent out. Only then was there heavy commerce. The colonies which the Ionian city-state, Miletus, for example, had planted on the southeastern and northern shores of the Black Sea would greedily buy Milesian woolen fabrics in exchange for wheat, timber, metals, salted fish, and slaves.

In order for this cycle of metal-hunting and trinket trade, of land settlement, and of heavy commerce to complete itself, two very special devices were badly needed and happily found: the art of writing, which the Phoenicians helped the Greeks to invent, and the art of coining money.

From Asia, the Greeks got the practice of coining money. By the early seventh century the kingdom of Lydia, which lay just behind Ionia in the mountains of western Asia Minor, had developed coins out of an earlier exchange token. This token was the bean-shaped 'dump' of electrum, an alloy of gold and silver sometimes called white gold, which the Lydians found in river beds, already blended by nature. The great empires of Egypt, Babylonia, and Assyria had made the transition from cattle as a medium of exchange to metal bars or ingots. But these, though more convenient than cattle, had to be weighed and their purity assayed if they were to fulfill their function. This problem had been met by having the government weigh and assay, and then stamp the metal as a guarantee of its value. The Lydian 'dump' was stamped in this way. But the royal Lydian government improved this little bean-shaped nugget of electrum by flattening it to a disk, placing it on an anvil, and striking it with an intaglio die which impressed a bas-relief design. It was this practice that spread from Lydia, first to neighboring Ionian city-states like Miletus and Samos, but soon to Aegina, the cities of Euboea, and the cities of Mainland Greece.[68] Since gold was scarce in the Greek world, the cities of European Hellas struck their coins from silver. Normally they were imprinted with the symbol of some god.

The spoken, wingèd word had now found its equivalent symbol in the written word; and the bar of metal had found its own equivalent symbol in the coin. These two transformations liberated both word and coin from serious limitations of space. The word could now be heard across the Aegean, across the whole Mediterranean, and to the farthest shore of the Black Sea, wherever another person lived who could read Greek. The coin traveled with greater ease and speed than ever metal bars could. But both symbols, the word and the coin, introduced complicated problems. In theory both were merely means of exchange, in the one case for images and ideas, in the other case for material objects. Together they promoted and enlarged the commerce in ideas, and the commerce in commodities. They should, therefore, have promoted community. But words, whether uttered or written, could lie, as well as tell the truth. Money, at first merely the means that would help a man exchange goods with his neighbor, to the advantage of both, could be turned from a means into an end. The exchange of goods could be carried on for the purpose of making money.

In the Greek city-states, and especially in those with easy access to the sea, coinage wrought a revolution. Slowly men shifted further and further from raising and making the things they used, to making and raising things in order to get coin, since it appeared that coin was the one thing that could always command other men's labor or possessions, whether in Hellas or in foreign lands. This shift produced disastrous consequences for the poor. It was only the rich, which at first meant only the nobles, who had enough surplus goods to acquire a share of the new power that coined money gave. Coin was still scarce, which meant that the few who had got hold of it could demand very high interest from those who needed money. Money developed the division of labor and special skills. The man who had been able in the old days to supply all his own wants, barring acts of the gods which might bring famine or pestilence, now began to need money to buy services as well as goods. The old family system of land ownership gave way to private personal ownership. Farms that had once rented for a fixed share of the crop now rented for a fixed sum of money: if the crop failed, the tenant was lost. And he was literally lost, because his creditor might legally seize, not only his personal possessions, not only the tools with which he labored, but his very person itself. In short, his creditor might sell him as a thing into slavery. When some city-states shifted from grain-growing to vines and olives, and when grain began to be imported from better grain lands abroad, the farmer without capital could not participate in this new division of labor. It took some five years for an olive tree to bear and it took nearer fifteen to get full production. The man without capital could not wait that long for his returns. Finally, since the laws were administered only by the nobles, since they were not even written down and were known only to the nobles, and since the revolution that was ruining so many of the poor was increasing the wealth and

41

power of the nobles, abuses were numerous and conditions were growing steadily more desperate.

The noble, who scorned the peasant because he could not find in him the virtues which he himself prized and was ready to die for, often felt the smoldering hate for the peasant that any normal man would tend to feel for the man he had wronged. In the early, vigorous days of the aristocracy, the noble discharged a genuine social function: the defense of the state and the administration of the state. His privileges were related to those functions and morally supported by them. But now something was happening that he could scarcely have foreseen, something that would rob him of his function and therefore something that would make his position and privileges seem unjust. Moreover, this happened just when the personal relationship that existed between noble and peasant in the old life together on the land was yielding place to the impersonal relationship, the cash nexus, of buyer and seller, of creditor and debtor. Yet it was just that personal relationship which must often have mitigated the inequalities of wealth. Now it was vanishing.

In the economic revolution through which Hellas passed not every man who prospered was a noble. Sometimes a Dustyfoot might through energy or shrewdness or sheer luck acquire some of the new power that movable wealth was introducing into a community where once power had come from land alone. Lacking the prestige of birth, of descent from the gods, of the right to rule the polis, such a merchant was nevertheless winning the prestige of wealth. At last this new power enabled him to play a new role on the field of battle. Around 700,[64] in the cities of Eretria and Chalcis, a new type of soldier appeared: the heavy-armed foot soldier, the hoplite. He fought, not as the half-armed, half-armored member of a rabble of peasants following the mounted nobles, but in a disciplined military formation known as the phalanx. He was able to find enough money to clothe himself in bronze armor, and he fought shield to shield with his hoplite comrades in a solid formation often eight lines deep. He learned to stand firm against pursuit by horsemen. He fought, not like Achilles for the glory of his lineage or himself, but to defend the polis where he lived and throve. It no longer took noble blood to defend that polis; and the hoplite inevitably came to wonder why it should take noble blood to rule it. The aristocratic republic, which in so many city-states had peacefully taken over or forcibly seized the duties and honors of the chieftain-king, now fought a rear-guard action against the new man whom trade had brought to birth, the well-to-do Dustyfoot who could defend his polis and longed to share in its rule to foster his own interests and to protect his way of earning his bread. The use of coin had increased the nobles' power to exploit their peasants' labor, and now it lost the nobles their exclusive power to rule the polis.

Here again, as in the case of so many similar revolutions in other civilizations, the new men lacked the confidence in themselves and in each other necessary to seize the government. But the discontent they generated, when added to the discontent of Dustyfeet less fortunate than themselves, was a standing invitation to some noble, more selfishly ambitious, or more clear-sighted, or merely more just, to lead a revolution. And thus arose the tyrant. In the beginning, it was the tyrant who led the peasant toward freedom.

When these revolutions first occurred, the term tyrant was not a term of abuse or opprobrium. It was morally neutral. The word itself came, as coins did, from the kingdom of Lydia, by way of Ionia.[65] It meant a person who had seized monarchical power by force. In the seventh century, in a number of Greek cities, tyrannies of this sort were established; and for obvious political reasons they favored the opponents of the nobles they had overthrown. They favored commerce and industry, and they might even see fit to lighten the lot of the peasants. Where the chieftain-king's power had rested on personal loyalty, religious sanction, and hallowed custom, the power of the new monarch, the tyrant, rested on popular hatred of the nobles and on money to pay the tyrant's personal bodyguard.

Despite all the Greeks who turned mariner, most Greeks still did what Greeks had done all through the Dark Ages and would keep on doing: they farmed. They found a poet who could speak for them as not even Homer had spoken, Hesiod. Later Greeks might think of him chiefly as the author[66] of the *Theogony*, in which he traced the lineage of the Olympic gods, and thereby expanded the divine lore which men had already learned from the *Iliad* and the *Odyssey*. But his greatest poem was a farmer's, not a warrior's, poem: *Works and Days*. It was written in the epic meter of the *Iliad*, and, although Homer's epics were greater than anything Hesiod ever wrote, *Works and Days* achieved a special greatness of its own.[67] Although the specific "works" described in *Works and Days*

43

are farm tasks, and the "days" discussed are largely those of good omen
or bad omen for farm operations, what Hesiod was really writing about was
justice, human and divine; and work, labor, the lot of man on earth. About
justice and about work he wrote with true poetic passion. The glory and
misery of war that Achilles knew did not directly interest him. Neither
did the "unfruitful sea,"[68] the "grey, discomfortable sea,"[69] which he
thoroughly disliked and feared, nor the restless drive of the explorer to
know. What he knew was the bountiful earth, "the wide-bosomed
Earth,"[70] from whom were descended both gods and men. What he knew,
or thought he knew, was that although once men lived on earth "free
from ills and hard toil,"[71] now they must work or perish. Was it some
dim folk-memory of Minoan wealth and power that led him to sing how
a golden race of men had once "lived like gods without sorrow of heart,
remote and free from toil and grief"[72]? Then had come a silver race. Then
a bronze race of men, who had strong, bronze armor, but no iron, and who
were destroyed by their own hands.[73] Could this, too, be a folk-memory?
A memory of the Mycenaeans, who weakened each other through incessant wars, who had finally fought at Troy, and who had been submerged
and thrown into disorder by the Northern Dorians, a race that according
to tradition had brought in iron? In any case, the bronze race was followed by a generation of "heroes," who also disappeared, but who now
dwelt on the Isles of the Blessed on the shore of the Ocean. At last a
generation of iron appeared, the men whom Hesiod saw about him; and
he cried out:

> Thereafter, would that I were not among the men of the fifth genera-
> tion, but either had died before or been born afterwards. For now truly
> is a race of iron, and men never rest from labor and sorrow by day, and
> from perishing by night.[74]

Centuries of turmoil had succeeded the fall of Mycenae and its world,
centuries of labor and sorrow by day and perishing by night. Those centuries were ending now: many a chieftain-king had founded a settled polis,
and the polis had become a republic, though an aristocratic republic in
which few men ruled, and before long the colonists would go out, and
human existence, at least for those at the top, would become less full of
labor and sorrow. Even for some of the others, it would become in many
ways more significant and more exciting to live. But Hesiod had no way

of knowing all this. *Works and Days* was based on harsh personal experience, not on a colonial expansion that had not even begun. It was the experience of a smallholder, wringing a living from a farm at the foot of Mount Helicon, in southern Boeotia, in the eighth century.[75]

Hesiod's father had been a merchant sailor in the thriving port of Cyme on the coast of Asia Minor, and had failed in business. He salvaged enough to buy a farm, or clear one as a pioneer, here near the village of Ascra, and to leave it on his death to his two sons, Hesiod and Perses. *Works and Days* was addressed directly to Perses and sharply rebuked him for bribing the court of nobles which settled the inheritance. But the poem was also a hymn to Zeus, who ruled the invisible world of the gods as well as the hard world of those men who belonged to a race of iron; to Zeus who loved justice, and who in the long run would punish those who bought and sold crooked judgment. Hesiod was as indignant at being legally robbed of land that was rightfully his as Achilles was when his superior, Agamemnon, robbed him of his meed of honor, the woman Briseis. But he was sure that injustice would be punished. For the Fates

> pursue the transgressions of men and of gods; and these goddesses never cease from their dread anger until they punish the sinner with a sore penalty.[76]

Zeus had

> thrice ten thousand spirits, watchers of mortal men, and these keep watch on judgements and deeds of wrong as they roam, clothed in mist, all over the earth.[77]

Indeed, Justice herself, also

> wrapped in mist, follows to the city and haunts of people, weeping, and bringing mischief to men, even to such as have driven her forth in that they did not deal straitly with her.[78]

It was to right these injustices that Zeus "humbles the proud and raises the obscure."[79]

Hesiod rebuked the nobles for accepting bribes and seizing what was not their own and dealing out crooked justice. He made no explicit objections to government by the Best People. He was a moral reformer, but not a political one. More than either, he was a poet, heavyhearted at man's injustice to his fellow man, and at violence as a substitute for justice.

Heavyhearted, and indignant. On this earth, sang the farmer, man's destiny was to work, and then work. Neither begging nor robbing would substitute for *ergon*, work. This was why he explained to Perses, his brother, how the farmer's work was done and on which days it was likeliest to be best done. The warning of the thrice ten thousand spirits who kept watch on judgments was brusquely addressed to the nobles themselves.

Fighting would not help. Zeus

has ordained this law for men, that fishes and beasts and winged fowls should devour one another, for right is not in them; but to mankind he gave right which proves far the best.[80]

Evil action was easy and the road to it was smooth. "But between us and Goodness the gods have placed the sweat of our brows."[81] "Both gods and men are angry with a man who lives idle."[82] Wealth should not be seized: "god-given wealth is much better."[83] This was why he urged his rapacious brother to "work upon work,"[84] and to "work the work which the gods ordained for men."[85]

As for *Eris*, or Strife, she was not one goddess but two, a good Eris and a bad. The Eris who led neighbor to vie with neighbor in productive work was wholesome for men.[86] But Hesiod hated the Eris who fostered war, the Eris Achilles followed, as he hated the sea Odysseus followed. And in the *Theogony*, a poem in which, taught by the Muses whom he invoked, he told which god was descended from which, or married which, or gave birth to which, he told also where this second, evil Eris came from and what her evil progeny was. This second and "hard-hearted Strife"[87] was born of Night, who also bore Deceit and hateful Age.

But abhorred Strife bare painful Toil and Forgetfulness and Famine and tearful Sorrows, Fightings also, Battles, Murders, Manslaughters, Quarrels, Lying Words, Disputes, Lawlessness and Ruin, all of one nature . . .[88]

Despite the hardness, the toughness, and the peasant grumbling about the crops and the farmer's life, *Works and Days* could have been written only by a man who loved the earth, this earth that he was forced to till if he would eat. The country images of the weather, the hills, the birds, the flowers kept bursting through the dour descriptions of man's plight. In the *Theogony* Hesiod[89] said he saw a divine vision. The Muses, who danced on soft feet atop Mount Helicon about the altar of Zeus, were in the habit of going abroad by night, veiled in thick mist, to utter their song.

And one day they taught Hesiod glorious song while he was shepherding his lambs under holy Helicon, and this word first the goddesses said to me—the Muses of Olympus, daughters of Zeus who holds the aegis:

"Shepherds of the wilderness, wretched things of shame, mere bellies, we know how to speak many false things as though they were true; but we know, when we will, to utter true things."

So said the ready-voiced daughters of great Zeus, and they plucked and gave me a rod, a shoot of sturdy laurel, a marvelous thing, and breathed into me a divine voice to celebrate things that shall be and things that were aforetime; and they bade me sing of the race of the blessed gods that are eternally, but ever to sing of themselves both first and last.[90]

They were veiled, as the Homeric gods so often were, in thick mist; and none would expect a wretched thing of shame, a mere belly, to pierce through that mist with his eyes. But Hesiod did.[91] Nor would one expect the Muses to hand him the rod that would authorize him to speak, that would literally inspire him with a divine voice. But this the Muses did. And the divine voice celebrated things that would yet be and things that had already been.

This, of course, was Hesiod's interpretation of what happened to him that night at the foot of holy Helicon. But he himself stated that the goddesses were veiled in a thick mist. The later Greeks, whose memories were the *Iliad* and the *Odyssey*, firmly believed that, after Homer, the other great authority on the immortal gods was Hesiod. And the manner of life the small aristocratic republics fought to defend and carried in their hollow ships to the other small cities that they founded all over the Mediterranean world was a manner of life shown to them by the gods, largely through Homer and Hesiod. That manner of life would make the Greeks an inspired race and not mere bellies and wretched things of shame. And thanks in large measure to Hesiod, they would learn not only to die gloriously, not only to search ceaselessly for man's home, but to work the work which the gods ordained for men. Indeed, some of them would even learn, in the very midst of war and slavery and oppression, to accept the law that Zeus had ordained for men, that they differed from fishes and beasts and winged fowls, who devoured one another, for right was not in them; but to man he gave right, which proved far the best.

47

THE LAWGIVERS,
LYCURGUS AND SOLON

IT WAS on the Asian shore of the Aegean, not on the European, that the Hellenes first emerged from the Dark Age that followed the Dorian invasion. In Europe, where Minos the Cretan lawgiver had become a confused memory and where even Tiryns and Mycenae had turned into legend, men had re-entered the womb of their mother, the earth. And from that spacious womb a new agrarian, feudal society had been born, lived out its rough childhood, and was still uncouth when the cities of Asian Greece began to develop something that Minos himself would have recognized as a good life for men. The Dorian invasion that had thrown Mycenaean Greece into chaos had driven many of its victims to flee across the Aegean to the nearby coast of Asia Minor. Because of the many islands, the refugees at no time needed to lose sight of land. In Asia Minor they found a balmier climate than the one they had left, and a relatively wide and fertile littoral to settle. Some of the refugees were Achaeans, some were the Pelasgians whom the Achaeans had conquered. They may well have taken with them a larger share of Mycenaean ideas and skills than could survive in Mainland Greece. On the Asian shore they may well have found more of those ideas and skills. In the north, Aeolians settled the littoral of Phrygia and Mysia, and their settlements came to comprise Aeolis. In the center, Ionians who would claim to have sailed from Attica founded settlements that came to be called Ionia. But all of these refugees, and even a thrust of Dorians who followed the Cyclades islands to found Doris on the southernmost portion of this same inviting shore, were exposed to the fertilizing influences of the great and ancient civilizations of the Middle East, like Babylonia and Assyria. Their new home turned out, therefore, to be a hothouse in which their own skills, images, and ideas went through a rapid forcing stage. Ionia, especially, developed powerful and wealthy and luxurious cities when the city-states of Mainland Greece were by comparison small and rustic communities. In Europe, on the other hand, Greeks of the young cities for long came into contact only with their uncouth cousins to the north, such as the tribesmen of Macedonia or Epirus. Even in the western Mediterranean the Greek colonists met mostly with barbarous tribes and confronted few civilized foreigners except their trade competitors: seafaring men of Phoenicia, Carthaginians, Etruscans.

One of the Homeric Hymns, this one the Hymn to the Delian Apollo, described a religious festival of the Ionians in the Isle of Delos, the land the god loved best:

> for there the long robed Ionians gather in your honour with their children and shy wives: mindful, they delight you with boxing and dancing and song, so often as they hold their gathering. A man would say that they were deathless and unaging if he should then come upon the Ionians so met together. For he would see the graces of them all, and would be pleased in heart gazing at the men and well-girded women with their swift ships and great wealth.[92]

A goodly portion of this great wealth was concentrated in the Ionian city of Miletus. Strategically situated on a promontory, this city had four sheltered harbors and easy communications inland by the Meander River. There was flat, fertile land for wheat, flanked by hillside vineyards and orchards. On the plateau behind, there was ample pasturage for the sheep whose wool nourished the city's famous cloth manufacture. With a mixed but thoroughly Hellenized population, Miletus became by the sixth century the busiest and most populous of Greek cities anywhere. For two centuries Milesians had colonized the Black Sea. They had established a special trading post on the coast of Egypt. Everywhere they traded their famous goods for the food, the raw materials, and the slave labor they required. They processed the skins and precious metals of neighboring Lydia, the wool of Phrygia, the hemp of Colchis at the foot of the Caucasus, and iron from the Chalybes, a little south of Colchis. The Milesians turned out furniture, especially beds. Except in Mainland Greece, their customers not only wanted pottery; they wanted pots that were filled with oil or wine. Wealthy customers in Western Greece—especially southern Italy and Sicily—bid for Milesian rugs and the Milesians' magnificent purple cloth.

In the sixth century this great wealth of the long-robed Ionians came under the gentle protectorate of a partially Hellenized monarch, Croesus of Lydia. The Ionians had steadily refused to convert the Panionian League, a primarily religious association, into some sort of political and military unit capable of defending them. So, one by one, Croesus had conquered their cities. Lydian garrisons took over the Ionian cities, and those cities paid Croesus an annual tribute; otherwise, they governed themselves. Croesus enforced a peace between them, a peace which their mutual jealousy had hitherto prevented. Their rustic cousins across the Aegean might affect to despise them for surrendering their freedom; but they admired them, too, and envied them their wealth. The Ionians loved money and luxury and elegance. In their trailing robes, fastened with golden grasshopper pins, their arms loaded with finely wrought gold and jewels, the men promenaded along their cities' handsome avenues. Their wives, escorted by many slaves, displayed their elaborate costumes, their hair and their breasts perfumed. Pleasure had conquered them quite as much as Croesus had; but, while they feasted and sang, Croesus descried a mounting danger in the East.

However, Ionia was more than pleasure, and more than business. In the plastic arts, in architecture, in music, in poetry, in natural philosophy Ionians pioneered; and their dialogue in the arts and sciences penetrated Mainland Greece and involved the Western Greeks as well. Mainland Greece was still building Doric temples out of wood and brick long after

Ionia had learned to use marble. The Ionian sculptor likewise learned to use marble, and to cast hollow bronze statues too. The sculpture helped the architect develop the narrow, fluted marble column with the gracefully voluted Ionic capital. He invented the caryatid, or marble statue of a woman, placed to serve as a temple column; and, in order to portray the long-robed Ionians, he pioneered in the study of elaborate drapery. At its worst, his art struck the Mainlander as luxurious, fussy, prettified, effeminate; but at its best, the Mainlander found it gracious, smiling, delicate, and utterly charming. Throughout the sixth century, Mainland Greece went to school to Ionian sculptors and architects.

Greece-in-Asia, which had dreamed the first great poems, the epics of Homer, now originated another kind of poetry, a poetry of short songs sung to a lyre, or to a cithara, or to a flute. In the case of the choral lyric, both musical notes and dance steps went with the poem. The poet departed from the dactylic hexameter of Homer and Hesiod and invented various metrical forms. He no longer sang, one after another, tales about the great heroes of the past. Increasingly, the poet talked about himself, about the deeds he himself had done, the passions he himself had suffered.

This poetry could be savagely satirical and morally revolutionary. To a Greek, for example, to throw away one's shield in battle was the very hallmark of cowardice. Yet in the seventh century Archilochus of Paros could cry:

> The shield I left because I must, poor blameless armament! beside a bush, gives joy now to some Saian, but myself I have saved. What care I for that shield. It shall go with a curse. I'll get me another e'en as good.[93]

Or he could be tersely witty:

> The Fox knoweth many things, the Hedgehog one great thing.[94]

Later in the same seventh century, the Aeolian poet, Alcaeus of rich Lesbos, sang his aristocratic disdain of the new merchant class, in which "money maketh man,"[95] his aristocratic hatred of the tyrant Myrsilus, and his savage exultation at news of the tyrant's death:

> Now must a man get drunk and pledge with strength since Myrsilus is dead.[96]

The poems of Alcaeus called on his friends to drink sweet wine, to pile up the fire while a winter storm raged outside—or in summer to drink wine in the grateful shadow of some sheltering rock.

Early in the sixth century Ionia gave Hellas Anacreon of Teos, although a Persian invasion would eventually drive him to emigrate from Ionia to Thrace. A love affair with a Thracian girl led Anacreon to sing naughtily:

> Pray, why do you look askance at me, my Thracian filly, and shun me so resolutely as though I knew nothing of my art? I would have you to know I could bridle you right well and take rein and ride you about the turning-post of the course. But instead you graze in the meadows and frisk and frolic to your heart's content; for you have not a clever breaker to ride you.[97]

Anacreon visited the court of Polycrates, the celebrated tyrant of Samos, who also played patron to a poet of southern Italy, Ibycus of Rhegium. When the Persians captured and crucified Polycrates, Anacreon went to the court of Hipparchus, tyrant of Athens, where he charmed men with his drinking songs and love lyrics. Like so many of the melodious, witty, sensual poems Ionian poets sang, Anacreon's poems were haunted by the remembrance of oncoming Death. But he lived to be eighty-five.

Neither Anacreon nor Alcaeus nor Archilochus, with all their wit, with all their beauty of image, could match the torrential force of an Aeolian poet, born like Alcaeus in lovely Lesbos. But this other Lesbian was a woman, Sappho, a friend of Alcaeus, an aristocrat like him. She was born about 612. In Lesbos she directed a sort of school, based on the cult of Aphrodite, in which girls were educated and prepared for marriage. Sappho's deep attachments to her young charges would survive only in slight fragments, but in fragments burning with passion. A Mainland Greek might find Lesbos sophisticated, worldly-wise, half-mocking, pleasure-loving; at best, gracious, smiling, melodious. But these few remaining words out of Lesbos, sung by one woman, would always live, searing and terrible words, words inspired by the great Goddess of Love, so that it was rightly that Alcaeus, and others too, called Sappho "holy." It was as if an Aeolian woman had suddenly reminded her hearers that Aphrodite was first worshiped in Eastern lands and that the soul of Asian Greece was most truly itself when it stood stricken, not indeed by the pleasant desire for wine, women, and song, but by all-destroying love. For Asia Minor knew, more clearly than Mainland Greece, the frightening power of this Great

Goddess, whether men called her Aphrodite, or Astarte, or Ishtar. It was this dread goddess that holy Sappho served. She wrote:

> It is to be a God, methinks, to sit before you and listen close by to the sweet accents and winning laughter which have made the heart in my breast beat fast, I warrant you. When I look on you, Brocheo, my speech comes short or fails me quite, I am tongue-tied; in a moment a delicate fire has overrun my flesh, my eyes grow dim and my ears sing, the sweat runs down me and a trembling takes me altogether, till I am as green and pale as the grass, and death itself seems not very far away. . . .[98]

And again:

> The Moon is gone
> And the Pleiads set,
>   Midnight is nigh;
> Time passes on,
> And passes; yet
> Alone I lie.[99]

Ionia and Lesbos gave Greece these early poets, but Ionia gave her also her earliest philosophy. For most of her first philosophers either lived or wrote in Ionia; or left Ionia to teach in Mainland Greece or in the West; or came to Ionia from elsewhere. At Miletus, Thales, Anaximander, and Anaximenes devoted themselves to natural philosophy, to a search for a common material principle or base to which the varied and changing phenomenal world about them could be reduced. Pythagoras fled Polycrates' tyranny in Samos to teach in Croton, in southern Italy, and to found there a sort of ascetic order of both men and women. This Pythagorean order for a while governed Croton. Its master taught the necessity of purifying the soul, largely through intellectual discipline. He sought to explain the phenomenal world by applying mathematics to it. Also to Western Greece, to Elea, came Xenophanes from his native Colophon; he was another political refugee. Although Xenophanes admitted more than one god in his pantheon, he was certain that one of those gods was supreme over all others. He blamed Homer and Hesiod, who had "ascribed unto the Gods all that is reproach and blame in the world of men, stealing and adultery and deceit."[100] He declared that rainbows were not the goddess Iris but merely "a cloud, purple and red and yellow to view."[101]

And he scorned the Greeks' habit of making their gods in their own image:

> Now if horses or oxen or lions had hands or power to paint and make the works of art that men make, then would horses give their Gods horse-like forms in painting or sculpture, and oxen ox-like forms, even each after its own kind.[102]

And:

> The Aethiop saith that his Gods are snub-nosed and black, the Thracian that his have blue eyes and red hair . . .[103]

"There's one God," wrote Xenophanes again, "greatest among Gods and men, who is like to mortals neither in form nor mind."[104]

In Ephesus, Heraclitus speculated on the unity-in-change of the world about him. Some of these Ionian thinkers wrote in verse; but in the sixth century others became the earliest writers of Greek prose, a medium that was proving useful to another intellectual venture, the first writing of history.

All in all, Greece-in-Asia, and especially Ionia, had by the end of the sixth century played an extraordinary role in the history of Hellas. These Asian Greeks had moved from the simplicity of children to adult awareness, and sometimes even to middle-aged disillusionment, in three brief centuries. That they made that passage early was natural, given their contact with the old ways and thoughts and dreams of Asia, an Asia past her full bloom. Ionian artists, Ionian poets, Ionian musicians, Ionian philosophers would scatter westward through the Greek world and guide that tardier world's first steps toward more beautiful images, more expert crafts, profounder thoughts. If it was primarily in Ionia that the Hellenic world had encountered the immemorial ways of Asia, how would Asia affect the political life of Hellas? That question was answered, at least provisionally, when Croesus, the wealthy and half-Hellenized king of Lydia, made himself suzerain of the semi-autonomous city-states of Greece-in-Asia. Politically, it seemed, Asian Greeks were destined to be ruled by non-Hellenic Asians. Meanwhile, Mainland Greece had received the gift of Ionia's vision. And Mainland Greece was more sheltered than Ionia, from annexation by non-Hellenic military states, from the too swift absorption of non-Hellenic ideas, and from the confusion bred by wealth too speedily acquired.

By the sixth century no other city-state in Mainland Greece enjoyed such prestige as Lacedaemon, or Sparta. In the first place Sparta directly ruled a larger territory than even Athens, her nearest competitor. Hollow Lacedaemon, the land from which Helen of Troy had fled with Paris when she deserted her husband, King Menelaus, for that Trojan prince, lay in the southeast portion of the Peloponnese, between two mountain ranges. Geologically, Lacedaemon had been a lake bottom. When the Dorian invasion came, a band of Dorians seized this fertile valley and united four small villages into a polis, officially "the City of the Lacedaemonians," informally "Sparta." The entire territory which the Spartiates first governed was named Laconia. Two leading families shared the government: from early times Sparta had two kings, one from each of these two families.

As the number of Spartans increased and as land grew scarce, Sparta followed the usual pattern of the Greek polis: the nobility managed to monopolize most of the land. But Sparta did not attempt to solve her problem as did Corinth, another leading Dorian state, by repeatedly sending out colonies. Instead, toward the end of the eighth century, she attacked Messenia, across the mountains to her west, a populous state with even more fertile farm land than Laconia had. The First Messenian War took some twenty years of hard fighting. The dispossessed Messenians were subjected. As Sparta's fighting poet, the lame Tyrtaeus, would later put it, they were "galled with great burdens like asses, bringing to their lords under grievous necessity a half of all the fruit of the soil."[105] Each Spartiate family was assigned its portion of the land and its fruits in addition to what the family had been assigned at home in Laconia. But violence between conqueror and conquered broke out again: Messenia revolted about 640 and was with difficulty quelled in the Second Messenian War; and by the sixth century Sparta had been transformed into an aristocratic, conservative state unique in Greek history.

According to tradition this conservative state had been shaped by a great lawgiver named Lycurgus, who had lived long before, though tradition was uncertain as to just how long before. Lycurgus' father, one Eurypon, was one of the two kings of Sparta. In Sparta too, the usual tensions developed between the wealthy landowner and the poorer citizen; and Lycurgus' father was stabbed while trying to make peace during a riot. Lycurgus' elder brother, Polydectes, inherited his family's crown; but Polydectes himself died shortly afterwards without issue, and the crown passed to Lycurgus. Then Lycurgus discovered that his brother's widow was with child and he insisted that, if this posthumous child of the late king should be a boy, this boy must reign; he himself would step aside and would act as regent to his nephew-king. The child did turn out to be a boy, and Lycurgus did step aside and was greatly admired for acting on his just decision.

But there were also Spartans who accused him of secretly aiming to recover royal power. To avoid suspicion, Lycurgus determined to travel abroad until his nephew should come of age, marry, and beget a son to succeed him. He traveled in Crete, the storied land of Minos, the law-giver.[106] From Crete, with its excellent laws, he voyaged to luxurious Ionia, in order to understand what happened when the laws of a polis did not impose a simple and severe regime on its citizens. There he discovered the poems of Homer, which he copied to take home with him to Sparta. Some historians claimed that he visited Egypt, too, and one even insisted that he had gone as far as India and talked with the gymnosophists, or naked philosophers, there. Meanwhile, this inquiring traveler, this ex-regent of Sparta who could have remained king had he been a little less scrupulous, was longed for in his own polis. The people considered their present kings undistinguished and lacking in leadership and wanted Lycurgus back. Even the kings wished for his return, on the chance that he could control their subjects' insolence. From Egypt or from India or from elsewhere Lycurgus returned. Judging that Spartan society was sick and that only the most drastic reforms would save the polis, he went to Delphi and consulted Apollo. The priestess gave him an oracle:

> Dear to Zeus thou hast come to my well-stored temple, Lycurgus,
> Dear to Zeus and to all who dwell in the courts of Olympus.
> Art thou a man or a god? 'Tis a god I deem thee, Lycurgus.[107]

According to one tradition, Apollo then gave him a constitution for Sparta. He returned to Sparta, put down the unruly populace, strengthened the aristocracy, and established his new order. He retained Sparta's two kings, who continued to perform the offices of high priest and, at least to some extent, those of supreme judge, and who commanded Sparta's army in the field. But he set up also, by a *rhetra*, or compact, especially obtained from Delphi, a Council of Elders, or Senate, the *Gerousia*. This Senate contained the two kings and twenty-eight other members at least sixty years old, elected for life. The Senate wielded enormous powers, especially in foreign affairs. It was the Spartan version of the aristocratic council which replaced kingship in most Hellenic states. As for the restive populace, those men over thirty formed the *Apella,* or Assembly. They could initiate no laws. They cast no ballots. They did not deliberate. They merely acclaimed by shouts those measures of the Senate that they approved. Indeed, at some period later than Lycurgus' day, two kings of Sparta were said to have changed the famous compact so that, if the popular Assembly tried to amend the laws submitted to it, the Senate could dismiss the Assembly. Apollo, the Spartans claimed, sanctioned this change too. But now the Senate grew tyrannical and, more than a century after Lycurgus, the kings managed to establish a board of five Ephors, or Overseers, to check the insolence of the Senate and to defend the rights of all Spartans. The Overseers were elected by the people, from the people, for a term of one year.

Lycurgus also judged that one of the principal causes of the disorder Sparta had suffered from was the fact that land was concentrating in the hands of the rich. His remedy was heroic: he would do away with the bad eris, or strife, of competitive money-making, of greed, and luxury, and recover the good eris, the competition for honor. He persuaded his fellow citizens to turn over all land to the polis. Then he assigned equal lots of land to all Spartiates and equal lots of other land in Laconia to the *Perioeci,* or Dwellers-round-about. The subject population, what survived of the pre-Dorian stock,[108] became state serfs called Helots. These Helots were assigned to the lots of the Spartiates and were compelled to produce a modest, fixed amount of food for their masters. All beyond their masters' rations they might keep for themselves.

But Lycurgus knew that money was the great cause of the tensions between rich and poor that had threatened to destroy the polis, and here too his remedy was heroic. He caused all gold and silver coin to be withdrawn and he issued in its place a clumsy iron money, too heavy and of too little value to invite hoarding or other misuse. The new currency had the further advantage of isolating Sparta from the merchants of luxuries, the teachers of rhetoric, the wandering soothsayers, the pimps, the goldsmiths, the silversmiths, in short from all those who had swarmed in from abroad when there had been real money, current throughout Greece, to be made there. As for craftsmen, Lycurgus turned their attention to the few useful

57

articles like chairs, tables, and beds that his new-style Spartan would still need: let them make these few things beautiful and not waste their time on baubles.

Tradition recounted that the rich were outraged by losing the luxuries which gold and silver had once bought for them; that they stoned Lycurgus from the market place, and that he fled to a temple. Before he reached sanctuary, a youth named Alcander smote him with his staff and blinded one eye. When the Spartans saw him bloody and half-blinded, they repented, and delivered Alcander to him to punish. Lycurgus commended them, led Alcander home, dismissed his servants, and bade Alcander tend his needs. In doing so, Alcander discovered that Lycurgus was neither rough nor self-willed, but gentle, calm, self-disciplined, and diligent. He became Lycurgus' devoted disciple. Moreover, the contrite Spartans ceased henceforth from carrying staves into their Assembly.

Lycurgus counted on training and ingrained habits, rather than legal statutes, to maintain his and Apollo's polis. One of his Delphic compacts even forbade written laws, when once his basic rhetras had established *eunomia*, the state of being well-lawed. Another rhetra, rather than forbidding luxurious dwellings, forbade the citizen to build his house with any tools but the ax and the saw. With no fine house to furnish, who would want silver-footed couches, purple coverlets, or gold drinking cups? Another compact forbade frequent expeditions against the same foe; why school that foe to fight better next time? Tradition would ascribe all these compacts to Delphi and to Apollo, who knew the will of his father, Zeus. They were *themis*, the will of the gods, made *diké*, or human justice, by the mediating wisdom of Lycurgus the lawgiver.

When his polis had been reconstituted and was healthily functioning, Lycurgus announced to his fellow Spartans that one great matter remained, and on this matter he must go to Delphi again. Then he made them swear an oath to keep his laws until his return, and set out for Delphi. There he sacrificed to Apollo and asked if his laws were good. Apollo answered that they were, and that the city would continue to be held in highest honor so long as it remained faithful to the laws of Lycurgus. Lycurgus wrote down this oracle and sent it back to Sparta. He had performed man's highest function: by translating *themis* into *diké*, divine law into human law, for the common good of his fellow men, he had in some sense joined earth to heaven. His one remaining problem was to hold his fellow men to his divinely dictated compacts; and, since they had sworn not to subvert his laws until he returned to Sparta, he could bind his countrymen for all time only by ending his life. He therefore abstained from food until he died of starvation. His body was brought home to his polis and buried. According to tradition, a bolt of that lightning which only Zeus could wield struck his tomb. The Spartans built a temple to him and worshiped him as a god.

This, men said, was how Sparta had won her eunomia, her state of being well-lawed. It was true that on many points traditions conflicted; but at least as myth they were true: they contained the high poetic truth that Homer's tale of Achilles contained. In part, at least, they were supported by historical fact, as Homer's Achilles was.

Sparta had never turned to the sea, as Corinth had done. Corinth, like Sparta, was a Dorian state; but Corinth straddled an isthmus, with a port on either side. Her port of Nisaea looked toward rich Ionia and the Aegean trade; her port of Pagae, toward Italy, Sicily, and all the Western Greeks; and her famous *diolkos*, a track with rollers for moving ships across the high ground between, connected two seas that beckoned forth to trade. No wonder Corinth became for a time the leading center of trade in Mainland Greece. No wonder she sent out colonies that grew to be important cities and even to be rivals of their mother-city. But Sparta's coast was bare of good harbors, and much of it lay between two capes, Malea and Taenarum, which all Greek sailors dreaded. Indeed, Cape Taenarum was one of the entrances to Hades.[109]

Nevertheless, in the seventh century Sparta was open to ideas and skills from many lands. She welcomed foreigners. She had relations with Rhodes, Cyprus, Cyrene. Samos aided Sparta in her second struggle with Messenia. The powerful kingdom of Lydia sought her friendship. Sparta practiced the arts of peace too: she had her own architects, her celebrated potters, her weavers, her leather-workers, her metal-workers, her sculptors in wood, although many of these artists were indeed foreign-born. Like rich Miletus, she dyed purple cloth. She had her famous temples, like the Brazen House of Athana—as the Spartan called Athena in his broad Dorian Greek. Sparta's dancers, her singers, her musicians were renowned. Indeed, the choral lyric flourished at Sparta as nowhere else. It was, for example, for Spartan maidens that Alcman, although he came from Sardis in Lydia, wrote his famous choral lyrics. Spartans won numerous victories at the various panhellenic games. At the Olympics between 720 and 576, out of eighty-one athletes who won the victor's laurel crown, forty-six were reported to be sons of Sparta.

That was in the eighth and seventh centuries, long after the period to which tradition assigned Lycurgus. Yet by the sixth century, the arts seemed to disappear and the laws of Lycurgus were firmly entrenched. By then the City of the Lacedaemonians contained three classes of men. First came the Spartiates, who ruled and fought but never labored. Next came the Dwellers-round-about, who governed their own cities, but were forced to pay tribute to Sparta, to farm the royal domains and temple domains, and to serve in the Spartiates' army in the lower ranks. These Dwellers-round-about were forbidden to intermarry with their Spartiate masters. They earned their living by farming, raising stock, fishing, mining; by producing woolen cloth, lumber, and pottery; and above all by supplying the army. They held a monopoly of all the business life of the state, such as still existed; and some of them acquired wealth. Lastly came the Helots, or serfs, owned by the polis and each assigned to a Spartiate to farm the piece of land allotted for his support. The Helot's master could neither sell him nor free him, since he belonged to the state. He was forced to deliver to his master annually an amount of barley, of fruit, of olive oil, and of wine sufficient to free his master of all economic functions. But since his master was required to live simply, this placed no heavy burden on the Helot. The rest of what he produced he kept, and some Helots were quite well off. The Helot might be compelled to follow his Spartiate master to war, as a servant or even as a light-armed infantryman; but if he was, he was allowed to pillage freely.

To each his function. Whether or not the relations of these three classes reflected in part the original Dorian conquest, those relations were by the sixth century essentially relations of force with a minimum of consent. It is true that, at least in theory, all classes served the state. It is true that the dominant class received for its service honor, danger, no private property, harsh discipline, a daily and arduous military training, and stark subsistence. But the Dwellers-round-about were at their mercy and were looked down upon; the Helots were held under by a reign of terror. The Helots might, indeed, eat better food than their Spartiate masters, but they had no rights at law whatever. They were forbidden to carry arms except on campaign. They were forbidden to assemble after nightfall.

Once a year the five Overseers proclaimed a state of siege under which any Spartiate was permitted to murder a Helot with impunity.[110] Young Spartiates hunted down Helots at night as part of their military training. A secret police, known as the *Krypteia*, watched the Helots constantly for signs of revolt and quietly murdered any serf who seemed likely to start trouble.

Sixth-century Hellas was still a basically aristocratic society, and the Greek aristocrats' forebears, whether Achaean or Dorian, had been hardy Northern barbarians, who had fought their way into Mycenaean Greece and had ultimately wrecked a civilization. In the Dark Age that followed they had become landed nobles, fighting, ruling, and living on the labor of those whose lives they had spared. Their image was Achilles, the descendant of Zeus, who chose a brief life and the immortality of fame over a long life of ease—Achilles, who chose, not to live long, but to live well, and to obey his father's command "to be ever the best and to excel all other men."[111] But the sea, trade, and money had softened these nobles and, in many cities, even robbed them of the right to rule. Here, now, was Sparta, which had restored Achillean glory to the polis, and had created a school of virtue—of aristocratic virtue. She had placed courage in battle first. But she had also banned intemperance, the love of pleasure that had so largely transformed the warrior class elsewhere. She had forbidden gold and silver and had continued the use of her ancient iron money. The gay Ionian poets and musicians were gone from Sparta, and poetry had been put to its proper use: the inculcation of the aristocratic virtues. Her lame poet-general, Tyrtaeus, had sung:

> For 'tis a fair thing for a good man to fall and die fighting in the van for his native land ... to a young man all is seemly enough, so long as he have the noble bloom of lovely youth, aye a marvel he for men to behold, and desirable unto women, so long as ever he be alive, and fair in like manner when he be fallen in the vanguard. So let each man bite his lip with his teeth and abide firm-set astride upon the ground.[112]

Let Dwellers-round-about and Helots fear pain and follow pleasure! Shorn of private property and taught to obey the law at all costs, was the Spartiate not the just man? Practical, shrewd, and even cunning, could he not fairly be considered wise?

Was not Hellas right to admire a kind of man who was fair in his dealings with his fellow citizens, self-controlled, brave unto death, pious? And this in a world so full of men who were unfair, greedy, cowardly, and foolish? If Lycurgus' laws were not the best in Hellas, why could no other army in the Hellenic world stand up to the Spartans in battle? To do so would be to count on green troops against a seasoned and expert regular army, the only regular army of any size in the Greek world. In other Hellenic states it was not only the aristocrats who looked on the City of the Lacedaemonians as the school of Hellas, even though it was a school that most men would have lacked the courage to attend.

Hellas could admire Sparta all the more because, around 550, under the guidance of one of her famous Overseers, Chilon, she ceased her aggressive expansion and intervened in other Hellenic states only to help put down tyrants and restore freedom—the traditional freedom of the nobles, who were normally pro-Spartan. Her policy, domestic and foreign, became a stubborn rear-guard action against change. Old ways were best. A nation of soldiers, she avoided wars wherever she could with honor. Could any war be fought without leaving an enemy at her back—her sullen Helots? And in that sea of Helots, there in hollow Lacedaemon, watchful Sparta lay, proud that she was unwalled. Or rather, proud that her only wall consisted of the tough, willing bodies of her ceaselessly drilled citizens, bodies trained to obey by a city that claimed to be a school of moral virtue.

The man who was born into that school passed through many ordeals. When he was born, he was presented not only to his father—as were Greek babies elsewhere—to decide whether he was to live or die; here, the elders of his father's tribe had to decide also. Would he make a strong man? Would his father's allotment and its fixed yield suffice to support this newcomer? If he was spared, he was turned over to his mother until he was seven—for his father lived, not at home, but among his fellow soldiers. At seven he was placed, along with other little boys, in the hands of a young man to train. There followed a rigorous instruction and test after test. If successful, at the age of twenty he too was placed in charge of a group of boys to train. He taught them to bear pain, to speak only when spoken to, and then only to the point, to respect their elders, to obey absolutely, to harden their bodies, to eat sparingly, to forage by night for any additional food they might need, and to suffer flogging if caught— not because they had stolen but because they had clumsily allowed themselves to be detected. Lycurgus, noting that it was rivalry which produced good athletes at the games and good choruses, had determined to match the young men of Sparta "in an eris of valor,"[113] in that kind of eris that was dearest to the gods, and in the highest sense political—the eris that would set the standard of a brave man's conduct, and in which each party would exert itself to the end that it might never fall below its best, and that, when the time came, every member of it might support the Polis with all his might.

When a young man became a trainer of boys, he applied for admission to an eating club, for Lycurgus had decreed that all Spartan citizens should mess together daily, on the simplest of food, and in groups or clubs of about fifteen members. A young trainer could gain admission to a club only by the consent of all its members, but once admitted he would belong to his club for forty years, if he lived that long, unless degraded for cowardice or inability to keep up his subscription. At mess, the trainer had the right to eat Lycurgus' black broth, which was said to be palatable only to those who had first plunged into the cold waters of the River Eurotas.

To the club mess-tables the boys in training were brought as part of their education. There they heard the conversation of men who lived hard lives and were proud of it, who knew how to die but not how to surrender. Laconians prided themselves on speaking laconically, and they treasured and quoted terse, pithy, acid repartee, and the rough, soldierly jest that a soldier should know how to take. If war came, the members of each club would march off together to the sound of the flute, wearing heavy bronze armor, a crimson[114] tunic, and a plumed helmet, their hair long in the old way, and on their lips perhaps one of Tyrtaeus' marching songs.

Now a full-fledged member of the army, a young man could hope to earn promotion by serving with distinction. If his performance was brilliant, he might even gain membership in the special royal guard, the Three Hundred. If he married, the State would make sure that he married a strong and healthy woman, able to bear future soldiers, nor could he quit his barracks to sleep at home until he was thirty. If he failed to beget children, he might invite a companion to sire children for him. His wife, who had herself received strenuous athletic training in order to fit her to mother strong future soldiers, would be expected to consent to be loaned out in this fashion. If the men went off to war, their wives assumed considerable political responsibilities in their absence. At sixty, the Spartiate would be released at last from his military service, would live at home, and would be eligible for that highest elective honor, membership in the Senate.

There was room in this somewhat hierarchical society for a perverse brutality, but could not its admirers claim that brutality existed everywhere? There was also room for the kind of immortality Achilles sought and perhaps for a better kind than he sought. For besides the individual immortality of deathless fame for heroism in battle, there was a subtler ideal of immortality: one might die oneself, but that would not so much matter if one's own death served the continuing life of Sparta, the City of the Lacedaemonians. To that second aim all had been sacrificed: pleasure, even bare comfort, gaiety, gentleness, most of the beauty of the arts, much of the free motion of the human mind. But, in return, the Spartiate achieved the heroic life of danger, the taut will, the sense of triumph that drove the daring horseman to choose the dangerous horse. The horse that Sparta was riding was each Spartan's own subordinates; was Sparta's restless allies; was jealous, neighboring Argos, with memories of her mighty, Mycenaean past; was the rebellious Helots, sullenly dreaming of freedom or rising in desperate revolt; was each man's own fears, each man's own appetites, conquered at last or at least cowering in silence. Living under this tension, a man gained the respectful companionship of brave and expert warriors. A man gained Sparta, a city like no other.

In the seventh century the aristocratic republic of Athens governed more territory than any other state in Hellas except Sparta. But, whereas the Dorians who settled Sparta had subjected by military conquest first Laconia and then neighboring Messenia, Athens had long ago persuaded the rulers of the various small communities throughout Attica to merge their governments with that of Athens.[115] The citizens of those communities received full rights as citizens of Athens. The Athenian government now controlled some thousand square miles, although about two-fifths of it was mountainous[116] and therefore yielded little but timber, charcoal for fuel, and some pasturage. This decision of Attica to unite may have been partly responsible for the Athenian legend that the people of Attica had always lived there. Partly responsible, too, was the fact that the destructive Dorian conquest, which had created Sparta, had bypassed Attica—perhaps because the Attic land was conspicuously poorer than some of the areas the Dorians seized, such as Laconia and the even richer Messenia.

Although less rich in good land than hollow Lacedaemon, Attica possessed what Laconia signally lacked—a number of excellent harbors. Moreover, it was a peninsula thrust into the Aegean and therefore thrust toward Asia Minor and rich Ionia. Attic traditions agreed with Ionian that it was from Attica that the Ionians had emigrated to Asia Minor. Athens had sent out no colonies in the eighth or seventh century. When the sea did at last call her to trade, Miletus in Ionia and her own near neighbors, Corinth, Chalcis, and Aegina, were already trading far and wide.

As with all the more advanced Hellenic cities, Athens had moved early from a monarchy, in which a normally hereditary king governed with the advice of a council of nobles, to an aristocratic republic in which the king lost all but his priestly functions. In the seventh century the nobility not only deliberated but decided. By 686 three archons, or rulers, each elected for one year, and themselves nobles, formed the executive. One of them, the king-archon, had taken over the monarch's last remaining duties, which were chiefly religious. Another, the *polemarch*, or leader in battle, directed the armed forces. The third archon was civil head of the state. But it was the nobles who controlled the Athenian republic. Were they not the Eupatrids, the "Well-fathered"? They alone owned war horses. They alone enjoyed the right of "iron-bearing"—the right to bear arms in life, and later in their tombs. They alone could do justice because they alone knew *themis*, they alone *diké*. Of written law there was none. The popular Assembly, which in Athens was called the Ecclesia, exercised little power.

In Attica as in many other city-states, the shift from growing food to eat to growing crops for money, from barley and wheat to exportable wine and olive oil, brought greater wealth to the wealthier nobles and increased misery for the bulk of the peasants. At some time in the seventh century, blue blood made a partial concession to silver money. Political rights began now to reflect wealth—but only wealth in land. The nobility remained dominant. But since family ownership and inalienability of land were giving way, since more and more land could be individually owned and could be bought and sold, those who made money in commerce could secure greater rights by buying land. The nobles began marrying non-noble heiresses. Social barriers were crumbling. To protect her commerce, Athens developed a fleet. Those who rowed in that fleet were most certainly not nobles. The effect was like the effect of the shift all over Greece from cavalry to heavy-armed infantry. Those who defended the commonwealth with their bodies would more and more demand the right to help govern it with their minds. It appeared less and less likely that the noble, by mystic right of blood, was alone able to read the will of the gods, alone able to apply that will by interpreting unwritten customary law which he alone knew, alone able to deliberate on essential measures for the good of the whole polis. The Greek colonists who had gone out to Italy and Sicily had broken with so many customs; had indeed often included in their number men from so many different states with so many differing customs, and so many poor men who sought not only land but an escape from the scorn and oppression of the Best People; had, finally, met so many new conditions to which the good old ways were irrelevant, that they were compelled to contrive constitutions and laws in writing for all to read. The experience of these Western colonists shook in turn even the stay-at-homes in the mother-cities of Mainland Greece.

As the Athenian nobles turned more and more into merchants, their ancient privileges seemed less and less to operate in the common interest; their monoply of law and justice seemed correspondingly less justified, their decisions less and less to be trusted. Under pressure, the nobles made a concession: they placed the surveillance of the legal system in the hands of a special commission. But social discontent continued. A young noble named Cylon, son-in-law of Theagenes, the tyrant-ruler of neighboring Megara, tried with Theagenes' help to seize the Acropolis and restore by force the disappearing privileges and prestige of the Athenian nobility. Cylon's attempt to seize power was put down by a popular insurrection, led by a nobleman of the pro-reform family of Alcmeonid. Nevertheless, enough disorder followed, and enough private vendettas, to force action. The archon Dracon was furnished in 621 with extraordinary powers to reform criminal justice.

Dracon's principal achievement was to substitute public trial and punishment for family vendetta and private vengeance. To ensure that necessary shift he made public punishment so severe that later generations, not faced by his problems, would declare that Dracon's laws were written, not in ink, but in blood. But, thanks to Dracon, the force of the whole Athenian community was placed behind law. Legal evidence and reasoned argument replaced endless and unreasoning vendetta; law was no longer the monopoly of the Well-fathered but of the polis; and, to that end, it was written law.

Despite this triumph of human reason, the land of Attica continued steadily to fall into fewer and fewer hands. The peasant fell further into debt. Sometimes he sold his land, paid his debt, and went into exile. Sometimes he could not meet his debt, and under traditional law his creditor had legal power to seize him, his wife, and his children, and sell them all as slaves. Finally, the peasant might sometimes yield up his land, remain as tenant, and accept the status of serf, required to turn over to his lord five-sixths[117] of his harvest; the sixth share, he retained, and he was therefore called a *hectemor*, or sixth-sharer.

Throughout Attica discontent ripened toward rebellion. The peasants demanded that the lands of the nobles be confiscated, as had happened in certain other city-states, and redistributed among those who tilled it. The rich, whether noble or non-noble, wanted to develop further their monopoly of the land. Athens, "the oldest land of Ionia," was "being slain."[118] Only eunomia,[119] the state of being well-lawed, could save her from falling into that wrong kind of strife, of physical violence, of eris, that Hesiod had so much dreaded for man.

Lycurgus had tried to find eunomia for Sparta. He had shut Sparta off from the ideas that were current in Greece, from the silver and gold coins that were current, and had shut her in with her iron money and her iron thoughts and, above all, with her iron will. He had turned her citizens into a professional standing army imposing its will on Dwellers-round-about and Helots alike. He had tried to abolish all inequality of wealth for his citizen-soldiers by reducing all to a subsistence wage, supplied in kind by state serfs. What was left of industry and commerce he delegated to the Dwellers-round-about. He gave the gods their due, the kings their due, and his warriors theirs.

Other cities, commercial ones like Athens' neighbors, Megara and Corinth, had turned to tyranny to guide the state from rule by landed nobles to rule by trade and money, to economic development, to the arts of Ionia on which Sparta had turned her back, to the future, not the past.

Between the Scylla of Spartan renunciation and the Charybdis of popular dictatorship the Athenians tried to steer their political course into the unknown future. They sought Hesiod's other kind of eris, when neighbor vied with neighbor in productive work, the eris that is wholesome for men. To reach their goal they freely elected, about 594, a leader to show the way. His name was Solon. They made him archon and they gave him extraordinary powers to find eunomia for Athens.

Solon was a noble, whose family had been wealthy landowners; but he was no rustic conservative. His father had been openhanded toward others and had impaired the family fortune: Solon's response was not to join those of his fellow nobles who wanted to squeeze Dustyfoot harder, but to take to commerce and the sea and repair his inheritance by his own work. He became a successful merchant, who understood the economic problems Athens now faced. He was also a poet, whose poems were political pamphlets, written in the elegiac[120] couplets which Ionia had invented. He was an undoctrinaire reformer, who sought political equilibrium for a polis that was reeling from dissension between large landowner and peasant. Naturally, many of his fellow landowners hoped he would put down popular discontent with a firm and ruthless hand. Naturally, many of the peasants hoped he would redistribute the land. He neither repressed the poor nor confiscated the lands of the rich. What he did do was to abolish the peasants' debts, to forbid enslavement for debt, to limit the size of landed estates, to bring back those whom debt had driven into exile and those who had been carried there as slaves—"men," he wrote in one of his pamphleteering poems, "that no longer spake the Attic speech because they had wandered so far and wide."[121] "By fitting close together right and might"[122] he did these things—that is, he made force the servant of justice and of law.

The Athenian census already distinguished between the *hippeis*, or cavalrymen, men rich enough to report for military service mounted on their own horses, and the *zeugitai*, men rich enough to keep a yoke of oxen and to serve as heavy-armed infantry. To these two classes, Solon added two more, the Five-hundred-Bushelers, whose title reflected their annual income, and the *thetes*, or Wage-earners. Eligibility for office was no longer based on birth and wealth, but on wealth alone, though in general the wealthy were still the Well-fathered. Which offices a man was eligible for depended on which of the three top classes he belonged to. The fourth class, the Wage-earners, could not hold office. Alongside the aristocratic Senate, or Council of the Areopagus, Solon established a Council of Four Hundred to prepare the agenda for the popular Assembly, in which even the Wage-earner sat, could join in debate, and could vote. Finally, Solon established courts, whose membership was selected by lot from the popular Assembly.

Solon clearly did not judge the Wage-earners ready for equal political rights, but his new constitution permitted every citizen to take some part in the political process of self-government, and it rendered inevitable a growth in that participation. By imposing severe penalties for idleness, he reflected Hesiod's respect for ergon, for work, and he encouraged Hesiod's good kind of eris. He encouraged the same good strife by reforming the currency and by reforming weights and measures. In his new constitution, he also invited all Athenians to a higher form of this good strife, the eris of making law and of judging cases under the law the citizen helped make. Athens would inevitably move nearer to a community of free men, able by fitting close together right and might to seek justice together in an open society. For such a society, however dimly Solon may have descried it in the future, he laid the strong foundations; and, although he was a widely traveled man, he could have found no model for such a society in any land he had come to. In his own Odyssean imagination and intellect he had found the route to a kind of home for free beings. On this home, precisely because it was free, some of the divine light of another home was shed—the home of the gods, Olympus.

He could appeal in his poems to Zeus, who punished human violence, and to the other Olympians whom the Achaean and Dorian invaders had discovered and worshiped before they ever entered Greece. But in the poem in which he claimed to have fitted close together right and might, he spoke of quite another god, or rather goddess. She was that goddess whom the Pelasgians of the great days of Crete and Mycenae had worshiped for centuries, before the Achaean and Dorian war bands had swarmed in from the North. She was the Great Mother, the Earth. Solon had removed the boundary stones on which farm mortgages were recorded and had loosened the strangle hold of the rich upon the life-giving land. And "Right good witness shall I have in the court of Time," he wrote,

> to wit the Great Mother of the Olympian Gods, dark Earth, whose so many fixed landmarks I once removed, and have made her free that was once a slave.[123]

He had freed the energies of the earth as he had freed the energies of his fellow Athenians—their political energies, their commercial energies, their industrial energies. He offered no vast blueprint of some future human equality. From time to time, he even made an aristocrat's hard judgment on the folly and envy of the classes beneath his own. But he did know how to detect energy, divine or human, actual or potential.

Lycurgus the Lawgiver had taken the stubborn stance of godlike Achilles, who could pray and fight and love and hate, but who lacked wily Odysseus' will to think and skill to think. As for the work that Hesiod glorified, and that Odysseus had also will and skill to do, Lycurgus left that to ungodlike underlings, whose task it was to live unhonored lives. Meanwhile the Polis would be the armed and disciplined Spartiates, each of whom knew how to "bite his lip with his teeth and abide firm-set astride upon the ground." It was the ideal of an aristocrat, and of an aristocrat hard pressed by the changes coming over Hellas.

Although in the seventh century Sparta was open to the arts of other lands, in the sixth she turned in on herself, broke off almost all friendly contact with other Greek cities, and became a garrison state, fearful of foreign attack, and, if anything, yet more fearful of rebellion by those whom the Spartiates had brutally subjected. Paradoxically, the society she then proceeded to construct, a society men ascribed to Lycurgus the Lawgiver—Did he indeed live? If he did, when? Was he god or man?—became the admiration of Hellas, and not merely of the rich or the Well-fathered. The Greek mind was fascinated by Lycurgus' eunomia; by a certain symmetry in the Lycurgan constitution; by the laconic repartee of these Laconians—a repartee full of suppressed violence; by their single-minded courage on behalf of their polis; by their readiness to die in the grand manner of Achilles; by their self-control in the face of corrupting pleasures, their freely chosen life of hardship, their swift obedience to lawful authority; and by their whole air of time-honored virtue such as men had displayed in the good old days.

Solon of Athens, though himself an aristocrat, was a poet, a man of imagination and intellect, a man whom later generations would place among the Seven Sages of Greece. He followed, not Achilles, but wise Odysseus. He discovered and invented. The Spartans whom Lycurgus had molded by his stern discipline said that Homer was a poet for warriors, Hesiod for serfs.[124] But Solon the Lawgiver by a gentler discipline molded

70

his Athenians toward both the justice and the work that had inspired Hesiod to sing.

As one of the Seven Sages, he commonly got credit for two epigrams as famous as any that Greece had yet produced: "Know thyself" and "Do nothing too much"[125]—that is, moderation in all things. He had sought to apply this second formula to Athens' most basic problem: how to change peacefully from a polis in which men husbanded the feminine earth, plowed her yielding body, sowed seed in her womb, and from her womb received the things their own bodies required—from a polis in which noble blood and ancient custom and family ties ruled, to a new polis that men could scarcely yet comprehend. In this new polis men produced olive oil and wine to sell for money and to ship to distant lands. The oil and wine were shipped in exquisitely painted pots of Attic clay. The money from their sale abroad bought grain to make bread with or dried fish or leather hides from grazing countries or better timber for ships than one could any longer hope to find on the cut-over mountainsides of Attica. Somehow, in this change from growing things for use to growing things to sell, the rich seemed to get richer and the poor to get poorer. In other Greek cities some man, usually a noble, had used force to make himself tyrant, and in the name of justice for the poor had destroyed freedom. Solon strove hard to protect the poor against the greed of the rich and the rich against the envy of the poor without resort to the usual Greek device: tyranny, a dictatorship, violence instead of reason. Before he laid down his powers, he made all citizens swear an oath to support the new constitution which had disappointed so many. Further to forestall violence, he ingeniously required that if violence did break out every citizen must openly take sides: he feared the withdrawal of moderates when and if the hotheads acted. Then he deliberately withdrew from Athens and voyaged to Egypt and Cyprus.

In the short run, Solon failed. Violence between rich and poor quickly broke out. Parties formed: the People of the Plain, composed of nobles and successful peasants, who wanted to abolish Solon's reforms; the People of the Coast, composed of men who lived by commerce, shipping, and fisheries, of craftsmen, and of poor but free peasants; and the Mountaineers, composed of the goatherds in the mountains of Attica but also of the poorest men everywhere, who were still determined to confiscate and redistribute the land. An ambitious noble, Pisistratus, seized the leadership

71

of the Mountaineers. Solon, who had returned to his disordered polis and was watching the shrewd moves of Pisistratus, launched more of his pamphlet-poems to warn Athens that Pisistratus wanted to be tyrant; but he warned to no avail. At the opportune moment Pisistratus used the true and tried device: he rushed into the Agora, covered with blood and crying out that his political opponents had sought to assassinate him. A confederate promptly proposed that he be given a guard of fifty men armed with clubs. Once he secured his personal guard, he of course seized the Acropolis, and Athens had her tyrant at last.

That was in 561, thirty-three years after Solon had first assumed power—constitutionally. Now he had to watch this comedy played to its expected, bitter end. The aged statesman hung up his shield and spear before the door of his house, as a symbol that other men, perhaps younger men, must take over the defense of freedom. But Solon knew how much easier it was to permit a tyrant to seize power than to get rid, not only of a tyrant, but of the political habits tyranny might breed. Was his dream of a free society, of citizens seeking justice together through common deliberation, a dream beyond the power of men to realize? Would Pisistratus rule the men of Athens as animals are ruled, and then Pisistratus's sons, and his sons' sons?

Meanwhile, Pisistratus showed him great deference. A year or two after freedom fell, Solon died.

4

FOR NONE
SAVE ONLY ZEUS
IS FREE

SOLON had been no mean poet, but he may not have completely read his own symbolic act when he hung up his arms before the door of his dwelling. For it was basically by bringing arms to Solon's peaceful revolution that Pisistratus, tyrant of Athens, defended the gains of that revolution. He, too, fitted close together right and might, as Solon had done; but he increased the proportion of might in Solon's formula. Even then, during the thirty-three years between his seizure of power in 561 and his death in exile in 528, his political opponents succeeded in exiling him twice, for a total of fourteen years. The first time he was exiled, his property was confiscated and sold; but he maneuvered his way back to power by marrying the daughter of his political opponent, Megacles. Exiled a second time, he later landed on the coast of Attica at the head of an army of mercenaries, occupied Marathon, reconquered his country, and ruled it.

The sequence of events had been instructive. The Athenian aristocracy had tried, and failed, to govern Athens under Dracon's written laws. As violence mounted, the aristocrats had agreed with their opponents to elect Solon as dictator[126] with extraordinary powers to arbitrate differences. Although extraordinary, these powers had been strictly constitutional. Despite the oath which all citizens had sworn to obey Solon's new laws, tensions between rich and poor had again produced anarchy. Thereupon Pisistratus had secured his bodyguard of men with clubs, by deception but without openly violating the constitution; then he had ignored the constitution and had seized the citadel on the Acropolis. Driven from Athens twice, he had hired mercenary troops and conquered power by force of arms.

The fact remained that he used that power to protect and develop Solon's reforms. In effect, he forced the rich and Well-fathered of Athens to keep the oath that Solon had exacted of all citizens before he deliberately went on his travels. It was as if the doctor had failed through the obstinacy of the patient and a ruthless surgeon had taken over. Pisistratus gained the reputation of a wise and moderate ruler, a reputation not many Greek tyrants had gained. He kept the forms of Solon's constitution, merely seeing to it that only his supporters held office. He guarded the interests of the peasant, redistributed the lands of exiled nobles, built an aqueduct and undertook other public works that employed the poor in the city of Athens. Since Athens could now count on grain from her Black Sea trade, he encouraged the farmer to produce wine as well as olive oil for export.

Moreover, Pisistratus and the two sons who succeeded him built temples and altars to the gods, especially a new temple to Athens' divine patroness, Athena, goddess of wisdom; and began a great Doric temple to Olympian Zeus. To decorate these temples and altars, they brought over famous sculptors from Ionia and from the Aegean Isles; and painters decorated the walls of these buildings with frescoes. The Ionian sculptors, and the Athenian sculptors who learned their art from them, turned from brilliantly painted statues of limestone to statues carved from marble. Both statues and temples, first of wood and then of limestone, had invited paint, if only to hide the irregularities of the material. But when the Ionians taught the Athenians to carve their statues and build their temples out of marble, the painters less and less often covered them with their brilliant and varied colors. The sculptor noted that the more regular surface did not need color; besides, the better Greek marbles were simply too beautiful to spoil by concealing their translucent radiance. Instead, he tinted the statue, enough to give a flush to the portions that represented human skin, and colored perhaps the hair and eyes and lips. Or he contented himself with the waxing process called *ganosis*, to bring out the mellow tone. The statues in low relief or high relief that decorated the pediments of temples and the friezes along their sides were no longer brightly colored against a plain background. At about the time that potters changed from black figures on red ground to red figures on black, the artists who created the statues on pediment or frieze left their white marble statues uncolored against a solidly painted ground.

But what most distinguished the statues of this period was not a matter of technique, not a matter of gay color, or of ganosis, or of their stiff, formal, almost Egyptian style. It was their aristocratic bearing, shown alike in god and godlike youth, in goddess and in girl. It was the fact that the sculptor ignored the transient, the particular; what he sought was the universal and eternal. He saw, for example, in a child, not the large head and half-formed features of childhood but only another case of man, and he carved the boy merely as a small man. And for the fleeting emotion on the human face, he substituted the mysterious, discreet smile,[127] the smile a god might wear, or even a godlike youth, even a godlike youth who was wounded, who was dying. These marble gods and youths were not concerned with the obvious but with what was, for most men, hidden. And yet, alongside this aristocratic and reticent and radiant sculpture, artists were painting delicately shaped pots and jars and amphorae and lamps, some indeed displaying the heroic but many of them covered with the scenes of everyday Hellenic life, with its work, its play, its pleasure and vices, its comedy, and its laughter.

To Athens came the artists; to Athens came the poets. From the nearby Aegean island of Ceos came the lyric poet Simonides to the court of the tyrant sons of Pisistratus. When the gay poet, Anacreon, came, Athens even sent a trireme to conduct him from Samos. Not content with making more impressive the Great Panathenaic festivals, in which athletes from all over Greece competed, chariots raced, rhapsodes recited Homer, and musicians sang or played, Pisistratus also founded the Great Dionysiac

75

festivals to appeal to the people—for Dionysus was a favorite god of Dusty-foot.

A central feature of the Great Dionysiac was a chorus of singers, disguised as followers of Dionysus and chanting tales of his adventures. Then it became a custom to have the leader step forward and sing responses to the dithyrambic verses of the rest of the chorus. Later, from being merely the leader of a chorus, he took to impersonating a god—and a kind of dramatic dialogue was born, a dialogue in words and in dance, a dialogue between god and man. Pisistratus organized these performances and established prizes for which their authors might compete in yet another eris.

Pisistratus and his two sons were not the only tyrants who favored those gods and heroes whom the populace most loved. Periander of Corinth and Clisthenes of Sicyon went further: they frowned on the ancient religious family rites of the nobles. In favoring Dionysus, the god of the grape, of wine, of the union of man with god, of death and resurrection, in favoring Demeter, who made the peasants' crops grow, Pisistratus was drawing on the deepest beliefs of the poor, on ancient religious hopes and fears that the nobles, with their Olympic deities, in general did not share. The Eleusinian mysteries were celebrated each spring at Eleusis, a town near Athens that dated back to ancient Minoan days; and the secret rites to Demeter promised eternal life to all initiates, even slaves.

In their foreign policy the Pisistratids gained a firm grip on the Helles-pont to secure Athens' access to Black Sea grain, and they also staked out claims in Thrace where precious metals and timber were to be had. Athens began to crowd out Corinth as the leading commercial city of Greece. Her wine, her olive oil, and her pottery were now shipped out to every part of the Mediterranean.

Pisistratus was succeeded in 527 by his eldest son, Hippias, who was assisted by his brother, Hipparchus. Fourteen years after the father's death an attempt was made to assassinate both brothers, and the younger one was indeed killed. Four years later still, Hippias was driven out of Athens by a Spartan army, co-operating with exiled Athenian nobles. The long tyranny had ended, partly because of certain setbacks in foreign policy, but partly because tyranny had largely lost its function by doing its work too well. It had lasted, with interruptions, from 561 to 510—over half a century. It had fostered, against the landlords, a commercial and industrial society, a society self-confident and ready to govern itself in freedom.

Backed by Spartan military intervention, the nobles now tried to abolish Solon's reforms, which Pisistratus and his sons had retained, and to re-establish the aristocratic republic. But Solon's reforms and Pisistratus's administration had created a new Athenian republic and one whose problems the landed noble was ill equipped to solve. The new society soon found a leader—Clisthenes, member of the aristocratic family of Alcmeonid, a family which, like Solon's, had long looked to the future, toward the sea and adventure; not back toward the land or custom or the past. The nobles found means of banishing Clisthenes, but this counter-revolution of the old nobility was stopped in its tracks by a popular rising. The Spartan garrison and the intransigent nobles were forced to quit Athens. Clisthenes then returned to Athens and completed the revolution in which Dracon, Solon, and Pisistratus, whose work had covered more than a century, had each played a vital role. In a few months he had reorganized the constitution of Athens. In particular, he effected three major reforms.

The first of these reforms was to divide Attica into one hundred districts known as demes. Citizenship in the deme, not membership in one of the four Ionic tribes, now gave citizenship in the polis. This freed the polis and its common good from the bad eris between ancient tribes and families. With their powerful religious traditions and passionate loyalties, these groups had kept Athena's Polis the contested prize of great families.

Clisthenes' second reform was to admit to citizenship many of the metics, foreigners whom the laws protected but who could not help make law, and he admitted many former slaves as well. He provided that henceforth the son of a citizen should inherit citizenship regardless of his mother's status. He then divided his hundred demes into ten new 'tribes' of ten demes each; but he saw to it that each tribe should contain nearly the same number of demes from each of the characteristic regions of Attica, regions that had already produced three opposing factions: the Mountain, the Plain, and the Coast. The effect of forming his new, artificial tribes out of scattered demes was to prevent any one tribe from representing in concentrated form a single, basic economic interest. To the rich he left their family rites and even the ancient rites of the four Ionic

77

tribes that he had just superseded politically. But by composing his new tribes of widely scattered demes and by enrolling many metics and freedmen as citizens he fatally weakened the power of the great landed families, with their local retainers and clients.

Clisthenes' third reform was to introduce the legal device of ostracism. Once a year the popular Assembly deliberated on whether any citizen should be required to go into exile for ten years on the grounds that his presence in Athens was a threat to the constitution. If the Assembly voted to hold an ostracism, a second vote was taken. Then, if six thousand citizens[128] wrote the same name on an *ostrakon*, or potsherd, the man named must leave Athens for ten years. But he did not lose his citizenship, his goods were not confiscated, he did not even suffer disgrace. In fact, it was only the man of great ability who was likely to be ostracized, yet the possibility of ostracism was a constant deterrent to overweening political ambition.

The reforms of Clisthenes completed Solon's work for him, and their success proved that Solon's failure had been more apparent than real. The result was a kind of eunomia that no Greek ever heard of as existing outside Hellas. In Athena's Polis women, children, slaves, foreign residents, and some of the sons of non-citizens were still excluded from a share of making law, of administering it, and of judging those accused of infringing it. Yet Athens came nearer to being a self-governing community than anything man had dreamed of in the Mediterranean world. Every citizen lived in freedom under law, and this law was the fruit of debate, of argument, of reason, of Hesiod's good kind of eris in action. The rivalry of Athenian potters and other craftsmen had already produced a standard of workmanship famous throughout the Mediterranean. But now the clash of political argument was leading Athenians of every class to a constant, responsible consideration of the common good. The good potter sought beauty in his work. In the Assembly the same potter could seek the good by taking part in the city's search for good law. But that kind of search involved an intellectual discipline that encouraged men to search together by eris for what was true, regardless of whether this truth appeared immediately applicable to the making of a beautiful, useful pot or even to the making of a good and useful law.

By fitting close together right and might, Athens was learning to seek and to understand, to make and to demonstrate. But during the same

78

period she was doing two other things. Inside the Polis, she was growing rich. Outside, in the ever larger area of her expanding commercial interests, she was fighting and imposing her will. On the one hand, by multiplying her material means she risked losing sight of her moral ends. Would the acquisition of wealth serve to underwrite this free society, or would it become an end in itself? On the other hand, she was threatened from abroad. Her dethroned aristocracy was inciting Sparta to put down the democratic revolution at Athens. The expelled tyrant, Hippias, was trying to stir up Persia. The Boeotian League which Thebes headed was trying to rob Athens of the support of Plataea. The commercial oligarchies which governed Megara, Chalcis, and Aegina were frightened by Athenian competition in their foreign markets. In the spring of 506, a Peloponnesian army under Spartan command marched northward and invaded Attica from the west; a Boeotian army invaded from the north; and a Chalcidian army, from the east. But at a crucial moment, Sparta and her Peloponnesian allies withdrew. The Athenian democracy defeated Boeotia and Chalcis and planted colonies in the island of Euboea, as Athens had settled colonists in the island of Salamis half a century before. These colonists in Salamis and Euboea were not of the traditional type, groups of emigrants spontaneously organized to seek new lands and new homes —emigrants who had normally set up their own sovereign polis connected with the mother-city only by filial piety and religious rites. Colonies of this new kind, known as cleruchies, were composed of Athenian citizens who nominally retained their Athenian citizenship. Their resettlement relieved the hunger for land in Attica and at the same time furnished Athens with advanced outposts in case of war.

The democratic revolution at Athens, headed by an aristocrat, had done away with oppression by aristocrats and then with oppression by an anti-aristocratic tyrant, and had substituted for aristocrats and tyrant alike freedom through law for all citizens. Aristocrats, tyrant, and foreigners had then combined to destroy by violence this new and strange community of men who had so largely replaced force with reason, blind obedience with common deliberation for the common good. But the common good they deliberated about was the common good of a single polis, Athens. That polis now faced those who would destroy such deliberation. It faced émigré nobles who despised Dustyfeet and their rebellious efforts to decide by arguments public questions that the Well-fathered could de-

79

cide better. It faced an exiled tyrant who was determined to rule again by his own will and by force. It faced the oligarchs now of one neighboring polis, now of another, oligarchs intent on their own common good. All these opponents had appealed to the sword. To defend her area of freedom for all under law made by all, the Polis of Athena, too, took up the sword. Her war of defense turned into a war of conquest. She seized land from her assailants. By sending out cleruchs, or outsettlers, she gained for her poorer citizens a freedom from want which at least in theory gave them the right to help make the laws they were committed to obey. In practice, of course, an outsettler in the island of Lemnos could hardly deliberate with his fellow citizens in Athens. In practice, too, Athens was learning to impose her will by the sword, outside Attica.

In 552, about the time that Pisistratus was being driven out of Athens into exile for a second time, the head of an obscure people in the Iranian plateau, Cyrus, king of Persia, revolted against Astyages, king of Media, overthrew him, and took over the Median Empire. During the sixth century, that empire had been accounted the most powerful state in Asia— or, at least, in the only Asia the Greeks knew anything about, the Middle East. To achieve that power, the Median Empire had helped Babylonia destroy the terror of the seventh century, Assyria.

The Mede whom Persian Cyrus had overwhelmed was a brother-in-law of Croesus, the rich king of Lydia. Though Croesus had conquered and annexed Greece-in-Asia, he had come to be accepted in some degree as a member of the Greek community; and one of his first moves toward restoring his Median brother-in-law to the throne from which Cyrus had hurled him was to consult the various oracles of Greece. Of those oracles, the one through which Apollo spoke at Delphi was by now the most famous. That of Zeus at Dodona, farther northwest in Thesprotia, was indeed older. But both Dodona and Delphi were holy places even before the Achaean and Dorian invasions, and at Delphi in Mycenaean days men worshiped an earth spirit. Now, in the Hellenic era, Apollo gave his oracle there. From all over the Hellenic world men came to seek his advice and the advice of the other Olympic gods for whom he spoke. They came to seek counsel on their private affairs; they came to seek guidance for their governments. Both Lycurgus and Solon were reported to have sought counsel from the Delphic oracle of Apollo on the proper laws to give their respective cities. In the eighth and seventh centuries many Greeks wanted advice on where to colonize. They did not see Apollo himself at Delphi. He spoke through the lips of a priestess. Seated on a tripod, she went into a kind of trance, and uttered incoherent words. A prophet stood by, who translated her words into verse. All over the Hellenic world men quoted these verses.

Sometimes the oracles thus issued were fairly specific. More often, their language was dark, ambiguous, ironic—in short, oracular. The truth they purported to convey was poetic truth and required interpretation. It came to men disguised, as Athena so often came to Odysseus. Specific questions were likely to elicit general answers or answers which, like so many other poems, wore an air of being specific yet irrelevant.

Faced with the question of whether to attack Cyrus the Persian and try to restore his brother-in-law to the Median throne, Croesus sent rich gifts of gold and silver to the god Apollo at Delphi together with this message: "Shall Croesus send an army against the Persians . . . ?" The Delphic oracle's reply was characteristic: "that if he should send an army against the Persians he would destroy a great empire."[129] Croesus was delighted. Like many other men who consulted the Delphic oracle, he was eager that Apollo should advise him to do what he, Croesus, had already made up his mind to do. He attacked Cyrus, and by doing so he promptly destroyed a great empire—his own. After his defeat, he sent another delegation to Delphi. Its members were instructed to ask Apollo "if he were not ashamed that he had persuaded Croesus to attack the Persians, telling him that he would destroy Cyrus' power . . ."[130] Apollo retorted that he had but prophesied that

> if he should lead an army against the Persians he would destroy a great empire. Therefore it behoved him, if he would take right counsel, to send and ask whether the god spoke of Croesus' or of Cyrus' empire. But he understood not that which was spoken, nor made further inquiry: wherefore now let him blame himself.[181]

Should he not have made further inquiry? At a minimum, Apollo had challenged him to recognize that it was easier to start a war than to predict its outcome. A god could scarcely have given more important advice, and the advice was more important, because more general, than the answer Croesus imagined he heard. His willfulness not only cost him an empire: it cost the Greek states in Asia their easy Lydian yoke and left them to face the rapidly expanding Persian Empire. That was in 546.

Faced with the threat of Persian conquest, the Ionians and Aeolians sent embassies to Sparta, renowned as the most powerful state in Greece, to get help, but none came. The city of Lycurgus was never given to distant and dangerous expeditions. Thales of Miletus, the philosopher, proposed that the Ionian city-states form one large state, as the various tiny states of Attica had done centuries before; that the religious alliance known as the Panionian League convert itself into a government capable of the common defense. Bias of Priene, a statesman accounted one of the Seven Sages, advised that all the Ionians quit Asia, sail west to the great island of Sardinia, and there set up a common polis. And in fact most of the citizens of Phocaea did emigrate to Alalia, a colony which they had already founded in Corsica, while the citizens of Teos sailed to the coast of Thrace and founded Abdera.

But Thales' advice was ignored; no common defense was achieved; and, one by one, Cyrus picked off the Greek cities of Asia, along with those on the Hellespont. Then Cyrus turned eastward and conquered various peoples clear to the Jaxartes River. By 538 he had turned back and had taken Babylon. Persia was preparing to conquer Egypt when Cyrus died. His son and successor, Cambyses, conquered Egypt and annexed it. From the Hellespont to the Pamir Mountains, northeast of modern Afghanistan, from the Nile to the Caucasus and to the Jaxartes River beyond Samarkand, a single mighty empire stood. The lands that several empires had once governed—the Egyptian, the Babylonian, the Assyrian, the Hittite— were all governed now by the King of Kings. The whole Fertile Crescent was his, and the Arabian tribes of the desert were his allies. Nothing like this political colossus had ever been known to the Greeks.

The Persian Empire, though it could brutally repress rebels and could transplant whole populations if need be, gave on the whole just government. Above all, the laws of the Medes and Persians brought a kind of universal peace to the Middle East. The Empire also improved agriculture, irrigated dry lands, built needed roads. It respected local religions and local customs. But, to the Ionian cities, it was a sorry substitute for Croesus of Lydia. Croesus had been halfway adopted into the Hellenic family and so had many of his Lydian subjects. The Ionians were now a tiny fringe of a vast empire, ruled from remote Susa by a Great King, an empire with no leanings toward Greek gods or Greek ways. Worse still, the Great King had seized control of the grain route from the Black Sea and had opened it to Ionia's ancient Phoenician rivals, Tyre and Sidon. The Phoenicians were also subjects of the Great King and now after all these decades they were again competing in the commerce of the Aegean itself.

Cyrus the Great had built most of this empire, except for Egypt, which his son Cambyses had added. When Cambyses died, his conquering army was still in Egypt. A Persian noble, Darius, led that army home. Three years later Darius was King of Kings. Less than a decade later he turned to his northern and western frontiers. He crossed the Bosphorus on a pontoon bridge built by an Ionian engineer of Samos, and conquered the tribes of eastern Thrace. In 512 he reached the Danube River. An Ionian fleet serving the Great King sailed through the Black Sea and up the Danube to join Darius' army. There the fleet formed another pontoon bridge. While the Ionians held the bridge, Darius warred against the nomadic Scythians on the steppes.[132] But the Scythian horsemen were too much for him: the quick attacks of the Scythians and their instant disappearances into vast and empty steppes left the Persian army in sore straits, and Darius at last retreated to the pontoon bridge across the Danube. Even so, after he returned to Asia, his empire still extended to the Danube. News of his disasters on the steppes caused Byzantium and several neighboring Greek city-states to revolt; but a Persian army shortly reconquered them, and the Greek cities of Asia saw their vital grain route from the Black Sea again under the control of Persia, again open to their competitors, the merchants of Phoenicia.[133]

In 499 the cities of Ionia rose against Darius' world empire. The revolt was not well organized or even well planned. It was occasioned in large part by the political intrigues of Aristagoras, tyrant of Miletus. Once it had broken out, Aristagoras surrendered his tyranny and voyaged to Greece to secure the aid of the two leading states there, Sparta and Athens. The Spartan kings refused to move: their state was interested in retaining its hegemony over Mainland Greece; it was neither a colonizing nor a trading state; one of its kings, Cleomenes, was at odds with the other king, Demaratus; Aristagoras admitted that Persia was so vast that it took three months to march from the sea to the Great King's capital at Susa; and finally, Cleomenes correctly judged that the Ionian Revolt was militarily doomed.

Though Sparta refused to budge, the democratic Assembly of Athens saw the matter differently. According to tradition the Ionian cities had been founded hundreds of years before by colonists from Attica. Darius, who had ruled the Ionian cities through local tyrants, now harbored the last of the tyrants at Athens, the hated Hippias, son of Pisistratus; and Hippias was busily if vainly trying to persuade the King of Kings to restore him by force as tyrant of Athens. Moreover, by closing off the Black Sea, Darius had endangered not only Ionia's trade but the trade of Athens. In that region Athens sold her olive oil, her wine, her now famous pottery, and the other works of industrious Athenian minds and hands. And Athens bought timber, fish, and grain from the Black Sea states. For Athens, as for Ionia, the Black Sea was a larder. So the Assembly voted to send twenty triremes. To these twenty, Eretria in Euboea added five: Miletus had once aided Eretria in a war against Chalcis. Between them, Athens and Eretria brought the Ionian rebels some 2,000 fighting men.

In the spring of 498 the expedition reached Ionia, where the Persians were getting ready to besiege Miletus. Thereupon the Ionians, with their Athenian and Eretrian allies, marched on the provincial capital of Sardis and took it. During the sack of Sardis, fire broke out and largely destroyed the city, including the temple of Cybele, the Earth Mother. But the Greek army was decisively beaten that summer; the Spartan judgment on the revolt appeared to be confirmed; and the Athenian force sailed home. Cyprus now joined the Ionian Revolt. So did the Greek cities of the Hellespont and the Propontis, clear up to Byzantium. So did Caria. But in the summer of 494 an Imperial Persian fleet composed of Phoenicians, Egyptians, Cilicians, and loyal Cypriots decisively defeated a smaller Ionian fleet off the island of Lade. The King's forces assaulted Miletus, ringleader of the rebellion, captured it, and razed it. They slaughtered or deported most of its male citizens; they enslaved its women and children and resettled them at the mouth of the Tigris River, where it emptied into the distant Persian Gulf. By the following summer the rebellion had been everywhere put down.

"Lord, remember the Athenians!" This admonition, according to reports, a slave of Darius' had been ordered to pronounce three times whenever the Great King dined. Certainly, there seemed little to prevent Darius from launching a punitive expedition against Athens and Eretria for aiding their Ionian cousins to rebel against the King of Kings. Sparta's two kings, Cleomenes and Demaratus, quarreled on. Athens was torn by faction: the oligarchic party was back in office and pro-Persian, although Clisthenes' constitution remained intact. It was the oligarchs who had insisted on recalling the expedition sent to aid Ionia. The Athenian democracy was badly shaken by the news of the destruction of Miletus; and when the Athenian dramatist Phrynichus represented the fall of Miletus in a tragedy, the audience wept. The government thereupon fined Phrynichus and forbade the tragedy to be played. Meanwhile, Corinth was having trouble with her colonies. Aegina was brooding over her defeat in a war with Athens; Argos, over a recent defeat by Sparta. The northern city-states were clearly leaning toward Persia. Thessaly and Phocis were distrustful of each other. Greek colonies on the shores of the Black Sea, of the Propontis, of the Hellespont, and of Thrace had fallen to the Great King. The various city-states, intent on their wars with each other, from time to time appealed for Persian support against their neighbors. Clisthenes himself, when Athens' neighbors had attacked her in 506 and enemy forces had started to close in upon her, had sent an embassy to solicit Persian aid. These ambassadors even consented to offer the traditional earth and water to the Great King, but on their return to Athens they were disavowed. The Athenians therefore got no Persian aid against their Greek neighbors. When Hippias was expelled from Athens and sought Persian help to re-establish his tyranny, he was only one of a succession of Greeks who had gone up to Sardis to persuade the Persian governor there to intervene, either to help their polis against other Greek states or to help their faction against another faction in their own polis.

In Western Greece, the Hellenic city-states, weakened by wars with one another and by civil wars inside many states, were threatened by the Etruscans, the Italiots, and above all by the mighty Phoenician city on the African coast, Carthage. The Western Greeks were now being pushed back by Carthage in Corsica, in Sardinia, in Gaul, in southern Spain; and even in Sicily the Greeks were in danger. If Darius should indeed "remember the Athenians" and strike—at them, at Eretria too, or perhaps at all of Mainland Greece—the home countries could hardly expect their colonists in the western Mediterranean to come to their rescue. Whether Darius negotiated with Carthage or not, events would negotiate for him. A Graeco-Persian war would furnish Carthage her best chance of sweeping

Greek merchants from the western seas at a moment when no restless Athens or Eretria could bother about Sicily.

Greece-in-Asia had been reconquered and swallowed up in the maw of the mighty Persian Empire. And Mainland Greece might well have seemed to Darius a cauldron of anarchy. It was a cauldron that had boiled over once already to Persia's hurt, when Athens and Eretria had insolently aided the Great King's Greek subjects in Ionia to rebel against the laws of the Medes and Persians. It might boil over again. Mainland Greece was a serious frontier problem for a world empire. Yet the anarchy it presented might be expected to simplify the problems of a punitive expedition.

In 492 Darius struck. His young son-in-law, Mardonius, led a large army and fleet through Ionia to the Hellespont. In view of the fact that the tyrants who governed the Ionian cities had fomented the recent Ionian Revolt against the Persian Empire, Mardonius had deposed most of them and had established democratic governments in their place. After all, Persia's interest in Ionia was not in the forms of local government: Persia merely wanted tributary governments on whose loyalty she could depend. Arrived at the Hellespont, Mardonius first used his navy to ferry his army across to the European shore, and then to reduce the nearby island of Thasos, while his army conquered much of Macedonia and annexed it to the Empire. Next, the fleet coasted down to Acanthus, on the north shore of the first of the three peninsulas which Chalcidice thrust southeastward into the Aegean Sea. This first finger, called Acte, began with an isthmus about a mile and a quarter wide and fairly level. Then a spine of hills started down it and turned into a range of mountains. As the Persian ships moved down the coast, the mountains on their right grew higher until there loomed up at the tip of Acte a huge shape, like a vast pyramid. It was Mount Athos, towering over 6,000 feet out of the sea. Among the Greek sailors who plied the route to the Black Sea, Mount Athos was greatly feared.

On a momentous day Darius' navy started to round this cape to punish Athens and Eretria for aiding his rebellious Ionians, and perhaps to sub-ject other Greek states as well. Immediately, a violent north wind sprang up and shattered his fleet against Athos. It was later reported[134] that al-most 300 vessels were destroyed and nearly 20,000 men. Some of the men were dashed against the rocks; some died of exposure; many of them did not know how to swim and were drowned; the survivors gazed on the

Aegean Sea blossoming with dead men.[135] Boreas, the god of the north wind, had saved Hellas from the Persian fleet. But it was Thracian tribesmen who meanwhile attacked and defeated the army. Even Mardonius, its commander, was wounded. Mardonius fought the Thracians again, conquered them, and made them subject to Persia. But, with his fleet shattered, he postponed the punishment of Athens and retreated to Asia.

Darius did not forget the Athenians: he merely made more careful preparations. He now sent out heralds to various states in Mainland Greece and in the Aegean Isles to demand earth and water, the symbols of obedience. At the same time he ordered his seaport towns, including those in Ionia, to provide warships and horse transports. Many of the Greek states sent earth and water, despairing of defense against the Eastern colossus. Then, in the spring of 490, two years after Mardonius had lost his ships off Athos, Darius launched a second punitive expedition against those two meddling cities, Athens and Eretria. With the expedition went Hippias, the deposed tyrant of Athens, ready to serve as the Great King's local governor. This time there would be no Athos: this second army, cavalry and all, would proceed straight across the Aegean by way of the islands, conquering them as it went. The expedition included some 50,000 men.[136] The island of Naxos was taken by surprise. Those inhabitants who did not flee to the mountains were captured and sold as slaves; their houses and temples were burned. Apollo's holy island of Delos was, indeed, spared; but other islands were subdued. At last the conquerors reached the southern tip of Euboea, a few miles from Athens, and ravaged Carystus. Sailing northward up the strait, they assaulted Eretria.

Athens had intended, if Eretria were attacked first, to dispatch to her aid 4,000 Athenians whom she had sent as outsettlers[137] to nearby Chalcis on the Euboean coast. But there was clearly a group of pro-Persians in Eretria who favored surrender; other Eretrians had fled to the mountains of Euboea; and Athens ordered her colonists back across the strait to help defend Attica, whose turn to receive the blow was evidently next. After six days of fighting, Eretria was betrayed by two of her citizens, and fell. The temples were burned in revenge for those that had been burned at Sardis when Ionia revolted. The people were taken captive and eventually resettled near Susa, the capital of the Great King. The island of Euboea, just off the coast of Attica, now became the advanced base of Persia's expeditionary force. From Euboea Hippias guided the conquerors to the nearby Attic shore where a plain would give scope to the Persian cavalry. Half a century before, Hippias had landed here with his father, Pisistratus, who was then returning from his second exile. Now that he was an old man, he was about to win his throne again.

Some twenty miles away, news reached the Athenian generals that the Persians had beached their ships on the shore below Marathon and had pitched camp. Should the Athenians attack them there or await their onslaught? On September 3, 490, the generals dispatched a professional runner to Sparta, some 140 miles away over rough country. His name was Phidippides. He finished his Marathon race in two[138] days; and even so he had time left for a conversation with the god Pan, whom he met en route—or so he reported when he returned to Athens. Pan had asked the runner why the Athenians neglected him; he had often helped them, and would do so again. Phidippides also reported that, for reasons connected with a religious festival, the Spartans could not march to battle before the next full moon. Luckily, Plataea, a small Boeotian town just across the frontier, which had sought alliance with Athens as a protection against Thebes and her Boeotian confederacy, promised to send prompt help.

Ten thousand heavy infantry marched from Athens to the high ground northwest of the Plain of Marathon. One thousand Plataeans joined them there. They camped in the holy grounds of a temple built to Heracles, high up a rocky valley, where they could readily guard the two roads that led to Athens. Below lay the Plain of Marathon between the small but rugged mountains and the Bay. The plain was over four miles long, but marshes occupied each end. The Persians had chosen—or Hippias had chosen for them—a camping spot next to the northeastern marsh. The distance from the mountains to the shore varied from one and a half to two miles, which gave the Persian cavalry room for maneuver against an army without cavalry. The Imperial fleet was anchored along the northeast end of the crescent-shaped shore, snugly protected by the hilly promontory of Cynosura.

Neither side was in a hurry to fight. The best strategy for the Persians was to watch for a signal, flashed by a shield in the sunlight to tell them treason had done its work in Athens and that their sympathizers were ready to help them take the city, preferably while the Athenian army was still absent. So they waited. The obvious strategy for the Athenians and their Plataean allies was to wait until the Spartans could join them. So they, too, were willing to wait. But, even so, the Athenians were the better placed. If the Persians chose to attack them, they would have to come up a narrow valley where numbers would not count and where cavalry could not do its proper work. If they started for Athens, they would expose their right flank to sudden assault from high ground. If they re-embarked, they would be, for a brief time at least, highly vulnerable. For about a week the Athenian army waited, and both sides watched.

The Athenian polemarch, or battle chief, had called a council of war with his ten generals, one from each Clisthenic tribe. Some of them argued that the Greeks were heavily outnumbered. Given the delay at Sparta, they ought to return to Athens, some twenty-four miles away, and protect the city. But one of them, Miltiades, argued for fighting it out on the Plain of Marathon. Miltiades had come recently from the Thracian Chersonese, where he had inherited a frontier kingdom from his uncle of the same name and had also ruled as tyrant over colonists from Athens. He knew the Persians well. Pisistratus had at one time banished his father. The sons of Pisistratus had hired assassins to kill his uncle. Now Hippias, one of Pisistratus's sons, had guided a Persian fleet to the shore a few miles down the valley where Miltiades argued for attack.

Miltiades persuaded some of his fellow generals and he persuaded Callimachus, the battle chief, who presided over the military council. He won his argument. In accordance with Athenian law the ten generals took turns, each for one day, as field commander. Those who had voted with Miltiades yielded their days to him. Even so, perhaps because he knew that his tyranny in the Chersonese rendered him suspect at Athens, he waited for his legal day. Or perhaps he chose that day because it was then that the Persians chose to move, both by land and sea. Persian forces started southward down the shore of the Bay of Marathon, and other Imperial forces started re-embarking to take the ninety-mile sea route around Cape Sunium to Athens. When part of the latter forces and all of the cavalry mounts had re-embarked, Miltiades' army started down the valley.

Within a mile of the Persian forces they formed for battle. Callimachus commanded the right wing. The Plataeans took the left. To cover the longer Persian formation, and perhaps also because he had ideas of his own, Miltiades made his two wings heavy and stretched his line between them perilously thin. The Imperial command had placed its picked troops,

Persians and Sacans, opposite that weak center. Miltiades' chief danger was not enemy cavalry—they were now safely in the ships. His chief danger was from the Persian arrows until his heavy infantry could close hand-to-hand and make its superior weapons and superior armor felt. So he ordered his line forward at a run[139] for this last mile. The Persian forces, seeing this smaller army[140] attack them at a run, thought the Greeks must have lost their senses. The elite Persian center fought steadily, broke Miltiades' weak center, and started to chase the Athenians back toward the hills. For a long time the two armies fought. Then Miltiades closed the pincers upon the victorious Persian center.

At this point the god Pan put into the hearts of the Persians one of those sudden, irrational, Panic fears, which taught Hellenic armies to pray to him. There was wild disorder, and the Imperials fled toward those ships that were still beached or were anchored in shallow water. The Athenian soldiers were calling for fire in order to destroy the enemy ships, now ready to carry the foe against their sacred polis. The ships tried to shove off. In the melee on the beach, Callimachus the battle chief performed doughty deeds, then gave his life for his polis. Cynegirus, brother of the tragedian, Aeschylus, seized the stern of an escaping ship; an enemy ax chopped off his hand; and he died on the beach. But seven ships were captured. The rest of the fleet escaped; a distant shield flashed in the sunlight and gave the sign of treason; and the Great King's fleet started for Phalerum, the port and arsenal of Athens. On the blood-stained beach they had left behind them were 6,400 dead. The Athenians lost only 192, for the battle had ended in Panic slaughter.

But Athens was still in danger: the Persian fleet could still sail around Cape Sunium at the tip of Attica and hope to reach Athens in nine or ten hours. Despite their long battle, the little Athenian army made a forced march back to their threatened polis. Who had flashed the bronze shield from the summit of Mount Pentelicus? What friend of Hippias or what aristocratic opponent of the new democracy at Athens? Nobody ever found out. When the Persian fleet reached Athens, the very Athenian army that had just that day destroyed an army of the Great King at Marathon, grimly awaited a second round. The Persian fleet sailed back to Asia.

A second time, the mighty Persian Empire had failed to conquer Greece. Two years before it had been Boreas, the north wind, or perhaps

Posidon, great god of the sea, who had destroyed the fleet of the Great King off Mount Athos. Now it was Athens, unaided by the leading military state in Greece, Sparta. When 2,000 Spartans did reach Attica after a forced march of three days, the mighty invaders had already sailed away, defeated; and the Spartans marched to Marathon, not to risk their lives but to view the dead warriors from Asia. Athens had indeed been supported on the day of Marathon by 1,000 Plataeans. But, according to the reports of her army, the gods had fought on her side too, as some of the gods had once fought for the Achaeans from Greece on that other plain centuries ago beneath the walls of Troy. The god Pan had kept his promise to the runner, Phidippides, that he would help Athens, and the Athenians showed their gratitude by setting up a shrine to Pan in a cave on the slope of the Acropolis. The hero, Theseus, who as king of Athens long ago had, according to tradition, peacefully united all Attica, had been seen fighting in the Athenian ranks at Marathon. An unknown warrior, dressed like a countryman and armed only with a ploughshare, fought there too. Later, when he could not be found, the Athenians sent to Delphi to ask Apollo's oracle who this could have been. Apollo replied that they should worship the hero Echetlus, him of the Ploughtail.[141]

Darius, King of Kings, was angered by the defeat of his army on the plain below Marathon and by his second failure in two years to subdue Mainland Greece. This second failure was bound to make for restlessness in Thrace and Macedonia, so recently brought under Persian law, and even in recently reconquered Ionia. But Egypt was first to revolt. Darius thereupon set about mustering enormous forces, sufficient to reconquer Egypt and to avenge Marathon too by annexing Greece. This time, he proposed to command his forces himself. Then, suddenly, after a reign of thirty-six years, he died. Although he had conquered less territory for the Persian Empire than Cyrus the Great, its founder, yet Darius the Great had done much to reorganize its administration; and he had ruled his empire well. At his death he had already designated which of his sons should rule: Xerxes now mounted the throne. Along with that throne he inherited the Empire's Greek problem and its Egyptian problem.

Egypt he reconquered. The Greek problem was more complex, if only because, unlike Egypt, Greece was not itself an empire but a collection of small states torn by wars among themselves, by the bad eris between rich and poor inside many of the individual states, and by intervention in each other's internal strife. On all three counts Xerxes could have truthfully declared that Mainland Greece did not know how to govern itself, and that in addition the intervention by Athens and Eretria in Ionia had proven that Mainland Greece was determined to prevent the Persian Empire from governing Greece-in-Asia. Meanwhile, he was being urged to settle this Greek problem once and for all by the powerful family of the Aleuadae, who ruled Larissa in Thessaly and longed to rule more; by Demaratus, the Spartan king, who had finally been deposed, had fled to the court of Darius, and now wanted Darius' son Xerxes to restore him to power; by another deposed king, Scythas of Zancle in Sicily; by the descendants of Pisistratus, who longed to be restored as the reigning dynasty of Athens; and by these Pisistratids' oraclemonger, Onomacritus, who kept finding—or forging—oracles which promised Greece to Persia.

Xerxes now spent three years in the most thorough preparations for massive war that the Mediterranean and Middle Eastern world had ever witnessed. He made an alliance[142] with Carthage that was calculated to keep the Greeks of the western Mediterranean too busy defending their own states to answer any calls for help that might come from Mainland Greece. He sent his ambassadors throughout Mainland Greece, demanding earth and water. Most of the states in northern Greece, uncertain that Athens could, or that Sparta would, defend them, promptly medized— that is, submitted to a Persian Empire which the Greeks had traditionally called Median. But, even in central Greece, the oligarchic rulers of many cities in Boeotia medized too. And in more distant Peloponnesus, Argos, always against the Spartans, who had robbed her[143] of her Homeric hegemony, made a secret treaty with Xerxes. To Athens and Sparta Xerxes sent no ambassadors. Both cities had once killed heralds whom his father had sent.

The army and navy which Xerxes proposed to hurl at Greece would be far too large to transport straight across the Aegean, on the pattern of 490 and Marathon. Neither would Xerxes risk rounding dangerous Mount Athos, where his father, Darius, had already lost a fleet in 492. He would not even try to ferry his army across the Hellespont as Darius had done in that same catastrophic first attempt on Greece. Instead he set Phoenician and Egyptian engineers to work to construct a double pontoon bridge across the Hellespont at Abydos, a matter of less than two miles. Persian engineers bridged the Strymon River in Macedonia. To avoid Athos, the same Persian engineers cut a canal across the isthmus of the peninsula of Acte which wholly bypassed Athos and was wide enough to allow two triremes to pass through abreast. Moles at each end extended into the sea to keep the two mouths of the canal from silting up.

The Greeks were puzzled that Xerxes should dig this canal, since their own ships crossed the Isthmus of Corinth on a wooden track with rollers, Corinth's famous *diolkos*. They suspected ostentatious pride. But they overlooked two facts. First, a canal at Corinth would have needed to be perhaps three times as long as the one that Xerxes dug across Acte and would have had to run through higher ground at that. Second, Xerxes had ampler labor power at his disposal than anything the Greeks could command. In addition to his canal and his bridges, Xerxes also established huge depots of supplies in a line that extended clear to the mouth of the Axios River in Macedonia.

Nevertheless Xerxes' problem of moving several hundred thousand men from all over his vast empire on foot, on horse, on camel, and of keeping them supplied with food and water, was formidable. Besides, the divine powers which had destroyed his father's fleet twelve years ago struck, too, at him. A tempest smashed the two parallel pontoon bridges that were to bring his monstrous herd of men across the Hellespont from Asia into Europe. The huge cables, cables of flax made by the Phoenicians, cables of papyrus made by the Egyptians, that bound the anchored ships together in lines for nearly two miles, had snapped.

Xerxes ordered the Hellespont scourged with three hundred lashes and addressed defiant words to it; he commanded that a pair of fetters be thrown into it to bind it to his will; he sent it word that it was but just that no man offer it sacrifice, since it was a turbid and briny river. For the briny water flowed from the Black Sea; that sea was constantly increased by great rivers like the Danube, the Dniester, the Dnieper, and the Don; and the scourged and fettered waters ran down to the Mediterranean at some seven knots. The Greeks, when they heard that Xerxes had scourged the Hellespont, were horrified by his hybris, by this insolence in the face of divine powers. As this huge army, this human war-tempest, moved under arms toward their lovely land, were they heartened by the fact that its leader was defying not only Athens, not only Greece, but the

93

gods that watched over both and that would surely punish pride and blasphemy?

The pontoon bridge was rebuilt, and it was a Greek engineer who rebuilt it, an Ionian of Samos named Harpalus. Three hundred sixty ships, anchored side by side, composed the floating base of one bridge; three hundred fourteen, the other. Again they were bound together with cables. On these cables plank was laid, and over the plank, first brush, then earth. Fences were built on both sides of each bridge so that the animals would not be frightened of the briny, rebellious river that flowed beneath. Xerxes had yoked the neck of the sea.[144]

The day fixed for beginning the crossing arrived. At dawn Xerxes himself poured a libation from a golden phial into the sea he had earlier scourged and fettered. He then prayed to the Sun for the success of his expedition into Europe. Now he cast the golden phial into the waters of the Hellespont, and with it a golden bowl and a Persian sword. Then Xerxes and his Persian warriors crossed; and of these the 10,000 picked troops known as the Immortals wore garlands on their heads. Finally, the contingents of his subject provinces started crossing under the lash, and later tradition would recount that it took this polyglot army seven days and seven nights to complete its crossing.

At Doriscus Xerxes ordered his army and navy renumbered. The army may have contained some 360,000 combatants. A confused throng of servants, concubines, and supply men followed it. And the navy that supported it contained 1,207 triremes, mostly from Egypt, Phoenicia, or Ionia, although perhaps only 700 or 800 were fighting ships, as distinguished from supply ships and transports. It was a formidable force.[145] It is true that the higher naval officers were Persians with no naval tradition; that the loyalty of the recently rebellious Ionians might depend only on fear for their families, in Asia, and therefore at the mercy of the Great King; that, with the exception of the Persians, few of the soldiers or sailors of Xerxes showed enthusiasm for the war. They had come against Europe because they had to come. Finally, even if the gods should not grow jealous of this one man's godlike power, there were two great enemies to be dreaded, the land and the sea: the largely unknown land ahead might lead these vast forces to famine, and the uncertain sea might strike this fleet off a coast with two few harbors to shield it from storms. Such was the warning of the Great King's uncle, Artabanus. In any case, the invasion

army embodied might rather than right, brute force rather than an appeal
to justice, blind will rather than questing intellect, and its strategy tended
toward the hammer blow rather than the planned maneuver or the skillful
thrust. How can man will the waves of the sea to calm? How can he make
food spring from a strange and mountainous and none too fertile land?
They were entering a hard land, a treacherous sea, to fight hard men who
were preparing to defend their hearths. In their favor, they had overwhelming numbers, though marching under the lash and preparing to fight under
the lash. This multitude was supported or hindered by cooking women,
concubines, and eunuchs. Persian hybris and confidence in force, wealth,
and luxury—on a scale never dreamed of by Cyrus, founder of this empire
—were preparing to drive a mammoth army of conquered subjects from
many lands against desperate courage and the ingenuity that necessity
might mother.

On the beach near Doriscus, Xerxes, riding in a chariot, reviewed his
vast army. He rode past his Persians with their coats of mail and their
breeches, their wicker bucklers and their quivers, their short spears, long
bows, and reed arrows, and their daggers hanging from their girdles. The
Medes were equipped in the same way and so were the Cissians, and the
Hyrcanians who came from the southeastern shore of the Caspian Sea. The
Assyrians wore bronze helmets, with Egyptian-style shields and spears and
daggers. They carried wooden clubs studded with iron, and wore linen
breastplates. Xerxes' chariot passed the Bactrians, carrying bows made of
reeds and short spears; and the Sacans, a Scythian folk, with tall, stiff-
pointed caps on their heads and breeches on their legs, and carrying their native bows, daggers, and axes. He drove past troops from India, wearing
garments of 'tree-wool,' or cotton, and armed with reed bows and iron-
tipped arrows; past Areians, Parthians, Caspians, Pactyes, and past Sarangas
with knee-high boots. His Arabian contingent carried bows which, when un-
strung, curved backward. His Ethiopians wore leopard skins and lion skins;
their long-bows were made of strips of palm wood, and their short arrows
were tipped with sharpened stone; the Ethiopians carried also spears tipped
with the horn of the gazelle, and their clubs were studded. Half of each
Ethiopian's body was painted white with gypsum and half was red with
vermilion. The eastern Ethiopian soldiers each wore the skin of a horse's
head on his, with the mane for his crest, and the horse's ears erect; his
shield was made from the skin of a crane. The Libyans wore leather cloth-

ing and charred their wooden javelins. The Lydians were equipped more or less in the Greek style. The Thracians wore fox-skin caps, many-colored mantles, fawn-skin boots on their feet and legs. They were armed with javelins, daggers, and shields. Of all these peoples, the Persians were the most richly adorned. They brought with them an abundance of gold. Carriages bore their concubines and servants. Camels and other pack animals bore their food.

Of the various national contingents many, but not all, included cavalry. The Sagartian cavalry used lassoes. The cavalry of India rode swift horses; they also used chariots drawn by horses and wild asses. The Arabians were mounted on camels, and rode in the rear so that their animals would not panic the horses.

When Xerxes had reviewed his army, he reviewed the linen-winged warships of his Imperial navy. The ships were drawn down the beach, launched, and anchored in a line. Xerxes alighted from his chariot, boarded a Sidonian vessel, and sat under a golden canopy while he was carried past the prows of the ships and while on each trireme his marines stood to arms.

The Imperial navy's 1,207 triremes came from Phoenicia, Egypt, Cyprus, Cilicia, Pamphylia, Lycia, Caria, Doris, Ionia, and the Aegean Islands. The best ships were brought by the Phoenicians, and the best of the Phoenician ships had sailed out of Sidon. Besides the 1,207 triremes, there were ships of thirty oars and of fifty oars, light galleys, and huge transports for horses. On all the triremes there were fighting marines: Persians, Medes, and Sacans.

Xerxes was well satisfied. He summoned Demaratus, the deposed Spartan king.

"You are a Greek, . . ." said Xerxes. "Now therefore tell me this: will the Greeks offer me battle and abide my coming? . . ."[146]

"O King," answered Demaratus, the Spartan,

seeing that you bid me by all means speak the whole truth, and say that which you shall not afterwards prove to be false,—in Hellas poverty is ever native to the soil, but courage comes of their own seeking, the fruit of wisdom and strong law; by use of courage Hellas defends herself from poverty and tyranny. Now I say nought but good of all Greeks that dwell in those Dorian lands; yet it is not of all that I would now speak, but only of the Lacedaemonians; and this I say of them; firstly, that they will never accept conditions from you that import the

96

enslaving of Hellas; and secondly, that they will meet you in battle, yea, even though all the rest of the Greeks be on your side. But, for the number of them, ask me not how many these men are, who are like to do as I say; be it of a thousand men, or of more or of fewer than that, their army will fight with you.[147]

Xerxes was smiling but incredulous. Demaratus reminded him that Sparta had made him, Demaratus, an exile without a polis, while Xerxes' father, Darius, had received, protected, and supported him. As to the Spartans:

> fighting singly they are as brave as any man living, and together they are the best warriors on earth. Free they are, yet not wholly free; for law is their master, whom they fear much more than your men fear you. This is my proof—what their law bids them, that they do; and its bidding is ever the same, that they must never flee from the battle before whatsoever odds, but abide at their post and there conquer or die. If this that I say seems to you but foolishness, then let me hereafter hold my peace; it is under constraint that I have now spoken. But may your wish, O king! be fulfilled.[148]

Xerxes made a jest of Demaratus' answer, but treated the Spartan kindly.

Under the presidency of Sparta, thirty-one of the warring states of Greece had met at the Isthmus of Corinth to concert a common defense in the autumn of 481, before Xerxes' monstrous herd of men had even crossed the Hellespont. Those northern states which were most exposed, like the states in Thessaly, were cautious about promising to fight until they could judge whether the states of central and southern Greece were prepared to help defend them. A defensive alliance, the Panhellenic League, was formed. Feuds between states were hastily patched up. Athens and her neighbor, Aegina, were persuaded to end their war. It was inevitably agreed that Sparta would lead the army. But who would lead the navy? Sparta had the strongest army in Greece; however, under the guidance of a statesman of genius, Themistocles, a man of relatively obscure origins but with an imagination and wiliness worthy of Odysseus, Athens had just built the strongest navy. The urgent necessity of her war with Aegina had happily coincided with a chance strike at her state-owned silver mines at Laurium. By this year of invasion Athens had built, with her new funds, 147 ships[149] ready for action and was holding 53 more in reserve. If Sparta had the right to command the Allied armies, Athens had the same right to command the Allied navies. But the rapid rise of Athenian power had aroused so much jealousy and fear that the congress at the Isthmus demanded that Sparta should command the Allied navies too, even though Sparta was no sea power. The congress was able to muster some 35,000 heavy infantry and some 40,000 light-armed followers.[150]

If only the Thessalians would join, the Allies could send cavalry too, against the formidable cavalry of the invader. Out of all the states of Mainland Greece, only Thessaly, and to a far lesser extent Boeotia, bred horses extensively and maintained a real cavalry. And most of the Boeotian cities had already followed Thebes's example and medized. As Xerxes approached the Hellespont, those Thessalians who opposed the medizing Aleuadae of Larissa announced that they would join the Greek alliance provided the Allies would fight on their northern border. The Allies therefore sent 10,000 heavy infantry to hold the narrow Pass of Tempe. The Vale of Tempe led for nearly five narrow miles from Macedonia, between Mount Olympus, home of the Twelve Great Gods, and the less imposing Ossa, into Thessaly. Here in the Vale of Tempe, the Allies were joined by Thessalian horse. But learning there were alternate routes from Macedonia into Thessaly, the Allies withdrew at just about the time that Xerxes' army marched triumphantly across that briny river, the Hellespont. Thessaly now medized and added her cavalry to the monster army that was headed south for Athens.

One of the most alarming aspects of the coming storm was the attitude of the gods. Not only was a man of godlike power[151] now marching against Athens, but the Delphic oracle was apparently advising the embassies of various Greek states that their governments should medize. When an Athenian embassy sought Apollo's counsel, he replied through the mouth of the Pythoness:

> Wretches, why tarry ye thus? Nay, flee from your houses and city,
> Flee to the ends of the earth from the circle embattled of Athens! . . .[152]

and Apollo went on to predict that fortresses and temples would alike be burned. The two Athenian envoys were dismayed. But where Croesus of Lydia understood not that which was spoken, nor made further inquiry, the envoys from Athens took suppliant boughs in their hands and made further inquiry, praying aloud to Apollo:

Lord, regard in thy mercy these suppliant boughs which we bring to thee, and give us some better answer concerning our country; else we will not depart out of thy temple, but abide here till we die.[158]

Confronted by this obstinate and urgent faith, Apollo spoke a second oracle. His language was full of the poetic ambiguity and obscurity that clothed so many of his famous oracles; but he seemed to be saying that Athena, divine protectress of Athens, was trying in vain to secure the help of Zeus for her city; that all Attica would be lost to Xerxes, but that Zeus would permit a wood-built wall to protect the Athenians; that they should withdraw from Athens rather than await there the armies of Xerxes; that, even then, they would meet him in battle; and, finally, that "Salamis, isle divine" would "destroy children of women."

This second oracle sounded at least more merciful than the first, so the envoys wrote it down and took it back to Athens. Then, when they read it before the Athenian Assembly, the argument began. Some of the older citizens, who had lived on, and loved, the Attic soil before the younger citizens of Athens had turned to the sea, to ships, and to commerce, thought that the wood-built walls were the thorn hedge that had once upon a time fenced in the Acropolis. They should therefore retire to the Acropolis and defend that. But others insisted that the wood-built walls were the walls of their ships. They should flee all of Attica and take to the sea. Then they should fight Xerxes' fleet near Salamis, isle divine, which lay a quarter of a mile off the Attic coast a short distance above the Piraeus and indeed near to Athens itself. The professional interpreters of oracles pointed out that Salamis would destroy them. No, said the wily Themistocles, who had caused Athens to build her present excellent fleet and who had moved her naval base from exposed Phalerum to the now partially fortified and nearer harbor at Piraeus, if the children of women whom Salamis would destroy were Athenians, Apollo would not have called that island "divine" but would have called it by some word like "cruel." Apollo, he declared, meant that Salamis would destroy the Persian fleet, if the Athenians would but quit Attica, Acropolis and all, and take to their ships. Themistocles won the debate.

But the Greek states were troubled not only by those other oracles of Apollo that seemed to urge submission. They were also troubled because in most states the aristocrats, who were fighting a losing battle against rising democracies, were defecting to Persia. The Best People were unmoved by the heroic opposition of the Athenian democrats. If the people who were not Best, instead of turning sailor or shipbuilder, merchant or politician, had stayed on the land and tilled the farms of the landowning nobles; if they had left law to the nobles, who knew from of old how to translate divine law into civil law and how to govern the polis; then there might well have been no Athenian or Eretrian intervention in aid of the Greek King's rebellious Ionian subjects and no invasion of Greece.

Among the aristocrats who remained unmoved by the efforts to rally Hellas against the invading Xerxes was the famous Theban poet, Pindar. Pindar wrote victory odes for nobles and even tyrants, for men descended from gods, men who strove in the ancient, traditional, athletic contests like the Olympic Games; who won crowns of laurel for their skill and endurance; and whose excellence in sport reminded Pindar of the excellence their ancestors had shown in war. But it was excellence for the sake of excellence, not for the sake of grain routes to the Black Sea or of timber from Thrace. It was an excellence that strove, not for progress, but for perfection. Even the aristocrat, the descendant of a god, could not excel but by the grace of the Olympian.

> Creatures of a day, what is anyone? What is he not? Man is but a dream of a shadow; but when the Zeus-given gleam of sunlight comes, a radiance rests on men, and a gentle life.[154]

Pindar looked, for significance, not outward beyond the sea, but upward, toward the gods; not toward a prosperous future but toward the permanent and immortal, contained and reflected in the present, heroic, striving moment. The god-descended noble, the god-descended runner or chariot-driver at the Olympic Games, or at the Pythian, the Nemean, or the Isthmian, could fulfill himself and make his life a sign of eternity only because he lived the present moment to the full, and because a radiance rested on him. That Pindar might remain neither the dream of a shadow nor the creature of a day, but endure, that those victorious athletes for whom he wrote his odes might also endure, he looked to the gleam of Zeus-given light that had brought courage to Achilles, that he also might endure, and he did not look to the restless cunning of Odysseus.

As to Apollo, who spoke the will of Zeus through his oracles at Delphi, was it so sure that, as many charged, his priests were corrupted into medizing? The Athenian envoys who would not take no for answer had inquired further, and Apollo had told them that Zeus would permit a wood-built wall to protect the Athenians. There all inquiry ceased, and whether they or their sons or their sons' sons would prove but creatures of a day and what would ultimately befall their Polis if they fought, and which children of men Salamis, isle divine, would ultimately destroy, was never disclosed to them, if only because they did not ask.

Despite the hope in Apollo's second oracle, given when the envoys of Athens had insisted on making further inquiry—assuming Themistocles had read the oracle rightly—the men of Athens could hope for little either from the gods or from the gods' descendants, the nobles, in most of the cities of Greece. When the Allies fell back from the narrow Pass of Tempe and abandoned Thessaly, the next obvious place to defend eastern Greece south of the Malaic Gulf was a narrow pass between sheer mountains and the sea, connecting Malis and Locris. The pass ran from east to west for about a mile along the south shore of the Malaic Gulf, near the western cape of the long island of Euboea. At each end of the mile, the pass became so narrow as to suggest two gates. In fact, the gates were scarcely wider than a cart road. The area between them widened somewhat, but the flow from a number of hot mineral springs created a morass. Many years before, the Phocians had deliberately guided the hot, sulphurous water into the pass so as to keep the pass from being used by Thessalian raiders who might come against them. For the same reason, they had built a wall, which was now in ruins, across the path near the western gate. Because of the hot springs and the two narrow gates, the whole pass was called Thermopylae, or the Hot Gates. At Thermopylae a huge army would enjoy little advantage over a small force of men who knew how to die. It is true that a circuitous, little-known path over the mountain that flanked the pass could furnish a detour, but this mountain trail could also be guarded.

The Allies, in congress at the Isthmus, decided to guard the Pass of Thermopylae and at least to delay the enemy there. They also decided to send the Allied fleet to Artemisium, on the northernmost coast of Euboea. There it could guard the entrance to the strait that separated that island from the mainland. In case of necessity, it could fight the Great King's fleet inside the strait, where the narrow waters would serve as a naval Thermopylae for a small but determined force. And it could keep an eye on the coast to the rear of the men who must hold Thermopylae.

In the summer of 480 Leonidas, one of the two kings of Sparta, marched a force of 300 chosen Spartans from the Isthmus to Thermopylae. All his men were mature citizens who had already fathered sons to defend Sparta in future years. With them marched upwards of 4,900 men from other Greek cities, even including 400 Thebans, unsympathetic with the medizing policy of the oligarchs who governed Thebes, and perhaps some Helots from Lacedaemonia and other light troops. The Allied command claimed that this was only an advance guard. Sparta delayed sending more men for the moment, because a religious festival detained them at home. Unkind critics would later declare that, since she really wanted to hold the line, not in central Greece, but at the Isthmus of Corinth, she had sent only a token force to the coming battle at the Hot Gates. But Sparta was not alone in delaying. Other states delayed on the grounds of another religious festival, the Olympic Games. In any case, given the size of Xerxes' army and given the remarkable strategic value of Thermopylae, Leonidas commanded only token forces.

Meanwhile, the Allied fleet was posted off Artemisium, but when some of their scouting vessels reported that the much larger Persian fleet was following down the east coast of the peninsula of Magnesia, the Allies somewhat fearfully withdrew down the strait between Euboea and the mainland. Then, according to later report, Posidon, the sea god, and Boreas, the north wind, suddenly raised a fearful storm off Magnesia, where most of the enemy fleet were anchored, and for three days the sea rose in waves of death, as it had risen against the Achaean conquerors, homeward bound from fallen Troy.[155] Four hundred warships were destroyed, together with unnumbered supply ships and transports. The gods had struck an even deadlier blow at the navy of Xerxes than the blow they had struck twelve years earlier at his father's navy off Mount Athos. After the storm, the still formidable Persian fleet withdrew for a few days to the Gulf of Pagasae.

The huge Persian land forces now arrived outside the Hot Gates and encamped. At sight of this overwhelming host, this "mighty flood of men,"[156] many of Leonidas's army lost heart. Most of the Peloponnesian contingents wanted to fall back to the Isthmus of Corinth where with reinforcements they might at least save the Peloponnese. This proposal naturally angered the contingents of Phocians and Locrians, whose little countries would instantly fall to the Persian host. Leonidas decided to stay, and sent messengers to the Allied cities to demand reinforcements, since he and his forces were too few to stand against Xerxes' huge army, even in the narrow pass between the Hot Gates.

Xerxes sent a mounted scout to spy out the Greek position. Most of the Greeks were hidden behind the ancient wall which the Phocians had built and which Leonidas's men had now repaired; but the Lacedaemonians were posted outside the wall. Here, on this mid-August day, between the mountain's rock cliffs and the sea, some of them were practicing gymnastic exercises. Others were busy combing their hair, which they wore long, as did all Spartans, in the fashion of their forefathers. When the scene was reported to the Great King, he found it so laughable that he summoned the deposed Lacedaemonian king, Demaratus, whom he had brought with him to Greece, and demanded an explanation. Now it was Demaratus' fellow king Cleomenes who had brought about his deposition. Cleomenes was now dead, and a few miles away his son-in-law Leonidas held the narrow pass. To the Great King's questions about his amusing handful of opponents, combing their hair and ignoring certain doom, Demaratus answered, with due deference but with Spartan stubbornness, that "these men are come to fight with us for the passage, and for that they are preparing"[157]; the Lacedaemonians, he added, always adorned their hair before risking their lives.

But Xerxes would not believe him. Four days he waited for the Greeks to withdraw and save themselves—as indeed most of the contingents under Leonidas wished to do. Then he grew angry. He ordered his Median and Cissian troops to attack, capture the Greeks, and bring them alive into his presence. For a whole day the Medes and Cissians fought the Greeks and lost many men, but to no avail. The second day, Xerxes ordered out the Immortals. But the Lacedaemonians, favored by the narrowness of the pass, by greater length of spear, and by cleverer tactics, slew many of the Immortals, lost relatively few men themselves—and held the pass. The third day Xerxes hoped to find the Greeks exhausted; but the contingents of the various cities took turns fighting. And they held the pass.

Meanwhile, a Greek from Malis, a state abutting Thessaly which had medized when the Allies abandoned Tempe and left the northern states to their fate—this Greek, whose name was Epialtes, informed Xerxes of the mountain trail that detoured the Hot Gates. The Phocian contingent had been ordered by Leonidas to hold this trail. Xerxes thereupon sent his Immortals by night and by this trail across the mountain that flanked Thermopylae. They were guided by Epialtes.[158] On this still August night, the Phocians' first warning that Persians were at hand was the noise of dried oak leaves beneath Persian feet. Under a rain of arrows and convinced that the Persians had come especially to attack them, they fled to the top of the mountain and prepared to die. The Immortals let them flee and hurried on to trap Leonidas from the rear.

Leonidas was warned by his seer, Megistias, that he and his little band were to die next morning. Then deserters brought them word that they were outflanked. When day dawned, their own sentries rushed down from the heights to tell them that they would soon be bottled up in the pass.

Following their custom, the Greek forces held a council, and many advised retreat. Leonidas thereupon sent back those who were eager to return to their respective cities. Leonidas and his Spartans remained at the post to which they had been ordered. The Thespian contingent chose to remain at their side. The Thebans, his most dubiously loyal contingent, Leonidas detained against their will. Did he have hopes of reinforcements? Or was he merely determined to obey when someone had blundered? Or did he recall an oracle which the Spartans had received from Delphi at the beginning of the war? Apollo had told them that Xerxes, mighty as Zeus, would either lay waste Sparta or else kill one of their kings. Perhaps Leonidas thought his death at Thermopylae would save his polis. Finally, Leonidas may have sent back the other contingents, not to their cities, but to attack the Persian Immortals and to protect the contingents that still held the pass.

Xerxes rose when the sun rose, and offered libations, but he delayed the assault until later in the forenoon to give his Immortals time to make their detour and to strike simultaneously with his own forces at the eastern gate from the rear of Leonidas. Having chosen to die, Leonidas and his little band shifted tactics. On the three previous days they had fought from behind the Phocian wall. Now they went beyond it; and, while the Persian officers scourged their men to advance, the Greeks mowed them down. Most of the Greeks had by now broken their heavy spears and were working with swords. In that work Leonidas fell, and over his body the Greeks fought, as the heroes in Homer had fought to retrieve the body

of Patroclus. Just then word came that the Persian Immortals were approaching from the rear. The Greeks promptly withdrew behind the
Phocian wall and took position on a hillock near the eastern gate. During
the withdrawal, the Thebans suddenly threw down their arms and surrendered. Of those on the hillock, the men who still had swords worked
with them; the others worked with their fists and their teeth. But Persian
arrows rained down; to the west the Phocian wall was breached; the hillock
was now ringed round; and, to a man, the Greeks fell. After the war, the
Amphictyonic League would erect pillars where they fell, one to all the
Peloponnesians who died at Thermopylae and one to the Spartans alone.
Each pillar would bear an inscription, a laconic inscription, composed by
the poet Simonides. For all those who fell, Simonides would write:

> Here four thousand of the Peloponnese once fought with three
> thousand thousand.[159]

And for the Spartans alone:

> Stranger, go tell the Lacedaemonians that we lie here obedient to their
> word.[160]

When Xerxes examined the bodies of the fallen Greeks, the body of
Leonidas was identified. Xerxes ordered the head struck off and the body
crucified. Twenty thousand men of Xerxes' army had been slain.

While Leonidas fought at the Hot Gates, things were happening at sea
too. For a while Xerxes' battered navy licked its wounds in the Gulf of
Pagasae, but it was still large enough to strike dread in the Allied fleet off
Artemisium. Several of the Greek contingents wanted to draw back, and
the people in the island of Euboea were begging for time to evacuate their
children and slaves before Euboea was abandoned. Luckily, the Euboeans
hit on the plan of giving Themistocles, who commanded the Athenian
contingent, a handsome bribe of thirty talents. Themistocles promptly
distributed modest fractions of this sum to the recalcitrant Allied commanders. The fleet stayed.

The Persians now decided that, before attacking the Allied fleet, they
should close the southern end of the Euripus, the strait that lay between
Euboea and the mainland, in case the Allies should attempt to use it as
an escape corridor. So they detached 200 ships and sent them around

Euboea. Then the main Persian fleet sighted the Greek ships approaching from Artemisium. There was a battle, and by superior tactics the Greeks captured thirty ships from the Persians. Night put an end to the fighting, and the Allies returned to Artemisium.

But with night the sea once more rose in waves of death, and in this new storm it was the 200 Persian ships on their voyage around Euboea that were entirely lost. Cheered by news of this event and by the timely arrival of 53 additional ships from Attica, the Allies struck again, this time at some Cilician ships from the Persian navy, and destroyed them. At the end of this second day, they withdrew again to Artemisium.

On the third day the two main fleets fought a pitched battle and both were badly mauled, with no clear victory for either side.

Shortly thereafter, an Athenian ship that had waited offshore near Thermopylae to obtain news of the outcome reported back that the pass was lost. Central Greece now lay open to the Great King's land forces and the Allied fleet hurriedly withdrew to that divine isle, Salamis, to cover the evacuation of Attica. But the wily Themistocles found time as his Athenian contingent sailed round Attica to cut inscriptions on the rock cliffs wherever the Persian fleet was likely to stop for fresh water. The inscriptions read:

> Men of Ionia, you do wrongly to fight against the land of your fathers and bring slavery upon Hellas. It were best of all that you should join yourselves to us; but if that be impossible for you, then do you even now withdraw yourselves from the war, and entreat the Carians to do the same as you. If neither of these things may be, and you are fast bound by such constraint that you cannot rebel, yet we pray you not to use your full strength in the day of battle; be mindful that you are our sons and that our quarrel with the foreigner was of your making in the beginning.[161]

Whether or not Xerxes believed that the Ionians would change sides, he would be likely to distrust them, perhaps to the point of not sending them into battle.

Meanwhile, the huge Persian army was moving south toward Athens. But part of it made a detour to seize the rich votive offerings of Apollo's temple at Delphi. The Delphians asked the god whether they should bury his treasures, but he replied through his priestess that it was unnecessary: he was able to protect his own. The Delphians ferried their women and children across the Gulf of Corinth to Achaea, while most of the men sought refuge on the heights of Mount Parnassus. On came the Persians. A frightful storm burst. Two crags split off from Mount Parnassus, and rolled down on the Persian forces, killing a large number.[162] The Persian forces fled; the Delphians dashed from their hiding places and slaughtered many of the Great King's men; and it was later reported that two armed warriors, of more than human stature, joined in the chase and in the slaughter.

The Peloponnesian land forces, under the command of the dead Leonidas's brother, were now busily building a wall across the Isthmus of Corinth. They were determined not to defend anything north of that point. The Persians therefore occupied Boeotia, collected fresh cavalry there, and reached the frontier of Attica with so many Greek reinforcements as to be stronger than before Thermopylae.

The ships of Athens now proceeded to remove the inhabitants of Attica —some to Salamis, some to Troezen in the Argolid, and some to the land of their recently reconciled enemy, the Aeginetans. From various parts of the Greek peninsula and from some of the islands, more ships hurried in. There was even one ship from southern Italy, from the Greek city of Croton. At the Allied base at Salamis there were now 378 triremes, not counting a number of the old-fashioned penteconters.

A council of war was held, and most of the commanders of contingents urged moving the Allied fleet to the Isthmus, since Attica was lost. Indeed, word came that the Persians had marched through Boeotia, where they had burned Plataea—whose men alone had fought beside the men of Athens ten years before at Marathon. The Persians had also burned Thespiae, whose men had stood by Leonidas and fallen with him at Thermopylae. They were now ravaging Attica and burning everything. At Athens they found a deserted city: the polis, the human community, had quit this sacred ground on Apollo's advice. A few citizens had disobeyed the proclamation to quit Attica and had taken refuge in the Acropolis, which they had boarded up with wooden plank, apparently wagering their lives that they had read the oracle's phrase better than Themistocles and that a wood-built wall would protect them. The Persians came; despite a long and heroic resistance the wager was lost; the Persians slew every Athenian; and they burned Athena's temple in vengeance for those temples of Sardis in Lydia that had been burned when Athenians and Eretrians had aided the Ionian rebels against the King. Marathon, too, was avenged: Lord, remember the Athenians. Many captains of Greek naval contingents, when they heard the fate of Athens, quit the council, went on board their ships, and made ready to fall back to the Isthmus.

But they reckoned without the cunning of Themistocles. First he persuaded the Spartan admiral to call them again into council, and Themistocles argued. To no avail. The commander of the Corinthian fleet pointed out bitterly that a man with no polis should have no vote. Themistocles declared that he had a polis greater than Corinth so long as Athens had 200 fully manned ships, for no other polis in Greece could beat them off. Then he played his trump card: the Athenians would collect their households, voyage to Siris in Italy, and settle there, leaving the rest of them to face the Persians alone. At that, the Spartan admiral came about.

Themistocles and the captains of the contingents from Megara and Aegina, city-states which, like Athens, were faced with desertion by the Peloponnesians, seemed to have won the argument. But the Peloponnesians managed to call another council of war and threatened to outvote them. Thereupon, Themistocles slipped quietly out of the meeting and sent a messenger to the Persians, declaring himself a secret friend of the Great King and urging Xerxes to attack quickly and bottle up the Allied fleet in the narrow straits between Salamis and the mainland. During the night, the Persians took his advice.

But now, while the Allied captains still argued, Themistocles was called out of the meeting by the Athenian, Aristides. Aristides had been a political opponent of his, had been ostracized by the democratic Assembly, and had gone into exile. He came now from Aegina to inform Themistocles that the Allied fleet was encircled. Themistocles told him of his ruse and pointed out that if he, Themistocles, conveyed Aristides' message to the wrangling captains, they would not believe him: Aristides himself should tell them. Even then, most of the wranglers were incredulous, until a deserter from the Persian fleet confirmed the news. It was dawn now. There was nothing left but to fight.

A recent earthquake, a deep bellowing thunder beneath the earth,[163] had caused the Allied Greek captains to offer prayers to the gods; to beg help of those two brother heroes, Ajax and Teucer, who had sailed from Salamis to fight at Troy; and to send a trireme to Aegina to fetch statues of other members of their family. At sunrise of the morning after Xerxes

sealed the strait, the Greeks manned their ships, and at that moment
the trireme returned from Aegina with the sacred images. The Allied fleet
had scarcely put out when the Great King's navy attacked. Most of the
Greek triremes began to back water; but one charged an enemy ship. It
was later reported, too, that the vision of a woman appeared and demanded of the Greeks, "Sirs, what madness is this? how long will you
still be backing water?"[164] Then the vision issued commands in a voice
loud enough for the whole Greek fleet to hear. A Greek trumpet sounded.
The Greek paean rose and echoed against the hills of Salamis. A Greek
voice cried out:

> O Greek sons, advance! Free your fathers' land, free your sons, your
> wives, the temples of your fathers' gods, the tombs of your forefathers.
> Now you fight for all you love.[165]

The Greeks, especially the men of Aegina and of Athens, now found
the rhythm of their oars and drove the bronze beaks of their triremes
against the sides of the enemy ships or sheared off their oars. Between the
craggy Isle of Salamis and the nearby Attic shore, they did their skillful
work. The Aeginetans faced mainly the Great King's Ionian ships; and,
despite the message of Themistocles inscribed on the sea cliffs and urging
them to change sides or at least fight halfheartedly, most of the Ionian
ships fought well, far better than at Artemisium a few weeks before. The
Athenians faced Xerxes' best contingent, the Phoenicians. Back of the
Phoenicians, high on the shore of Attica, with Mount Aegaleos towering
behind, the Great King himself sat on a white marble throne with silver
feet, to watch the Greeks' defeat, while his scribes stood at his side to write
down the names of whichever of his captains should distinguish themselves most. Farther to the right rose the Acropolis of the city they had
left; and from the Acropolis looked down upon their ships the half-burned
temples of their gods. The massive Imperial navy, crowded into narrow
waters, fell into disorder and the Great King's ships through mischance
rammed and smashed each other. His ships capsized and showed their
bellies. Their bronze jaws gaped. The narrows became a bloody mass of
wreckage. Corpses

> glutted beaches and the rocks.
> Every warship urged its own anarchic
> Rout; and all who survived that expedition,

Like mackerel or some catch of fish,
Were stunned and slaughtered, boned with broken oars
And splintered wrecks: lamentations, cries
Possessed the open sea, until the black
Eye of evening, closing, hushed them . . .[166]

The Athenian squadron under Themistocles drove many of the Phoenician warships against the tiny, rocky island of Psyttaleia, that lay between Salamis and Athens' port city, the Piraeus. From dawn to twilight the battle had raged. It was on tiny Psyttaleia that Xerxes had posted some picked fighters with orders to rescue any men they could who might survive a wrecked Imperial ship and to kill any Greek sailors or infantry who might survive a wreck of their own. When the Imperial fleet fled in disorder, Aristides ferried Athenian infantry to Psyttaleia and slaughtered the Imperials to the last man. The victorious Allies towed to Salamis all the wrecks they could find. Although the beaten Imperial fleet had withdrawn to Phalerum, the Allies assumed that they would have to fight again. Night fell, while "the sea-dyed corpses" still whirled "vagrant on cragged shores."[167]

The battle of Salamis was fought on September 29[168] in the year 480. It lasted all day, and it went as Themistocles expected it to go. It was he who had created the Athenian navy. The "fountain of silver"[169] at Laurium had nourished it. Long and hard practice had taught it skill and a kind of discipline at which the dogged Spartan army could barely guess. Athenian ingenuity and flexibility made it a terrible instrument. The war with Aegina had tempered it, and it was not by chance that the navies of Aegina and Athens distinguished themselves at Salamis above all others. Though the ships were manned by oarsmen who were not descended from the gods, yet they looked on themselves as free-born sons of Athens, governing themselves by reason and law, no victims of oligarchic or tyrannical force. They and their scattered, exiled families were part of a polis torn loose from its native soil, but with the image of lovely Attica in their hearts and the promise of Apollo to protect them.

The Persian fleet was defeated, demoralized, and disaffected. During the battle, some of the Phoenicians who escaped from the melee in the narrow straits accused the Ionians of treason and of destroying Phoenician vessels. Xerxes, watching the defeat from his marble throne near the Attic shore, just then happened to witness the heroic behavior of an Ionian ship. Turning on these Phoenician informers in one of his sudden rages, he ordered their heads cut off, that cowards like themselves should no longer be able to accuse better men. By the time the battle was lost, it was doubtful whether either of the main elements in his navy, the Phoenician or the Ionian, could be fully counted on.

Would Thrace and Macedonia rebel? If so, would they break the bridge at the Hellespont? And what of Ionia? The warships of the Great King fled toward the Hellespont. Unsupported by a fleet, the army withdrew northward. A message had already gone to Susa that Athens had been burned. By a stretch of the royal imagination, the destruction of Athens could be pictured, along with the sack of Eretria and the submission of many Greek states, as the real point of the whole horrible enterprise. Now another message went to inform Susa of the catastrophe at Salamis. Mardonius, brother-in-law of Xerxes, persuaded the King to give him a force[170] of picked men and to return to Asia with the rest. Mardonius chose the Persian Immortals and other Persian troops, including the Great King's personal guard of a thousand horse; the contingents of Medes, of Sacans, and of Bactrians from northwest Afghanistan, and Indians from the Punjab; and certain distinguished fighters from other provinces of the empire. Then he and his army wintered in Thessaly. The bridge over the Hellespont had been destroyed by another storm, but the fleet ferried the Great King and his army back to Asia. Mardonius planned the campaign of 479.

The Greeks divided the booty, built temples to the gods who had saved them, set up captured Phoenician ships as trophies of their great victory, and of their booty sent the first fruits to Apollo at Delphi. As to the prize of valor for the captain who had most distinguished himself, the wrangling captains again could not agree; but all of them voted the second prize to Themistocles.

The Great King's fleet was ordered to Samos to watch restless Ionia. The Athenians returned to their empty city and countryside and began reconstruction. The Allied fleet withdrew to Aegina. The Ionians sent envoys to Sparta and begged the Spartans to lead the Allies to Asia and liberate Ionia. Cautious Sparta did not budge. So the Ionians went to Aegina. They succeeded in getting the Allied fleet to move as far eastward as the island of Delos.

Sparta, at the command of a Delphic oracle, sent heralds after Xerxes. They were given an audience and solemnly announced: "The Lacedaemonians . . . demand of you, King of the Medes! that you pay the penalty for the death of their king, whom you slew while he defended Hellas."[171] The King of Kings never had been able to understand the Greeks. Now he laughed. Pointing to Mardonius, he said, "Then here is Mardonius, who shall pay . . . such penalty as befits them."[172] The irony was worthy of a Delphic oracle; but might this irony raise questions for Xerxes as well as for the Spartans?

From Athens the wily Themistocles sent a secret message to Xerxes that, as a service to the Great King, he had persuaded the Allies not to pursue his navy northward nor to break down the bridges at the Hellespont. The message was untrue of course, but who could tell whether Xerxes might not be useful some day to Themistocles? Then Themistocles, who seemed to possess an equal talent for giving and accepting bribes, secretly blackmailed some of the island states in the Aegean that had medized by threatening them with punishment for their treason to Greece.

Mardonius was convinced that his picked force, now wintering in Thessaly, could reduce Greece if only he could detach the Athenians and thereby break the sea power of the Greeks. He therefore sent Alexander,[173] king of the Macedonians, to propose an alliance between Athens and the Persian Empire. When news of this proposal reached Sparta, the Lacedaemonians were thoroughly alarmed and rushed envoys to Athens. They pointed out to the Athenians that Athens had really started the war by aiding the Ionian revolt a dozen years earlier, and had done it without consulting Sparta. How could Athens, which loved freedom, now help the Persians reduce all other Greeks to slavery? The Spartans promised to see that the Allies should bear the expense, for the duration of the war, of supporting Athens' civilian population, since Athens had lost two years' harvest at Persian hands.

To Alexander the Athenians replied:

So long as the sun keeps its course, we will never join alliance with Xerxes. Nay, we shall oppose him unceasingly, trusting in the aid of those gods and heroes whom he has lightly esteemed, whose houses and whose images he has burnt with fire.[174]

They then rebuked the Spartan envoys for suspecting that the Persians could bribe them. Because the Persians had destroyed their temples and their images of the gods, because of their common brotherhood with other Greeks, their common language, their common altars, and their common way of life, it would ill become Athenians to be false. They thanked the Spartans for offering to help them, but declined to be a burden to the Allies. But they pointed out that by rebuffing Mardonius's offer, they invited a second invasion. They therefore begged Sparta to hurry and join them in occupying Boeotia.

The Athenians were right in their fear of a second invasion. When Mardonius received their refusal of his offer, he quickly occupied Boeotia himself. The Lacedaemonians, relieved of their alarm, were busily celebrating another religious festival. More important, they were now completing the wall across the Isthmus, which was to shelter the Peloponnesians from invasions such as Athens had to endure. Athens, Megara, and Plataea, all of them situated beyond the protecting wall, sent envoys to Sparta to reproach her and beg help, but the Spartans played for time.

The Thebans urged Mardonius to stay in Boeotia and to break up the Greek alliance by a judicious distribution of bribes to the Allied states. But with Sparta and her Peloponnesian allies delaying, Mardonius chose to move into exposed Attica and, for the second time in ten months, the Persians seized Athens. For the second time they captured an empty city: the Athenians had taken to their ships again and had placed their families on Salamis. Again the Athenians pleaded with Sparta to help them fight the Persian army, this time in Attica. At last Sparta, reflecting however tardily that if Athens really should in despair switch her sea power to the side of Persia, the wall Sparta had built at the Isthmus would do her little good, sent her army to the Isthmus. Medizing Argos promptly warned Mardonius that a Peloponnesian army which the Argives were too weak to attack was on its way. In June, 479, Mardonius leveled partially rebuilt Athens, wasted the countryside, and withdrew to Boeotia: Attica, with its mountainous frontiers, could have proved a trap for his army; and besides, Attica offered his powerful cavalry no advantage comparable with the plains of Boeotia.

In August of 479 the two armies converged near Plataea. Mardonius commanded an army of some 125,000 men, including 24,000 Greek heavy infantry and 1,000 Greek cavalry. Pausanias, the Spartan regent, commanded around 40,000 Greek heavy infantry, including contingents he had picked up from Megara, Athens, and Pataea.[175] But Pausanias was without cavalry, and Herodotus reported[176] that the Persian and Theban cavalry, especially the mounted archers, sorely harassed the Allied forces. From Lacedaemon Pausanias had brought 5,000 heavy-armed Spartan infantry, with 35,000 light-armed Helots to attend them and 5,000 Dwellers-round-about, who formed his right wing. The left wing was held by 8,000 heavy-armed Athenians, under the command of Aristides. Spartan and Athenian were preparing now to fight shoulder to shoulder at Plataea because they needed each other. The Allied army that faced Mardonius included contingents—some of them very small—from Lacedaemonia, Athens, Tegea, Corinth, Potidaea, Orchomenos, Sicyon, Troezen, Lepreum, Mycenae, Tiryns, Phlius, Hermione, Eretria, Styreia, Chalcidice, Ambracia, Leucas, Anactorium, Pale, Aegina, Megara, and Plataea.

Mardonius's cavalry continually harassed the Allied army and even succeeded in badly disorganizing its lines of supply. But for days there was no general pitched battle, while prophets on both sides consulted the auspices. Cut off from water, Pausanias was forced to withdraw by night more than a mile farther westward. But he handled his withdrawal badly. The Megarians, Phliasians, and Corinthians fell back on Plataea. The Athenians failed to effect complete junction. One of the Spartan battalion commanders decided it was dishonorable to withdraw, as Pausanias had ordered, and the other leaders lost hours trying to persuade him. Indeed, when dawn broke, Persian scouts found only his battalion still near the original line.

On August 27, 479, Mardonius attacked. His picked Persian troops closed with the Lacedaemonians and Tegeans; the Athenians were not even in sight. The Boeotians and the other medizing Greeks in his army followed but in some disorder. Pausanias, when the Persian cavalry attacked him, sent word to the Athenians, beseeching their prompt aid. But the Athenians by this time were fighting off Mardonius's Greek allies and could send no help. Pausanias prepared therefore to defend himself with only some 50,000 Lacedaemonians and 3,000 Tegeans, but few of these were heavy infantry, and most of them were light-armed Helots. The Spartans were sacrificing to the gods but could not get favorable auspices. The Persians set up their shields for a fence and rained arrows on Pausanias's men.

Pausanias lifted his eyes to the temple of Hera in nearby Plataea and prayed to her for help. The men of Tegea did not wait for him to finish: they charged the Persians. Just then the Spartans' sacrifices started showing favorable omens, and they too charged the Persians. The Persians threw away their bows and fought now at the line formed by their fence of shields. When the fence was overthrown, they seized the Spartans' spears and broke them off: they fought bravely, but were less well armed than the Spartans and less skilled at close combat. As at Marathon ten years earlier, they were more dangerous when shooting arrows from a distance than they were when fighting hand to hand. Where Mardonius, riding a white charger, fought, surrounded by a thousand especially chosen Persians, the Lacedaemonians bought their ground dear.

Then Mardonius was slain, along with his picked troops, and Spartan heavy armor and Spartan skill in close combat and Spartan discipline began to tell. The Imperial army fled and took refuge in its fortified camp outside Thebes, a camp surrounded by a wooden stockade with towers. The Theban cavalry covered the Persian retreat; and, indeed, of all the Greeks who had medized and who had served in Mardonius's army, the Thebans alone fought hard, bravely, and skillfully. Meanwhile one of the Great King's favorite generals, Artabazus, who had disapproved when Xerxes granted Mardonius his army and had again disapproved when Mardonius insisted on a pitched battle instead of holding Thebes and counting on bribery to dissolve the Greek Alliance—Artabazus now, when he approached the battleground and found Mardonius's men already in flight, turned the 40,000 men in his corps toward the Hellespont and home, leaving the remains of Mardonius's forces to their fate in the wooden fortress outside Thebes.

Pausanias and his Lacedaemonians assaulted the fortress, but made little headway, for the Spartans lacked skill in assaulting walls. Then the Athenians, who possessed that skill, arrived. After several days, they scaled the wall and breached it too, and the Greek Allies poured in. The rest was massacre—a

> sacrificial cake of clotted gore
> Made at Plataea by Dorian spear.
> And corpses piled up like sand . . .[177]

Mainland Greece was free at last.

The Allies buried their relatively few dead. Of the heavy infantry who fought, 91 Spartans lost their lives, 52 Athenians, and 16 Tegeans. The Mantineans arrived too late for the battle. They begged Pausanias to let them pursue Artabazus and his 40,000 men, now fleeing toward the Hellespont, but the Lacedaemonians refused to allow them to pursue fleeing men.

In fulfillment of the oracle, Mardonius had paid with his life for the death of Leonidas. The men of Xerxes' ruined army were either dead or enslaved or streaming toward the Hellespont and Asia, leaving an immense and rich spoil, of which the Greeks awarded a tithe to Apollo's temple at Delphi. Thebes was forced to surrender its pro-Persian oligarchs, whom Pausanias took to Corinth and put to death without trial. Plataea, on whose soil the victory had been won, was voted heavy compensation. She, on her part, undertook to render religious honors yearly at the tombs of the Greeks who had fallen and to hold every fifth year athletic contests like the Olympic Games, to be known as the festival of Eleutheria—that is, of Freedom. The Allies exchanged oaths to protect the sovereignty of Plataea against the Thebans' constant efforts to rule her. And they dissolved the Boeotian federation. The Allies then solemnly swore to maintain the Panhellenic League against Persia and to meet annually at Plataea.

Five centuries later the Eleutheria would still be held. At break of day a trumpeter would sound the signal for battle and then lead the procession. Behind him would come the wagons loaded with myrtle wreaths, then the black bull, then the freeborn youths bearing the jars of wine and milk for the libations and the pitchers of oil and myrrh. No slave would be allowed to help, for the men whom this procession would honor died for freedom. Then would come the chief magistrate of Plataea, robed in purple, carrying on high a water jar from the city's archive chamber, and in his other hand a sword. Arrived at the graves of those who died for freedom, he would take water from the sacred spring and wash their gravestones with his own hands and anoint them with myrrh. Then he would slaughter the black bull at the funeral pyre; pray to Zeus the Liberator, and to Hermes as guide of the dead;[178] and summon the brave men who died for Hellas to come to the banquet and drink its copious draughts of blood. Finally, he would himself drink wine and would pour a libation saying: "I drink to the men who died for the freedom of the Hellenes."[179]

After Salamis, word had come that Greeks in Sicily had won another victory for Hellas. It was even reported that they had done it on the very day that the Greek Allies had battered Xerxes' fleet at Salamis. For, presumably in concert with Xerxes, Carthage had struck at Sicily. Like Persia, Carthage was constantly being invited by Hellenic cities to aid them in their ferocious quarrels with each other. Like Persia's Phoenician subjects of Tyre and Sidon, Phoenician Carthage keenly felt the competition of Greek merchants. In 480 a Greek tyrant, whom the city of Himera on the northern coast of Sicily had recently expelled, appealed to Carthage to help him regain his lost throne—as Hippias, son of Pisistratus, had got Persian help in order to win back the tyranny of Athens. Carthage exploited the occasion. One of the two magistrates who headed the oligarchic republic of Carthage was the general-in-chief, Hamilcar, son of a Carthaginian father and a Syracusan mother. He now convoyed a large army[180] of mercenaries, recruited from Carthage, Libya, Spain, Sardinia, Corsica, and from Liguria, south of the Alps, to Panormus, a Greek city on the future site of Palermo. He then marched on nearby Himera and laid siege to the city. Himera appealed to Gelo, tyrant of Syracuse, for help. At this time Syracuse was, along with Athens and Sparta, one of the three great cities of Hellas; and Athens and Sparta had vainly solicited Gelo's aid when Xerxes was preparing to strike. Gelo marched against Hamilcar's mercenaries, destroyed his army, enslaved thousands of prisoners, and captured immense booty.

When the Allied fleet had moved from Aegina to the island of Delos, envoys from Ionia promptly followed it there and again begged its Spartan admiral to liberate Ionia. The Persian fleet was still based on the island of Samos, where it was keeping an eye on Greece-in-Asia. When the Ionian fleet went to Samos to defeat it, the Persian fleet dismissed the disaffected Phoenicians and cautiously withdrew to the mainland promontory of Mycale. There a Persian army of 60,000 men was stationed to forestall a second Ionian revolt, like the revolt that had precipitated the three attempts to conquer Mainland Greece. Under protection of these forces, the sailors of the Persian navy beached their ships and threw up a rampart of stones and tree trunks to protect both the ships and themselves. There the Allied fleet found them. The Spartan commander immediately repeated the stratagem of Themistocles on the sea journey from Artemisium around Attica to Salamis; but he did it by a herald's voice rather than by inscriptions.

Men of Ionia, you that hear us, take heed of what I say! for in no
case will the Persians understand aught of my charge to you: when we
join battle, let a man remember first his freedom, and next the watchword "Hebe": and let him that hears me not, be told of this by him
that hears.[181]

This stratagem the Persians met by disarming the Samians, whom they
rightly suspected of conspiring with the Allies. Since they suspected the
Milesians also, they sent them up into the heights of Mycale, allegedly
to guard the approaches to the Persian camp.

Just as the Greek Allies prepared to attack, a *phēmē,* or voice from
heaven,[182] sped through all the army, and a herald's wand was observed
lying on the shore where the waters of the sea began, as if it had floated
over with news from Greece. According to the phēmē, the Allies had
defeated the Persians in Boeotia. The Allies at Mycale had been de-
pressed by the knowledge that even now Mardonius might be overwhelming their comrades at home. They were aware that if their comrades had
won at home and if Mycale should prove a victory too, then the Aegean
Isles would be liberated and the Hellespont could be shortly cleared.
Heartened by the phēmē and by the herald's wand, the Greeks grew eager
for battle. Their line was so established that the Athenians had either
beach or other level ground before them, but the Lacedaemonians had
to advance through a ravine and among hills. The Persians prepared to
fight outside their stockade; and, just as at Plataea, they stood their shields
upright in a line to form a barrier. The Athenians, and the contingents that
flanked them—the men of Corinth, of Sicyon, and of Troezen—saw a
chance to break through the Persian shields before the Lacedaemonians
could make contact with the enemy, and they went to work in earnest.

The Persians fought hard behind their barrier of shields. Even after the
barrier was broken down, they stood their ground for a long time. But
they finally retreated inside the palisade where the ships lay beached.
However, the Athenians and Corinthians and Sicyonians and Troezenians
managed to crowd in after them and, unlike the stockade outside Thebes
that furnished temporary refuge for the Great King's men after the battle of
Plataea, this wall at Mycale never demanded Athenian skill at breaching.
When the Allies had once rushed inside the fortified area, all the Imperial
troops surrendered except the native Persians. The Persians fought on.
But then the Lacedaemonians arrived; the Samians turned on the Persians

with whatever weapons they could seize; and, finally, the other Ionians turned on them too. Some of the Persians managed to escape from this slaughterhouse of men and to flee to the hills where they had posted the Milesians, who knew the country, to act as guides in case of disaster. But the Milesian guides deliberately led the Persians into ambushes and in the end joined the Allies in slaughtering the refugees. Some managed to escape. The Greek losses were not light, but the Persian losses were frightful.

Ionia was once more free. And according to later tradition,[188] the Allies had won the battle of Plataea in the morning, and their comrades in Asia had won the battle of Mycale toward evening, of that same day, August 27, 479.

It was now some twenty years since Athens and Eretria had intervened in the Ionian Revolt and had thereby drawn down Darius' wrath on Mainland Greece. Shipwrecked at Athos, beaten at Marathon, halted at Thermopylae, badly defeated at Salamis by Greek triremes, routed at Plataea by Greek infantry, the Persians had failed even in Asia, and the second Ionian revolt was on.

But what was to prevent the mighty Persian Empire from quelling the second revolt, as she had quelled the first, once the Mainland Greeks had sailed home? The Peloponnesians answered this problem in their traditional way. They urged that all Greeks should be removed from this lovely, luxurious, but perilous coast. How could the Mainland Greeks, even after Salamis, even after Plataea, even after Mycale, hope to protect Greeks in Asia against the vengeance of the King of Kings? Why should the Greeks not content themselves with holding the sea, the islands, and the Hellespont? But where could the Greeks of the Asian coast be resettled? The Peloponnesians suggested seizing for their use the seaport towns of those Mainland Greeks who had medized in the hour of Greece's awful peril. But the Athenians objected that Ionia had been settled by men from Attica centuries ago and that Ionia must be defended. It was not only sympathy and Ionian pride that led Athens to refuse to evacuate Ionia. It was to the Ionians' and to her mutual advantage that the Persian Empire be shut off from the Aegean Sea as well as from the Hellespont and the Black Sea beyond it. The Ionians, like the Athenians, and quite unlike most Peloponnesians, were seafarers, sea fighters, and merchants; and Athens had the word of Apollo himself that in the hour of gravest danger her polis must be based on ships. The Peloponnesians yielded.

The first task was to break down the bridges at the Hellespont. The Allies thought these were still standing and were still inviting Asians to invade Europe, but when they reached Abydos on the Hellespont, they found the gods had done their work for them some ten months before.

The Spartan commander and the Peloponnesians under him now considered the war closed. But not the Athenians. Athens had long possessed important interests in the Chersonese, the peninsula that formed the western shore of the strategic Hellespont. It was from this Chersonese that Miltiades, later the hero of Marathon, had fled the Persians a year before their first invasion. The Chersonese was still held by a Persian governor; and its strongest fortress was Sestos. So while the Peloponnesians sailed away to their homes in triumph, the Athenians toiled through the autumn of 479, laying siege to Sestos. When the city had been reduced to stark famine, the Persian garrison managed to escape and their victims inside joyfully opened the gates of the city wall. The Athenians seized the treasures of the Persian governor, including the massive cables of hemp and the cables of papyrus that had borne the Great King's yoke of continents.[184] These they took home as trophies to dedicate in their temples to those gods who had so often saved the freedom of Hellas.

THE SCHOOL OF HELLAS

IN 489, when Miltiades, hero of Marathon, had suffered fiasco in his attack on Paros, it was Xanthippus who prosecuted him for deceiving the Athenian people. Xanthippus was a noble. He had married Agariste, niece of the great constitutional reformer, Clisthenes. Like him, Xanthippus opposed the return either of oligarchy or of tyranny. In 485 Athens ostracized Xanthippus, as she exiled Aristides two or three years later. Like him, Xanthippus was recalled under the general amnesty of 480, when Thermopylae had fallen and when the Athenians had left their city silent and deserted and had set forth for Salamis, for heroism, and for triumph.

About 490, the year of victory at Marathon, a son was born to Xanthippus and was named Pericles. He was about five when his father went into exile. The boy's uncle, Megacles, had been ostracized two years earlier. Pericles was ten when the women and children were hurried from Athens, some to the divine isle of Salamis, some to Aegina, some to Troezen. The young Pericles was taken to Salamis, that island so near Athens, which, ninety years before under the urging of Solon, Athens had seized, colonized, and made part of Athena's Polis. According to later tradition,[185] beside the trireme that bore Pericles swam his dog, refusing to be left behind. He made the island and then, exhausted, fell dead. In Salamis Pericles must have witnessed, as Xerxes did, the fleet of Xerxes and the fleet of the Greek Allies confront each other at dawn in the narrow waters. He must have heard the paean rise from the Allied fleet; have heard the trumpets' blast; have seen the even stroke of foaming oars. He may even have caught the Greek words ringing across the sounding straits and calling on the sons of Greece to free their fathers' tombs.

The next year, 479, Xanthippus was elected archon; then *strategos*, or commander. He commanded the Athenian contingent at the battle of Mycale, which freed the Ionians from Persian rule. It was Xanthippus and his Athenian troops who opposed the Spartans' plan of evacuating the Ionians to Greece. In the spring of 478, it was Xanthippus who besieged Sestos on the Hellespont, when the Peloponnesians had returned to Greece. The Persian garrison fled, Sestos surrendered, Xanthippus pursued the Persians, massacred many of them at Aegospotami and crucified their leader for his many cruelties while governor. It was Xanthippus who brought back to Athena's temple those two eloquent trophies—the cable of hemp and the cable of papyrus, which had supported Xerxes' impious bridge from Asia into Europe.

An Athenian boy of Pericles' clan would spend his first seven years in the women's quarters with his mother. He was then schooled by men. First he learned to read and write and reckon, on his little wooden tablet covered with soft wax to take the stylus' mark. Then he studied music, which included not only melody, not only the flute, the lyre, singing, and the dance, but the epic poets, Homer and Hesiod, and lyric poets like Solon, Mimnermus, Theognis. Music and poetry were expected to form his soul, to gentle and to civilize him. Was not music the lore of the Muses of Olympus, daughters of Zeus, who danced on soft feet about his altar on holy Helicon where Hesiod shepherded his lambs? Hesiod heard them sing and learned from them. But most men clearly did not. Hesiod saw them; but they often went abroad, clothed in thick mist, through which most men could not see. The poems and melodies they could teach to men must open the heart of the young Athenian to things mere reasoning could not fathom; must bring his heart into harmony with wiser minds and deeper knowledge than any race of iron could hope to find without the Muses' aid.

The boy Pericles was also taken to an outdoor gymnasium, the *palaestra*, where he learned to run, to leap, to wrestle, to throw the discus and the javelin, his body stripped beneath the Attic sun. In such fashion he would be hardened; he would learn courage and endurance. A young noble like Pericles, who could expect some day to serve in the cavalry, would in addition learn to ride and handle horses. From eighteen to twenty, he did his military service—a year of active duty, followed by a year of garrison duty. Then he was a full-fledged citizen with all the rights of a free man, member of a free polis.

In Pericles' boyhood the barbarians had come, bent on destroying freedom, on restoring a tyrant to Athens, on reducing Athens to the status of a subject city. The Athenians had closed ranks. The polis had twice uprooted itself and taken to the fleet and to Salamis. Twice its members had swarmed home to the smoking ruins of their temples and their homes. Tensions there still were, between rich, landowning nobles harking back nostalgically to their lost feudal power, and the new, raw democracy, bred by commerce and the sea, disciplined by the potter's wheel, the flaming forge, the shipyard, and the grueling work on the rowing pads of the swift, bronze-beaked triremes. But shared disaster, shared hardship, and shared ultimate triumph over tyranny and barbarism alike had redefined for all Athenians the very words tyrant and barbarian. Tyrant no longer meant merely a man who had seized power to rule in the interest of merchant and wage-earner against a decadent and rapacious nobility: tyrant meant the foe of freedom. Rich and poor alike had gazed in admiration at the bronze group of the two tyrannicides who had assassinated Pisistratus's younger son and had planned to assassinate Hippias too—gazed in admiration, that is, until this famous bronze had been stolen from the polis by Xerxes and taken to Susa, capital of the barbarians. As for this other word, barbarian, it no longer meant merely non-Hellene;[186] it was beginning to mean a man incapable of establishing a free polis or even of knowing what polis meant.

The schoolboy Pericles had watched free men, rich and poor alike, defeat overwhelming numbers of barbarians, mere slaves of one master, of him they called the King of Kings. Athenians, too, had a master, the Law.

But they demanded *isonomia,* equality before the law. And they demanded *isegoria,* equality in discussion, the free competition of ideas in the agora, the market place, before a rule was voted into law. In short, they governed themselves, and that was a new and exhilarating thing to do. They were learning to substitute reason for force, right for might. Or, more accurately, they were determined that the might of Athena's Polis should clearly serve the right, and that what was right should be determined by reason and free debate. They were determined to achieve, not only freedom, but law and justice.

In this democratic dream, men's minds and bodies were alike provided for. Through the medium of money they freely exchanged the material objects their bodies might require. Through the medium of words they freely exchanged the ideas their minds required. Yet not all the might of the polis had been tamed and made to serve right. Some money was used to oppress those who had none; some words were used to deceive the ignorant. And there were many persons in the polis still who did not share isegoria or help to make the laws they were nevertheless forced to obey. Athenian boys like the young Pericles were carefully taught to speak wingèd words. But their sisters were not. Athenian women were taught the domestic arts and could expect neither to hold office, nor to vote, nor even to participate in public discussion. Nor could the metic, or foreign resident, do any of these things, no matter what wealth he might amass in the business life of the Piraeus. Nor could the slaves; and, as the wealth of Athens grew, slaves became more and more numerous. Finally, although the common hardships of all Athenians, twice driven to abandon Attica, had created politically a kind of sacred union of democrats and aristocrats, yet nobles with permanent democratic leanings, nobles such as Pericles' father, Xanthippus, were rare. The Areopagus, that most conservative body in the machinery of government, in which only ex-archons could sit but where these had seats for life, regained some of its ancient rights to supervise the entire operation of government. In the Persian crisis, the Areopagus had behaved well. When that crisis was over, would the nobles not use it again to thwart the progress of equality? Would the nobles not feel in their bones, as they had always felt—these descendants of Achaean invaders who had bought Hellas with their blood and who commonly claimed descent from the very gods they had taught the conquered to worship—would these nobles not feel that they could make juster laws than ignorant and ignoble peasants and craftsmen? Might they not again feel justified in using might to assert their right, the right of the Best to rule? Inside the Polis of Athena, then, the dream of equal freedom under law was far from realized: the poor man, the man who was not Well-fathered, the slave, the woman, the metic were all in varying degrees shut out.

But what of the relations between the free men of Athens and the citizens of some other Hellenic polis, who spoke approximately the same tongue, who worshiped the same gods, not to mention the outer world of non-Hellenes, of barbarians? The other Hellenes lived under other laws, perhaps under laws like those of Sparta, perhaps, in backward northwestern Greece, under a form of monarchy or a later form of landed aristocracy. If the men of Athens and the men of Sparta disagreed on right, to what court could they turn? Both cities were sovereign states, obeying no human law but their own. Would disputes between those cities have to be settled by force and fraud? In default of a court, administering equal law, made by citizens in equal and free debate, must Athenians and Spartans turn to diplomatic deception and, at the last, to war? To Ares, whom Homer's Zeus clearly declared the most hated of all the gods on high Olympus? To Ares, who is "just and slays him who slays"[187]? If so, what of the fact that the nobles of Athens, or most of them, were frankly pro-Spartan and even imitated the Spartans' dress and manner? Neither the simmering hatred between rich and poor nor the constant threat of foreign war with some neighboring sovereign Greek state promised well for Solon's dream of fitting right with might. A new Hellenic community was emerging, knit together by growing commerce and relatively speedy transportation. Although individual city-states had achieved law internally, Hellas had not yet achieved law.

After the second occupation of Athens had ended and after what was left of the Persian army had fled northward from destruction at Plataea, the Athenians returned a second time to find their houses, except for those which Persian leaders had lately occupied, largely destroyed, Xanthippus' house among them. Xanthippus himself was still besieging Sestos on the Hellespont, when Pericles was taken home from Salamis to the city.

Themistocles now enjoyed, as a result of the victory off Salamis in 480, something of the prestige which had come to Miltiades after the battle of Marathon ten years before. It is true that men distrusted his cleverness, his wiliness; but his lively imagination and his ingenuity in practical affairs compelled them to follow him. In any case, they did trust Aristides, and Aristides was working with him to restore their common polis. On the eve of Salamis, in Themistocles' darkest hour, when the squadrons of the Peloponnesians seemed bent on deserting the Athenian fleet, it was Aristides, the recalled political exile, who had brought his political enemy the glad tidings that the Persians had bottled up the Greeks in the very spot where Themistocles wanted them. Because the Allies distrusted the man of many wiles, he had persuaded Aristides to convince them they must seek decision off Salamis. It had taken little persuasion. With or without Hesiod's help, Aristides could distinguish between the two strifes: the blind strife between two lusts for power and the good strife of common rivalry for the common good, the rivalry in excellence that stirred the aristocratic poet Pindar, the rivalry not for private gain but for the materially worthless laurel wreath the Olympic victor won. And therefore Aristides had said, "Let the rivalry between us be now as it has been before, to see which of us two shall do his country more good."[188] The Greek word he used for "rivalry" was the same word Hesiod had used when he spoke of the good kind of strife: *eris*. Now with both Themistocles and Aristides back in their ruined common city, Aristides stood by the good strife.

Themistocles imagined the Athenian polis as an island, a peninsula no more—an island defended by the wooden walls of her swift, beaked ships. He "wished to attach the whole city to the sea,"[189] where its new strength lay, by building a new wall for Athens, as he had fifteen years before built a wall for her new port at the Piraeus. The first task was not to rebuild private homes, but to make the polis an island. So all set to work— old men, women, and children, every able-bodied person not with the fleet. They traced a wall some five and a half miles long around their polis, to enclose a bigger space than the old wall had. Along that line, they dug a ditch some five feet deep and seven or eight feet wide. They filled it with heavy stones, some of them stones from their ruined homes, some from the city's public buildings, even some columns from grave monuments; and they cemented these stones together. Then they continued the wall upward with unfired brick—for the present to a height of ten or eleven feet. The width varied from seven or eight feet to fifteen. In nine days, the foundations were done. In a month their city was stoutly walled against further attack.

When Athens' new wall began to rise, other states grew alarmed and persuaded Sparta to protest. Spartan envoys urged the Athenians not to wall their city, but on the contrary to help her raze the walls of all cities that stood north of the Isthmus. Then, if the barbarians should come again, they could not shelter their forces behind city walls as they had done at Thebes before the battle of Plataea. It was the old Spartan policy of abandoning everything beyond the Isthmus if and when danger should strike Hellas. But the Spartans reckoned without Themistocles. He persuaded the Athenians to send him to Sparta to negotiate, and meanwhile to delay sending Aristides and a third ambassador. By one ruse after another he stalled for time, while the old men, the women, and the children of Athens feverishly walled their polis in. At last, he was able to face the Lacedaemonians and tell them frankly that Athens was already walled and quite able to look out for her own interests. He reminded them that Athens had shown better judgment than the Spartans had in the night before Salamis. Either all the cities in the Panhellenic League, which had been formed to fight Xerxes, would dismantle their fortifications—which unwalled Sparta knew, alas, they would not do—or Athens would keep hers too. He insisted that a walled Athens was an advantage to all Hellas. The Spartans, outwitted as usual, swallowed their resentment.

Then Themistocles turned to his true love, the Piraeus, with its three superb ports less than five miles from Athens. He had begun a wall around the Piraeus some years before, when he was archon. Now he finished it. He also enlarged the town of Piraeus in modern style. Athens, like other cities, had emerged from the Dark Ages of Greece with little, crooked, unplanned streets. Now Hippodamos of Miletus laid out a new Piraeus with three straight, parallel avenues, intersected at right angles by a fourth. Also he furnished the new port town with a spacious agora, or market place, in the Ionian manner. Did Themistocles secretly wish the Athenians would move their capital to up-to-date Piraeus? Whether he did or not, religious piety as well as simple sentiment would have blocked any such proposal. So Themistocles, always with his inward eye fixed on that image of an island, "fastened the city to the Piraeus, and the land to the sea."[190] The city's patron-goddess, Athena Polias, now stood armed to defend her people. The walls of Athens and Piraeus were her shield; the Athenian fleet was her spear.

In the summer of 478, when Xanthippus, father of Pericles, had taken Sestos, the Spartans in their turn again took up the sword. An Allied army left for Thessaly under the command of Leutychides, one of Sparta's two kings and commander of the Allied forces at Mycale when Xanthippus commanded the Athenian contingent there. But, whereas Xanthippus succeeded at Sestos, the Spartan king's expedition against the Persians failed. Sparta then sent out a small naval force under Pausanias, who had commanded the Greek Allies at Plataea and who was regent for the young son of Leonidas, the hero of Thermopylae. Pausanias subjected part of the island of Cyprus; then headed north and took Byzantium. But success promptly went to Pausanias's head. At the temple of Posidon on the Black Sea, he dedicated a bronze crater describing himself as "Pausanias, ruler of vast Hellas."[191] Then men remembered that when the Panhellenic League had set up a gold tripod at Delphi as a trophy and votive offering for the victory at Plataea, Pausanias on his own authority had inscribed it,

> When as captain of the Hellenes he had destroyed the Persian host,
> Pausanias dedicated this memorial to Phoebus [Apollo].[192]

The Lacedaemonians had promptly chiseled off his inscription and replaced it with the names of all the cities whose men had fought at Plataea. Now, on the Hellespontine shore, he was making himself generally hated by the Allies. They found him overbearing, as the Spartans often seemed, with that discourtesy which the Spartans often paraded as masculine candor and soldierly brevity. He was accused of conspiring with the King of Kings in order that he might be ruler of all Greece. He dressed in the Persian manner and maintained a bodyguard of Medes and Egyptians. He scandalized his carefully frugal subjects at home by having his table served in the Persian style. It was rumored that he was intriguing with the Helots and fomenting a rebellion. Sparta ordered him home. There he was caught corresponding with Persia; he took sanctuary in the Spartan temple to 'Athana' called the Brazen House; he was starved into weakness; he was dragged out lest his death defile Athena's holy ground; and he died.

Pausanias's command of the expeditionary forces was turned over to an obscure Spartan, a ship's captain; but the Allies had had enough and rejected Sparta's traditional claim to hegemony. The islanders of Samos, Chios, and Lesbos demanded that Athens lead them. More specifically, they demanded that the trustworthy Athenian, Aristides, organize the common Hellenic defense. For Pausanias's absurd and treasonable behavior had merely dramatized Sparta's unfitness to lead in a war whose purposes she could not share and perhaps did not wholly grasp: the common defense, not merely of the Peloponnese, but of the whole Aegean community.

In the spring of 476, when Pericles was fourteen, delegates from Ionia and the Isles began arriving in Athens to concert the common defense of Hellas and of freedom. From their deliberations emerged the League of Delos. It was not a government, not even a federal one. Its member states remained sovereign; and in its deliberative assembly each state, no matter how small or weak, was to have one vote. The common assembly would sit once a year on the Isle of Delos, birthplace of Apollo, where for centuries the long-robed Ionians with their swift ships had gathered for their religious festivals, for boxing and dancing and song. There, too, the League would establish a common treasury, a thing never done by Sparta's Peloponnesian Alliance nor even by the Panhellenic League formed to fight off Xerxes.

The program of the League of Delos was to free those Hellenic cities which the King of Kings still held and, meanwhile, to pillage his empire. The means to carry it out included a joint army and, above all, a joint navy. Ships cost money, and the League Assembly had to decide the painful question of naval quotas. Since everybody trusted Aristides, the delegates turned over to him the allocation of quotas. The important islands of Samos, Chios, Lesbos, and Naxos contributed ships. But most of the new League's member states possessed only obsolete war vessels; most of them lacked timber with which to build new ones; some of the smaller states would have had to combine resources to furnish even one modern trireme; and most states preferred to make a fixed money contribution. Aristides calculated their joint contribution at 460 talents a year. This *phoros*, or tribute, they would pay to the League's Treasury at Delos. Then he assessed each member state's contribution according to its capacity to pay. The Treasury would turn over all these funds to Athens, with her shipyards, her imported timber, and her skilled shipwrights; and Athens would recruit the ships' crews from her own population and from the other cities of the League. Everybody was well satisfied with Aristides' handling of an unpopular task.

The decision to commute the tribute from ships to money perhaps implied more than the delegates at Athens guessed; as, indeed, the shift long before from subsistence agriculture to a money economy had implied more for Athens than Athens herself had guessed. Money had turned out to possess an unexpected tendency to concentrate economic and even political power. It was now agreed that Athens would in effect serve as the executive branch of this new shadow government of Aegean Hellas. It was true that the power of the purse would be in the hands of something that resembled a legislative branch, the League Assembly at Delos. The tribute would indeed flow to Delos, but no Samian or Chian or Lesbian or Naxian ship would report to Delos for active duty. Instead, they would report to Themistocles' new port town of Piraeus with its three harbors. If Solon's element of right in politics remained at holy Delos, the money tribute of most League members placed Solon's element of might in Athens' hands. Finally, the delegates who established this lopsided League with Athens made no provision for secession from it. The urgent fact was still Persia, and no member state could be spared from the war of liberation born at Marathon and Salamis. Hellas was riding a wild beast.

Meanwhile, Themistocles faced a new political rival, young but able. His name was Cimon. He was the son of Miltiades, hero of Marathon, by a Thracian princess whom Miltiades had married when he was tyrant of the Chersonese. Cimon was around twenty when his father died in prison, to which the Athenians had sent him after the fiasco of his expedition against the island of Paros. The son was tall, handsome, curly-haired, with a soldierly eloquence of the sort practiced by the Spartans and by those Athenian aristocrats who wistfully imitated them. He loved to drink, to sing, to make love. The ruin of his father's fortunes left him poor. But he married off his sister to a mineowner named Callias, perhaps the richest man in Athens at the time, and Callias paid the heavy fine Miltiades had bequeathed to his son. Cimon then married a wealthy heiress. A second wife was a granddaughter of Megacles, who, like Clisthenes and Pericles' mother, was a member of the Alcmeonid family. Cimon had fought brilliantly at Salamis, had been elected general about a year later, had showed himself a born military leader like his father and an ingenious ship's architect besides. Like other noblemen, he had served in the cavalry; but when Themistocles was persuading the Athenians to take to their ships, and when the land-loving nobles had hesitated, Cimon had gaily led a procession of them up to the Acropolis, carrying in his hands his horse's bridle. This he dedicated to Athena; he took down a shield which hung on the wall, made a prayer to the goddess, and led his noble fellow horsemen down to the sea.

When this half-Thracian, aristocratic, picturesque kinsman by marriage of the young Pericles entered active politics at Athens, there was little danger that he would collide with Aristides, who was engrossed with the League of Delos and its difficult new problems. But he could hardly hope to co-operate with the social newcomer, Themistocles, devious, slippery with money, distrusted, brilliant, overbearing, sarcastic, a hater of Cimon's beloved Sparta. Themistocles, too, had a foreign mother, some even said a Thracian; but she was no princess. His father was indeed an Athenian, but he was not among the Well-fathered.

Cimon's rise was swift. When he was elected general, the Spartan regent, Pausanias, had not yet been ordered home; he had taken possession of Sestos, the town which Xanthippus' Athenians had finally reduced, and had seized Byzantium. Cimon managed to force him out of both, and in 475 drove the Persians out of nearby Eion. Then he planted a colony of Athenian cleruchs, or citizen outsettlers, to hold it; but the colony was massacred by Thracians a few years later.

Cimon tried in vain to clear the Persians from Doriscus. Then he turned to the island of Scyros, where a nest of pirates had been preying on Aegean shipping. Inevitably one of the tasks of Athens, as head of the League of Delos, would for some years remain that of making the Aegean safe for Hellenic commerce. Scyros, once cleared of pirates, could also complete a chain of ports from Attica to Euboea to Scyros to the Hellespont. The island was conquered, the pirates were sold as slaves, and another cleruchy, this one successful, was established. Then Cimon somehow found on the island, or claimed to find, the bones of Athens' early king, Theseus; for Theseus, men said, had died four centuries before in Scyros and had been buried there. Cimon took the hallowed bones of the hero in his own trireme and bore them triumphantly to Athens. It was the military and political career of Cimon which unfolded itself before the eyes of a kinsman by marriage, a youth still under twenty, Pericles, son of Xanthippus.

Cimon's clash with Themistocles was not long in coming. For Cimon, Athens' policy was clear: to finish defeating Persia, and, through the League of Delos, to control the Aegean, leaving Sparta predominant on land in

Mainland Greece. But Themistocles wanted to use Athens' new power to confound her only Hellenic rival, Sparta. The clash ended in a vote of ostracism, in 472, and it was Themistocles who was forced into exile. He went to Argos, that city of ancient jealousy toward Sparta, and proceeded to carry on a one-man diplomatic duel with Lacedaemon.

Themistocles in his duel with Sparta and with oligarchy seemed to be winning. Argos underwent a democratic revolution. The oligarchs were driven out of Elis, which proceeded to adopt a democratic constitution modeled on that of Athens. The imitation went further than popular government even: Elis achieved a synoecism, as Athens had done centuries before, and made Elis the polis of many neighboring towns which had previously been sovereign. In Arcadia, the city of Mantinea did the same thing: she organized democratic government and collected the citizens of five little cities into one polis. In 473-472, Tegea, in Arcadia, declared war on domineering Sparta, but met defeat. Most of the small cities of Arcadia adopted a common coinage and defied Sparta. But aid from Argos failed to arrive, and this coalition, too, was suppressed by Sparta. Sparta now reorganized her reluctant allies and placed their military contingents under Spartan officers. What role did the exiled Themistocles play in these rebellions against Lacedaemon? In any case, he conspired with Pausanias, before the regent's death on holy ground beside Athana's Brazen House in Sparta. When the Spartans uncovered their conspiracy, they demanded that Athens punish the ostracized Themistocles with death, and Themistocles was summoned back to Athens. He promptly fled to Corcyra; was refused refuge there; went to the king of the Molossians, a half-civilized Hellenic folk in the western part of Mainland Greece; with the king's aid reached Pydna, a Macedonian port; and then shipped to Ephesus in Ionia. Athens sentenced the refugee to death. When Xerxes died in 464 and Artaxerxes succeeded him as King of Kings, Themistocles went to the Great King's court. There he reminded Artaxerxes that he had warned his father that the Greek Allies would destroy his Hellespontine bridge and cut off his escape; and Artaxerxes greatly honored him as the King's friend. He was even assigned, as a gift, the revenues of three Ionian cities. His long and arduous odyssey ended at Magnesia near the Meander River in Asia Minor, where he lived until his death.

For Themistocles was indeed an Odysseus. True, he was no king as Odysseus was: he was even considered baseborn. But he possessed the wily

Odysseus' quick mind, his capacity for ruse, his audacity, and an almost animal cunning against his antagonists. He would have gladly risked the boasts Odysseus made as the Ithacans' ship bore him to sea and Cyclops raged. Had Themistocles not annoyed Athens by his arrogance in the days before ostracism drove him forth? For example, he had built a temple near his dwelling, dedicated to Artemis, Best Counselor, to remind the Athenians that it was his advice in the days of Salamis that had saved their skins.

Themistocles' exile, followed in a few years by Aristides' death, left Cimon pre-eminent in Athens. He continued his task of destroying the pirates that infested the Aegean Sea. He forced the city of Carystus, in southern Euboea, to join the Delian League. Naxos tried to secede from the League, and Cimon conquered her and reduced her, not to her old status of member, but to the new status of subject city. Naxos was the first member of the League to lose its formal sovereignty. At the head of 200 warships, Cimon liberated the coasts of Caria and Lycia from Persian control. About 468 he destroyed a fleet of the Great King's ships at the mouth of the Eurymedon on the southern coast of Asia Minor; disembarked and defeated a land army; re-embarked and captured a Phoenician fleet that was coming to the rescue of the Great King's now destroyed naval force. He returned to Athens in triumph. After the battle of the Eurymedon, the Delian League controlled most of the Greek cities from Euboea to the Bosphorus, from Pamphylia to the Black Sea, some 200 cities in all. Athens meanwhile had become the commercial metropolis of the eastern Mediterranean. Cimon and his moderate conservatives now seemed beyond political attack, and the rehabilitated Council of the Areopagus, that constitutional bastion of the Best People, bore daily witness to the forces back of Cimon.

Those were the political facts that confronted Pericles, now nearing thirty. But he discerned also a less well-recognized fact. The Athenian workingmen, who belonged to the fourth category of citizens in Solon's constitution and were still excluded from high offices, were growing restless. It is true that, since Solon's categories had long been calculated in money and since the value of money had steadily declined, more and more voters had graduated to a higher category. But there were still many in the lowest grade who had manned the oars at Salamis and yet remained at a political disadvantage in the polis they had risked their lives to save. These men were rallying to the standard of Ephialtes, a political leader of good family but democratic beliefs, who was now ranged against the powerful Cimon and his conservative aristocrats. Pericles, though rich, belonged both by preference and family tradition to the minority of nobles in favor of the emergent democracy. He was slow to enter the fray: he belonged to a suspect social class and both his father, Xanthippus, and his uncle, Megacles, had suffered the ostracism that brilliant leaders so often incurred.

In the spring of 472, Pericles had gained some public fame as choregus of a successful tragedy—the *Persians* of Aeschylus, which dramatized the insolence of Xerxes and his catastrophe at Salamis. As choregus, Pericles had assumed the duty of providing and training the chorus. But eight years later, he took the real plunge into public life. Cimon, triumphant at the Eurymedon, had undertaken to clear out the few remaining Persian garrisons in Thrace. In the process he collided with one of Athens' most powerful allies, Thasos, a city which had commercial and mining interests in Thrace. Thasos thereupon seceded from the League of Delos. The League Council declared her in rebellion; and Cimon, after an arduous siege of two years, forced Thasos to surrender, seized her fleet, and levied a heavy cash indemnity. However, despite this triumph, Ephialtes and the democrats charged him with coddling Alexander, the king of Macedonia, and with dragging out the siege of Thasos to please his beloved Sparta. But it was Pericles who formally called him to account on a charge of accepting bribes from Alexander. And, although Cimon won acquittal and with it the first round of a struggle with the democrats, the fight continued.

In the summer of 464 a frightful earthquake destroyed Sparta. Thereupon, the Helots rose in rebellion; two cities of the Dwellers-round-about revolted; Messenia rose. After a long, hard fight the Spartans drove their rebellious subjects back to the stronghold of Mount Ithome. Here some of the ancestors of the rebels had made their last desperate stand over two centuries before, when Sparta had first conquered Messenia. Now in the fifth century, a Spartan army again laid siege to the natural fortress of Ithome. But the Spartans were notoriously inept at sieges, where the Athenians were clever, and perhaps men once more remembered that it was wily Odysseus, not staunch Achilles, who ended the ten long years of siege when Troy fell. The Spartans appealed to Athens for aid, not against Persians, not on the sea, but on the land, Sparta's own element, and against Sparta's own rebellious subjects.

In the Athenian Assembly, Ephialtes argued that Sparta should be left to her fate. But Cimon argued for sending aid. The moderate aristocrats whom Cimon led had accepted the sea, and commerce, and war with the Persians, and even a League of Delos that excluded the ancient military city they admired and often imitated. But they were unwilling to accept the democratic view of men like Ephialtes and Pericles that now, when Persia had been pushed back, Sparta was the rival to be feared and watched. The alliance of Athens with Sparta had for long been an uneasy one, held together by the common fear of the Persian invasion. Even so, they had in fact fought shoulder to shoulder against the polyglot army of Asia at Plataea; and under the common mound at Thermopylae the men of Sparta lay, obedient to her commands. When Cimon exhorted the Athenians "not to suffer Hellas to be crippled, nor their city to be robbed of its yoke-fellow,"[193] he won his debate and led an army of 4,000 heavy infantry, including the Best People, to Ithome. This middle-aged, conservative, landowning noble had won, even with the use of a farmer's metaphor, not a seaman's. Yet, only the earthquake and the Helot revolt had prevented Athens' yoke-fellow from fulfilling her secret promise to aid Thasos in its revolt against Athens by invading Attica. Sparta's secret promise[194] to Thasos remained an unread footnote to the thesis of Ephialtes and of his political lieutenant, Pericles, that the true enemy of Athenian sea power was Sparta and that with a trireme no ox could be yoked.

At Ithome the Spartans grew suspicious: might not these revolutionary Athenians, even Athenian aristocrats, change sides and aid the rebels? The Spartans requested them, and them alone among all the allies who had come to Sparta's rescue, to go home. The Assembly at Athens was furious. While the more aristocratic Athenians were serving at Ithome, Ephialtes took advantage of their absence to push through the Assembly laws removing from the Areopagus its recently recovered powers to supervise the operation of the state, to punish officials, and to inquire into the private lives of citizens. It retained only certain religious functions, including the right to judge those accused of polluting their polis with premeditated murder. Cimon led back his humiliated forces from Ithome and promptly made an ill-timed effort to restore to the Areopagus the powers the democrats had just removed. In 461, a few months after his humiliation at Ithome, Cimon was charged with being a friend of the Lacedaemonians and an enemy of the people[195] and was ostracized. Athens then prepared to ally herself with Thessaly and Argos. The Panhellenic League, which had won the great battles of Salamis, of Plataea, and of Mycale, was finished. Shortly after the ostracism of Cimon, his chief political opponent, Ephialtes, was assassinated.

The aristocratic party lay in ruins. Many members of that party had lost their lives in battle. Sparta's insult at Ithome had destroyed the party's prestige. Cimon was in exile, and there was no leader capable of replacing him. On the democratic side, Themistocles, ostracized too, had died in exile a year before Cimon's ostracism. Now Ephialtes was gone, and his leadership had been inherited by Pericles, who had helped him curtail the powers of the Areopagus and to place the state in the hands of the whole body of citizens. Now, at last, the whole Assembly made the laws; the Council of Five Hundred executed them; the popular courts judged those who broke them. The Confederacy of Delos, headed by the people of Athens, controlled and policed Aegean Hellas; Persia had been pushed back; the uneasy alliance with Sparta was broken; and, by land, the people of Athens leaned on two new allies: Thessaly in the north with her formidable cavalry; Argos in Peloponnese, the traditional enemy of neighboring Lacedaemon.

The new Hellas coming to birth inside the old was conceived by fear of Persian might. It loved justice; and its enthusiastic choice of Aristides the Just to apportion the contributions of its sovereign members expressed its Solonian determination to bind right to might. But, alas, the necessities of war gave might a persistent advantage. The Council of the League did indeed meet, not at Athens, but in holy Delos; and the Treasury of the League was kept in Delos too. But Athens controlled the League's navy. When, about 469, Naxos tried to secede, Cimon had not only crushed her, but degraded her from ally to subject city. In 454 the Treasury of the League was transferred to Athens. True, it was transferred by consent and not by force. It was Samos, not Athens, which moved that it be transferred on the grounds that it would be safer there. For Athens controlled the League's ships and the League's money: in short, Athens controlled the might, as her own aristocracy had controlled the might in Athens before Solon joined it to the people's right. What Athens was tempted to do, and did, was to place both ships and money at the disposal of the Athenian Assembly: the Council of the League ceased to meet and its functions were taken over by that Assembly. Athens joined the League's might to the Athenian democracy's right. The inevitable result was a growing resentment among her Allies.

The truth is that democratic Athens, victorious over Persia and in control of the new League of Delos, displayed that same exultant pride and overweening ambition that had led the Odyssean Themistocles to ostracism from Athens and that had also led Pausanias to death at Athana's Brazen House in his native Sparta. Solon's commands, "Know thyself" and "Nothing too much," were forgotten, as limitless prospects of glory and profit opened up. For sixteen years the Athenian democracy tried its hand at military conquest.

Athens seized Naupactus from the Ozolian Locrians, which gave her considerable control over the westbound traffic of her commercial rival, Corinth. Megara quarreled with Corinth about their common frontier and made alliance with Athens. Athens promptly built a double line of walls from the citadel of Megara to its southern port, Nisaea, and garrisoned Megara. Athens thereby blocked the east road from Sparta into central Greece. She besieged her other chief commercial rival, Aegina; captured that city; and forced Aegina to join her League of Delos, to surrender her fleet, and to pay tribute. While doing all these things, Athens audaciously launched a large expedition to aid a revolt against Persia which had broken out in the Egyptian delta, a rich granary for an Athens always interested in grain. But, in 457, Sparta forced the cities of Boeotia back into a league under Theban domination, to serve as a counterpoise to the growing power of neighboring Athens. A Spartan army in Boeotia was stirring up trouble for Athens, whose citizens were now busy connecting Athens with the Piraeus by a double line of walls like those they had built between Megara and her port, Nisaea. The ostracized Cimon came to the Athenian army, which was encamped on Boeotian soil, and begged to fight again for Athens. But the democrats refused his plea. A battle followed at Tanagra; Athens' Thessalian cavalry deserted, and the Athenians lost. On a motion of Pericles, the Athenian Assembly recalled Cimon, and Cimon negotiated a five-year truce with Sparta.

Two months later, Athens conquered all of Boeotia except Thebes, and the vanquished cities were required to furnish contingents to her armies. She also subjected Phocis and Opuntian Locris. Now, in addition to her maritime empire, which had evolved out of a voluntary league of sovereign states, she controlled most of her near neighbors and had protected her land frontiers, so often crossed in the past by hostile armies. She dominated the eastern, civilized portion of central Greece from Thessaly to the borders of Corinth. She had not only gained a new protection for the frontiers of Attica; she had won a Mainland empire which Themistocles could scarcely have approved. Nevertheless, she prudently completed the Long Walls. One wall connected Athens to her port, Piraeus, some four miles away. A second wall ran from Athens to Phalerum, the ancient harbor to the east of triple-harbored Piraeus. The triangle Athens-Piraeus-Phalerum was now a single island of the sort Themistocles had always longed for.

But in 454 a Persian army attacked and defeated the force which Athens had sent to Egypt to aid rebellion there. The Athenian army was then surrounded, and burned its ships to keep them out of Persian hands. At last the Athenians capitulated on condition that they should be allowed to withdraw in peace from Egypt. They started by foot across the Libyan desert, but only a handful reached the Greek city of Cyrene on the Libyan coast. Meanwhile, a fleet of fifty triremes, sent to Egypt as reinforcements, was almost completely destroyed by the Persians. According to later tradition, the Egyptian expedition cost Athens some 35,000 men, of whom 6,000 were Athenian citizens. No Greek army had ever suffered so catastrophic a defeat. It was precisely this catastrophe and the fear that a Persian fleet would once more appear in the Aegean that had prompted Samos to propose moving the Treasury of the League of Delos from Apollo's exposed island to the temple of Athena in Athens.

Another, and a subtler change, was coming over the League of Delos. Athens' policy toward her allies had been relatively free of political doctrine. When, in 457, she had liberated the Boeotian cities from Thebes, she recalled their exiles, oligarchs included. She was not fighting to spread democracy but to build a continental empire north of the Isthmus. In the years that followed, however, and in many of her subject cities, pro-Spartan oligarchs led rebellions against Athenian imperial control, and democratic Athens found herself aiding the local democratic opponents of these oligarchs. If, therefore, she robbed other cities of their sovereignty, she at least found herself liberating democrats in them from the oligarchs who oppressed them.

The Egyptian disaster and the restlessness in Athens' new empire led Pericles to set Cimon the task of negotiating another peace with Sparta; and, in the spring of 450, Cimon effected his five-year truce. Then Pericles turned to Persia again: Artaxerxes' Phoenician fleet, which had put down the rebellion in Egypt, was under orders to restore the Great King's authority in Cyprus. Athens sent Cimon to the rescue with 200 ships. But Cimon, already ill, died during the campaign of 450-449; and, although his forces gained a face-saving victory at Salamis in Cyprus, a costly campaign netted Athens nothing more substantial than a chance to negotiate with Persia. Cimon's rich brother-in-law, Callias, was sent to Susa. Whether a formal treaty was in fact drawn up or not, in 449-448 began the Peace of Callias, characterized by the following abstentions. Persia would send no Black Sea warship of hers west of the Bosphorus. She would send no Mediterranean warship of hers nearer the Aegean than Phaselis on the southern coast of Asia Minor. Athens, on her side, would attack no territory of the King of Kings. Athens' lonely battle for freedom had begun four decades before on the shore of Marathon, and tradition would recount that Callias had taken part in the battle. The new Athenian Empire and the Persian Empire had now, by long trial of strength and great military disasters on both sides, found their common frontier. Pericles and the Athenian democrats were left free to deal with the city which the late Cimon had called Athens' yoke-fellow, Sparta.

But Themistocles' urge toward the sea and away from the land seemed justified: Athens' Mainland empire, so recently won, began to dissolve. Anti-Athenian oligarchs seized control of some of the cities of Boeotia, and Athens intervened. In the summer of 447, a small army of volunteers—which Pericles deemed quite inadequate—marched into Boeotia: near the town of Coronea, it suffered complete disaster. Boeotia was lost; and with Boeotia gone, it became strategically impossible to hold either Phocis or Opuntian Locris. By the end of 447, all central Greece was lost. The next summer most of the cities in the neighboring island of Euboea rose, and Pericles himself led an army to Euboea to restore Athenian control. They had hardly disembarked when news came that Megara, on Attica's western flank, had massacred its Athenian garrison and allied itself with Corinth. The Isthmus was open again to Sparta and her Peloponnesian allies; the five-year truce with Sparta, negotiated by Cimon, expired; and Sparta promptly led her Peloponnesian allies into Attica. Then, somewhat mysteriously, they withdrew. Pericles returned to Euboea; subjected it, confiscated the lands of the anti-Athenian oligarchs, planted colonies of Athenian cleruchs, and tightened Athenian control of Euboea's city-states. Meanwhile, those who had led the Peloponnesians against Athens were charged on their return with having accepted bribes to withdraw. They fled Sparta and were condemned to death in contumacy.

Both yoke-fellows were now exhausted. Late in 446, Callias once more went on embassy, this time with nine other envoys, this time to Sparta. A Thirty Years' Peace was negotiated. Athens gave up all claim to her continental empire, except for Naupactus, that strategic station at the mouth of the Gulf of Corinth. Aegina would stay in the League of Delos, but as a sovereign, not a subject, state. Athens agreed not to receive any dissatisfied allies of Sparta into her League of Delos, and Sparta agreed not to receive into her Peloponnesian League any state that seceded from the League of Delos. Any neutral state might join either league it wished to join. Argos, which had recently broken with Athens and made her peace with Sparta, had nevertheless not formally joined the Peloponnesian League, and Athens was left free to treat with her.

But, with Megara gone, and the eastern coast road to Attica once more open, Athens would be exposed to Spartan attack if the Thirty Years' Peace should collapse. Her country population might, of course, take refuge in the Themistoclean island formed by Athens, Piraeus, and the Long Walls. But though the North Wall ran to Piraeus and the South Wall met the sea at Phalerum, yet the marshy shore of the bay that lay between was inconveniently long to defend against attack by sea. Pericles thereupon replaced the South Wall with a middle wall, paralleling the North Wall and leaving a corridor between them some 200 yards wide, like the bar of a dumbbell, connecting ancient Athens with her triple-harbored port of Piraeus. The man-made island became safer than ever, and it still ruled an Aegean empire largely composed of islands made by nature. For the first time since 480, for the first time since Thermopylae, Artemisium, Salamis, and Plataea, there was peace in Greece.

Athens' meteoric career of conquest and violence had lasted fourteen years and had ended in defeat on the Mainland and catastrophe in Egypt. If this catastrophe did not bring recognition and understanding to all her citizens, yet her chief citizen, Pericles, had learned. He himself had led some of his city's recent campaigns, and not without success. But he now left to others the dream of assaulting Egypt again, or of attacking grain-rich Sicily or even Carthage or Etruria in central Italy. His own plan was to consolidate Athens' grip on the basically maritime League of Delos; and to enlarge it by persuasion, not by force. Four times he had been elected general—in 458, in 454, in 448, and now in 446, the year the Thirty Years' Peace began. Ever since 461, when Cimon, leader of the aristocrats, had been ostracized and Ephialtes, leader of the democrats, had been assassinated, Pericles had led the Athenian democracy. When Cimon died in 450-449, a relation of his by marriage, Thucydides—not the historian of that name—took over the leadership of the rich and Well-fathered; but in 443 or 442 Thucydides was ostracized. The democracy then governed Athens without serious challenge. Athens in turn virtually governed the League of Delos. Culturally, though not politically, she even governed Hellas. She had achieved peace with Persia and at least a truce with the state that Pericles most distrusted—Sparta, with her Peloponnesian League, with her fear and hatred of Athenian democracy, of Athenian wealth, of Athenian prestige, above all, of Athenian expansion.

To preserve this new Athenian Hellas, Pericles increased the navy of the League of Delos and kept one squadron always on maneuver for eight months of the year. He developed grappling irons to aid in boarding enemy ships. The booty his father's army had taken at Sestos on the Hellespont after the final liberation of Ionia had been used in part to convert Athens' so-called cavalry from a contingent of mounted infantry with very limited functions to a genuine cavalry, trained to fight on horseback. Pericles therefore developed horse transports. The oarsmen who manned his navy were now paid three obols a day, in addition to their cash allowance for food. They were recruited from the thetes, the fourth and lowest class of citizens, the Wage-earners; but they were recruited also from the poorer class in the cities of Athens' allies, a class that was usually pro-Athenian. From the thetes also he recruited an enlarged force of light infantry, and the number of archers was increased from the 700 who fought in the Persian War to 1,600, plus 200 horse-archers. Even the heavy infantry came to be paid; and the state provided an allowance for feeding the cavalryman's mount.

As usual, the poor man who was invited to risk his life for the state demanded a greater share in governing it. That had happened in the old days in the aristocratic republics of Greece, when heavy infantry started usurping the role of the nobles who went to war on horseback. Now in the middle of the fifth century the highest office, the archonship, was opened to the third class of citizens, the zeugitai, and in practice to the fourth, the thetes. But if all classes were to participate in government, the juryman must be compensated in part for the workday lost. The aristocrats, with their tradition of free service to the state, objected to the large courts of paid jurymen, whom the nobles regarded as too lazy to work and as drunk with self-importance. But the large juries had at least the great virtue of being too numerous to bribe in a society where bribery was a serious problem. In general, Athens' cash economy and her economic inequality made payment for both civil duties and military duties inevitable, if freedom was indeed to mean that a man must obey only those laws which he had first had a chance to vote on, after free debate, open to all. Finally, the prestige and superior education of aristocrats like Pericles gave them still a near-monopoly of high office provided they showed themselves loyal to the ideas of equality of debate and equality before the law.

This dream of a free society guided a polis of perhaps 410,000-420,000,[196] of whom a good half lived in the city of Athens and its port, the Piraeus. Of this total, there may have been around 208,000 slaves and 70,000 metics, or foreign residents. There may have been some 138,000 free Athenians. But of these only the adult males voted and were eligible for office: there may have been some 41,700 of them. Few as these full citizens were, in 451 on the motion of Pericles they reversed the slow expansion of freedom that Dracon, Solon, and Clisthenes had striven for, that had inspired Athens' heroic courage under the onslaughts of a vast, despotic Persian Empire, that men had died for at Marathon and at Salamis, that had rallied Ionia and the Isles to Athenian leadership, that attracted to Athens the admiration and even the emulation of most of Hellas. In 451 wealth, comfort, and enjoyment were increasing; the number of metics and slaves was increasing; the control of her allies by Athens was increasing. It is true that some metics were gaining citizenship, though not always by honest methods. And the son of an Athenian citizen had always been a citizen, even though his mother might be a foreigner. In 451 a law proposed by Pericles provided that no man should be a citizen of Athens unless both parents had been citizens—though the mother, of course, would in any case neither have voted nor held office.

This closure of naturalization was highly symbolic. The new law would have denied citizenship to Clisthenes, to Miltiades, to Themistocles, to Cimon, to the great historian, Thucydides. All of them had had foreign mothers. Indeed, Athenian aristocrats had always been quick to marry the daughters of other aristocrats—or, anyhow, of rich men—whether native or foreign: high birth transcended frontiers. Against the privilege of birth or wealth the Athenian democracy had waged political war; today the Athenian citizen, rich or poor, enjoyed legal equality and freedom. But under Pericles' new law the political and economic benefits of freedom would be reserved to those who had inherited freedom, as a new privilege, a kind of property. It would be reserved by force: by the enforced law of the polis against metic and slave, by the enforced will of Athens against ally and commercial rival and military rival alike. Athens, which had so long explored with Odysseus, would now dig in her heels with Achilles—so far, at least, as her political life was concerned.

Her closed citizenry would not only determine to have and to hold Athens against all newcomers. By the system of cleruchies, so detested by the Allies, this closed citizenry would establish colonies recruited from its own ranks, colonies in the Thracian Chersonese, in Lemnos, in Imbros, in Andros, in Naxos, in Eretria, in Thracian Brea, in Oreus, in Amisus and Astacus on the Black Sea, in Aegina. The land for Athenian settlers was at first paid for by a reduction in tribute, but later Athens merely seized it. It is true that the land she seized was often confiscated from anti-Athenian oligarchs. But it was seized; and often the new Athenian landlords allowed the former owners to work the land for the landlords' benefit. Surely these cleruchies must have reminded at least a few Athenians of the Messenians the Spartans had reduced to helotry when they had conquered Messenia centuries ago. By the will of Athens, some 10,000 Athenians in all were settled as cleruchs, to help find livelihood for the poor of Athens, to solve Athens' population problem, to keep an eye on restless allies and to guard trade routes.

However, under the guidance of Pericles, the yoke of Athens was not a crushing one. Her government brought a considerable measure of economic unity to the new Aegean Hellas, encouraged the exchange of commodities and hence the wiser use of local resources, and enriched her own unenfranchised metics. Athens became the undisputed emporium of Aegean Hellas; and her oil and wine and pottery were going even to Western Greece, even to distant Etruria. Her ships policed the seas that had once been preyed upon by pirates.

She brought also a kind of intellectual unity, and she was the center of the literary and artistic life of the Hellenes. Her rich Attic dialect was beginning to serve as the common tongue of Hellas, the medium for the exchange of ideas. Her coin, bearing the famous image of Athena's sacred owl, was beginning to serve as the common coin of the Aegean, the medium for the exchange of Greek commodities. Her imposing system of law was being widely copied by her Allies. That system spread in part because she took over a portion of the judicial function of the governments of her Allies. Athenian courts came to handle acts against the League and to hear appeals against sentences of death, of exile, of confiscation of goods—if only to protect her supporters in Allied lands from discontented oligarchs. Still, her Hellenic subjects were not free in Athens' own sense of freedom.

Was it Pericles' sense of how far Athens was substituting might for right that led him in 448 to call a Panhellenic Congress at Athens? Or, since he had every reason to expect that jealous Sparta would refuse, was it mere diplomatic maneuver, an effort to convey to Hellas that Athens sought consensus and not a Spartan blind obedience? In any case, he proposed that all Hellenes take common counsel on a plan to rebuild the temples the Persian barbarian had destroyed and to police the seas that connected their city-states together. Sparta refused, and nothing came of Pericles' plan for a Panhellenic Congress. Hellas remained dangerously cleft in three parts: Athens' League of Delos, Sparta's Peloponnesian League, and a neutral and hesitant and divided world of shifting petty alliances.

Five years later, in 443, Pericles launched another common effort, of a kind that had a long and familiar tradition, though for a new purpose. He founded Thurii, near the ancient site of Sybaris in southern Italy. He invited Hellenes, not only from Athens, but from all Greece to join in the settlement. The new city of Thurii was laid out by that same Hippodamos of Miletus who had laid out the geometrical avenues of Piraeus. It grew rich. Its citizens included famous men: Herodotus, the historian; Protagoras, the sophist, who became its official lawgiver; Empedocles, the natural philosopher; and others. But within a decade Thurii was drifting away from Athenian political influence.

Late in 441, Athens' most powerful ally, Samos, quarreled with one of Athens' subject cities, Miletus, and defeated her in battle. Miletus appealed to Athens for help, and Athens demanded that Samos submit her quarrel to Athenian arbitration. Samos refused. Thereupon Pericles sailed for Samos at the head of forty vessels, and the oligarchs who had governed

Samos withdrew to the mainland to seek Persian aid against Athens—against Athens, which had taken the leadership only a few short decades before in rescuing Samos and the other Ionian states from their Persian rulers. In 441 Pericles placed a democratic government in power and withdrew. But the oligarchs, with their Persian mercenaries, returned to Samos and declared the independence of Samos. Pericles had already written off Athens' briefly held land empire in order to control more securely the League of Delos. When Byzantium followed Samos and revolted, he struck hard. But it was not until the spring of 439, after a most costly war, that Pericles and his fleets forced Samos to capitulate. She was forced to surrender her fleet, raze her fortifications, pay a heavy indemnity, accept a democratic government, and become a subject city. Pericles returned to Athens in triumph. Byzantium, and some of her restless neighbors, were promptly subdued; but during the war some of the Carian allies had ceased to pay tribute. Rather than risk a clash with Persia, Pericles avoided an immediate further suppression.

The Samian revolt was instructive. It was obvious that the voluntary League of Delos had turned into an Athenian Empire, in which Athens controlled the joint navy and the joint finances. In 434 she would even forbid her Allies to coin money, although the right of coinage was one of the Greek city-states' proudest sovereign prerogatives. On the other hand, Samos was not the only Allied city in which it was chiefly the wealthy class that hated Athenian control and in which the lower class tended to look on the imperial city as protector. Moreover, aside from championing the democrats and aside from policing the seas for the benefit of merchants everywhere, Athens held another and important advantage in her battle for Hellenic unity under her own hegemony. She had become the dazzling and exciting center of the cultural life, not only of her new empire, but of all Hellas. She represented a concentration such as no Hellene had known in any country anywhere, of architecture, sculpture, painting, music, philosophic inquiry, and especially of drama. If she had failed to expand the constitution of Clisthenes into some sort of true political union of city-states, if she had failed to develop the Council of the League from a diplomatic assembly of sovereign states to a common government of elected representatives, nevertheless she herself did represent every Hellene everywhere who wanted to enter the great conversation which Hellas was becoming. Even her fleet of fighting triremes looked, in the light of this achievement, less like naked force and tyranny, more like the might that must be joined to right if law and justice were ever to operate in fact. And although only the hated Athenian cleruchs could, by going to Athens, lawfully claim a seat in her Assembly, where free men governed themselves, yet plenty of other Hellenes could, and did, go to Athens to help build the temples and paint the pictures and carve or mold the statues that made human existence come alive, that made the earth a more luminous dwelling place for man; or to argue about those intangible but powerful things the Athenian called ideas, things that only the mind's eye could see. It is true that neither these Hellenic visitors, or immigrants, nor—since the Periclean law of 451—their sons nor their sons' sons could ever help make law at Athens. Yet they could be sure of a welcome to all who cared about what was good or what was true or what was beautiful. They could be sure of a certain civilized gentleness, a certain courtesy in human intercourse, that marked off Athens from Sparta.

It was thus that Polygnotus, the painter, could come from Thasos to work beside Phidias, the native Athenian sculptor, and watch him plan with Pericles a temple to Athena. And what other temple in Hellas made so noble a home for a god as the Parthenon? Ictinus would help design it; Callicrates would carry out his plans. Mnesicles would design the magnificent approach to it—the Propylaea. Phidias, already famous for the colossal statue of Zeus at Olympia, would create inside the Parthenon the colossal statue of Athena, her flesh formed of ivory, her vesture of pure gold. Around the outside walls not only would the sculptor carve in marble bas-relief the figures of gods and men but the painter would decorate the background in brilliant red and blue. And painters like Polygnotus and Micon would paint life-size frescoes on the walls of the Painted Portico in the market place and on temple walls too, in the city that lay below Athena's hill. When the fleets returned to Athens from their sweeping cruises through the Aegean or the Black Sea, and long before they sighted the Acropolis, they would see on the high cliffs at the southern tip of Attica the tall marble columns of a temple to Posidon. And as they approached Athens on a sunny day they would behold high on the Acropolis the spear point and plume of an heroic statue of Athena, Athena of Battles, standing jealous guard over the land she most loved.

The statues that Greek sculptors carved in marble, in the years when Pericles was leader of Athens and her Aegean empire, differed profoundly from those the tyrant Pisistratus had beheld. The stiffly formal figures with their long robes hanging in vertical lines; the masculine heads with their almost Assyrian ringlets; the mysterious, secret smile; even the brilliantly painted limestone from which these gods and goddesses, these godlike youths and maidens, had been formed—all these things gave way now before a different sort of god, a different sort of youth or maid. The sculptor evoked them from exquisite marble, often the marble of Paros, from which sunlight did not glance away but into whose translucent outer edges sunlight caressingly melted. This marble was painted little or not at all. But what stirred the wonder of the beholder was not the superior matter in which the sculptor found his image or the exquisite skill with which he could now guide his questing chisel. It was rather the image he discovered, the incredibly graceful naked youth in all his muscled strength and sudden glory; the gently curved body of goddess or woman, draped in garments that fell in curved folds of exquisite harmony. It was the grave, serene face, so often lightly tinged with melancholy. Perhaps there was something that soared invisibly upward from those older and ruder statues of the sixth century, as if it would quit an imperfect world for a world where all would be perfection, and perhaps this something was missing from the technically perfect statues of Periclean Athens. But at least that other perfection, that no man's naked eye would ever see, had somehow, if incompletely, come down from where the gods dwelt, as radiant light comes down, and had clothed itself in marble and in bronze. If these later statues hinted less at beauty eternal, they now embodied more, here and now in Athens and in the other cities of Hellas. What spring had promised, summer had almost fulfilled. And if summer in turn appeared to promise autumn, summer was still a gift whose beauty could come but from the gods themselves.

But it was not only her temples and her statues and her paintings that gave meaning to life at Athens. It was also her music, her dancing, her literature. Pericles reorganized the Great Panathenaic Festival, which rejoiced Athena and her people for ten days of every fourth year. In Festival time a great procession of the people followed the maidens who bore the yellow wool garment they had woven for the goddess. They climbed the high Acropolis to the old temple which Athena shared with Erechtheus, whom she herself had reared—him, the son of Earth herself, who had ruled Athens as king in her half-remembered past. Animal sacrifices were held and the people ate meat with their goddess; then they clothed her in her newly made robe. There were competitions by those who recited, by those who played musical instruments and sang. The young men ran and leapt and wrestled; threw the discus and the javelin; engaged in the Pyrrhic dance of armed warriors to win the prize of an ox; raced on horseback; ran in the torch race, holding a flaming torch while protecting its flame with a shield.

Around 446, a Greek world traveler from Asia Minor read aloud to the Athenians something new in their experience and gained a prize of two talents. This composition, like a famous tragedy of Aeschylus, dealt with Xerxes' pride and punishment and with the leading role of Athens in the Hellenic fight for political freedom. But it was not poetry. It was not even written in meter but in prose. It began:

> What Herodotus the Halicarnassian has learnt by inquiry is here set forth: in order that so the memory of the past may not be blotted out from among men by time, and that great and marvelous deeds done by Greeks and foreigners and especially the reason why they warred against each other may not lack renown.[197]

Herodotus's word for inquiry was the Greek word *historia*, and without any adequate precedent he had just invented history—more specifically a history of the recent Persian War. Like Homer, he wrote about a war, and like Homer he wanted men to remember. As in Homer's *Iliad*, so in Herodotus's history the deathless gods sometimes appeared and aided the men who faced death, and who faced even the forgetfulness of later generations. It is true that Herodotus reported the divine interventions without always believing they occurred. Moreover the basic purpose had shifted from the purpose of Homer. Witnesses were called up and the causes of events were argued about. And the search for causes drove Herodotus back in time to Cyrus the Great and the rise of the Persian Empire; back, even, to Croesus of Lydia, who should have made further inquiry of Apollo before attacking Cyrus; back, even, to Homer's Trojan War. The search for causes drove him outward in space. He traveled to Egypt, to Libya, to Syria, perhaps to Mesopotamia, to the northern coast of the Black Sea. Throughout much of his work he was more the geographer and anthropologist than the historian. The strange customs he saw or heard of, the strange anecdotes he collected—these he repeated with contagious relish. He was often misinformed by those he questioned, but he clearly made enormous effort to learn what really did take place. His history became the first great prose work of Hellenic literature.

At the foot of the Acropolis stood the temple to Dionysus, the popular god of wine and ecstacy, who possessed his frenzied followers and who had died and been reborn to save them from their sins. Here, during religious festivals ever since the days of Pisistratus, a new kind of competition had been held, a competition by those who wrote tragedies. Here, in 472, the poet Aeschylus had presented his tragedy of the *Persians*, less than a decade after Xerxes had watched from his silver-footed throne while his fleet was destroyed in the narrow waters off the Isle of Salamis. This was the tragedy for which Pericles had served as choregus. Did Aeschylus make Salamis his scene of action or the Greek triumph his subject? On the contrary, he made the palace of Xerxes in Susa his scene, and he made his subject the insolent pride of Xerxes, his pride and its punishment by the gods, acting through the Greeks at Salamis. But Pericles was a young noble when he helped produce the *Persians*, and politically unknown; even Aeschylus was still in his fifties. Aeschylus continued to pour out tragedies: he may have written as many as ninety[198] dramas. During the early years of his career he, like other tragedians who competed before the temple of Dionysus, had to offer three tragedies, followed by a satyr play, a sort of grotesque farce. Each tragedy was complete in itself; but in Aeschylus's case the trilogy of tragedies often displayed an intelligible structure of its own. He first competed in 499, when he was twenty-six. In 484, four years before Salamis, he won his first victory. He may himself have fought at Salamis; he had certainly fought at Marathon. He remained the leading tragedian of Hellas until his death in Sicily in 455.

After Pericles came to power, Aeschylus's only performance at Athens was the trilogy known as the *Oresteia*, followed by a satyr play called the *Proteus*. The trilogy included the *Agamemnon*, the *Libation-Bearers*, and the *Eumenides*. The *Oresteia*[199] of Aeschylus exemplified the extraordinary role of tragic drama in Athenian and Hellenic life. Its performance was an act of religious devotion. It was presented to a god who was beloved by the common people and whose worship involved man's deepest and least understood longings more completely perhaps than did the worship of any other god on Olympus. It was presented to a god, son of Zeus, born of a mortal woman. In it, the arts of the poet, the musician, the choreographer were harmoniously combined. This half-opera had to be played in the open air to an audience seated on wooden benches against the southern slope of the Acropolis, with an all-male cast of masked actors to whom special high shoes gave majestic stature. The drama had to come to life with only the simplest of stage settings. The *Oresteia* was a feast of awareness, in which citizens of every level of intelligence, of every political conviction, of every economic class, joined with their god.

The plot of the *Oresteia* was not something Aeschylus had contrived in order to astonish a gaping crowd. On the contrary, he merely retold one of the best-known tales from the Homeric Cycle, from the corpus of epic poems that had nurtured Hellas for hundreds of years. It was a tale of those dimly remembered Mycenaean days before the eruption of the Dorians into Greece more than half a millennium ago. It was a tale of dynastic families, of bloody violence, of vengeance blindly trying to serve the function of public law; a tale of greatness brought low; and, above all, a tale of the suffering through which a man might win understanding and release. The plot did indeed come from Homer's world, and Aeschylus himself, according to later tradition, remarked modestly that his tragedies were but slices of meat from Homer's mighty dinners.[200] But where the *Iliad* merely told, through the mouth of the rhapsode who sang or declaimed it, what the men of old had done and said and suffered, the *Oresteia* made them do and say and suffer these things before the spectator's very eyes, while their cadenced, magic words rang out against the steep slope of the holy Acropolis itself. The *Oresteia* carried the spectators back through the centuries to the day when Agamemnon, having sacked Troy, returned in triumph to his palace so few miles south of where the spectators sat, only to be done to death by his queen, Clytemnestra. But, if it carried the spectators back in time to the return of the conquerors from Troy, it carried Mycenae forward too. Agamemnon's palace at Mycenae was magically transported to neighboring Argos, which has just made common cause with Athens to hold the Spartans in check.

The bloody vendetta of which Clytemnestra's murderous act was but a part would proliferate hopelessly until her son Orestes would kill her; until the tormented matricide, pursued by the frightful Furies of the nether world, would seek Apollo's advice at Delphi; until Apollo would escort Orestes to Athens, home of law and justice; until Athena herself would preside over a formal court, whose judges would be members of the Areopagus—of that Areopagus whose traditional power to judge blood-guilt not even Ephialtes or Pericles had torn from it; and until this court, presided over by Divine Wisdom herself, would acquit the matricide, Orestes. Nor could the tragic cycle end until Athena had assigned the avenging Furies, now robbed of their prey, to sanctuary in a cave, a cave in the side of the very hill on which the Areopagus still heard such cases when the *Oresteia* was played. The Furies were given a new name, the Gracious Goddesses,[201] and undertook to bless the city of Athens. Ancient vengeance for the blood that had been spilt, especially kinsman's blood, had been reconciled with wisdom and reason and law. Man as moral agent had through great suffering been purified; and through the direct intervention of the gods the Polis, the human community, had been saved from anarchy.

This was the trilogy, the tragedy-in-three-tragedies, that Athena's Polis was allowed to live in, to pass through, to understand, to remember. And it was this new art form, tragedy, fashioned and perfected in Athens out of ancient elements collected hither and yon, that conquered the Hellenic spirit. As for the *Oresteia* itself, it was the work of an aristocrat, born in the holy town of Eleusis, goal of pilgrims, of those who, burdened with sin, longed for a life beyond death. It was the work of an aristocrat who had fought at Marathon for a city already turning toward democratic rule, toward equality before Law, toward the right of every citizen to speak in the Assembly as an equal of all his fellows. Here in the Theater of Dionysus every citizen could see man face to face with his gods, face to face with his neighbor, speaking wingèd words, listening, thinking, acting. He could see man acting; he could see an actor acting. The actor in the play was a reflection of another man who acted, yet not in a theater. And by an effort of imagination, he could see the historical Agamemnon act, all unconscious that real acts in history might at some later day appear to men like mere reflections of the actions in a tragedy. This was an experience calculated to help the Athenian look at his own acts, to be aware of them, to live, not the life of the somnambulist, but the life of a man who was fully alive, alive to himself and to the persons about him. It was an experience calculated to give him not a childish optimism, not a foolish sentimentality, but the tragic sense of life that it was not a child's lot to possess.

Work of the caliber of Aeschylus's tragedies was well-nigh bound to provoke challenge; and it was chiefly Sophocles who responded. He was born in Colonus, a little town a little north of Athens, in 495, five years before Aeschylus fought at Marathon. When the Persian fleet met catastrophe in the narrow, crowded waters off Salamis, Sophocles was a lad of fifteen; and, when a trophy was dedicated after the battle, it was Sophocles who led the chorus that danced and sang around the trophy. Sixteen years after Aeschylus's first triumph in tragedy and only ten years before the Oresteia, Sophocles won first prize.[202] He was only twenty-seven, and his defeated opponent was Aeschylus. Sophocles lived about ninety years, and, according to later tradition, he wrote around 125 dramas,[203] of which some 24 won first prize. Like Aeschylus, he was an aristocrat and a soldier as well as a tragic poet. He held several public offices. When Pericles sailed in 440 to quell the revolt of Samos, one of his generals was Sophocles.

In Sophocles' hands, the structure of tragedy, with its high conventions, changed. The trilogy, or tragedy-in-three-tragedies, he attempted only once. Although gods and heroes might appear, the source of dramatic human action had somehow shifted from gods to men. But the men were likely to be the legendary kings and heroes of Hellas, who represented in their single persons the whole human community. This symbolizing of a community by a person enabled Sophocles, like Aeschylus, to deal with that community, with the political problems of war and peace, of tyranny and freedom under law, with law made by gods as against law made by men alone; and yet to deal at the same time with persons, not with faceless crowds. These were persons who loved, hated, thought, deliberated, made choices, acted, and suffered. As in the tragedies of Aeschylus, they were men who wielded power, who grew proud and misused power, who therefore grew blind and deaf, who listened less well, and who suffered the catastrophe that could bring understanding.

Technically, Sophocles increased the chances for listening and hence the opportunities for turning the deaf ear. He increased the chances for true communion with god and communion with other men. For where dialogue in Aeschylus might involve two characters at any given moment, besides the chorus, in Sophocles the dialogue might involve three. The point of interest correspondingly shifted still further from the chorus, which took less and less part in the action, but rather observed and commented. Although there were now more characters ready to speak, they seemed readier to speak with each other than with the gods. In place of the tremendous religious tension that led the spectator of Aeschylean drama up from human action to the action of the gods, the tension in Sophoclean drama often led the spectator more from one man's act and purpose to the clashing purpose and counter-act of other men.

The tragedy that won Sophocles his most enduring fame was *Oedipus the King*. Like Croesus, king of Lydia, Oedipus consulted the oracle at Delphi. Like Croesus, he consulted him inadequately. For Oedipus wanted to keep buried memories hidden. He had been brought up to consider himself the legitimate son of the king and queen of Corinth. A fellow reveler at a banquet cast doubt on his parentage. When he consulted the oracle, he was told only that he would slay his own father and wed his own mother. He jumped to the conclusion that the oracle alluded to the king and queen of Corinth—although whether he was indeed their son was precisely the problem that had taken him to Delphi in the first place. He determined to avoid Corinth; he rushed blindly off toward Thebes. On the road he met an old man and his servants; he quarreled over the right of way; he slew the old man. He arrived at plague-ridden Thebes; freed it from plague by reading the riddle of the sphinx; gained, by way of reward, the hand of its middle-aged, recently widowed queen, Jocasta, and became king of Thebes. All this happened before the action of Sophocles' tragedy began: Oedipus's precipitate misreading of the oracle; his failure to make further inquiry; the slaying where three roads met of a man old enough to be his father; his triumphant reading of the riddle; his consequent marriage with the widowed queen; the coming of a new plague to Thebes. Then the action of the drama itself began.

The blind prophet Tiresias announced that the plague was a moral pollution: Jocasta's first husband, the late king, had been murdered. The murderer must be identified and banished if the Polis was to be cleansed and the plague driven out. Oedipus, with enormous pride in his power to read dark words, with enormous recurrent suspicion that his kingly authority was being threatened by treason, and with a proud determination to find the murderer, to do justice, and to save his people for a second time, embarked on his quest to find—himself. But such was his overweening pride that, though the dialogue of the drama offered him many opportunities to learn the hideous truth and to know himself, to know who he was, he could not listen, he could not understand, but threatened those who, wittingly or unwittingly, provided the clues he needed.

In the end he found the murderer—and himself, but not before his mother, wife, and queen had discovered who she and he both were and had taken her own life. He found himself murderer of his own father, husband of his own mother, half-brother of his own sons, father of his two half-sisters, nephew of his brother-in-law, Creon, who now became his king and not his subject: he found himself a man with eyes who could not see. Thereupon he tore out his offending eyeballs and went into banishment.

Among many others things, the *Oedipus* recalled Solon's command ment, "Know thyself." It suggested strongly that this commandment was hardest to obey for those who wielded power, since power tended to blind. In recalling this commandment of Solon's, it pictured these blinding effects of power just as Athens was becoming the most powerful state in Greece, an imperial city quick to scotch rebellion, the wealthy market place of the eastern Mediterranean. To her were crowding the artistic talents of Hellas; to her were crowding the masters of Hellenic literature. And to her crowded the sophists, lecturers and publicists who taught what was known or believed about the world the Greek inhabited and, above all, the art of rhetoric, that would enable their pupils to face political debate or judicial prosecution alike and win the war of words. Some pupils adopted from the sophists who taught them the convenient conviction that knowledge was but opinion, that everything was relative, that morals were but mores, that law was a convenient human convention, that the ancient myths about the gods were old wives' tales, and that might made right.

It was in the context of Aeschylus's tragic vision of the will of Zeus and the will of other gods fulfilling itself through the free choices of men; and it was even more in the succeeding tragic vision of Sophocles, of men who have seized the initiative but must still consult the will of Zeus, as transmitted by Apollo and his oracle at holy Delphi;—it was by this prismatic light that Pericles ruled democratic Athens, but by persuasion, not by force. From Damon he had learned music and the curious personal harmony, serenity, gentleness, and courtesy that contrasted so strongly with the bluff, hearty manner of his fellow aristocrat, Cimon, that cavalryman turned successful admiral. A statesman, a soldier, and an admiral himself, Pericles yet appeared strangely withdrawn and aloof, so that his political enemies derisively called him Olympian Zeus; but he was so cogent in debate, in a polis more and more attentive to the appeal to reason and to the charm of skillful speech, that his gentle mastery of that polis could not be overthrown. Like Solon, he was a man of both thought and action, and this at a moment in Athenian history when war and violence more and more threatened the marriage of thought and action. As to his gentleness, a tale was told that when a scurrilous and uncouth citizen followed him all day long, heaping insults upon him, he made no reply; and, when this stream of abuse followed him clear to his own doorway that evening, he still made no comment, except to order his servant, now darkness had fallen, to light a torch and escort his assailant safely home.

From Zeno the Eleatic, Pericles learned the power of close argument. Indeed, Zeno was sometimes called its inventor. But Zeno also sought the One, to which the many shifting phenomena of an ever-changing world might be reduced. So did, according to some, the founder of the Eleatic school in southern Italy, Xenophanes of Colophon, that enlightened Ionian poet, philosopher, and theologian who made such sport of Hellenic polytheism. Besides Damon's music and Zeno's brilliant dialectic, Pericles received for years the constant gift of Anaxagoras's thought. Anaxagoras had come from Clazomene in Ionia in 456 and was Pericles' intimate companion. He was learned in mathematics and medicine; he speculated in natural philosophy; and he taught the doctrine that neither air, nor fire, nor earth, nor water had originated our universe but that this universe had been made out of such elements by *Nous*—that is, by mind, intellect. Certainly it was to intellect that Pericles turned as to a court of last resort.

And yet, despite this Ionian tendency to trace all things to one primal cause, despite this Odyssean tendency toward intellectual light, toward quiet reflection, the question, and attentiveness, it was Pericles who sponsored the exhilarating program of housing the traditional, numerous gods of Athens in magnificent new temples. It was Pericles who worked intimately with Phidias to crown the Acropolis and Athens and Hellas with marble that could speak, with columns that would soar, with bas-relief that would remember the community of gods and men, that would glorify and validate a polis as something other than a herd of clever animals; that would certify it as other for all men at all hours of the day wherever the eye glanced and regardless of their varying intellectual powers; that would give work to the unemployed and would thereby consecrate Athens' surplus labor to an expression of adoration for the gods, of adoration from all the men of all the cities of her new empire, of adoration from all Hellenes ready to adore.

The tongues of many lands were now spoken on the busy docks of the Piraeus. The compelling might of the Athenian fleets patrolled the Aegean and kept the allied and subject cities obedient to the Athenian people. The delicate foods and delectable luxuries that flowed in on Athens tempted at least her richer citizens with a new vision that might blur the tragic sense or the rule of intellect, a vision of comfort and pleasure and a high standard of living, far from the stark simplicities of food and clothing and shelter amidst which she had fought for human freedom. Nevertheless, life in Pericles' Athens possessed an extraordinary luminous significance. There was plenty to worry about; most men were still poor; many had lost through slavery their full rights as men; yet human existence in Athens was at least phosphorescent with meaning, as it was in the great tragedies of Aeschylus and Sophocles.

Even the men of birth and money were partially won over by Pericles, by his moderation, by his prudence, by his obvious loftiness of spirit. Their aristocratic claim that quality be recognized, Pericles so clearly met; but they still regretted the breach with aristocratic, conservative Sparta and its rigorous, simple life. They challenged their own city's right to use the tribute of other League members, not for defense but to deck out Athens in baubles like some harlot. They were rendered uneasy by the Periclean democracy's growing tendency to overthrow their fellow nobles and fellow rich in Allied cities, to confiscate their lands, and to settle Attic rustics and craftsmen as cleruchs on those lands.

To the charge that Athens had no right to use the tribute of the League members, levied for the common defense, in order to beautify the capital city of a single member, Pericles replied that the Allies had no right to object so long as Athens protected them from Persia. They now contributed only money and they received protection. Besides, the construction program brought employment to the needy. Had Aristides,[204] who first divided the burden of the common defense, been alive now, would he have accepted the first of these arguments? But the Allies were in no condition any longer to object, and the work went on.

In 453, when he was nearing forty, Pericles married. Two sons were born of this marriage; but the parents separated by mutual consent when the boys were still small, and the mother remarried. Pericles did not remarry. He took into his home Aspasia, an extraordinary, highly cultivated woman from Miletus, who presided for years over a salon for the writers and artists and thinkers and statesmen of Athens, at a time when Athenian women, even of high family, were given little formal education and could provide little intellectual companionship for men like Pericles. He kept his two sons with him, and ultimately had a son by Aspasia. By virtue of Pericles' own law of 451, since Aspasia was not an Athenian, her son could not look forward to citizenship in his native polis. In addition to these three boys, Pericles took into his own home as wards two other boys, whose father, Clinias, a kinsman of Pericles, had fallen in the battle of Coronea in 447, the battle in which Athens lost control of Boeotia. These two wards were named Alcibiades and Clinias. Of these two, Alcibiades early showed brilliance of mind, a headstrong will, and a soaring ambition.

In 443, the aristocratic opponents of Pericles formed a coalition with the more radical democrats. This coalition dared not attack Pericles personally: his superior abilities were too obvious. He was a less great soldier than Cimon had been; he lacked the infallible animal cunning of a Themistocles and Themistocles' marvelous talent for improvised solutions. But he was as incorruptible as Aristides the Just; he was a prudent commander in the field; and, once he and Athens had surrendered their territorial ambitions to landward, both his foreign and domestic policies were essentially those of Themistocles. Above all, his intellectual attainments were conspicuously higher than those of either Cimon or Aristides or Themistocles, at a time when Athenian hegemony in Hellas was as much intellectual as military. He was the great persuader in a polis more sensitive to argument and persuasion than perhaps any other in Hellas.

Invulnerable in himself, he was forced to watch his opponents attack him in the persons of his intimates. His teacher of music, Damon, had already been ostracized around 444. In 432 Anaxagoras, who had taught him that Intellect ordered the universe and who had kept Pericles' own intellect active and inquiring in areas closed to his opponents, was prosecuted for atheism toward the many gods of Hellas and for pro-Persian sympathies. Pericles helped him escape from Athens to Lampsacus on the Hellespont, where he founded a school. When Pericles' mistress, Aspasia, was prosecuted on the same two counts, Pericles managed to get her acquitted. Phidias, his great collaborator on the Parthenon and other temples, was accused of misappropriating some of the gold destined for his colossal gold and ivory statue of Athena, in the inner sanctum of the Parthenon. But the gold had been applied in thin, removable plates. When removed and weighed, it was not found wanting. The political opposition thereupon prosecuted Phidias for impiety. When he had designed a frieze on a wall of the Parthenon, showing the Battle of the Amazons, could not he and Pericles too be discovered in the design that decorated Athena's shield? Still in prison and under trial, the greatest of Athens' sculptors died—and the scandalmongers whispered that Pericles had poisoned him to forestall incriminating testimony.[205]

Meanwhile the comic poets like Cratinus were deriding Pericles, his policies, his mistress, his friends. He was the Olympian, withdrawn, arrogant. He was Squill-head, Onion-head; for despite the grave beauty of his features, his head was unduly elongated, and this defect caused sculptors to portray him with his helmet unvisored but in place.

While his opponents crowded in upon him, like hounds around a stag, war came nearer. The growing power of Athens caused a growing fear in Sparta. It caused even more fear in Athens' commercial rival, Corinth. Even among Hellenic states outside both power blocs, the sense of impending collision was driving the weak to take sides. The brutal fact was that the Hellenic community, united by common gods, by common religious shrines, by a common literature and common plastic arts, by a growing philosophic tradition and a growing commerce in material goods, had as yet found no way to establish a common government. Hellas lived in that deceptive and dangerous anarchy in which the community was ungoverned but in which its parts—in the case of Hellas, each city-state, each polis—had made the difficult transition from private vendetta to public law, based on court evidence, on general published rule, and on judicial application of that rule by reasoned argument. This was the transition that the *Oresteia* of Aeschylus recorded, in all its agony and in all its final triumph. This was the law of which the exiled Spartan king, Demaratus, spoke, on that Samothracian beach, to Xerxes, when the Great King had passed in review his vast, polyglot army and his magnificent navy: "What their law bids them, that they do."[206]

But Simonides' terse epitaph on the Three Hundred who fell at Thermopylae referred the reader not to Hellas but to the Spartans: "Obedient to their word we lie." One could not lie down in death, obedient to the word of Hellas, because Hellas possessed no government to make laws. Hellas was armed against herself: private vendetta between city-states still gave Hellas rule by violence—the violence of one polis against another.

The nearest thing to Hellenic law that had been devised was the law of Athens. It was imposed on the city-states that now formed her empire. It was imposed partly by the Hellenic community's desperate need of a common government, partly by the high reputation of Athenian courts, and in the last analysis by force of arms, as witness the end of the Samian revolt. But those who made that law were citizens neither of Samos nor of any other ally; they were citizens of Athens. And the essential point of the freedom for which men had died at Marathon, at Thermopylae, at Salamis, at Plataea, at Mycale, the essential point of the recent war that had freed the Boeotians and other Hellenes from Athenian domination was that a man should help make the laws he lived under if he were to be truly free. Only then could law rightly be his master.

Athens stood for the unity of Hellas under law, and, if necessary, under imposed law. Sparta stood for the independence of every polis against a law imposed by force from outside its community of citizens. The clash between them drew ominously nearer. It was predictable that the necessary military incidents would not be lacking. One of them happened in 433 at Corcyra, an island state off the west coast of Greece, on the grain route from Sicily. A second occurred in the same year at Potidaea, a tributary city of Athens in the Chalcidic peninsula, not many miles from the canal that Xerxes had dug to avoid the dangerous cape at Mount Athos. Both Corcyra and Potidaea were originally colonies of Athens' enemy, Corinth. A third incident occurred when Megara, so recently part of Athens' Mainland empire, allied herself with Corinth, and when, as a counter-measure, Athens closed the markets of her whole empire to Megara's goods in the spring of 432. That autumn Sparta's allies persuaded her to demand that Athens make concessions to Corinth and Megara or fight. Pericles, convinced that war with Sparta was inevitable, persuaded Athens to reject this ultimatum and to offer to submit to arbitration by a third party, as provided for in the Thirty Years' Peace. The Athenian offer to arbitrate was not accepted.

In 431 an army of Spartans, other Peloponnesians, and Boeotians occupied Acharnae, the most populous Attic deme outside of Athens. Some six miles away in Athens many Athenians wanted to attack, but Pericles had determined to follow where the wily Themistocles had led. He abandoned the Attic countryside and packed the country population inside the walled island that comprised Athens, its triple port of Piraeus, and the corridor that connected them. Their cattle and sheep and goats were sent across the strait to Euboea and to other islands. Athens still controlled the sea. She could live on imported foodstuffs. Meanwhile, she would harry the coasts of the Peloponnese until Sparta and her Peloponnesian League should tire of the war and should sue for peace.

Inside the walls the country people crowded wretchedly, in this city whose clever folk they so much distrusted. They slept in temples, in the towers on the city wall, in Piraeus, in the long walled corridor that connected Athens with her port. They huddled sorrowfully among the household furnishings they had salvaged and watched with horror from the walls while the enemy ravaged their orchards and vineyards and grain fields, so toilsomely husbanded over the decades. They outnumbered the city-dwellers. The polis that Pericles ruled, that the sea and the distant lands obeyed, with its foreign slaves and busy docks, its luxury and its power, its idle and garrulous and litigious citizens—this polis was still, if one merely counted heads, mainly a rural polis, a polis of ploughing and reaping, of herding, of pruning the vine, of beekeeping, and of the relentless work of the sort that Hesiod had prescribed in song. Conservative, pious, fond of their ancient traditions, slow-moving and slow-speaking, what could the men who carried on this work know of the clever, greedy, lazy, restless, skeptical city and its ways? Only the old could remember how, nearly fifty years before, with the vast armies of the Great King approaching, they had abandoned their fruitful countryside, had abandoned even Athens itself, to take to the ships and die for the right of the survivors to come home. Now, crowded in their unsanitary quarters, uprooted and homesick, they grumbled and lamented. Pericles tried to conciliate them by sending out raiding parties of cavalry to protect the fields nearest Athens. But he declined to convoke the Assembly for fear the hotheads would force a military blunder. Then, when the long summer campaign was over, he followed Athenian custom and held a state funeral for those who had fallen for Athens in the first year of the Peloponnesian War.

It was he who had pronounced, nine years before, a funeral oration over the bones of those who had fallen in the Samian revolt, and men still repeated his phrases. One could not see these fallen heroes now, he had then declared; neither could one see the gods, "but from the honors which they receive, and the blessings which they bestow, we conclude that they are immortal."[207] And so it was with the heroes who died suppressing the rebels at Samos. And in that same oration, he had cried that the Polis had lost its youth and the year had lost its spring. Now it fell to his lot to pronounce another oration, this one over the bones of those who had fallen in the first year's fighting of another, more ominous war.

Like a victory ode of Pindar that leaped upward from victory in the games to the victor's god-descended ancestors who also won victories and won them on storied battlefields, the funeral oration of Pericles leaped from the present occasion and the newly fallen heroes to their heroic ancestors who had kept Athens free, to their fathers who had won for her an empire, and to the battles which those present had fought to extend that empire. But, he asked, under what kind of government and out of what sort of habits and customs had such greatness grown? "It is true," he answered,

that our government is called a democracy, because its administration is in the hands, not of the few, but of the many; yet while as regards the law all men are on an equality for the settlement of their private disputes, as regards the value set on them it is as each man is in any way distinguished that he is preferred to public honours, not because he belongs to a particular class, but because of personal merits; nor, again, on the ground of poverty is a man barred from a public career by obscurity of rank if he but has it in him to do the state a service. And not only in our public life are we liberal, but also as regards our freedom from suspicion of one another in the pursuits of every-day life; for we do not feel resentment at our neighbour if he does as he likes, nor yet do we put on sour looks which, though harmless, are painful to behold. But while we thus avoid giving offense in our private intercourse, in our public life we are restrained from lawlessness chiefly through reverent fear, for we render obedience to those in authority and to the laws, and especially to those laws which are ordained for the succour of the oppressed and those which, though unwritten, bring upon the transgressor a disgrace which all men recognize.[208]

And our city is so great that all the products of all the earth flow in upon us, and ours is the happy lot to gather in the good fruits of our own soil with no more home-felt security of enjoyment than we do those of other lands.[209]

We are also superior to our opponents in our system of training for warfare. . . . In the first place we throw our city open to all the world and we never by exclusion acts debar any one from learning or seeing anything which an enemy might profit by observing . . . for we place our dependence, not so much upon prearranged devices to deceive, as upon the courage which springs from our own souls when we are called to action.[210]

For we are lovers of beauty yet with no extravagance and lovers of wisdom yet without weakness. Wealth we employ rather as an opportunity for action than as a subject for boasting; and with us it is not a shame for a man to acknowledge poverty, but the greater shame is for him not to do his best to avoid it. . . . We alone regard the man who takes no part in public affairs, not as one who minds his own business, but as good for nothing; and we Athenians decide public questions for ourselves or at least endeavour to arrive at a sound understanding of them, in the belief that it is not debate that is a hindrance to action, but rather not to be instructed by debate before the time comes for action. For in truth we have this point also of superiority over other men, to be most daring in action and yet at the same time most given to reflection upon the ventures we mean to undertake . . .[211]

Then came an extraordinary statement. Pericles was, after all, making a patriotic oration. It was scarcely surprising that the Athens he described did not exist concretely, either in the now abandoned Attic countryside or behind the walls of the man-made island Themistocles had imagined, or even in the wooden walls of Athens' watchful fleets. It existed only as an ideal, yet an ideal toward which Athens had steadily been tending. Even if his oration were construed as an effort to console by flattery, it was extraordinary by what high and central point in his discourse he chose to flatter—he who knew his audience so well, knew what they wanted to be or even to seem to be.

In a word, then, I say that our city as a whole is the school of Hellas . . .[212]

He said more: he spoke of those things that such an oration had to speak of before he dismissed his fellow citizens:

grief, I know, is felt, not for the want of the good things which a man has never known, but for what is taken away from him after he has once become accustomed to it.[213]

But he had already summed up in a sentence his hopes for his city, in a universe ruled by Nous, by Intellect.

When the winter of 431-430 closed, the Spartans and their allies again invaded Attica and ravaged it; but a worse enemy than Sparta struck an even harder blow at the school of Hellas: a frightful plague broke out in the crowded city, and, during the hot and stifling summer that followed, turned Athens into a city of horrors. Men believed the epidemic had started on the upper Nile; that it had swept Egypt and Libya and most of the Great King's empire. Then it broke out in the Piraeus, for it came from the sea that Hesiod so much dreaded, from the sea whence so many modern ills had come. Thucydides, who contracted the disease himself but recovered, carefully set down its symptoms, its fearful crisis, and the ghastly death that frequently followed. With it came a frightening demoralization that loosened the bonds that held the polis together. Crowded in their stifling, improvised cabins, idle, disconsolate, the refugees from the Attic countryside died like flies. Faced with probable death, and hence with a probable escape from retribution, at least in this life, many Athenians did things they had always feared to do or had always been ashamed to do.

Meanwhile Athens struggled on with the war. She sent a fleet to ravage the coast of Peloponnese, but the plague attacked the fleet. She sent an army to conquer rebel Potidaea, but the plague attacked the army. Pericles himself lost his two legitimate sons. He lost his sister. He lost most of his friends. His eldest son had, in any case, quarreled with him over money matters and was publicly slandering him. But when the younger son died too and the moment came for Pericles to lay a wreath upon the dead, he did what he had never yet done in public: he wept.

Nevertheless the Olympian kept his courage. The Athenians, watching their city fill with corpses and their countryside with enemy troops, murmured against his leadership. At last, in despair, they insisted on suing for peace, but failed to secure it. Then they turned on Pericles. He called an assembly. He rebuked them for breaking under their private misfortunes and reminded them that

> even though a man flourishes in his own private affairs, yet if his country goes to ruin he perishes with her all the same. . . . Since, then, the state may bear the misfortunes of her private citizens but the individual cannot bear hers, surely all men ought to defend her.[214]

"Nor must you think," he warned,

> that you are fighting for the simple issue of slavery or freedom; on the contrary, loss of empire is also involved and danger from the hatred incurred in your sway . . . for by this time the empire you hold is a tyranny, which it may seem wrong to have assumed, but which certainly it is dangerous to let go.[215]

This very point the Corinthians had made on the eve of the war when they were urging hesitant Sparta and her other allies to combine against imperial Athens. The Peloponnesians, they had cried, ought not to prove

> degenerate sons of our fathers, who liberated Hellas, whereas we, so far from making this liberty secure, should be allowing a city to be established as a tyrant in our midst, though we claim the reputation of deposing the monarchs in single states.[216]

Pericles won the debate on policy, but resentment against him for Athens' disasters was so high that he was prosecuted for embezzlement. His accounts were examined for a period of fifteen years. There was one sum of some ten or twenty talents that he could not account for and that he had probably used to bribe an invading Spartan king in 446. He was fined some fifty talents and lost his civic rights. But his integrity was perfectly well known; his wisdom was desperately needed; and he was shortly restored to power. Indeed, a few months later, the Assembly at his request granted rights of citizenship to the son whom Aspasia, his Milesian mistress, had given him, a son now some sixteen years old. He, too, was named Pericles.

In the autumn of the following year, 429, the Olympian fell ill. According to later tradition, it was the plague; and though it was but a light attack, it slowly used him up. According also to tradition, when a friend visited him, Pericles ruefully showed him an amulet the women of his household had hung around his neck. Pericles had so hated superstition and had always so serenely followed reason. As he lay dying, he might well reflect that he had not even wholly completed the group of buildings that crowned the Acropolis—for example the new temple known as the Erechtheum, and even certain details of the queenly Parthenon itself. The Hephaesteum, erected to the glory of Hephaestus, blacksmith son of mighty Zeus, and to Athena Hephaestia, patron god and patron goddess of the busy artisans of Athens, especially of her blacksmiths and her potters—

even the Hephaesteum had not yet been formally dedicated. Pericles had learned by grim experience to expect that, once he was gone, the Athenian democracy would most likely lose its head, would perhaps commit some fatal folly in the war that now raged into its third year. He left no political heir capable of guiding and restraining the Assembly.

While he lived, Athens was the school of Hellas in a double sense. She incited other Hellenic states by her contagious example to achieve democratic freedom, a freedom in which law was the conclusion of debate, of deliberation on the common good by all citizens, regardless of birth or wealth. But she was a school also for her own Athenian citizens, a learning polis, where men learned to make useful and beautiful objects and to defend the polis with their swords, their oars, and their lives; where men could listen to great music in the Odeum that Pericles had built near the Acropolis, partly from the masts and spars of captured Persian ships; could listen to rhapsodes recite Homer and to Herodotus the Halicarnassian read his history of the Persian Wars; could sit in the open-air theater of the god Dionysus and watch the heroes of Aeschylean tragedy act, suffer, and learn; could look up to the Acropolis and gaze on as lovely temples as man had ever built; could wrestle naked in the Attic sunlight in the palaestra and make their bodies strong and swift and skillful and beautiful, like the bodies of the gods themselves; could make law in the Assembly and render judgment under law in the courts; could stroll in the Agora and argue about the nature of man and his destiny, or listen to lectures by sophists, or simply talk with the merchants and sailors from strange and distant lands who crowded the water front of Piraeus. And yet, the citizens of Athens had clearly not developed the wisdom to govern their polis without unusual leadership. When Pericles had died, who would be competent to lead? Above all, when he died, he would bequeath this lovely city, this school of Hellas, but, alas, this tyrant-city too, a most deadly war. That war now threatened to bring Athens at last to her knees and to destroy once and for all the semblance of Hellenic unity which she had built out of her blood, out of her toil, out of her overweening pride.

In the autumn of 429 Pericles died.

THE AGONY OF HELLAS

THE WAR the dying Pericles bequeathed to his successors was a war in which both sides fought for Hellenic freedom. Half a century earlier both sides had fought, shoulder to shoulder, for the right of Hellenes to make the laws which they themselves obeyed and not to obey those of the Great King. On the beach at Marathon, in the bloody Pass of Thermopylae, between the rock cliffs and the sea, in the waters north of Artemisium, and in the narrow straits of divine Salamis, men had died for that freedom. And, when the Asian army of Mardonius had broken at Plataea, it was to Zeus Eleutherius, Zeus the Liberator, that the Hellenes dedicated annual sacrifices; for Mainland Greece was free. Then Athens willingly, and Sparta with hesitation, had freed Greece-in-Asia, on another beach, at Mycale. The two leading cities of Mainland Greece now diverged. For Sparta, freedom had been saved; but Athens and the Asian Greeks first fought to open the Hellespont and then formed the League of Delos to protect Aegean Hellas and the sea lanes that made Aegean Hellas possible.

From a league to defend Hellenic freedom Aegean Hellas evolved into an Athenian Empire. The thrust of that empire was toward trade, money, sea power, and government by the people, the Demos—that is, toward democracy. More and more, whatever support Athens found for her rule she found among the populace in each of the cities she governed. More and more, the Well-fathered and the wealthy in each subject city, sure of their right to rule their own polis, conspired against the imperial capital of this new Hellenic empire.

Aegean Hellas flourished. Its political unity brought, within its jurisdiction, something approaching peace. Freed by Athenian naval power from the piracy that had cursed the Aegean, freed from the competition of the Great King's Phoenician merchants, Hellenic trade expanded. The standard of living in Athens' empire rose. If an ordinary citizen in one of the subject cities could not always find work and bread in trade or industry, he might hope to find a bench and a seaman's wage in one of the imperial triremes that Athens built with the tribute from his own, or another, city. As for the intellectual, the artist, the philosopher, he would find a gracious welcome at Athens, the undisputed capital of thinking, feeling Hellas. Even the enterprising merchant might move his business there. Though he could no longer hope, except by a special grant from the Assembly, to become a citizen, he might certainly hope to grow rich and to enjoy life in the loveliest and liveliest city in all Hellas. The statues and temples, the mural paintings, the music, the soaring tragedies and ribald comedies, the exciting conversation, and the civilized, courteous daily life of Athens were his.

The price of this new order was the loss of sovereignty, though not the loss of local self-government. For the ordinary citizen of a polis in Aegean Hellas, the part he played in governing his city might actually be increased. The noble, and the rich merchant too, who wanted to make the laws this humbler citizen must obey, threatened his freedom far more than Athens seemed to do. Even his polis, if it happened to be a small one, was protected by Athens against its more powerful neighbors, as the merchant and dock-worker of Athens had once been protected by the tyrant Pisistratus against the rapacious Athenian noble. The brutal fact remained that this small polis, if it should decide to secede from the League of Delos, now become an empire, must reckon with the might of Athens. Indeed, this polis was at the mercy of the triremes and infantry of Athens precisely as every single Athenian had once been at the mercy of the tyrant Pisistratus's bodyguard. If a subject polis claimed it suffered from injustice, such as Athens' doubling the tribute in 425, the only court it could carry its grievance to would be a court in Athens. Was this freedom?

Opposed to Athens and her Aegean empire stood Sparta and her Peloponnesian League. Sparta fought, at least in theory, for the sovereignty of each polis. But she maintained her leadership by supporting the Well-fathered and the well-to-do against the mob in each polis with which she was allied. Although some of her allies, such as Corinth and Megara, lived by trade rather than by the plough, Sparta herself did not. She still put her faith in the eunomia of Lycurgus, in tradition, in the shield and spear of the heavy infantry, in the courage and iron discipline of that infantry, in the virtues of the aristocrat. She still counted on the terror her army inspired both at home and abroad. In short, Sparta stood guard over an older Hellas, a Hellas that was dying, but a Hellas that was still a glorious and moving tradition. For the new problems of adventurous, enterprising, commercial Aegean Hellas she offered no solutions; she promised only freedom from Athens.

Both Spartan and Athenian, then, loved freedom under law. If ever in Hellenic history there had been need of a good strife, a good eris, a fruitful dialogue, it had been during the last years of peace as the hundreds of Greek city-states watched and as war, the evil eris, approached. If Pericles could have assembled his Panhellenic Congress, could its delegates have explored freedom by means of the good eris? Could they have devised a Solonian joining of right with might throughout the new Aegean Hellas?[217]

A new, emerging Hellenic community, with not only a common tongue, common gods, and common customs, but with an economy that was more and more common too, remained a collection of small city-states, each one a sovereign polis. The polis remained the largest area of man-made law. Of necessity, the polis, when it differed with a neighbor, took law into its own hands and fought for what it believed was justice, was freedom under law. At best, both sides sometimes submitted their disputes to arbitration. In short, they behaved toward each other as noble families had done before the polis had replaced vendetta with a court of law. It was as if that important step, which Aeschylus, in the *Oresteia*, had shown men taking under the guidance of Athena, goddess of wisdom, required more imagination, perhaps more mutual confidence, more spiritual energy, than Greeks could any longer muster. It was as if they had, with the help of the gods, expanded their comprehension of the human community from family

168

to polis, but could not win through to a vision of a still wider human community, of free men living by reason and not violence. What blinded them? Was it the residual violence, the bad eris, between rich and poor that still smoldered beneath the surface of community life, or wildly erupted and threatened to destroy life, liberty, property, and polis? Or was it the other way around? Did the eris between Demos, the People, on the one hand, and on the other the Oligoi, the few—that is, the Best People and especially the rich people—did this evil eris of democratic revolution and oligarchic counter-revolution spring from the artificial assumption that, though man clearly needed law, yet one's own small polis was somehow the whole of mankind?

By the autumn of 429, when Pericles lay dying, War was taking over from Law, "but war, which robs men of the easy supply of their daily wants, is a rough schoolmaster and creates in most people a temper that matches their condition."[218] From the beginning of the war, whomever the Lacedaemonians caught in ships off the coast of Peloponnese, whether soldier, sailor, or civilian, whether Athenian or neutral, they put to death. In reprisal, in 430, when Athenians in Thrace captured envoys from Sparta and her allies, bound for the Great King's court to beg for money and other help against Athens, they killed them without trial. When the Athenians besieged and blockaded Potidaea, hunger within that city led to cannibalism. When Potidaea surrendered, the entire population was driven into exile. The plague in crowded, besieged Athens brought not only a loss of some one-third of her population, including 4,400 hoplites and 300 cavalry, but a terrifying demoralization of those who remained. Plataea, for nearly a century the ally of Athens, and sole sharer of Athens' glory at Marathon, was betrayed by her own oligarchs to Thebes. But she held out for four years. When Athens failed to send the aid she had promised, the Plataeans surrendered to a Lacedaemonian army on condition they would be tried. Five Lacedaemonian judges, determined to please their Theban allies, asked the Plataeans one by one, only one question: whether they had done the Lacedaemonians and Lacedaemon's allies any service in the war. The Plataeans could only answer no, and they were led out singly and slain to a man.

War was indeed taking over, and even the original policy for the war itself, laid down by Pericles, grew blurred, as violence led to violence. Pericles had wanted to collect the people of Attica into the man-made island of Athens and Piraeus, to allow the Peloponnesians to ravage the countryside, and never risk battle against Sparta's vastly superior land forces; meanwhile to keep firm control of the sea, and to make sudden and damaging raids on the coasts of Laconia and the Peloponnese. He wanted Athens to hold tight her subject allies and above all not to attempt fresh conquests. Sparta would soon grow sick of a futile war, which she had not the money to prolong, and would make peace. The war would have demonstrated that Sparta's professionalized citizen-army was indeed supreme on land but that Athens' imperial navy was equally superior at sea.

What that navy could do, the Athenian admiral Phormio had shown in the last months of Pericles' life. Other Greek navies were still using the trireme in the way that Athenian cavalry had until recently used the horse: to transport infantry. Arrived at the battlefield, this mounted infantry had dismounted and had fought it out, as other men fought it out. But Greek triremes too, once they had come to battle, used grappling irons on the enemy triremes while the marines they carried fought it out. Later, Greek cavalry had learned to fight from horseback and had learned to turn its horses into combat weapons. And Phormio's triremes had turned into weapons, too. Pericles' training routine that kept 60 battle craft constantly at sea during the best eight months of the year had created crews with such consummate skill that Phormio, with 20 ships, could outmaneuver 47 Peloponnesian ships, later increased to 77, in the Gulf of Corinth, could row rapidly around them in a steadily constricting circle, then wheel and ram their wooden flanks with the bronze beaks of his vessels or shear off their oars, or merely crowd them into colliding fatally with each other. Or, with one daring, wheeling ship, he could throw them into utter confusion. His crews went at their hard, skillful work in silence, that they might hear their officers' commands. Their officers learned to exploit the familiar behavior of wind and current, to co-ordinate their own work with the work of the sea, and so to destroy their enemies. Those officers knew their work and watched for the propitious day just as surely as had Hesiod, who knew the land but feared the sea. The ships of Athens inspired in men the same awe and admiration as the heavy infantry of Sparta. Sparta's naval disasters nonplused her, and she suspected misconduct and cowardice. But Phormio knew that Spartan courage was based on hard-won knowledge, knowledge of the spear and sword. The knowledge the Spartan lacked was a knowledge equally hard to win, knowledge of what the sea was and of what a ship could do about it. As the arts of peace declined, the arts of war developed. War, that rough schoolmaster, taught men not only how to die like heroes, but how to kill other men efficiently.

In the year after Pericles' death, Mitylene, a city on the coast of Lesbos facing the Asian mainland, revolted against Athens and appealed to Sparta and Boeotia for aid. The other towns of Lesbos, with the single exception of Methymna, joined in the revolt, and indeed set up a common polis with Mitylene. Mitylenian envoys attended the Olympic Games of 428, stood in the temple of Zeus, and put their case. So Sparta sent a fleet; and simultaneously she ravaged Attica more thoroughly than before to distract Athens from her problem in Lesbos. But the Spartan fleet loitered; provisions failed at Mitylene; and Salaethus, whom Sparta had sent ahead of the fleet to take charge of the city's defense, now decided to provide even the democrats with heavy arms and armor in order to fight his way out of the beleaguered city. Once armed, the democrats promptly mutinied against their oligarchic government, demanded that the oligarchs distribute the provisions they were hiding, and threatened that otherwise they would surrender the city to the Athenians. Fearful that the democrats would turn them over to a besieging Athenian army for instigating rebellion, the oligarchs themselves surrendered the city, on condition that they be allowed to send an embassy to Athens before anyone should be punished. The Athenian general, Paches, agreed. Along with the envoys, he sent to Athens the Spartan Salaethus and the oligarchs who had instigated the revolt.

The democratic party which still governed Athens was no longer led by Periclean appeals to reason. The war had brought to the top the rope merchant, Eucrates; Lysicles, a sheep dealer; Hyperbolus, a lamp manufacturer; and above all, a rich tanner named Cleon. Cleon was widely denounced by his opponents as a harsh and violent demagogue, ill-born, vulgar, domineering, cynical, venal, a master of invective. But he was a militant leader of Demos against a conservative party that did not relish the war. He was a militant imperialist, because imperial expansion brought economic benefits to Demos.

Cleon saw the Mitylenian revolt in black and white. In addition to the execution of Salaethus, the Spartan, he demanded of the Assembly that they decree the death of the oligarchic Mitylenians now imprisoned in

Athens, the death of every adult male in Mitylene, and slavery for the women and children. Diodotus, a moderate, opposed his motion. The prospect that rebellion might spread throughout their empire and leave them at the mercy of Sparta frightened the Athenians. Mitylene had revolted even though Chios and Lesbos were the only parts of the Athenian Empire still allowed to supply a quota of ships as against money tribute. This fact angered the Athenians, and they carried Cleon's motion. Orders were sent to Paches at Mitylene to execute the murderous decree.

But the Athenians shortly repented of their cruelty, another meeting of the Assembly was called, and a hot debate ensued. Then Cleon spoke again. He declared that Athens was a tyrant-city, obeyed by her allies out of fear, not love. The term tyrant, of course, had been applied by the Olympian himself to his beloved School of Hellas. But Pericles would not have agreed with Cleon's next point: that Athens ruled by force alone and that her allies obeyed her not out of loyalty but out of fear. Cleon's point was that the Athenian Empire was governed by might, a might that need not be joined with right. He rebuked his fellow citizens for not holding more firmly to their decisions and declared he had often observed that a democracy was incompetent to govern others; that "simpler people for the most part make better citizens than the more shrewd."[219] He attacked those who wanted to review the decree against Mitylene. These orators, he declared, were acting for gain. Or, at best, they were taking advantage of the Assembly's great weakness: to vote for the more eloquent, not the more cogent speaker. The members of the Assembly were prone to confuse legislative deliberation with contests for orators, to be "spectators of words and hearers of deeds."[220] There was no reason to punish only the aristocrats at Mitylene; the democrats had participated in the rebellion. Cleon warned the Athenians against pity, delight in eloquence, and clemency: they were the chief threats to an imperial state.

> I can sum up what I have to say in a word. If you take my advice, you will do not only what is just to the Mytilenaeans but also at the same time what is expedient for us; but if you decide otherwise, you will not win their gratitude but will rather bring a just condemnation upon yourselves; for if these people had a right to secede, it would follow that you are wrong in exercising dominion. But if, right or wrong, you are still resolved to maintain it, then you must punish these people in defiance of

equity as your interests require; or else you must give up your empire and in discreet safety practise the fine virtues you preach.[221]

Next Diodotus, the man who had spoken against Cleon's brutal motion, spoke again. He first parried Cleon's attack on that glory of Athens, free speech. He insisted that wise action must be based on deliberation; haste made for folly. If frank advice was to be met with the charge of bribery, then orators would have to resort to deceit to win the Assembly to even the wisest proposal: even "the man whose proposals are good must lie in order to be believed."[222]

Then the man whose proposals were good perhaps lied in order to be believed. Instead of appealing to the compassion which he might have assumed in many members of his audience and then showing how that compassion was a reflection of wisdom and for that reason practical, Diodotus bowed to the lesson which war had taught the Athenians: to be realistic, without compassion; to serve only their immediate interests; to sit in Athens and mete out cold-blooded massacre; to treat other men not as opponents in a dialogue, not even in the dialogue of battle and death, but as objects; not as ends, like themselves, but as means. After all, that was what these freedom-loving democrats considered their own slaves, at least in law. They were means to the good life of their free masters. Either Diodotus was now himself holding this view of such things as force and freedom, right and might; or he was afraid to risk statesmanship against a cynical politician. The issue, he declared, was not what wrong Mitylene had done but what was the wise course for Athens. Mitylene and Athens were not involved in a lawsuit: the problem was how best to make Mitylene useful to Athens again. Diodotus denied that the mass death sentence would deter other allies from rebellion: the death sentence had never yet deterred men from crime. If rebellion was to spell death, other rebels in the future would merely be more desperate fighters.

And do you consider, too, how great a mistake you would make in another point also by following Cleon's advice. At the present time the populace of all the cities is well disposed to you, and either does not join with the aristocrats in revolting, or, if forced to do so, is hostile from the beginning to those who stirred up the revolt; and so, when you go to war, you have the populace of the rebellious city as your allies. If, however, you destroy the populace in Mitylene, which took no part in the revolt, and which voluntarily put the city into your hands as soon as it got hold of arms, in the first place you will be guilty of killing your benefactors, and, in the second place, you will bring about what the influential men most wish: the next time they instigate a revolt among our allies they will at once have published it abroad that the same punishment is ordained for the innocent and for the guilty. Why, even if they were guilty, you should pretend not to know it, to the end that the only class that is still friendly to us may not become hostile.[228]

Then Diodotus again denied appealing to either pity or clemency; urged passing sentence on those rebels who had been brought to Athens for punishment, advised letting the others alone; and sat down. The debate went on. But, in the end, Diodotus's plea for the higher realism, combined perhaps with a compassion which neither he nor any other man dared to show, won by a bare majority. Cleon's decree for massacre was repealed. By this time the trireme they had sent to Mitylene, bearing death and slavery in its hold, had gained a start of about twenty-four hours, but it was bent on so horrible a mission that its crew had rowed halfheartedly. A second trireme was sent after it, bearing life and mercy. The Mitylenian envoys had provided wine and barley for the crew and had promised a large reward if they should reach Mitylene in time. So the oarsmen, as they rowed, ate their barley cakes, kneaded with wine and oil, and they took turns sleeping and rowing. When they arrived, Paches had received the decree of death and was about to start the butchery. The butchery never took place.

The Athenians did not impose tribute on Lesbos. Instead, they confiscated all the land of the island, except that held by loyal Methymna, and divided it into 3,000 allotments. A tenth of these they turned over to the gods. The rest were assigned to Athenian outsettlers, chosen by lot; and the outsettlers rented them to their former owners to work. Athens demolished the walls of Mitylene and seized her navy.

The revolt of Mitylene was suppressed in 427, in the fifth year of the war, but not before Plataea, faithful ally of Athens in Boeotia, had fallen that same summer and had been razed to the ground by the Peloponnesians. In this same year, the plague broke out a second time in Athens, although this time it lasted not two years, but one. Attica was invaded again. Yet, when Leontini, a city in Sicily, sent Gorgias, the famous rhetorician, to beg for Athenian help against Syracuse, Athens sent twenty triremes. In 433, two years before war with Sparta began, she had renewed her treaties with Leontini and Rhegium, a city just across the strait from Messina; and before the war began she was already active in the waters off the west coast of Mainland Greece, where the route to Sicily lay. Now that war had come, Sicily and southern Italy were more interesting than ever to Athens, since some of the Peloponnesian cities depended on grain from those areas. But in this same eventful year, 427, something else happened off the west coast of Mainland Greece that shed a lurid light on one aspect of the war, an aspect that was steadily growing in importance. Civil war broke out in Corcyra.

Corcyra, on the island now called Corfu, had been founded, or taken over from Eretrians, about 625, by colonists from Corinth. With the help of Corinth, Corcyra had founded a colony called Epidamnus, at the site of modern Durazzo, on the coast of Illyria. By 435 the democrats of Epidamnus had expelled the oligarchs, and the oligarchs joined the barbarous Illyrian tribesmen of the mainland to harass the democrats. The democrats appealed for help to their mother-city, Corcyra. When aid was refused, they asked Apollo at Delphi whether they should appeal to Corcyra's mother-city, Corinth, and Apollo advised them to do so. Corinth helped Epidamnus; and Corcyra, annoyed by Corinthian meddling, defeated a Corinthian fleet at sea. Corcyra then proposed a defensive alliance with Athens. Since Athens did not want the second naval power of Hellas aligned against her, she agreed. When Corinth attacked Corcyra's fleet, Athens helped her ally. This collision in 433 between Athens and Corinth led to the revolt of Potidaea in Chalcidice, a city which paid tribute to Athens but was closely bound to its mother-city, Corinth. The affair of Epidamnus and the affair of Potidaea had done much to precipitate the war between Athens and the Peloponnesians. For it was chiefly Corinth that had persuaded Sparta to issue her ultimatum to Athens.

In 427, a group of Corcyrean oligarchs whom Corinth had taken prisoner in a naval battle were released on condition that they should detach Corcyra from her alliance with Athens. These oligarchs entered the Senatehouse of Corcyra, attacked the leaders of the popular party and slew them. Then a street battle between oligarchs and democrats broke out, and both sides sent into the countryside and offered freedom to any slaves who would join them. Most of the slaves joined the democrats; whereupon the oligarchs hired 800 mercenaries from the mainland. Another street battle broke out: the democrats fell on the oligarchs, while from the tops of houses women pelted the oligarchs with tiles.

Next day an Athenian general, Nicostratus, arrived with 12 ships and with 500 heavy infantry from Messene. Nicostratus tried to make peace and bring the ringleaders of these riots to trial. But violence again broke out. The pro-Athenian democrats began killing the pro-Spartan oligarchs. Next, they

> went into the temple of Hera, persuaded about fifty of the suppliants there to submit to trial, and condemned them all to death. But most of the suppliants, not having consented to be tried, when they saw what was happening set about destroying one another in the sacred precinct itself, while a few hanged themselves on trees, and still others made away with themselves as best they could. And during the seven days that Eurymedon [an Athenian admiral sent to reinforce Nicostratus], after his arrival, stayed there with his sixty ships, the Corcyraeans continued slaughtering such of their fellow-citizens as they considered to be their personal enemies. The charge they brought was of conspiring to overthrow the democracy, but some were in fact put to death merely to satisfy private enmity, and others, because money was owing to them, were slain by those who had borrowed it. Death in every form ensued, and whatever horrors are wont to be perpetrated at such times all happened then—aye, and even worse. For father slew son, men were dragged from the temples and slain near them, and some were even walled up in the temple of Dionysus and perished there.[224]

Thucydides at this point noted that the war propagated revolution:

> for afterwards practically the whole Hellenic world was convulsed, since in each state the leaders of the democratic factions were at variance with the oligarchs, the former seeking to bring in the Athenians, the latter the Lacedaemonians. And while in time of peace they would have had no pretext for asking their intervention, nor any inclination to do so, yet now that these two states were at war, either faction in the various cities, if it desired a revolution, found it easy to bring in allies also, for the discomfiture at one stroke of its opponents and the strengthening of its own cause. And so there fell upon the cities on account of revolutions many grievous calamities, such as happen and always will happen while human nature is the same, but which are severer or milder, and different in their manifestations, according as the variations in circumstances present themselves in each case. For in peace and prosperity both states and individuals

have gentler feelings, because men are not then forced to face conditions of dire necessity; but war, which robs men of the easy supply of their daily wants, is a rough schoolmaster and creates in most people a temper that matches their condition.[225]

War not only made men's deeds brutal; it twisted men's words:

The ordinary acceptation of words in their relation to things was changed as men thought fit. Reckless audacity came to be regarded as courageous loyalty to party, prudent hesitation as specious cowardice, moderation as a cloak for unmanly weakness, and to be clever in everything was to do naught in anything.[226]

The cause of all these evils was the desire to rule which greed and ambition inspire, and also, springing from them, that ardour which belongs to men who once have become engaged in factious rivalry. For those who emerged as party leaders in the several cities, by assuming on either side a fair-sounding name, the one using as its catch-word "political equality for the masses under the law," the other "temperate aristocracy," while they pretended to be devoted to the common weal, in reality made it their prize; striving in every way to get the better of each other they dared the most awful deeds, and sought revenges still more awful. . .
The result was that though neither had any regard for true piety, yet those who could carry through an odious deed under the cloak of a specious phrase received the higher praise. And citizens who belonged to neither party were continually destroyed by both, either because they would not make common cause with them, or through mere jealousy that they should survive.[227]

So it was that every form of depravity showed itself in Hellas in consequence of its revolutions, and that simplicity, which is the chief element of a noble nature, was laughed to scorn and disappeared, while mutual antagonism of feeling, combined with mistrust, prevailed far and wide. . . .
And it was generally those of meaner intellect who won the day; for being afraid of their own defects and of their opponents' sagacity, in order that they might not be worsted in words . . . they boldly resorted to deeds. Their opponents, on the other hand, contemptuously assuming that . . . there was no need to secure by deeds what they might have by wit, were taken off their guard and perished in greater numbers.[228]

. . . At this crisis, when the life of the city had been thrown into utter confusion, human nature, now triumphant over the laws, and ac-

177

customed even in spite of the laws to do wrong, took delight in showing that its passions were ungovernable, that it was stronger than justice and an enemy to all superiority. . . . Indeed, men do not hesitate, when they seek to avenge themselves upon others, to abrogate in advance the common principles observed in such cases—those principles upon which depends every man's own hope of salvation should he himself be overtaken by misfortune.[229]

In 426, the year after Mitylene fell and the Peloponnesians razed Plataea and civil war broke out in Corcyra, Athens sent a general named Demosthenes around the Peloponnese to ravage the western coast and outlying islands of Mainland Greece. There Demosthenes was persuaded by the Messenians to attack neutral Aetolia and eventually to pass eastward through Phocis and attack Boeotia from the rear. Meanwhile Nicias and an Athenian army were attacking Boeotia from the east. Aetolian tribesmen were, indeed, numerous and warlike; but they used only light armor and lived in unwalled villages scattered far apart. Almost untouched by the commerce in goods and ideas that had civilized the cities on the Aegean coast of Mainland Greece, they still lived the sort of life all Greeks had once lived. Some of them spoke a Greek which the Athenians could barely understand. Some of them ate their meat raw. Even civilians carried arms. This plan of Demosthenes to conquer central Greece was a reversion to the land imperialism that had followed Cimon's death, that had dazzled Pericles in his younger days of power, that had ended in instructive disaster, and that violated the formula of Themistocles, which Pericles had fervently adopted: Athens was an artificial island whose destiny lay on the sea. The lesson was now learned all over again, and it was written in blood. Among the wooded mountains of Aetolia, tribesmen armed with bow and arrow and familiar with the terrain fell on the heavy infantry of Athens as they wandered in pathless gullies. At last Demosthenes' men lost their way in a forest and the wild tribesmen set the forest afire. The survivors escaped to the sea and took ship back to Athens. Demosthenes, afraid of punishment in Athens, stayed behind. Luckily, a little later, at the head of a force of Acarnanians, he retrieved his military reputation, first by saving the city of Naupactus from an army of Peloponnesians and Aetolians, and then by defeating an army of the Peloponnesians and Aetolians at Olpae on the Ambracian Gulf.

In this sixth year of the war, numerous earthquakes occurred, some of which caused destructive tidal waves on the coasts. In consequence an army of Peloponnesians which was preparing to invade and ravage Attica as usual, when it had reached the Isthmus, turned back, and Attica was spared. Three years earlier, the plague at Athens had apparently shortened a similar invasion. These invasions, which happened in five of the first ten summers of the war, had failed to provoke Athens to the land battle Sparta desired. Nor could the Peloponnesians face a decisive battle with Athens by sea. But the confused struggle in many theaters of war was teaching Athens more than improved naval tactics. Demosthenes, at least, was learning about forests, forest fires, and what light infantry could do with the somewhat despised bow against the traditional heavy infantry of Greece. On their side, Spartans were acquiring some knowledge of the sea and of the skills that sea power could teach. If they were learning their new art more slowly than Athens was learning hers, that was because Athenian infantry could drill not only on islands but on any other land Athenian triremes could defend, while Sparta's raw navy was largely barred by Athens from the drill ground it needed—the sea.

In general, however, the war was destructive, demoralizing, and indecisive. Sparta's traditional caution and conservatism lost her many valuable opportunities, such as the chance to liberate Mitylene. Her bad political judgment in foreign affairs often cost her the support of potential allies. But the Athenian democrats were capable of the same bad judgment, as Diodotus pointed out in his debate with Cleon. And Athens' chief mistake was worse: after the death of Pericles, her cleverness, her quick-wittedness, her inventiveness, her Themistoclean talent for brilliant improvisation repeatedly led her to gallop in all directions, as it were; to fail to concentrate on her main objective, victory through attrition. Pericles had wanted only to convince Sparta that Athens' empire could not be taken from her. The constant use of force was dulling the intelligence of both sides and reducing statesmanship to cunning tactics, far too short-ranged to achieve a solution of the problems common to all Hellas. And it was in Hellas, after all, that both Athens and Sparta were privileged, or condemned, to live.

It was not until 425, the seventh year of the war, that Athens unexpectedly won a serious advantage over Sparta. In the previous year, Athens' allies in Sicily requested help against the growing power of Syracuse and in 425 Athens sent out forty ships, with orders to stop off at Corcyra on their way. For Corcyra, now under democratic government, was suffering from raids by some 500 of her exiled oligarchs who had stationed themselves on a nearby mountain and were receiving help from the Peloponnesians. The Athenians also allowed Demosthenes, the hero of tribal warfare in Acarnania, to go with the Athenian squadron and use it on the Peloponnesian coast if opportunity beckoned. The fleet was forced by a squall to take shelter behind the small peninsula of Pylos, which lay off the western coast of Messenia in southwest Peloponnese. It had been Demosthenes' plan to fortify the hill at the tip of this peninsula. Pylos lay some forty-five miles from Sparta. There was abundant stone and timber with which to wall it off. Moreover, this was the ancient country of Demosthenes' friends, the Messenians, whose ancestors Sparta had "galled with great burdens like asses"[230] nearly a century earlier. Only three decades before, the Athenians had rescued some Messenian exiles and had settled them at Naupactus to guard the narrowest part of the Corinthian Gulf. They were now Athens' most loyal allies in the west country. Only the year before they had shared Demosthenes' disaster among the wild Aetolian tribesmen. Only the year before they had taken the chief honors when he defeated the Peloponnesians and their Ambraciot allies at Olpae. He now believed that, with their help, he could raise a Messenian rebellion against the hated Spartan overlords, provided he could make a fortified Pylos, with its ample harborage, a safe base for insurrection.

The commanders of the fleet failed to share his vision. They wanted to hurry on to Corcyra and then to Sicily. But the storm raged on, and partly from boredom the Athenian soldiers suddenly set to work and in six days built the fort Demosthenes longed to see in being. Sparta, though nearby, lay quiet. Her army was, as so often at this season, invading Attica. A religious festival was in progress, as religious festivals so frequently were. Anyhow, the Spartans were confident they could drive off the Athenians whenever they chose to do so. The Athenian commanders now left Demosthenes five of their ships, to which were added two Messenian privateers, and a garrison for his new fort. Then they hurried toward Corcyra. South of his little fortified hill on Pylos lay an island, Sphacteria, nearly three miles long, about half a mile wide, hilly and wooded like Pylos. The Spartans came. They occupied Sphacteria with 420 heavy infantry and their attendant Helots. Though Demosthenes had sent after the Athenian fleet for help, a Peloponnesian fleet from Corcyra got there first and blocked the narrow[231] inlets to the harbor behind Pylos and Sphacteria. The outer shore of Pylos offered no harborage and the Athenians could not hope to base a fleet on it. The Lacedaemonians then prepared to attack Pylos both by land and sea, and Demosthenes manned his land fortifications and the rocky outer shore of Pylos. Ship after ship tried to force a landing, even at the cost of wrecking itself on the rocks. The Spartan who most distinguished himself was a ship's captain named Brasidas, who was severely wounded trying to force his way ashore. All one day and most of the next a spectacle continued that amazed contemporaries: an Athenian army was fighting from the land, where usually Sparta's power was overwhelming—and was defending land that was part of Sparta's own domain at that—against Spartans coming from the sea, where normally the fleets of Athens were supreme. The Spartans failed to force a landing. Then the Athenian fleet returned from Corcyra.

The Peloponnesian fleet would not come out to meet it. But next day, for some reason, the Spartans neglected to close the inlet. The Athenian fleet sailed in, badly battered the Peloponnesians, and proceeded to blockade the Spartan forces on Sphacteria. Sparta was thoroughly alarmed. She requested an armistice to permit her to send envoys to Athens. Meanwhile, Sparta undertook to turn over to the Athenians what was left of her fleet at Pylos, together with all warships then in Laconia. Sparta agreed to make no attack on Demosthenes' fort, and Athens, no attack on the Spartan forces blockaded on Sphacteria. Sparta should be allowed to ship in provisions to Sphacteria. An Athenian ship should carry the Spartan envoys to Athens, and on the envoys' return, Athens would give back to Sparta all the ships now turned over to her. The armistice was accepted.

Arrived at Athens, the Spartan envoys addressed the Assembly with dignity and moderation. They proposed that Athens and Sparta make peace and insist that their allies respect the agreement. They even proposed an alliance between Sparta and Athens. Cleon, the leader of the democratic war party in Athens, persuaded the Assembly, which had recently longed for release from a war that stretched endlessly ahead, to take advantage of Sparta's predicament at Sphacteria and to demand back cities Athens had surrendered two decades ago in order to obtain the so-called Thirty Years' Peace. Since two of these cities were in Megara and none of them belonged to Sparta, the Spartan envoys were scarcely in a position to agree. What they proposed was that the Assembly appoint commissioners with whom they might try to negotiate mutually acceptable terms. Immediately, Cleon assailed them violently for wanting to go behind the backs of the Athenian people. Rather than lose credit with Sparta's allies by trying to negotiate in public with a popular assembly and convinced that the Athenians would agree to no acceptable terms anyhow, the envoys returned to Pylos and Cleon had his war.

When the Spartans now demanded their ships back, the Athenians refused to return them on the grounds that the Spartans had already broken the armistice by attacking Demosthenes' fort. This charge the Spartans denied, and hostilities were resumed. Many Helots won freedom by managing to carry provisions by night to the seaward shore of Sphacteria in small boats. Winter was coming on, and Athens began to worry. It would be difficult to convoy provisions in winter seas to her besieged garrison on Pylos and to the Athenian ships patrolling the inner shore of Sphacteria. The Assembly thoroughly regretted taking Cleon's advice. At this juncture Cleon rose to defend his policy. He pointed at Nicias, one of the ten elected generals of Athens and the leader of the conservatives in Athens ever since the death of Pericles. If, said Cleon tauntingly, the Assembly had men for generals, they could take Sphacteria and capture the Spartans now on it. If he, Cleon, were general, he could do it himself within twenty days. Nicias promptly rose and resigned his office in favor of Cleon. Cleon showed reluctance, but the Assembly clamored that he should go. Cornered, he went. Lacking military knowledge himself, he chose Demosthenes, who was still at Pylos, as his colleague. The conservatives were delighted: either the expedition would succeed and Athens would capture the Spartans, or, better still, it would fail, and Athens would get rid of their opponent, Cleon.

Demosthenes had not dared attack Sphacteria hitherto because the Spartans had the protection of a wood, and Demosthenes had learned the year before in Aetolia what that could mean. But, meanwhile, through an accident, the bulk of the forest on Sphacteria had burned and the danger of ambush was gone. Then Cleon arrived with reinforcements. In addition to his heavy infantry, Demosthenes threw into Sphacteria men from his ships' crews and—something which, again, Aetolia had taught him to value—archers, who would attack the flanks and rear of the Spartans. These light troops landed with sinking hearts at the thought of attacking the famous heavy infantry of Sparta, but they soon learned that they could succeed. The Spartans were not trained to cope with these nimble bowmen. Dust and ashes rose from the newly burned wood and blinded the Spartan infantry. They were exhausted from lack of adequate food. They were finally caught between a cross fire of arrows and began retreating. Cleon and Demosthenes, anxious to capture them alive and take them back to Athens, called on them to lay down their arms. A truce was arranged, and the Spartans sent to the Lacedaemonians on the mainland to ask for instructions. The reply came back: "The Lacedaemonians bid you decide your case for yourselves, but do nothing dishonorable."[232] The Spartans on Sphacteria surrendered. Of the 420 heavy infantry, 292 Lacedaemonians remained alive, of whom some 120 were Spartans.

Hellas was thunderstruck. A Spartan force had surrendered rather than die. What was it Demaratus had said to Xerxes on the beach near Doriscus? The Spartans "must never flee from the battle before whatsoever odds, but abide at their post and there conquer or die."[233] Those words were signed at Thermopylae. But now, when someone tauntingly asked of one of the Spartans who had surrendered on Sphacteria whether his slain comrades were brave men, the Spartan answered that any arrow which could distinguish a brave man from a coward would be a very valuable weapon.[234] Some of the exiled Messenians in Demosthenes' army were making incursions on the mainland of their ancient country. Helots were deserting from the Spartan army. Again Spartan envoys went to Athens, but Athens was in no mood to negotiate. Cleon had made good his boast that he himself could capture Sphacteria and bring its defenders alive to Athens within twenty days; he had done so; and the democratic war-party was drunk with victory.

In the same year, 425, the Athenian fleet continued to Corcyra and helped the democrats force the surrender of the Corcyrean oligarchs on the mountain nearby. Formally, they surrendered to Athens, but the democrats tricked them into breaking an agreement they had made with the Athenians and the oligarchs were given up to their opponents, who

shut them up in a large building; afterwards they led them out in groups of twenty and marched them down between two lines of hoplites stationed on either side, the prisoners being bound to one another and receiving blows and stabs from the men who stood in the lines, if any of these perchance saw among them a personal enemy; and men with scourges walked by their sides to quicken the steps of such as proceeded too slowly on the way.

In this manner about sixty men were led out and killed without the knowledge of the men who remained in the house, who supposed that their companions were being led out in order to be transferred to some other place. But when they perceived what was going on, or were told by somebody, they appealed to the Athenians and urged them, if they wished to kill them, to do so with their own hands; and they refused thenceforth to leave the house, and declared that they would not allow anyone to enter if they could prevent it. Nor had the Corcyraeans themselves any intention of trying to force their way in by the doors, but climbing on to the top of the building and breaking through the roof they hurled tiles and shot arrows upon them from above. The men inside tried to defend themselves as best they could, and at the same time most of them set to work to destroy themselves by thrusting into their throats the arrows which the enemy had shot or by strangling themselves with the cords from some beds that happened to be in the place or with strips made from their own garments. Thus for the greater part of the night—for night fell upon their misery—dispatching themselves in every fashion and struck by the missiles of the men on the roof, they perished. When day came the Corcyraeans loaded the bodies on wagons, laying them lengthwise and crosswise, and hauled them out of the city; but the women who had been captured in the fort were sold into captivity. In such fashion the Corcyraeans from the mountain were destroyed by the popular party, and the revolution, which had lasted long, ended thus, so far at least as this war was concerned; for there were no longer enough of the oligarchs left to be of any account. But the Athenians sailed for Sicily, whither they had set out in the first place, and proceeded to carry on the war in conjunction with their allies in the island.[285]

The next year the Athenians, who still held their base at Pylos, managed, with Nicias as general, to seize the island of Cythera, about six miles south of Laconia, and from the island made repeated and unexpected raids on the coast of Laconia itself. Morale at Sparta sank. A famous rhetra of Lycurgus was being justified: they had fought Athens long enough for Athens to learn how to ravage more thoroughly at least the coasts of their own Laconia. The Spartans were alarmed by the possibility of a Helot revolt. They sent repeated embassies to Athens in a vain effort to negotiate peace. They had lost confidence in their own strategy. In desperation they organized a force of cavalry and even of archers—

they, citizens of an unwalled polis, who had from time out of memory counted on heavy infantry and despised light-armed bowmen. They were not even able to save their Aeginetan allies, whom they had settled in Thyrea on their Argolid frontier in the first year of the war, when the Athenians had driven them out of Aegina and converted that island into a colony of Athenian outsettlers. The Athenians raided Thyrea, killed many of the colonists from Aegina, captured the rest, and took them to Athens. There, out of their ancient hatred for Aegina, they slew without mercy all the Aeginetan prisoners. The same year, under the leadership of Hermocrates of Syracuse, the Sicilians assembled at Gela and put an end to the war in which Athens had for years taken part. The Athenian fleet sailed home to Athens; but there the Assembly banished two commanders and fined a third, Eurymedon, for having quit Sicily. By now the Athenian war party had reached that point of optimism where a setback could be ascribed only to treachery or cowardice.

Before the year 424 closed, the Athenians captured Nisaea, the port of Megara facing Salamis, with the help of a democratic faction in Nisaea. But they failed to win Megara itself, since just then a Peloponnesian force moved up, led by that Spartan who had most distinguished himself in the attack on Demosthenes at Pylos, Brasidas. But the success at Nisaea set the Athenians dreaming again of the land empire they had once won and lost when Pericles was young. Supported by democrats in Boeotia, they launched a three-pronged attack on that country. At Delium they suffered overwhelming defeat. Meanwhile, Brasidas had managed to march northward through Thessaly with 1,700 infantry. The people of Thessaly were pro-Athenian, but the country was governed by pro-Spartan oligarchs. Even so, Brasidas needed tact and speed if Sparta were to reach Perdiccas, a Macedonian king, and Athens' subject cities in Chalcidice. Both Perdiccas and these cities were soliciting Sparta's aid. Perdiccas wanted help against a neighboring Macedonian king, and the subject cities were eager to revolt.

The Spartans had sent Brasidas north for several reasons. They hoped to divert Athens from her raids on their coasts. They saw a chance to send 700 of their Helots out of the country, armed as heavy infantry. So frightened were they of a Helot insurrection that they even called on all Helots who claimed to have distinguished themselves against the enemy to come forward and receive their liberty. Some 2,000 did. Free at last, they crowned themselves and visited the temples. All of them disappeared, and no one seemed to know how. The Spartans had calculated that their ruse would deliver into their hands the most spirited and hence the most dangerous of their restless state serfs.

Brasidas was not only a brave fighter and a skillful strategist, who moved rapidly and decisively. He had the ability as a speaker as well as the tact that most Spartans notoriously lacked. But, above all, he had a policy, something beyond merely injuring the enemy. He promised in the name of Sparta that she would not interfere with the political constitution of any city she might help to free itself from Athenian domination. But, as Brasidas said at Acanthus,

> if you meet these offers of mine with the plea that you cannot join us, but, because you are well-disposed to us, claim that you should not suffer by your refusal, and maintain that the liberty I offer seems to you to be not without its dangers, and that it is right to offer it to those who can receive it but not to force it on anyone against his will, I shall make the gods and heroes of your country my witnesses that, though I come for your good, I cannot persuade you, and I shall try, by ravaging your territory, to compel you; and in that case I shall not consider that I am doing wrong, but that I have some justification, for two compelling reasons: first, in the interest of the Lacedaemonians, that with all your professed good-will toward them they may not, in case you shall not be brought over, be injured by the money you pay as tribute to the Athenians; secondly, that the Hellenes may not be prevented by you from escaping bondage. For otherwise we should not be justified in acting thus, nor are we Lacedaemonians bound, except on the plea of some common good, to confer liberty on those who do not wish it. Nor, again, are we seeking after empire, but rather we are eager to stop others from acquiring it; and we should do wrong to the majority, if, when we are bringing independence to all, we permitted you to stand in the way. In view of these things, deliberate wisely, and strive to be the first to inaugurate freedom for the Hellenes and to lay up for yourselves undying fame; thus you will save your own property from injury and confer upon your whole state the fairest name.[236]

On into the cold Macedonian winter he fought. He liberated Acanthus and a number of Athens' other subject cities. At last he reached Athens' most valuable possession on the northern coast of the Aegean, the city of Amphipolis, on the Thracian bank of the river Strymon. Amphipolis commanded the resources of nearby Mount Pangaeus. Three miles downstream, at the mouth of the Strymon, lay the port of Eion. Across the river from Amphipolis lay the smaller city of Argilus. Argilus admitted Brasidas, and Spartan sympathizers in Argilus were in secret correspondence with fellow conspirators inside Amphipolis. There were two Athenian commanders charged with protecting the area. One of them, Eucles, was inside beleaguered Amphipolis. The other, Thucydides, the historian, was at the Isle of Thasos, half a day's sail away. Eucles got word to Thucydides to come quickly and help defend Amphipolis, and Thucydides with seven ships sailed promptly to Eion. But by that time, Brasidas had persuaded Amphipolis to admit him. He failed to dislodge Thucydides from Eion.

Athens was thoroughly alarmed. The navy counted heavily on Amphipolis for the timber it constantly needed, and the gold and silver mines Amphipolis also commanded had helped finance the war. The bridge at Amphipolis now gave Peloponnesians access to the Thracian coast and perhaps to the Hellespont itself, Athens' life line to Black Sea grain. Brasidas, by proclaiming the liberation of Hellas and by acting with model clemency, was encouraging Athens' Mainland possessions to revolt, where Spartan tactlessness and brutality during the revolt of Mitylene had produced the opposite effect. Torone fell. Lecythus fell. By the spring of 423, the Athenians were ready to sign a one-year armistice with Sparta. This would give them a chance to plan defenses against Brasidas. The Spartans hoped to convert the armistice into a peace and thereby get back the Spartan prisoners whom Cleon and Demosthenes had triumphantly brought home from the island of Sphacteria.

The one-year armistice was concluded, but Brasidas's political warfare had now so shaken Athenian rule in Chalcidice that city after city came over to him. When the armistice terms officially reached Chalcidice, Brasidas objected that one of the cities he had acquired, Scione, had revolted two days before the date on which the armistice had been signed; he accordingly refused to give Scione back. This point of Brasidas's Athens denied, and Cleon got a decree from the Assembly that Scione should be reduced and all its citizens put to death. Brasidas had now become entangled in the politics of his ally, Perdiccas the Macedonian. Athens sent Nicias and another commander to Chalcidice with 50 ships and over 1,700 troops. Perdiccas suddenly changed sides, allied himself with Athens, and persuaded the Thessalians not to allow Peloponnesian reinforcements for Brasidas to pass through. For Sparta to reinforce him by sea was, of course, impossible: as usual, the sea belonged to Athens' navy. Straight through the one-year truce the struggle in Thrace continued. Elsewhere, the armistice proved effective.

The next year, 422, when the armistice had ended, Cleon persuaded the Athenian Assembly to let him go to Thrace. He took 1,200 heavy infantry, 300 horse, and 30 ships from Athens, and a larger land force of allies. His brilliant success at Pylos, when his political opponent, Nicias, had resigned as general, made him confident he could drive out Brasidas, who had first won fame at Pylos too, and that he could regain Athens' jewel, Amphipolis. Outside of the walls of Amphipolis, he awaited reinforcements of troops from Perdiccas of Macedonia as well as a contingent of Thracian mercenaries. The impatience of his troops to attack induced him to lead them near the city walls. Brasidas made a sudden sally; Cleon's troops panicked; he himself fled and was killed. But Brasidas, too, was wounded. He was carried back into the city and lived long enough to learn that once more he was victorious. He had been the most intelligent, and therefore the most dangerous, opponent the ten years of warfare had brought against Athens. He had won his first fame in the Spartan assault from the sea on Pylos and died three short years later at Amphipolis in Thrace. Sparta had never given him adequate support, partly because Athens held the sea and because sending reinforcements to Brasidas by land was not always possible, given Thessaly's dubious and fluctuating attitude; but partly also because he was envied by other Spartans at home. He had been skillful, tactful, gentle, modest, honest, and loyal to Sparta. But he had also been those things in Thrace; and two generations before, Pausanias, another Spartan general, had taught Sparta caution in exporting generals there. Pausanias had been arrogant, harsh, foolish, and treasonous. Now Brasidas was dead and, with Sparta's allies standing to arms, he was buried at public expense in the market place of Amphipolis. The citizens of this polis that he had liberated ceased to pay public honors to their Athenian founder and decreed those honors now to the Spartan hero, Brasidas, with annual games and offerings.

With Cleon and Brasidas dead, Athens and Sparta negotiated a peace, to be binding for fifty years. The treaty was largely the work of Nicias, the Athenian general, and Pausanias's son, Plistoanax, the restored king of the Lacedaemonians. The conservative Nicias was now the most influential leader in Athens. He had, for years, even when Cleon defeated him in matters of policy, been more respected than Cleon, largely because he was above bribery, whereas few Athenian politicians were. He was well-fathered, he was rich, he was no oligarchic schemer against democracy, he had won an excellent record as a general, and he discharged his political and religious duties to the polis with zeal and generosity. It is true that his religion seemed to incline him to superstition and to an inordinate interest in auguries and prophecies, that he was timid when faced with demagogues like Cleon, and that he was quick to buy off informers and blackmailers. Much of his income he derived from the state silver mines at Laurium, which he leased and worked with a large number of slaves at a handsome profit. The peace he negotiated with Sparta brought him immense popularity in war-weary Athens and was commonly called the Peace of Nicias.[237]

Just before the Thirty Years' Peace a quarter of a century earlier, Plistoanax had been deposed as one of Sparta's kings. With the recently built land empire of Athens crumbling, and Plistoanax about to invade Attica, the king had unaccountably led his army home again. He had therefore been charged with accepting a bribe from Pericles. He had fled to western Arcadia and had built a house for himself, half of which lay conveniently within the sanctuary of a temple to Zeus. But, whenever the Lacedaemonians sent envoys to Delphi to consult Apollo they were told by the god to bring home the seed of the demigod son of Zeus—Plistoanax, the Heraclid, the descendant of Zeus's hero son, Heracles. The Spartans had finally brought him back. His enemies were now murmuring that he had bribed the prophetess at Delphi and that his unjust restoration was the cause of their many disasters in the present war with Athens. Plistoanax could hope to end the accusation by ending the disasters, and the best way to end the disasters was to negotiate a peace with Athens. He and Nicias made peace.

The Peace of Nicias provided that Amphipolis would be given back to Athens. Certain other cities were to be restored. Any citizens of these places who did not wish to remain under Athenian leadership would be permitted to emigrate, taking their property with them. The cities were to be self-governing, provided they paid their contributions to Athens as originally assessed by Aristides. Athens was to free certain other cities, though she retained her strong point at Pylos. All prisoners on both sides were to be released, including of course the Spartans captured at Sphacteria. It was Sparta's determination to recover these last that had made her return Amphipolis. The ten-year butchery seemed to be over at last, but it was a bad sign that when Sparta and her allies voted to accept the treaty, Boeotia, Corinth, Elis, and Megara voted nay.

Hellas lay exhausted and demoralized; but meanwhile, three famous Athenians had been commenting on the war. When the Peloponnesian War began, Thucydides judged it would be the greatest war Hellenic man had yet known, and he had begun to chronicle its events. He displayed in his history neither the buoyant confidence nor the charming, childlike curiosity nor the zest for anecdote of Herodotus, who had so recently won his prize from the Athenians for his history of Persia's invasion of Hellas. "The absence of romance in my history," wrote Thucydides,

> will, I fear, detract somewhat from its interest; but if it be judged useful by those inquirers who desire an exact knowledge of the past as an aid to the interpretation of the future, which in the course of human things must resemble if it does not reflect it, I shall be content. In fine, I have written my work, not as an essay which is to win the applause of the moment, but as a possession for all time.[238]

Thucydides served in the war he wrote about. An aristocrat, like Pericles, he rallied early to Pericles' leadership and democratic program. When he was around the age of thirty, Pericles died, and Thucydides watched with disgust the self-interest and fumbling of the Olympian's successors. When Amphipolis fell, Thucydides and his fellow commander in Thrace, Eucles, were banished for their failure to save the city from the Spartan, Brasidas. In exile, Thucydides had a chance to watch the progress of the war from the new vantage point of neutral and even enemy lands. Had the drama of Aeschylus and Sophocles taught him the tragic sense of life that matured to intellectual adulthood so many citizens of Athens? Had Aeschylus and Sophocles taught him to discern in the hurrying events of the Peloponnesian War the pattern of a vast tragedy of which Athens was the hero? As a polis suddenly risen to power and pride, Athens developed the blindness of power, the faith in violence, the necessity to give hostages to fortune, the hybris of Agamemnon on his return from Troy and of Oedipus at Thebes. The attempt of Athens to solve one problem led to the creation of other problems. She grew confused, lost her purpose, redoubled her efforts, and arrived at the Peace of Nicias, a peace that promised more violence to come. There would be suffering that would inspire in Thucydides and his readers both pity and terror, and perhaps bring in the end frightful and chastening catastrophe and, through suffering, a kind of knowledge. Just such knowledge had come also, if not always to the tragic heroes of Aeschylus and Sophocles, then at least to some of those who watched their tragedies before the temple of the god Dionysus.

Herodotus, too, had found in a chain of historic events the same tragic pattern. Herodotus's hero had been Xerxes, or Xerxes and his powerful empire. Xerxes had hurled the strength of that empire at the little city-states of Greece, had exulted in his pride, his hybris, had affronted the gods themselves, and had suffered great catastrophe. But there was an exuberant faith in human existence in Herodotus, a gaiety and serenity reminiscent of the mysterious smile on the faces of those painted limestone statues which Ionia and Athens had created in the sixth century. And his confident faith in the power and justice of Zeus recalled somehow the robust and soaring faith of Aeschylus in the midst of the horror and disaster he projected in his plays.

Thucydides, on the other hand, with heavy heart was watching his beloved Athens pick up the power and cares and cruelties of empire. He was watching freedom turn to license and folly. He was watching Hellas tear itself to pieces, as it polarized into pro-Athenian demos and pro-Spartan oligarchy, and as polis after polis was torn apart and plunged into civil strife. His history exhibited therefore some of the gravity as well as some of the elaborate skill that his readers could see in some marble statue of the days of Pericles, with its still serene but slightly melancholy face. His careful account of events displayed the intricate plot and the skillful, sophisticated study of human motive and human conflict that Sophocles had exhibited more than Aeschylus; and, just as in many of Sophocles' tragedies, so in this history by Thucydides, the gods were somehow in the background and even there did not transcend their reported interventions. In Thucydides' sober report, oracles certainly affected decisions of state. Professional diviners certainly influenced men like the rich and pious Nicias. Oaths were often kept because men believed the gods existed, or might exist. But the necessities of man's own existence, his urgent and clamorous physical existence, reduced the gods to stage properties more than they did in Herodotus's history of an earlier war. Herodotus's tragedy of Xerxes, unlike Thucydides' tragedy of the School of Hellas, was rendered luminous by the triumph of human freedom, which Zeus the Liberator granted as boon to those who stood ready to die for freedom's sake.

Thucydides' tragic sense of life did not lead him away from concern for historical fact, but it did supply him with a sure and severe sense of relevance: he knew which of his many facts held permanent significance for his own and for future generations.[239] It led him also to use a kind of dramatic dialogue, in the shape of formal speeches, that gave a due content of thought and purpose to both sides in the bloody conflict and kept that conflict from sinking to the level of mere animal violence. He warned his readers in advance that he could not vouch for the strict accuracy of the speeches, even when he had heard them personally; but he adhered "as closely as possible to the general sense of what was actually said."[240]

Another Athenian who found himself living through this war did not try to write its history, for he was born a poet. Euripides started life around 485, a year before Aeschylus won his first prize for tragedy, and Euripides was already around thirty when Aeschylus, now in his last years, departed for Sicily. That had left Sophocles unrivaled in tragic poetry at Athens. Euripides presented his own first tragedy in 455, the year Aeschylus died. Out of some ninety plays[241] he wrote, only four won him victory. In his latter years he lived in Thessaly and at the court of King Archelaus in Macedonia, where he died about 406. Sophocles, though a decade older, outlived him a year. Tragedy did not normally treat of contemporary themes, except by implication; and Euripides therefore commented on these war-torn years only in a very special sense. But, compared with the slightly older Sophocles, who after all lived through the same horrors, his tragedies reflected in curious ways the disintegration of Hellas. The very plots of his plays faltered when compared with those of Aeschylus and Sophocles, as if life were becoming less intelligible, less whole. Euripides excelled less in plot than in character; and, even here, where his two elder fellow poets showed the heart of man by what man did and thought as well as felt, Euripides psychologized and analyzed. He was often less interested in those who performed great actions than in those who suffered great passions. He was especially interested in the weak and oppressed—in women, in children, in slaves. It was not the heroic, masculine, ruthless courage of Achilles that shone from a tragedy like the

Trojan Women, but the agony and grief of the victims, such as the dead Hector's mother, Hecuba, who lived through the deliberate murder of Hector's tiny son, hurled from the walls of Troy when Troy was sacked and burned. In the *Trojan Women* the old queen held the tiny corpse of her grandson in her arms and cried:

Lay down the circled shield of Hector on the ground:
a hateful thing to look at; it means no love to me.
Achaeans! All your strength is in your spears, not in
the mind. What were you afraid of, that it made you kill
this child so savagely? That Troy, which fell, might be
raised from the ground once more? Your strength meant nothing, then.
When Hector's spear was fortunate, and numberless
strong hands were there to help him, we were still destroyed.
Now when the city is fallen and the Phrygians slain,
this baby terrified you? I despise the fear
which is pure terror in a mind unreasoning.

O darling child, how wretched was this death. You might
have fallen fighting for your city, grown to man's
age, and married, and with the king's power like a god's,
and died happy, if there is any happiness here.
But no. You grew to where you could see and learn, my child,
yet your mind was not old enough to win advantage
of fortune. How wickedly, poor boy, your fathers' walls,
Apollo's handiwork, have crushed your pitiful head
tended and trimmed to ringlets by your mother's hand,
and the face she kissed once, where the brightness now is blood
shining through the torn bones—too horrible to say more.
O little hands, sweet likeness of Hector's once,
now you lie broken at the wrists before my feet;
and mouth beloved whose words were once so confident,
you are dead; and all was false, when you would lean across
my bed, and say: "Mother, when you die I will cut
my long hair in your memory, and at your grave
bring companies of boys my age, to sing farewell."
It did not happen; now I, a homeless, childless, old
woman must bury your poor corpse, which is so young.
Alas for all the tendernesses, my nursing care,
and all your slumbers gone. What shall the poet say,

what words will he inscribe upon your monument?
Here lies a little child the Argives killed, because
they were afraid of him. That? The epitaph of Greek shame.
You will not win your father's heritage, except
for this, which is your coffin now: the brazen shield.

O shield, who guarded the strong shape of Hector's arm:
the bravest man of all, who wore you once, is dead.
How sweet the impression of his body on your sling,
and at the true circle of your rim the stain of sweat
where in the grind of his many combats Hector leaned
his chin against you, and the drops fell from his brow!

Take up your work now; bring from what is left some robes
to wrap the tragic dead. The gods will not allow us
to do it right. But let him have what we can give.

That mortal is a fool who, prospering, thinks his life
has any strong foundation; since our fortune's course
of action is the reeling way a madman takes,
and no one person is ever happy all the time.[242]

This was Euripides' comment on war's glory. It was as if the Peloponnesian War had broken him, had broken his dramatic plots, had left his sweetly lyrical choruses without dramatic function, had left his most typical tragedies filled with pathos whenever they did not border perilously on melodrama. It was as if the gods—or Aeschylus's gods, anyhow—had withdrawn for all time to Olympus, and could be introduced on the stage now only by a derrick[243] which let them down from above. It was as if even then the gods could not convince all of the spectators, could not, perhaps, convince Euripides himself. Did he not make Heracles, own hero son of Zeus, speak with blasphemous melancholy to Theseus?

Then Zeus—whoever Zeus may be—begot me
for Hera's hatred. Take no offense, old man,
for I count you my father now, not Zeus.[244]

Further on in the same tragedy, Heracles made another Euripidean statement to Theseus. And if all agreed that Heracles was the son of Zeus, many believed that Theseus was the son of Posidon, Zeus's own brother. Faced with the gods of Homer and Hesiod, faced with the gods of his con-

temporaries, Aeschylus and Sophocles, this time Euripides made Heracles
say:

> but I do not believe the gods commit
> adultery, or bind each other in chains.
> I never did believe it; I never shall;
> nor that one god is tyrant of the rest.
> If god is truly god, he is perfect,
> lacking nothing. These are poets' wretched lies.[245]

Whether it was his religious skepticism or the weakened structure of
his dramatic plots, his four victories in the contests for tragedies were
disappointingly few. But may not his deepest frustration have derived from
the fact that, as Hellas moved into what looked like a death agony of
vengeance and violence and as fear and hate and even bloodshed tore
the Polis itself apart, the audience for real tragedy began to disintegrate?
That audience had formed, in the great days of Aeschylus, a Polis in the
ancient sense, a community of gods and men engaged in a dialogue
of words and deeds, in full personal encounter: persons all, divine and
human, never mere things. There had indeed been nameless crime, searing
remorse, but also redemption from pollution, for god, for man, and for
the Polis too. But there had always remained community, whether in hus-
banding the meager, crowded land, or in seeking a like home far beyond the
sea, or in fighting Asians at day's end on some bitter battlefield, or in
the rhythm of the oars as the triremes charged, or in the great religious pro-
cessions when men broke bread with their gods, or here in the Theater
of Dionysus where, with high and ancient ritual, with painted scenery,
with dance and song, men who had acted in all these dramas of their
common life watched others act out before them in formal mask and
costume the actions that made men what men were, a community of
feeling, thinking, speaking persons, and not a lonely herd of dumb beasts.

The decade of blood that bought the fragile Peace of Nicias provoked
a comment also from a third Athenian, this time neither an historian nor
a tragedian but the comedian, Aristophanes. He brought out his first
comedy[246] in 427, the year in which Cleon argued for mass murder in
Mitylene, in which Plataea fell, and in which civil war broke out in Corcyra.
His comedy won first prize and by the time the Peace of Nicias came,
six years later, he had already surpassed in fame older and more famous
rivals such as Eupolis and Cratinus.[247] While Attic tragedy portrayed the

noble and the great and the godlike, Attic comedy portrayed the ignoble, the low, the coward afraid of his own shadow, the glutton and the womanizer, the absurdly impractical man, the inveterate cheat. It showed these petty people and their acts and laughed at them hilariously and infectiously. Precisely because men had the power to learn how to be brave, to exercise self-control, to make wise practical decisions, to treat their fellow men justly—in short, precisely because a man could learn to let his mind and will guide his bodily appetites—the all too familiar sight of the man whose bodily appetites guided his mind and will into petty catastrophe awoke ridicule and restored sanity.

Comedy had sprung from the ancient village comus, or revel, in which buffoons fought, in which actors hurled ribald insults at each other or at members of the audience, in which the chorus sang and danced, often with obscene gestures, and in which the action was likely to end with the comic hero being borne off in hilarious triumph to the bed of his new bride. In Athens, comedy had inherited or developed as many conventions as tragedy: the comic mask, the grotesque costume, the painted scenery, the song of the chorus, gloriously bawdy, or sometimes a movingly beautiful lyric that pictured the Attic countryside, the unrestrained dance, and the frequent gibes at contemporary events, at the very important people who gave themselves airs, even at persons in the audience. The obscenity that abounded in most comedies was not something slipped in to spice dull lines, it was integral to the play. That any animal as godlike as man should remain so much an animal as to be constantly fornicating, urinating, and defecating—especially if he defecated from terror—struck Athens as enormously funny.[248]

To achieve his Olympic laughter, Aristophanes had to submit to the strenuous discipline of Thalia, the comic muse.[249] For example, when the *Acharnians* showed a private citizen of Athens, weary of the war, now in its seventh year, making a private peace with Sparta, Aristophanes got good comedy. The year that Nicias was negotiating his peace with Sparta, Aristophanes' laughter came loud and clear. He presented the *Peace* at the Great Dionysia, and on the day after that festival Athens and Sparta agreed on the terms of peace. In the *Peace* a low character named Trygaeus, despairing of ever seeing the long war end, had determined to climb to heaven and try to get Zeus himself to stop the war. But Trygaeus' ladder had broken, so now he tried riding to heaven on a huge dung beetle.

At this point the stage derrick Euripides so often used to lower a god to earth was employed to help the dung beetle, with Trygaeus astride him, to soar above the theater and to reach Zeus in heaven. Yet, on his precarious voyage, Trygaeus had time to cry out:

Ah! machinist, take great care of me. There is already a wind whirling round my navel; take great care or, from sheer fright, I shall form food for my beetle.[250]

To portray the cowardice of a comic hero by making him fear that he would defecate was a typical Aristophanic device. And the freedom for an actor to address the audience or a stagehand without fear of destroying the dramatic illusion was also Aristophanic. For in a sense there was no illusion to destroy. The spectators lost themselves in tragedy, lived it with the persons represented before them, and could not safely be reminded that they were only at the theater. But a comedy could remind them. They were not expected to identify themselves too profoundly with the characters represented: these characters were obviously too contemptible, too ridiculous, for real sympathy. Comedy mocked the great men who controlled war and peace. It mocked the spectators who let them do it. It mocked itself. It even mocked the gods.

Trygaeus reached Zeus's palace in heaven only to learn from Hermes that Zeus and the other gods had become so annoyed with the follies of the Greeks that they had retired to the farthest end of the dome of heaven and had placed Polemos, or War, in their own dwelling with full power to do as he pleased with the Greeks. But why? asked Trygaeus. "Because," answered Hermes,

they have afforded you an opportunity for peace more than once, but you have always preferred war. If the Laconians got the very slightest advantage, they would exclaim, "By the Twin Brethren! the Athenians shall smart for this." If, on the contrary, the latter triumphed and the Laconians came with peace proposals, you would say, "By Demeter, they want to deceive us. No, by Zeus, we will not hear a word; they will always be coming as long as we hold Pylos."[251]

Moreover, War had cast Peace into a pit and had now brought a huge mortar in which to pound up all the cities of Greece. But War needed a pestle. He sent his slave, Tumult, to Athens to fetch one, but Athens' pestle, "the tanner who ground Greece to powder,"[252] was lost, for

Cleon had fallen at Amphipolis. Tumult was then sent to Sparta, but Sparta had lent her pestle to the Thracians, who had lost it; for Brasidas, the spectators in the theater knew, had died at Amphipolis too.

Then the Chorus, composed of laborers and farmers from various Greek states, helped Trygaeus hoist Peace out of the pit where War had thrown her. At last she emerged; and with her, Opora, goddess of Fruitfulness, and Theoria, goddess of Spectacle. But Peace was angry. After the battle of Pylos, she complained, she had offered Athens a truce three times, only to have the Assembly vote each offer down. Trygaeus finally persuaded Peace that Athens was really done with war. Then he returned to Athens and to the spectators of the play, accompanied by the two lovely companions of Peace: Fruitfulness and Spectacle. And Trygaeus remarked,

> Ah! it's a rough job getting to the gods! my legs are as good as broken through it.

Then, turning to the spectators,

> How small you were, to be sure, when seen from heaven! you had all the appearance too of being great rascals; but seen close, you look even worse.[258]

A delegation of armorers arrived, terrified by the prospect of losing their swollen war profits, but Trygaeus scorned them. He offered to buy a couple of helmet crests to use for dusting the table and to buy a breastplate to use as a thunder-mug. Then the beautiful Fruitfulness, whom Hermes had given Trygaeus to wed, appeared onstage. The bridegroom was borne triumphantly off, to the traditional bridal cry, "Oh! Hymen! oh! Hymenaeus!"

In some ways, the commentary of Aristophanes the comic poet on the ten terrible years of massacre, vengeance, betrayal, and brutalization was more pregnant than either the somber account of Thucydides the historian or the tragic pathos of Euripides, as first Hellas and then the Polis itself began to disintegrate. For through sane laughter Aristophanes achieved a godlike view of the war. His comic hero had ridden on a dung beetle to the palace of Zeus himself and had seen men as the gods could always see them, and "How small you were, to be sure, when seen from heaven!" It was a rough job getting to the gods. Possibly Aeschylus himself could no longer have done it; for the audience, the Polis, had too far lost the tragic sense of life. In a measure, Euripides did it, but his tragic world lacked the wholeness of the tragic deed, and, anyhow, did the gods exist? Thucydides got nearer, if not to the gods, then at least to ideas, to intelligibility, by writing, not tragedy, but history. But, when the Polis had slipped; when, seen from heaven, it looked smaller and smaller; when, seen close, it looked worse; then, perhaps, only a dung beetle could take one to the gods for help. Not to see the face of Zeus, who had withdrawn from men in disgust, but at least to talk with the caretaker of his palace, Hermes. And Hermes could give crucial information on how to find Peace.

Since the Peace of Nicias was never signed by Sparta's chief allies, Athens agreed to an alliance with Sparta for fifty years, under which Athens gave back the prisoners from Sphacteria. This was Nicias' idea, and by it Athens lost her chief means of exerting pressure on Sparta to fulfill Sparta's part of the bargain. Foremost of those at Athens who wished to cancel the new treaty with Sparta was Alcibiades, the former ward of Pericles and now a political rival of Nicias.

Alcibiades was still in his early thirties. He came of illustrious lineage, and although the people of Athens insisted on political democracy, a famous family name was still a help to a young man ambitious to lead. Alcibiades' father, Clinias, had fallen at Coronea in 447, the battle Pericles would have chosen not to fight, the battle that symbolized the end of his early dream of expansion on the mainland. This Clinias was not only a eupatrid, one of the well-fathered; he belonged to a clan whose actual name was Eupatrid. His wife was an Alcmeonid, as was the mother of Pericles, and as Clisthenes had been.

The home in which Alcibiades grew up was not only the political center of Athens: it was also a center of philosophy and of art and of letters. Moreover, his brilliant, restless mind led him to join the young men who gathered around the philosopher Socrates. Socrates recognized his brilliance; fell under the spell of his personal beauty and the enormous personal charm for which the young man was famous throughout Athens; tried to strengthen him in his search for wisdom; and recognized his dangerous love for applause. This exuberant, dazzling, handsome youth, by turns ingratiating and imperious, drunken reveler and victorious athlete, adored by women, imitated—even to a slight speech defect—by other young dandies about town, attracted older men to the romantic homosexual relation which Hellenic custom allowed, but did not attract Socrates.

Socrates wanted, not the young man's body, but his mind. He wanted to provoke that mind to do its proper work. In the summer of 432 both of them left with the heavy infantry for Potidaea, which was rebelling against Athens. There, muffled miserably against the cold of a northern winter, its soldiers' feet wrapped in fleeces, the army conducted its siege; there Socrates and Alcibiades were messmates. Socrates saved Alcibiades' life in battle; and, when the generals wished later to award the prize of valor to the famous young blood, Alcibiades insisted in vain that it should go to Socrates. Eight years later they met on another battlefield, when the Boeotians defeated the Athenians at Delium. The heavy infantry was in rout. This time Alcibiades was serving in the cavalry and was able to protect Socrates on the retreat.

That same year, 424, Alcibiades, still under thirty, tried his hand at private diplomacy. Trading on the fact that his father's father, also named Alcibiades, had served as proxenus, or honorary consul, for Sparta, the youthful politician tried to negotiate a peace that would include a return of the prisoners from Sphacteria. Sparta preferred to deal with his political opponent, Nicias. When the Peace of Nicias was signed and the alliance with Sparta had been concluded, and when Sparta had proven unable or unwilling to persuade her allies to carry out her side of the agreement, Alcibiades vigorously attacked Nicias for having given back the prisoners, and entered into private negotiations with Argos to stir her up against Sparta. Argos had stayed out of the ten-year war, had thereby grown prosperous, was in the hands of her democratic party, and was interested. Alcibiades now urged Argos that she, Mantinea, and Elis ally themselves with Athens as protection against Sparta's domination of the Peloponnese.

Sparta became alarmed and sent envoys to Athens with full power to negotiate with the Council there. Alcibiades, to save his Argive alliance, thereupon promised the Spartan envoys that if, when they should appear before the popular Assembly, they would state that they lacked full powers, he would undertake to secure the withdrawal of the Athenian garrison from Pylos. This time, his private diplomacy succeeded. When asked in the Assembly if they had full powers, the envoys denied that they had them. Alcibiades thundered out a denunciation of them. In the end, Alcibiades got his anti-Spartan alliance. Shortly thereafter he was elected one of the generals of Athens.

During the next year Alcibiades led 1,000 heavy infantry to the Peloponnese to defend Argos, but his plans foundered on the complexities of Peloponnesian politics and nothing decisive came of them. In fact, in 418, when Nicias was elected a general again, Alcibiades failed to win a third annual term. Also, his Peloponnesian Alliance was decisively defeated by Sparta at Mantinea in August of 418, and Argos made a treaty with the Spartans. Athens was once more learning that she had no future as a land power in Mainland Greece. Sparta's prestige, shattered by the surrender of her heavy infantry on the island of Sphacteria, was restored throughout Hellas. Tension between Nicias and Alcibiades grew, and for the first time in 26 years an ostracism was held. When the voting was over, it was the popular leader, Hyperbolus the lamp manufacturer, who was ostracized. But Hyperbolus seemed to the Athenians so unworthy of the penalty inflicted on some of their greatest, and hence potentially dangerous, leaders that the device lost its function. In 417-416 Alcibiades was again elected a general.

Since the war had broken out in 431, the Dorian islands of Thera and Cythera had both been annexed by Athens. Even the island of Melos, colonized by Laconians long ago, had been pillaged by Nicias in 426, but the city of Melos had held out. In 416 an Athenian fleet of thirty-eight ships sailed to the island with 3,420 troops and tried to negotiate admission to the city of Melos. Thucydides, whom Athens had eight years before banished for arriving too late from Thasos to save Amphipolis from Brasidas, recorded the negotiations of the Athenian commanders for a peaceful surrender of the city. The Melian oligarchy would not allow the Athenians to address their popular assembly, perhaps because in most islands the populace was pro-Athenian. So the Athenian envoys presented their case to the magistrates:

> Well, then, we on our part will make use of no fair phrases, saying either that we hold sway justly because we overthrew the Persians, or that we now come against you because we are injured, offering in a lengthy speech arguments that would not be believed; nor, on the other hand, do we presume that you will assert, either that the reason why you did not join us in the war was because you were colonists of the Lacedaemonians, or that you have done us no wrong. Rather we presume that you aim at accomplishing what is possible in accordance with the real thoughts of both of us, since you know as well as we know that what is just is arrived at in human arguments only when the necessity on both sides is equal,

and that the powerful exact what they can, while the weak yield what they must.[254]

Melians: As we think, at any rate, it is expedient (for we are constrained to speak of expediency, since you have in this fashion, ignoring the principle of justice, suggested that we speak of what is advantageous) that you should not rule out the principle of the common good, but that for him who is at the time in peril what is equitable should also be just. . . . And this is not less for your interest than for our own, inasmuch as you, if you shall ever meet with a reverse, would not only incur the greatest punishment, but would also become a warning example to others.

Athenians: But we on our part, so far as our empire is concerned, even if it should cease to be, do not look forward to the end with dismay. For it is not those who rule over others, as the Lacedaemonians also do—though our quarrel is not now with the Lacedaemonians—that are a terror to the vanquished, but subject peoples who may perchance themselves attack and get the better of their rulers. . . . what we desire is to have dominion over you without trouble to ourselves, and that you should be saved to the advantage of both.

Melians: And how could it prove as advantageous for us to become slaves, as it is for you to have dominion?

Athenians: Because it would be to your advantage to submit before suffering the most horrible fate, and we should gain by not destroying you.

Melians: And so, you mean, you would not consent to our remaining at peace and being friends instead of enemies, but allies of neither combatant?

Athenians: No; for your hostility does not injure us so much as your friendship; for in the eyes of our subjects that would be a proof of our weakness, whereas your hatred is a proof of our power.

Melians: Do your subjects regard equity in such a way as to put in the same category those that do not belong to you at all and those—your own colonists in most cases and in others revolted subjects—who have been subdued by you?

Athenians: As to pleas of justice, they think that neither the one nor the other lacks them, but that those who preserve their freedom owe it to their power, and that we do not attack them because we are afraid. . . .

Melians: . . . And in this what else are you doing but strengthening the enemies you already have, and bringing upon you, against their inclination, others who would never have thought of becoming your enemies?

Athenians: Not so, for we do not reckon those as the more dangerous to us who, dwelling somewhere on the mainland and being free men, will defer for a long time taking any precautions against us, but rather those who dwell in some of the islands, both those who, like you, are subject to no control, and those who are already exasperated by the necessity of submission to our rule. . . .

Melians: Surely, then, if you and your subjects brave so great a risk, you in order that you may not lose your empire, and they, who are already your slaves, in order that they may be rid of it, for us surely who still have our freedom it would be the height of baseness and cowardice not to resort to every expedient before submitting to servitude.

Athenians: No, not if you take a sensible view of the matter . . . rather the question before you is one of self-preservation—to avoid offering resistance to those who are far stronger than you.

Melians: But we know that the fortune of war is sometimes impartial and not in accord with the difference in numbers. And for us, to yield is at once to give up hope; but if we make an effort, there is still hope that we may stand erect.

Athenians: Hope is indeed a solace in danger, and for those who have other resources in abundance, though she may injure, she does not ruin them; but for those who stake their all on a single throw—hope being by nature prodigal—it is only when disaster has befallen that her true nature is recognized, and when at last she is known, she leaves the victim no resource wherewith to take precautions against her in future. This fate, we beg of you, weak as you are and dependent on a single turn of the scale, do not willingly incur; nor make yourselves like the common crowd who, when it is possible still to be saved by human means, as soon as distress comes and all visible grounds of hope fail them, betake themselves to those that are invisible—to divination, oracles, and the like, which, with the hopes they inspire, bring men to ruin.

Melians: We, too, be well assured, think it difficult to contend both against your power and against fortune, unless she shall be impartial; but nevertheless we trust that, in point of fortune, we shall through the divine favour be at no disadvantage because we are god-fearing men standing our ground against men who are unjust; and as to the matter of power, that the alliance of the Lacedaemonians will supply what we lack, since that alliance must aid us, if for no other reason, because of our kinship with them and for very shame. . . .

Athenians: Well, as to the kindness of the divine favour, neither do we expect to fall short of you therein. For in no respect are we departing from men's observances regarding that which pertains to the divine or from their desires regarding that which pertains to themselves, in aught that we demand or do. For of the gods we hold the belief, and of men we know, that by a necessity of their nature wherever they have power they always rule. . . . But as to your expectation regarding the Lacedaemonians, your confident trust that out of shame forsooth they will aid you—while we admire your simplicity, we do not envy you your folly. We must indeed acknowledge that with respect to themselves and the institutions of their own country, the Lacedaemonians practise virtue in a very high degree; but with respect to their conduct towards the rest of mankind . . . one may declare that of all men with whom we are acquainted they, most conspicuously, consider what is agreeable to be honourable and what is expedient just. . . .[255]

The argument continued. Then the Athenians urged the Melians to think it over, and withdrew. The Melians decided not to yield and to hope for help from Sparta and the gods. The siege began. Twice the Melians made fairly successful sorties. But, after some months, the city was betrayed from within, and the authorities surrendered unconditionally. All the grown men were put to death. The women and children were sold into slavery. Athens resettled the island with 500 outsettlers. The strong had done what they could, and the weak had done what they were forced to do. Prophecies and oracles seemed what the envoys of Athens had claimed they were, inventions that delude. Whether the gods the envoys professed did, as they claimed, rule wherever they could, whether, indeed, all men did it, at least, in this case, the Athenians did. By their own professed theology, their deed was godlike.

Hesiod, who hated the wrong kind of eris, the eris of violence and war, had declared that Zeus "has ordained this law for men, that fishes and beasts and wingèd fowls should devour one another, for right is not in them, but to mankind he gave right which proves far the best."[256] But Melos was devoured. In 427 Mitylene had barely escaped the same fate. Mitylene was indeed in theory a free city, supplying ships, not tribute, and she had turned against her own ally. In 421 Scione had defected and had received the punishment of Melos. But Melos was a neutral, and the negotiations at Melos which Thucydides reported went further than to countenance massacre: they enunciated doctrine, about men, about the gods, including Zeus whose daughter was Justice.

The punishment of Melos was voted on the motion of Alcibiades. At Athens, Alcibiades had attained new heights of popularity. He won office, he won prizes for choruses, he entered seven four-horse chariots in the races at the Olympic Games. Euripides, who could write so movingly of the vanquished, could write of victors too. Pindar's great odes had celebrated the athletic victories of those whose ancestors had won great victories on the field of battle. Euripides sang of Alcibiades:

> But I will sing thy praises, son of Cleinias. A noble thing is victory, noblest of the noble to do what no Greek had ever done, be first and second and third in the chariot-race, and go unwearied yet, wreathed in the olive of Zeus, to make the herald cry you.[257]

No man in Athens was more gossiped about. His luxurious manner of life, his drunken revels, his courtesans, his highhandedness and studied insults, the Ionian effeminacy of his dress, his trailing purple robes, his golden shield shocked and angered his conservative elders. If the young blades followed and imitated him, what of Athens as a whole? The god Dionysus would answer that question in Aristophanes' comedy, the *Frogs*: "She loves and hates, and longs still to possess."[258] And, when the poet Aeschylus appeared in the same comedy, he advised Athens how to treat her hero:

> No lion's whelp within thy precincts raise;
> But, if it *be* there, bend thee to its ways![259]

The very year of the massacre of Melos, Alcibiades saw opportunity for greatness open: Segesta, Athens' Sicilian ally, was calling for help against its neighbor Selinus, and Selinus was backed by Syracuse, which had recently swallowed up Leontini. Athens had been allied with Segesta for 38 years and with Leontini for 17. Only 11 years earlier, the year Athens crushed the Mitylenian revolt, she had sent 20 ships to help Leontini against Syracuse, but Syracuse had persuaded her neighbors, including Athens' allies, to make peace. Now Segesta was pointing out that powerful, Dorian Syracuse, daughter of Athens' enemy, Corinth, was likely some day to unite all Sicily and come to the aid of the Dorians of Peloponnese against Athens. Less hypothetical than that aid was the fact that the Peloponnese counted on grain from Sicily as Athens counted on grain from the Hellespont and beyond.

The Athenian Assembly voted an expedition of 60 triremes to go to

Sicily. They appointed Nicias, Alcibiades, and Lamachus to command, and granted them full powers. Their instructions were to help Segesta against her neighbor Selinus; to restore Leontini, which Syracuse had depopulated; and "to settle all other matters in Sicily as they might deem best for the Athenians."[260] Nicias argued against the expedition. He pointed out that the peace which bore his name was ignored by some of Sparta's allies; that Athens' tributary allies in Chalcidice were still in rebellion; while Sicily, even if conquered, would be difficult to hold and govern. "And," added Nicias,

> if there be anyone here who, elated at being chosen to command, exhorts you to sail, considering—especially as he is too young to command—only his own interest, how he may get admiration for his raising of fine horses, and then, because that is very expensive, how he may also get some profit from his command, do not afford this man, at the cost of the state, opportunity to make a personal display, but rather consider that such men damage the public interest while they waste their own property, and that the matter is one of great seriousness, and not such as a youth may decide and rashly take in hand.
>
> It is of such youths, when I see them sitting here in answer to the appeal of this same man, that I am afraid; and I make a counter-appeal to the older men, if any of you sit by one of these, not to be shamed into fear lest he may seem to be a coward if he do not vote for war, and not, though that may be *their* feeling, to have a morbid craving for what is out of reach, knowing that few successes are won by greed, but very many by foresight; on the contrary, on behalf of our country, which is now running the greatest risk it has ever run, hold up your hands in opposition ... and let us not make allies, as we are wont to do, whom we must assist when they fare ill, but from whom we shall get no help when we are ourselves in need.[261]

Clearly, Alcibiades, the warmest advocate in the Assembly for the Sicilian expedition, had to reply:

> It belongs to me more than to others, Athenians, to have command— for I must needs begin with this, since Nicias has attacked me—and I think, too, that I am worthy to command. For those things for which I am railed at bring glory to my ancestors and myself, as well as advantage to my country. For the Hellenes, who had previously hoped that our state had been exhausted by the war, conceived an idea of its greatness that even transcended its actual power by reason of the magnificence of my

display as sacred deputy at Olympia, because I entered seven chariots, a number that no private citizen had ever entered before, and won the first prize and the second and the fourth, and provided everything else in a style worthy of my victory. For by general custom such things do indeed mean honour, and from what is done men also infer power. And again, although whatever display I made in the city, by providing choruses or in any other way, naturally causes jealousy among my townsmen, yet in the eyes of strangers this too gives an impression of strength.[262]

Moreover, he continued,

look at my public acts and see whether I execute them worse than another. I brought together the greatest powers of the Peloponnesus without great danger to you or expense and forced the Lacedaemonians to stake all upon a single day at Mantinea; and in consequence of this, though victorious in the field, even yet they have not firm confidence.

Thus did my youthfulness and my seemingly abnormal folly cope with the power of the Peloponnesians in fitting words and with a spirit that inspired faith win assent. And now be not afraid of it, but while I am still in the flower of youth, and Nicias has the reputation of good luck, make the most of the services of us both.[263]

Far from not helping Athens, Alcibiades insisted the Segestaeans did help by keeping Syracuse too preoccupied in Sicily to aid her Dorian cousins in the Peloponnese against Athens.

And it is not possible for us to exercise a careful stewardship of the limits we would set to our empire; but, since we are placed in this position, it is necessary to plot against some and not let go our hold upon others, because there is a danger of coming ourselves under the empire of others, should we not ourselves hold empire over other peoples. And you cannot regard a pacific policy in the same light as other states might, unless you will change your practices also to correspond with theirs.

Calculating, then, that we shall rather strengthen our power here if we go over there, let us make the voyage, that we may lay low the haughty spirit of the Peloponnesians, as we shall if we let men see that in contempt of our present peaceful condition we even sail against Sicily; and that we may, at the same time, either acquire empire over all Hellas, as in all probability we shall, when the Hellenes there have been added to us, or may at least cripple the Syracusans, whereby both ourselves and our allies will be benefited. . . . In short, I declare that a state which is accustomed to activity would very quickly be ruined by a change to inactivity; and that those men live most securely whose political action is least at variance with existing habits and institutions, even when these are not the best.[264]

To discourage the Assembly, Nicias shifted tactics and demanded more ships and men than had been proposed. To his dismay, the Assembly promptly and enthusiastically voted them. The Athenians, their decision now made, longed to see their great armada sail. The city, so recently impoverished by the plague, was rich again and ready to invest its wealth in war. The older citizens believed so great a force would either win or at least escape disaster. A new generation had grown up that had seen little or no battle, and the young men were excited by the prospect of distant adventure. With so many Athenians eager for the attack on Sicily, the few who feared disaster feared also to appear disloyal if they voiced their doubts.

The poorer citizens, who did not live on mining concessions like the wealthy Nicias, had learned from Cleon and from experience the economic benefits of empire; it meant employment, as soldier, as sailor, as ship-builder, or as paid juror in the courts. They knew that these wages were paid out of tribute received from Athens' subject cities and that more subject cities meant more tribute. In the old days many of them lived on the land. Since then they had been forced into the city by Spartan invasions or drawn there by the prospect of wages in a thriving city. They were now uprooted, urbanized, and anxious to share in the luxuries they saw about them. Many of them lived by their wits in a society that was teaching them daily how easy and pleasant it was for the strong to exploit the weak. Conquests in this distant island in the west meant relief from want and maybe, even, a chance for wealth and ease.

While the polis prepared its grand armada, it was suddenly thrown into hysterical panic by a mysterious event. In a single night, around June 7 of 415, most of the traditional Herms, the blocks of stone carved at the top into a bust of the god Hermes and left uncarved in the lower portion, which commonly stood in the doorways of both temples and private dwellings, were badly mutilated. This sacrilege was taken as an evil omen for the great expedition. Rewards were offered for the desecrators. Informers were busy. Just then some resident aliens and slaves testified that other sacrileges had occurred. Other images had been mutilated by young men in a drunken frolic, and mock celebrations of the Eleusinian mysteries had been held in private houses. The enemies of Alcibiades promptly tried to incriminate him: it was all a scheme of this insolent and notorious flouter of ancient convention to overthrow the Athenian democracy.

Alcibiades denied the charges and demanded trial. But his opponents were afraid the army would support him. The Argives and Mantineans who had joined in the expedition had done so out of confidence in his leadership. The expedition was now nearly ready to sail. So his opponents insisted on deferring the trial until after the campaign. It was about midsummer. Most of the allies and the supply ships had been ordered to muster at Corcyra, on the route to Sicily.

But the Athenians themselves and the allies that were present went down to the Peiraeus at dawn on a day appointed and proceeded to man the ships for the purpose of putting to sea. And with them went down also all the general throng, everyone, we may almost say, that was in the city, both citizens and strangers, the natives to send off each their own, whether friends or kinsmen or sons, going at once in hope and with lamentations —hope that they would make conquests in Sicily, lamentations that they might never see their friends again, considering how long was the voyage from their own land on which they were being sent. And at this crisis, when under impending dangers they were now about to take leave of one another, the risks came home to them more than when they were voting for the expedition; but still their courage revived at the sight of their present strength because of the abundance of everything they saw before their eyes. The strangers on the other hand and the rest of the multitude had come for a spectacle, in the feeling that the enterprise was noteworthy and surpassing belief.

For this first armament that sailed for Sicily was the costliest and most splendid, belonging to a single city and with a purely Hellenic force, that had ever up to that time set sail. . . . And the fame of the armament was noised abroad, not less because of amazement at its boldness and the splendour of the spectacle than on account of its overwhelming force as compared with those whom they were going against; and also because it was the longest voyage from home as yet attempted and undertaken with the highest hopes for the future as compared with their present resources.

When the ships had been manned and everything had at last been put aboard which they were to take with them on the voyage, the trumpeter proclaimed silence, and they offered the prayers that were customary before putting out to sea, not ship by ship but all together, led by a herald, the mariners as well as the officers throughout the whole army making libations with golden and silver cups from wine they had mixed. And the rest of the throng of people on the shore, both the citizens and all others present who wished the Athenians well, also joined in the prayers. And when they had sung the paean and had finished the libations, they put off, and sailing out at first in single column they then raced as far as Aegina. The Athenian fleet, then, was pressing on to reach Corcyra, where the rest of the armament of the allies was assembling.[265]

In Syracuse opinion was divided on whether to attack the Athenian fleet before it could cross the Ionian Sea to Italy, to call on Carthage to help defend Sicily, to call on Sparta to invade Attica again, or whether to await the armada's coming and then defend Syracuse. Meanwhile, the armada met with a chilly reception from the Greek cities on the coast of Italy; in Sicily Segesta turned out to be quite unable to supply the funds she had promised: Alcibiades, Nicias, and Lamachus held a council of war. Nicias urged that they try to settle Segesta's dispute with Selinus, coast past the port cities of Sicily to display their power, and go home. Alcibiades wanted to negotiate for allies before striking Syracuse. Lamachus, who was a more experienced soldier than either of his colleagues, correctly guessed that Syracuse had not completed her preparations for defense, and was for striking now. The three men compromised on the plan of Alcibiades. But the cities of Sicily were distrustful of the Athenian armada and almost all of them refused to co-operate. The armada was ominously big. Its purpose was ill-defined, even in the minds of the Athenians at home. Its purpose was divided in the minds of those who led it. It necessarily wore an air of blind force and one could not argue with blind force. Where one could not argue, what was there to negotiate?

At Athens, the hysteria over the mutilated Herms and the parody of the holy mysteries had continued; rumor flew that oligarchic subversives planned a tyranny. About a hundred suspects were rounded up, some were executed, and others escaped abroad with a price on their heads. The tyrant-state which had so often imposed its will by force on other states and which had declared through the mouths of its generals at Melos that, in the eyes of gods and men, might made right, now wondered if it was itself destined for the fate of Corcyra: civil war. There appeared to be men inside the polis who were prepared to apply the Melian formula at home, godless men who would enthrone might over right in the School of Hellas itself. But where were they? The enemies of Alcibiades made it clear that in all likelihood he was one of them. They persuaded the Assembly to summon him home for trial. The official city trireme, the Salaminia, was ordered to Sicily to escort Alcibiades' trireme back to Athens, bearing Alcibiades himself and some others who were accused. At Thurii, in Italy, the group of suspects jumped ship and disappeared. Alcibiades, now an outlaw, crossed in a trading vessel to Cyllene, a port in Peloponnese; the Salaminia returned to Athens; and the Assembly passed sentence of death on all the refugees from justice.

The armada was now in the hands of Nicias, who had never at any point approved of the expedition; and of Lamachus, a good soldier but without prestige in the army. The general who really believed in the expedition was in exile with a price on his head. The advice Aristophanes had put in the dead Aeschylus's mouth concerning Alcibiades had been ignored: Athens, having reared a lion in the state, had failed to humor him. The rest of the summer was frittered away by Nicias and his remaining colleague. The Syracusans recovered from their earlier alarm. Winter came. Nicias and Lamachus by a stratagem lured the Syracusan army to nearby Catana to attack them there. Then they swiftly embarked with their whole army by night; landed on the coast north of Syracuse; and seized Epipolae, or Overtown, a long hill overlooking Syracuse and its Great Harbor. Epipolae was now fortified; and when the Syracusans returned from their wild goose chase to Catana, Nicias defeated them. But Nicias despaired of taking Syracuse without more cavalry, without more money, and without the Sicilian allies he hoped his recent victory would now bring him, and he therefore led his army back to Sicilian Naxos and Catana for the winter. Under the leadership of Hermocrates, Syracuse began to rebuild her armed forces and to urge Corinth and Sparta to send help. Corinth agreed to help, and sent envoys along with the Syracusan envoys to Sparta. Arrived there, they found unexpected support—from Alcibiades, who had audaciously taken refuge in the city he had so much harmed.

The Spartans agreed to help; but, as usual, they delayed. Whereupon Alcibiades addressed them. He defended himself for stirring up Sparta's allies against her five years before: had Sparta not snubbed him when he tried to help her get back the prisoners from Sphacteria? He defended himself for co-operating with the Athenian democracy: he gladly admitted that democracy was absurd, as witness what the extreme democrats had just done to him; but he had had to adjust to the facts of political life. Then he came to the business at hand:

> We sailed to Sicily, first, to subdue the Siceliots, if we could, and after them the Italiots also; and then to make an attempt upon the empire of the Carthaginians and upon the city itself. If these things, either all, or at least the greater part of them, succeeded, then we intended to attack the Peloponnesus, bringing here the whole Hellenic force that had joined us there, hiring besides many barbarians, both Iberians and others of the peoples there that are admittedly the most warlike of the barbarians at the present day, and building many triremes in addition to our own, as Italy has timber in abundance. Laying a blockade with these triremes round the Peloponnesus, and at the same time attacking it with our infantry by land, having thus taken some of its cities by assault and walled in others, we expected easily to reduce it, and after that to have sway over the whole Hellenic race. As to money and food, for making any of these projects more feasible, the additional territory acquired in Sicily would of itself furnish these in sufficient quantity, independently of our home revenues.[266]

But now, he continued, unless Sparta acted quickly, Sicily would fall to Athens and the Peloponnese would be in grave danger. Sparta should send heavy infantry to help Syracuse. Even more important, she should send a Spartan to organize the resistance. Then they must occupy Decelea in Attica, the move Athens had always feared most. It would cut off Athens from her silver mines at Laurium and encourage her subject allies to neglect paying their tribute.

> The accomplishment of any of these projects promptly and more zealously depends, men of Lacedaemon, upon you. . . . And I claim that no one of you shall think more harshly of me because I, who once seemed to be a lover of my city, now make assault with all my might upon her, in concert with her bitterest enemies; nor do I think that my word should be suspected on the score of the outcast's zeal. . . . the worse enemies are not those who, like you, have merely hurt their enemies, but those who have forced their friends to become foes. And as to love of country—I have it not when I am wronged, but had it when I possessed my civil rights in security. . . . And the true patriot is not the man who, having unjustly lost his fatherland, refrains from attacking it, but he who in his yearning for it tries in every way to get it back. So I urge you, Lacedaemonians, to use me without misgiving for any danger and for any hard-

ships, recognising that, according to the saying which is on everybody's lips, if as an enemy I did you exceeding injury, I might also be of some sufficient service to you as a friend, in so far as I know the affairs of the Athenians, while I could only conjecture yours. And I urge, too, that you yourselves now, convinced that you are deliberating about interests that are of the greatest importance, shrink not from sending an expedition into Sicily, and also into Attica, in order that, by keeping a small detachment on the island, you may preserve the large interests you have over there and may overthrow the power of the Athenians both present and prospective, and after that may yourselves live in security and be accepted by all the Hellenes of their free will, not by force but through affection, as their leaders.[267]

The Spartans took Alcibiades' advice. Although they did not immediately fortify Decelea in Attica, they did send a Spartan general, Gylippus, to command the Syracusans and to find out in Syracuse what other help must be sent. Nicias, meanwhile, received money and cavalrymen from Athens, with instructions to find their mounts in Sicily. He had had almost no luck in rallying the civilized coast cities to his banner, but he did get men and even some money from the interior. He now began, in the summer of 414, to run a wall from the Bay of Thapsus, north of Syracuse, where his own fleet was stationed, to the Great Harbor of Syracuse, south of the city. He built a circular fort and from that point started one wall north toward the bay and another south toward the harbor. Cut off from help by land, Syracuse could then be cut off by his fleet from help by sea and must be forced to surrender. The Syracusans started building a counter-wall to prevent Nicias' south wall from reaching the Great Harbor. This counter-wall the Athenians succeeded in destroying. The Syracusans then attempted a palisaded trench to prevent Nicias' wall from reaching the Great Harbor. This, too, the Athenians attacked and destroyed. But they paid a price: Lamachus was killed in action. Of the three commanders under whom the grand armada had sailed, one was in Sparta, a second was dead, and the only one left had disapproved of the expedition. But provisions and even some allies were coming in, and victory seemed to beckon. Morale inside Syracuse was sinking. Where was the help from Sparta? The Syracusans started proposing terms to Nicias. They began to accuse each other of treachery. They appointed new commanders.

Word reached Nicias that Gylippus, the Spartan commander, had touched Tarentum in Italy. But Gylippus apparently had so few ships that Nicias concluded he must be bent only on piracy. Gylippus therefore sailed unhindered to Himera on the north coast of Sicily, collected some troops, and marched on Syracuse. After losing one battle and winning another, he managed to build another counter-wall that effectually destroyed Nicias' last hope of leading his own wall, which had now reached the Great Harbor in the south, all the way to the Bay of Thapsus in the north.

Nicias appealed to Athens. From being the besieger, he was now the besieged. He was cut off by Gylippus from obtaining supplies by land, and even supply by sea was becoming precarious. Slaves were deserting from the Athenian fleet. So were other sailors who had signed on merely for high pay and in the hope of booty. Some of the latter had bribed their captains to accept Sicilian slaves in their places and were themselves scattering to engage in trade. Nicias appealed for another fleet and another army as large as those he had led to Sicily; for more money; and for a general to replace him, since he was suffering from a serious disease of the kidneys.

The Athenian Assembly voted another army and navy, money, and two new generals, but they refused to accept Nicias' resignation. His two new colleagues were to be Demosthenes, who had fought in Aetolia and shared with Cleon the glory of capturing the Spartans on Sphacteria, and Eurymedon, who had co-operated with the democrats in the revolution at Corcyra and who had later been involved in Athens' unsuccessful efforts in Sicily.

Gylippus, the Spartan, was showing some of the prompt strategy and deft diplomacy that no Spartan had shown abroad since the death of Brasidas; but Gylippus was not Nicias' only enemy. At Sparta, Alcibiades was tirelessly inciting action. It was largely due to Alcibiades that Gylippus had gone to Sicily. Now, in the winter of 414-413, he was still urging the Spartans to invade Attica, in order to discourage Athens from sparing too much help for Nicias, and to seize and fortify Decelea as a permanent base from which to ravage Attica more systematically. In the spring, Agis, one of Lacedaemon's two kings, wasted Attica and fortified Decelea. The new fort was no more than fourteen miles from Athens and about the same distance from the frontier of Athens' bitter enemy, Boeotia. It blocked off a supply route from Euboea, Athens' nearest breadbasket, through the port of Oropus. It blocked communications with Laurium, where Nicias' mining interests lay, and where a fountain of silver had nourished Athens' war against the Peloponnesians, as it had once nourished her war against Xerxes. More than 20,000 slaves, including many artisans, escaped from the Athenians to the Spartans.

Sparta also sent 1,600 heavy infantry to Gylippus in Sicily: men from Boeotia, Corinth, Sicyon, together with Helots and emancipated Helots from Lacedaemonia. Meanwhile, Demosthenes left Athens for Syracuse with 65 ships, 1,200 Athenian heavy infantry, and as many islanders as Athens could muster.

The Great Harbor was some three miles across from north to south, with a mouth about a mile wide. North of the mouth lay 'the Island,' the oldest part of Syracuse. South of it, the land extended to a point called Plemmyrium. Here Nicias had built three forts where he could base his ships. Gylippus, backed by Hermocrates, the Syracusan commander, persuaded the Syracusans to attack the dread Athenian fleet; and though the Athenians won, a simultaneous land assault by Gylippus captured Plemmyrium and the supplies stored there. The Athenian fleet fell back on the northern shore of the harbor, near where their north-south wall reached the water's edge. Syracusan vessels could not guard both sides of the harbor mouth, and any ships that brought in supplies for Nicias were subject to attack.

Meanwhile, Demosthenes and his reinforcements had joined forces with an Athenian fleet of thirty ships, had picked up some heavy infantry from Argos, troops from the western coast of Mainland Greece, and from Thurii in southern Italy, and were said to be approaching Syracuse. The 1,300 Thracian archers he had hoped to include in his forces had reached Athens too late to join the expedition, so the Athenians sent them home by ship with orders to do what harm they could to the enemy. Landing on the northern coast of Boeotia, they attacked a small town called Mycalessus and butchered all the men, women, children, and even animals that they could find. In particular, they attacked a boys' school and massacred all the students. In the eyes of Hellas the massacre brought no glory to the School of Hellas. The massacre sprang from orders to wild tribesmen to do the enemy all the harm they could, and those orders caricatured the original orders to the three commanders of the Sicilian armada to settle all other matters in Sicily as they might deem best for the Athenians. It caricatured even the massacre of Melos: why spare the women and children and animals? Athenian purpose was less and less defined and could command less and less respect in Hellas. War as skillful surgery had turned into war as butchery and buccaneering. Small wonder that Sicily began to rally to Gylippus against what felt more and more like an explosion of arrogant and mindless violence from Athens.

The Syracusans had finally dared to meet an Athenian fleet and, though they had suffered defeat, it was a defeat that fell far short of catastrophe. Heartened, they now prepared to attack again by sea and land. Besides, a Corinthian squadron had recently fought an Athenian squadron in the Corinthian gulf, where the latter had been stationed to guard the supply line from Athens to Sicily. Although here again the results slightly favored the Athenians, a new naval device of the Corinthians had proven itself brilliantly. The device consisted of strengthening the prow and cheeks of the Corinthian triremes so that they could be used with devastating effect in prow-to-prow collisions. The prows of seven Athenian triremes were thus staved in. The Syracusans now copied this device. The skillful Athenian crews, already rendered less skillful by desertions, lacked space for their customary maneuvers, which generally ended with ramming the sides of the enemy ships. The Syracusan triremes simply charged head-on, and their newly enforced bronze beaks staved in the weaker bronze beaks of the Athenian vessels. The darters on the decks of the Syracusan triremes did their work well. And, worst of all, darters in small boats dashed in close to the Athenian ships and attacked their sailors. The Syracusans won a decisive victory and drove the Athenians back to their improvised base.

Then, to the dismay of Syracuse, Demosthenes and Eurymedon arrived from Athens with a new fleet of over 70 triremes, with nearly 5,000 heavy infantry, with Hellenic and barbarian darters, and with slingers and archers as well. Demosthenes did not propose to imitate Nicias, who had wasted a whole winter while Syracuse grew strong. He urged that the army immediately attack Gylippus' counter-wall, take it, and complete Nicias' wall from the Great Harbor clear to the Bay of Thapsus. If this effort succeeded, it ought to be possible to starve out Syracuse. If it failed, they should return to Athens instantly and not risk losing both army and fleet. In short, for Nicias' paralysis, he wanted to substitute decisive action.

The Athenian army attacked the counter-wall by night. A confused struggle ensued; for a while the Athenians were gaining; but in the end they met severe defeat. Demosthenes now voted to quit Sicily and fight in Mainland Greece, where Sparta's occupation of Decelea was pressing hard on Athens. But Nicias, though he had not approved of the war in the first place and had frittered away the period during which Syracuse might have been taken, insisted on staying. He did not want to face the Athenian Assembly and the usual accusations of bribery and malfeasance. The pro-Athenian party in Syracuse was secretly encouraging him to believe that Syracuse was in an even worse plight than its besiegers. The besiegers stayed.

Then Gylippus returned from recruiting a fresh army among the Sicilian cities, and fresh infantry also reached him from the Peloponnese. The Athenian army, encamped on marshy ground beside the Great Harbor, was ravaged by sickness and thoroughly discouraged. At last even Nicias agreed to withdraw from Sicily. At that moment an eclipse of the moon occurred, which was taken as a bad omen. The army wanted to delay. Nicias' soothsayer declared they should wait "thrice nine days" before departing, and Nicias had never in his career failed to exhibit the most pious respect for divination. The besiegers stayed.

The Syracusans got wind that the Athenian armada planned to quit the siege of Syracuse, but they did not propose to let the Athenians retreat to some other point on the island only to make trouble later. They launched another sea and land attack on the besiegers. The land attack by Gylippus was indecisive, but the Athenian fleet was again defeated and its ships driven ashore. During the battle Eurymedon, whom Athens had sent out with Demosthenes to help Nicias, was slain. Athens, confronted with cities in Sicily which were already ruled by democrats, had been unable to seduce them by offering to free them from oppressive oligarchs. She had been unable to crush them by force. Not only her land forces but also her fleet had been decisively defeated. The failure of the expedition was clear for all to see. What was left of it would, when the omens permitted, go home. But the Syracusans, who had only recently despaired of saving their city, no longer wanted to drive the armada off: they wanted to destroy it. Now would come the kill; now would come the freeing of Hellas from the tyrant-state, Athens. The Syracusans began to block up the Great Harbor by mooring vessels across its mouth.

The Athenians fortified their little base on the harbor shore and staked their fleet on a final naval battle. They planned, if they lost, to burn their ships and fight their way by land to the nearest friendly place they could reach. They succeeded in manning some 110 ships for the final struggle. To protect their ships against the strong-beaked Syracusan triremes, they prepared grappling irons. They would close quickly and fight, in the antiquated style, a land battle on the decks of ships. Nicias made a last appeal to his Athenians and to their allies, then ranged his land forces along the shore at his base, while Demosthenes led his fleet toward the blocked mouth of the harbor. The Syracusans stretched hides over the prows and gunwales of their ships so that the grappling irons of the Athenians would slip harmlessly off and leave them free to ram Athenian prows, back water, and ram again. The Syracusans, with around ninety ships, deployed their fleet at various points around the Great Harbor and posted their land forces around the shore. In this vast arena, with the two armies looking on, the two fleets fought long and hard. The Athenian soldiers watched from the shore in an agony of fear and hope, their bodies swaying with the fortunes of their comrades, who were victorious at one point in the melee of ships, overwhelmed at another. Some Athenian spectators were overjoyed that they might once more behold Athens and at the same moment other spectators wailed aloud their grief and despair. Then, at last, the Athenian fleet broke, and its triremes fled for shore. There was complete panic.

Demosthenes convinced Nicias that they should try again next morning to force their way through the blockade at the mouth of the Great Harbor. They still had about sixty ships left to the enemy's less than fifty. But the men were now wholly demoralized and refused to go on board. The fleet was lost. The Athenians burned the few triremes that the enemy, after the Athenians panicked, had not seized and towed away. There remained the problem of getting as many men as possible, both from the army and the navy, out of the area before Gylippus should block the roads. The Syracusan Hermocrates sent men who would pose as pro-Athenian to warn Nicias against a night march on the grounds that the roads were already blocked. So the besieged besiegers stayed on.

> After this, when it seemed to Nicias and Demosthenes that adequate preparations had been made, the departure of the army at last took place —on the third day following the sea-fight. And it was terrible, not in one aspect only of their fortunes, in that they were going away after losing all their ships, and, in place of high hopes, with danger threatening both themselves and their State, but also in that, on the abandonment of their camp, it fell to the lot of each man to see things that were painful both to sight and mind. The corpses were still unburied, and whenever a man saw one of his own friends lying dead, he was plunged into grief commingled with fear; and the living who were being left behind,

wounded or sick, far more than the dead seemed piteous to the living, and were more wretched than those that had perished. For turning to entreaty and lamentation, they drove the men to distraction; begging to be taken along and calling aloud upon each one if they saw anywhere a comrade or a kinsman, clinging to their tent-mates now going away and following after them as long as they were able, and then, when the bodily strength of one or another failed, falling behind, though not without faint appeals to the gods and lamentations; so that the whole army, being filled with grief and in such perplexity, found it hard to depart, even out of a country that was hostile, and though they had endured already sufferings too great for tears and feared for the future what they might still have to suffer. There was also a general feeling of dejection and much self-condemnation. For indeed they looked like nothing else than a city in secret flight after a siege, and that no small city; for in the entire throng no fewer than four myriads were on the march together. And of these, the rest all bore whatever each could that was useful, while the hoplites and the horsemen, contrary to their wont, carried their own food, some for want of attendants, others through distrust of them; for there had been desertions all along and in greatest numbers immediately on their defeat. But even so they did not carry enough, for there was no longer food in the camp. Furthermore, the rest of their misery and the equal sharing of their ills—although there was in this very sharing with many some alleviation—did not even so seem easy at the moment, especially when one considered from what splendour and boastfulness at first to what humiliating end they had now come. For this was indeed the very greatest reversal that had ever happened to an Hellenic armament; for it so fell out that in place of having come to enslave others, they were now going away in fear lest they might rather themselves suffer this, and instead of prayers and paeans, with which they had sailed forth, were now departing for home with imprecations quite the reverse of these; going too as foot-soldiers instead of seamen, and relying upon hoplites rather than a fleet. And yet, by reason of the magnitude of the danger still impending, all these things seemed to them tolerable.[268]

But the roads and fords were now blocked. Cavalry and archers harassed the retreating Athenians. Food and water were scarce. So they abandoned their westerly route into the interior of Sicily. Then they tried by a night march to throw Gylippus off the scent, and struck for the coast and Catana. They reached the sea, but again they found the Syracusans blocking the ford of a river they must cross. Demosthenes' rear guard had meanwhile during the night march lost contact with the forces under Nicias, was ambushed in a walled olive orchard, and was showered with murderous arrows. At last Demosthenes surrendered, on condition that the lives of his men would be spared. Some 6,000 men laid down their arms.

Then the forces of Nicias, exhausted and suffering from thirst, pushed on toward the Assinarus River.

> And when they reached it, they rushed in, no longer preserving order, but everyone eager to be himself the first to cross; and at the same time the pressure of the enemy now made the crossing difficult. For since they were obliged to move in a dense mass, they fell upon and trod one another down, and some perished at once, run through by their own spears, while others became entangled in their trappings and were carried away by the current. The Syracusans stood along the other bank of the river, which was steep, and hurled missiles down upon the Athenians, most of whom were drinking greedily and were all huddled in confusion in the hollow bed of the river. Moreover, the Peloponnesians went down to the water's edge and butchered them, especially those in the river. The water at once became foul, but was drunk all the same, although muddy and dyed with blood, and indeed was fought for by most of them.[269]

Nicias finally surrendered and begged Gylippus to stop the butchery. The official prisoner list was not long. Many prisoners had been hidden by their captors to be sold as slaves. Of these, some escaped later to friendly Catana. The slaughter had been the worst of the war. Nicias and Demosthenes, against the will of Gylippus, were executed by Syracuse and her allies. And despite Nicias' fatal blunders at Syracuse, Thucydides judged him "a man who, of all the Hellenes of my time, least deserved to meet with such a calamity, because of his course of life that had been wholly regulated in accordance with virtue."[270] The remaining official prisoners were deposited in some stone quarries. There, exposed to broiling sun by day and autumnal chill by night, to the cries of their wounded and dying, and to the stench of their dead, they were allowed a daily ration of one pint of water and one pint of grain. After seventy days some of the survivors were sold, but the Athenians and those from Sicily or Italy who had been guilty of joining the Athenians remained in the stinking quarries a total of eight months.

The great expedition was over. As at Melos, Athens had appealed to the principle that the strong do what they can and the weak suffer what they must, to the law of the pack, not of the polis. At Melos they had declared, in defiance of Zeus, who had reputedly taught men justice: "of the gods we hold the belief, and of men we know, that by a necessity of their nature wherever they have power they always rule."[271] It took Thucydides only a few lines to weigh the fruits of their policy:

> This event proved to be the greatest of all that had happened in the course of this war, and, as it seems to me, of all Hellenic events of which we have record—for the victors most splendid, for the vanquished most disastrous. For the vanquished, beaten utterly at every point and having suffered no slight ill in any respect—having met, as the saying goes, with utter destruction—land-force and fleet and everything perished, and few out of many came back home.[272]

When news of this vast catastrophe reached Athens, of this greatest event of all that had happened in the course of the war, her citizens at first declined to believe it. But when they became convinced, they passed, through rage at those who had persuaded them to send their armada to Sicily, to unprecedented panic. They had lost not only an experienced army; they were almost without ships or money to build ships, and almost without crews to man them if built. Would the Syracusan fleet now close in on Athens?

The subject cities of Athens dreamed of freedom from the tyrant city at last. Some of them sent envoys to seek aid of Agis, the Spartan king who held Decelea in Attica; others sent to Sparta itself. The neutrals in the war reflected that it would have been their turn next had Syracuse fallen and began to consider joining in the crusade against the oppressor before it was too late to share in the coming victory. Sparta levied contributions of ships from among her allies. The Persian governor Tissaphernes was promising Sparta to subsidize an army if she would send one to liberate the Ionian subject cities of Athens. The Persian governor Pharnabazus was bidding against him, to get Sparta to liberate Athens' subject cities on the Hellespont instead. The oligarchs of Chios, who wanted help, seconded Tissaphernes. So did Alcibiades. The Spartans sent seven ships to Chios and Alcibiades went with them.

He had stayed in Sparta some two years. As usual, he had ingratiated himself with many persons. He who had trailed a purple robe at Athens left his hair untrimmed in Spartan style, took cold baths, ate coarse bread and Sparta's famous black broth. But with King Agis away and occupying Decelea, Alcibiades seduced his wife, Queen Timaia, and she bore him a son. Spartan custom had always condoned the loan of a wife to a friend as the means of obtaining an especially fine son, and Alcibiades now mockingly declared that he had neither been misled by passion nor by a desire to insult the king but by the wish that descendants of his might be kings of the Lacedaemonians. He went unpunished, but the Spartan authorities may well have been glad to see the end of him. Since the queen had not been loaned by her husband but requisitioned like that other queen of Sparta, Helen of Troy, King Agis, on campaign in Attica, was furious.

Ionia turned out to be a paradise for a man with Alcibiades' gift for intrigue. Tissaphernes wanted to use the Spartans and their allies as mercenaries to recover from Athens Ionian cities whose tribute would then go to him. Sparta wanted to use Tissaphernes as paymaster for her navy in order to deprive Athens of her Aegean empire, since tribute from that empire was Athens' only means of tyrannizing over Mainland Greece and even threatening Sparta's hegemony in the Peloponnese. Pharnabazus hoped to wean the Spartan fleet away from Tissaphernes so that it might enable him to replace Athens in the region of the Hellespont. Out of this complex of cross purposes, Alcibiades was determined to find leverage that would force Athens to recall him in triumph to the city he loved and wanted to possess. The method he chose was to convince the Athenians that he enjoyed Tissaphernes' complete confidence and that, if they wanted to defeat Sparta and save their empire, they must make him, their condemned exile, their agent. His method of retaining the confidence of Tissaphernes was to urge him privately to subsidize the Spartan fleet enough to keep it fighting the Athenians but not enough to let it win. When both sides were exhausted, Tissaphernes could, unmolested, gather up the stakes. Alcibiades would still have to face the problem of deceiving the Spartans, but a few months after he reached Ionia the Spartan government grew weary of his schemes and his effrontery and sent orders to its commanders to kill him. Alcibiades got wind of the orders and instantly fled to Tissaphernes.

Meanwhile, a democratic revolution occurred at Samos; and Athens, confident the new democratic regime would yield her fidelity and aid, decreed that Samos should be independent. Alcibiades then entered into secret negotiations with the officers of an Athenian force stationed at Samos and persuaded them with ease that if only Athens would get rid of "the villainous mob-rule that had banished him"[273] he would return to Athens and make Tissaphernes help her against Sparta. With some difficulty, these officers persuaded their soldiers and sailors that Athens should modify her constitution. The men grumbled, but the prospect of good pay from a Persian subsidy was tempting and they made no trouble. The officers then sent envoys to Athens; and these addressed the Assembly. The vision of a Persian subsidy persuaded the Assembly to adjust their constitution at least until peace could be won. Alcibiades' officer friends returned to Samos, put it back into the hands of its oligarchy, ignored Alcibiades, and started again for Athens, restoring oligarchies in a number of the subject states as they went. At Athens political murders had begun, and the officers called an Assembly at Colonus, just outside Athens, and persuaded it to set up a Council of Four Hundred, who would rule in the emergency and would eventually call into being a citizenship of Five Thousand, all of whom must be able to serve their country without pay. The Four Hundred disposed of troublemakers by execution, prison, or exile, and opened negotiations for peace with Sparta.

Meanwhile, at Samos, the democrats seized power again, with the help of soldiers and sailors from the Athenian camp. Then news came of the oligarchic seizure of power in Athens by the Four Hundred. The soldiers and sailors held an Assembly, deposed their oligarchic officers, and elected officers they felt they could trust. In effect they declared that they, encamped in Samos, were the Polis, and not the Four Hundred who now oppressed Athens. It was they who owned a fleet, not the Four Hundred. It was therefore they and not these oligarchic tyrants in Athens who could collect the tribute from the islands. As for the war with Sparta, the base for that was in any case not Athens but Samos. If the oligarchs at home did not restore the democratic constitution, the camp at Samos would exclude Athens from the sea. If the camp brought Alcibiades back from exile, he would in return bring it alliance with the Great King. And if all else failed, the camp possessed a fleet strong enough to win its members new lands to settle.

Once, long before, as Xerxes marched southward, the whole Polis, noble and democrat, rich and poor, man, woman, and child, had left Athens and gone to divine Salamis. Now, a democratic army and navy had appropriated the Polis and located it on another and more distant island, Samos. Themistocles at Salamis, within sight of silent, deserted Athens and reproached by an Allied captain that he could no longer speak for a city, had also seen that so long as Athens had her fleet her citizens could settle where they pleased.

The leaders of this new, democratic Polis-in-exile then, in effect, invited that general-in-exile, Alcibiades, to the camp at Samos. Alcibiades continued his bluff of many months and reported that Tissaphernes had solemnly promised him to subsidize the Athenian forces "if he could but trust the Athenians'" and that "he could place confidence in the Athenians only on condition that he, Alcibiades, should be restored in safety and become surety to him."[274] The army believed him and promptly elected him a general; and in effect he took charge of the Polis-in-exile. Its Assembly now clamored to go to Athens and put down the oligarchs. But Alcibiades refused: he must immediately see Tissaphernes and concert strategy. He was determined to show his new constituents in the Athenian camp that he enjoyed the Persian governor's confidence. He was also determined to show the Persian that he could now speak from military strength. He was no longer a lonely exile. He was head of an army and a fleet. To get those things, he had had to lie, to betray, and above all to bluff.

On his return to Samos envoys from the Four Hundred arrived and tried to conciliate the Athenian forces. They failed, and there were cries from the audience to kill the envoys and sail against the Four Hundred in Athens. It was Alcibiades who dissuaded them and pointed out that, while they were sailing against Athens, the enemy would certainly seize their empire in Ionia and around the Hellespont. When the envoys returned to Athens, the Four Hundred made a desperate attempt to obtain peace from Sparta on almost any terms. But, in the autumn of 411, Euboea revolted, all of the island except Oreus was lost, and a fleet of 36 triremes which the oligarchs had sent to defend Euboea was overwhelmed by 42 Peloponnesian ships and suffered the loss of 22 vessels. The fall of Euboea struck home as not even the great catastrophe at Syracuse had done: with Attica in the hands of King Agis at Decelea, food from Euboea was more desperately needed than ever. The camp at Samos was in full revolt. Athens had too few ships to defend Piraeus against the attack they felt sure was imminent. An Assembly was called. The Four Hundred were deposed. All who could afford a suit of armor were to belong to 'the Five Thousand,' a body the

Four Hundred had always talked about but had never actually created. Nobody should receive pay for public office. And the Assembly voted to recall Alcibiades and other exiles. A message was sent him, beseeching him and the camp at Samos to keep pressing the enemy. Most of the hated Athenian oligarchs fled to Decelea and the Spartan king. The Peloponne-sian fleet, sick of hearing Tissaphernes' promises of a Phoenician fleet, which never came and which quite possibly was never available to him, deserted its paymaster for Pharnabazus, whose province included the Hellespont.

The naval campaign now shifted to the Hellespont. But Tissaphernes went there too; Alcibiades visited him—and was arrested and sent to Sardis. He escaped. In the spring of 410 a Peloponnesian fleet, now under the command of Mindarus, was badly defeated by the Athenians, off Cyzicus on the Propontis. Alcibiades, Theramenes, and Thrasybulus slipped a fleet of 86 ships through the Hellespont, unseen, and surprised Mindarus. They sank or captured about 60 triremes, and Mindarus was killed. The Athenians intercepted a laconic message to Sparta from Mindarus' suc-cessor: "The ships are gone. Mindarus is dead. The men are starving. We know not what to do."[275] When news of the victory at Cyzicus was re-ceived, the old democratic constitution was restored. Under Alcibiades' leadership, the Athenian forces won back complete control of the grain route, including the Bosphorus. But while Alcibiades won glory in the north, affairs nearer home presented a sharp contrast. King Agis still held Decelea and therefore Attica. Euboea was gone. Megara had won back her eastern port, Nisaea. Chios was lost again. Corcyra threatened to become neutral. And, after all these years, Sparta had at last regained Pylos. In the spring of 407 Alcibiades learned that the Athenian Assembly had once more elected him a general.

Now he chose to come home, not because he had been grudgingly re-called in 411 when the Four Hundred fell, but because he was a conquering hero who had again secured his city's life line to the grain supply of the Black Sea. Or did Athens look on him as a hero? As a matter of fact, opinion was still divided. He collected troops at Samos and twenty ships. He sailed to the Ceramic Gulf in southwest Asia Minor and collected a hundred talents. Then he cautiously sailed near Athens to learn for himself how he would be received. When his ship reached Piraeus, after his exile of eight years, a crowd awaited him. On seeing a group of his relatives and personal friends, he was reassured, and went up to Athens, with his friends protectively surrounding him, and addressed the Council and Assembly. He denied the old charge of sacrilege and claimed he had been unjustly treated. No one spoke in opposition: by now the Assembly would not have tolerated it. He was voted extraordinary powers[276] to save his polis. His first act was to conduct in person the procession of the Eleusinian mysteries.

There was no question either of the death sentence or of the curse placed upon him for sacrilege, when toward the end of October, 407, he sailed with a fleet of a hundred triremes. Eight years before, he had sailed out of Athens with 134 ships, bound for Sicily and conquest, but he had been only one of three commanders of that doomed expedition and he had sailed under a cloud, accused of desecrating the holy mysteries of Eleusis. This time, before he sailed, he had organized and led the first annual pilgrimage that Athenians had made in years, by land along the Sacred Way to Eleusis, his troops guarding the holy procession. He had made it under the nose of the Spartan King Agis at Decelea—of Agis, whose queen he, Alcibiades, had seduced, while conspiring in Sparta against Athens, to bring Athens to her senses again. There were indeed dissenting voices, but, as he sailed from Piraeus with his hundred ships, he was the hero of his polis. He had already opened the Hellespont; now he must reconquer those of the Ionian cities still in a state of revolt. On the way, he attacked Andros, but failed to take the city, and returned to Athens' main base at Samos.

But fate had pitted against him two new and formidable antagonists. One was Lysander, whom Sparta had sent out to command her forces, perhaps the ablest man she had sent out since Brasidas. The other was the Persian prince, Cyrus, to whom the Great King had turned over most of Tissaphernes' province and a mandate to finish the war with Athens. Cyrus was much struck with Lysander's ability and honesty and raised the wage of the seamen in Lysander's fleet, settled arrears of pay, and gave the seamen a month's pay in advance. In 407, Alcibiades, finding it necessary to be away from his fleet, committed it to the care of a favorite of his, Antiochus, captain of Alcibiades' own ship. He also ordered him not to attack Lysander's fleet, now lying at Ephesus. During his absence, Antiochus disobeyed, allowed Lysander to trap him into a battle, and lost. Opinion in Athens turned against Alcibiades, the Assembly replaced him, and Alcibiades fled to one of his private castles on the Hellespont, built on his last campaign in those regions.

Meanwhile, things were going badly for Athens too. With the backing of Cyrus, the Peloponnesians built their fleet up to 140 ships. The Athenian commander, Conon, with only 70 vessels, was attacked outside Mitylene and lost 30 precious triremes, and the rest of his fleet was blockaded in the harbor. Athens was now desperate. She borrowed the gold and silver dedications from the temples on the Acropolis, melted them down, built a new fleet of 150 triremes, and sent it to relieve Mitylene. The Peloponnesians met the new Athenian fleet near the Arginusae, a cluster of tiny islands between Lesbos and the mainland. Lysander's term of office had expired and now, in 406, his successor Callicratidas commanded the Peloponnesians. He was overwhelmed; 70 of his ships were sunk or captured, and he himself was killed. But the eight Athenian commanders in charge were accused at Athens of criminal negligence: they had delayed rescuing the crews of 25 triremes that had been wrecked in battle, until a rising storm had rendered rescue impracticable. Two commanders had since fled. The other six were illegally tried in a group, before the Assembly itself and not in court. Although Alcibiades' friend, Socrates, who happened to be presiding that day, refused to put the illegal motion to the vote, a vote was nevertheless taken, and all six of the commanders were executed. One of them was Pericles, son of Aspasia and the great Pericles.

The battle of Arginusae had given the eastern Aegean back to Athenian sea power, so Sparta sued for peace. Athens, elated by her newly re-won power, rejected Sparta's proposals. Again Sparta turned to Lysander. Under Spartan law he could not officially serve as admiral a second time, but he was sent as secretary to his successor in office with real power to direct operations. Toward the end of summer, 405, Lysander sailed to the Hellespont and captured Lampsacus. An Athenian fleet which followed him beached across the Hellespont from Lampsacus at Aegospotami, or Goat's River. From his neighboring castle Alcibiades noted the Athenian camp and rode over to urge the commanders in charge to fall back on Sestos, about two miles downshore, so that the crews could secure provisions without leaving their fleet. The commanders paid no heed and ordered him off: it was they who were in charge, not Alcibiades. Soon thereafter his fears were realized. Lysander, with some 200 vessels, fell on the Athenian fleet when it was unprepared: only nine ships escaped. Most of the men were captured. Lysander then called together his allies and invited proposals on what was to be done with the Athenian prisoners. The allies charged the Athenian Assembly with having declared that, if their fleet won, their commanders would cut off the right hand of every man they might capture. One Athenian commander, Philocles, who had captured two ships, was accused of having thrown every man on them overboard. It was decided to execute every prisoner who was an Athenian, except one man who had opposed the motion made in the Assembly. As to Philocles, Lysander ordered his throat cut.

The man-made island, Athens-Piraeus, would now learn the price islands had to pay when they lost the sea. But news of her final defeat did not immediately reach Athens.

> It was at night that the Paralus [an official State trireme] arrived at Athens with tidings of the disaster, and a sound of wailing ran from Piraeus through the long walls to the city, one man passing on the news to another; and during that night no one slept, all mourning, not for the lost alone, but far more for their own selves, thinking that they would suffer such treatment as they had visited upon the Melians, colonists of the Lacedaemonians, after reducing them by siege, and upon the Histiaeans and Scionaeans and Toronaeans and Aeginetans and many other Greek peoples. On the following day they convened an Assembly, at which it was resolved to block up all the harbours except one, to repair the walls, to station guards, and in all other respects to get the city ready for a siege. They busied themselves, accordingly, with these matters.[277]

Lysander of Sparta now held the sea, and Lysander was made of iron. Unlike some other commanders Sparta had sent out, he scorned personal gain, avoided luxury, and wore his hair long. Incorruptible himself, he freely corrupted others. He lied, he bribed, he was notorious for his cruelty. He conquered city after city, abolished democratic government everywhere, and installed oligarchies backed by Spartan garrisons. He methodically rounded up every Athenian he could find and offered him safe-conduct to Athens or the risk of death if caught elsewhere. He had determined to blockade Athens by sea, while King Agis held it blockaded by land, until famine should open it; hence, the more people it had to feed the better.

King Pausanias marched an army up from Sparta to join King Agis, and Lysander closed his sea blockade of Piraeus with 150 ships. With no fleet, no allies, and little food, Athens closed ranks and restored political rights to those she had disfranchised. People had begun to starve, but for a while she made no effort to negotiate. Then, when all her supplies of food were exhausted, she sent ambassadors to Agis. She offered to become the ally of Sparta, if only she might keep Piraeus and her walls.

Sparta insisted the Athenians must tear down a portion of the Long Walls for about a mile and a quarter—enough, in short, to convert the man-made island into a peninsula, accessible to control by Spartan land forces for the first time in over half a century. The negotiations dragged on, while famine gripped Athens harder. Then the Athenians grew more amenable and gave their ambassadors full powers to go to Sparta and negotiate with the Lacedaemonians and their allies. Thebes, Corinth, and many other allies opposed a treaty: they favored destroying Athens. But the Spartans retorted that they would not enslave a Greek city which had done so much for Greece. Had not Athens first defeated the Persian invaders at Marathon? And fought at Sparta's side at Salamis, at Plataea, at Mycale? Athens could now have peace if she would destroy the Long Walls and the walls of Piraeus, surrender all but twelve of her ships, allow her exiled oligarchs to come home, and subordinate her foreign policy to Sparta's.

So Theramenes and his fellow-ambassadors brought back this word to Athens. And as they were entering the city, a great crowd gathered around them, fearful that they had returned unsuccessful; for it was no longer possible to delay, on account of the number who were dying of the famine. On the next day the ambassadors reported to the Assembly the terms on which the Lacedaemonians offered to make peace; Theramenes acted as spokesman for the embassy, and urged that it was best to obey the Lacedaemonians and tear down the walls. And while some spoke in opposition to him, a far greater number supported him, and it was voted to accept the peace. After this Lysander sailed into Piraeus, the exiles returned, and the Peloponnesians with great enthusiasm began to tear down the walls to the music of flute-girls, thinking that that day was the beginning of freedom for Greece.[278]

It was April of the year 404, twenty-seven years after Sparta had invaded Attica and thereby precipitated the Peloponnesian War.

And Alcibiades? The thirty oligarchs who ruled Athens after her fall from power were nominally charged by the Assembly, acting under pressure from their conqueror, Lysander, with drawing up a new constitution. But first the thirty inaugurated a reign of terror. Now that Sparta, which had condemned Alcibiades to death, was taking over the Hellespont, he fled to the Persian governor, Pharnabazus. So the 'Thirty Tyrants' officially banished him. Then one of them, Critias, persuaded Sparta that the democrats in Athens would never willingly submit to government by their betters so long as they could hope that some day Alcibiades might come home. Once more Sparta sent orders, this time to Lysander, to see that Alcibiades was killed. Lysander persuaded Alcibiades' Persian host to have him slain. The men sent to kill him found him in a village in Phrygia, where he was living with a courtesan. They went at night to his house and, not daring to enter it, they set it afire. Alcibiades dashed out and scattered them with his sword, but they slew him with javelins and arrows. His mistress wrapped his body in her own garments and gave him the most brilliant funeral she could provide. But this whole story of his death survived as only a dubious legend. Some men said that it was neither Lysander nor the Spartans nor the Persian, Pharnabazus, who took his life. These men claimed it was not a courtesan with whom he was living but the daughter of a well-known family; that Alcibiades had seduced her; and that it was her brothers who fired the house and killed him. Others claimed that he went to Pharnabazus with the project of imitating that earlier famous exile from Athens, Themistocles; and that he also, Alcibiades, planned to go up to Susa to the palace of the Great King. There he would offer to help the King put down his new rival for power in the Aegean, Lacedaemon. In any case,[279] Alcibiades died when he was about forty-six years old, in the year 404, the same year the Athenian Empire died.

Indeed, he and the Athenian democracy mirrored each other. He was beautiful, and so was Athens; he loved beauty, and so did she; he had taste, and so had his city. He displayed a captivating charm at a time when the charm of Athens captivated all Hellas. He had the quick adaptability of Odysseus, and Athens had it too. He was courageous, and often rash. Was not Athens both? Like his city, he struck hard at his enemies. He displayed an insolence, a hybris, such as the gods hated, and so did his polis. And like her, he was dramatic, both in word and deed. He had an imagination that led him to dream of conquering Italy and Carthage when Amphipolis still defied her metropolis, and tradition would record that in those same months, before their splendid armada sailed off for Sicily, the people of Athens also dreamed dreams of unlimited glory. For both Alcibiades and Athens desperately wanted fame and always wanted money. In the west, could they not find both? Both he and she were quickly diverted if opportunity suddenly beckoned. They were changeable in fortunate times, obstinate and persevering when the times seemed hopeless.

When dark days came, they both refused to give up. After complete catastrophe in Sicily, to the amazement of all Hellas Athens won a naval victory at Cynossema in 411 and an overwhelming victory off Cyzicus in 410. After her defeats in 407 at Notion and off Mitylene, she melted down the gold and silver ornaments in her temples, built a new fleet, and overwhelmed her foes again at Arginusae in 406. But in that terrible summer of 405 and in the hungry winter that followed, she came at last to know that the sword and the oar had failed her. And in April, 404, her Long Walls came down. For his part Alcibiades had repeatedly risen from disaster. After his city had placed a price on his head, he taught Sparta to humble her. After he had left Sparta for Ionia and had got news that Sparta, too, had condemned him to death, he went alone to Tissaphernes, the Persian governor; he bluffed the Athenian forces at Samos into believing that he could bring Athens the subsidies Persia now gave Sparta, if only Athens would get rid of the extreme democracy that had banished and condemned him; was elected a general; led the reconquest of the route to the Black Sea and Athens' daily bread; returned in triumph to Athens; lost Athens' confidence and was replaced; retreated to his Hellespontine castle; tried to rescue an Athenian fleet from its folly and bad strategy; saw that fleet's ruin; and then—according to at least one of the traditions that grew up about him—planned to find new leverage as an advisor to the Great King himself. Where the city had been surrendered and forced out of its sheltering walls by famine, Alcibiades had been surrounded and forced out of his house by fire—if another of the legends of Alcibiades was correct. And he was forced out to die, sword in hand, under a hail of arrows.

Athens was his mistress, not his wife, and he loved her with possessive passion. She would be his, or nobody's. They were capable of doing each other great injury, but they longed with passion for each other. And, indeed, where else but Athens could he hope to be happy? Where else but in this witty polis would he find the conversation that could feed his mind? Where else the beauty that shone down from the Acropolis? Where else so sophisticated a community of men, "feeding on the most illustrious wisdom," as Euripides wrote, "and walking delicately in the most radiant air"[280]? In short, what other place than Athens was truly civilized? What could one do in the long months at Sparta, except perhaps eat black broth, take cold baths, and seduce a Spartan queen? Then, at least, Sparta would have a half-Athenian king to reign over her dour, laconic, cautious army of drill sergeants. In Athens, in the Agora, there was something no Spartan would ever grasp, something he would scorn as idle chatter: there was good talk, a communion of men's minds, a duel of wits, and if Socrates happened to be present, a joint search into the invisible realm of ideas, vaster and more mysterious than Sicily itself.

THE PHILOSOPHER KING

IN APRIL, 404, when the twenty-seven years of butchery and devastation, of hatred and deception, of suspicion and betrayal, of heroic sacrifice and black grief had ended, when to the sound of flutes the Long Walls came down that Hellas might be free, and when empire was gone, Socrates of Athens was sixty-six years old. He had been a boy of about ten when Pericles and democracy came to power in Athens. He had been a young man of twenty-four when Pericles abandoned the idea of empire in Mainland Greece and focused on sea power, islands, and distant coasts. He was thirty-one when the revolt of Samos was quelled; and at thirty-seven he served in the heavy infantry at the siege of rebel Potidaea. He was thirty-nine when Sparta and her allies invaded Attica, and the Great War, the long agony of Hellas, began. Then came Pericles' famous funeral oration, in which he declared that this polis of Socrates was the School of Hellas; then the frightful plague; the drop in Athenian morale; and another great speech from Pericles, in which he warned the Athenians that their polis was a tyrant-city, ruling her allies by force, and that it was too late to turn back from the path of empire. Now, a quarter of a century later, when Socrates was an old man, the Long Walls came down. In a sense, he too had followed the path of empire. It had led him not only to Potidaea, but also to take part in the Athenian rout at Delium in 424. In 422 it led him to fight in the battle of Amphipolis, in which fell both Cleon of Athens and Brasidas of Sparta, those two 'pestles' who had ground up the cities of Hellas in the mortar of war.

But Socrates' understanding had already been formed in pre-war Periclean Athens, in the polis which created the Parthenon to crown its holy Acropolis; which created the music one heard in the Odeon at the foot of that same Acropolis; which created in the nearby theater of the god Dionysus the majestic religious tragedies of Aeschylus and the more complex tragedies of Sophocles; and which created the mural paintings in the arcaded Agora. It was the polis in which Herodotus read aloud his history of the defense of Hellenic freedom against the vast imperial forces of Xerxes; the polis which gathered up the philosophers from all over Hellas, with their speculations on the nature of matter and the universe; the great sophists, ready to lecture, for a fee, on rhetoric and on many other subjects, the great artists—and the great merchants. For Athens' port, the Piraeus, joined to her by the impregnable Long Walls in a man-made island ruling natural islands, was now the main emporium of the Mediterranean world, an emporium where money was no longer a mere medium for the exchange of commodities but was often an end in itself, an emporium where strange tongues could be heard and strange costumes seen. Athens was also the headquarters of a powerful fleet of swift triremes, ready to police the trade routes against pirates, ready to collect the tribute imposed on her subject cities, ready to guarantee the grain route from the Black Sea that a polis which Attic farms could no longer feed might continue nevertheless to eat. She was the most populous polis in Hellas: counting her slaves and her metics, she contained perhaps over 400,000 souls. She was the richest city in Hellas, richer even than her jealous commercial rival, Corinth. To impose her will, she had easily the most powerful navy, much stronger than that of her nearest competitor, Corcyra.

If the Piraeus was the Mediterranean's leading center for the exchange of commodities, Athens was its leading center for the exchange of words. For, among other things, this polis was an unending conversation. At its best, it was a noble conversation, the noblest that Hellas had achieved.

It was a communion of men's minds that sought communion with the gods themselves, a conversation through which a community of men learned together. When Simonides had written that "Polis teaches man,"[281] might he not have had in mind that the true polis was in essence a conversation, a conversation about important matters? Perhaps he even knew that conversations were conducted not merely in speculative words that jointly sought a truth common to all men in the polis, nor in deliberative words that sought their common good in council, assembly, or court of justice. Perhaps he knew a conversation could also occur between architects, not in words but in temples, between sculptors who carved or modeled statues, between painters who spoke on walls or only on vases and kitchen pots, between all artists and their other fellow citizens; and that it raised questions and essayed answers in a common search for beauty.

Yet, either because the docks and warehouses and shops of the Piraeus were too close, or because the physical appetites of philosopher, statesman, or artist were too clamorous, the citizens of Athena's Polis bought and sold, not only oil and wine and pots and woolen cloth, but words and statues too. The sophist might turn word merchant to teach men the false argument that deceived, that bore false witness in assembly or court, the poet might write what was neither true nor beautiful but what would gain a prize, the artist might consciously or unconsciously build or carve or paint the meretricious.

These were some of the problems that faced the polis into which, in 470, Socrates had been born. His father was a sculptor in stone and a friend of Lysimachus, son of Aristides the Just. The mother of Socrates, Phaenarete, was in her later years an expert midwife. When Socrates was young, he studied, as other Athenian boys did, music and gymnastic. Music meant Homer and other poetry as well as music in the usual sense; gymnastic trained one in grace of movement as well as in strength and endurance. Socrates also acquired some knowledge of geometry and astronomy. He started out in his father's occupation, sculpture or stone-cutting. But he became enamored of the speculations of the Ionians on the nature of matter, and together with a friend named Chaerephon and other young men tried to acquire the natural science of his day.

However, his interest slowly shifted to the intellectual and moral nature of man, to man's place in his polis, to what made the polis itself good or evil. Finally, he combined a deep interest in religion with a ceaselessly questing mind. Did his interest in religion spring, at least in part, from a direct and powerful intuitive experience he had known intermittently since childhood? This intuition took the form of a kind of voice, a divine spirit that dwelt within him, a sign, that often warned him not to do something he was about to do, but never gave positive advice.

During the period of his friendship with Socrates, Chaerephon was so impressed with his friend's intellectual powers that he journeyed to Delphi and boldly asked Apollo to tell him whether anyone was wiser than Socrates. The oracle replied that there was no man wiser. When this reply was reported to Socrates, he was troubled:[282] he did not believe he was wise at all, but neither did he believe that the god would lie. That Apollo should appear to speak in a riddle was of course no cause for astonishment: everybody knew that oracles were often ironical. Cassandra, the Trojan prophetess in Aeschylus's *Oresteia* spoke in that style; so did the prophet Tiresias in Sophocles' *Oedipus the King*. The problem was to keep the conversation going, to assume the oracle made sense, to assume therefore that one must discover in what sense the words were delivered. When Croesus, king of Lydia, had lost an empire to Cyrus of Persia and had then sent envoys to rebuke Apollo for deceiving him with the promise that, should he attack Cyrus, a great empire would fall, had not Apollo calmly pointed out to the Lydian envoys that Croesus should have inquired further? That was precisely what Socrates now proposed to do. He would try to find another man who was clearly wiser than himself and then go to Delphi and confront Apollo with his discovery. He would say to the god, "Here is a man who is wiser than I am, but you said that I was the wisest."[283]

Socrates picked out a leading Athenian politician and questioned him narrowly. But though the politician he had picked out "was thought wise by many, and still wiser by himself,"[284] his confused and conflicting answers to Socrates' questions made it clear that he was anything but wise. Also he apparently realized he had made a fool of himself, for he was angry. So Socrates left him, saying to himself as he went away:

> Well, although I do not suppose that either of us knows anything really beautiful and good, I am better off than he is,—for he knows nothing and thinks that he knows; I neither know nor think that I know. In this latter particular, then, I seem to have slightly the advantage of him.[285]

He went to others, with the same result. They always started the conversation sure of their wisdom. Then they became confused and contradicted themselves. Then they felt shown up and became angry. Socrates concluded from a series of such examinations "that the men most in repute were all but the most foolish; and that others less esteemed were really wiser and better."[286] After the politicians, he tried poets, whom he questioned about "some of the most elaborate passages in their own writings,"[287] only to discover that poets apparently wrote out of inspiration, not out of their own wisdom. Yet, because they really had written good poetry, they imagined they were the wisest of men in other matters also. He tried artisans, with the same results.

The method of close, logical questioning that Socrates used normally led the answerer to self-contradiction. Socrates did not denounce the answerer's opinions. He merely elicited from him, step by logical step, opinions which conflicted so glaringly that the answerer grew furious. Yet Socrates was faultlessly courteous. He treated the firmly announced opinions of other men as he had treated the oracle of Apollo: their answers often appeared to him false, but he assumed, for the purposes of the discussion, that the fault lay in him, not in them. He continued, patiently and apologetically, until they fell into pitfalls that not even their pride of authorship could protect them from seeing. They thereupon guessed that Socrates had all along seen these pitfalls coming; yet it was not Socrates, but their own words that landed them in a refutation. The Greek word for refutation, *elenchos*,[288] had an older and primary meaning: disgrace, dishonor. When their own words refuted them, they felt disgraced and dishonored, and by Socrates, or at least in front of Socrates. It was with Socrates that they remained angry.

And Socrates? He concluded that the riddling words of the oracle which had been given to his friend, Chaerephon, really meant that no man was truly wise, that only God was wise, and that the only human wisdom that Socrates or any other man could possess was to know that his own wisdom meant nothing. In that case, what could a mere man do? He could inquire further. This was what Socrates invariably and persistently did and it was his unique characteristic. Indeed, he construed the oracle given to Chaerephon as a mission given to him, Socrates, to keep inquiring further. "Obedient to the god,"[289] he kept inquiring. To do so, he accepted the poverty that Pericles, in his great funeral oration, had declared was no disgrace in Athens. To continue to inquire, he joyfully embraced poverty, which Pericles had declared it was disgraceful not to do something about. Pericles was of course talking about material possessions, those that satisfy the body's wants. But Socrates, by focusing on possessions that satisfied the mind's wants, in effect restated the Periclean formula: ignorance was no disgrace; the only disgrace was not doing anything about ignorance. Socrates had not always been poor: as late as 431, when he fought at Potidaea, he had fought in the heavy infantry, which the very poor could not enter because of the cost of equipment. But, at least in the later years of his mission, he wandered about Athens in a single garment, in all weather, and without sandals. The diet of Athenians, excepting some of the rich, was a matter of bread, mixed wine and water, olives, vegetables, salads, dried fish, and all of them scantly rationed with perhaps a piece of meat on the days of public sacrifice. Yet even in Athens Socrates' diet was conspicuously scant and simple. Antiphon, the sophist, once remarked to him:

> you are living a life that would drive even a slave to desert his master. Your meat and drink are of the poorest: the cloak you wear is not only a poor thing, but is never changed summer or winter; and you never wear shoes or tunic.[290]

"But," objected Socrates, "my belief is that to have no wants is divine; to have as few as possible comes next to the divine."[291]

He embraced poverty, partly to gain freedom from the preoccupations that a higher standard of living would have brought him, partly to gain the leisure for a kind of inquiry that was clearly a full-time job, partly because he found it brought him a sort of health which physical pleasures would have quickly stolen away. He had observed that doctors were busy chiefly with treating the effects of overindulgence. Most Athenians would inevitably regard Socrates as a barefoot, garrulous eccentric but essentially one of the sophists or teachers of wisdom. But the other sophists tended to lecture and to teach others to make speeches too: Socrates disliked speech-making and monologuing and preferred a very special form of conversation, dialectic, in which one person—either person of the two who consented to play the game of dialectic—questioned the other. In this game, skillful play normally started with a request for a definition, a request meant to invite a brief answer. Then the questioner asked a second brief question and got a second brief reply. By brief question alternating with brief reply, the game went on. The skillful questioner would try to make his question elicit the implications of the first reply—of the first, tentative definition, the first hypothesis, as it were—until, short logical step by short logical step, the answerer reached a conclusion so palpably absurd that he himself either rejected it or else refined his first hypothesis and tried again to survive in this trial by ordeal.

This game of dialectic was none other than old Hesiod's good eris, that good strife, or free competition, that set potter against potter and minstrel against minstrel. But in dialectic it was clear ideas that must be shaped, not pots, argument that must vie with argument, not song that must outdo song.

Alongside of this good eris, again as in Hesiod, stood an evil eris that superficially resembled it. Indeed, eristic was its common name. Both were contests. But in true dialectic, questioner and answerer alike came out victorious. Both of them at the end were likely to discover that the original definition or opinion with which the cross-examination had started was false. If they were concerned with truth, they were glad to be rid of a false opinion. Socrates learned early that the ignorant man abounded in unexamined opinions: the ignorant man was the opinionated man. If the falseness of one of his opinions neared the surface of his mind, he fell into a psychic panic, as the hero of Sophocles' Oedipus the King did when-ever his search for the man who had murdered the former king confronted him with troubling words that might have meant not only that it was he who had murdered, but that the victim was his own father, and his wife, Queen Jocasta, his own mother. At the end of·a dialectical process, Socra-tes' opponent in the good eris all too often assumed that the elenchos which meant refutation was really the elenchos that meant dishonor and disgrace. Since the habits of Socrates' opponent had usually been the habits of eristic dispute, not of a common dialectical search, the opponent often valued his opinions not because they were demonstrably true but because they were his own. It was therefore a point of honor or prestige to get them agreed to, true or false though they might be. When the intellectual wrestling match ended in the opponent's logical fall, the op-ponent was concerned with his single defeat, Socrates with their joint victory. The examined opinion had for Socrates passed through an ordeal of its own, like the ordeal of a tragic hero in one of the plays of Aeschylus or of Sophocles. It had met catastrophe, and out of catastrophe might come understanding; out of hybris and defeat, a kind of victory.

By such encounters Socrates made many bitter enemies, especially among the very important people in his polis. The more important they were, the more face they had to lose. And they often lost it in front of others. As the questions and answers continued and his victims felt the jaws of logic closing on them, they somehow mistook the grip of logic for the grip of Socrates. Was their increasing discomfiture precisely the disgrace and dishonor which they, with their eristic habits, had hoped to inflict on Socrates? That Socrates was unusually courteous, even in a polis renowned for courtesy, mysteriously added insult to injury—or smugness to injury. That he was gay and humorous, with the gaiety and humor that sprang from freedom, freedom from wealth and the hostages given to wealth, made him still more insufferable, like an executioner who put men to the rack while jesting about no laughing matter. Those whom he questioned accused him of knowing in advance the correct answers to his questions. For example, in 404, when Sparta installed an oligarchical government in defeated Athens, a member of this government, Charicles, ordered Socrates to stop asking questions of young men.

"Suppose," asked Socrates gently, "I want to buy something, am I not even then to ask the price if the seller is under thirty?"

"Oh, yes," answered Charicles, "you may in such cases. But the fact is, Socrates, you are in the habit of asking questions to which you know the answer: so that is what you are not to do."[292]

But Charicles, too, was judging Socratic dialectic by eristic: he was judging argument as a means to discover the truth or falsity of an opinion by argument for the sake of apparent victory regardless of the truth. The same basic misunderstanding made men doubt the kind of statement Socrates once made to his friend, Charmides:

> And at this moment I pursue the argument chiefly for my own sake, and perhaps in some degree also for the sake of my other friends. For is not the discovery of things as they truly are, a good common to all mankind?[293]

The same misunderstanding made men doubt even the kind of statement Socrates once made to Callicles:

These truths . . . would seem now to have been fixed and riveted by us, if I may use an expression which is certainly bold, in words which are like bonds of iron and adamant; and unless you or some other still more enterprising hero shall break them, there is no possibility of denying what I say. For my position has always been, that I myself am ignorant how these things are, but that I have never met any one who could say otherwise, any more than you can, and not appear ridiculous.[294]

Socrates clearly stood ready to re-examine the issues.

The intellectual good manners of Socrates, the courtesy and even the deference he showed to all comers, were the courtesy and deference he owed formally to a fellow inquirer. This formal courtesy sprang from his deference to truth. He never offered deference to birth or fame or wealth, except with a kind of gentle irony, which the eristic debater, if he detected it, would be likely to interpret as sarcasm. But it was irony, and Socrates loved and used irony because it raised a question, as Apollo's irony in his first answer to Croesus had raised a question, and because, as in a good oracle, irony therefore invited thought. Irony to a wealthy and important Athenian would at least raise the question of whether either the wealth or the importance of a man need have any relevance either to the correctness of his opinions or to his desire to learn; of whether, indeed, a man's worldly status need bear at all on his ordeal by question.

In a polis where famous sophists taught for high fees, Socrates steadfastly refused to accept money for his teaching. How could he, since he did not teach?[295] And how could he teach, since he claimed no knowledge? He was merely trying to learn and maybe to help others to learn, though he sometimes admitted he did know one or two things: for example, that one must try to know. He remarked once to his friend Meno,

Some things I have said of which I am not altogether confident. But that we shall be better and braver and less helpless if we think that we ought to enquire, than we should have been if we indulged in the idle fancy that there was no knowing and no use in seeking to know what we do not know;—that is a theme upon which I am ready to fight, in word and deed, to the utmost of my power.[296]

He knew too, or firmly believed he knew, what he meant by the word knowledge. Speaking to Meno on the same occasion, he said:

I too speak rather in ignorance; I only conjecture. And yet that knowledge differs from true opinion is no matter of conjecture with me. There are not many things which I profess to know, but this is most certainly one of them.[297]

The level of Socrates' irony was general and universal, a level of the permanent and timeless. There was no climbing to that level by syllogisms, since syllogisms could lead only downward from the general to the special, from the universal to the particular. To help his companions up, he cast down rope ladders of analogy, of metaphor; he played the poet; he jested; he teased when they tired and he caressed them with his words when they struggled to climb up; he punctured their vanity when they were complacent. He wanted them to think, as he wanted himself to think. When Theaetetus struggled vainly to answer a difficult question the argument had posed, Socrates comforted him:

> These are the pangs of labour, my dear Theaetetus; you have something within you which you are bringing to the birth.
> *Theaet.* I do not know, Socrates; I only say what I feel.
> *Soc.* And have you never heard, simpleton, that I am the son of a midwife, brave and burly, whose name was Phaenarete?
> *Theaet.* Yes, I have.
> *Soc.* And that I myself practise midwifery?
> *Theaet.* No, never.
> *Soc.* Let me tell you that I do though, my friend: but you must not reveal the secret, as the world in general have not found me out; and therefore they only say of me, that I am the strangest of mortals and drive men to their wits' end. Did you ever hear that too?
> *Theaet.* Yes.
> *Soc.* Shall I tell you the reason?
> *Theaet.* By all means.
> *Soc.* Bear in mind the whole business of the midwives, and then you will see my meaning better:—No woman, as you are probably aware, who is still able to conceive and bear, attends other women, but only those who are past bearing.
> *Theaet.* Yes, I know.
> *Soc.* The reason of this is said to be that Artemis—the goddess of childbirth—is not a mother, and she honours those who are like herself; but she could not allow the barren to be midwives, because human nature cannot know the mystery of an art without experience; and therefore she assigned this office to those who are too old to bear.
> *Theaet.* I dare say.

Soc. And I dare say too, or rather I am absolutely certain, that the midwives know better than others who is pregnant and who is not?

Theaet. Very true.

Soc. And by the use of potions and incantations they are able to arouse the pangs and to soothe them at will; they can make those bear who have a difficulty in bearing, and if they think fit they can smother the embryo in the womb.

Theaet. They can.

Soc. Did you ever remark that they are also most cunning matchmakers, and have a thorough knowledge of what unions are likely to produce a brave brood?

Theaet. No, never.

Soc. Then let me tell you that this is their greatest pride, more than cutting the umbilical cord. And if you reflect, you will see that the same art which cultivates and gathers in the fruits of the earth, will be most likely to know in what soils the several plants or seeds should be deposited.

Theaet. Yes, the same art.

Soc. And do you suppose that with women the case is otherwise?

Theaet. I should think not.

Soc. Certainly not; but midwives are respectable women who have a character to lose, and they avoid this department of their profession, because they are afraid of being called procuresses, which is a name given to those who join together man and woman in an unlawful and unscientific way; and yet the true midwife is also the true and only matchmaker.

Theaet. Clearly.

Soc. Such are the midwives, whose task is a very important one, but not so important as mine; for women do not bring into the world at one time real children, and at another time counterfeits which are with difficulty distinguished from them; if they did, then the discernment of the true and false birth would be the crowning achievement of the art of midwifery—you would think so?

Theaet. Indeed I should.

Soc. Well, my art of midwifery is in most respects like theirs; but differs, in that I attend men and not women, and I look after their souls when they are in labour, and not after their bodies: and the triumph of my art is in thoroughly examining whether the thought which the mind of the young man brings forth is a false idol or a noble and true birth. And like midwives, I am barren, and the reproach which is often made against me, that I ask questions of others and have not the wit to answer them myself is very just—the reason is, that the god compels me to be a midwife, but does not allow me to bring forth. And therefore I am not myself at all wise, nor have I anything to show which is the invention or birth of my own soul, but those who converse with me profit. Some of them appear dull enough at first, but afterwards, as our acquaintance ripens, if the god is gracious to them, they all make astonishing progress; and this in the opinion of others as well as in their own. It is quite clear that they never learned anything from me; the many fine discoveries to which they cling are of their own making. But to me and the god they owe their delivery. And the proof of my words is, that many of them in their ignorance, either in their self-conceit despising me, or falling under the influence of others, have gone away too soon; and have not only lost the children of whom I had previously delivered them by an ill bringing up, but have stifled whatever else they had in them by evil communications, being fonder of lies and shams than of the truth; and they have at last ended by seeing themselves, as others see them, to be great fools. Aristeides, the son of Lysimachus, is one of them, and there are many others. The truants often return to me, and beg that I would consort with them again—they are ready to go to me on their knees—and then, if my familiar [daimōn] allows, which is not always the case, I receive them, and they begin to grow again. Dire are the pangs which my art is able to arouse and to allay in those who consort with me, just like the pangs of women in childbirth; night and day they are full of perplexity and travail which is even worse than that of the women. So much for them. And there are others, Theaetetus, who come to me apparently having nothing in them; and as I know that they have no need of my art, I coax them into marrying some one, and by the grace of God I can generally tell who is likely to do them good. Many of them I have given away to Prodicus, and many to other inspired sages. I tell you this long story, friend Theaetetus, because I suspect, as indeed you seem to think yourself, that you are in labour—great with some conception. Come then to me, who am a midwife's son and myself a midwife, and do your best to answer the questions which I will ask you. And if I abstract and expose your firstborn, because I discover upon inspection that the conception which you have formed is a vain shadow, do not quarrel with me on that account, as the manner of women is when their first children are taken from them. For I have actually known some who were ready to bite me when I deprived them of a darling folly; they did not perceive that I acted from good will, not knowing that no god is the enemy of man—that was not within the range of their ideas; neither am I their enemy in all this, but it would be wrong for me to admit falsehood, or to stifle the truth. Once more, then, Theaetetus, I repeat my old question, 'What is knowledge?' —and do not say that you cannot tell; but quit yourself like a man, and by the help of God you will be able to tell.

Theaet. At any rate, Socrates, after such an exhortation I should be ashamed of not trying to do my best. Now he who knows perceives what he knows, and, as far as I can see at present, knowledge is perception.

Soc. Bravely said, boy; that is the way in which you should express your opinion. And now, let us examine together this conception of yours, and see whether it is a true birth or a mere wind-egg:—You say that knowledge is perception?[298]

When the famous sophist, Protagoras of Abdera, visited Athens shortly before the Great War began, one of Socrates' young friends awoke him at dawn. Protagoras had gone to the home of the wealthy Callias; so had Hippias of Elis, Prodicus of Ceos, and several other wise men. Hippocrates persuaded Socrates to take him to Callias' home and present him to the great sophist. Arrived at the vestibule of Callias' house, Socrates and Hippocrates fell into philosophic argument and argued long before knocking. The porter had already had enough of sophists: when they knocked, he grumbled that Callias was not at home and slammed the door in their faces. But they finally got in. Socrates later described what they saw:

When we entered, we found Protagoras taking a walk in the cloister; and next to him, on one side, were walking Callias, the son of Hipponicus, and Paralus, the son of Pericles, who, by the mother's side, is his half-brother, and Charmides, the son of Glaucon. On the other side of him were Xanthippus, the other son of Pericles, Philippides, the son of Philomelus; also Antimoerus of Mende, who of all the disciples of Protagoras is the most famous, and intends to make sophistry his profession. A train of listeners followed him; the greater part of them appeared to be foreigners, whom Protagoras had brought with him out of the various cities visited by him in his journeys, he, like Orpheus, attracting them by his voice, and they following. I should mention also that there were some Athenians in the company. Nothing delighted me more than the precision of their movements: they never got into his way at all; but when he and those who were with him turned back, then the band of listeners parted regularly on either side; he was always in front, and they wheeled round and took their places behind him in perfect order.[299]

The irony Socrates put into describing Protagoras and his adoring disciples invited his companion to gauge the distance between the peripatetic lecture and the healthily rough give-and-take of dialectic. Physically as well as intellectually, the great Protagoras was followed. Physically and intellectually, those who followed him got out of his way when he and his thought turned. And once more, "in perfect order," they followed.[300]

Then, casually, the famous, elderly Protagoras and the then young Socrates engaged. But Protagoras quickly threw aside the brief give-and-take of dialectic and soared into a long and rhetorically skillful oration. At last it ended, and Socrates remarked that many orators, including Pericles, could pronounce a fine discourse,

> but then when one has a question to ask of any of them, like books, they can neither answer nor ask; and if any one challenges the least particular of their speech, they go ringing on in a long harangue, like brazen pots, which when they are struck continue to sound unless some one puts his hand upon them; whereas our friend Protagoras can not only make a good speech, as he has already shown, but when he is asked a question he can answer briefly; and when he asks he will wait and hear the answer; and this is a very rare gift. Now I, Protagoras, want to ask of you a little question, which if you will only answer, I shall be quite satisfied.[301]

Now, at least for a short while, Socrates held the great man to the brief answer. But as the going began to get rough for a man with great face to lose, and fees, too, Protagoras grew hesitant, evasive, then ruffled and excited—and made a longer speech, so eloquent that his adoring followers broke into a cheer. Then Socrates:

> Protagoras, I have a wretched memory, and when any one makes a long speech to me I never remember what he is talking about. As then, if I had been deaf, and you were going to converse with me, you would have had to raise your voice; so now, having such a bad memory, I will ask you to cut your answers shorter, if you would take me with you.
>
> What do you mean? he said: how am I to shorten my answers? shall I make them too short?
>
> Certainly not, I said.

But short enough?

Yes, I said.

Shall I answer what appears to me to be short enough, or what appears to you to be short enough?

I have heard, I said, that you can speak and teach others to speak about the same things at such length that words never seemed to fail, or with such brevity that no one could use fewer of them. Please therefore, if you talk with me, to adopt the latter or more compendious method.

Socrates, he replied, many a battle of words have I fought, and if I had followed the method of disputation which my adversaries desired, as you want me to do, I should have been no better than another, and the name of Protagoras would have been nowhere.

I saw that he was not satisfied with his previous answers, and that he would not play the part of answerer any more if he could help; and I considered that there was no call upon me to continue the conversation; so I said: Protagoras, I do not wish to force the conversation upon you if you had rather not, but when you are willing to argue with me in such a way that I can follow you, then I will argue with you. Now you, as is said of you by others and as you say of yourself, are able to have discussions in shorter forms of speech as well as in longer, for you are a master of wisdom; but I cannot manage these long speeches: I only wish that I could. You, on the other hand, who are capable of either, ought to speak shorter as I beg you, and then we might converse. But I see that you are disinclined, and as I have an engagement which will prevent my staying to hear you at greater length (for I have to be in another place), I will depart; although I should have liked to have heard you.[302]

Socrates had early in life displayed a memory for complicated conversation that was extraordinary, yet his plea of a bad memory contained an element of truth: he found it hard to remember the unrelated items in a rhetorical explosion set off for purposes of display; and he could not imagine how a series of such explosions could advance the dialectical search he had drawn Protagoras into. But his wealthy host, Callias, begged him to stay. At last Socrates said:

Let me tell you then what I will do in order that the conversation and discussion may go on as you desire. If Protagoras is not disposed to answer, let him ask and I will answer; and I will endeavour to show at the same time how, as I maintain, he ought to answer: and when I have answered as many questions as he likes to ask, let him in like manner answer me;

and if he seems to be not very ready at answering the precise question asked of him, you and I will unite in entreating him, as you entreated me, not to spoil the discussion. And this will require no special arbiter—all of you shall be arbiters.

This was generally approved, and Protagoras, though very much against his will, was obliged to agree that he would ask questions; and when he had put a sufficient number of them, that he would answer in his turn those which he was asked in short replies.[308]

Protagoras promptly shifted the theme of their argument to a doubtfully relevant passage of the poet Simonides; tried to trip Socrates up in argument; and again elicited cheers from his followers. Thereupon Socrates made a very long speech, delicately parodying the intricate literary criticism which sophists like Protagoras loved. Indeed, Hippias quite missed his irony and was so inspired that he asked permission to propound his own interpretation of the passage in Simonides. "Nay, Hippias," said Alcibiades; "not now, but at some other time." Then Socrates said:

I wish Protagoras either to ask or answer as he is inclined; but I would rather have done with poems and odes, if he does not object, and come back to the question about which I was asking you at first, Protagoras, and by your help make an end of that. The talk about poets seems to me like a commonplace entertainment to which a vulgar company have recourse; who, because they are not able to converse or amuse one another, while they are drinking, with the sound of their own voices and conversation, by reason of their stupidity, raise the price of flute-girls in the market, hiring for a great sum the voice of a flute instead of their own breath, to be the medium of intercourse among them: but where the company are real gentlemen and men of education, you will see no flute-girls, nor dancing-girls, nor harp-girls; and they have no nonsense or games, but are contented with one another's conversation, of which their own voices are the medium, and which they carry on by turns and in an orderly manner, even though they are very liberal in their potations. And a company like this of ours, and men such as we profess to be, do not require the help of another's voice, or of the poets whom you cannot interrogate about the meaning of what they are saying; people who cite them declaring, some that the poet has one meaning, and others that he has another, and the point which is in dispute can never be decided. This sort of entertainment they decline, and prefer to talk with one another, and put one another to the proof in conversation. And these are the models which I desire that you and I should imitate. Leaving the poets, and keeping to ourselves, let us try the mettle of one another and make proof of the truth in conversation. If you have a mind to ask, I am ready to answer; or if you would rather, do you answer, and give me the opportunity of resuming and completing our unfinished argument.

I made these and some similar observations; but Protagoras would not distinctly say which he would do. Thereupon Alcibiades turned to Callias, and said:—Do you think, Callias, that Protagoras is fair in refusing to say whether he will or will not answer? for I certainly think that he is unfair; he ought either to proceed with the argument, or distinctly to refuse to proceed, that we may know his intention; and then Socrates will be able to discourse with some one else, and the rest of the company will be free to talk with one another.

I think that Protagoras was really made ashamed by these words of Alcibiades, and when the prayers of Callias and the company were super-added, he was at last induced to argue, and said that I might ask and he would answer.

So I said: Do not imagine, Protagoras, that I have any other interest in asking questions of you but that of clearing up my own difficulties. For I think that Homer was very right in saying that

'When two go together, one sees before the other,'

for all men who have a companion are readier in deed, word, or thought; but if a man

'Sees a thing when he is alone,'

he goes about straightway seeking until he finds some one to whom he may show his discoveries, and who may confirm him in them. And I would rather hold discourse with you than with any one, because I think that no man has a better understanding of most things which a good man may be expected to understand, and in particular of virtue. For who is there, but you?—who not only claim to be a good man and a gentleman, for many are this, and yet have not the power of making others good— whereas you are not only good yourself, but also the cause of goodness in others. Moreover such confidence have you in yourself, that although other Sophists conceal their profession, you proclaim in the face of Hellas that you are a Sophist or teacher of virtue and education, and are the first who demanded pay in return. How then can I do otherwise than invite you to the examination of these subjects, and ask questions and consult with you?[804]

249

So again they tried, Socrates asking, Protagoras answering. But Socrates led the argument to a certain stage and then pointed out to Protagoras that somehow they had shifted sides and must start again. "And," he added, "if you have no objection, as I said at first, I should like to have your help in the inquiry."

But Protagoras had throughout the long discussion aimed at another goal than Socrates. Socrates contested with Protagoras as a means to their jointly discovering the truth. Had Protagoras accepted his invitation to a joint search because the search was a contest he had hoped to win? And because the contest was held before an audience of fellow sophists and prospective pupils? He had been, after all, as Socrates had pointed out, the first sophist to "proclaim in the face of Hellas" that he was a sophist, that he taught virtue, and demanded pay for his teaching. This particular contest, or exhibition of his skill, had not proven wholly satisfactory. So he excused himself:

> Socrates, I am not of a base nature, and I am the last man in the world to be envious. I cannot but applaud your energy and your conduct of an argument. As I have often said, I admire you above all men whom I know, and far above all men of your age; and I believe that you will become very eminent in philosophy. Let us come back to the subject at some future time; at present we had better turn to something else.[305]

Had the compliment to Socrates been not ironical, as had been those of Socrates to him, but conciliatory? If it was a shade patronizing—well, was not Protagoras the older man and a great deal the more famous? If Socrates' courtesy to him had been wholly ironical, it nevertheless showed him deference because Protagoras was a human being and he might therefore at any moment rise from eristic to dialectic, from the bad eris to the good.[306] Perhaps Protagoras's courtesy to Socrates was a generous invitation to share personal glory and professional prestige, the polite offer of one professional intellectual to conspire with another. Perhaps it suggested an offer to split with a famous colleague the limited fund of respect and money which a lay public was prepared to afford to intellectuals as a group.

This conspiracy of the intellectuals did not escape the sharp eyes of Aristophanes. At the Great Dionysia of 423 he presented the *Clouds*. It won only third prize. In the *Clouds* Aristophanes pilloried the sophists, those wise men who taught for pay and who especially taught men to argue successfully, whether they wished to debate in the Assembly or the Council on public measures or whether they wished to prosecute others or defend themselves in the courts. In the *Clouds*, a rustic from the Attic countryside named Strepsiades, who had married above himself socially and now lived in Athens, was struggling with the unpaid bills of his spend-thrift son Phidippides. Phidippides was mad about horses and loved the expensive, aristocratic sport of chariot-racing, the sport at which the great Alcibiades excelled. Next door to Strepsiades' home the spectators beheld a house full of learned sophists who studied under the direction of Socrates. They studied natural philosophy, astronomy, geography, geometry, and especially the air: had not Anaximenes, the Ionian, and his followers found in air, not only the basic substance of the material universe, but the source of mind itself? Here now was Socrates, suspended in a basket from the derrick that enabled the gods in Euripides' tragedies still to appear to men. Here was Socrates observing loftily:

> I have to suspend my brain and mingle the subtle essence of my mind with this air, which is of the like nature, in order clearly to penetrate the things of heaven. I should have discovered nothing, had I remained on the ground to consider from below the things that are above; for the earth by its force attracts the sap of the mind to itself. It's just the same with the water-cress.[307]

This house of Socrates and his studious companions was "the Thoughtery of wise souls."[308] And they not only studied nature; like other sophists they could teach one how to present a bad policy in the Assembly and make it sound like a good one, to go to court with guilty hands and yet persuade the judges to acquittal. So Strepsiades wished to enroll and to learn the skill that could defraud his creditors. In the Thoughtery Socrates presented him to the Clouds, or to the chorus dressed as clouds, as "the only goddesses; all the rest are pure myth."[309] But what of Zeus? Does he not make it rain? Not at all: the Clouds do, by bumping against each other. But doesn't Zeus cause them to bump? Not at all: the aerial Whirl-wind does that.

But Strepsiades turned out too stupid to learn the esoteric knowledge of the Thoughtery. The chorus of Clouds advised him to send his son instead. Strepsiades went home, informed his son that Whirlwind had driven out Zeus and was now King, and persuaded him to study at the

Thoughtery; meanwhile he himself staved off his creditors with his newly acquired sophistry and with threats of force. Phidippides returned home fully corrupted by the Thoughtery, gave his father a sound thrashing, and calmly defended his action with elaborate sophistry. This was too much for the old man. "Oh!" he cried, "what madness! I had lost my reason when I threw over the gods through Socrates's seductive phrases."[310] He called his servants and burned the Thoughtery over the heads of these evil men, crying:

> Ah! you insulted the gods! You studied the face of the moon! Chase them, strike and beat them down! Forward! they have richly deserved their fate—above all, by reason of their blasphemies.[311]

The real Socrates, of course, was conspicuous for declining pay; he did not scoff at the gods of his polis, although he did reject, as degrading, myths about them which he thought unworthy of the godhead; he was punctilious in prayer and sacrifice; he early turned from Ionian speculations on the nature of matter; he turned instead to the mission Apollo had placed on him to ask questions and to seek the good life for man and the good life of the polis. Yet any ordinary spectator who witnessed the *Clouds* was most likely accustomed to think of Socrates as a sophist—a word which was originally as free of obloquy as the word tyrant had once been. If asked to name a sophist, such a spectator would have been likely to name Socrates—that ubiquitous, eccentric, talkative fellow, with his bare feet, his single garment, his snub nose, flanging nostrils, thick lips, and bulging eyes. True, the other sophists did not wander the streets exchanging ideas with all comers. On the contrary, they lectured in private to young men who could afford to pay well for instruction. It was also true that this well-known eccentric did not conduct a school. But in the years when Chaerephon's admiration for Socrates' intellectual abilities had driven him to Delphi to consult Apollo about him, he and Chaerephon and other young men really had studied natural philosophy together.[312] So the eccentric Socrates came to personify in the *Clouds* those sophists who marketed ideas as commodities, those who taught men to use words not as the medium of exchange for the ideas that might lead to a common truth but as weapons in the war of words, weapons fitted to deceive, to confuse, to injure. The Athens of Aristophanes, now in the ninth year of a demoralizing war, was more and more inclined to use words in just that way. Did not the great Thucydides, speaking of the bloody revolution at Corcyra and of those which followed elsewhere, note one of the effects of substituting violence for reason: that ordinary words lost their traditional meanings and took on new and more cynical meanings?

If Aristophanes' caricature was somewhat irresponsible in those dangerous years, it did not reflect a lack of friendship for Socrates. Indeed, when Socrates' friend Agathon gave a banquet[313] to celebrate his having won first prize for his first tragedy, both Socrates and Aristophanes were among his guests. The banquet was held a few months before the great armada was to sail against Syracuse. Alcibiades, who came late to the party, had already been named one of the three generals to command the expedition which he, more than any other man, was responsible for launching. Socrates even wore sandals to celebrate the occasion, finery, as he explained, because Agathon was such a fine man. After dinner, when the drinking began, the usual flute girl appeared, but was told to leave: they wanted to talk. They had met for a banquet, and their Greek word for banquet was symposium, a drinking together. But, being Athenians, they wanted to think together too—or, at a minimum, to talk together. They decided to take turns at making an extemporaneous eulogy of the great and glorious god, Love, or Eros. Phaedrus delivered a highly rhetorical speech in praise of the homosexual love which Dorian states like Sparta encouraged in their armies as an incitement to valor and which the laconizing aristocrats of Athens tended to cultivate. Pausanias's speech demanded that love be more than merely sensual. The turn of the comic poet Aristophanes came next, but he had developed hiccoughs; so Eryximachus, who was a doctor, exchanged turns with him, meanwhile ordering him to hold his breath. The doctor then gave an ingenious and playfully pedantic speech likening love between persons to other forms of attraction in matter, animate and inanimate. Then Aristophanes, his hiccoughs now cured, delivered a thoroughly Aristophanic discourse, picturing the sexual union of man and woman as a reunion of the two halves of a previously round animal with two faces, four arms, and four legs. Zeus, it appeared, had sliced these monsters in two, and sexual desire was their longing for the wholeness of which Zeus had deprived them. Then the host, Agathon, the tragic poet, gave a wordy speech in purple prose, a dithyrambic glorification of Eros, god of love. And Socrates' turn came.

Socrates began with a few simple questions to Agathon, and the dialectic disclosed that erotic love was a desire, a want, a need, a lack. Before Socrates was through, he had pictured Love as the longing of the soul for the eternal and the divine. Love was not himself beautiful, but longed for the beautiful, a *daimōn*, "the mediator who spans the chasm"[314] between man and God—or so Socrates claimed to have learned from a wise woman, Diotima of Mantinea, who came once to Athens to purify the polis and thereby delayed the coming of the great plague for ten years. Nor was Love wise: he was a lover of wisdom, a philosopher. The soul's longing that men called Love could lead a man to the fair woman who might bring him a sort of immortality through posterity, or even to the vision which led Homer to father a great poem and Lycurgus and Solon to father wise laws. Love could lead a man up a kind of ladder from perceiving and loving a beautiful form to loving all beautiful forms, to the beauty of institutions and laws, to the beauty of the various sciences, to a science of beauty everywhere, until at last such a man could behold pure beauty itself, beauty bare, unspecified, simple, everlasting. This, too, was only what the wise Diotima had told him, but Socrates claimed to believe her. Just as he finished delivering his encomium, they heard a great knocking at the door and the notes of a flute girl.

"A little while afterwards," according to Plato's later report,

> they heard the voice of Alcibiades resounding in the court; he was in a great state of intoxication, and kept roaring and shouting "Where is Agathon? Lead me to Agathon," and at length, supported by the flute-girl and some of his attendants, he found his way to them. "Hail, friends," he said, appearing at the door crowned with a massive garland of ivy and violets, his head flowing with ribands. "Will you have a very drunken man as a companion of your revels? Or shall I crown Agathon, which was my intention in coming, and go away? For I was unable to come yesterday, and therefore I am here to-day, carrying on my head these ribands, that taking them from my own head, I may crown the head of this fairest and wisest of men, as I may be allowed to call him. Will you laugh at me because I am drunk? Yet I know very well that I am speaking the truth, although you may laugh. But first tell me; if I come in shall we have the understanding of which I spoke? Will you drink with me or not?"[315]

They begged him to stay. Alcibiades drank deep and bade Socrates drink the same quantity.

"Observe, my friends," he said, "that this ingenious trick of mine will have no effect on Socrates, for he can drink any quantity of wine and not be at all nearer being drunk."[316]

Then the drunken general-elect of the coming expedition to Syracuse threatened an encomium of his own, and what he proposed to praise was Socrates.

> What are you about? said Socrates; are you going to raise a laugh at my expense? Is that the meaning of your praise?
>
> I am going to speak the truth, if you will permit me.
>
> I not only permit, but exhort you to speak the truth.
>
> Then I will begin at once, said Alcibiades, and if I say anything which is not true, you may interrupt me if you will, and say 'that is a lie,' though my intention is to speak the truth. But you must not wonder if I speak any how as things come into my mind; for the fluent and orderly enumeration of all your singularities is not a task which is easy to a man in my condition.
>
> And now, my boys, I shall praise Socrates in a figure which will appear to him to be a caricature, and yet I speak, not to make fun of him, but only for the truth's sake. I say, that he is exactly like the busts of Silenus, which are set up in the statuaries' shops, holding pipes and flutes in their mouths; and they are made to open in the middle, and have images of gods inside them. I say also that he is like Marsyas the satyr. You yourself will not deny, Socrates, that your face is like that of a satyr. Aye, and there is a resemblance in other points too. For example, you are a bully, as I can prove by witnesses, if you will not confess. And are you not a flute-player? That you are, and a performer far more wonderful than Marsyas. He indeed with instruments used to charm the souls of men by the powers of his breath, and the players of his music do so still: for the melodies of Olympus are derived from Marsyas who taught them, and these, whether they are played by a great master or by a miserable flute-girl, have a power which no others have; they alone possess the soul and reveal the wants of those who have need of gods and mysteries, because they are divine. But you produce the same effect with your words only, and do not require the flute; that is the difference between you and him. When we hear any other speaker, even a very good one, he produces absolutely no effect upon us, or not much, whereas the mere fragments of you and your words, even at second-hand, and however imperfectly repeated, amaze and possess the souls of every man, woman, and child who comes within hearing of them. And if I were not afraid that you

would think me hopelessly drunk, I would have sworn as well as spoken to the influence which they have always had and still have over me. For my heart leaps within me more than that of any Corybantian reveller, and my eyes rain tears when I hear them. And I observe that many others are affected in the same manner. I have heard Pericles and other great orators, and I thought that they spoke well, but I never had any similar feeling; my soul was not stirred by them, nor was I angry at the thought of my own slavish state. But this Marsyas has often brought me to such a pass, that I have felt as if I could hardly endure the life which I am leading (this, Socrates, you will admit); and I am conscious that if I did not shut my ears against him, and fly as from the voice of the siren, my fate would be like that of others,—he would transfix me, and I should grow old sitting at his feet. For he makes me confess that I ought not to live as I do, neglecting the wants of my own soul, and busying myself with the concerns of the Athenians; therefore I hold my ears and tear myself away from him. And he is the only person who ever made me ashamed, which you might think not to be in my nature, and there is no one else who does the same. For I know that I cannot answer him or say that I ought not to do as he bids, but when I leave his presence the love of popularity gets the better of me. And therefore I run away and fly from him, and when I see him I am ashamed of what I have confessed to him. Many a time have I wished that he were dead, and yet I know that I should be much more sorry than glad, if he were to die: so that I am at my wit's end.

And this is what I and many others have suffered from the flute-playing of this satyr. Yet hear me once more while I show you how exact the image is, and how marvellous his power. For let me tell you; none of you know him; but I will reveal him to you; having begun, I must go on. See you how fond he is of the fair? He is always with them and is always being smitten by them, and then again he knows nothing and is ignorant of all things—such is the appearance which he puts on. Is he not like a Silenus in this? To be sure he is: his outer mask is the carved head of the Silenus; but, O my companions in drink, when he is opened, what temperance there is residing within! Know you that beauty and wealth and honour, at which the many wonder, are of no account with him, and are utterly despised by him: he regards not at all the persons who are gifted with them; mankind are nothing to him; all his life is spent in mocking and flouting at them. But when I opened him, and looked within at his serious purpose, I saw in him divine and golden images of such fascinating beauty that I was ready to do in a moment whatever Socrates commanded: they may have escaped the observation of others, but I saw them. . . .[317]

Then Alcibiades remembered their days at the siege of Potidaea:

there we messed together, and I had the opportunity of observing his extraordinary power of sustaining fatigue. His endurance was simply marvellous when, being cut off from our supplies, we were compelled to go without food—on such occasions, which often happen in time of war, he was superior not only to me but to everybody; there was no one to be compared to him. Yet at a festival he was the only person who had any real powers of enjoyment; though not willing to drink, he could if compelled beat us all at that,—wonderful to relate! no human being had ever seen Socrates drunk; and his powers, if I am not mistaken, will be tested before long. His fortitude in enduring cold was also surprising. There was a severe frost, for the winter in that region is really tremendous, and everybody else either remained indoors, or if they went out had on an amazing quantity of clothes, and were well shod, and had their feet swathed in felt and fleeces: in the midst of this, Socrates with his bare feet on the ice and in his ordinary dress marched better than the other soldiers who had shoes, and they looked daggers at him because he seemed to despise them.

I have told you one tale, and now I must tell you another, which is worth hearing,

'Of the doings and sufferings of the enduring man'

while he was on the expedition. One morning he was thinking about something which he could not resolve; he would not give it up, but continued thinking from early dawn until noon—there he stood fixed in thought; and at noon attention was drawn to him, and the rumour ran through the wondering crowd that Socrates had been standing and thinking about something ever since the break of day. At last, in the evening after supper, some Ionians out of curiosity (I should explain that this was not in winter but in summer), brought out their mats and slept in the open air that they might watch him and see whether he would stand all night. There he stood until the following morning; and with the return of light he offered up a prayer to the sun, and went his way. I will also tell, if you please—and indeed I am bound to tell—of his courage in battle; for who but he saved my life? Now this was the engagement in which I received the prize of valour: for I was wounded and he would not leave me, but he rescued me and my arms; and he ought to have received the prize of valour which the generals wanted to confer on me partly on account of my rank, and I told them so (this, again, Socrates will not impeach or deny), but he was more eager than the generals that I and not he should have the prize. There was another occasion on which his behaviour was very remarkable—in the flight of the army after the battle of Delium, where he served among the heavy-armed,—I had a better opportunity of seeing him than at Potidaea, for I was myself on horseback, and therefore comparatively out of danger. He and Laches were retreating, for the troops were in flight, and I met them and told them not to be discouraged, and promised to remain with them; and there you might see him, Aristophanes, as you describe, just as he is in the streets of Athens, stalking like a pelican, and rolling his eyes, calmly contemplating enemies as well as friends, and making very intelligible to anybody, even from a distance, that whoever attacked him would be likely to meet with a stout resistance; and in this way he and his companion escaped—for this is the sort of man who is never touched in war; those only are pursued who are running away headlong. I particularly observed how superior he was to Laches in presence of mind. Many are the marvels which I might narrate in praise of Socrates; most of his ways might perhaps be paralleled in another man, but his absolute unlikeness to any human being that is or ever has been is perfectly astonishing. You may imagine Brasidas and others to have been like Achilles; or you may imagine Nestor and Antenor to have been like Pericles; and the same may be said of other famous men, but of this strange being you will never be able to find any likeness, however remote, either among men who now are or who ever have been—other than that which I have already suggested of Silenus and the satyrs; and they represent in a figure not only himself, but his words. For, although I forgot to mention this to you before, his words are like the images of Silenus which open; they are ridiculous when you first hear them; he clothes himself in language that is like the skin of the wanton satyr—for his talk is of pack-asses and smiths and cobblers and curriers, and he is always repeating the same things in the same words, so that any ignorant or inexperienced person might feel disposed to laugh at him; but he who opens the bust and sees what is within will find that they are the only words which have a meaning in them, and also the most divine, abounding in fair images of virtue, and of the widest comprehension, or rather extending to the whole duty of a good and honourable man.

This, friends, is my praise of Socrates.[318]

There was laughter. They jested a little. Then a stray band of revelers entered and great confusion ensued. Aristodemus, who had come with Socrates to the banquet, fell asleep:

he was awakened towards daybreak by a crowing of cocks, and when he awoke, the others were either asleep, or had gone away; there remained only Socrates, Aristophanes, and Agathon, who were drinking out of a large goblet which they passed around, and Socrates was discoursing to them. Aristodemus was only half awake, and he did not hear the beginning of the discourse; the chief thing which he remembered was Socrates compelling the other two to acknowledge that the genius of comedy was the same with that of tragedy, and that the true artist in tragedy was an artist in comedy also. To this they were constrained to assent, being drowsy, and not quite following the argument. And first of all Aristophanes dropped off, then, when the day was already dawning, Agathon. Socrates, having laid them to sleep, rose to depart; Aristodemus, as his manner was, following him. At the Lyceum he took a bath, and passed the day as usual. In the evening he retired to rest at his own home.[319]

Perhaps the truth which Alcibiades spoke in his cups, that Socrates' words cast an enchantment on him; that his dialectic reduced him to shame; that he had often wished Socrates were dead; but that, though he often fled, he was inexorably drawn back—perhaps this experience was based chiefly on the fact that, when he talked with Socrates, he found another human mind fully meeting his own mind to a degree he never experienced in conversation with any other man. Perhaps, also, this exhilarating sense of communing with another was based on one thing more than on any other: Socrates listened. He listened to Apollo's oracles; he listened to the opinions of other men; he listened as the poets and artists of Athens must have listened to the Muse, in quietude of spirit. He listened to—or gazed inward at—ideas, standing at Potidaea for twenty-four hours, lost in thought, while the light-hearted, pleasure-loving Ionians in the besiegers' camp gazed at him curiously. This boon companion at banquets, this rigorous master of deductive argument, had somewhere learned the even rarer art of contemplation, perhaps from listening to the voice of his own *daimōn*, a voice that had spoken to him intermittently since childhood. His listening was not of the sort that flattered the vanity of the chatterer. On the contrary, he was renowned for deflating vanity.

But, for the young men who came to him, his attentiveness gave a dimension to human intercourse that brought them alive. His awareness awakened those who were intellectual sleepwalkers. Had not Heraclitus once written that the world was one and common to those who were awake?[320] The conversations these young men had taken part in over the years so often had been blind collisions. Now there was no collision, but engagement. This man listened. In a city more given to listening than most, he out-listened all competitors: the result was a kind of communion that gave back to the polis some of the ancient excitement Simonides had expressed, when he had written, "Polis teaches man."[321]

Indeed, in the most famous of all his conversations, Socrates imagined and he caused his companions to help him imagine, what a truly listening polis would be like, and hence what a truly human community would be like, a community seeing by intellectual light. At some time around 421[322] he and Glaucon, the elder brother of Plato, went down to Piraeus to attend the festival of Bendis, a Thracian goddess corresponding to the Hellenes' Artemis. Polemarchus, son of a wealthy metic named Cephalus, persuaded them to stay for the evening and for good talk. Included among the guests was a famous sophist from Chalcedon, Thrasymachus. The company fell to talking about justice, about what a just man was. Various definitions ran the dialectical gauntlet: that the just man was one who spoke the truth and paid his debts; that he was one who did good to his friends and evil to his enemies; or perhaps one who did good to his friends only when his friends were good, and evil to his enemies only when his enemies were evil. None of the definitions survived the short questions which Socrates so gently and persistently put.

But the famous sophist of Chalcedon was growing restless. As Socrates reported next day, in recounting the conversation to a friend,

> Several times in the course of the discussion Thrasymachus had made an attempt to get the argument into his own hands, and had been put down by the rest of the company, who wanted to hear the end. But when Polemarchus and I had done speaking and there was a pause, he could no longer hold his peace; and, gathering himself up, he came at us like a wild beast, seeking to devour us. We were quite panic-stricken at the sight of him.
>
> He roared out to the whole company: What folly, Socrates, has taken possession of you all? And why, sillybillies, do you knock under to one

another? I say that if you want really to know what justice is, you should not only ask but answer, and you should not seek honour to yourself from the refutation of an opponent, but have your own answer; for there is many a one who can ask and cannot answer. And now I will not have you say that justice is duty or advantage or profit or gain or interest, for this sort of nonsense will not do for me; I must have clearness and accuracy.

I was panic-stricken at his words, and could not look at him without trembling. Indeed I believe that if I had not fixed my eye upon him, I should have been struck dumb: but when I saw his fury rising, I looked at him first, and was therefore able to reply to him.

Thrasymachus, I said, with a quiver, don't be hard upon us. Polemarchus and I may have been guilty of a little mistake in the argument, but I can assure you that the error was not intentional. If we were seeking for a piece of gold, you would not imagine that we were 'knocking under to one another,' and so losing our chance of finding it. And why, when we are seeking for justice, a thing more precious than many pieces of gold, do you say that we are weakly yielding to one another and not doing our utmost to get at the truth? Nay, my good friend, we are most willing and anxious to do so, but the fact is that we cannot. And if so, you people who know all things should pity us and not be angry with us.

How characteristic of Socrates! he replied, with a bitter laugh;—that's your ironical style! Did I not foresee—have I not already told you, that whatever he was asked he would refuse to answer, and try irony or any other shuffle, in order that he might avoid answering?

You are a philosopher, Thrasymachus, I replied, and well know that if you ask a person what numbers make up twelve, taking care to prohibit him whom you ask from answering twice six, or three times four, or six times two, or four times three, 'for this sort of nonsense will not do for me,'—then obviously, if that is your way of putting the question, no one can answer you. But suppose that he were to retort, 'Thrasymachus, what do you mean? If one of these numbers which you interdict be the true answer to the question, am I falsely to say some other number which is not the right one?—is that your meaning?'—How would you answer him?

Just as if the two cases were at all alike! he said.

Why should they not be? I replied; and even if they are not, but only appear to be so to the person who is asked, ought he not to say what he thinks, whether you and I forbid him or not?

I presume then that you are going to make one of the interdicted answers?

I dare say that I may, notwithstanding the danger, if upon reflection I approve of any of them.

But what if I give you an answer about justice other and better, he said, than any of these? What do you deserve to have done to you?

Done to me!—as becomes the ignorant, I must learn from the wise—that is what I deserve to have done to me.

What, and no payment! a pleasant notion!

I will pay when I have the money, I replied.

But you have, Socrates, said Glaucon: and you, Thrasymachus, need be under no anxiety about money, for we will all make a contribution for Socrates.

Yes, he replied, and then Socrates will do as he always does—refuse to answer himself, but take and pull to pieces the answer of some one else.

Why, my good friend, I said, how can any one answer who knows, and says that he knows, just nothing; and who, even if he has some faint notions of his own, is told by a man of authority not to utter them? The natural thing is, that the speaker should be some one like yourself who professes to know and can tell what he knows. Will you then kindly answer, for the edification of the company and of myself?

Glaucon and the rest of the company joined in my request and Thrasymachus, as any one might see, was in reality eager to speak; for he thought that he had an excellent answer, and would distinguish himself. But at first he affected to insist on my answering; at length he consented to begin. Behold, he said, the wisdom of Socrates; he refuses to teach himself, and goes about learning of others, to whom he never even says Thank you.

That I learn of others, I replied, is quite true; but that I am ungrateful I wholly deny. Money I have none, and therefore I pay in praise, which is all I have; and how ready I am to praise any one who appears to me to speak well you will very soon find out when you answer; for I expect that you will answer well.

Listen, then, he said; I proclaim that justice is nothing else than the interest of the stronger. And now why do you not praise me? But of course you won't.

Let me first understand you, I replied. Justice, as you say, is the interest of the stronger. What, Thrasymachus, is the meaning of this? You cannot mean to say that because Polydamas, the pancratiast, is stronger than we are, and finds the eating of beef conducive to his bodily strength, that to eat beef is therefore equally for our good who are weaker than he is, and right and just for us?

That's abominable of you, Socrates; you take the words in the sense which is most damaging to the argument.

Not at all, my good sir, I said; I am trying to understand them; and I wish that you would be a little clearer.[323]

The year of 421, when these men talked together about justice, was the year of the Peace of Nicias. Six years before, the Assembly had debated on whether to massacre all the adult males of reconquered Mitylene. In another five years Athens really would massacre the conquered Melians after warning them of what the sophist Thrasymachus was already shouting at Socrates: that might made right. But Socrates remained unconvinced, not because he was unable to face the harsh realities of his brutalized world but because he rejected the childish notion that brute force could successfully parade as logical proof. He therefore quietly continued to question Thrasymachus, who now cried out that Socrates argued like an informer.

Indeed, Thrasymachus, and do I really appear to you to argue like an informer?

Certainly, he replied.

And do you suppose that I ask these questions with any design of injuring you in the argument?

Nay, he replied, 'suppose' is not the word—I know it; but you will be found out, and by sheer force of argument you will never prevail.

I shall not make the attempt, my dear man; but to avoid any misunderstanding occurring between us in future, let me ask, in what sense do you speak of a ruler or stronger whose interest, as you were saying, he being the superior, it is just that the inferior should execute—is he a ruler in the popular or in the strict sense of the term?

In the strictest of all senses, he said. And now cheat and play the informer if you can; I ask no quarter at your hands. But you never will be able, never.

And do you imagine, I said, that I am such a madman as to try and cheat Thrasymachus? I might as well shave a lion.

Why, he said, you made the attempt a minute ago, and you failed.

Enough, I said, of these civilities. It will be better that I should ask you a question: Is the physician, taken in that strict sense of which you are speaking, a healer of the sick or a maker of money? And remember that I am now speaking of the true physician.[324]

And so it went: brief, probing question followed brief, probing question; with Thrasymachus entangled in his own contradictions, yet sure of his practical experience of a wicked world; with Socrates gently coaxing him on, throwing down his ladder of analogies from everyday life, trying to help him climb to a clear idea, to some recognizable principle:

> And the pilot likewise, in the strict sense of the term, is a ruler of sailors and not a mere sailor?
>
> That has been admitted.
>
> And such a pilot and ruler will provide and prescribe for the interest of the sailor who is under him, and not for his own or the ruler's interest?
>
> He gave a reluctant 'Yes.'
>
> Then, I said, Thrasymachus, there is no one in any rule who, in so far as he is a ruler, considers or enjoins what is for his own interest, but always what is for the interest of his subject or suitable to his art; to that he looks, and that alone he considers in everything which he says and does.
>
> When we had got to this point in the argument, and every one saw that the definition of justice had been completely upset, Thrasymachus, instead of replying to me, said: Tell me, Socrates, have you got a nurse?
>
> Why do you ask such a question, I said, when you ought rather to be answering?
>
> Because she leaves you to snivel, and never wipes your nose: she has not even taught you to know the shepherd from the sheep.
>
> What makes you say that? I replied.
>
> Because you fancy that the shepherd or neatherd fattens or tends the sheep or oxen with a view to their own good and not to the good of himself or his master; and you further imagine that the rulers of states, if they are true rulers, never think of their subjects as sheep, and that they are not studying their own advantage day and night. . . .[325]

Then Thrasymachus, conscious that his argument was breaking down, hurried into one of those long and complicated tirades, such as Protagoras, too, had launched, and concluded emphatically:

> And thus, as I have shown, Socrates, injustice, when on a sufficient scale, has more strength and freedom and mastery than justice; and, as I said at first, justice is the interest of the stronger, whereas injustice is a man's own profit and interest.
>
> Thrasymachus, when he had thus spoken, having, like a bathman, deluged our ears with his words, had a mind to go away. But the company would not let him; they insisted that he should remain and defend his position; and I myself added my own humble request that he would not

leave us. Thrasymachus, I said to him, excellent man, how suggestive are your remarks! And are you going to run away before you have fairly taught or learned whether they are true or not? Is the attempt to determine the way of a man's life so small a matter in your eyes—to determine how life may be passed by each one of us to the greatest advantage?

And do I differ from you, he said, as to the importance of the enquiry?

You appear rather, I replied, to have no care or thought about us, Thrasymachus—whether we live better or worse from not knowing what you say you know, is to you a matter of indifference. Prithee, friend, do not keep your knowledge to yourself; we are a large party; and any benefit which you confer upon us will be amply rewarded. For my own part I openly declare that I am not convinced, and that I do not believe injustice to be more gainful than justice, even if uncontrolled and allowed to have free play. For, granting that there may be an unjust man who is able to commit injustice either by fraud or force, still this does not convince me of the superior advantage of injustice, and there may be others who are in the same predicament with myself. Perhaps we may be wrong; if so, you in your wisdom should convince us that we are mistaken in preferring justice to injustice.

And how am I to convince you, he said, if you are not already convinced by what I have just said; what more can I do for you? Would you have me put the proof bodily into your souls?

Heaven forbid! I said; I would only ask you to be consistent; or, if you change, change openly and let there be no deception. . . .[326]

Again, the gentle, gentle, relentless questions, the faultless memory for the thread of argument, the attentive ear that heard the word, but also the mind's eye that saw the idea, half-clothed in mist, behind the word, until the crucial admission was made, and Socrates could say,

Then the just has turned out to be wise and good and the unjust evil and ignorant.

Thrasymachus made all these admissions, not fluently, as I repeat them, but with extreme reluctance; it was a hot summer's day, and the perspiration poured from him in torrents; and then I saw what I had never seen before, Thrasymachus blushing. As we were now agreed that justice was virtue and wisdom, and injustice vice and ignorance, I proceeded to another point:

Well, I said, Thrasymachus, that matter is now settled; but were we not also saying that injustice had strength; do you remember?

Yes, I remember, he said, but do not suppose that I approve of what you are saying or have no answer; if however I were to answer, you would be quite certain to accuse me of haranguing; therefore either permit me to have my say out, or if you would rather ask, do so, and I will answer 'Very good,' as they say to story-telling old women, and will nod 'Yes' and 'No.'

Certainly not, I said, if contrary to your real opinion.[327]

More questions. An admission. And Socrates:

Then the just is happy, and the unjust miserable?
So be it.
But happiness and not misery is profitable.
Of course.
Then, my blessed Thrasymachus, injustice can never be more profitable than justice.
Let this, Socrates, he said, be your entertainment at the Bendidea.
For which I am indebted to you, I said, now that you have grown gentle towards me and have left off scolding. Nevertheless, I have not been well entertained; but that was my own fault and not yours. As an epicure snatches a taste of every dish which is successively brought to table, he not having allowed himself time to enjoy the one before, so have I gone from one subject to another without having discovered what I sought at first, the nature of justice. I left that enquiry and turned away to consider whether justice is virtue and wisdom or evil and folly; and when there arose a further question about the comparative advantages of justice and injustice, I could not refrain from passing on to that. And the result of the whole discussion has been that I know nothing at all. For I know not what justice is, and therefore I am not likely to know whether it is or is not a virtue, nor can I say whether the just man is happy or unhappy.[328]

As so often before, he had not found what he was looking for—in this case, the true nature of justice. The whole of Hellas was being torn to pieces by men who charged each other with injustice: had the charge no meaning? True, those who conversed that summer night had found some of the things justice was not, things men had mistaken for justice itself, and there was some negative gain in that. The argument had once more done for Socrates what his *daimōn* had often done for him: it had vetoed, but it had not yielded the secret of what he ought to do, what he ought to believe. Except that, by implication, it told him to inquire further. And that is precisely what one of his young companions, Glaucon, begged him to do. So at it they went again, while the long night wore on—at this game of dialectic. Wild Thracian to the north, laconic Spartan to the south, would have looked on this game with an equal disdain. But this was Athens.

Socrates then somewhat playfully proposed that since men spoke not only of a just man but of a just polis, and since a polis was bigger than a man, maybe they could first locate justice in a polis and then the more readily locate it in the individual man. And so it came about that for most of the night Socrates, with what help he could conscript, imagined an ideal polis, a polis that was just because its citizens were just and that was in turn capable of educating citizens to be just. Polis teaches man.

First, thought Socrates, a polis was brought into being because men needed each other's skills and because a division of labor between them and an exchange of their products made human life better. The farmer could produce food; the builder, houses; the weaver, clothing; and, asked the barefoot Socrates, "shall we add to them a shoemaker, or perhaps some other purveyor to our bodily wants?"[329]

Slowly the list of craftsmen grew: carpenters, smiths, toolmakers, herdsmen, wage-laborers, even merchants and sailors. For this simple polis would want to exchange products with other communities. For exchange there would need to be money. Playfully, Socrates embarked on a lyrical description of a happy polis with a primitive economy. But Glaucon cut in:

> Yes, Socrates, he said, and if you were providing for a city of pigs, how else would you feed the beasts?
> But what would you have, Glaucon? I replied.
> Why he said, you should give them the ordinary conveniences of life. People who are to be comfortable are accustomed to lie on sofas, and dine off tables, and they should have sauces and sweets in the modern style.
> Yes, I said, now I understand: the question which you would have me consider is, not only how a State, but how a luxurious State is created; and possibly there is no harm in this, for in such a State we shall be more likely to see how justice and injustice originate. In my opinion the true and healthy constitution of the State is the one which I have described. But if you wish also to see a State at fever-heat, I have no objection. For I suspect that many will not be satisfied with the simpler way of life. They will be for adding sofas, and tables, and other furniture; also dainties, and perfumes, and incense, and courtesans, and cakes, all these

not of one sort only, but in every variety; we must go beyond the necessaries of which I was at first speaking, such as houses, and clothes, and shoes: the arts of the painter and the embroiderer will have to be set in motion, and gold and ivory and all sorts of materials must be procured.

True, he said.

Then we must enlarge our borders; for the original healthy State is no longer sufficient. Now will the city have to fill and swell with a multitude of callings which are not required by any natural want; such as the whole tribe of hunters and actors, of whom one large class have to do with forms and colours; another will be the votaries of music—poets and their attendant train of rhapsodists, players, dancers, contractors; also makers of divers kinds of articles, including women's dresses. And we shall want more servants. Will not tutors be also in request, and nurses wet and dry, tirewomen and barbers, as well as confectioners and cooks; and swineherds, too, who were not needed and therefore had no place in the former edition of our State, but are needed now? They must not be forgotten: and there will be animals of many other kinds, if people eat them.

Certainly.

And living in this way we shall have much greater need of physicians than before?

Much greater.

And the country which was enough to support the original inhabitants will be too small now, and not enough?

Quite true.

Then a slice of our neighbours' land will be wanted by us for pasture and tillage, and they will want a slice of ours, if, like ourselves, they exceed the limit of necessity, and give themselves up to the unlimited accumulation of wealth?

That, Socrates, will be inevitable.

And so we shall go to war, Glaucon. Shall we not?

Most certainly, he replied.

Then, without determining as yet whether war does good or harm, thus much we may affirm, that now we have discovered war to be derived from causes which are also the causes of almost all the evils in States, private as well as public.[330]

Was Socrates' picture of a primitive polis designed merely to tease his listeners into demanding a more Periclean polis, a high human culture? Certainly what Glaucon called a city of pigs would have furnished Socrates himself with all the material goods he needed or desired, plus the finery of a pair of sandals. But he assented gaily enough to expand his city of pigs into a luxurious city, with an army ready to make war. Indeed, as he ironically observed, it might be easier in a luxurious city to see how justice and injustice originated. In passing, one could note one consequence of "the unlimited accumulation of wealth": "And so we shall go to war, Glaucon. Shall we not?"[331] In any case this conversation contained not only taut logical necessities but humor and satire and repartee. In the hands of this sculptor and son of a sculptor, or in his words and the words of his companions, the image of a polis slowly took shape, a polis in which the boys who would one day have to defend it would study music and poetry, as the present company had done themselves, to make their souls gentle and receptive; to teach them, in fact, to listen. But the music and the poetry would have to be of the right kind. Not even Homer, whom Socrates revered and appeared to know by heart, would be allowed to tell to the young base stories about the gods and heroes, nor would there be the Lydian music that relaxed and over-softened. There would be stirring Dorian music. Then, of course, there must be gymnastic, to discipline and free the body's strength and grace, to school the youth in courage and endurance.

From among these Guardians of the Polis, the ablest would be picked out and trained in wisdom that they might know how to rule. Those who remained merely soldiers, Socrates speculated, might better be renamed Auxiliaries. The bulk of the population, requiring neither the wisdom to rule nor the courage and endurance to fight, would produce and exchange the material goods the polis would need. Their special virtue should be temperance or self-control. The polis Socrates had now imagined was an aristocracy, a government by the Aristoi, the Best People. But they were best, not because of the military virtues of the ancient, feudal aristocracies of Hellas; they were best because they had been tested and found wisest. The ancient aristocracies had forfeited their right to rule, partly by their avarice, which had led them to monopolize the wealth of the polis, partly by family vendettas that had bred faction and split the polis. Socrates forbade his Guardians to own private property, as Lycurgus had forbidden his Spartiates. But where Lycurgus merely put severe limits on marital life, Socrates—laughing at the audacity of his prescription—forbade marriage, in order to prevent his rulers from substituting the private good of the family for the common good of the polis. These Guardians whom he had called into being would be assigned by their magistrates temporary mates from among women as rigorously educated as themselves, in order to procreate their class. Except for this eugenic breeding, male and female Guardians alike would remain chaste. Neither artisan nor laborer nor businessman could participate in governing the polis, although they alone could hold private property. Only the wise must govern.

But there were things not even the wise knew, such as the services and rites and sacrifices due to the gods. For this last kind of knowledge, suggested Socrates, we must turn to the oracle of Apollo. Was not Apollo "the spokesman of his father, Zeus"[332]?

Even if the wise ought in fact to govern, how find the wise? And how secure the consent of the less wise to be governed by the wise? To the second question Socrates in effect imagined a myth worthy of Hesiod. His future citizens would be isolated in childhood and would be taught that the Earth was the common mother of them all; that they were therefore all brothers; but that some of them were golden and destined to rule, some were silver and destined for the army, and some were of iron or bronze and would neither rule nor fight. As to the first problem, the problem of finding the wise, that would have to be done through the most strenuous education.

They had built their imaginary state. It was ruled by the wise, defended by the brave, obeyed by those concerned with its material needs. These three functions were performed by specialized classes: golden Guardians, silver Auxiliaries, and the men made of baser metals. When each of the three classes performed well the function for which it was responsible, then, they decided, there was a just polis.

Turning from the polis to the single human being, Socrates and his colleagues in political sculpture saw the human intellect as corresponding to the ruling Guardians, with wisdom as its specific virtue; saw spirit, or drive, as corresponding to the Auxiliaries, with courage as its virtue; and saw the physical appetites as corresponding to the producing, exchanging, money-making class, with self-control as the specific virtue of the appetites. The man whose intellect governed his spirit or drive, as well as his physical appetites—the man, otherwise stated, who was wise and courageous and self-controlled—would be a just man who would choose to act justly, regardless of rewards and punishments, either in this life or another.

But how should these wise Guardians be educated? Most of this long night's conversation had been lighthearted, humorous, fanciful, free of literal-mindedness, part debate and part story-telling, emphatically not constitution-making of a schematic sort. But on the point of education for wisdom, Socrates grew earnest. He reminded his companions that they lived in two interpenetrating worlds, the world of things the physical eye could see by the light of the sun and the world of ideas which only the mind's eye could see—and then only by virtue of an intellectual light, shed by something he preferred to call the Idea of the Good. To educate Guardians wise enough to govern a polis was to help them to move freely between this visible world and that intelligible world—and thereby to find intelligibility in the concrete world they must deal with. An unprincipled man could not govern wisely; no man could deal with cases without knowing what they were cases of. Socrates now suggested, as so often, an analogy that might help his companions to intuit—in fact, an analogy that fruitfully burst forth into a cluster of analogies and proportions.

Imagine a line, he suggested, and divide it unequally, so that AB is to BC as AD is to DB and as BE is to EC. Let BC represent things the body's eye can see and let AB represent the things which only the mind's eye can see—the intelligibles. Imagine EC to represent only images and reflections, like the reflections in water and in mirrors. The objects they reflect, he suggested, the objects his companions called real, could be represented by BE. Now Socrates invited them to enter AB, the world of the intelligibles, the world of understanding—the world, he might have added, in which Oedipus saw more clearly once he had destroyed his physical eyesight. But that world, too, had a higher and a lower division. In DB there dwelt abstract ideas like triangle and circle—perfect triangularity and perfect circularity—which the intellect of the geometer had seized, or abstracted, from the imperfect triangles and circles the physical eye had seen in BE. The triangles in BE, however, were merely approximate and never permanent, because they were made out of changing matter. Those in DB were immaterial, eternal, perfect, unchanging. Such was the world of every mathematician. But the sciences which dealt with the eternal objects of DB all depended, as geometry did, on certain basic assumptions, certain axioms, which everybody took for granted.

Now he invited his audience to ascend to the last subdivision of the line

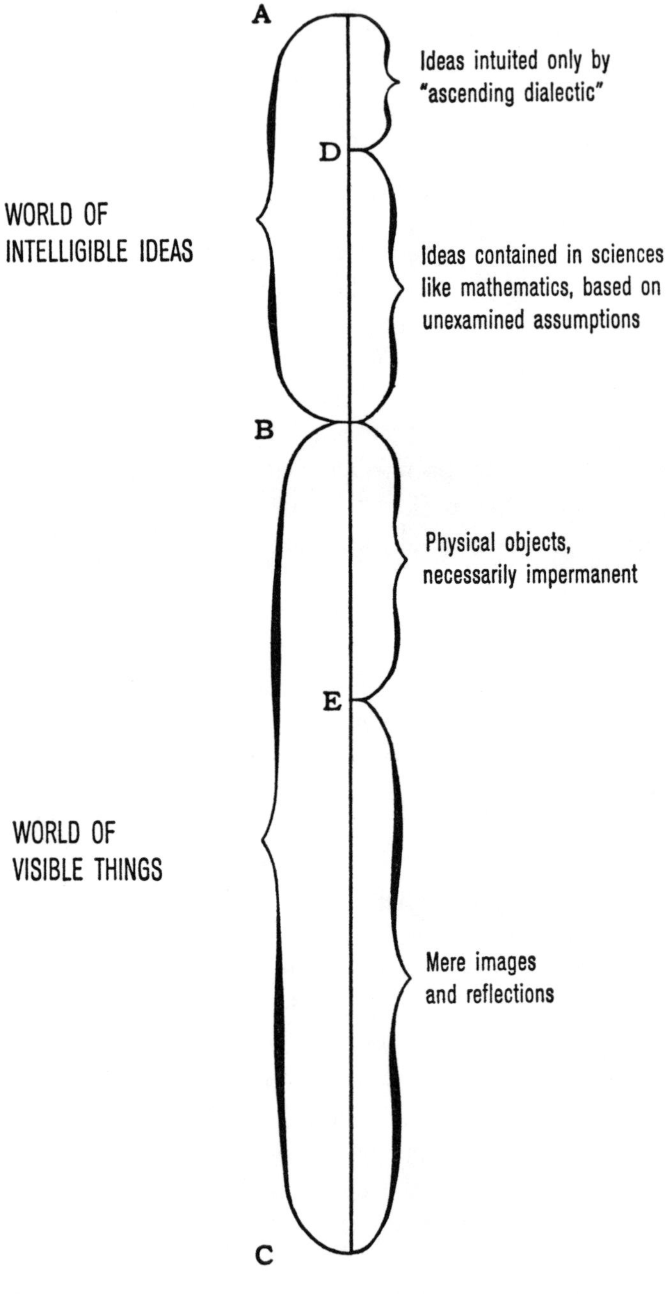

A

Ideas intuited only by
"ascending dialectic"

D

WORLD OF
INTELLIGIBLE IDEAS

Ideas contained in sciences
like mathematics, based on
unexamined assumptions

B

Physical objects,
necessarily impermanent

E

WORLD OF
VISIBLE THINGS

Mere images
and reflections

C

SOCRATES' "DIVIDED LINE"

he had imagined, a subdivision where the deductive logic of DB could not suffice, and where only dialectic could guide:

And when I speak of the other division of the intelligible, you will understand me to speak of that other sort of knowledge which reason herself attains by the power of dialectic, using the hypotheses not as first principles, but only as hypotheses—that is to say, as steps and points of departure into a world which is above hypotheses, in order that she may soar beyond them to the first principle of the whole; and clinging to this and then to that which depends on this, by successive steps she descends again without the aid of any sensible object, from ideas, through ideas, and in ideas she ends.[333]

Socrates' ladder that led from the world of sensory perception and unexamined opinion to the world of clear ideas and knowledge led toward truth itself, as another ladder he had described to the drunken Alcibiades and his fellow revelers led toward beauty itself. Glaucon thought he understood, though by no means perfectly. Glaucon, though he came of an aristocratic family, was a child of Periclean democracy, a society whose love of free speech and equality before the law was not unconnected with Socrates' willingness to talk with anybody who was willing to search, but a society which inevitably misled the ignorant into supposing that what they could not understand was not understandable. Had Glaucon, then, contracted from his master some of the art of listening that made it possible to learn, some of the intellectual courtesy that made Socrates formally assume that, when another man seemed to be talking nonsense, it was his, Socrates', fault that communication failed? And that the cure for such failure, whether one conversed with an apparent dolt or with Apollo himself, was to inquire further and find out if what seemed to have no sense could be important truth if only the riddling word, the dark saying, were understood in another sense? In any case, Glaucon continued now to listen. And, as if to rescue him from groping, Socrates shifted his figure of speech and cast down another ladder:

And now, I said, let me show in a figure how far our nature is enlightened or unenlightened:—Behold! human beings living in an underground den, which has a mouth open towards the light and reaching all along the den; here they have been from their childhood, and have their legs and necks chained so that they cannot move, and can only see before them, being prevented by the chains from turning round their heads. Above and behind them a fire is blazing at a distance, and between the fire and the prisoners there is a raised way; and you will see, if you look, a low wall built along the way, like the screen which marionette players have in front of them, over which they show the puppets.

I see.

And do you see, I said, men passing along the wall carrying all sorts of vessels, and statues and figures of animals made of wood and stone and various materials, which appear over the wall? Some of them are talking, others silent.

You have shown me a strange image, and they are strange prisoners.

Like ourselves, I replied; and they see only their own shadows, or the shadows of one another, which the fire throws on the opposite wall of the cave?

True, he said; how could they see anything but the shadows if they were never allowed to move their heads?

And of the objects which are being carried in like manner they would only see the shadows?

Yes, he said.

And if they were able to converse with one another, would they not suppose that they were naming what was actually before them?

Very true.

And suppose further that the prison had an echo which came from the other side, would they not be sure to fancy when one of the passers-by spoke that the voice which they heard came from the passing shadow?

No question, he replied.

To them, I said, the truth would be literally nothing but the shadows of the images.

That is certain.

And now look again, and see what will naturally follow if the prisoners are released and disabused of their error. At first, when any of them is liberated and compelled suddenly to stand up and turn his neck round and walk and look towards the light, he will suffer sharp pains; the glare will distress him, and he will be unable to see the realities of which in his former state he had seen the shadows; and then conceive some one saying to him, that what he saw before was an illusion, but that now, when he is approaching nearer to being and his eye is turned towards more real existence, he has a clearer vision,—what will be his reply? And you may further imagine that his instructor is pointing to the objects as they pass and requiring him to name them,—will he not be perplexed? Will he not fancy that the shadows which he formerly saw are truer than the objects which are now shown to him?

Far truer.

And if he is compelled to look straight at the light, will he not have a pain in his eyes which will make him turn away to take refuge in the objects of vision which he can see, and which he will conceive to be in reality clearer than the things which are now being shown to him?

True, he said.

And suppose once more, that he is reluctantly dragged up a steep and rugged ascent, and held fast until he is forced into the presence of the sun himself, is he not likely to be pained and irritated? When he approaches the light his eyes will be dazzled, and he will not be able to see anything at all of what are now called realities.

Not all in a moment, he said.

He will require to grow accustomed to the sight of the upper world. And first he will see the shadows best, next the reflections of men and other objects in the water, and then the objects themselves; then he will gaze upon the light of the moon and the stars and the spangled heaven; and he will see the sky and the stars by night better than the sun or the light of the sun by day?

Certainly.

Last of all he will be able to see the sun, and not mere reflections of him in the water, but he will see him in his own proper place, and not in another; and he will contemplate him as he is.

Certainly.

He will then proceed to argue that this is he who gives the season and the years, and is the guardian of all that is in the visible world, and in a certain way the cause of all things which he and his fellows have been accustomed to behold?

Clearly, he said, he would first see the sun and then reason about him.

And when he remembered his old habitation, and the wisdom of the den and his fellow-prisoners, do you not suppose that he would felicitate himself on the change, and pity them?

Certainly, he would.

And if they were in the habit of conferring honours among themselves on those who were quickest to observe the passing shadows and to remark which of them went before, and which followed after, and which were together; and who were therefore best able to draw conclusions as to the future, do you think that he would care for such honours and glories, or envy the possessors of them? Would he not say with Homer,

'Better to be the poor servant of a poor master,'

and to endure anything, rather than think as they do and live after their manner?

Yes, he said, I think that he would rather suffer anything than entertain these false notions and live in this miserable manner.

Imagine once more, I said, such an one coming suddenly out of the sun to be replaced in his old situation; would he not be certain to have his eyes full of darkness?

To be sure, he said.

And if there were a contest, and he had to compete in measuring the shadows with the prisoners who had never moved out of the den, while his sight was still weak, and before his eyes had become steady (and the time which would be needed to acquire this new habit of sight might be very considerable), would he not be ridiculous? Men would say of him that up he went and down he came without his eyes; and that it was better not even to think of ascending; and if any one tried to loose another and lead him up to the light, let them only catch the offender, and they would put him to death.

No question, he said.

This entire allegory, I said, you may now append, dear Glaucon, to the previous argument; the prison-house is the world of sight, the light of the fire is the sun, and you will not misapprehend me if you interpret the journey upwards to be the ascent of the soul into the intellectual world according to my poor belief, which, at your desire, I have expressed—whether rightly or wrongly God knows. But, whether true or false, my opinion is that in the world of knowledge the idea of good appears last of all, and is seen only with an effort; and, when seen, is also inferred to be the universal author of all things beautiful and right, parent of light and of the lord of light in this visible world, and the immediate source of reason and truth in the intellectual; and that this is the power upon which he who would act rationally either in public or private life must have his eye fixed.

I agree, he said, as far as I am able to understand you.

Moreover, I said, you must not wonder that those who attain to this beatific vision are unwilling to descend to human affairs; for their souls are ever hastening into the upper world where they desire to dwell; which desire of theirs is very natural, if our allegory may be trusted.

Yes, very natural.

And is there anything surprising in one who passes from divine contemplations to the evil state of man, misbehaving himself in a ridiculous manner; if, while his eyes are blinking and before he has become accustomed to the surrounding darkness, he is compelled to fight in courts of law, or in other places, about the images or the shadows of images of justice, and is endeavouring to meet the conceptions of those who have never yet seen absolute justice?

Anything but surprising, he replied.

Any one who has common sense will remember that the bewilderment of the eyes are of two kinds, and arise from two causes, either from coming out of the light or from going into the light, which is true of the mind's eye, quite as much as of the bodily eye; and he who remembers this when he sees any one whose vision is perplexed and weak, will not be too ready to laugh; he will first ask whether that soul of man has come out of the brighter life, and is unable to see because unaccustomed to the dark, or having turned from darkness to the day is dazzled by excess of light. And he will count the one happy in his condition and state of being, and he will pity the other; or, if he have a mind to laugh at the soul which comes from below into the light, there will be more reason in this than in the laugh which greets him who returns from above out of the light into the den.

That, he said, is a very just distinction.

But then, if I am right, certain professors of education must be wrong when they say that they can put a knowledge into the soul which was not there before, like sight into blind eyes.

They undoubtedly say this, he replied.

Whereas, our argument shows that the power and capacity of learning exists in the soul already; and that just as the eye was unable to turn from darkness to light without the whole body, so too the instrument of knowledge can only by the movement of the whole soul be turned from the world of becoming into that of being, and learn by degrees to endure the sight of being, and of the brightest and best of being, or in other words, of the good.

Very true.

And must there not be some art which will effect conversion in the easiest and quickest manner; not implanting the faculty of sight, for that exists already, but has been turned in the wrong direction, and is looking away from the truth?

Yes, he said, such an art may be presumed.

And whereas the other so-called virtues of the soul seem to be akin to bodily qualities, for even when they are not originally innate they can be implanted later by habit and exercise, the virtue of wisdom more than anything else contains a divine element which always remains, and by this conversion is rendered useful and profitable; or, on the other hand, hurtful and useless. Did you never observe the narrow intelligence flashing from the keen eye of a clever rogue—how eager he is, how clearly his paltry soul sees the way to his end; he is the reverse of blind, but his keen eye-sight is forced into the service of evil, and he is mischievous in proportion to his cleverness.

Very true, he said.

But what if there had been a circumcision of such natures in the days of their youth; and they had been severed from those sensual pleasures, such as eating and drinking, which, like leaden weights, were attached to them at their birth, and which drag them down and turn the vision of their souls upon the things that are below—if, I say, they had been released from these impediments and turned in the opposite direction, the very same faculty in them would have seen the truth as keenly as they see what their eyes are turned to now.

Very likely.

Yes, I said; and there is another thing which is likely, or rather a necessary inference from what has preceded, that neither the uneducated and uninformed of the truth, nor yet those who never make an end of their education, will be able ministers of State; not the former, because they have no single aim of duty which is the rule of all their actions, private as well as public; nor the latter, because they will not act at all except upon compulsion, fancying that they are already dwelling apart in the islands of the blest.

Very true, he replied.

Then, I said, the business of us who are the founders of the State will be to compel the best minds to attain that knowledge which we have already shown to be the greatest of all—they must continue to ascend until they arrive at the good; but when they have ascended and seen enough we must not allow them to do as they do now.

What do you mean?

I mean that they remain in the upper world: but this must not be allowed; they must be made to descend again among the prisoners in the den, and partake of their labours and honours, whether they are worth having or not.[334]

Each of the Guardians of the Republic, each of the future rulers of the polis they were imagining, must somehow in his education be "liberated

278

and compelled suddenly to stand up and turn his neck round and walk and look towards the light." This turning round, this conversion, was the essence of liberal education. Compared with the practical instruction the famous sophists were offering to would-be politicians and exhibitionistic young gentlemen, Socrates' words were the words of a mystic. What was this invisible world? Was it there that he went during those fits of abstraction like the one at Potidaea? Was he really lost in thought? Or merely trying not to be lost in feckless action, merely trying to find himself—or, in the words inscribed at Delphi, to know himself? If the Guardians would also know themselves, they must come out of the underground den and begin to see things in their true light. Already taught to listen by music and poetry, already toughened by strenuous gymnastic, they must now enter the difficult world of the intelligibles—not yet its subdivision where dialectic would be learned but that less arduous area, the mathematical sciences. When they had learned there to deal skillfully with such easily abstracted ideas as triangle and circle, there would be time—say, when they were thirty—to pass upward to the much more difficult abstractions, like man, or polis, or justice.

But even when men who had undergone long training in both mind and body should have been magically placed in power in this polis Socrates had imagined, the ideal polis could not hope to endure. The aristocracy of the wise and brave would degenerate into a timocracy; the lover of wisdom would yield place to the lover of *timē*, honor. In effect, the gold men would yield authority to the silver, the philosophers to the soldiers. And these silver men, lacking wisdom, would slowly discover the delights of private property, of money, of faction—as indeed the timocrats of seventh-century Hellas, who of course called themselves aristocrats, had turned to money; then timocracy would yield to oligarchy, or rule by the Oligoi, the few—which in practice would mean the rich. Socrates had that very evening pointed out[335] that not a single Greek polis of his day was actually one polis. It was two: the polis of the rich and the polis of the poor. The oligarchy, with or without civil war or foreign intervention, would in the end give way to democracy. And, where the principles of oligarchy were thrift and avarice, the principles of democracy were liberty and pleasure. Democracy hated discipline and authority. Socrates remarked:

> By degrees the anarchy finds a way into private houses, and ends by getting among the animals and infecting them.

How do you mean?

I mean that the father grows accustomed to descend to the level of his sons and to fear them, and the son is on a level with his father, he having no respect or reverence for either of his parents; and this is his freedom, and the metic is equal with the citizen and the citizen with the metic, and the stranger is quite as good as either.

Yes, he said, that is the way.

And these are not the only evils, I said—there are several lesser ones: In such a state of society the master fears and flatters his scholars, and the scholars despise their masters and tutors; young and old are all alike; and the young man is on a level with the old, and is ready to compete with him in word or deed; and old men condescend to the young and are full of pleasantry and gaiety; they are loth to be thought morose and authoritative, and therefore they adopt the manners of the young.

Quite true, he said.

The last extreme of popular liberty is when the slave bought with money, whether male or female, is just as free as his or her purchaser; nor must I forget to tell of the liberty and equality of the two sexes in relation to each other.

Why not, as Aeschylus says, utter the word which rises to our lips?

That is what I am doing, I replied; and I must add that no one who does not know would believe, how much greater is the liberty which the animals who are under the dominion of man have in a democracy than in any other State: for truly, the she-dogs, as the proverb says, are as good as their she-mistresses, and the horses and asses have a way of marching along with all the rights and dignities of freemen; and they will run at any body who comes in their way if he does not leave the road clear for them: and all things are just ready to burst with liberty.

When I take a country walk, he said, I often experience what you describe. You and I have dreamed the same thing.

And above all, I said, and as the result of all, see how sensitive the citizens become; they chafe impatiently at the least touch of authority and at length, as you know, they cease to care even for the laws, written or unwritten; they will have no one over them.

Yes, he said, I know it too well.

Such, my friend, I said, is the fair and glorious beginning out of which springs tyranny.[336]

Socrates now proceeded to give a hideously accurate picture of the cruelty and violence that tyranny did often bring. The tyrant was a man who made the interest of the stronger serve for justice, and he was wretched. So were his enslaved fellow citizens. No, the happy polis was the just polis; and the happy man, the just man. Of this wise man he spoke:

He will look at the city which is within him, and take heed that no disorder occur in it, such as might arise either from superfluity or from want; and upon this principle he will regulate his property and gain or spend according to his means.

Very true.

And, for the same reason, he will gladly accept and enjoy such honours as he deems likely to make him a better man; but those, whether private or public, which are likely to disorder his life, he will avoid?

Then, if that is his motive, he will not be a statesman.

By the dog of Egypt, he will! in the city which is his own he certainly will, though in the land of his birth perhaps not, unless he have a divine call.

I understand; you mean that he will be a ruler in the city of which we are the founders, and which exists in idea only; for I do not believe that there is such an one anywhere on earth?

In heaven, I replied, there is laid up a pattern of it, methinks, which he who desires may behold, and beholding, may set his own house in order. But whether such an one exists, or ever will exist in fact, is no matter; for he will live after the manner of that city, having nothing to do with any other.

I think so, he said.[337]

The long discussion was ending. Socrates had convinced his hearers that treating others unjustly made one even unhappier than being treated unjustly by them; that, whether or not there was an after-life with rewards and punishments, the just life was the happier life here and now. But having convinced them, he chose to assume that the soul of man was indeed immortal. He did not try to prove it: on more than one occasion he made it clear that he knew no proof, but only signs and evidence. So now, instead of presenting an argument, he told a tale, to finish off the evening. A man named Er, a Pamphylian, had been slain in battle, but his body did not decay, and ten days after he died he returned to life and told his friends what he had seen in that other world. A kind of purgatory he had seen; he had seen the mouth of a kind of hell; from other souls he had heard news of a kind of heaven, where there were visions of inconceivable beauty.

The evening at the Piraeus ended. Socrates had imagined a kind of polis, a kind of human community, that he had never seen except with the mind's eye. Would it ever exist? One had no proof that it was impossible.[338] But neither was it likely. Meanwhile, as he observed to Glaucon, there was one thing a man could do, even in a most imperfect polis. He could order that city within him, his own soul, after the pattern laid up in heaven of the polis they had just imagined.

During these same years, Socrates' friend, Aristophanes, was having his say, too, on man and his polis. The very year after he and Socrates banqueted at Agathon's and heard the drunken Alcibiades declare his subjection to Socrates, the comic poet presented the *Birds*. With Nicias besieging Syracuse and with Athens dreaming of conquests that would cut off Sicilian and Italian grain from her enemies in Peloponnese, Aristophanes imagined two Athenian rogues founding Cloudcuckooland in the sky, a city of birds, a pattern laid up in heaven by two ridiculous, cowardly clowns, where the animal appetites could rule supreme, unhampered by reason and wisdom. This delightful polis intercepted the smoke that rose from men's sacrifices to satisfy the gods. So the gods were quickly reduced by famine and one of the Athenian rogues received as his bride a beautiful young woman, Basileia, or Sovereignty, who made Zeus's lightning bolts for him. Their marriage would place him on the throne of Zeus.

So much for a heavenly city far from the wise and virtuous community Socrates would imagine for Glaucon and his other friends. But by the time Socrates and Glaucon had imagined their just polis, Aristophanes presented another utopia, this time his own Athens, but an Athens in which a woman named Lysistrata had persuaded the women of Hellas to stop sleeping with their husbands until their husbands should put an end to the Great War. And in 392, when Socrates was dead, Aristophanes built still another imaginary polis, the *Ecclesiazusae*, in which women ruled instead of men and property was held in common.

By then, Euripides, whom Aristophanes and the other comic poets mocked so often for his newfangled tragedies, had withdrawn from Athens, which never till after his death was generous with prizes for his drama. About four years before the fall of Athens, Euripides left for Magnesia in Thessaly and then for the court of King Archelaus in Macedonia, where he wrote his *Bacchae*. There he shortly died, some two years before Lysander laid the Long Walls of Athens low and made the School of Hellas subject to Sparta.

Democracy had fallen. The exiled or refugee oligarchs swarmed joyfully home. Theramenes, the moderate, who had established in 411 a moderate constitution only to see an Athenian victory the next year at Cyzicus restore the old democratic constitution, now tried again. His party combined with the extreme oligarchs who had returned from exile. Their leader Critias had been one of Socrates' companions, a disciple of the Sicilian sophist Gorgias, an orator and poet. Cowed by their brutal conqueror, Lysander, the Athenian Assembly voted to establish a provisional government of thirty men, charged with establishing a constitution and meanwhile governing Athens. Each of Athens' ten tribes would supply three men, one chosen by Critias, one chosen by Theramenes, and one by the Assembly. In the summer or fall of 404, the Thirty were chosen. Technically, Athens was again a sovereign state, while the cities subject to her, despite Brasidas' promises of liberation and autonomy, were now governed by small groups of vengeful oligarchs, generally committees of ten called decarchies, chosen by Lysander. But when Lysander had seen the Thirty safely installed and the rest of the Long Walls and the walls around Athens and Piraeus pulled down, and when he had set forth with his fleet for a triumphant return to Sparta, he took all but twelve of Athens' warships with him. Then the Thirty, to make sure of their rule, managed to secure a Spartan garrison, which they undertook to maintain until, as they said, "they could put the 'scoundrels' out of the way and establish their government."[339]

Critias and his extremists promptly turned the Thirty into an engine of terror. At first they arrested and executed the political informers under the previous democracy and other men hateful even to the democrats. Then they began killing men for no reason other than their support of the democracy which had exiled Critias. His moderate colleague, Theramenes, demurred. When the extremists began to kill from personal enmity or merely to confiscate property, the strain between Critias and Theramenes increased. The extremists even made up a list of metics, or resident aliens, to kill and despoil, among them one Leon of Salamis. To implicate as many citizens as possible in their crimes and thereby give their terrified subjects a motive for supporting them, they ordered groups of citizens to arrest these innocent metics. Socrates was one of five citizens ordered to produce Leon. Socrates refused. And Critias did not punish him. In a few months, according to later reports, 1,500 victims met their death; 5,000 others were banished.

Of the moderates among the Thirty, Theramenes alone dared protest publicly against Critias and his terror. He counted on persuading the newly created Council to back him up in his demand that the Thirty produce their constitution and end their interim government. In October, 404, by a show of force, Critias frightened the Council into striking Theramenes' name from the list of citizens. Then the Thirty condemned him to death. The executioner handed him the cup of poison. He threw out the last drops, exclaiming: "Here's to the health of the noble Critias!"[340] One of the young Athenians who backed the provisional government until its violence and injustice alienated them later reported the death of Theramenes and added: "I deem it admirable in the man that when death was close at hand, neither self-possession nor the spirit of playfulness departed from his soul."[341] In that same autumn, the exiled Alcibiades was hunted down in Asia Minor and slain.

Meanwhile, a group of exiled Athenian democrats were gathering in Thebes, under the leadership of Thrasybulus, one of the heroes of the Athenian naval victory of Cynossema seven years earlier. Other refugees from the terror in Athens were in Corinth and Megara. All these cities had fought alongside Sparta against democratic, imperialist Athens. But Sparta's high-handed refusal to share the spoils of their joint victory, combined perhaps with the tales of horror coming out of prostrate Athens, predisposed them to shelter the intended victims of the Thirty. In December, 404, Thrasybulus set out from Thebes with a little band of seventy intrepid exiles and seized a mountain fortress on the Athenian frontier. The Thirty tried to reduce it, but a violent snowstorm caused them to withdraw to Athens. From all sides volunteers now poured in to Thrasybulus. The Thirty sent against them the Spartan garrison and two squadrons of cavalry, only to have these forces ambushed by night. Thrasybulus killed 120 of them and, best of all, seized provisions and the arms of the fallen. The Thirty next sent an offer to Thrasybulus to join their government. He refused. With opinion at Athens rising against them, the Thirty seized Eleusis and Salamis as refuges in case they were driven from Athens. Meanwhile they evacuated from Athens to Piraeus some 5,000 men not of their party. Thrasybulus and his force promptly joined the 5,000 there and took possession of the heights of Munychia.

Every city in Hellas, Socrates had once said on an evening in the Piraeus, near where Thrasybulus' army of exiled democrats stood, was not one city, but two: a city of the rich and a city of the poor. That had become cruelly apparent at Corcyra, at the beginning of the long war which had ended a year ago. During that war city after city had split into two cities, the poor turning to Athens for help, the rich, to Sparta. In Athens, Pericles had held the two cities together. Even after his death, when Nicias timidly led one city and Cleon the other, the struggle between them had remained a battle of words, often eristic and violent words, in the Assembly, not of weapons in the Agora. After the frightful disaster at Syracuse, when the subject cities of the Athenian Empire revolted, the strain in Athens increased. In 411, the democratic Assembly had been persuaded, at least for the duration of the war, to establish an oligarchic government. The extremists in that government appealed to Sparta for help. There was disorder; there was even political murder. But the oligarchic government lost Euboea; a moderate democracy took its place; and the extreme oligarchs fled to Decelea, the Attic fortress the Spartans then held. Thrasybulus' naval victory at Cynossema and the overwhelming victory which he and Theramenes and Alcibiades won the next year off Cyzicus enabled the democrats to upset Theramenes' moderate government and restore full democracy. The extreme oligarchs had now executed Theramenes at Athens, had perhaps caused the murder of Alcibiades in Asia Minor, and watched from Athens, the city of the rich, while Thrasybulus and his city of the poor held that hill in Piraeus.

Critias led his city of the rich against Munychia, and stormed up the hill. But his forces were badly defeated and he himself was slain. When a truce was declared so that the two armies might gather up their dead, some men from both sides fraternized. Then, reported Xenophon, one of Thrasybulus' men cried out to those from Athens:

Fellow Citizens, why do you drive us out of the city? why do you wish to kill us? For we never did you any harm, but we have shared with you in the most solemn rites and sacrifices and the most splendid festivals, we have been companions in the dance and schoolmates and comrades in arms, and we have braved many dangers with you both by land and by sea in defence of the common safety and freedom of us both. In

285

the name of the gods of our fathers and mothers, in the name of our ties of kinship and marriage and comradeship,—for all these many of us share with one another,—cease, out of shame before gods and men, to sin against your fatherland, and do not obey those most accursed Thirty, who for the sake of their private gain have killed in eight months more Athenians, almost, than all the Peloponnesians in ten years of war. And when we might live in peace as fellow citizens, these men bring upon us war with one another, a war most utterly shameful and intolerable, utterly unholy and hated by both gods and men. Yet for all that, be well assured that for some of those now slain by our hands not only you, but we also, have wept bitterly.[342]

Those who listened, over the bodies of their common dead, were hastily marshaled back to Athens by their oligarchic officers, but it was too late. Opinion in Athens now sharply divided those who were afraid of punishment for their crimes if the Thirty were deposed from those who were sick of the Thirty and of their unbridled, cynical violence. The Thirty were voted out. Their worst violence had lasted eight months. Some of the extremists who had followed Critias then withdrew to Eleusis. There they composed an epitaph for Critias and the other oligarchs who had fallen at Munychia: "In memory of the brave men who once lanced the swollen pride of the damned democrats at Athens."[343]

The civil war between oligarchic Athens and democratic Piraeus continued, with metics, other foreigners, and even slaves joining Thrasybulus' democratic army, and with Athens' communications increasingly difficult. In despair, Athens and extremist Eleusis sent an appeal to Lysander. But the Ephors of Sparta declined to rescue those who had perpetrated the notorious terror at Athens. They sent one of their two kings, who bore the famous name Pausanias, and Pausanias set to work to reconcile the moderates in the Athenian Assembly with the motley army of democrats under Thrasybulus at Piraeus. By August, 403, he had succeeded. A general amnesty was declared. It excluded only the Thirty and a few others. Then Pausanias discreetly withdrew from Athens. On September 2, 403, the men from Piraeus returned to Athens, went up to the Acropolis, and offered sacrifice to Athena. When a united Assembly had been convoked, Thrasybulus read the terms of agreement and they were unanimously sworn to. Then he offered some advice, both to his late enemies, the city of the rich, and to his own city of the poor, now reunited with their goddess and their common polis:

"I advise you," he said, "men of the city, to 'know yourselves.' And you would best learn to know yourselves were you to consider what grounds you have for arrogance, that you should undertake to rule over us. Are you more just? But the commons, though poorer than you, never did you any wrong for the sake of money; while you, though richer than any of them, have done many disgraceful things for the sake of gain. But since you can lay no claim to justice, consider then whether it is courage that you have a right to pride yourselves upon. And what better test could there be of this than the way we made war upon one another? Well then, would you say that you are superior in intelligence, you who having a wall, arms, money, and the Peloponnesians as allies, have been worsted by men who had none of these? Is it the Lacedaemonians, then, think you, that you may pride yourselves upon? How so? Why, they have delivered you up to this outraged populace, just as men fasten a clog upon the necks of snapping dogs and deliver them up to keepers, and now have gone away and left you. Nevertheless, my comrades, I am not the man to ask you to violate any one of the pledges to which you have sworn, but I ask you rather to show this virtue also, in addition to your other virtues,—that you are true to your oaths and are god-fearing men. . . ."[344]

The reconciliation proved extraordinary. Athens' love of free speech, her long tradition of equality before the law, her civilized manners, her skill and wise political compromise, her gift for commerce and industry magically revived. It was as if the vast tragedy which Thucydides described had brought her the Aeschylean wisdom that only suffering could bring. The tyrant-state that Pericles' clear eyes had seen in his beloved polis had been deposed: Sparta was tyrant now, a far harsher and more irresponsible tyrant than Athens had ever been, except at rare moments and in a few places. What remained was Pericles' other image, the School of Hellas, that and a conscious effort to get back to the laws of Solon, which sought to build a just polis, a common home for all free men, for rich and poor alike.

It was in this restored and chastened democracy, in this reconciled polis, that a charge was preferred against Socrates by a rich tanner named Anytus. He was a partisan of the moderate oligarch, Theramenes, whom the brutal

Critias had liquidated, and had played a leading role in the great reconciliation. He was deeply convinced that back of Athens' military catastrophe, back of her recent political disintegration, lay a religious and
moral decline. He was convinced that for that decline the atheistic natural
philosophers and morally skeptical sophists were largely responsible. Here
was Socrates, whom all the comic poets, not just Aristophanes, had
lampooned as an eccentric sophist. Socrates had once advised this tanner
not to confine his son's education to hides.[345] What was wrong, Anytus
had wanted to know, with this boy's taking over a business his father's
father had run before him? But Socrates' young men were always criticiz-
ing their elders. And who had his disciples been? A Critias, of all the
Thirty the greediest and most violent. An Alcibiades, licentious, insolent,
sacrilegious, traitor to his country. A Charmides, who had aided Critias
and had fallen when Critias fell in the unsuccessful attempt to storm the
hill that Thrasybulus held at the Piraeus.

Anytus left the formal prosecution to Meletus, an unsuccessful tragic
poet,[346] who had been angered[347] by Socrates' comments on poets and poetry. The indictment read to this effect: "Socrates is guilty of rejecting the
gods acknowledged by the state and of bringing in strange deities: he is
also guilty of corrupting the youth."[348] The penalty proposed was death.
It soon became apparent that the object of the indictment was not to
take Socrates' life; it was to frighten him into withdrawing from Athens
and accepting exile. The trial took place in February, 399, before a tribunal
of 501 citizen judges. Among those present were a number of Socrates'
most devoted disciples, and among these disciples was a young aristocrat
named Plato, still under thirty, who would later report his master's speech
in his own defense.

The great ironist had rarely faced a more deeply ironical situation. His
judges assumed that they were judging him, and Socrates was completely
aware that the case was judging them. His judges were trying to determine his relation to the gods of their polis: Socrates was well known for
his piety, yet he constantly raised questions which his judges might well
deem impious. Under cross-examination, of the usual Socratic variety, he
easily led Meletus on the one hand to accuse him of being a complete
atheist and on the other of believing in new gods—but gods just the same.
So he brushed the accusation aside. He had always insisted that he did
not teach, since he laid no claim to knowledge. If lectures by sophists were

teaching, he of course spoke the truth; but his midwifery of ideas was a far more powerful form of teaching, and he knew it. Indeed, at one point in his speech, he dropped that particular irony and stated calmly that he would always practice and teach philosophy, a word which in the Greek he spoke meant, at least etymologically, not the wisdom, or *sophia*, that so many sophists professed to teach, but the love of wisdom.

Then this indicted atheist announced:

> For I do nothing but go about persuading you all, old and young alike, not to take thought for your persons or your properties, but first and chiefly to care about the greatest improvement of the soul. I tell you that virtue is not given by money, but that from virtue comes money and every other good of man, public as well as private. This is my teaching, and if this is the doctrine which corrupts the youth, I am a mischievous person. But if any one says that this is not my teaching, he is speaking an untruth. Wherefore, O men of Athens, I say to you, do as Anytus bids or not as Anytus bids, and either acquit me or not; but whichever you do, understand that I shall never alter my ways, not even if I have to die many times.[349]

That statement caused such a stir that he had to request his judges not to interrupt him. He continued:

> And now, Athenians, I am not going to argue for my own sake, as you may think, but for yours, that you may not sin against the God by condemning me, who am his gift to you. For if you kill me you will not easily find a successor to me, who, if I may use such a ludicrous figure of speech, am a sort of gadfly, given to the state by God; and the state is a great and noble steed who is tardy in his motions owing to his very size, and requires to be stirred into life. I am that gadfly which God has attached to the state, and all day long and in all places am always fastening upon you, arousing and persuading and reproaching you. You will not easily find another like me, and therefore I would advise you to spare me.[350]

He spoke of his military service to the state, only to make the point that he ought not here in court any more than in battle to fear death. He reminded his judges that, after the battle off Arginusae seven years before, in the days of the democracy, when they wanted to try the generals in a batch and therefore illegally, he alone had refused to vote to submit their cases to the Assembly in that form. He reminded them that, in the later days of the oligarchy, when the Thirty had ordered him and four others to arrest Leon of Salamis, he alone had risked his life by refusing.

Then he switched back to a meaning of the word teach that he was fond of and, in a context that made his meaning clear, stated that he never taught or professed to teach anybody: he conversed with people, with anybody who wanted to converse with him. He identified companions of his in the court and challenged his accusers to produce a witness who could testify to his having morally damaged some youth.

He reminded his judges that sometimes the accused produced his children or relations in court to weep and thereby move the judges. He had a wife, too, and three sons, one almost a man and two small ones, but he felt that leading them in now would be "discreditable to myself, and to you, and to the whole state."[351] It was not his function as the accused to ask a favor of the judges; it was his function to inform and convince them. It was their function "not to make a present of justice, but to give judgment."[352] They had sworn to the gods to do justice; and if— the old irony returning like bubbling waters from some inexhaustible spring—

> if, O men of Athens, by force of persuasion and entreaty I could over-power your oaths, then I should be teaching you to believe that there are no gods, and in defending should simply convict myself of the charge, of not believing in them. But that is not so—far otherwise. For I do believe that there are gods, and in a sense higher than that in which any of my accusers believe in them. And to you and to God I commit my cause, to be determined by you as is best for you and me.[353]

The judges prepared to vote. Were his friends in the court moved by his running so true to form? He had been calm, humorous, gentle in his personal behavior, but his line of argument had been as rigorous, as inexorable, as disquieting as always. His accusers had hoped he would flee Athens before his trial came up. He had not only stayed. He had forced his judges to face up to the issue. He had forced them to make a genuine choice. For it was his accusers, not he, who wanted to evade the issue, who wanted not to choose, who merely wanted the gadfly to go away and stop stinging. He had encountered them physically in court and he had done his best to encounter their minds there as well. He showed no signs of wanting to die, although the young Xenophon, who loved and admired him but who was absent in Asia Minor, would later guess in his own, secondhand account of the trial, that, being now around seventy, Socrates dreaded grievous old age and wanted to die. If his judges should now vote him innocent, he would know that the trial had taught them something, about law, about a polis, about membership in a polis. That would be a triumph, not because he feared to cease living physically, but because learning and thinking were always a triumph for man.

The judges voted by 281 to 220 that he was guilty. Under Athenian law he was now required to propose a penalty alternative to the one Meletus had proposed. Legally, the judges must choose one of the two penalties proposed. If he proposed one that showed a little contrition, 31 votes might shift in his direction and he would escape death. This would be his last chance. But the irony of the trial continued: on his own premises, it was his judges who should be given one last chance—to see the point, and so in effect to reverse an unjust decision.

Socrates gave them that last chance:

> Reflecting that I was really too honest a man to be a politician and live, I did not go where I could do no good to you or to myself; but where I could do the greatest good privately to every one of you, thither I went, and sought to persuade every man among you that he must look to himself, and seek virtue and wisdom before he looks to his private interests, and look to the state before he looks to the interests of the state; and that this should be the order which he observes in all his actions. What shall be done to such an one? Doubtless some good thing, O men of Athens, if he has his reward; and the good should be of a kind suitable to him. What would be a reward suitable to a poor man who is your benefactor, and who desires leisure that he may instruct you?[354]

The answer: free meals at the expense of the polis—a reward sometimes given to citizens who had deserved well of their country. Nor, he hastened to add, was he trying to be impudent, any more than when he refused to bring his family to court to weep and beg for mercy. He was merely trying to state truthfully what he, Socrates, considered a just penalty, or rather a just return for what he had actually done. He was, he went on, not afraid of death, since he did not have knowledge of what followed this present life. Would the just penalty be imprisonment? But why? A fine? He had no money. Exile? If Athens could not tolerate him, what other polis would? Unless, of course, he stopped examining himself and others:

but precisely this sort of inquiry was the greatest good of man and, besides, "the unexamined life is not worth living."[355] Then he said:

> Well, perhaps I could afford a mina, and therefore I propose that penalty: Plato, Crito, Critobulus, and Apollodorus, my friends here, bid me say thirty minae, and they will be the sureties. Let thirty minae be the penalty; for which sum they will be ample security to you.[356]

It was as if he had relented and had offered to join a game that children were playing, rather than appear to them incomprehensibly obstinate.

The judges again sustained his accuser, this time by a larger vote: 360 to 141. His companions, who had tried to purchase his life, recognized this sort of outcome from long experience: his persistent return to what he regarded as the true issue had once more aroused anger.

A third time he spoke. He prophesied to those who had voted his death that they would get the polis an evil name by killing him. And he informed them that by pleading his case in the manner they would have approved he could have escaped death.

> The difficulty, my friends, is not to avoid death, but to avoid unrighteousness; for that runs faster than death. I am old and move slowly, and the slower runner has overtaken me, and my accusers are keen and quick, and the faster runner, who is unrighteousness, has overtaken them. And now I depart hence condemned by you to suffer the penalty of death,—they too go their ways condemned by the truth to suffer the penalty of villainy and wrong; and I must abide by my award—let them abide by theirs. I suppose that these things may be regarded as fated,—and I think that they are well.[357]

To those who voted for his acquittal he wanted to show "the meaning of this event"[358]—he who had always sought for meaning. He told them that the divine sign within him, which had so often checked him from some word or deed, had today not checked him once. And as to death, if it was not merely an eternal sleep, it might lead him to another place where he could converse with Orpheus, Hesiod, Homer, Ajax, Agamemnon, and Odysseus.

> What infinite delight would there be in conversing with them and asking them questions! In another world they do not put a man to death for asking questions: assuredly not. . . . I am not angry with my condemners, or with my accusers; they have done me no harm, although they did

not mean to do me any good; and for this I may gently blame them. . . .

The hour of departure has arrived, and we go our ways—I to die, and you to live. Which is better God only knows.[859]

But he could not legally be executed until a sacred ship which had been sent to Apollo's Isle of Delos should return. In his prison cell, his devoted friend Crito tried to persuade Socrates to let him bribe his jailers and spirit him away to friends of Crito's in Thessaly. Desperately Crito advanced every conceivable argument, and Socrates—questioned him, of course. The arguments would not stand up. Granted that the judges who voted him guilty had done evil, he himself could not escape now without breaking the laws of his polis. Should he, too, do evil? The distraught Crito yielded.

On his last day a group of devoted companions visited his cell and they argued the day away on the subject of immortality. Once more, according to Phaedo's eye-witness account to Echecrates, he let down his ladder of analogies, not to prove anything but to provoke insights. Once more he charmed them with poetic myth. It was clear that he had faith in the immortality of the soul. It was equally clear that he knew of no way to construct a logical proof of immortality:

A man of sense ought not to say, nor will I be very confident, that the description which I have given of the soul and her mansions is exactly true. But I do say that, inasmuch as the soul is shown to be immortal, he may venture to think, not improperly or unworthily, that something of the kind is true. The venture is a glorious one, and he ought to comfort himself with words like these, which is the reason why I lengthen out the tale. Wherefore, I say, let a man be of good cheer about his soul, who having cast away the pleasures and ornaments of the body as alien to him and working harm rather than good, has sought after the pleasures of knowledge; and has arrayed the soul, not in some foreign attire, but in her own proper jewels, temperance, and justice, and courage, and nobility, and truth—in these adorned she is ready to go on her journey to the world below, when her hour comes. You, Simmias and Cebes, and all other men, will depart at some time or other. Me already, as a tragic poet would say, the voice of fate calls. Soon I must drink the poison; and I think that I had better repair to the bath first, in order that the women may not have the trouble of washing my body after I am dead.

When he had done speaking, Crito said: And have you any commands for us, Socrates—anything to say about your children, or any other matter in which we can serve you?

Nothing particular, Crito, he replied: only, as I have always told you, take care of yourselves; that is a service which you may be ever rendering to me and mine and to all of us, whether you promise to do so or not. But if you have no thought for yourselves, and care not to walk according to the rule which I have prescribed for you, not now for the first time, however much you may profess or promise at the moment, it will be of no avail.

We will do our best, said Crito: And in what way shall we bury you?

In any way that you like; but you must get hold of me, and take care that I do not run away from you. Then he turned to us, and added with a smile:—I cannot make Crito believe that I am the same Socrates who have been talking and conducting the argument; he fancies that I am the other Socrates whom he will soon see, a dead body—and he asks, How shall he bury me? And though I have spoken many words in the endeavour to show that when I have drunk the poison I shall leave you and go to the joys of the blessed,—these words of mine, with which I was comforting you and myself, have had, as I perceive, no effect upon Crito. And therefore I want you to be surety for me to him now, as at the trial he was surety to the judges for me: but let the promise be of another sort; for he was surety for me to the judges that I would remain, and you must be my surety to him that I shall not remain, but go away and depart; and then he will suffer less at my death, and not be grieved when he sees my body being burned or buried. I would not have him sorrow at my hard lot, or say at the burial, Thus we lay out Socrates, or, Thus we follow him to the grave or bury him; for false words are not only evil in themselves, but they infect the soul with evil. Be of good cheer then, my dear Crito, and say that you are burying my body only, and do with that whatever is usual, and what you think best.

When he had spoken these words, he arose and went into a chamber to bathe; Crito followed him and told us to wait. So we remained behind, talking and thinking of the subject of discourse, and also of the greatness of our sorrow; he was like a father of whom we were being bereaved, and we were about to pass the rest of our lives as orphans. When he had taken the bath his children were brought to him—(he had two young sons and an elder one); and the women of his family also came, and he talked to them and gave them a few directions in the presence of Crito; then he dismissed them and returned to us.

Now the hour of sunset was near, for a good deal of time had passed while he was within. When he came out, he sat down with us again after his bath, but not much was said. Soon the jailer, who was the servant of the Eleven, entered and stood by him, saying:—To you, Socrates, whom I know to be the noblest and gentlest and best of all who ever came to this place, I will not impute the angry feelings of other men, who rage and swear at me, when, in obedience to the authorities, I bid them drink the poison—indeed, I am sure that you will not be angry with me; for others, as you are aware, and not I, are to blame. And so fare you well, and try to bear lightly what must needs be— you know my errand. Then bursting into tears he turned away and went out.

Socrates looked at him and said: I return your good wishes, and will do as you bid. Then turning to us, he said, How charming the man is: since I have been in prison he has always been coming to see me, and at times he would talk to me, and was as good to me as could be, and now see how generously he sorrows on my account. We must do as he says, Crito; and therefore let the cup be brought, if the poison is prepared: if not, let the attendant prepare some.

Yet, said Crito, the sun is still upon the hill-tops, and I know that many a one has taken the draught late, and after the announcement has been made to him, he has eaten and drunk, and enjoyed the society of his beloved; do not hurry—there is time enough.

Socrates said: Yes, Crito, and they of whom you speak are right in so acting, for they think that they will be the gainers by the delay; but I am right in not following their example, for I do not think that I should gain anything by drinking the poison a little later; I should only be ridiculous in my own eyes for sparing and saving a life which is already forfeit. Please then to do as I say, and not to refuse me.

Crito made a sign to the servant, who was standing by; and he went out, and having been absent for some time, returned with the jailer carrying the cup of poison. Socrates said: You, my good friend, who are experienced in these matters, shall give me directions how I am to proceed. The man answered: You have only to walk about until your legs are heavy, and then to lie down, and the poison will act. At the same time he handed the cup to Socrates, who in the easiest and gentlest manner, without the least fear or change of colour or feature, looking at the man with all his eyes, Echecrates, as his manner was, took the cup and said: What do you say about making a libation out of this cup to any god? May I, or not? The man answered: We only prepare, Socrates, just so much as we deem enough. I understand, he said: but I may and must ask the gods to prosper my journey from this to the other world—even so—and so be it according to my prayer. Then raising the cup to his lips, quite readily and cheerfully he drank off the poison. And hitherto most of us had been able to control our sorrow; but now when we saw him drinking, and saw too that he had finished the draught, we could no longer forbear, and in spite of myself my own tears were flowing fast; so that I covered my face and wept, not for him, but at the thought of my own calamity in having to part from such a friend. Nor was I the first; for Crito, when he found himself unable to restrain his tears, had got up, and I followed; and at that moment, Apollodorus, who had been weeping all the time, broke out in a loud and passionate cry which made cowards of us all. Socrates alone retained his calmness: What is this strange outcry? he said. I sent away the women mainly in order that they might not misbehave in this way, for I have been told that a man should die in peace. Be quiet then, and have patience. When we heard his words we were ashamed, and refrained our tears; and he walked about until, as he said, his legs began to fail, and then he lay on his back, according to the directions, and the man who gave him the poison now and then looked at his feet and legs; and after a while he pressed his foot hard, and asked him if he could feel; and he said, No; and then his leg, and so upwards and upwards, and showed us that he was cold and stiff. And he felt them himself, and said: When the poison reaches the heart, that will be the end. He was beginning to grow cold about the groin, when he uncovered his face, for he had covered himself up, and said—they were his last words—he said: Crito, I owe a cock to Asclepius; will you remember to pay the debt? The debt shall be paid, said Crito; is there anything else? There was no answer to this question; but in a minute or two a movement was heard, and the attendants uncovered him; his eyes were set, and Crito closed his eyes and mouth.

Such was the end, Echecrates, of our friend; concerning whom I may truly say, that of all the men of his time whom I have known, he was the wisest and justest and best.[360]

Crito had decently closed the eyes of a man who had spent his life learning to see things no physical eye could see. That man had clearly believed that, after death, he would see those things more clearly, as Oedipus saw them more clearly once he had blinded himself, and as Tiresias, the blind seer, could so perfectly see. Crito also closed the dead man's mouth, the lips that Athens had been so determined to seal. But those questioning lips had already done their work. The questions they framed had thrown a new light on the whole history of Hellas from the Dark Ages to the tranquil death in the prison cell, on Hellenic man's effort to achieve a polis that participated in two worlds. It must be a community of both gods and men. It must express the will of eternal gods, who only half revealed themselves to men; of invisible ideas that could, though only with humility and travail, be embodied in concrete things; of universal freedom and justice applied to practical politics and the unruly passions of men; of the kind of intellect for which every answer posed the next question. It must be an anagogical polis, in which all things led the understanding upward, in which the thing was read as sign, in which symbol soared, and in which to live, though often painful, must never be meaningless. It must be a polis in which not only the mind's eye should see but the heart could feel, and in which carved temple, statue of cast bronze, mural panel, or note of flute or lyre, should open the heart of man, guide his foot in delicate dance and his voice in exultant song. It must be a polis in which person intimately confronted person, a polis whose citizens were not things.

All those longings of Hellas had been brought to focus in the Athens that gave Socrates birth, in the polis that Pericles proudly called the School of Hellas. And though she was also a tyrant-state, which compelled physical submission, yet her intellectual and aesthetic vocation compelled the minds and souls of Hellenes from Spain to Cyprus, from Libya to the Russian steppes. For Athens represented Hellas; she was the mouthpiece of Hellas, even when Hellas fought against her. And the mouthpiece of Athens was Socrates, even when Athens slew him. If the whole history of Hellas, all the way up to 399, was a kind of Aeschylean tragedy, in which understanding must be won through suffering, then of that tragedy Socrates was the hero.

Other characters represented more perfectly than he specific aspirations and achievements of the Hellenic spirit. Though he started life as a sculptor, he was no Phidias. Though he sometimes wrote poetry, as when alone in his prison cell he turned Aesop's *Fables* into verse, he was no Aeschylus. He loved jest, but he was no Aristophanes. He understood what law was, but it was Solon and Clisthenes, not he, who in some sense legislated Athens into existence. He imagined a polis, and Pericles ruled one. He was a good soldier, but no Themistocles. He was as just as Aristides the

Just, but he held no high office. Yet essentially, Hellas was quest. Hellas sought to know and to understand. And in tireless quest Socrates stood supreme, the key actor in the great drama called Hellas.

At the Piraeus with Glaucon and the others, when they had imagined a more perfect polis, he had not greatly cared whether final decision rested with one philosopher king or a number. In a very real sense he himself was the uncrowned philosopher king of Athens. There was an ancient myth in Hellas, though not only in Hellas, that the king must die. Now he had died. In his court defense he had not sought death, whether, as Xenophon later guessed, in order to avoid the ills of grievous old age, or to call attention to his ideas on man and the polis. The philosopher king died because he refused to quit his quest. Did not his death perfect his reign and extend it to men of all times and in all places? Did not his wingèd words before an Athenian court reach even to Achilles, who had willed, not to live long, but to live well? Did they not reach beyond Athens to Hellene and barbarian alike? For they had put the enduring and ironical question, to man, in polis: Who am I?

8

THE POLIS IN FLIGHT
AND
THE THIRTEENTH GOD

IN THE SPRING of 401, some two years before his death, Socrates was asked for advice by one of his young friends, Xenophon. Xenophon had received a letter from an old family friend, a Theban named Proxenus. Cyrus, younger brother of Artaxerxes II, new King of Kings, had induced Proxenus "to get as many men as he could and join him, since he was about to attack the Pisidians, who were making themselves a nuisance to his country."[361] So Proxenus had raised a force of mercenaries and had gone to Cyrus. If Xenophon would join him there, he promised

> to introduce him to Cyros, who was, he said, more than home and country to himself. Xenophon read his letter, and consulted Socrates the philosopher about this trip. Socrates had a suspicion that there might be

some state objection to his being friendly with Cyros, because Cyros had favoured the Lacedaimonians in their war against Athens; so he advised Xenophon to go to Delphi and inquire of the oracle about this journey. Accordingly Xenophon went and asked Apollo what god he should sacrifice and pray to, that he might best accomplish the journey he had in mind, and come back safe and successful. Apollo named the gods to whom he must sacrifice.

When he came back he told the oracle to Socrates. But Socrates blamed him because he had not asked first whether it was better for him to go or to stay, but just decided to go, and then asked how he could best do it. "But," said he, "since you did ask that, you must do what the god bids."[362]

So Xenophon sacrificed to the gods whom Apollo's oracle had named and joined Proxenus and Cyrus of Persia in Sardis.

The decision was a fateful one. It was the subsidies of Cyrus that had enabled the Spartans to destroy the Athenian Empire, to starve Athens herself to her knees, to place a Spartan garrison on the holy Acropolis, and to back up the bloody Critias in his anti-democratic terror. Xenophon, then in his early twenties, son of a landowner from an estate some nine miles northeast of Athens, member of the class of knights, politically conservative and glad to have Athens again allied to her yoke-fellow Sparta, had served in the cavalry under the Thirty. Now the democracy was back in power. Now he was joining his Theban friend, to whom Cyrus the Persian was "more than home and country." And, from Socrates' point of view, Xenophon had consulted the oracle, as Croesus and so many others had done, the wrong way. He had not asked what he should do but which gods he should conscript to help him do what he had already made up his mind to do.

The Greek mercenary force he joined at Sardis contained some 12,900 infantry, of whom 10,600 were heavy-armed. On March 6, 401, Cyrus led them eastward out of Sardis. Not even Proxenus knew that it was not the hill tribes of Pisidia whom Cyrus was leading them against but the King of Kings himself. Of the Greeks, only the Spartan Clearchus, their commander, knew.

However, when they got as far as Cilicia, it seemed to be clear to all that they were marching against the king. Most of them followed for shame of one another and Cyros, although they feared the journey and went against their will; and one of these was Xenophon.[363]

At Tarsus the Greeks balked, and some of the mercenaries even stoned Clearchus. But Clearchus cleverly succeeded in convincing them it was unsafe to turn back, and Cyrus lied about his reasons for wanting to reach the Euphrates River. Although the Greeks were still suspicious, a 50-per-cent increase in pay decided them to follow on. At Thapsacus on the Euphrates, Cyrus told the higher Greek officers the truth: they were marching against the King and against Babylon. This time it took a bonus to get the Greeks in motion again, but they crossed the river and followed Cyrus down the left bank toward the famous city, marching through the Syrian desert with its sweet-smelling plants, hunting the wild asses, whose meat tasted like venison but was tenderer, hunting the ostrich, the bustard, the gazelle. When they neared the King's army, Cyrus made fresh promises in case of victory and then reviewed his forces. Cyrus had his Greek mercenaries, a much larger number of Asian troops, a few scythe-bearing chariots. His brother, King Artaxerxes, had a much larger force than his, more scythed chariots, but no Greek mercenary force.[364] On a September morning at the village of Cunaxa, a few miles from the site of modern Baghdad, the Great King struck. The Greek mercenaries of Cyrus raised the paean, charged at the double, and completely scattered the forces opposite them. But Cyrus himself was less lucky. He managed to attack the King his brother personally, and even to wound him, but he himself was killed. Instead of attacking the Greeks, Artaxerxes then withdrew: anyhow the death of Cyrus had brought the Greek expedition to ruin. When the Greeks returned to their camp for breakfast, there was nothing to eat: the camp had been pillaged.

When the Great King sent word that they were to lay down their arms, they refused. They wanted to get home to Greece, but how? They had marched nearly 1,500 miles from Sardis. They could not possibly go back the way they had come: they lacked the necessary provisions to cross the desert. Tissaphernes, the royal governor whom Cyrus had replaced at Sardis, offered to guide them northward toward the Black Sea. And so, with Tissaphernes' army leading, the Greeks started up the left bank of the Tigris toward the great eastern mountains of modern Turkey. They reached the Great Zab, which flowed into the Tigris.

But there was distrust between the two armies. Where, wondered the

Greeks, was Tissaphernes guiding them? Would they be ambushed? On the Persian side, there was fear of this desperate army of Greek mercenaries, which, like some hostile polis, moved through the heart of the Persian Empire. How get rid of them? At last Clearchus, the Spartan commander, decided to seek a conference with Tissaphernes and to try for some sort of firmer understanding. Tissaphernes invited the Greek leaders to his quarters; there he seized Clearchus, Proxenus, Menon, and two other Greek leaders and sent them to the Great King; the remainder of the delegation were massacred. Then he sent fresh demands to the Greek army to lay down their arms.

In Xenophon's judgment, Clearchus the Spartan, principal commander of the Greeks, had been a harsh, cruel, but efficient leader. After refusing to return to Sparta with an expedition he was leading to the Hellespont, he had been sentenced to death for disobedience, and had turned soldier of fortune. War was his passion. He was about fifty when the Great King beheaded him. Xenophon's friend Proxenus was likewise beheaded; he was only about thirty. Xenophon mourned Proxenus as a man too gentle and too honorable to command his mercenary force. Of Menon, the Thessalian general, Xenophon had a low opinion, and he heard without sorrow that he had not merely lost his life like the other generals but had met slow death by torture. When Xenophon came later to write the history of their Anabasis, their March Up Country, he pictured the army, now largely bereft of leadership:

They could not sleep for sorrow, longing for home and parents, for wives and children, which they never expected to see again. In this state they all tried to rest.[365]

There was a man in the army named Xenophon, an Athenian, who was neither general nor captain nor private . . .[346]

And now in their desperate plight, he was unhappy like the rest and could not sleep; but he did snatch a nap, and then he saw a dream. He thought there was lightning and a thunderbolt fell on his father's house, and all was in a blaze. He woke at once in terror; the dream he judged to be good in one way, because amid troubles and dangers he seemed to see a great light from Zeus, but in another way he feared, because he considered the dream to come from Zeus the king and the blaze of fire seemed to be all round, so he feared difficulties would fence him in all round, and he might not be able to get out of the country of the king.[367]

Xenophon called together the officers who had served under his friend Proxenus, pointed out that the Persians had broken their oaths and thereby aligned the gods on the side of the Greeks, and said:

They are men easier to wound and to kill than we are if the gods give us victory as before.

Perhaps others are now thinking the same, but in heaven's name don't let us wait for someone else to come and pat us on the back and say, Go it. Here's a grand enterprise! Let us take the lead and show the others how to be brave! Show yourselves the best of officers, and as worthy to be captains as the captains themselves! Count on me, if you are willing to make the start; I will follow you, or if you order me to lead, I will not make my youth an excuse, but I think I am old enough to keep danger from myself![368]

With one dissenting vote, the subordinates of Proxenus chose this young Athenian to lead their contingent. Then they collected officers from the other contingents and by midnight about a hundred officers were in council. Xenophon was called on to speak. He urged them instantly to appoint new officers to replace those the army had now lost. This was done, and then they convened a general assembly of the whole army, just as the Council at Athens might have convened the Assembly of all citizens. A Lacedaemonian officer addressed them, then the newly appointed general of the Arcadian contingent spoke.

Then Xenophon rose; he was arrayed for war in his finest dress. "If the gods grant victory," he thought, "the finest adornments are most proper for such a victory; if I must die, after grand ambitions I would meet my end in grandeur."[369]

He insisted that with God's help there were many good hopes of safety. Someone in the audience sneezed. This was a good omen; the soldiers recognized it as such by kissing their hands to heaven; and Xenophon instantly cried:

While we were speaking of safety came an omen of Zeus the Saviour! Then I think we should vow to this god a thanksgiving for salvation as soon as we reach the first friendly country, and vow a sacrifice to the other gods according to our ability. Whoever agrees with this, let him hold up his hand.[370]

All held up their hands. Then they made their vow and chanted the paean. Xenophon now spoke at length. He reminded them that the Persians had come long ago to punish Athens. At Marathon the Athenians had beaten them. Then Xerxes had come by land and sea with an innumerable host. The ancestors of this audience he was addressing had beaten them. The Greeks would beat them again. No cavalry? They would need none. No provisions? They would seize provisions. Rivers impassable? All rivers could be passed if you went far enough toward the source. Even if the army could not escape, it was strong enough to settle down and defy the King, as some of the hill tribes had in fact done.

> But I am afraid that if we once learn to live idle in luxury, and to dally with the fine big women and girls of the Medes and Persians, we may be like the lotus-eaters and forget the way home!
> I think, then, that we must first try to reach Hellas and our own people, and show the Hellenes that they are poor only because they want to be, when they could bring their paupers over here and see them rich. But don't forget, men, that all these good things belong to the conquerors; and now it is necessary to say how we can travel most safely and fight most successfully.[371]

Next he proposed that they burn their baggage train. All hands would be needed to fight. But the chief thing was complete obedience to discipline. The Persians had treacherously killed the Greek leaders: the Persians must find that the Greeks could obey new leaders. He called for a vote approving his plans.

> Or if anyone has anything better, let him speak up boldly and say so, even if he is a private soldier, for our common safety is our common need.[372]

The Greek army started north toward the high mountains, a Greek polis on the march, a panhellenic polis like the one Pericles dreamed that Thurii might be, a footloose polis like Athens herself, but one prepared to move much further than Salamis, into the towering, unknown mountains. Nearly a century and a half before, when Cyrus had conquered Lydia, had not the Phocaeans deserted their hearths and planned their city elsewhere, on some islands off Chios? Had they not then sworn a solemn oath to move to Corsica? For their common safety had been their common need. Only a few weeks before Cyrus had known that if he could but slay his brother, the Great King, the leaderless Imperial host would rally to himself. When Cyrus was slain, the Persians assumed that his Greek followers could only lay down their arms. But Clearchus and the other Greek generals had taken charge. Surely, if these too could be got rid of, their army would be forced to surrender. Not at all: the army turned polis and struck out for the mysterious highlands. Their common safety was their common need; their habits of self-government bound them together, their sneezes were omens, and their trust was in Zeus the Savior.

The long ordeal began. The Persian archers could outrange the Cretan archers who served in the retreating polis. And Xenophon had been wrong about not needing cavalry. Persian cavalry constantly harassed the rear guard, which Xenophon and Clearchus' successor, the young Timasion, commanded. Xenophon concluded that slingers and horsemen must be found. Some 200 men of Rhodes were collected who understood slings and whose leaden bullets had twice the range of the stones, as big as a human fist, which the Persian slingers hurled. Horses hitherto used as pack animals were examined and some fifty were found fit for cavalry. By the time the retreating army reached the ruins of Nineveh, the Rhodian slingers and the newly formed cavalry were holding Tissaphernes at bay. The Cretans were collecting and using the spent arrows of the Persians. Moreover, in some of the villages they found lead to make bullets for the slings and plenty of gut to use in the slings themselves. The moving polis was in some sense importing the goods it required, but importing them by moving to where they were. Sometimes it found a well-provisioned village and spent a few days there, partly to let its surgeons tend the wounded, partly to eat the good wheat meal stored there and drink the wine and let their horses feed on the stored-up barley.

It took them seven days of constant fighting to pass through the mountainous country of the wild Kurds, at whose hands they suffered more losses than all those Tissaphernes had been able to inflict. Then they started across Armenia, shadowed by Tiribazus, the King's local governor, who kept an eye on them but did not attack. It was now late autumn and the heavy snowfalls began. Once they marched through snow six feet deep. The army lost animals, slaves, soldiers.

Men also were left behind who had been blinded by the snow or lost their toes by frostbite. It did some good to the eyes if the men marched holding something black before their eyes; for the feet, to keep them moving without rest all the time and to take off the shoes at night. But if any slept with shoes on, the straps worked into the feet and the shoes froze; for the old shoes were gone, and they had to make them of raw leather from untanned hides newly flayed.[373]

They came to underground houses, filled with people and animals. There they got provisions, including an unfamiliar drink, beer:

barley-wine in tubs; there were barley-grains floating on the wine at the rim, and straws lay there, large and small, without knots. If you were thirsty, you picked up one of these and sucked through it. It was very strong wine if drunk neat, and the taste was delicious when you were used to it.[374]

A village headman proved hospitable. And he also taught Xenophon how to wrap bags round the hooves of his horses so they would not sink to their bellies in the snow. In some villages the people feasted them:

everywhere on the same table were piles of lamb, kid, pork, veal, fowl, with all sorts of cakes, both wheaten and barley. When one would show goodwill by drinking your health, he dragged you to the bowl, and you must duck your head and gulp it up like a bullock.[375]

Through the countries of the Taochians and the Chalybeans they stumbled on until they reached a sizable city called Gymnias. Thence they marched five days to Mount Theches.

When the first men reached the summit and caught sight of the sea there was loud shouting. Xenophon and the rearguard, hearing this, thought that more enemies were attacking in front; for some were following behind them from the burning countryside, and their own rearguards had killed a few men and captured others, and taken wicker shields, covered with raw hairy oxhides, about twenty. But when the shouts grew louder and nearer, as each group came up it went pelting along to the shouting men in front, and the shouting was louder and louder as the crowds increased. Xenophon thought it must be something very important; he mounted his horse, and took Lycios with his horsemen, and galloped to bring help. Soon they heard the soldiers shouting "Sea! sea!" and passing the word along.

Then the rearguard also broke into a run, and the horses and baggage animals galloped too. When they all reached the summit then they embraced each other, captains and officers and all, with tears running down their cheeks. And suddenly—whoever sent the word round—the soldiers brought stones and made a huge pile. Upon it they threw heaps of raw hides and sticks and the captured shields . . .[876]

And so they sacrificed to their gods. They still had to get through the country of the Macronians, but luckily a man in the Greek army, who had been a slave in Athens, recognized these highlands as his native land and was able to negotiate safe passage. They now reached the Colchians, those distant barbarians Jason had reached when his Argonauts had sought the Golden Fleece, barbarians whose passionate princess, Medea, Euripides had immortalized. The Colchians massed their forces in order to hold a mountain pass. Xenophon formed the Greek army in company columns and prepared them to fight their way through. Then he addressed the soldiers:

> "Men, these whom you see alone are left in the way, to keep us from reaching at once the place we have been seeking so long. These men, if we can, we must devour raw!"[877]

> Then the word went round to offer their prayers; they prayed aloud, and chanted the battle-hymn, and advanced.[878]

The enemy fell into panic. In two more days the Greeks were in Trapezus, on the shore of the Black Sea, that vast water the Greeks had always called the Euxine, the Hospitable[879] Sea.

They had left Sardis, so near the Aegean, in spring. They had fought the fateful battle of Cunaxa, outside the mighty walls of Babylon, in September. They had crossed the highlands of eastern Turkey in the dead of winter. Now it was February, and they had gained the sea, and to a Greek the sea was the road home. Meanwhile, the citizens of Greek Trapezus provided them with a market, and made them gifts; and, with the encouragement of their hosts, the wandering army spent about thirty days despoiling the nearby Colchian tribes.

> After this they prepared the sacrifice which they had vowed; they had cattle enough to sacrifice fully to Zeus Saviour and Heracles and the other gods, all they had vowed.
> They held also a contest of games and sports on the hill where they were encamped. To find a racecourse and superintend the games they chose one Dracontios, a Spartan noble who had been banished as a boy for striking a boy with his knife and killing him by accident.

After the sacrifice they gave over the hides to Dracontios, and told him to take them to his ground. He pointed to the hill where they stood, and says he, "This hill is the best possible place to race wherever you like." "Oh," said they, "and how can they wrestle on this hard bushy ground?" He said, "So much the worse for the man who gets a fall." There was the two hundred yards for boys, mostly captives; in the long race the Cretans ran, more than sixty of them; others did wrestling and boxing and both combined, and it was a fine sight; there were plenty of entries, and plenty of rivalry with all their comrades looking on. There was horse-racing too; they had to ride down the precipice into the sea, and back again to the altar. On the way down most of them rolled along; on the way up the horses could hardly walk up that sheer steep. What shouts, what roars of laughter, what cheers![380]

After the sacrifices and games, the moving, pillaging panhellenic polis met and deliberated on the best way to get home.

First Leon, a Thurian, rose, and spoke as follows:
"To speak for myself, sirs, I'm tired out by this time, with packing up and marching and doubling and carrying arms and falling in and keeping guard and fighting. I want a little rest now from these hardships. We have the sea, then let's go by sea the rest of the way, lying flat like Odysseus, till we get to Hellas."
There was great cheering at this, "Good! Good!" and someone else said the same, and so said all of them. Then Cheirisophos rose, and said:
"I have a friend, sirs, Anaxibios, who is now Lord High Admiral at home, as it happens. If you will send me there, I think I shall bring you back ships of war and transports to carry you. If you want to go by sea, wait until I return; I won't be long."
On hearing this, the men were delighted and voted that he should sail, the sooner the better.[381]

But suppose Chirisophus should fail to secure sufficient sea transport? Xenophon persuaded the army to borrow warships from Trapezus and seize merchant vessels. They would pay and maintain the crews. He also tried to organize the pillage on which the army counted for food. He persuaded the coast cities to repair the roads, so they could march to the Hellespont if they had to; and the cities acceded, because they were all fearful of this mercenary force and eager to be rid of them. When Chirisophus did not return and when they themselves failed to capture enough transports and when provisions grew scarce, they put on board the ships they had those who were sick, those over forty, the boys and women they had seized during the long march, and most of the baggage, and sent them westward to Cerasus, another colony of Sinope. The rest of the army made the journey on foot in three days. At Cerasus the generals reviewed and numbered their troops. There were 8,600 men left, about two-thirds of those who had fought at Cunaxa. The rest had been killed in action, or lost in the mountains, or had perished in the snow, or had been captured, or had died of disease. They now divided the booty. They reserved a tithe for Apollo and Artemis, and entrusted shares of it to their generals, including Xenophon.

The army started westward again. Then men marched through strange lands, among people who used dolphin blubber in place of olive oil.

When they were among friends on this march the people held shows for them of rich men's children, fatted children fed on boiled chestnuts, tender and very white, and almost as broad as they were long, with backs and breasts variegated and tattooed all over in flower patterns. They ran after the women in the camp and wanted to lie with them in broad daylight, which was their own custom. All the men and women were fair-skinned. The army said that these were the most savage of all they had seen in their travels, and the farthest away from Hellenic customs. They would do in public what other human beings would do in private, and when they were alone they did what people do in company, talk to themselves and laugh at themselves, stop and dance anywhere as if they were showing off.[382]

They tried to get more ships from the city of Sinope to come and fetch them.

Meanwhile, Xenophon looked upon all these men-at-arms, and all those targeteers, and the bowmen and slingers and horsemen, too, and all fit from long practice—he saw all these on the Euxine, where so great a force could never have been collected without vast expense, and he thought it would be fine to found a city there, and to add territory and power to Hellas.[383]

The army heard of his desire and murmured. They wanted to go home. But, now that their common danger had decreased, discipline was declining fast. The Greek cities of the coast were increasingly alarmed, as Sicily had once been alarmed by Athens' grand armada, with its concentration of

force and its ill-defined purpose. This same combination now gave Xenophon's army of mercenaries the appearance of a very large animal with
a very small brain. Repeatedly, during the summer of 400, as the army
slowly made its way toward the Bosphorus, Xenophon toyed with the
idea of colonizing, especially at Calpe's Haven, which lay on the Black
Sea coast only a score of miles east of Byzantium, only half a day's journey
by oar. He would give this brainless, thrashing animal a purpose. Xenophon
later wrote:

> Calpe's Haven lies halfway on the voyage between Heracleia and Byzan-
> tion. It is a promontory jutting out into the sea; the part by the sea being
> a sheer cliff, height where it is least no less than twenty fathoms, and
> facing the land a neck about four hundred feet wide. The space inside
> the neck is enough for ten thousand inhabitants. The harbour under the
> cliff has a beach towards the west. There is a spring of plentiful sweet
> water close beside the sea commanded by the promontory. There is
> abundance of all sorts of wood, and particularly a great deal of fine
> wood for shipbuilding close to the sea. The highland stretches into the
> country some two or three miles, good soil without stones; and the
> part along the seashore is longer still, set thick with much timber of all
> sorts. The rest of the country for a long way round is good, and has many
> villages full of people; the land bears barley and wheat and pulse of all
> sorts, millet and sesame, figs enough, plenty of grapes, good wine-grapes
> too, and everything else except olives. So much for the country.
> They encamped on the beach beside the sea. They would not camp
> on a place which might be turned into a city, and they thought indeed
> that they had really been brought there by some scheme of persons who
> wanted to found a city. For most of the soldiers had not been driven
> by poverty to this expedition; but it was the fame of Cyros which had
> brought them, some had followers with them, some had spent money
> themselves, and a few others had run away from home—they had left
> father and mother, or even children too, hoping to return with wealth
> for them, since they had heard how others had made their fortunes with
> Cyros. Men such as these wished to return safe to Hellas.[884]

When at last they reached Byzantium and the Spartan admiral Anaxibius
closed the city's gates against them, they forced their way in. Xenophon
had to remind them that the Lacedaemonians now controlled Hellas. If
the Lacedaemonians had but recently brought his own city, imperial
Athens, to her knees, they could certainly reduce Byzantium and they

could punish any mercenary army that had seized it. To everybody's relief, at that moment

a certain Coiratadas arrived; he was a Theban on his travels, not a banished man but one with a fever for generaleering, ready with his services if army, city, or nation wanted a good commander. He came and said he was ready to lead them to what is called the Delta of Thrace, where they could get all sorts of good things; until they got there, he would find plenty of food and drink. While he was speaking, the answer came from Anaxibios: that if they were obedient they should never be sorry for it; he would report it to the authorities at home, and he would himself do all he could for them. Accordingly, the soldiers accepted Coiratadas for their general, and went outside the walls. Coiratadas arranged to be there the next day with victims for sacrifice, and a seer, and food and drink for the army. When they were outside, Anaxibios closed the gates and proclaimed that any soldier caught inside would be sold as a slave.[385]

A new Spartan governor arrived and found 400 sick men from Xenophon's army whom his predecessor had quartered in Byzantium. The new governor promptly sold them as slaves. The Theban buccaneer, Coiratadas, who had hired the army, sacrificed repeatedly in a vain effort to get favorable auspices; then he disappeared. The generals could not agree where to lead their rootless, hungry polis next. An exiled Thracian prince named Seuthes hired the army in hopes of winning back his father's kingdom. All through the harsh Thracian winter they served him, but the pay was irregular; and so, hearing that Sparta had decided on war with their old enemy Tissaphernes and would willingly pay them well, some 6,000 followed Xenophon across the Hellespont back into Asia Minor. They passed near Troy and then marched to Pergamos. There in March, 399, Xenophon turned over his 6,000 men to the Spartan commander, Thibron. Scarce fifty miles to the southeast lay Sardis, whence Cyrus had led them bravely forth two long years before. It was an expedition that had taken them some 4,000 miles.

Meanwhile, several things had happened to Xenophon. A month before his old master, Socrates, had been condemned to death in Athens. A month later the city that condemned Socrates would condemn Xenophon himself, in his absence, to exile:[386] had he not served under Cyrus, whose pay had enabled Sparta to destroy the Athenian Empire? According to Xenophon's own later account of the great expedition, he reached Pergamos with scarcely more worldly goods than Socrates, and had to sell his horse in order to pay his passage home. But luckily the wife of a Greek exile at Pergamos told him of a wealthy Persian who lived in a nearby castle. Xenophon led his followers against this fat prey, bagged the Persian, his wife and children, many other captives, horses, and cattle. Of this rich plunder Xenophon was voted the lion's share. But there was more booty in the Persian provinces yet to be won, and fame too: he stayed on in Persia's Aegean provinces to serve in the Spartan army.

During the first four decades of the fourth century the disintegration of the Hellenic state system that had produced the Peloponnesian War continued unabated. Athens had failed to give her lost empire a workable constitution. Sparta and her Peloponnesian allies had fought the long war to liberate Athens' subject allies. Sparta promptly garrisoned those she liberated and collected for herself the tribute they had before paid Athens. She restored oligarchies in them. She dominated and bullied her allies in Mainland Greece. She lacked any real interest in the new economic problems of the Aegean and Asian Greeks. Sparta still vaunted the laws of Lycurgus, but Lysander's conquests had flooded her with the gold and silver which Lycurgus the Lawgiver had strictly forbidden. Inequalities of wealth bred discontent and Sparta was even forced to nip an incipient revolution within the ranks of the Spartiates themselves, while always the Dwellers-round-about and the Helots sullenly nursed their grievances. Her principal allies in the Peloponnesian War, states like Thebes and Corinth, had been ruthlessly shouldered aside when Sparta appropriated the empire of fallen Athens.

In less than a decade from the fall of Athens, Sparta's allies in Greece were ready to rise against her. A Spartan army was plundering Phrygia, nominally to complete the liberation of Greece-in-Asia. It was Persian money that had enabled Sparta to destroy Athens; now, with a Spartan army ravaging her western provinces, Persia used her money again, but this time to subsidize Sparta's discontented allies in Mainland Greece. Thebes, Athens, Corinth, and Argos thereupon headed an insurgent alliance. Within three years Sparta was so hard pressed that she solicited Persia to impose peace on the warring Greeks. She failed; but there was still hope, for the Great King was bound to be alarmed by signs of Athenian recovery in the Aegean.

In the fourth century the problem of every state that aspired to power was money. In one of the last comedies Aristophanes wrote, a querulous old man declared to Wealth:

> See here, everything that's done is done through you. You and you alone are the cause of everything. Why, even in war, it's the side you're on that wins.[887]

Even under Pericles it had been money that had built and manned the fleet. During the Peloponnesian War both sides more and more often hired mercenaries, either Greek or barbarian. When the long war ended in 404, all Hellas was flooded with men who had never mastered any trade but war. A whole generation had grown up amidst violence, violence between polis and polis, between rich and poor inside the polis. Returning from war to a ravaged homeland, to its disrupted commerce, and to unemployment, the former soldier looked, as Xenophon had looked, to foreign service: under a Persian prince eager to seize his brother's crown, or under a Thracian princeling like Seuthes, or even under an unknown Theban buccaneer with a fever for generaleering, full of promises of good pillage in the Thracian countryside. Hundreds of years ago, Hellas had been founded by marauding bands. The new marauders of the fourth century, unlike their remote Achaean or Dorian ancestors, fought for money. They plundered village storehouses and made off with cattle and kidnaped natives, but only in part to enjoy food or women. Much of what they seized, they sold for cash. Unlike their heroic ancestors they were the children of a cash economy, which even Sparta had now entered.

By the 380's, an Athenian captain of mercenaries named Iphicrates, who was born the son of a leather-worker, a little north of Marathon, had begun to revolutionize Greek warfare. Against this ingenious professional, the locked shields of the stubborn citizen soldiers of Sparta's heavy infantry proved an inadequate defense. For centuries Spartans had fought in ranks for a sacred polis, a little in the spirit of Homeric single combat. As early as 425, on the island of Sphacteria, Spartan heavy infantry had learned that this obstinate courage could not ward off arrows from lightly armed and swiftly moving troops under Demosthenes and Cleon. In the decades that followed, men like Xenophon were learning, often from

313

Persian opponents, the true uses of archers and slingers and cavalry. This Athenian professional, Iphicrates, now developed systematically both light infantry and cavalry. To his infantry he assigned the javelin, the bow, a lengthened lance, a lengthened sword, together with a light wicker shield covered with hide. Iphicrates' light-armed troops were trained to move fast, to surprise the enemy, to harass him, to maneuver rapidly. To his light cavalry he assigned the lance. Already on a winter's day in 390, near Corinth's port, Lechaeum, he had fallen on King Agesilaus' heavy infantry and taught all Greece what his own kind of light troops could do. Of the Spartan hero's heavy infantry 250 out of some 600 had been killed.

The new mercenary and the new warfare that money had created were subject to one important weakness. In Pericles' time, when a citizen Assembly voted for a campaign, a citizen general was likely to get the funds he required to win it, if only because the men who voted, or their relatives, or their immediate friends, would have to fight it. But a fourth-century Assembly might vote the campaign and then vote quite inadequate sums to some professional like Iphicrates. The professional had then to hire an army of mercenaries and embark on the campaign, only to find later that he must resort to brutal requisitions abroad or even encourage pillaging an ally to keep his professionals from quitting.

Faced with the Aristophanic fact that in war the side the money was on would win, and knowing from experience that Persia was where the big sums of money were, by 386 Sparta became in a sense herself a mercenary. For she induced the Great King to put Persia's money on Sparta once again, or in any case to publish the fact that she would do so if the Greek states did not make peace. No confederation or alliance except Sparta's Peloponnesian League would be permitted. To obtain those terms, Sparta abandoned the Asian Greeks. In effect she sold Greece-in-Asia to the Great King in return for the right to dominate Mainland Greece. The many little leagues that were springing up had to be dissolved. The anti-Spartan coalition knew it could not confront Sparta's Peloponnesian League backed by Persian gold. To make war, they would have required mercenaries, and only money could buy them. The meeting of interests between Sparta and Persia took the form, not of a treaty, but of a terse announcement made in 386 by the King of Kings:

> King Artaxerxes thinks it just that the cities in Asia should belong to him, as well as Clazomenae and Cyprus among the islands, and that the

314

other Greek cities, both small and great, should be left independent, except Lemnos, Imbros, and Scyros; and these should belong, as of old, to the Athenians. But whichever of the two parties does not accept this peace, upon them I will make war, in company with those who desire this arrangement, both by land and by sea, with ships and with money.[888]

The Great King's announcement ended with the right words: *kai chremasin*, and with money. Persian money had started the war. The power of Persian money now stopped it. Was it the memory of Leonidas standing firm at Thermopylae while Thebes and many other Greek states medized and either helped Xerxes assault Greece or did not hinder him, that caused a bystander to cry out to Xenophon's Spartan hero, King Agesilaus: "Alas for Greece, now that the Spartans are medizing." "Are not," replied the king, "the Medes the rather spartanizing?"[389] Agesilaus' reply was in the great Spartan tradition of the pithy, laconic epigram. But it concealed a brutal fact: that the monetizing of war had just led to the sale of Greece. Scarcely ninety years before, Persian gold had failed to prevent the catastrophe of Xerxes at Salamis, at Plataea, at Mycale, or even his loss of Greece-in-Asia.

Persia had often subsidized Greek against Greek to keep them from meddling in Persian affairs. But, more than once in the fourth century, the Great King needed Greek soldiers in order to put down rebellion, in Egypt or in some other province. Peace among the Greeks was then needed. With the rise of the mercenaries, one of diplomacy's functions was to regulate the market in mercenaries. War was an industry that consumed mercenaries, and therefore money; it produced captives, therefore slaves, therefore money from the sale of slaves. War also produced booty, which again produced money when mercenaries sold it. Slaves made life comfortable for free citizens, which made free citizens less willing to face war, which created a market for mercenaries. Free citizens were often unwilling to tax themselves sufficiently to provide adequate pay for the armies they hired, and so their armies plundered. These sudden shifts in military campaigns prolonged old wars and started new ones. To keep all these processes going, one prime mover was required: money.

After the King's declaration of 386, the Spartans grew more highhanded than ever, and it was their hybris, their insolence, that undid them. Theban oligarchs betrayed Thebes to a Spartan army; a resurgent, democratic Thebes, led by Pelopidas, ejected its Spartan garrison. Within a decade,

A military genius, Epaminondas, had reorganized the Theban army. The new Theban phalanx, fifty shields deep, met the famous Spartan line, which was only twelve shields deep, at Leuctra in July, 371, and by its weight the phalanx broke the line. Then Epaminondas began periodic invasions of Laconia. Indeed, having just missed capturing Sparta, he laid waste southern Laconia itself, stirred up a serf rebellion in Messenia, and refounded the city of Messene on the slopes of famous Mount Ithome. Persia, having subsidized Sparta, then Athens, then Sparta again, chose now to place her money on Thebes. The year after Sparta's defeat at Leuctra, the tyrant Jason of Pherae, Epaminondas' ally, who had united all Thessaly and might have disputed the hegemony that Epaminondas was wresting from Sparta, was assassinated, and his death cut short the further growth of Thessalian power. In 362, Epaminondas fought a great battle at Mantinea. Although he once more beat a Spartan army, he lost his own life, and the pre-eminence of Thebes did not long survive him. Athens, too, had made another bid for hegemony. She had constructed a confederacy for the second time. She had tried to avoid features like the tribute and the cleruchies, which had aroused revolt against her former confederacy once it had turned empire. But she failed a second time to devise political institutions through which her new union might govern itself in freedom. She was constantly weakened by the revolts of her allies.

Throughout the confused events that marked successive bids for power by Sparta, by Thessaly, by Thebes, by Athens again, one fact was clear. Greek city-states could be briefly brought into alliance, and sometimes on a small scale into political union, only by a common fear of conquest or else by a common hatred of arbitrary force and a common rebellion against it. The kaleidoscopic shifts in alliances that went on during these four decades were basically scrambles for security in a constantly shifting balance of power. The shifts continued not only between alliance and alliance but also inside most states between oligarchy and democracy.

Xenophon, the Athenian exile, tried to give in his *Hellenica* an account of Greek history from 411, the point at which Thucydides broke off, to 362, when Epaminondas the Theban defeated Sparta at Mantinea and fell in action. Xenophon had served under King Agesilaus in Asia in 396-394. When Sparta's allies rose against her and the Ephors swiftly recalled Agesilaus and his army to save Sparta, Xenophon, still an exile from Athens, followed him to Greece. When Agesilaus won an empty victory over the Thebans and Athenians at Coronea, in Boeotia, Xenophon fought under him and then retreated with him to Peloponnese. The Spartans gave the exile an estate near Olympia. There, with a wife and two small sons, he lived the life of a retired army officer and country noble and there he wrote a book on the *Republic of the Lacedaemonians*, praising the laws of the wise Lycurgus, at least a portion of his *Memorabilia*, recounting the actions and sayings of Socrates, and began a treatise on estate management, and another on horsemanship.[390]

Plato had written his *Apology*, a report of Socrates' defense in court. So Xenophon also wrote an *Apology*, his own defense of their common master. His writings about Socrates showed a less luminous person than the person revealed in the *Dialogues* of Plato. But there was no essential contradiction between them. Like Plato he saw in Socrates great goodness. Unlike Plato, he moralized about that goodness. He assumed that Socrates chose death, not—as Plato's Socrates himself declared—because he had no other right choice open, but because he feared the evils of old age. His portrait of Socrates was the picture of a philosopher painted by a gallant soldier, a wily strategist, a practical man of action, a country gentleman, conventional, unspeculative, ambitious, uncritical of his own motives, a man who was not greedy or covetous but who valued money and position, though he valued fame and honor even more. In place of the dialectical view of virtue that interested the Socrates whom Plato presented, Xenophon displayed a sort of basic decency, supported by a naïve casuistry. He possessed an enormous zest for life and a great capacity for friendship and loyalty. He looked outward, not inward. All these traits were reflected in his easy, simple, sometimes rather circumstantial style.

His knack for straightforward narrative and his eye for vivid detail made his *Anabasis* a delight to read. But his more ambitious effort to relate the political and military history of Greece for the half-century following the period which Thucydides covered lapsed for the most part into something more like chronicle than history. The *Hellenica* did indeed contain brief passages that were memorable; but the important questions were often not only unanswered, they even went unasked. For this, Xenophon was only in part responsible. Even Thucydides had flagged in the latter portion of his own history. After the great catastrophe at Syracuse, the Peloponnesian War increasingly lost its inner meaning. The confrontation of ideas that kept its early stages dialectical and tragic and therefore human and intelligible, more and more gave way to mere violence and counter-violence, to the conflict of passions rather than of ideas. Was it death that made Thucydides break off his writings seven years before the flutes had played and the walls of Athens had come down? Or had the later years of the war so lost meaning that his subject began to bore and depress him? The vast tragedy he had mounted for the readers of all time had stupidly refused to end. It was at that perilous moment in the plot that Xenophon tried to take up the history of Greece. In theory he could have traced Sparta's seizure of Athens' empire, the hybris Sparta showed as oppressor of Mainland and Aegean Greece, her cynical recourse to the Great King to guarantee her supremacy, and finally the loss of her hegemony; but Sparta's statesmen worked by the light of too few ideas for even a Thucydides to have cast their polis as tragic hero. The rise and fall of Spartan hegemony furnished a pattern that Xenophon could have used to greater advantage in the *Hellenica* than he did, but even if he had so used it, he could not have achieved the universal human significance of Thucydides.

With the weakening of Sparta's power after the battle of Leuctra in 371, Sparta relinquished to Elis the district near Olympia where the pleasant estate of Xenophon lay. He accordingly moved to Corinth. Two years later Athens, alarmed by the rise of Theban power, allied herself with Sparta; and two years after that, Athens revoked the decree which had exiled Xenophon. A year or two later he returned to Athens, after an absence of nearly forty years. Then, at the battle of Mantinea in 362, the point at which he left off his history of Greece, one of his sons was killed in action while serving in the Athenian cavalry, fighting for the two cities his father loved best, Athens and Sparta, for the moment yoke-fellows once more, as Cimon had long ago prescribed.

Two years after his son's death at Mantinea, Xenophon's old commander, King Agesilaus of Sparta, died. Xenophon wrote a laudatory biography of the man under whom he had fought in Asia and at Coronea. He continued and completed an historical romance about another king, another leader of men: the *Education of Cyrus*. The hero of this tale was not the Cyrus whom Xenophon had followed to the waters of Babylon but Cyrus the Great, who founded the Persian Empire. Even before King Agesilaus died, Xenophon had written of that other master of his, that very different hero, Socrates. Did he wish to emulate Plato's picture of Socrates in the *Symposium*, in which Socrates and others had praised love and the riotous Alcibiades praised Socrates? In any case, Xenophon wrote his own *Symposium*, in which the conversation was more boisterous, often trivial, sometimes flat. Shortly after Agesilaus died, he wrote, not too skillfully, a dialogue dealing with the life of the typical tyrant. He finished his essay on horsemanship and wrote another on the cavalry commander. He finished his history of Greece, the *Hellenica*, down to that battle at Mantinea, in which one of his own sons had fallen; and he finished his *Memorabilia* of Socrates. Around 354 Xenophon died.

Xenophon was a child of the Peloponnesian War. He had seen imperial Athens humbled. He had seen Sparta, Thebes, and Athens fail successively to unite Mainland Greece. It had been Athens' second failure to find a common purpose and common political institutions for herself and for her allies that had lost her much of the power which she had in part recaptured. But it had been also a desperate lack of money. And so the last work Xenophon composed was his *Ways and Means*, apparently addressed to his city's Council of Five Hundred. In it he urged an income tax; hotels, erected by the state for foreign merchants and visitors; a fleet of state-owned merchant vessels; and better exploitation of the state silver mines at Laurium. Also he prescribed peace. He was a cavalryman and he had loved adventure, but he had always prided himself on being practical and useful to others. He admired Socrates because he was so practical, so useful.

The Hellenic world in which Xenophon died was a far different world from the one that had formed his mind and character. Protagoras the sophist had scandalized Hellas in the fifth century by announcing that man was the measure of all things; but by the fourth, a man's money seemed to be a simpler, more concrete measure. The old landed nobility that had created the polis as an aristocratic republic ruled by the Best People had now been partly killed off in the perpetual wars between polis and polis. Its specific virtue had been courage; its aim, honor in this life and fame after death. But, as Socrates implied, it lacked the wisdom that transcended even honor; and when the sea opened and trade grew and money multiplied, it came to love money. It retained some traditional prejudices against trade; its members would still have preferred to seize rather than to haggle and save and scheme like a merchant. But as generation followed generation, blue blood and silver coin mixed; an aristocracy that had really been a timocracy was transformed into an oligarchy; the Best People became merely the richest, the few, *hoi Oligoi*. Beneath them were the many, *hoi Polloi*, the poor.

The blooded aristocrat like Cimon, or Pericles, or even, potentially, Alcibiades, had attracted the many, the poor, by a certain nobility of soul. These aristocrats had displayed a grandness of manner, some mysterious power to represent the aspirations even of the lowly. Their wealth was their perquisite, not their essence. Their scorn of vulgarity and pettiness and servility struck some resonance even in the vulgar, the petty, and the servile. But the man who was merely rich, especially if he happened to be clearly vulgar too, was distinguished not by what he was but by what he had. What he had, any other man could have who was strong enough or sly enough to get it away from this rich man or to get wealth like it elsewhere. By the time Xenophon died, then, class cleavage in Hellas existed more explicitly between rich and poor than it had ever done before. In some oligarchies the oligarchs actually took an oath: "And I will be hostile to the people and will plan whatever evil I can against them."[391] The aristocrat had excited admiration; the oligarch ruled by economic force. If the oligarch thought of himself as an aristocrat, few of those who hated or feared or used him shared his opinion. Few were taken in by his romantic love of Sparta: he would have loathed its black broth and grueling physical drill. The oligarch was no Spartan ascetic. On the contrary, the oligarch was learning the uses of physical luxury; and ever since Lysander had flooded Sparta with booty and money the oligarch had been learning luxury even in Sparta.

The fourth century was marked by a sharp drop in population. In 431 Athens had scarcely more than 40,000 voters. By 390 she had only 30,000; by 310 she would have 20,000. Constant wars, the famines and plagues caused by wars, the destruction of productive capital such as olive trees and vines and farm houses and draft animals, took their toll. Thousands of Greek captives were sold into slavery, often abroad, although by way of compensation thousands of foreign slaves were imported. Exposure of unwanted children had always been acceptable practice and had always been legal.[392] In most states the father decided; in Sparta, the state. In Sparta, in 480, the Spartiates furnished over 8,000 heavy infantry; on the eve of the terrible defeat at Leuctra in 371, there were less than 2,000; less than half a century later Aristotle[393] would put them at 1,000.

Not only was the population diminishing; what was left of it was migrating from the countryside to the city. The farmers whom Pericles had summoned into his walled, artificial island when Sparta invaded Attica had been homesick and unhappy in the city. But, as the long war had gone on and as the ravages of Attica had increased, many of them had learned to be city folk in Athens, or port folk or sailors in Piraeus. At Athens, also, thousands of outsettlers who had farmed in the islands had been driven back to hungry, besieged Athens to give her more mouths to feed. In Attica they had found no land to take up and became city men. Finally, the smallholder, whose ancestors had lived a hard life and sold only the small surplus of food they and their household did not need for themselves, could not compete in cash farming with the men of means who were buying up small plots here and there or seizing them for debt; who could carry these plots in years of lean crops; and who could squeeze profit out of them with slave labor or cheap labor and by improved methods and equipment. For methods did improve: rotation of crops, a metal point for the ancient wooden plow, legumes in place of fallow, better irrigation, better manuring, seed selection, better choice of crop according to soil. But all these improvements called for money. A technical literature on agriculture sprang into being, but for capitalist investors in land, not for smallholders.

In the city, industry and commerce were growing also. In industry cloth production, flour production, and bread baking were partly shifting now from home to shop, and shops were likely to be manned by slaves. The father of the orator Demosthenes, for example, operated a sword factory manned by some thirty-two slaves and a couch factory manned by twenty slaves.[394] In commerce navigation was improving, especially whenever Athenian sea power was in a position to police the seas for pirates. Commercial companies were forming. Banking facilities were increasing. Attic pottery was sold from one end of the Mediterranean to another. Not only Athens, but Ephesus in Asian Greece, Cyzicus on the Propontis, Byzantium at the southern entrance of the Bosphorus, Olbia on the Scythian coast of the Black Sea, Cyrene on the coast of Libya, Massilia on the present site of Marseilles, and scores of other ports prospered. Above all, strategically placed as a port of call, Syracuse became the most populous city in Hellas.

In this new, money-loving Hellas, the upper class had lost much of its social function. Its members no longer looked on military service as a duty or even, what it had originally been, the prerogative of a fighting aristocracy. The status of mercenary had caused a shift in army nomenclature.[395] In the fifth century a mercenary was an *epikouros*, or helper, a skilled professional assisting amateur citizen-soldiers. The term signified nothing about the money the helper earned. In the first half of the fourth century he was less reticently called a wage-earning peltast, or light infantryman. By the close of the fourth century he was merely a *stratiōtes*, a member of an army, a soldier. Being hired was no longer a distinguishing characteristic. It was natural that, with the professionalizing of warfare, athletics tended to turn professional too. The hard, sunburnt body of the free Athenian often turned white and soft, like the body of an upper-class Asian. One took one's ease.

Political leadership, like military leadership, was no longer a function of noble blood. Like generalship, it tended to fall into the hands of the professional, as the operations, especially the fiscal operations, of the polis grew more complex. As to the statesman's problem of public persuasion, that task went more and more to the professional persuader, the phrasemaker, the paid speech-writer, the orator. In 354, about the year Xenophon died, a thirty-year-old orator named Demosthenes made his first speech in a court trial and his first oration before the Athenian Assembly. The speeches of the new orators were not delivered on the Olympian level of the speeches the great Pericles had made. They reminded one more of the violent style and personal invective which, according to Thucydides, the tanner Cleon first introduced into the Assembly. These orators spoke before an audience of connoisseurs, who were too often guilty of the civic crime Cleon had charged the Assembly with in his day: they voted not for what they deemed wisest for the polis but for the speaker they most enjoyed hearing. Indeed, the speeches which men like Demosthenes wrote, learned by heart, delivered before the Assembly, and then published became perhaps the most characteristic form of literature in the fourth century.

Both literature and art ceased to be the confident enterprise of a close-knit polis and began to express a population of lonelier individuals than before, of less intuitive individuals, more analytical, harder to lead to the heights, more eager for pleasure and for the one thing that seemed to buy pleasure with the least effort. Money could propitiate the gods, pay the speech-writer, bribe the statesman, buy the use of beautiful women, buy the richest food, the best wine, the most skillful cook, and even pay the doctor who repaired the harm these pleasures might do the body. Money could buy the soldier's courage, or anyhow the mercenary's skill, and within the polis mercenaries might win their paymaster a tyrant's throne. Even for the least ambitious and the least daring, money could purchase ease and comfort and pleasure, and even friends, or at least parasites, to share one's pleasures.

As the invisible world of revealed gods and intuited ideas receded from most men's experience, and as the attention of most men focused with a feverish new interest on the world the senses knew, literature and art faithfully recorded the shift. Great tragedies were no longer being written. The theater sometimes revived Euripides, whose plays were more admired now than when he was still alive. There were even revivals of Sophocles. But to the fourth century Aeschylus appealed less than either. The things Aeschylus was most concerned with, the gods, the justice the gods taught men, the polis that bound men together, the truly heroic man or woman, seemed more and more remote. Aeschylus was too deeply religious, too deeply aristocratic, too bound by—or freed by?—conventions no longer comprehended. He was too intellectually strenuous.

Comedy had had to change too. Aristophanes had laughed uproariously, but at things he considered central and important: at man's failure to find his true relation to the gods, at man's failure to achieve polis, community —in short, his failure to find a genuinely human existence, a life worthy of being lived. And since Aristophanes believed such a life could be lived only in a polis that intimately associated man both with his gods and with his fellow citizens, some of his finest comedies were profoundly political. But now, in the fourth century, the polis, and the sense of polis, were in decline. Both the relation between god and man and the relation between man and his political community interested audiences less. The successors of Aristophanes wrote less of the citizen and more of the individual and his private affairs. These later writers were less joyous, less confident, less boisterous, less bawdy. For the infinitely playful, they substituted the cleverly contrived, the technically expert. For high-spirited obscenity they substituted wittily suggestive innuendo. They parodied the myths about the gods, myths that had lost much of their power to move and could be handled now as amusing scandal. The literary conventions of comedy, which had sprung out of forgotten religious rites, in part distintegrated, and comedy was left free to be merely amusing. It could help the relieved spectator to descend comfortably from the sublime to the foolish, from wisdom to knowledgeability, from a troubling, striving faith to amused and self-flattering incredulity. It diverted. It relaxed.

The architect and the sculptor followed the same descent. Now that both tragedy and comedy carried a lighter load of significance, now that both had lost some of their ancient ritual power to unite and lift, the architect compensated in part for that loss by building magnificent marble tiers to replace the rude wooden seating of the outdoor theater and by designing more elaborate staging. Athens might have no great tragedians left, but those she still had could be heard in more elegant surroundings. In these splendid surroundings an Athenian could hear his favorite actor, regardless of the play. It had once been unimportant what actor spoke from behind his conventional mask, and an Aeschylus might himself write the play and also act in it. But now the professional actor flourished and found his enthusiastic followers able to applaud his virtuosity even in a second-rate tragedy or comedy.

The architect still built temples as dwellings for the gods, but his vision of beauty had somewhat changed. One of the marvels of the fifth-century Parthenon was its perfect marriage of Dorian masculinity with the feminine grace of Ionia. In the fourth century, it was as if the softer, more delicate spirit of Ionia had finally won out. And why not? Athenian life now resembled the life of sixth-century Ionia far more than Periclean Athens had resembled it. The aesthetic solutions of Ionia found a resonance in the new Athens. Softness, delicacy, daintiness, ornateness, and even prettiness were the marks of that resonance. Even by 407, alongside the Parthenon with its strong Doric columns, Athens had completed another temple, the Erechtheum, a temple with tall, slender Ionic columns. The roof of one of its porches rested on the heads of a row of young maidens in marble: caryatids, priestesses of Artemis, and caryatids too were first carved in Ionia. The solution was devised with technical brilliance; but compared with the grave and masculine Dorian columns of the nearby Parthenon, it remained a bit contrived, a bit forced, its emphasis more on means than on ends. The Erechtheum lacked the wholeness of the Parthenon. Its sculptured details exhibited skill, delicacy, and sensuous grace rather than the majesty one saw in the friezes of Athena's stately dwelling. The shift exemplified in the Parthenon and the Erechtheum continued in the fourth century.

But the architects did not stop at making the new dwellings for their gods more human, more delightful. They were also building costlier, hand-somer homes for men, or rather for rich men. The fifth-century aristocrats of Athens had kept their homes in the country and had maintained only humble dwellings in town for their occasional use. The soaring temples of Athens' gods had once stood in marked contrast with the simple dwellings of the men, whether rich or poor, who worshiped those gods. But in the fourth century the rich lived more continuously in the city, even if they owned farmland outside, and they now employed architects to build them more elaborate dwellings. Moreover, when the architect or sculptor or painter went to other lands, it was less now to build other temples to the same great gods of Hellas than to build a palace or a splendid tomb for the truly rich man, the monarch or tyrant. In general, the artist was treating men as if they were gods.

Sculptors, too, turned from the gods to men. They did indeed continue to model or carve statues of Apollo and Aphrodite and the other gods, but their gods were more and more like men: the Apollo of sculptors like Praxiteles was likely now to display a beauty that was merely human and a grace that was even slightly effeminate; and their Aphrodite was less a superhuman being than a voluptuous, desirable, and even coy woman. On the other hand, portrait statues and busts of the rich or famous multiplied and were made more specifically true to life. In earlier days, gods were shown as larger then men; small boys looked like diminutive men. But now the sculptor carefully distinguished between the fully developed features of a man and the more blurred features of a child.[396] Also, he took pains to note that the child's head was larger in proportion to his body than a man's would be. The earlier sculptors had thought of the boy as a man, imperfectly developed but essentially a man. Their successors saw in a boy something different from a man, and something different from other boys of the same age. It was the same story with the transient emotion reflected on a human face. Instead of the masklike smile of the sixth century and the serenity of the fifth, sculptors like Scopas now por-trayed not only transient emotions but even violent emotions. Finally, just as the fourth-century actor emerged, metaphorically, from behind his mask and became no longer anonymous but a personal favorite of his public, so the architect and sculptor strove to be original: a so-called school or style might be associated less with a polis than with a famous and admired virtuoso in his art.

In art, as in literature, the individual had been freed from his polis. Otherwise stated, he had lost his community and stood alone. Was it this aloneness that made him look for a man, some man who could save Hellas, some man of the very type that would have provoked a legal ostracism from an earlier polis? As life grew more urban, more complex, more impersonal, the yearning for a person grew concurrently. Was this yearning connected with Xenophon's hero-worship of King Agesilaus? Was it connected with Xenophon's constant obsession with the charismatic qualities of the true military leader? With the ability of Epaminondas and Pelopidas to lead Thebes and Boeotia in a few years to the brief hegemony of Mainland Greece? With Xenophon's historical romance about Cyrus the Great? With the fascination exerted at Athens and elsewhere by the orator, who knew how to exalt his audience to a sense of at least emotional community? More importantly, did this search for a person in part account for the mingled dread and hope with which Mainland Greece watched the sudden rise of a new king of barbarous Macedonia to the north, a king whose name was just becoming famous at Athens during the last few years of Xenophon's life?

That king was Philip II. The Macedonia into which he was born was mountainous, like Greece. But the lowlands around the Thermaic Gulf north of Thessaly and a number of plains on the plateaus upcountry supplied plentiful grain for bread and ample pasturage for farm stock and specifically for horses. Like Thessaly and Boeotia, Macedonia had never been forced by hunger to turn to the sea. Besides, Greek maritime states like Chalcis and Corinth had early planted colonies on its coasts, especially on the trident-shaped peninsula which had come to be called Chalcidice. It was they, and not the Macedonians, who exploited and exported the country's timber and metals to Greece. Later it was imperial Athens. Macedonia remained, therefore, like the western portion of Mainland Greece, archaic, tribal, monarchical, and largely feudal, a country of horses rather than of ships, a country more like the past self of Greece than Greece was.

The Greeks looked down on Macedonians as backward, as lacking true arts or letters or politics, as not being Greek, although Herodotus reminded the Greeks that Alexander I of Macedonia had claimed to be Greek, had demanded and obtained the right therefore to compete in the Olympic Games; and although Thucydides reported that Alexander's family, the Temenid dynasty, came from Argos. The kings of Macedon not only claimed to be of Greek stock. In the true style of the Greek king or noble, they claimed descent from the same savior hero as the Spartan kings: Heracles, son, by a human mother, of Zeus himself. The king's subjects could manage to talk with Greeks without an interpreter, whereas a Thracian could not. The Macedonian dialect indeed contained Illyrian words, words like *sarissa*, the name for a very long pike used by Macedonian soldiers; but these same soldiers could not understand the language of the dangerous neighbors from whom they had borrowed such words. Some of their place names, like the names of their months, bore witness to the fact that, like the more civilized Greeks to the south, they were the racial product of the Achaean and Dorian invaders and of a population these conquerors had subdued. Alexander I not only competed at Olympia: he cultivated the great Theban poet Pindar, who knew how to write victory odes worthy of royal competitors, and he received the historian Herodotus at his court.

Alexander's son Perdiccas reigned during the Peloponnesian War and had his hands full maintaining his kingdom's independence while Brasidas was on campaign. Perdiccas' successor, Archelaus, built roads and fortresses, moved his capital from Aegae to Pella, reorganized his army. Like his father, Archelaus tried to bring Greek civilization to Pella. He commissioned the famous painter Zeuxis to decorate his palace with murals; brought in Timotheus of Miletus, famous for his reforms in music; attracted from Samos the epic poet Choerilus and from Athens the young friend of Socrates, the tragic poet Agathon. Certainly Zeuxis was no Polygnotus; his painting sometimes strove for a realism and a pathos that Polygnotus would not have sought. But Zeuxis was praised for his improved techniques; and, in any case, Polygnotus was not available: his painting days belonged a generation before, and the hellenizing Perdiccas took what the Hellas of his own day could still offer. Agathon, too, was a far cry from Aeschylus or Sophocles; but, a few years before Athens finally surrendered to Lysander in 404, Euripides had moved to Thessaly, and Archelaus

327

brought him to his court. There Euripides composed his last tragedies, including the *Bacchae* and *Archelaus*, and there he died.

It was Archelaus' grandfather who had won for his family the right to participate in the panhellenic games at Olympia. The grandson set up new games in Macedonia at Dion, where men would compete in racing, in music, and in drama. Appropriately, Dion lay in Pieria, traditionally considered a favorite abode of the Muses, those daughters of Zeus whom Hesiod had heard singing on holy Helicon. Just south of Dion towered Mount Olympus, where Zeus himself dwelt, on the frontier between Macedonia and Hellas. About 399, the year in which Athens executed Socrates, Archelaus was assassinated, and for seven years coronations and assassinations alternated rapidly. Then Amyntas III came to the throne. By 370, when he died, Amyntas had managed to rescue his kingdom from pressure by the wild Illyrians, had skillfully maneuvered his way through the tangled antagonisms of Greek politics, and had reduced his feudal princes in the highlands to obedience.

Amyntas' eldest son, Alexander I, reigned two years; then his mother arranged his assassination so that she and Ptolemy, her son-in-law and lover, might rule. But the Chalcidian League was backing another candidate for the throne. The murderous queen called in Athens' brilliant professional general of mercenaries, Iphicrates, as support against the League. Her husband had adopted Iphicrates as his son, to please a Thracian king whose daughter the Athenian general had married. Aside from this somewhat personal tangle, Athens was opposed to the Chalcidian League, which was supporting Amphipolis against reconquest by Athens. But then friends of the Macedonian queen's dead husband called on Pelopidas of Thebes to lead an army of mercenaries against the queen and her lover Ptolemy. Ptolemy bribed the mercenaries and agreed to serve only as regent and as guardian of the queen's two remaining sons, Perdiccas and Philip. He also turned over to Thebes fifty hostages, including Philip. Philip was about fifteen when he went to Thebes, and he stayed there for some three years. In 365, Perdiccas came of age and demanded the crown. Ptolemy refused; Perdiccas contrived his assassination and his mother, the queen, having caused the murder of her eldest son in order that she and her lover might reign, consoled her widowhood by learning to read.

Her second son, Perdiccas III, carried on the hellenizing tradition of his court at Pella, interested himself in philosophy and geometry and received at his court a pupil of Plato's. He was an able administrator; and with the aid of an Athenian exile, he reorganized his kingdom's finances. The Illyrians again started trouble in the northwest. In 359 he led an army against them, but he was overwhelmingly defeated. Some 4,000 Macedonians fell in battle; among them was the king. His infant son succeeded him, with Philip as regent. The Paeonians were attacking from the north; the Thracians were attacking from the east and backing a claimant to the throne; and Athens was backing another claimant with her fleet.

Philip was only twenty-three when he became regent of Macedonia. He had been born the year the Spartans seized by treachery the citadel of Thebes. He was eleven when news came that Epaminondas, the Theban general, had decisively defeated a Spartan army at Leuctra. Epaminondas had smashed through the famous Spartan line, twelve shields deep, with his newly developed phalanx or wedge of heavy infantry, fifty shields deep. At the front of the phalanx he had placed the Sacred Band, led by his friend Pelopidas. Four years after Leuctra, Philip, as one of the hostages to Thebes, came to know both Epaminondas and Pelopidas, and there he was lodged in the home of another great Theban general, Pammenes. By then Epaminondas had three times invaded the Peloponnese, had broken all precedent by ravaging the heart of Laconia itself, and had barely missed taking Sparta. Pelopidas had twice invaded Thessaly. Although Athens still headed her second maritime league, it was Thebes that dominated Mainland Greece. She dominated largely through the military genius of Epaminondas and his ingenuity in developing new tactics.

Although Thebes, too, sometimes used mercenaries, her victories were won primarily by citizen-soldiers fighting as heavy infantry or as cavalry, citizen-soldiers who had spent their lives largely as the Macedonians had done, in farming, hunting, and fighting, citizen-soldiers who were neither merchants nor seamen. Boeotia, unlike Macedonia, had produced a Hesiod and even a Pindar; the men of Attica nevertheless looked down on Boeotians as not living what Pericles had described as the good life. Despite her two coasts, Boeotia kept her hand from the ship's tiller, kept her hand on the plow. By turning her back on the sea, she partially turned her back both on commerce in goods and on commerce in ideas. Her name itself suggested cow country, and precisely so Athenians viewed her. While Philip was living in Thebes, Epaminondas did make a precipitate effort to match Athens at sea, but Thebes's naval career, though not inglorious, was brief. Given the Boeotian economy, a navy was essentially artificial; and money soon failed.

A young, hellenized Macedonian prince could learn lessons here in Thebes. He could admire Athens at a distance as a city of ideas, as a city of ships, a city turned toward the sea. He could admire the aristocratic, military tradition of Sparta and her extraordinary hold on the imagination of aristocrat and oligarch throughout Greece. But he would remember that Thebes had humbled Sparta, and that it was in Thebes that men were really thinking about the occupation of princes, war. For Thebes was effecting her own revolution in warfare and it was a different revolution from that of Iphicrates. Were Macedonia to acquire this new Theban knowledge, could she not put it to even more effective use than Thebes?

In 359, Philip became regent, then king, of Macedonia. He bought off, or fought off, the various foes that threatened her. Between his return from Thebes and his assuming the post of regent, he had been assigned a semi-independent principality. There he had trained in the latest Theban fashion 10,000 infantry and 600 cavalry. They had crushingly defeated the Illyrian clans. But he had learned in Thebes that the new warfare, even with his citizen-soldiers, would require a standing army, professionally trained, able to keep the field the year round, and that this took money. His brother, Perdiccas, had deserted an alliance with Athens and had, to the fury of Athens, defended against Athenian troops Amphipolis, guardian of the gold mines of Mount Pangaeus and guardian too of the ship's timber that could be floated down the Strymon River. To pacify Athens, Philip declared Amphipolis an independent polis. He also returned without ransom the Athenians he had captured in a battle with Athens' claimant to his throne and even made a secret treaty with Athens. Under that treaty Philip himself was to conquer Amphipolis and then turn her over to Athens, while Athens was to turn over her ally, Pydna, a free Greek city on the Macedonian coast, to Philip. In 357 he marched to Amphipolis and demanded that it surrender. The Amphipolitans begged for Athenian help. But Athens, neutralized by her secret treaty with Philip, delayed. Philip brought up his rams, breached the walls of Amphipolis, and the city fell. He then declined to keep his promise in the secret treaty to yield his prey to Athens.

Athens, faced with a revolt among her allies, did nothing to recover

Amphipolis. Since she was either morally or physically unable to deliver Pydna to Philip, a few months later he marched on Pydna, secured help from traitors inside, and seized the city. Philip now converted the nearby mining town of Crenides, on Mount Pangaeus, into the city of Philippi, and began to exploit the gold. Before long, he was receiving the immense revenue of a thousand talents a year. No other state that he would have to deal with, except Persia, enjoyed a revenue anywhere near that figure. By 348-347 Philip was striking a new gold coin, the *philippeion*. Had he learned in his Greek exile why the right of coinage, the right to emit the medium which made possible the commerce in things, was prized almost as much by the polis as was the word, the medium which made possible the commerce in ideas? Or that it took coins as well as words to support a commercial community?

Whether or not he reflected on such things, Philip now held the means to do what neither Pericles of Athens nor Lysander and Agesilaus of Sparta nor Epaminondas and Pelopidas of Thebes could possibly have done. No one of these three sovereign city-states, even considered along with its subject states, could properly be called a nation. No one of them ever devised institutions capable of making Hellas a nation in the political sense. But Philip now led a kind of nation, and that nation held nearly twice the territory of its Greek neighbor Thessaly, and, on the rare occasions when Thessaly was united, it was the most extensive single political unit in Mainland Greece. Once Philip had finally integrated his wild highlanders of the western hinterland into his kingdom, Macedonia was not only extensive but populous, and Philip could muster 80,000 fighting men able to equip themselves at their own expense. In terms of Greek warfare, this was an immense force. Nor were they the subject slaves of a King of Kings, fighting unwillingly under the lash. They loved fighting. They were a nation of fighting nobles and peasants, owing allegiance to a king who, given Macedonia's troubled history, was primarily commander-in-chief. It was a nation that had passed through none of the frustrations and disillusionments, none of the intellectual skepticism and debilitating ease, of most of the Greek city-states to the south. Its new monarch knew Greek life at first hand, admired the Athens Pericles had called the School of Hellas, had every reason to be wary of the imperializing city which Pericles had called a tyrant state. Philip knew the Greeks' increasing love of money; he knew their increased respect for force and fraud; he knew both the skill and the fickleness of the Greek mercenary. His money brought to his court the Greek knowledge and Greek administrative skill he wanted, and Greek administrators and civil servants were spreading in Macedonia the Attic dialect in which Xenophon wrote, the dialect that had now become the common tongue of educated Hellenes everywhere.

Not only was Philip's army large. It combined the patriotic loyalty of Epaminondas' Thebans, the constant drill that had once made Spartan infantry supreme over her neighbors' citizen levies, the innovating tactics of the new mercenaries of Athens. But where the Athenian general of mercenaries, Iphicrates, had already lengthened the pike of the light infantryman, Philip lengthened the traditional Macedonian lance, the sarissa, to over twenty feet for the men in the rear rank. And since the length of the sarissa varied with the rank its user marched in, a formidable porcupine of spear points held off Philip's enemies while his other infantry and his cavalry deployed and maneuvered for attack. The flood of golden philips from the mines of Mount Pangaeus kept Philip's armies in the field the year round, sure of the regular wage on which Athens' expert mercenaries could never depend. Thus Philip's army was a knife that never turned and cut his hand, as Athens' mercenary armies turned and cut hers when, lacking pay, they pillaged their city's own allies.

Philip never used force unless amicable negotiation, fraud, and bribery had all failed. In diplomacy he lied as fast as the Greeks did, if not even faster; but he lied with much more method and in terms of the long view. In his handling of his army he was a ruthless disciplinarian, a generous rewarder of merit, and expert in choosing the right man for the right task. Above all, he had clear-cut policies, and his opponents had not. He had single-minded purpose, and his purpose dictated means and ends. His most persistent opponent, Athens, followed conflicting purposes, and the conflict kept her means and ends confused. Philip's purpose was to unite under his leadership Hellas and Macedonia. He would thereby bring political order to the Greeks and Hellenic culture to his half-barbarous Macedonians. His golden philips bore on one side a head of Apollo, who interpreted to men the will of his father Zeus, and on the other a two-horse chariot with its ambiguous Pindaric overtones of Achilles' eris against the Trojans and the eris of the holy races held at the Olympic Games.

By the summer of 356 Philip had taken Potidaea and had eliminated the Athenians from the Chalcidic peninsula, he had put an end to the inroads of the Illyrians and Paeonians, and he had pushed his eastern, Thracian frontier from the Strymon River to the Nestus River, to the far side of gold-laden Mount Pangaeus. In that same single summer[397] he received news that Parmenion, one of his generals, had won a final victory over the Illyrians; that his horses had won the chariot race at the Olympic Games; that his wild Epirote wife, Olympias, had borne him a son and heir, whose name would be Alexander.

Except for the city of Methone on the Thermaic Gulf, Philip had cleared his coast of colonial control by Athens and he had done it without open war. He did not want war with Athens. Athena's polis remained the symbol of Hellenic culture, and his overriding aim was to merge that culture with the semi-barbaric vitality, the military power, and the economic resources of Macedonia. In his own phrase Athens was the Theater of Glory.[398] However, he wanted Methone, and in 353 he laid siege to it. Athens, as usual, delayed too long, and Methone fell. In the battle Philip lost one eye; he also lost his troubled peace with Athens.

Philip was now ready for intervention in Greece. Happily, an ideal opportunity arose. In 356 Thebes had become involved in the affairs of Phocis and persuaded the Amphictyonic League, an organization of neighboring states formed to protect Delphi and its oracle, to fine certain rich Phocians on a charge of sacrilege. When the fines were not paid on time the Amphictyons assigned the lands of the accused to the temple of Apollo. The victims determined to resist, appointed one Philomelus general, and hired mercenaries. Philomelus then seized Delphi and used the treasures of the temple, treasures he insisted he was merely borrowing from Apollo, to raise mercenaries and defend Phocis. He insisted also that the little town of Delphi belonged to Phocis and was not a sovereign holy enclave, and he got promises of help from Athens, from Sparta, and from some other Greek states. But one forced loan from Apollo led to another, as more and more mercenaries were hired. The war, being a holy war, was fought with extraordinary ferocity. At last, in 354, whether or not because the god objected to forced loans, Philomelus was disastrously defeated and committed suicide.

His lieutenant Onomarchus took over. Onomarchus not only continued to borrow from the god in order to raise mercenaries. A dream convinced him that the gods were on his side.[399] He melted down the gifts of bronze and iron accumulated by Apollo and made armor of them. He melted down the gold and silver gifts Apollo had received since the time of Croesus of Lydia, and minted them; and some 10,000 talents sufficed to bring him the mercenaries he needed and to corrupt the leaders in other states. The sacred war to protect Apollo had brought an unexpected result: Apollo was being turned into money.

It was the culmination of a long process. The Hellenes had more than once become confused over the relation of Apollo and money. Whether or not Apollo correctly informed men of the will of Zeus, the information had to pass through several corruptible human agents. There was, first, the Pythia, the priestess, who sat on her tripod, went into a trance, and murmured or mumbled the god's message or cried it out in words that often sounded quite unintelligible. Secondly, there were the priests, who commonly put the message into hexameter verse, the ancient meter of Homer and Hesiod. More than once in Greek history the priests had been charged with accepting bribes. But even if the priests were faithful translators, their messages had a way of sounding like riddles, cynically calculated to cover all contingencies. Wooden walls might conveniently have meant either ships or the stockade around the Acropolis. A Croesus eager to attack Cyrus, or a Xenophon eager to serve another Cyrus, might jump to conclusions instead of really listening, really questioning. Obviously, if bribes could deflect the oracle, whether Apollo's part in it, or the Pythia's, or the part the priests played, there was room for cynicism. If the final oracle was ambiguous, was its ambiguity merely a cloak for ignorance, an effort to cover all contingencies? Ever since those terrible days nearly a century and a half before when Xerxes and his monstrous herd drew nearer and nearer and when Apollo had issued more than one warning not to oppose the invader, Apollo—or his temple servants—had been accused of medizing in Hellas' greatest hour of peril; and Delphi had lost face correspondingly.

In any case the gods themselves had in some sense withdrawn from among men. Xenophon, who must have remembered how they helped the heroes fight at Troy and who may have read in Herodotus of how they still appeared to men when Xerxes struck, could have found no such theophanies in Thucydides' history, the very history he himself completed; he was able to find only the religious hysteria over the mutilated Herms at Athens, the costly pride of piety that Nicias displayed before Syracuse,

334

and the auspices and omens that the least pious general always had to respect. Xenophon himself wrote:

> If anyone is surprised at my frequent repetition of the exhortation to work with God, I can assure him that his surprise will diminish, if he is often in peril, and if he considers that in time of war foemen plot and counterplot, but seldom know what will come of their plots. Therefore there is none other than can give counsel in such a case but the gods.[400]

And he had, of course, earned the rebuke of Socrates by conscripting Apollo at Delphi when he was bent on serving Cyrus in Asia. But if it was not to learn the will of Zeus that one now went to Delphi, if one no longer listened in quietude of spirit, if Delphi was something to be used, along with the god who dwelt there, a case could be made for melting down the god and minting him into coin, the medium through which all things could be obtained, including victory in war.

The relation of Phocis to the panhellenic shrine within her territory was also a debatable point; and if the Phocians were now correct in asserting that Delphi, with its profitable pilgrim trade, had always belonged to them, was Onomarchus in principle doing more than the Athenians had done during the Pelponnesian War when they borrowed the holy statues and other gifts from the Parthenon to save Athena's city? The Phocians had firmly declared they would return the equivalent of Apollo's treasures as soon as they had fought off the invasion of the busybody Amphictyonic League. Still, the ransacking of Delphi had reached the proportions of an orgy of plunder. A god was indeed being melted down and minted, a god not merely of the Phocians but of Hellenes everywhere.

Philip saw his chance. When the Thessalian League joined the Boeotians against the sacrilegious Phocians, Onomarchus allied himself with the rulers of Pherae in Thessaly, enemies of the League, and the League appealed to Philip. Philip marched south into Thessaly. But Onomarchus, on whom Apollo's gold had temporarily conferred the military supremacy of central Greece, marched into Thessaly too and defeated Philip twice, so severely that Philip withdrew into Macedonia. The following year Philip returned and, in a battle fought near the Thessalian port of Pagasae, he killed or captured a third of the Phocian army. Among the slain lay Onomarchus, who had minted a god. Onomarchus had been a formidable soldier and a skillful statesman. But Philip was now busy defending Apollo against sacrilege: he ordered his prisoners thrown into the sea and he crucified the corpse of Onomarchus. That was in 352. Then he organized the quarreling cities of Thessaly in a league under his own control and thereby imposed a peace which Thessaly had badly needed for half a century. Her cities would govern themselves, on condition that their armies would stand ready to serve Philip. He especially needed Thessalian cavalry, which had always been the best in Greece.

Strengthened by his new resources, Philip dedicated a statue to Apollo, collected the combined forces of Macedonia and Thessaly, and started for the Pass of Thermopylae to continue the war on Phocis. But the allies of Phocis got to the famous Hot Gates first. Even Athens acted promptly this time; she sent a fleet, 5,000 heavy infantry, and 400 horse. Sparta sent 1,000 men; Achaea, 2,000. The Thessalians of Pherae, whom Philip had defeated, also arrived with 2,000 mercenaries. Even assuming that Philip had found the means of outflanking Thermopylae and attacking its defenders from both ends, as Xerxes had, it would have been a politically stupid move. The image which Philip was busily and carefully presenting to Greece was that of the ruler of the largest state in Greece leading a panhellenic holy war against the violators of Greece's holiest shrine. The image he was determined not to present was that of a barbarian king leading, like Xerxes, an assault on Hellas. Philip did not want to conquer Greece, least of all Athens. He wanted to rally Greece to his leadership. If he marched on Phocis, he must somehow march in Greece's name. His path could lead through Thermopylae; or, if need be, through bloodshed; but not through both at once.

Meanwhile, the sacrilegious but determined Phocians fought on against the Thebans, under a brother of Onomarchus, until that brother fell ill and died, then under their crucified leader's son. Even when Thebes secured a subsidy from Persia in return for a promise of mercenaries, the minted god kept Phocian mercenary guerillas in the field. At last, in 347-346, the temple treasure was exhausted, the mercenaries were grumbling, and the war petered out. Meanwhile Philip had defeated Cersobleptes, king of Thrace, and forced him into an alliance. The Athenian Assembly hurriedly voted an armament to prevent Philip from cutting off her grain route from the Black Sea. But then word came that Philip was dead, and Athens postponed her expedition.

Though Philip was not dead, he was at least temporarily ill. He was now violently attacked in an oration delivered before the Assembly of a Greek polis. Worse still, the polis was Athens. The orator's name was Demosthenes. He was young: he was the same age as Philip. His father had been a well-to-do Athenian businessman, who produced among other things swords for the army. But the father died when Demosthenes was but seven, and the boy's guardians betrayed their trust. Demosthenes determined to sue his guardians in court when he came of age and he prepared himself by studying under the orator Isaeus. He was too delicate to follow the usual course of gymnastics. He haunted the courts and the Assembly and practiced rewriting the speeches he heard there. He studied Thucydides' history and relived the glories of his polis in the great days of Pericles. When he came to speak publicly, he noticed his defects. So he practiced declaiming with pebbles in his mouth, and he practiced gesticulation before a mirror. He pleaded his case against his guardians and won back at least a part of his inheritance. He became a professional speech-writer and made considerable money at the profession. He served repeatedly as trierarch, or officer charged with fitting out a trireme for the state; and, armed with his gift for speaking, he entered politics.

Most men of Demosthenes' economic class followed the conservative statesman Eubulus, who stood for sound fiscal policy and peace at almost any price. Mercenary warfare fell heavily on the rich. It even threatened the pleasures of the poor, for it soon became evident that the polis could not continue its custom of free tickets to the great religious dramatic festivals if its resources must go to war. Demosthenes set himself against this peace policy on the grounds that Philip clearly proposed to conquer Greece. His oratory won him enormous acclaim but not the prompt action he pleaded for. By 351 he was excoriating the Assembly for its apathy, in his first great philippic:

> Or tell me, are you content to run round and ask one another, "Is there any news today?" Could there be any news more startling than that a Macedonian is triumphing over Athenians and settling the destiny of Hellas? "Is Philip dead?" you ask. "No, indeed; but he is ill." And what is that to you? Even if something happens to him, you will soon raise up a second Philip, if that is the way you attend to your affairs; for even this Philip has not grown great through his own unaided strength so much as through our carelessness.[401]

Demosthenes' forensic war on Philip continued tirelessly. His orations were enormously admired. But, even when he could arouse the Athenians to action, the action was usually too little and too late to stop Philip. Undoubtedly, Demosthenes fought under a great handicap. As he himself later complained to the Athenian Assembly, Philip's advantages were many:

> In the first place, he was the despotic commander of his adherents: and in war that is the most important of all advantages. Secondly, they had their weapons constantly in their hands. Then he was well provided with money: he did whatever he chose, without giving notice by publishing decrees, or deliberating in public, without fear of prosecution by informers or indictment for illegal measures. He was responsible to nobody: he was the absolute autocrat, commander, and master of everybody and everything. And I, his chosen adversary—it is a fair inquiry—of what was I master? Of nothing at all! Public speaking was my only privilege: and that you permitted to Philip's hired servants on the same terms as to me. Whenever they had the advantage of me—and for one reason or another that often happened—you laid your plans for the enemy's benefit, and went your ways.[402]

Philip did indeed have more money, an army he could keep in the field the year round, the secrecy of dictatorship, and a dictator's power to command. And Demosthenes was justified, when he cried to the Athenian Assembly in his first philippic:

> in your present condition you would be unable, even if the opportunity offered, to take over Amphipolis, having neither a force nor a policy ready to hand.[403]

But, while Demosthenes himself gave good advice about mobilizing the force, his own policy was to stop Philip, as Athenians of another generation had stopped Xerxes at Marathon, at Salamis, at Plataea, at Mycale. Those other Athenians, however, had been poorer, tougher men than these; they had been full of boundless hope and spiritual vigor. They had not known the glories and miseries of imperial power, nor the treasons and brutalities of the Peloponnesian War, nor the disillusionments of an empire's collapse. They had not seen the rise of their own polis to power, nor its corruption by that power, nor its failure to bring peace and justice to a Hellas still dispersed in its many small, sovereign city-states. The Athenians who had stopped Xerxes had not seen Sparta take her turn and fail, or Thebes take hers. They had not witnessed Athens' effort to reconstitute her old Aegean empire, nor the second disintegration of that empire. Granted that the Athenians of Philip's time no longer wanted to serve in battle, their unwillingness was not all cowardice: war had become professionalized and Greece was awash with expert fighters looking for employment. Granted they loved the pleasant life of Athens and its civilized ease; that they liked listening to the brilliant rhetorical fireworks of Demosthenes and the other professional orators better than the hard work of real political life. To do that hard work intelligently, they needed a cogent purpose; yet they, like Demosthenes, lacked a real policy. Was not the problem that called aloud for a policy the political organization of Greece? Yet Demosthenes never dealt with that problem.[404]

Demosthenes' orations, therefore, though they exhibited great skill and intricate workmanship, fell short of their target. Moreover, in their personal vituperation of Philip and of those Athenian orators who opposed Demosthenes, they often sank to the level of bitter impotence. On his own assumptions, indeed, Demosthenes proved a better prophet than his opponents did: when Philip deceived them as to his determination to gain control of Mainland Greece, he did not deceive Demosthenes. Demosthenes therefore tasted some of the agony that Cassandra tasted in Aeschylus's *Agamemnon*: it was Apollo's cruel gift to her that she should see future events but should always fail to persuade others that she saw them. Demosthenes had something of the same cruel gift, which lent him at least the appearance of lonely grandeur. But was not the future he saw partly the product of his own incapacity to find a solution to the real problem?

Lacking the procreative idea, Demosthenes redoubled his rhetorical flourishes; and thereby managed unwittingly to justify the cutting remarks on rhetoric which Socrates had once made[405] to the famous sophist, Gorgias. Rhetoric inflated Demosthenes, as it had the sophist Protagoras, whom Socrates was dragged at dawn to admire. How much inflated it left Demosthenes, he himself discovered afresh whenever Phocion, the statesman and general, the pupil of Socrates' disciple Plato, would rise and make one of his simple, laconic statements. Then it was as if Lycurgan Sparta herself were rebuking the garrulity, the flattery, the florid excitement of this Athenian, with his carefully elaborated, studiedly emotional, thoroughly memorized calls to greatness, each gesture in its proper place. Demosthenes dreaded Phocion. According to later tradition, when Phocion would approach the rostrum, the great orator would remark to his friends: "Here comes the pruning-knife of my speeches."[406]

It was Isocrates of Athens who nearly saw the problem. He was eighty-five years old when Demosthenes delivered his first philippic before the Athenian Assembly. He was born in the great age of Pericles in 436, five years before the long Peloponnesian War broke out. He was the son of a prosperous manufacturer of flutes. He knew Gorgias the sophist, and Socrates too. But where Plato was attracted by Socrates' questioning mind, Isocrates saw chiefly the side of him that Xenophon saw, the moral side. Like Demosthenes, Isocrates was drawn toward oratory and the political life. But a weak voice and a certain lack of assurance diverted his ambition, and he therefore wrote speeches for others. More importantly, he started a school, which became the only institutional rival of the Academy set up a few years later by Plato. There he taught the art of discourse. He conceived of this art as not merely the composition of speeches, but the liberal education that alone enabled the orator, not merely to say things well, but to know what should be said. Indeed, he thought of himself as a philosopher. Although Socrates had prophesied, when Isocrates was young, that he would go beyond all other speech-writers because he already showed some impulse toward philosophy, yet Isocrates had turned from the intellectual rigors of philosophic thought to the realm of the practical. His school attracted students from all over Hellas, from the Black Sea to Sicily. He was a true Athenian in his love of the word. Writing autobiographically when he was an old man of eighty-two, he praised the art of discourse:

> We ought, therefore, to think of the art of discourse just as we think of the other arts, and not to form opposite judgements about similar things, nor show ourselves intolerant toward that power which, of all the faculties which belong to the nature of man, is the source of most of our blessings. For in the other powers which we possess, as I have already said on a former occasion, we are in no respect superior to other living creatures; nay, we are inferior to many in swiftness and in strength and in other resources; but, because there has been implanted in us the power to persuade each other and to make clear to each other whatever

we desire, not only have we escaped the life of wild beasts, but we have come together and founded cities and made laws and invented arts; and, generally speaking, there is no institution devised by man which the power of speech has not helped us to establish. For this it is which has laid down laws concerning things just and unjust, and things honourable and base; and if it were not for these ordinances we should not be able to live with one another. It is by this also that we confute the bad and extol the good. Through this we educate the ignorant and appraise the wise; for the power to speak well is taken as the surest index of a sound understanding, and discourse which is true and lawful and just is the outward image of a good and faithful soul. With this faculty we both contend against others on matters which are open to dispute and seek light for ourselves on things which are unknown; for the same arguments which we use in persuading others when we speak in public, we employ also when we deliberate in our own thoughts; and, while we call eloquent those who are able to speak before a crowd, we regard as sage those who most skilfully debate their problems in their own minds. And, if there is need to speak in brief summary of this power, we shall find that none of the things which are done with intelligence take place without the help of speech, but that in all our actions as well as in all our thoughts speech is our guide, and is most employed by those who have the most wis-dom.[407]

The theory that speech was most employed by those who had the most wisdom would have seemed unlikely to Phocion, the laconic meat-cleaver of Demosthenes' forensic displays. Indeed, it would have seemed unlikely to Socrates.

Although Isocrates deserted early in life his profession of paid speech-writer, he became Athens' leading publicist, her leading commentator on political affairs. Even so, his writings were almost invariably cast in the form of speeches. Somewhat as Thucydides, writing in the great age of Greek tragedy, cast his history in the form of tragedy, so Isocrates, writing at a time when the oration was the leading literary form of Greece, cast his own comments in the form of speeches, although these speeches were never delivered from a platform. He believed that Athens had many rivals in contests of the body but that "in the training of the mind everyone would concede that we stand first."[408] He urged that Athenians "get our youth to look down upon a life of ease and be willing to give their minds to their own improvement and to philosophy."[409]

Miltiades won at Marathon, he reminded his readers, Themistocles led Athens to power, Pericles made both the Acropolis and the homes of Athenian citizens overflow with wealth, not only because they were well-born and well spoken of, but because they knew how "to think and speak."[410] Isocrates devoted his life to Greek culture, the kind of culture befitting a gentleman; to a broad, general education. But the role of philosophy in this training would be not architectonic, as in the life of Socrates, but in a sense ornamental, an amenity rather than a stern guide. Isocrates was no barefoot inquirer; he was a successful, well-to-do, somewhat vain, and kindly man. Like Xenophon, he wanted to be useful.

Like Xenophon, also, he wrote in the Attic dialect and helped make that dialect familiar in all corners of the Hellenic world as the Greek spoken by educated men. Where the Attic of Xenophon's *Anabasis* was used in simple, soldierly sentences to convey vividly events a soldierly man had witnessed, Isocrates elaborated a complex periodic sentence, full of subtle and graceful rhythms, and consciously aimed at giving to the ear some of the pleasure that poetry had once given. Attic shared the strength, without the harshness, of Doric; it shared the grace, without the softness, of Ionic. In the matter of coin, Macedonian philips might be competing hard with Athenian owls as the medium men now used to exchange commodities, or the medium they now misused in order to accumulate power without limit or to satisfy appetites that never ceased growing. But even Macedonians were learning the Attic words that men used when they exchanged ideas, as, alone among animals, men could do; or that men misused in order to substitute for common deliberation the virtuoso performance of the spellbinder. And now that poetry had yielded first place to prose, prose came to the rescue and served to stir emotions. Orators like Demosthenes and Isocrates became the literary models of Hellas.

In addition to presiding over his school, in which men could be taught to think and speak without the Socratic rigors of Plato's Academy, Isocrates for decades preached Hellenic unity through a joint attack on Persia. In 380, seven years before Athens had formed her second confederacy, shortly after the Great King's announcement of 386 in effect forbade the Greek states to unite, and in the very years when a Spartan garrison was occupying Thebes, Isocrates wrote a *Panegyric* to Athens:

And so far has our city distanced the rest of mankind in thought and in speech that her pupils have become the teachers of the rest of the world; and she has brought it about that the name "Hellenes" suggests no longer a race but an intelligence, and that the title "Hellenes" is applied rather to those who share our culture than to those who share a common blood.[411]

Isocrates urged Athens, guardian and transmitter of this culture, to lead Hellas on a sacred mission, the conquest of Persia. In 368 he urged Dionysius I, tyrant of Syracuse, to do it; in 356, he urged it on Archidamus, son of Xenophon's leader, King Agesilaus. Agesilaus had in some sense done it. In 342, he wrote a letter urging it on Philip. But four years before the letter to Philip, when Isocrates was ninety, he had written a much longer *Address to Philip*. For a third of a century he had been looking for a lever to raise Hellas from the anarchy and misery and bloodshed in which it had floundered. The aged Athenian publicist, who had based a long and famous career on his faith in words and their power to persuade, pointed out to the still young king that beyond any of the Hellenes he, the king, was

> possessed of both wealth and power, which are the only things in the world that are adapted at once to persuade and to compel; and these aids, I think, even the cause which I shall propose to you will need to have on its side. For I am going to advise you to champion the cause of concord among the Hellenes and of a campaign against the barbarian; and as persuasion will be helpful in dealing with the Hellenes, so compulsion will be useful in dealing with the barbarians. This, then, is the general scope of my discourse.[412]

Isocrates insisted that the mutual hatreds that separated so many Greek cities were counterbalanced by their willingness to ally themselves with former enemies in the name of expediency and by their common need of protection against one another. He retraced the confused, discouraging course of recent Hellenic history. He showed what certain leaders had accomplished against worse odds than would face Philip if, first, he composed the quarrels of the Greek cities, and, second, led them all against Persia. Look at what Xenophon and his fellow mercenaries had done against the Great King when they fought him at Cunaxa under Cyrus. There was now rebellion in the Persian Empire. Philip should

343

emulate his ancestor, Heracles, who helped the Hellenes. What fame would be Philip's if he conquered the Persian Empire or, at any rate, its western provinces and undertook

> to establish cities in this region, and to settle in permanent abodes those who now, for lack of the daily necessities of life, are wandering from place to place and committing outrages upon whomsoever they encounter?[413]

If Philip would plant such military colonies on the eastern frontier of the Hellenic world in Asia, he would give an economic function to the mercenaries, the refugees, the uprooted, and he would at the same time restore order in Hellas. At a minimum he could free Greece-in-Asia from Persian control. There were other descendants of Heracles, but each clung to his own polis, while Philip was above cities and could, like Heracles, consider all Hellas his fatherland. And then the old man summarized his thesis, prompted by "the divine will"[414]:

> I assert that it is incumbent upon you to work for the good of the Hellenes, to reign as king over the Macedonians, and to extend your power over the greatest possible number of the barbarians. For if you do these things, all men will be grateful to you: the Hellenes for your kindness to them; the Macedonians if you reign over them, not like a tyrant, but like a king; and the rest of the nations, if by your hands they are delivered from barbaric despotism and are brought under the protection of Hellas.[415]

At his most thoughtful, Isocrates was urging that Philip restore order in Hellas and then maintain it by an economic and colonial expansion at Persia's expense. At his worst, was he trying to drain off the violence which now led Greek to murder Greek and to let it vent itself in the murder of the Great King's non-Hellenic subjects? Aeschylus had suggested in his *Oresteia* that, once violence was let loose, it required more than the counter-violence to purge it out of the human community. It required law. But Isocrates did not prescribe law. Unlike Demosthenes, he knew that the problem was not to stop Philip and restore the greatness of Athens under Pericles. He knew that the problem was anarchy in Hellas as a whole, the violence of polis against polis. Not having found a solution to the problem of violence, he ceaselessly advocated exporting it. But he was also exploiting a deep urge in Hellas.

The urge to emigrate, to colonize, sometimes man by man, more often

344

in bands, not only caused the citizens of Phocaea to swear a mighty oath to move their polis to Corsica, but permitted the men of the Athenian navy at Samos to fancy that they, and not the oligarchs at home, were the real polis. It was the same urge that had prompted Xenophon to gaze hungrily at Calpe's Haven on the Black Sea; that had led Aristophanes to imagine Cloudcuckooland, a comic paradise, a polis founded in between the world of the gods and the world of men. Even Socrates had imagined a heavenly polis in the clear world of ideas that every earthly polis could at best but imitate. Practically, poetically, philosophically, Hellas showed signs of flight from the polis which men had known to a polis poignantly sensed if dimly seen, a home that might be Ithaca or might be another shore Odysseus had not yet beheld.

While Demosthenes thundered out his denunciations of the barbarian, Philip, who was determined to put an end to Hellenic freedom, or more accurately to end the right of Greek cities to make war on each other and to subject each other—Philip continued methodically with his own plan to wed Macedonian strength and discipline to what was left of the Hellenic culture Isocrates admired and taught. He used and misused words quite as skillfully as Demosthenes. For Demosthenes' carefully written, brilliantly delivered orations, he substituted his diplomatic fencing, his personal charm, his golden philips. He played on the fears and hates that set Greek polis against Greek polis. He allowed his opponents to intercept messages which he had planted for the purpose. He spread rumors. He treated Athens as he might have treated one of his numerous mistresses: he courted her, he made her gifts, he slapped her when he felt he had to, he admired her and was fascinated by her. And Athens? Through Demosthenes' bitter, eloquent mouth she denounced and insulted him, she sent envoys and made up with him, she stirred up his neighbors against him. She still commanded the Aegean Sea and made what trouble she could for him with her fleet. But when by 348 Philip had reduced the Greek cities of Chalcidice, he controlled the coast from the border of Thessaly to the Chersonese.

In July, 346, Philip appeared again with an army at the Pass of Thermopylae. Opposing him was Phalaecus, son of Onomarchus, the Onomarchus who had minted the god Apollo to defend his country, Phocis. But internal squabbles in Phocis had driven out Phalaecus, and he and his mercenaries now held Thermopylae. Philip tried negotiation. Phalaecus asked for time, and sent to Athens for help. His mercenaries' pay was in arrears and they were growing restive. The Athenian Assembly was passing resolutions against Philip but would clearly not send adequate support. Thereupon Phalaecus sold the Pass to Philip. Philip marched south to help Thebes destroy the sacrilegious Phocians and to avenge Apollo. Phocis was devastated and the Delphians they had driven out ten years before were restored to their polis and its sacred temple. Through his oracle, Apollo thanked Philip, and the Amphictyons elected him to replace Phocis on their Council. By autumn he sat in the president's chair at the Pythian games.

Within four years, the cities of Thessaly had elected Philip archon of their League for life. He improved his navy and negotiated alliances in the Peloponnese with Messenia, Megalopolis, Elis, Argos. The polis he wanted most to conciliate was Athens, but at Athens Demosthenes was loudly charging that Philip was planning to destroy the city. Both Demosthenes and the orator Aeschines, bitter forensic foes, had served on Athenian embassies that had recently made peace with Philip, and both now engaged in mutual recriminations concerning the roles they had played while on mission. Demosthenes traveled through the Peloponnese trying to inflame people there against Philip. Meanwhile Philip marched into Epirus, where his Epirote wife's royal father had died, and secured the succession for his wife's brother. Then he conquered Thrace; dethroned Cersobleptes; made his kingdom a province of Macedonia; landed troops on the Chersonese; and attacked Byzantium. Athens' grain route was thereby endangered, and she sent a naval force that was able to save Byzantium. Demosthenes had by now so aroused Athenian fears that he was able to secure a law distributing more equitably the burden of fitting out triremes, and another law that diverted to military purposes the money previously reserved to buy admission for the poor to the great religious festivals. Having failed at Byzantium to secure the grain route and, with it, control of the food supply of Athens and other Greek cities, Philip struck northward and shattered an army of Scythians. But on the way home, he was attacked by wild tribesmen and was himself wounded in the thigh. The wound threatened to gangrene. He returned to his capital at Pella for the winter of 339-338.

In March a message arrived from the Amphictyonic League. Another political scuffle, involving the charge of another act of sacrilege, had broken out. The Amphictyons were in vain appealing to Athens and Thebes to punish the Locrian city of Amphissa. Now they appealed to Philip. Once more the defender of Apollo marched south to do his religious duty toward all Hellas. He went as far as Elatea in Phocis and then proposed to Thebes that she join him in pillaging Attica, or failing that, give him free passage through Boeotia. Athens sent envoys, including Demosthenes, who persuaded Thebes to desert her alliance with Philip and combine with Athens against him. Philip marched into Boeotia.

Near Chaeronea, around August of 338, he faced his Greek opponents: Thebans, with their Sacred Band in front, Athenians, mercenaries from Corinth, Achaeans, and contingents from a group of small cities. Philip himself faced the Athenians. His son, Alexander, now eighteen, faced the Thebans. The opposing armies were about equal in number: some 30,000 infantry and about 2,000 horse.[416] But Philip's troops were better trained, better armed, and much better commanded. Demosthenes finally had his hour: a Greek army was defending Greece against northern barbarians not many miles from Plataea, where a Greek army had defeated the Persian barbarians, and he, Demosthenes, stood in the ranks of the Athenians. On the Greek left the Athenians fought well, even though Philip badly outgeneraled them. But the Greek center gave way and suffered heavy losses. For a moment the right wing of the Athenians appeared to be gaining, and one of their generals, Stratocles, started yelling that they would push on to Macedonia. But the Athenian advance opened a gap in the Greek line. Into it Alexander and his cavalry promptly charged. Macedonian infantry followed the cavalry. And while the infantry by a flank attack rolled up the Greek line, Alexander's cavalry encircled the Thebans' Sacred Band. Philip threw the Athenians into a rout; some 1,000 were killed, some 2,000 were captured. The rest fled, Demosthenes among them. The Sacred Band, which had made the army of Thebes so formidable in the days of Epaminondas and Pelopidas, kept their tradition, to conquer or to die. They died to a man.

Chaeronea gave Greece to Philip, and he knew it. According to later tradition, he invited his officers to a feast, the sort his Macedonians loved, with plenty of women, plenty of music, plenty of wine. The usual heralds who came to seek permission to collect the Greek dead for burial were kept waiting. Athens had offered an alliance to Thebes on a motion by Demosthenes, and when the Macedonians had feasted,

> Philip waxed insolent for joy, and going forth in revel rout to see the bodies of the slain, and being in his cups, recited the beginning of the decree introduced by Demosthenes, dividing it into feet and marking off the time:—
>
> "Demosthenes, son of Demosthenes, of Paeania, thus moves."[417]

Among the Athenian prisoners stood Demades, an orator famed for his incisive speech. Now he spoke to Philip: "King, when Fate has cast thee for Agamemnon, art not ashamed to play Thersites?" The allusion to Homer, fount of the Hellenic culture which Philip had set out to win for his half-barbarian Macedonians, brought him to his senses. He tore the festive garlands from him; the wine cups and flutes were flung down and trodden underfoot; he ordered Demades to be set free, and went away ashamed.

The victor treated Thebes harshly. He garrisoned her citadel, the Cadmea, with Macedonian troops, and turned Thebes over to the tender mercies of some 300 men she had exiled for supporting Philip. It was from Thebes that, as a boy, he had learned the art of war. Now he repaid her in the coin war commonly used. For Philip had learned Homer, too: "Ares is just and slays him who slays."[418] But Athens must be an exception. He was determined not to appear her victor any more than she had forced him to play that role already. He gave back her prisoners; and, unlike Thebes, the city he still courted was not asked for ransom. Athens had strengthened her walls with tree trunks and even with gravestones, but her conqueror led no soldier across her frontier. When she sent envoys, he gave them an offer of alliance to take home, and sent Demades, his rebuker, with them. He also sent his regent, Antipater, and his son, Alexander, whose troops had broken the Thebans at Chaeronea. Even Demosthenes refrained from urging a last, desperate stand behind the walls: there were no besiegers to fight with. Freedom was lost, but at least he was chosen to pronounce an oration over those who fell at Chaeronea. As for Isocrates, he was now ninety-eight; and he wrote one last letter to Philip, in which he pointed out that

> on account of the battle which has taken place, all are compelled to be prudent and to desire that which they surmise you wish to do and to

say, namely, that they must desist from the madness and the spirit of aggrandizement, which they were wont to display in their relations with each other, and must carry the war into Asia. . . . No achievement could be more glorious, more useful to the Greeks, or more timely than this will be.[419]

Of the city-states of Mainland Greece, Sparta alone refused to submit. Philip ravaged Laconia, but the unwalled polis still would not recognize him as leader of the Greeks. He demanded the honor of Laconian citizenship for himself, and Sparta replied in her old grand manner, as Achilles might have done, that at least Philip could not prevent the Spartans from dying for their country. At last he diminished her territory and left her to sulk: to overwhelm her militarily would have blurred the image he wanted to present to Hellas.

Before the year of Chaeronea was spent, Philip convoked a congress of the Greek states to meet at Corinth. Early in 337, the delegates assembled. They represented all of Mainland Greece except Sparta, and even some of the islands and some of the Greek states in Thrace. Philip submitted a plan for a general peace between all the Greek states represented. They were to form a panhellenic league, and the league was to sign an offensive and defensive alliance with Macedon. All existing frontiers were confirmed. The league was charged with arbitrating all future disputes between member states. No member state could change its constitution by force, and no state was to permit the banished citizens of another state to organize on its soil a military expedition against their home government. In theory, therefore, both war and revolution, those twin evils of Hellas, each a contributing cause of the other, were quite simply abolished. Every state was to enjoy full local autonomy and full freedom of the seas. No city need accept a foreign garrison, except those cities already garrisoned by Macedonians to insure the common defense: Thebes, Chalcis, Corinth, and Ambracia. No city would be required to contribute money to the league, but all would be required to contribute military or naval contingents when needed. The king of Macedonia was to be ex officio Hegemon, or leader, of the Hellenes, and in theory would exercise the executive functions of the panhellenic league. In addition to its leader, the league would possess a council, called the Synhedrion of the Hellenes. This league council would be composed of delegates plenipotentiary, and each member state would be allowed delegates in proportion

349

to its military contributions. If any member state should break the peace, the league was to call on the executive—the king of Macedon—to mobilize the military contingents of the remaining members and to discipline the recalcitrant.

If the cities which established this council could have viewed it as the common representative assembly of all the citizens of all the member cities; if all the citizens of each state had elected their delegates to this panhellenic congress; and if the congress' new League of Corinth had been empowered to impose taxes; then might not a common government have made a genuine step toward freedom under law? In such a case, the idea of polis, which had already been twice extended, might have been extended once more, and a genuine, free, federal government might have emerged. But the weakness of the League of Corinth, together with its tight alliance with the king of Macedon, placed all real power in his hands. The dialectic between the freedom of Periclean democracy and the Spartan championship of sovereign independence for every polis had first been transformed into the eristic of the Peloponnesian War and of the increasingly senseless wars that followed, and the eristic had now ended in a peace imposed by a veiled despotism.

At Corinth Philip also announced his intention of invading the Persian Empire; and the member states of the new League of Corinth promised contingents for a crusade in which the Greeks no longer felt any real desire to take part. Their participation was clearly intended only as a token, but Philip still might hope that the joint enterprise would serve to weld together the force of Macedonia and the renowned culture of the Greeks. By the spring of 336 he had sent a fraction of his army to hold the Hellespont, in order that he might cross it into Asia, as Xerxes had crossed it a century and a half before, coming from that same Asia into Europe against the little city-states of Hellas. Philip of course consulted the Delphic oracle, not on whether to attack Persia, but on whether he would be victorious when he attacked. And Apollo answered: "The bull is crowned; the consummation is at hand; the sacrificer is ready."[420] Philip construed this oracle to mean that the crowned King of Kings was the bull and he, Philip, the man who would sacrifice him, the way one would sacrifice a real bull garlanded for slaughter at the altar.

He delayed leading the main force across to Asia. He had repudiated his Epirote wife Olympias, the mother of Alexander, on the charge of adultery. He himself, since their marriage, had acquired a number of wives, often for dynastic reasons. He now married Cleopatra, daughter of one of his generals, Attalus. He faced a long absence from his kingdom. Olympias had left in rage for the court of her brother, Alexander, king of Epirus. Would she stir up this brother against Philip while Philip was absent in Asia? To neutralize Olympias, Philip offered her brother the hand of his own and Olympias's daughter, who bore the same name as her new stepmother, Cleopatra. The offer was accepted. Olympias and Alexander returned to Macedonia for the wedding.

With the Delphic Apollo safely conscripted to his banner, Philip offered costly and magnificent sacrifices and solemnized the marriage of his daughter at Aegae, the capital of Macedonia before Archelaus had moved his court to Pella, and still the religious center of the royal family. Guests were invited from all over Greece. Many Greek cities sent golden crowns; and one crown came from Athens. She was grateful, or desired to appear grateful, for Philip's treatment of her in defeat and helplessness. Philip did his best to make the occasion one of reconciliation between Hellene and half-Hellene, between Greek and Macedonian. Neoptolemus, a famous tragedian, wrote verses on the coming expedition into Asia and gave a command recitation. There were music, dancing, feasting, athletic games, dramatic performances. Then, at a ceremony in the public theater, packed with guests, a pompous procession entered. Its members filed in, bearing twelve images of the Twelve Great Gods of Hellas, and "the image of Philip, clothed like the gods in every respect, made the thirteenth, hereby arrogating to himself a place, as if he would be enthroned among the gods."[421] Philip and his friends arrived. Philip commanded his friends to go before him into the theater and his guards to stand back. Then he prepared to enter alone, clothed in white, the admired conqueror, ruler of Macedonia and Hellas, the self-appointed sacrificer of the Bull of Persia. At that moment a youth, a favorite of Philip's, leapt forward, drew a dagger from beneath his cloak, and plunged it into the king's side. The Bull of Macedonia fell dead at his slaughterer's feet, and Apollo's oracle was fulfilled.

FROM THE VOYAGE OF PLATO TO THE EMPIRE OF ARISTOTLE

W HEN SOCRATES, in his prison cell, drank the cup of hemlock which his polis offered him, his followers were alarmed. It was the restored democracy of Thrasybulus that had condemned him and it was easy to picture him as anti-democratic. He had declared he could not teach because he had no knowledge; but he remained for many the Socrates of his friend Aristophanes' comedy, the *Clouds*, corrupting the young Phidippides for profit, a typical sophist among his disciples, aloft in his basket above his Thoughtery. And who were his disciples? The handsome, brilliant, insolent young aristocrat, Alcibiades, who had profaned the holy mysteries and defaced the Herms. Had not Socrates gone to his death on a charge of not believing in the gods of his own polis, he who in the *Clouds* had declared that Zeus was no longer king, but Whirlwind was king? Then his disciple Alcibiades, summoned home from Sicily, had fled to Sparta, that mainstay of oligarchs throughout all Hellas. Had this barefoot sophist not taught Critias too? Critias had been the bloodiest of the thirty tyrants who, with a Spartan garrison back of them, had established the oligarchic terror at Athens after her empire was lost and hunger brought her to her knees. Among Socrates' disciples also had been the young Charmides, Critias's nephew, who had fallen with his uncle in the battle of Munychia. It was over their dead bodies that the democrats who held the Piraeus had won the right to re-enter Athens and re-establish law, freedom, and democracy.

So it was that when Socrates died his friends were in fear, and a small group of them withdrew to neighboring Megara. There they were protected by Euclides, who had been with Socrates when he drained his last cup. Among those whom Euclides sheltered was Socrates' young friend Plato.

Plato was about thirty when he went to Megara. He had been born in 428-427, a year or so after Pericles died. His father, Ariston, was an Athenian noble whose family claimed descent from the ancient kings of Athens, and through them from Posidon, god of the sea and brother of Zeus himself. Plato's mother, Perictione, was a sister of Charmides, niece of Critias, and a collateral descendant of Solon, who gave law to Athens.

When the long Peloponnesian War finally ended, and when the Thirty, under Critias, seized power, they invited Plato to join them. He was twenty-three. He had been reared in a home where public service was taken for granted. He was a member of the Athenian landed aristocracy which now proposed to take back some of the power the rising commercial democracy had steadily acquired. Plato's stepfather, indeed, had been an active follower of Pericles. But after Pericles' death the democracy had gone from folly to folly and had led Athens to exhaustion and ruinous defeat. The young Plato enthusiastically backed the reforming oligarchs. But when he witnessed the executions and confiscations and when he saw the Thirty trying to force his "aged friend Socrates"[422] to share their guilt by fetching the innocent Leon of Salamis to his death, Plato was indignant and withdrew. When the Thirty fell, he once more wanted to enter public life. He was impressed by the moderation of the restored democracy; but when that democracy sentenced Socrates to death, he despaired of both political parties. He was convinced that the written laws as well as the customs of his own polis had become profoundly corrupted. There was nothing reassuring about the oligarchies which victorious Sparta had installed in the subject cities she seized from Athens; nor indeed about the Spartiates themselves, since Lysander's booty had vindicated the Delphic oracle that "love of money and nothing else will ruin Sparta."[423] Everywhere still, polis struggled against polis; within each polis the city of the rich and the city of the poor fought for the upper hand; and the struggle between classes stimulated and complicated the struggle between sovereign city-states. Plato was not the only Hellene to be horrified by the political chaos of Hellas or by the moral and intellectual chaos it reflected. Was the chaos curable? Plato concluded that there would be

> no cessation from evils until either the class of those who are right and true philosophers attains political supremacy, or else the class of those who hold power in the States becomes, by some dispensation of Heaven, really philosophic.[424]

The witnesses to the moral and intellectual chaos which Plato discerned behind the incessant wars and revolutions of the fourth century were numerous: skeptics, relativists, materialists, distrusters of civilization, romantics who sought in nature escape from what was artificial and conventional. The atomist, Democritus of Abdera, had written, "We know nothing in reality; for truth lies in an abyss."[425] As to the polis, that small, intense communion of gods and men, "to a wise man, the whole earth is open; for the native land of a good soul is the whole earth."[426] As for justice, Thrasymachus of Chalcedon, the famous sophist who argued so angrily with Socrates that evening at the Piraeus, was not the first to insist that justice was the interest of the stronger, that might made right. "Rule," said Democritus, "belongs by nature to the stronger."[427] To Protagoras's insistence that man was the measure of all things, Metrodorus of Chios added, "Everything exists which anyone perceives."[428] As for Socrates' brave faith that knowledge differed from mere opinion, this same Metrodorus held that "None of us knows anything, not even whether we know or do not know, nor do we know whether not knowing and knowing exist, nor in general whether there is anything or not."[429] As to the gods, Critias, the bloody leader of the Thirty and uncle of Plato's own mother, wrote a satirical play, a play in which one of the characters disposed of the gods as speedily as he himself disposed of his political opponents:

Then, when the laws forbade them to commit open crimes of violence, and they began to do them in secret, a wise and clever man invented fear of the gods for mortals, that there might be some means of frightening the wicked, even if they do anything or say or think it in secret. Hence he introduced the Divine, saying that there is a God flourishing with immortal life, hearing and seeing with his mind, and thinking of everything and caring about these things. . . . Thus, I think, for the first time did someone persuade mortals to believe in a race of deities.[430]

Socrates' old opponent, the sophist Antiphon, handled justice with sophistication:

Justice, then, is not to transgress that which is the law of the city in which one is a citizen. A man therefore can best conduct himself in harmony with justice, if when in the company of witnesses he upholds the laws and when alone without witnesses he upholds the edicts of nature. For the edicts of the laws are imposed artificially, but those of nature are compulsory. And the edicts of the laws are arrived at by consent, not by natural growth, whereas those of nature are not a matter of consent.

So if the man who transgresses the legal code evades those who have agreed to these edicts, he avoids both disgrace and penalty; otherwise not. But if a man violates against possibility any of the laws which are implanted in nature, even if he evades all men's detection, the ill is no less, and even if all see, it is no greater. For he is not hurt on account of an opinion, but because of truth. The examination of these things is in general for this reason, that the majority of just acts according to law are prescribed contrary to nature. . . .

We revere and honor those born of noble fathers but those who are not born of noble houses we neither revere nor honour. In this we are, in our relations with one another, like barbarians, since we are all by nature born the same in every way, both barbarians and Hellenes. And it is open to all men to observe the laws of nature, which are compulsory. Similarly all of these things can be acquired by all, and in none of these things is any of us distinguished as barbarian or Hellene. We all breathe into the air through mouth and nostrils, and we all eat with hands.[431]

When Plato turned in revulsion from the violence between polis and polis and the violence between rich and poor, he looked for causes, as

Socrates before him had looked. And what he saw in the thinking of men like Democritus, Thrasymachus, Protagoras, Critias, and Antiphon was that Hellas was sick. Wars and revolutions, demoralizing as they had been, were only symptoms. The real disorder was an intellectual and moral confusion which precluded both the search for truth and the making of good law. The real disorder lay deeper. Zeus was no longer king, but Whirlwind was king.

When Plato was about forty, he visited several Hellenic cities in southern Italy and Sicily. At Tarentum, according to later tradition, he observed the school which the Pythagoreans were setting up under Archytas. The Socrates of the Platonic dialogues had consistently shared the Pythagorean interest in mathematics as the door to philosophy. At Syracuse the tyrant, Dionysius I, had recently fought two successful wars against Carthage, had driven the Carthaginians out of all Sicily except its western corner and had gained control of every Hellenic polis in the island. He had recently crossed the Strait of Messina and subjected a group of cities in the toe of the Italian peninsula. He was the most powerful despot in Hellas when Plato visited Syracuse. There Plato met the tyrant's son-in-law, Dion, then about twenty years old. Plato was repelled by the high living and low thinking that cursed the wealthy cities of Italy and Sicily even more, in his judgment, than they cursed Mainland Greece. He was not surprised that a population of men who lived to satisfy their physical appetites should live also in a continual state of revolution, oscillating between tyranny, oligarchy, and a disordered democracy. But in the young Dion he found a lively intellect and a responsive one. Dion underwent something like a Socratic conversion, withdrew from the dissipated life of the tyrant's court, and started cultivating his mind. His decision naturally made him many enemies.

Meanwhile, Dionysius I extended the power of Syracuse up both coasts of Italy. The Celts had come down from the north and had invaded both Etruria and Latium. Dionysius also pillaged in Etruria and the garrisoned Corsica. In 387 the Celts seized Rome, a small republican city-state of Italic farmers, and sent an embassy to Dionysius, who now recruited Celtic mercenaries. Dionysius was working up the west coast of the Adriatic, founding Ancona, founding Hadria at one of the mouths of the Po, where the amber of northern Europe reached the Mediterranean. His power was felt even on the far shore of the Adriatic, among the Illyrians.

356

When, in 387, at Sparta's instigation, the Persian King of Kings laid claim to Greece-in-Asia and backed Sparta's hegemony over Mainland Greece, Dionysius I of Syracuse effectually controlled Western Greece. This man who had been born the son of a donkey-driver had risen fast. No wonder Isocrates of Athens saw in him, before he thought he saw in Philip II of Macedon, the savior who would bring peace and order to all Hellas.

But, like the Macedonian dynasts, this self-made Sicilian was not content with his military and economic power. Like them, he craved the culture, the artistic and intellectual aura, that only Mainland Greece could confer. This ruthless pillager of temples wanted to win personal fame at the holy games of Olympia, wanted to win first prize at Athens for a tragedy from his own pen. To import thinkers and writers and artists for Syracuse, as Hiero had done, would not satisfy him. The men he wanted at Syracuse were the engineers who built him powerful catapults for his armies and who understood the new science of ballistics. But Dionysius wanted to be his own poet. When the Olympics of 388 were held, he sent not only a magnificently equipped delegation and his best race horses; he also sent the best rhapsodes money could hire to recite the poems he himself had written. But the Athenian orator Lysias excited the throng at Olympia against this sacrilegious tyrant who subjected Hellenic cities with his barbarian mercenaries. The Syracusan delegation was not allowed to perform the sacrifices. Their splendid pavilion was attacked. Dionysius' horses failed to win prizes. When his poems were read, people refused to listen. It was a bitter cup, but the temple robber obstinately continued making gifts to the holy places of Mainland Greece.

After Thebes had defeated Sparta at Leuctra, and Athens shifted to the side of Sparta, both of these allies tried to get mercenaries from Dionysius to check the rising power of Thebes under Epaminondas. In 368 Dionysius sent Sparta a band of Celts, but Athens got no help until she fulfilled one of his highest ambitions. In no Hellenic competition had he ever won more than second or third prize with a tragedy until in February of 367 his *Ransom of Hector* was presented at Athens and won first prize. He celebrated his great victory with a drinking bout, took to his bed, and died.

The son of Dionysius succeeded him. Dionysius II was still a young man. He had been reared, not as a donkey-driver's son, but as son and heir of the most powerful Hellenic ruler of his day. Understandably, he lacked his father's drive; understandably, he shared his love of high living. But his brother-in-law, Dion, whom Plato had infected with such a love of justice and of reason, had successfully interested a few of his companions in mathematics and philosophy, and Dion hoped that the young monarch might vindicate Socrates' wistful statement, reported or imputed in Plato's dialogue, the *Republic*, that until philosophers became kings and rulers, "or until kings, or if not kings, the sons of kings or princes, are divinely inspired with a true love of true philosophy,"[432] then the miseries of the cities of Hellas must continue. Here was the son of a prince, who had inherited absolute power; his brother-in-law, Dion, believed he could be educated. Dion sent an urgent plea to Plato, in Athens, to come to Syracuse.

A score of years earlier Plato had visited Syracuse for a few months. If, as later tradition claimed, he met Dionysius I, he could hardly have seen in him a possible philosopher king. On the contrary, Dionysius displayed, despite his great abilities, most of the traits that the *Republic* ascribed to the typical tyrant. With no hope of converting this ruler into a philosopher, Plato on his return to Athens had followed the other route. He had bought a piece of property just outside the city walls in a grove sacred to the hero Academus. There he established a school, which from its location came to be known as the Academy. If he could not make an existing ruler philosophic, he could at least train philosophers capable of ruling, or of advising those who already ruled and who might seek advice. Isocrates' school had already been founded, and was also aimed at a more systematic preparation for public life than the lectures of itinerant sophists could furnish. But the Academy undertook to provide an intellectual discipline far more drastic than anything Isocrates wanted to give, or could have given. In fact, the Academy undertook a kind of study that Plato in the *Republic* had prescribed for the Guardians: mathematics and metaphysics. Isocrates could not see why a statesman should sweat over geometry or mathematical astronomy or engage in the, to him, insubstantial argument which some of Plato's later dialogues exemplified.

It was in this Academy that Plato's pupils learned to ascend the divided line from the world of visible things to the world of invisible ideas; from changing, physical objects, through the unchanging, abstract ideas of mathematics, to the investigation of the assumptions on which mathematics rested, to ideas that could only be intuited by dialectic, and at last to the Idea of Good itself. It was here in the Academy that men learned to turn around, or turn their minds around, away from the shadowland in which Demosthenes, and even Isocrates in large part, operated—from the world of practical men, of the struggle for political power, of aims that had not passed through the Socratic ordeal by dialectic. And having turned around, they left the semi-darkness of popular opinion and climbed out of the cave into daylight, and might even strengthen the mind's eye until it could gaze upon the sun itself, the Idea of the Good. By that sun's clear light they analyzed the principles of jurisprudence. And by that same light they recognized their duty to descend into the cave again when needed; so that more than one Hellenic polis turned to Plato's Academy for expert advice on constitutional reform. And more than one of Plato's pupils went forth from the Academy to study the practical problems which such cities faced; to fit principle to case and the idea of justice to concrete situation; and to make law.

It was from this Academy, too, that Dion now urged its founder to come forth, into the Sicilian and Italian world of power and insolence and self-will, the world which the donkey-driver's son had built out of the luxury-loving, money-getting cities of Western Greece. Dion insisted that he was not alone in desiring true law for this empire and that his brother-in-law, the new ruler, Dionysius II, was eager to educate himself to rule well under law. Dionysius himself seconded the plan, and Dion wrote that "now, if ever . . . all our hopes will be fulfilled of seeing the same persons at once philosophers and rulers of mighty States."[433]

Plato was wary. He still had great confidence in Dion, but it was not Dion who ruled at Syracuse. Years later he wrote:

Holding this view and in this spirit of adventure it was that I set out from home,—not in the spirit which some have supposed, but dreading self-reproach most of all, lest haply I should seem to myself to be utterly and absolutely nothing more than a mere voice and never to undertake willingly any action . . .[434]

Besides, Dion, who was his friend, was asking his help. By going, Plato said,

I freed myself from guilt in the eyes of Zeus Xenios and cleared myself from reproach on the part of Philosophy, seeing that she would have

359

been calumniated if I, through poorness of spirit and timidity, had incurred the shame of cowardice.[435]

At Syracuse those of Dionysius's friends who dreaded reform convinced Dionysius that Dion was plotting against him, and Dion was exiled. Plato thought Dionysius's suspicions were the fruit of monstrous slanders, but Dionysius's throne was a dangerous seat. It was at this court in his father's day that the sword of Damocles became legend. Could Dionysius help feeling that in an important sense, though not in a literal sense, Dion and even Plato wanted to use him? And was not the plan to use the sovereign, for no matter what high purpose, a form of usurpation? Somewhere in their hearts, perhaps unknown to themselves, might not disloyalty lurk? As it had lurked in the heart of Marsyas, whom Dionysius had advanced to positions of high command? Marsyas had dreamed that he had killed Dionysius, and Dionysius reasoned that the dream reflected a purpose and executed Marsyas.[436]

But Dionysius did not relish the reputation of having driven Plato from his court, and he begged Plato to stay. Indeed, he made it impossible for him to leave: he housed him in the citadel, from which no ship's captain would have dared accept Plato as passenger to Athens. He wanted Plato to praise him, Dionysius, rather than Dion; but his fear of the anti-reform element at his court made him chary of any serious study with Plato. At last the captive philosopher received permission to go home to Athens and his Academy. Naturally there were plenty of people to ridicule his adventure and to ascribe it to personal ambition, to vanity, to credulity, to the intellectual's naïveté when faced with the cruel realities of practical power politics. A tyrant had indeed turned to a philosopher, not to get his help in radically re-examining the function of ruler, but to get his advice on how to achieve his already chosen goals. In short, Dionysius had turned to Plato in the same way as the youthful Xenophon had turned to Apollo.

Dionysius's treatment of Dion went from bad to worse. He confiscated Dion's property. He gave Dion's wife to another man. In 361 Plato made his third voyage to Syracuse, in a special trireme sent by Dionysius to fetch him, and tried in vain to conciliate the two brothers-in-law, ruler and exile. At Syracuse, Plato worked on the draft of a common constitution for the Hellenic states of Dionysius's empire. But nothing came of it, and with difficulty he again got leave to return to Athens.

In 357 Dion landed with a small force in southwestern Sicily and won his way to the control of Syracuse. He had wanted to bring Syracuse a free constitution, but the political cross-currents were too much for him: he became himself tyrant. Then Callippus, one of Plato's pupils at the Academy, who had come with Dion to Sicily to liberate Syracuse, arranged for his murder and became tyrant. And so it went until the Syracusans begged Corinth, the mother-city of Syracuse, to rescue them. Corinth sent Timoleon, who restored order and even defeated an army Carthage sent into Sicily. Then he quietly laid down his powers and retired to a country estate, which the grateful Syracusans had given him.

Socrates had been executed in 399, and about 387 Plato had founded the Academy. During the dozen years that intervened Plato had written a group of dialogues[437] in which Socrates played the leading role. From the time Plato was forty to the time he entered his sixties, he wrote little or nothing and labored at his teaching and research in the Academy. Then he wrote more dialogues, but in a different tone. They were less dramatic, less poetic, more analytical; in some, Socrates played only a minor role; in some he did not even appear.

These later dialogues, like the earlier, simpler, more dramatic ones, were written for the general public. Plato's most serious teaching took place in the Academy, and he held to the Socratic reservations about written philosophy. Like Socrates, he was not interested in creating a philosophic system. Like Socrates, and despite his publication of the *Dialogues*, he was convinced that men could best seek truth together in the dialectical give-and-take of the spoken word, where the inadequacy of all words can most quickly be corrected, and where the powers of intuition are heightened. Perhaps he remembered Pindar's cry to men:

Creatures of a day, what is anyone? What is he not? Man is but a dream of a shadow; but when the Zeus-given gleam of sunlight comes, a radiance rests on man, and a gentle life.[438]

In any case he was sure that, in the higher reaches of Socrates' divided line, no written treatise could help. Contemplation and communion with ideas prepared the way for that gleam of sunlight Zeus could send to illuminate the shadow, man, and to shed the radiance of grace on his heart and mind. Knowledge of the ideas "is brought to birth in the soul on a sudden,"

361

Plato himself wrote, "as light that is kindled by a leaping spark, and thereafter it nourishes itself."[439]

Of the later dialogues, written in Plato's late sixties and seventies, the *Timaeus* was unique, because it dealt mainly with subjects Socrates had turned away from in his youth, cosmology, physics, physiology, and because no other Platonic dialogue did. Socrates appeared in it as a listener, while Timaeus speculated on the creation of the universe. Timaeus came from Locri, in southern Italy, and his speculation drew on the mathematical tradition of the Pythagoreans and the atomist tradition of Empedocles. Plato himself never appeared as a speaker in any of his dialogues. But this speculation on the origin of the material universe was not placed in Socrates' mouth either. Timaeus undertook to imagine or intuit the world in which any polis must operate, including the one Socrates had the day before imagined in the *Republic*.

God, as Timaeus imagined, created the cosmos; and this visible, tangible world he created according to an eternal and unchanging pattern; and being perfectly good himself, he desired that it should resemble him in goodness. He endowed the cosmos with soul and mind, so that it was a vast and living animal. He made it out of the four elements the Ionians had written of: earth, air, fire, and water. He made it spherical and rotating. It was impossible to make a material universe eternal and at rest, like the divine idea it copied. So he made a moving image of eternity, which men called time, and gave us past, present, and future, whereas God himself eternally is. He made the stars and planets, which were themselves gods and alive.

As for gods like Zeus and Hera, cosmogonies like that of Hesiod must be accepted. The men of old claimed to be descendants of the gods, and presumably these men knew their own family history. But these gods were not the Creator, the Demiurge, the Artisan, who created them and men and all. When these gods had been created, the God who created them commanded them to create other living creatures, men and animals; but the Creator reserved to himself the work of creating souls for men, since these souls, he told the gods, were

the part of them worthy of the name immortal, which is called divine and is the guiding principle of those who are willing to follow justice and you . . .[440]

Then the subordinate gods furnished men with mortal bodies and gave them food and made them grow and received them again in death.

Because man was given this double nature of soul and body, his youth was turbulent; later he became less subject to his appetites and if given proper education

> he attains the fulness and health of the perfect man, and escapes the worst disease of all; but if he neglects education he walks lame to the end of his life . . .[441]

The four traditional elements—earth, air, fire, and water—out of which men's bodies and all other matter were composed, were made of atoms that were regular geometrical solids, and the solids could all be reduced to triangles. And the triangles? The triangles, which were forms and hence knowable by the mind, were imposed on space. And space, having in itself no form, was not knowable. One could say only that it was the receptacle of all forms, the mother of all material things.

In this mathematical but live[442] universe, man moved and had his being—his double being. Because he had a mortal body, his mouth was designed to receive food; and because he had an immortal soul, it was designed to emit "the river of speech, which flows out of a man and ministers to the intelligence" and "is the fairest and noblest of all streams."[443] And "every man ought always to begin his speaking and his thinking with the gods,"[444] as if all true speech were a prayer and a communion. Because he had a mortal body, he was given eyes to guide him to what his body needed; and because he had an immortal soul his eyes could perceive the ordered movement of the stars in time—time, the moving image of eternity; his mind's eye could detect their mathematical harmony; and he could even order his own soul. And Timaeus concluded:

> We may now say that our discourse about the nature of the universe has an end. The world has received animals, mortal and immortal, and is fulfilled with them, and has become a visible animal containing the visible—the sensible God who is the image of the intellectual, the greatest, best, fairest, most perfect—the one only-begotten heaven.[445]

This tentative, humble, reverent, soaring account of the universe around Plato came from the ivory tower of the Academy, in which both the orator Demosthenes, crying defiance against Philip, and the publicist Isocrates, inviting Philip to lead Hellas, would alike have scorned to dwell.

But the *Timaeus* marked the Academy as not merely a withdrawal from the madness of Hellas' social disintegration but also as the expansion of mind from polis to universe, of mind probing the nature of man, the nature of matter, the most distant stars, the cunningly devised body of man, the ecology of the living earth. In time as well as in space the probing mind went, clear back to the Creation, to the dawn of time itself, to all that man remembered or half remembered. Had not the poet Alcman written long ago that Memory was "she that looks with the mind"[446]? Necessarily back to creation and necessarily forward to the future, since this living animal, the universe, bore everywhere the signature of purpose. And because all things were infused with purpose, all things were turned toward God and served his will. Man, having intellect, was created "the most religious of animals,"[447] but all animals were religious in the sense that their existence fulfilled the will of God. Necessarily backward to creation went Timaeus, necessarily forward; although it was not Timaeus but another and earlier Pythagorean who wrote that men perish because they cannot join the beginning to the end.[448] It was not Plato in the Academy but Demosthenes in the Assembly and Isocrates the political pamphleteer who sought neither the beginning nor the end. Demosthenes and Isocrates were both great talkers, either from a real platform or from an imaginary platform. They loved words and practical action. "The Athenian citizen," wrote Plato, "is reputed among all the Hellenes to be a great talker."[449] But they had never ascended from the cave to the light. It was one of the tasks of the Academy to induce this ascent.

The last dialogue the aged Plato wrote was the *Laws*. It was decades since he had written his *Republic*, in which Socrates imagined a polis on earth with some of the goodness that rendered luminous the heavenly pattern by which every polis must be judged. Now, in his old age, with a lifetime of reflection behind him and with the plight of Hellas far more parlous than in the days of Socrates, Plato set himself the task of sketching another, a more immediately realizable constitution for a new polis, for a colony. The *Laws* was technically a dialogue, in which a Cretan, a Lacedaemonian, and an Athenian Stranger discussed law, as they walked from Knossos, where Minos the lawgiver had ruled, to the grotto and temple of Zeus on Mount Ida. But there was little of the old sparkle that graced the dramatic dialogue in the *Republic*. Was the

Athenian Stranger the aged Plato himself? All three characters in the dialogue were elderly men. Crete and Lacedaemon were famous for their laws. It was Zeus himself who had given law to Crete; and if Lycurgus had received his rhetras from Apollo at Delphi, at least Apollo was reputed to interpret the will of Zeus. And so the three old men conversed; but the conversation threatened constantly to become a lecture delivered by the Athenian Stranger.

Law, the Stranger held, came from God, for not man, as Protagoras the sophist had proclaimed, but "God ought to be to us the measure of all things."[450] Man might well be a puppet of the gods, pulled by many cords this way and that. Some cords were of hard iron, but one cord alone was the golden cord of reason, soft because made of gold, beautiful and gentle, not violent. It was to this cord that a man must hold fast. For law was the expression of reason in the polis, "the distribution of mind"[451] in polis. And where mind was properly distributed, where law represented persuasion by reason and not mere brute force, men could develop not only the human goods of health, beauty, strength, and the proper amount of wealth, but the divine goods of wisdom, self-control in the face of pleasure, courage in the face of pain, and justice—the four kinds of virtue Socrates had talked of in the *Republic*. Long ago, Cronus, father of Zeus, had placed animals under the rule of divine spirits. Today, men ought to place themselves, through law, under reason, the golden cord which connected men with the gods.

In short, the Athenian Stranger, or Plato in his old age, had turned the talk from the *Timaeus* back to the double theme of the *Republic*: how to live a good, just, and happy life individually; and, since man could be wholly man only in the human community, only in polis, how to frame such laws for a polis as to make it a good, just, and happy human community. The Plato of the *Laws* was once more, like Socrates, overwhelmingly interested in finding answers to those two problems.

And yet so long as Hellas, or even Mainland Greece, could devise no law common to all the persons in it and able to put an end to the vendetta between polis and polis, there was little chance that any polis, no matter how good its laws, would escape being pulled apart by forces from beyond its own frontiers. But nowhere in his dialogues did Plato face that problem, not even in the *Laws*. His small city-state remained the only source of enforceable law, a polis armed against its neighbor, unable to protect its citizens except by a force in being that could not but cause a neighboring polis fear, could not but incite it to arm, could not but create, therefore, a peril to itself.

Socrates had sought the answers to the question of a good life for the polis and a good life for the citizen by starting conversations. And each conversation momentarily created, whether in the gymnasium, in the Agora, or even outside the city walls, a miniature, intense, and fleeting polis that seemed to some to threaten the tyrant-city, Athens. Plato had institutionalized that kind of conversation by creating the Academy, by providing something like the continuous, arduous education that Socrates himself had said the rulers of a just polis would need to have. And where Socrates had left in part to chance the persons he argued with, Plato had followed the path, in some ways harder, of trying to educate an actual ruler. When it came to setting up his ideal Republic, Socrates had playfully resorted to his old Phoenician tale of citizens born of a common mother the earth, some of whom were made of gold and hence were wise enough to rule. Plato, in the *Laws*, was prepared to launch his state if only an educable tyrant could be found.

If a truly wise legislator wanted to reform an existing society, Plato's Athenian Stranger thought the legislator's best chance was such a tyrant. A constitutional monarch would lack the necessary power. A democracy would be harder to persuade than either. Hardest of all to persuade would be an oligarchy, for here each member of the ruling group considered himself a potentate. Was Plato willing to compromise much further than Socrates in order to meet the more desperate moral and political chaos he now faced? He had hoped against hope that a tyrant like Dionysius, so like the evil portrait of a tyrant which Socrates had sketched in Plato's *Republic*, could become a philosopher king. But how free had Dionysius been to fulfill Plato's hope, to convert the corrupt power he held into the kind of power good law required? Was his distrustful treatment of Plato a confession, which perhaps a Socrates would have grasped, that he, Dionysius, was the chief slave of the system he had inherited? Socrates had never turned to the mighty for the redemption of polis. He and Plato both knew, what Solon had known before them, that the just polis required both right and might, that law had to be both just and enforceable. Either a philosopher must secure the might of a king; or else a king who already wielded might must be educated until he could discern justice and follow it. But Socrates went to no Syracuse. Plato did, though he went neither happily nor hopefully. In the *Laws* he was willing to forgo placing all authority in the hands of an aristocracy of wisdom and to seek a stable blend of monarchy and democracy, provided only the government was essentially a government of laws and not of men. There must be a consent of the governed. The laws should persuade even more by reason than by force: that is why the Athenian Stranger insisted that all laws should have preambles that would explain their legitimate purpose.

To the principle that men needed a government of laws, not merely of men, the slave was an exception. The laws did of course protect both master and slave, although the *Laws* proposed some very severe ordinances for slaves. But, within a legally defined area, the slave was governed, not by law at all, but by his master. Antiphon might insist that all men, barbarian and Hellene alike, were subject to the laws of nature; that they all breathed the air through mouth and nostrils and ate with their hands. And in the *Laws* the Athenian Stranger might hold that the sacred and golden cord of reason connected all men to gods; that law was to be obeyed because it expressed this reason; and that reason was beautiful and gentle, not violent. But did the golden cord reach the slave? Was his relation to the master who had bought him, who now owned him, and who might yet sell him, a relation of reason or of violence? The Athenian Stranger thought that the master should be even more scrupulously just to a slave than to his own equals; but he also knew that good, if firm, treatment helped to prevent revolt. It was better too not to have all slaves come from the same foreign country, speaking the same language. At most, the *Laws* urged softening what was in essence a relation of force. But the Athenian Stranger never asked what effect this relation of force— or, for that matter, the relation of force between sovereign polis and sovereign polis—was likely to have on the sacred and golden cord of reason.

The Athenian Stranger's laws sanctioned not only the use of force called war and the use of force called slavery but also the use of force called censorship. Like Socrates in the *Republic*, he censored poets. Indeed, unlike Socrates, he regulated beliefs about the gods. Those who denied that the gods existed, or that they took care of men, or that their actions were always just were to be prosecuted for impiety. Impiety would bring an imprisonment of at least five years; and a second offense would bring death, and death without burial at that. Would Plato have urged an attempt to control religion if in his last years he had not felt a desperate need to shore up the society he saw crumbling about him, a need which perhaps some of the judges who had voted for Socrates' death also had felt when they meted out death to Socrates, on a charge that included impiety? Certainly, the *Laws* tried to come to terms with an increasingly brutalized society, as the *Republic* had not. The freedom of speech, of which Pericles had boasted, assumed that men were adult. But could physically grown-up children, armed, greedy, and violent, be told things about the gods that sanctioned their own lawlessness?

As to the Athenian Stranger's censorship of the poets, Plato's fear of what poetry could do to the soul was based on direct experience. Many of the dialogues, notably the *Republic* and the *Symposium*, could have been written only by a man who was both a philosopher and a poet. Even in his last dialogue, the *Laws*, with its sometimes tedious lists of proposed statutes, his poetic gifts often broke through. Moreover, although neither he nor other writers of his generation any longer wrote their philosophic discourses in verse, as the early Ionians had often done, Plato himself wrote poems:

> Leaving behind the sounding surge of the Aegean we lie on the midmost of the plains of Ecbatana. Farewell, Eretria, once our glorious country; farewell, Athens, the neighbor of Euboea; farewell, dear Sea.[452]

Among other poems he wrote were:

> I am the tomb of a shipwrecked man, and that opposite is the tomb of a husbandman. So death lies in wait for us alike on sea and land.[453]

> I throw the apple at thee, and thou, if thou lovest me from thy heart, take it and give me of thy maidenhead; but if thy thoughts be what I pray they are not, take it still and reflect how short-lived is beauty.[454]

> Thou lookest on the stars, my Star. Would I were heaven, to look on thee with many eyes.[455]

> Some say the Muses are nine, but how carelessly! Look at the tenth, Sappho from Lesbos.[456]

He knew the magic power of poetry over those whose souls were open to poetry, and he knew that the fictions of poetry could both tell the truth and tell lies. It was as if he, not Hesiod, had met the Muses, the ready-voiced daughters of great Zeus, while he, not Hesiod, was shepherding his lambs under holy Helicon. And it was as if the Muses had sung to him, Plato: "we know how to speak many false things as though they were true."[457]

He bore the great epics of Hellas, sung or recited over the centuries, in his heart and memory. He bore there also, like an atavistic memory of the landed aristocracy from which he had sprung, the instinct to colonize, as the nobles of the eighth and seventh centuries had done. Western Greece, that land of opportunity for Mainland Greeks, where Plato went three times, had furnished the word Sybarite, the proverbial term for a man that lived in luxury. The cities of Western Greece had never become holy ground like Athens or Sparta or Argos or Delphi or Olympia. Most of them remained primarily centers of economic expansion. Intellectually, Syracuse excelled more in mechanics than in literature. Although great temples were built, as at Posidonia, the West tended to import its poets and philosophers and artists. Characteristically, the art in which the Sicilian cities most excelled was the designing of coins, and the education for which the West was most famous was training in rhetoric. It was somehow right that the coin and the word should be cultivated there. Both were means: means by which the men of a polis could exchange commodities and exchange ideas. But both could become means to power and almost ends in themselves. Even more than in Mainland Greece, the man of means had come into his own. Nevertheless, despite his revulsion from the Italians and Syracusans who spent their existence "in gorging food twice a day and never sleeping alone at night, and all the practices which accompany this mode of living,"[458] Plato went three times to Syracuse. And, had he achieved the success he never expected to achieve, he might himself have colonized in the somewhat raw but less tradition-bound world of Western Greece. He might have founded the polis, or at least have made Syracuse and its dependent cities into communities that would reflect the pattern Socrates saw laid up in heaven.

Plato never forgot poetry. He never forgot the need to colonize. Nor did he ever forget law. He admired the laws of Lycurgus, although he recognized that they made Sparta what Socrates in the *Republic* called a timocracy, whose goal was honor and whose special virtue was courage, and not what Socrates called an aristocracy, whose goal was justice and whose special virtue was wisdom. Sparta was governed by men trained as warriors rather than by men trained as statesmen, by Socratic auxiliaries rather than by Socratic guardians. Lacking wisdom, its timocracy had largely turned into oligarchy. Plato knew, as Solon had known, that the highest gift the gods could give to a polis was a just law. When Athens, "the oldest land in Ionia," was "being slain"[459] by class hatred, Solon had stood off envious pauper and grasping landowner alike, and had tried to bring his polis justice. Where Solon had hung up his armor at the door of his house when Pisistratus seized power, Plato, despite his scorching description of tyranny in the *Republic*, journeyed to Syracuse in the forlorn hope of educating a tyrant. Such a tyrant might add reason and law to naked force, might make laws that would bring reason and order to the life of his subjects, and

> these things, I say, the laws, as we proceed with them, will accomplish, partly persuading, and partly when natures do not yield to the persuasion of custom, chastising them by might and right, and will thus render our state, if the Gods co-operate with us, prosperous and happy.[460]

For Plato was certain that no polis could be free that did not hold fast to reason, the golden cord that joined the minds of men to the will of God. The forlorn hope perished, and he returned to Athens.

No polis could be free that would not use might to defend its freedom against outsiders who would subject it. In Plato's dialogue, the *Critias*, Critias—not to be confused[461] with the Critias who imposed a bloody terror on Athens in 405—recounted to Socrates and Hermocrates and Timaeus, who had finished describing the creation of the universe and its material structure, an ancient tale that Solon himself had brought back from Egypt. According to this tale, Athens had once, nine thousand years before, led the defense of the Mediterranean world against the wealthy and powerful peoples who dwelt in the vast island of Atlantis beyond the Pillars of Heracles, in the western ocean, an island later sunk by an earthquake. The tale brought memories of the gallant fighters at Marathon.

What disturbed Plato was not the heroic defense of Mainland Greece against Xerxes, but the Greeks' later betrayal of the freedom they had saved. Men exercised freedom not merely by rejecting the arbitrary will of invading despot or of domestic tyrant but by reverence for law, the polis' equivalent of self-control and justice in the soul of the individual citizen. No army, not even one of heroic Marathon fighters, could guarantee that internal freedom. For many years Sparta's freedom had survived precisely because, thanks to Lycurgus' reforms, "Law became with them supreme king over man instead of men being despots over the laws."[462] Aeschylus's statement, "For none save only Zeus is free,"[463] was echoed by Plato when he freely accepted one form of slavery for man:

> For as regards both slavery and freedom, when either is in excess it is wholly evil, but when in moderation wholly good; and moderate slavery consists in being the slave of God, immoderate, in being the slave of men; and men of sound sense have Law for their God, but men without sense Pleasure.[464]

Law "for their God" precisely because real law expressed reason, and reason was of God.

Plato could have drunk with a clear conscience the toast drunk annually at the graves of those who had fallen at Plataea, "I drink to the men who died for the freedom of the Hellenes."[465] But because of what Hellas had done with the freedom men died for at Plataea, Plato could have drunk another toast that would have stirred him even more deeply. In the cell in which Socrates had drunk of a cup not filled with wine, had Plato then been present with those other friends of Socrates, he could have drunk to the man who died for the freedom of the Hellenes, the man who loved freedom under law and bore witness to the end that the citizen who would be truly loyal would strive at the cost of life itself to use the reason God had given him. For Socrates had known what Plato declared in the Laws concerning the Hellenes who had freely died for freedom: "Education certainly gives victory, although victory sometimes produces forgetfulness of education."[466]

When the School of Hellas had passed through Melos, through Syracuse, to great catastrophe, to famine and surrender, and her conquerors had thought that tearing down her walls would prove to be "the beginning of freedom for Greece,"[467] it was not walls that kept freedom out of Greece. The bloody oligarchy that sought to silence the questioning Socrates and the restored democracy that silenced him forever taught Plato once and for all that the evil was radical and lay in the minds of those who governed, whether as democracy or oligarchy. Other Hellenic cities were busy documenting the same point. If freedom and justice were to be found, somebody's mind had to be changed—either the mind of a Dionysius or the minds of men who might advise the rulers of any given polis. The true nature of law had to be rediscovered, or the intolerable anarchy of Hellas would continue. The problem was not one of rhetoric or of orators; it was a problem of ethics and jurisprudence. It was one which only disciplined minds could solve. So Plato founded the Academy.

The Academy, which lacked the power of a government, was nevertheless the School of Athens, which was the School of Hellas. It dared turn toward high theory at a moment when the practical men of Hellas were diligently, if quite unintentionally, destroying Hellas. The Academy could hope to house a saving remnant and to become a miniature polis, a community of men sufficiently awakened intellectually to achieve communication. Could it save Hellas? The more relevant question was whether Hellas or any other community could find salvation by any other route. It was a miniature polis because, as Simonides had written, Polis teaches man.[468] Granted that it was another polis in flight, yet it had withdrawn in order to think. To leave the shadows in the cave for the clear sunlight outside was, as Socrates knew, a withdrawal that angered those whose necks remained chained, those who had never turned around, had never been converted to the question, the search, to faith in mind and in ideas.

Plato was no Pericles: he did not rule a state, much less an empire, while arguing with philosophers and planning with architects and sculptors. To unite thought and action in that pre-eminent degree was perhaps no longer possible in Hellas. But Plato also bore two worlds within him, the world of poetic insight and the world of close, cool-headed analysis. He was spiritual kith and kin to Homer and the great tragedians; he also wrote the most powerful philosophic discourses Hellas had known. In him were harmoniously blended rigorous thought and a lofty imagination; and his was at least the courage, if not often the chance, to enter the political arena.

The polis of Pericles had witnessed most of the great tragedies of the Athenian theater and the beginnings of its great comedies. According to later tradition Plato in his early youth wrote tragedies himself.[469] In the *Laws* he admitted into the polis both comedy and tragedy, though under careful censorship. Comedy he thought necessary, because "serious things cannot be understood without laughable things"[470]—a principle of which he himself had always made generous use in presenting his philosophic speculations, so often phrased with a deft sense of comedy. But comedy presented and laughed at vice; and he wanted no free citizen to act in comedies. To impersonate those who were cowardly or greedy or foolish or unfair was corrupting. To laugh at their weakness was to reject such weakness. As to tragedies, Plato's legislators should say to the poets who wrote them,

> we also according to our ability are tragic poets, and our tragedy is the best and noblest; for our whole state is an imitation of the best and noblest life, which we affirm to be indeed the very truth of tragedy. You are poets and we are poets . . .[471]

The well-ordered polis, in which and in which alone a man could live the noblest life, taught noble living even more adequately than tragedies enacted in some theater could do. But did he mean to imply also what he had reported or imputed in the *Republic*, that given the limitations of the human condition, even the most wisely governed polis must in the end, like a tragic hero, fail? In any case, the *Dialogues* were philosophy cast in dramatic form, comic or tragic or both by turns, as Thucydides' history had been cast in dramatic form. Plato could see human life as tragedy, but he could also see it through the laughing eyes of Aristophanes. And, although Aristophanes' caricature of Socrates, whom Plato loved, perhaps helped bring the cup of hemlock, Plato could nevertheless write a couplet:

> The Graces, seeking for themselves a shrine that would not fall, found the soul of Aristophanes.[472]

Finally, Plato loved not only drama but music and the plastic arts. Whether the tradition[473] that he painted was true or not, his writings were filled with brilliant and sensitive images, painted or sculptured in sensitive, musical prose.

But above all he was the child of war and revolution. The Peloponnesian War was only in its fourth year when Plato was born, and it was not until he was twenty-four that his famished polis surrendered, and the oligarchic terror began. He had been a mere baby when civil war had turned Corcyra into a cage of snarling animals. For the rest of his long life he watched the disintegration of Hellas by revolution and by war, a war in which he himself had fought with distinction, as Socrates had done.[474] He was still alive when Demosthenes stirred Athens with his *First Philippic*, but Plato felt a profound distrust for oratory. Like Xenophon and Isocrates, Plato dreamed of a ruler: of a king, or a malleable young prince, or even a tyrant. But in any case a man, a person, a mind. As for Demosthenes' eloquent pleas to Hellas to unite against Philip, Plato might have quoted to him that line from the *Agamemnon* of Aeschylus: "Great your design, your speech is a clamor of pride."[475] Better to lead a minute polis in flight from the Agora to the grove of the hero Academus, to remember, to reflect, to study, to understand, than to rally the planless power of Hellas against the planned power of Philip.

Plato died at the age of eighty, in 348-347. And centuries later it would be written:

> Plato, however, when he was now at the point of death, lauded his guardian genius [*daimōn*] and Fortune because, to begin with, he had been born a man and not an irrational animal; again, because he was a Greek and not a Barbarian; and still again, because his birth had fallen in the time of Socrates.[476]

Like Socrates, Plato had borne witness, although in a different fashion, to his love of the truth and to his vision of the Good. With the memory of that vision Socrates had descended into the cave most men inhabit, had seen their necks chained, had released them that they might climb with him out of the cave where the sun illuminated reality; and at the cost of his life had served notice on his judges that he would remove those chains again. But Plato, too, left the luminous upward search of the Academy and entered the shadowland of Sicilian politics in the barest hope of freeing other men. His descent into darkness was no less a witness to his faith in light than that of Socrates had been. His life was in danger at Syracuse. He courted ridicule in Athens as the impractical intellectual eager to play the statesman, as the professed lover of wisdom who was in fact the sycophant of power. Was the cup of failure which Plato drained at Syracuse less bitter than the hemlock in the cup of Socrates?

When the eighteen-year-old Aristotle entered the Academy around 366, he came as a foreign student. He entered the School of Hellas which Plato had founded inside Athens a score of years after it had first opened. In choosing Plato's Academy and not the celebrated school which Isocrates directed, Aristotle had chosen hard intellectual discipline and inquiry as against a course of studies designed to provide a general, if superficial, culture, and a preparation, especially in public speaking, for practical life. Though not an Athenian, Aristotle was a Hellene both by race and culture. He had been born in 384 in Stagira, a few miles up the eastern coast of the Chalcidic peninsula from the point where long ago Xerxes had dug his canal and a few miles from Amphipolis, which Thucydides, the admiral and historian, had reached too late. Stagira was originally a colony of Chalcis and Andros, and Aristotle's mother came from Chalcis itself. His father was a member of the medical guild, or clan, of Asclepius, and served at Pella as court physician to Amyntas III, father of Philip of Macedon. Both of Aristotle's parents died when the boy was young. Whether or not Aristotle spent any part of his boyhood at Pella, the growing power of Macedon was one of the facts of his youth. Whether or not his father's medical practice influenced him directly, his family background was neither aristocratic, like Plato's, nor socially humble: it was professional and scientific.

For twenty years, until Plato died, in 348-347, Aristotle studied and pursued his research at the Academy. At Plato's death, his nephew, Speusippus, succeeded him as head of the Academy. Was it because Speusippus tended from Aristotle's point of view to turn philosophy into mathematics that Aristotle, now about thirty-six, left the Academy? In any case, he and another member of the Academy, Xenocrates, joined a third Academic, Hermeias, on the Asian mainland near the island of Lesbos. Hermeias, once a slave, later a student at the Academy, had risen to be tyrant of Atarneus. Aristotle married the adoptive daughter, or perhaps the niece, of Hermeias and for three years lived at nearby Assus, where Hermeias had established a sort of philosophic institute and where Aristotle continued his studies in biology. Then, perhaps because Hermeias was betrayed, was sent to Susa, and was there executed by the Great King, Aristotle moved to nearby Mitylene on the coast of Lesbos. In 343-342, when Aristotle was around forty-one, Philip of Macedon offered him a post as tutor to his thirteen-year-old son Alexander. The post promised not merely honor and profit: the education of princes was one of the cardinal aims of the Academics. Had not Plato himself felt bound to go to Syracuse for the same purpose? Aristotle stayed at the Macedonian court until after the death of Philip. During his tutorship, he wrote at least two treatises for the young prince, one on monarchy and one on colonies.

Soon after Philip's death, in 336, Aristotle returned to Athens, but he did not rejoin the Academy, even though Xenocrates, his friend who had gone to Asia with him a dozen years earlier, had succeeded Speusippus as head. Instead, he started a school of his own. Outside Athens stood a grove sacred to Apollo Lyceius, or Apollo the Wolf God, and hence known as the Lyceum, a grove that Socrates had loved. In the Lyceum stood several buildings, and a covered colonnade. Not being an Athenian citizen, Aristotle could not purchase land. But he rented this property and started his school, and the Lyceum soon became famous. Like most schools it contained a *peripatos*, or walk, where the members of the Lyceum could stroll while conversing, and at the Lyceum they strolled enough to earn for themselves the title Peripatetics. When the Lyceum was founded, Isocrates had been dead for three years; the Lyceum succeeded his school as the chief rival of the Academy. The Lyceum was equipped with a considerable library, the largest yet formed in Hellas. It possessed maps and a museum of specimens for scientific study. Its members partook of common meals, and once a month held a symposium. Aristotle walked and discussed problems with his disciples, but above all he lectured. Although he had written dialogues, some of them bearing the same names as certain dialogues by Plato, the give-and-take of dialogue never played the role in his life which it played in the lives of Socrates and Plato. Those of Aristotle's works that would survive were essentially lectures or notes for lectures, and although these works commonly started off with a survey of the opinions of other thinkers on the subject and even of what the common man in the Agora opined, it was Aristotle himself who quickly took the floor, to rectify, to clarify, to render explicit.

Aristotle was indeed the intellectual son of Plato, as Plato in a somewhat different sense was the son of Socrates. But Aristotle's descent from Socrates was descent in a double sense. Socrates did of course insist on both the ascending and descending dialectic: on the motion of the mind from the thing to idea, from the visible to the invisible, from concrete to abstract, from the abstract idea itself to the more general idea implicit in it, and also on the motion by deduction from these high ideas back to things. He had reticently tried to describe this ascent and descent of the mind when he used the metaphor of the divided line. Socrates had tried to awaken reason in others, to play midwife to them when they conceived —when they conceived ideas, grasped concepts. But unlike the famous sophists he encountered, he denied that he had knowledge he could

376

transfer to others; denied that he was a teacher; took no pupils; accepted fees from no man. He inquired further, until his inquiries angered and alarmed the Athenians and they silenced him with death. He left no written philosophy behind him.

Plato institutionalized the dialectical search, accepted pupils, wrote and published. True, the writings he published were dialogues, though the later ones somewhat resembled lectures. Nevertheless, he remained Socratic in his dislike of the dogmatic, in his reverence for the truth still sought and not yet found, in his poetic insight, his humor, his commitment to his polis.

Aristotle, compared with either Socrates or Plato, was a professional intellectual, an alien resident at Athens, a distinguished professor. He neither practiced Socratic irony nor shrank, like Socrates, from publishing the written word. He eschewed the oracular, avoided the purposeful ambiguity of the poet. Though he wrote at least some verse, he was not a poet. His wit was sharp, but the sheet lightning of humor was missing. His genius was a superb common sense, a powerful and active mind, which observed tirelessly, described accurately, analyzed completely. For Aristotle, to know was to classify and systematize. Neither Socrates nor Plato built a philosophical system. Aristotle did. Socrates declared in his trial that he knew he knew nothing; Aristotle knew that he knew. What he knew, he was prepared to transmit. What he knew turned out to be a vast summary, an inventory, of Hellenic knowledge, corrected, ordered, made explicit.[477]

That knowledge he divided into three branches: the theoretical, the practical, the productive. To deal properly with any of them, a man must think logically, and in the *Organon*, or Instrument, Aristotle attempted to furnish the thinker with rules of thought that would enable him to think accurately and well. If a man thought theoretically, he would be seeking knowledge merely for its own sake, and because, as Aristotle himself stated in one of the most gallant Greek sentences yet written, "All men desire by nature to know."[478] But theoretical knowledge could itself be usefully divided. There was theology, the science of God, which he also called "first philosophy," since all other knowledge depended on it. His treatise on this first philosophy, later known as the *Metaphysics*,[479] dealt not with any class of material things such as men or animals or plants, which lived and moved and had their being on earth, but with abstract being as such.

A second theoretical science, or group of sciences, dealt with the objects of nature. A third dealt with mathematics: numbers and magnitudes. All these theoretical sciences were studied by man, not to learn what to do or how to make something, but merely to understand them.

Aristotle's theoretical sciences covered roughly what Plato's *Timaeus* had covered. But though it was not easy to find anything in Aristotle's treatises in theoretical science that had not been implied or suggested by the *Timaeus*, between them, nevertheless, a gulf yawned. For one thing, what the *Timaeus* stated poetically and provocatively, Aristotle stated at length, in detail, explicitly. Again, while the *Timaeus* portrayed God as the Creator, direct or indirect, of man and the world he dwelt in, Aristotle's God, the Unmoved Mover, had not created matter, which was co-eternal with God; and while the *Timaeus* imagined or intuited a God that found the world good, Aristotle's God neither intervened in nor gave a thought to the world. He contemplated the only thing worthy of his contemplation, himself. His only intervention in man's world was to exert an influence like the influence a loved person exerts on those who love him. As in the *Timaeus*, the whole earth and everything in it yearned toward him, and this fact gave to Aristotle's physics as well as his biology a strongly teleological cast. Finally, Aristotle's distrust of the Academy's tendency to mathematicize nature turned his physics and his astronomy away from number and quantity toward quality; and his distrust of the eternal forms of Socrates and Plato led him to insist that the form or essence of a class of things could exist only in concrete individuals, only in the matter they formed. For despite his metaphysical speculations, it was the downward dialectic of deductive science, not the upward dialectic of metaphysics, that occupied him most. He abstracted, he deduced, he applied, he observed, he classified.

His practical sciences dealt with *praxis*, with human action, with conduct. And since man was a "political animal,"[480] a polis animal, who could not achieve a good life alone, all ethical problems, all problems of how a man should act, were closely connected with the nature of the state and the science of politics. In the *Nicomachean Ethics* and the *Politics* Aristotle therefore studied the problems of man-in-polis, problems that Socrates had discussed in Plato's *Republic* and that the Athenian Stranger had expounded in Plato's *Laws*. It had been characteristic of Plato that in each of those two dialogues he had fused ethics and politics, and it was characteristic of Aristotle that, while insisting his two treatises made one whole, he nevertheless dealt with that whole in two treatises.

In the *Physics*, Aristotle created a network of terms with which the human intellect might grasp and hold the ceaselessly changing world of matter about him. There was Plato's "form," of course: the idea that made men call all things of a certain kind by the same name, like man, or animal, or plant. There was the matter in which this form was embodied. And there was the resulting substance. All the matter men had ever perceived was formed matter or substance, was in short matter of some kind: matter itself was therefore a mere abstraction like form. Nobody had ever seen or touched pure matter. But he declined to reduce this unsensed matter to mathematics, as Timaeus had invited Socrates to do.

These substances, these things, among which man lived, were in ceaseless motion: motion from place to place, or motion from small to large as in growth, the motion of being born and coming into being, of dying and passing out of being, of changing color or temperature or some other quality. It was this changing world of formed and reformed matter which the physicist, or philosopher of nature, studied.

These substances had powers, or potentialities. A learner had the power to learn, and this power was actualized, developed, realized, when he had used it and had learned. An unhealthy man had the power to be healed, and it was the doctor's function to actualize this power. Seeds had power to become plants, bronze to become a statue, bricks to become a house; and even a stone lying on the ground had the power to be moved. To understand learners and unhealthy men and raw bronze and stones, one needed to understand their powers and what causes could actualize those powers. There were, Aristotle held, always four causes in the material universe: the material, the efficient, the formal, and the final. In the case of a marble statue, the material cause was the block of marble from which a statue could be hewn. That marble had the power to become a statue only if other causes operated; nevertheless, without it, no marble statue could be caused. Unlike some of the early Ionian philosophers of nature, Aristotle declined to believe that matter could be the ultimate, sole cause of the universe. There had to be a sculptor, wielding a chisel: there had to be what Aristotle called the efficient cause. Even then, putting a man and a chisel and a block of marble together need not cause a statue. The man must have an idea, a Platonic form, of what he wanted to make: this was the formal cause of a statue's coming into being. But such a man could conceive such an idea or imagine such a statue, and still nothing would happen unless he had also the will and purpose to impress this form on the substance, marble, a substance which was itself a case of formed matter. His will and purpose were the end, the *telos*, which the sculptor had in view, and hence Aristotle could not envisage a physical universe that was purely mechanical and without purpose. This purposed end was the final cause. When the seed became a plant, nature, which Aristotle occasionally called God and nature, merged the formal cause and final cause, and out of a seed purposely formed a plant.

The skein of such terms as form, matter, power, actualization, and the four causes, which did such yeoman service in the *Physics*, Aristotle used also in the *Nicomachean Ethics* and the *Politics*. He concluded in the *Ethics* that the object of all men was happiness, though they differed as to the appropriate means to reach this end: some thought money would get them there, some thought honor would, some chose other means as their immediate, intermediary ends. Aristotle undertook in the *Ethics* to demonstrate that virtue, or, more precisely, a group of virtues, were the principal means. He undertook to name these virtues, to define them and classify them. The virtues, he argued, were essentially habits of making right choices, and their corresponding vices were habits of choosing wrongly. He assailed the view of Socrates and Plato, which appeared to him to reduce all virtue to knowledge, to trace all vice to ignorance. He insisted that a man sometimes knows what is right but does its opposite. In the sphere of practical action a man must actualize his power to act courageously by performing a courageous act. If he does this often enough he acquires the habit, or virtue, which men call courage, and he himself then and only then becomes a courageous man. It was the same with the other principal moral virtues: temperance, or self-control; prudence, or practical wisdom; and justice, or fair dealing. A man who lacked these four virtues would be cowardly, greedy, foolish, and crooked.

But, since the completely actualized man is one who can think well in the field of theory as well as act properly in practical life, a man should also actualize into habits his latent power to do certain things intellectually. Aristotle believed he could identify five ways in which the human intellect acted. It could make; and the habit of making skillfully, whether a man painted a picture or built a bridge, Aristotle identified as art, which he called one of the intellectual virtues. The intellect could also demonstrate, follow an argument, construct an ordered science like geometry; and the habit of doing these things well he called the intellectual virtue, science. The intellect could choose, in practical affairs, between things that were good and things that were bad for human beings; and prudence therefore had to be placed in this list of intellectual virtues, even though it had already been presented from another point of view as a moral virtue. The intellect had the power to intuit, and this power, when actualized by use into a habit, was the virtue of intuition. The intellect could, by subtly combining acts of intuition with acts of demonstration, or science, act wisely in the area of speculation and pure theory: such acts produced the virtue of *sophia*, speculative wisdom, as distinguished from practical wisdom, or prudence. The five intellectual virtues, then, were art, science, prudence, intuition, and speculative wisdom; and the last-named was man's highest and most godlike virtue. The virtuous man was the only man who could achieve happiness, because happiness was full activity, full operation, complete functioning; and only the virtuous man possessed the full use of the powers proper to man; the only man in full working order was the virtuous man.

Aristotle's conviction that the power to contemplate was the highest of human powers led him to another gallant statement. The great poets of the Hellenic past had warned man against the willful arrogance, the hybris, of imagining, in the intoxication of good fortune and success, that any man could wield the power the gods wielded. "Strive not," wrote Pindar, "to be a Zeus . . . Mortal aims befit mortal men."[481] And again, when Chiron the centaur restored a dead man to life, Zeus slew both of them, which led Pindar to cry: "Seek not, my soul, the immortal life."[482] But Pindar was talking about self-will, based on the lack of self-knowledge. Aristotle would have agreed, though in different terms perhaps, that a man ought not to set his will against the will of Zeus. But he knew of one act of God that, without hybris, man might and ought to imitate:

> If then the intellect is something divine in comparison with man, so is the life of the intellect divine in comparison with human life. Nor ought we to obey those who enjoin that a man should have man's thoughts and a mortal the thoughts of mortality, but we ought so far as possible to achieve immortality, and do all that man may to live in ac-

cordance with the highest thing in him; for though this be small in bulk, in power and value it far surpasses all the rest.[483]

And yet, if no peril of hybris lurked in contemplation, did the peril not confront the intellect the moment it re-entered the world of things? Aristotle himself had undertaken not merely to wonder at this intricate cosmos of concentric celestial spheres, of the earth, its plants and animals, its men, and the polis, that "partnership of free men"[484]; he had also undertaken to bring it to order, at least in his own mind, and to that extent to rule it. Plato's mind, too, had roved upward in space to the shining stars, moving on their appointed rounds, and backward in time to the lost continent of Atlantis, described to Solon by the priests of Egypt. But he had imagined and conceived undogmatically. He had seized no distant terrain as his own, as his colony, his empire of the intellect. Aristotle classified and defined and intellectually appropriated the marvels of this vast cosmos, this cosmos that yearned toward God. He divided and subdivided, often illuminatingly, sometimes a little obsessively and pedantically. If he warned Philip against imperialist adventures in Asia, was he not himself in some sense seizing the philosophic hegemony of Hellas? This sometimes gave his argument the eristic tone that Socrates always considered such a poor substitute for the dialectical.[485] But the note of professional rivalry in Aristotle's works suggested Philip's imperialism less than a related trait in his writings: his determination to achieve a certain neatness in his map of the cosmos, to make it conform to a system, and often to ignore the questions raised by his own answers to previous questions. By and large, his statements were those neither of a midwife nor a gadfly, but those of a judge rendering a verdict. By and large, they did not invite further dialogue from his reader. They invited him to fill in the detail of a world that Aristotle had made Aristotle's world. The conquest of that world wore the air of triumph, and what remained for the conqueror's successors was the work of mopping up, the work of pacification.

None the less, it was a brilliant conquest. Perhaps it was a necessary conquest, in the same sense that Philip's conquest of Mainland Greece was a necessary one. The dialectic of freedom had broken down in Hellenic politics, and Isocrates was not the only Hellene prepared to welcome Philip, to have him end the interminable eristic of war and revolution in Hellas. But back of that political breakdown was another crisis. The gods had largely withdrawn from Hellas, at least from its educated class. The relation of man to man was increasingly impersonal. Faith in ideas was yielding to skepticism, and free moral choices seemed to be narrowing toward animal survival. Hellenic man was lonely and frightened and he looked for shelter. Aristotle's system offered shelter. It was a better shelter than any other thinker offered, as Philip's empire was a better empire. If each in his way was an empire-builder, at least each responded to a genuine need.

To his *Politics* Aristotle brought the same diligent observation he had brought to his biological research. And though he, like his teacher and his teacher's teacher, was concerned to discover the ideal polis, the polis in which men could most fully develop both their moral virtues and their intellectual virtues, he wrote mostly in the vein of the *Laws*, not of the *Republic*. He wanted to apply sound political principle to the actual condition of Hellas. Like Socrates and Plato he discarded the notion that law was merely the rule of the stronger, that might made right, that laws were purely conventional and were not the embodiments of reason in the polis. The polis, he was convinced, was as essential to man's nature as the family. To function properly, the polis had to have a proper size. A polis of ten citizens could not be self-sufficient, but a polis of 100,000 would be absurd and no polis at all. Barbarians, ruled by despots, could live in huge cities; but no huge city could be a partnership of free men. Such partnerships permitted free men to govern themselves responsibly through reason and law and thereby provided the necessary conditions for the exercise of both the moral and intellectual virtues. Indeed, such freedom actualized man, made him most completely man, where the relationship of force or might did not. For that reason Aristotle looked on tyranny as a degradation of monarchy, on oligarchy as a degradation of aristocracy, on a democracy led by demagogues as a degradation of the sort of moderate, constitutional democracy Theramenes had briefly achieved in Athens in 411. He knew that revolution introduced force and tended to destroy the rule of reason even when its aim was to increase it.

A good polis, like a good man, needed good habits and a certain stability, and Aristotle's anxiety to restore such stability to the cities of Hellas, rent asunder by the ceaseless struggle of rich and poor, led him to prescribe a large middle class as the best device for steadying the state. He knew that the moral virtue of a good man is guided by intellect, that the moral act is voluntary and deliberate, not a mere reflex produced by animal training. But what he most emphasized in his *Ethics* was training and habit, and the fact that in practice courage, for example, was a mean between two extremes, rashness and cowardice; and he urged his reader to aim at the mean. Where Socrates sought the formal cause of virtue, knowledge, Aristotle tended to focus on its efficient cause. It was as if, in a world that threatened to brutalize its inhabitants and then collapse into final anarchy, he wanted not only to steady the polis with a middle class but also to steady the citizen by helping him acquire good civic habits, as a parent might help a child or a general might help raw recruits. Plato's talk about the moral virtues had reflected the aristocrat's insight into the heroic; Aristotle's, the middle-class professional man's insight into the advantages of moderate behavior. Where Plato's Socrates defined courage as knowing what is to be feared and not to be feared, Aristotle set for man the more modest, less inspiring goal of acquiring good moral habits with or without insight, by repetition and by the prudent rule of thumb: aim at the mean, or a little to whichever side of it would best compensate for one's recognizable failings.

But the kindred evils of war, slavery, and the money that came from booty and was invested in mercenaries remained in the *Politics* essentially unprescribed for. Had Aristotle's method been less that of the lecturer who already knew and more that of the questioner jointly exploring a problem with others, he might indeed have followed through on some of his own ideas, which, given his method, went unexplored. In explaining, for example, that a good polis needed citizens who were full of spirit like the barbarian peoples of Europe but who were also intelligent and skillful like the subjected peoples of Asia, he observed with satisfaction:

> But the Greek race participates in both characters, just as it occupies the middle position geographically, for it is both spirited and intelligent; hence it continues to be free and to have very good political institutions, and to be capable of ruling all mankind if it attains constitutional unity.[486]

But he was too full of his mean between two extremes to follow the insight contained in those last words, "if it attains constitutional unity," or to consider how Hellas might devise common political institutions. Or, if Macedonian hegemony had now rendered that question academic, to consider how such a political union might conceivably include Macedonia. And it was perhaps characteristic of a fourth-century Hellene, whether he were Aristotle or Isocrates, that when he thought of political union, capable of substituting law and reason for the interstate anarchy of Hellas, he should think of union not as a device for replacing force with reason so much as a device for joining forces and imposing the Hellenes' will upon their neighbors.

Again, if his readers sought his advice on that other glaring case where might made right in Hellas, on slavery, so largely itself a product of war and an incitement to make war, here too he lacked Socrates' capacity for detecting in an apparent irrelevancy an unexpected trail that might lead toward truth. Some thinkers, Aristotle observed,

> maintain that for one man to be another's master is contrary to nature, because it is only convention that makes the one a slave and the other a freeman and there is no difference between them by nature, and that therefore it is unjust, for it is based on force.[487]

But

> the manager of a household must have his tools, and of tools some are lifeless and others living (for example, for a helmsman the rudder is a lifeless tool and the lookout man a live tool—for an assistant in the arts belongs to the class of tools), so also an article of property is a tool for the purpose of life, and property generally is a collection of tools, and a slave is a live article of property. And every assistant is as it were a tool that serves for several tools; for if every tool could perform its own work when ordered, or by seeing what to do in advance . . . if thus shuttles wove and quills played harps of themselves, master-craftsmen would have no need of assistants and masters no need of slaves.[488]

It was clear that Aristotle was talking, not about the relatively few slaves employed in producing articles for sale, but about the large number the Hellenes used for domestic servants. But when he admitted that there would be no need of slaves if quills automatically played harps and if other less musical domestic services could be performed by automatic devices—an alternative he clearly considered absurd—did he not lay a poor groundwork for the rest of his argument?

> These considerations therefore make clear the nature of the slave and his essential quality: one who is a human being belonging by nature

not to himself but to another is by nature a slave, and a person is a human being belonging to another if being a man he is an article of property, and an article of property is an instrument for action separable from its owner. But we must next consider whether or not anyone exists who is by nature of this character, and whether it is advantageous and just for anyone to be a slave, or whether on the contrary all slavery is against nature. And it is not difficult either to discern the answer by theory or to learn it empirically. Authority and subordination are conditions not only inevitable but also expedient; in some cases things are marked out from the moment of birth to rule or to be ruled.[489]

Just as the soul ought to rule the body, and the king ought to rule his subjects; just as man ought to rule other animals, and it is an advantage to domestic animals to be ruled by their masters, "since this gives them security"[490]; just as, "between the sexes, the male is by nature superior and the female inferior, the male ruler and female subject"[491]; so

all men that differ as widely as the soul does from the body and the human being from the lower animal (and this is the condition of those whose function is the use of the body and from whom this is the best that is forthcoming)—these are by nature slaves, for whom to be governed by this kind of authority is advantageous, inasmuch as it is advantageous to the subject things already mentioned. For he is by nature a slave who is capable of belonging to another (and that is why he does so belong), and who participates in reason so far as to apprehend it but not to possess it; for the animals other than man are subservient not to reason, by apprehending it, but to feelings. And also the usefulness of slaves diverges little from that of animals; bodily service for the necessities of life is forthcoming from both, from slaves and from domestic animals alike. The intention of nature therefore is to make the bodies also of freemen and of slaves different—the latter strong for necessary service, the former erect and unserviceable for such occupations, but serviceable for a life of citizenship (and that again divides into the employments of war and those of peace); but as a matter of fact often the very opposite comes about—some persons have the bodies of free men and others the souls; since this is certainly clear, that if persons were born as distinguished only in body as are the statues of the gods, everyone would say that those who were inferior deserved to be these men's slaves. And if this is true in the case of the body, there is far juster reason for this rule being laid down in the case of the soul; but beauty of soul is not so easy to see as beauty of body. It is manifest therefore that there are

386

cases of people of whom some are freemen and the others slaves by nature, and for these slavery is an institution both expedient and just.[492]

Aristotle did not defend the subjection, as tools or mere means to another's will, of those who were slaves by law but not by nature. Only those who were slaves by nature, because they participated in reason so far as to apprehend it but not to possess it, were better off for being slaves. But why the hurried observation that, if only domestic tasks could be done by automatic tools, their services would not be needed? Was this relevant to the argument? Could not the fact that this observation was made, no matter how hurriedly, have suggested to a Socrates the question whether Aristotle's real reason for endorsing slavery as natural was that he felt a natural desire to enjoy the service of slaves, since that service freed his time and gave him leisure to think and teach and write?

Might not Aristotle's own conclusion, that man could secure the full use of his latent powers only by actualizing those powers into their appropriate moral and intellectual virtues, have suggested to him that what he called a natural slave was merely an unactualized man—that is, an uneducated one? That he did not take this step was all the more remarkable in that no Hellene, not even Plato, ever insisted more strenuously on the duty of the polis to educate its citizens if it was to govern by reason and consent and not by mere force.

When somebody asked him how the educated differed from the uneducated, Aristotle answered, "As much as the living from the dead."[493] The polis he wanted was a polis of living men. Had not Heraclitus written: "To those who are awake, there is one ordered universe common to all, whereas in sleep each man turns away from this world to one of his own"[494]? Because education actualized men's powers, it converted men from sleepwalkers into citizens. For only those who possessed the habits of acting justly, courageously, temperately, and prudently, and of using their intellects to purpose could hope to govern their own polis well, whether such persons were monarchs, or oligarchs, or democrats. Nor could any others use wisely those two extraordinary means to true community, those two powerful and easily misused media, those two sets of symbols: words and coins.

As to words, Aristotle's *Organon*, or treatise on logic, had gone far in examining words as well as ideas. And, in his grand encyclopedic arrangement of human knowledge into the speculative sciences, the practical sciences, and the productive sciences, he inserted among the productive sciences a treatise on *Rhetoric*, along with a treatise on *Poetics*. The *Rhetoric* was a handbook on how to make persuasive speeches, which the citizens of a free polis must know how to make if common deliberation was to proceed. The *Poetics* told how to make poems, in a society that lived in part by the epics men recited and the dramas, whether tragic or comic, that men needed if they were to be alive and awake.

On money, his thought followed the Platonic tradition: money was good when it served as a convenient medium for the exchange of material goods. But the use of money to make more money was an evil. Since the temptation to convert the means, money, into an end was an all too frequent phenomenon, Aristotle quoted Solon's warning: "But of riches no bound has been fixed or revealed to men."[495] Aristotle held that "a man cannot expect to make money out of the community and to receive honor as well."[496] Since of those who sought the good life many thought to find it in physical pleasure, and since physical pleasure could be bought with money, the many aimed in practice at piling up money. The aim of the military art was victory, but the mercenary often made that aim money. The aim of the medical art was to cause health in the patient, but the doctor could pervert its aim into the making of money. The management of money for the purpose of providing the necessities of life was the perfectly legitimate *oikonomikē*, or household art of economics, and Aristotle never attempted a treatise on political economy, the 'household art' of a whole polis. He noted that this household art was esteemed, but that trade for the purpose of making money was

> justly discredited (for it is not in accordance with nature, but involves men's taking things from one another). As this is so, usury is most reasonably hated, because its gain comes from money itself and not from that for the sake of which money was invented. For money was brought into existence for the purpose of exchange, but interest increases the amount of the money itself (and this is the actual origin of the Greek word: offspring resembles parent, and interest is money born of money); consequently this form of the business of getting wealth is of all forms the most contrary to nature.[497]

He then proceeded to discuss commercial practices, including monopoly, "a universal principle of business"[498]; and told a tale about Thales of

Miletus, who had founded the early Ionian philosophy and was commonly considered, like Solon, one of the Seven Sages.

> Thales, so the story goes, because of his poverty was taunted with the uselessness of philosophy; but from his knowledge of astronomy he had observed while it was still winter that there was going to be a large crop of olives, so he raised a small sum of money and paid round deposits for the whole of the olive-presses in Miletus and Chios, which he hired at a low rent as nobody was running him up; and when the season arrived, there was a sudden demand for a number of presses at the same time, and by letting them out on what terms he liked he realized a large sum of money, so proving that it is easy for philosophers to be rich if they choose, but this is not what they care about. Thales then is reported to have thus displayed his wisdom, but as a matter of fact this device of taking an opportunity to secure a monopoly is a universal principle of business . . .[499]

He had managed to come to terms with war and slavery, but not with the commercial and banking operations of Athens, operations which had done so much to create his Hellenic community. That community was still without common government, was a community of city-states, most of them split internally by democrat and oligarch, and divided externally from each other by a long history of battle and bloodshed. Aristotle in his detailed analysis of the varieties of government sometimes skirted the problem: the Greek race would be "capable of ruling all mankind if it attains constitutional unity."[500] But he did not follow that train of thought, since it did not fit into his arrangement of his material. He was discussing something else, as he was busy doing when his active mind opened that other trail, the relative uselessness of natural slaves if their work could be done by machinery.

He stuck to the polis; yet even Demosthenes the orator could have told him that Aristotle's former patron, Philip II of Macedonia, had already put an end to the polis by effectually robbing it of its sovereignty. Aristotle had performed a magnificent service in historical research by collecting his 158 city-state constitutions. But he did not think of political science as merely historical or descriptive or theoretical; he classified it as a practical science, to be studied as a guide to political action. It would have been fair to ask him, since the polis was in decline, how should men act politically once more?

When he passed from the practical sciences to the productive and faced the problem of analyzing drama, he was again in a sense too late. He wrote as if he admired Sophocles' *Oedipus the King* more than any other tragedy, but the days of Aeschylus and Sophocles and even Euripides were now long past. Their tragedies were presented in the Theater of Dionysus at Athens as revivals for a polis which could no longer write tragedies of that stature. Through the mind of this alien resident from the north, Athens was reflecting on a political organization that was no longer adequate to her problems and on dramas she could no longer conceive. The fact remained that the polis was one embodiment of that human community in which apparently all men must learn to dwell: in that sense polis could never die. And because man's destiny was tragic, Oedipus could not die, any more than Homer's Achilles could die. Aristotle undertook neither to write an epic nor a tragedy nor any other long poem; he undertook to analyze them as literary forms. How much analysis he could pack into few words he showed when he came to the problem of defining tragedy:

> Tragedy is, then, a representation of an action that is heroic and complete and of a certain magnitude—by means of language enriched with all kinds of ornament, each used separately in the different parts of the play: it represents men in action and does not use narrative, and through pity and fear it effects relief to these and similar emotions.[501]

Then, having offered his definition, he proceeded to expand and explain it. But the idea in his definition that perhaps shone most brilliantly came from the medical tradition, the tradition of his father's family. The relief which men got from their emotions when they witnessed tragedy Aristotle expressed by the Greek word *katharsis*, the regular medical term for a purge. The Athenian polis assembled twice a year under religious auspices, and tragedies were played, tragedies that stirred up the spectators' emotions and then by dramatic resolution drained them safely off. This was an insight Plato never had, or at least never put in his dialogues. And yet, Socrates in the *Republic* had used the medical metaphor in speaking even of a polis which neither he nor those who talked with him were ever likely to see on earth. For, once Glaucon had scorned Socrates' bucolic "city of pigs,"[502] Socrates had proceeded to imagine a fevered[503] state. Well, the fever men called civilization needed purging; tragedy was perhaps one of the cures.

If applying the medical notion of catharsis to his study of tragedy reflected Aristotle's most brilliant insight in his *Poetics*, then one of his most Platonic insights into narrative poetry in general was that "poetry is something more scientific and serious than history, because poetry tends to give general truths while history gives particular truths."[504] And finally, his most Hellenic insight was that what tragedy, and indeed all drama, essentially imitated or represented was not character or elevated diction, though these were needed. The essence of drama was action, human action. The very word drama, Aristotle asserted, came from the Dorians, who claimed to have invented both tragedy and comedy. The very word came from the Dorian word *dran*, to act, to do. It was what the characters did and not primarily what they were that made a tragedy dramatic. It was not characterization but plot. The point was profoundly Hellenic, as was for that matter Attic tragedy itself. For the Hellene loved action, including the action of the imagination and the reason. Achilles acted. It was through acts, Aristotle had insisted in the *Ethics*, that man acquired the moral virtues; it was through acts of choice. It was even by acts that he acquired the intellectual virtues. And it was precisely because it was an action of the intellect, moreover an action freed from the passions, relatively free from being acted upon through the body, that contemplation could be viewed by Aristotle as man's highest act. After all, the God he wrote about in his *Metaphysics*, a God completely immaterial, the Unmoved Mover of the whole cosmos, was pure Act.

For a dozen years Aristotle taught at his Lyceum and classified his universe. His wife died, leaving him a daughter. He remarried, and his second wife gave him a son, named Nicomachus for Aristotle's father, the royal physician to Amyntas III. Then, like Socrates, he was charged with impiety. Was his real crime his relations with his old pupil, King Alexander of Macedon, and with Alexander's regent for Hellas, Antipater? There was a wave of anti-Macedonian sentiment in Athens at the time. In any case, the evidence adduced against him was that he had written a hymn, a poem that could be properly addressed only to a god, and had indited it to Hermeias, the Academic, tyrant of Atarneus and Assus; and that he had also written an epitaph for a statue of Hermeias at Delphi. In 323, the year Alexander died, Aristotle left Athens for Chalcis in Euboea, his mother's native city, now under Macedonian control, observing that he would not permit the polis which killed Socrates to sin twice against philosophy.[505]

He left his old companion, Theophrastus, the botanist, in charge of the Lyceum. Aristotle's problem was different from that of Socrates. Socrates was an Athenian citizen and did not feel free to flout the laws of his own polis. Besides, Socrates, though he did not claim to know that man was immortal, expressed a lively faith that man was. Aristotle's writings were ambiguous on this point, but leaned away from personal immortality.

In 322 when he was sixty-two, and a year after he fled Athens, Aristotle died; and the tradition that grew out of his life would picture him as a bald man with thin legs, small eyes, and a lisp, a well-dressed man not given to ascetic living, a man with a mocking wit.

10

ALEXANDER'S
WORLD POLIS

WHEN Philip of Macedon, the Thirteenth God, was
murdered and his son Alexander mounted his throne, the young king was
twenty. He inherited more than a throne. Through his father he was
descended from Achilles; from the Argive hero, Perseus; and from Heracles,
the hero born of a human mother and of Zeus himself, a hero who by
arduous labors benefited the Hellenes and who by the will of Zeus was
raised to the rank of god. Philip bequeathed Alexander courage in battle,
the lessons in strategy and tactics learned in Thebes during the great days
of Epaminondas and the phalanx, and a magnificently trained, expertly
officered army.

From his mother Olympias, the rejected Epirote princess, Alexander
inherited a passionate and mystical nature. And though each of his
parents came from a dynasty which claimed to be Greek, Philip's own
mother had come from wild Illyria. Although Philip had made a number

of political marriages, he had married Olympias for love. He had met her on the Isle of Samothrace, during her initiation into a mystery cult, when he was twenty-seven and she was twenty. Tradition would report that, as an unusually zealous and inspired Bacchante, or woman worshiper of the wine god Dionysus, she used to distribute to her fellow revelers tame serpents, which coiled about the women's wands as they danced wildly, and that this spectacle terrified the men.

Through his tutor Aristotle, Alexander became heir to Greek poetry and to Greek political and ethical thought. He loved Aristotle, he used to say, more than he did his father Philip; for while Philip had given him life, Aristotle had taught him how to live a noble life.[506] He read Homer, loved Achilles, and learned sections of the *Iliad* by heart. He read Greek tragedy, especially Euripides, who had written his last plays at the Macedonian court. He read the great lyric poets. In a period when Greek thinkers were desperately turning toward monarchy and colonization, Alexander learned from Aristotle the problems which both ideas involved. After three years with Aristotle, at the age of sixteen he had served as regent in Philip's absence on campaign; had led an army himself against a Thracian tribe; and had founded a military colony, which he named Alexandropolis—the polis of Alexander. He had been eighteen when Philip and he had won control of Mainland Greece at Chaeronea, and it had been Alexander's cavalry charge that broke the Sacred Band of Thebes. After that battle, he had done what Philip had never done: he had entered holy Athens itself, the symbol of all poetry and philosophy, the unchallenged School of Hellas.

But if he inherited from Philip a greatly expanded kingdom and the hegemony of Mainland Greece, the inheritance had to be claimed in the Macedonian manner. Philip's death was the signal for some of the feudal lords of Macedon to rise and to conspire in favor of Alexander's infant half-brother, Philip's son by Cleopatra, the rejected Olympias's successor. There were, as usual, murders and executions before the throne could be guaranteed. Olympias herself saw to it that the infant claimant was murdered in Cleopatra's lap and that Cleopatra was forced to hang herself. Alexander of Macedon and Darius III of Persia ascended their thrones in the same year, 336. Both had waded through blood to be king.

In Athens, Demosthenes had received a secret message that his archfoe, the barbarian Philip, was dead. Demosthenes was at the time in mourning for his daughter, but on hearing the news he changed to his best clothes, placed a garland on his head, and offered a public sacrifice of thanksgiving. He spoke disparagingly of Alexander as a child and a silly madman.[507] Athens ordered a sacrifice of thanks to the gods and passed a decree in honor of Philip's murderer. The other Greek states prepared to defend themselves against Macedonia. With the promptness of a Philip, Alexander led his Macedonians southward; the Greek cities helplessly submitted. Alexander took no reprisals; the League of Corinth elected Alexander Hegemon in Philip's place; and the Greeks again agreed to support the crusade that Philip had planned to lead against the King of Kings, Darius III.

In 335, Alexander subdued the Triballians and the Getae in the northeast in a campaign that took him beyond the Danube; and subjected, with frightful slaughter, the Illyrians to his northwest. He was still in Illyria when news came that the Greek cities were in rebellion. Exiled democrats had seized Thebes, which Athens was promising once more to defend. Alexander led an army southward in fourteen days, collected contingents from Phocis and Boeotia, and laid siege to Thebes. In a single day's assault, Thebes fell. The League of Corinth conveniently voted for the city's destruction. Alexander razed it to the ground: except for the citadel, now garrisoned again with Macedonians, only the temples of Thebes were spared, her temples and the house of Pindar the poet. Some 6,000 Thebans were said to have been slain; some 8,000 men, women, and children were sold into slavery. The incipient Greek revolt ended in October, 335, and Athens sent Alexander congratulations. He replied by demanding the surrender of five anti-Macedonian politicians, including Demosthenes. But in the end, when Athens had agreed to prosecute them herself, Alexander relented. Like Philip, he was always gentle with Athens.

In the following spring he crossed the Hellespont into Asia, at the head of some 40,000 men, of which over 5,000 were cavalry. The great panhellenic crusade that Isocrates had longed for had begun at last. In the expeditionary force were 12,000 Macedonians; 12,000 Greeks, including Allied contingents and mercenaries, a mixed group of Thracians, Paeonians, Agrianians, Triballians, Odrysians, and Illyrians from beyond Macedonia's northern frontiers; and a contingent of archers from Crete. The panhellenic crusade was therefore about two-fifths Hellenic in race. Moreover, of that two-fifths many went, as Xenophon and his polis in flight had gone before

395

them, for pay and pillage and adventure. The rest reflected no enthusiasm on the part of Greek states for war with Persia.

Although Alexander had inherited from Philip a consolidated Macedon, a superb army, and the well-publicized project of a panhellenic crusade, he inherited neither an adequate navy nor an adequate war chest. Philip's navy was too weak to open and keep open communications by sea. Alexander's Greek allies had navies, but those allies were halfhearted and he chose not to exact naval contingents from them. Athens, for example, with a navy of 400 triremes, supplied him with only a token force of 20 ships. As to his finances, his long-term natural resources, notably his gold mines on Mount Pangaeus, were abundant; but when Philip died, the royal treasury was deeply in debt, and the booty Alexander's northern campaigns had brought in had only in part liquidated that debt.

In addition to his infantry and his cavalry, Alexander's army was supported by an artillery that included siege towers on wheels, rams for breaching walls, light catapults for hurling javelins, heavy catapults for launching huge stones. There were trained sappers and pontoon builders, architects, surveyors, geographers, botanists, and even historians. There was an excellent baggage train and commissariat. Aristotle, who had now returned to Athens to found his Lyceum, sent with Alexander his nephew, Callisthenes of Olynthus, philosopher and historian; and Alexander planned to send back to Aristotle scientific specimens and data. The empire Alexander proposed to win was not unrelated to the empire of the mind which Aristotle would win, and would win moreover with Alexander's financial support. Both master and pupil desired by nature to know,[508] and then to organize.

When Alexander crossed the Hellespont, he entered the vastest empire known to the Hellenic mind, an empire which had absorbed the earlier empires of Babylonia, Assyria, and Egypt, as well as Greece-in-Asia. Its wealth was a subject of fable. Although it had failed in the days of Xerxes to conquer Mainland Greece by force, it had in recent decades largely controlled Greece by judicious subsidy and bribe, and bribes and subsidies were still being offered to stir up the Greeks against Macedonia. But it was an empire which had grown fat with success; its provincial governors frequently revolted; and its most dependable soldiers were the mercenaries its gold drew from Mainland Greece. At the moment, it was defended by a huge polyglot army, containing hard fighters from the Persian and Afghan highlands and Greek mercenaries, but an army poorly organized, poorly disciplined, and poorly commanded. The Persian Empire was likewise defended by a navy of some 400 ships, drawn as usual from Phoenicia and Ionia, and commanded by an able Greek, Memnon of Rhodes. But Memnon's navy was never fully manned. The Empire, like its king, Darius III, was middle-aged, slow, hesitant, and purposeless.

Alexander had indeed inherited the project of a panhellenic war of revenge, but there were stronger practical reasons for attacking the Persian Empire than revenge for Xerxes' invasion. The Greek mercenaries under Darius III, the Persian gold that continued to buy friends in Greece, the Ionian ships in Memnon's navy, and Memnon's sea power in the Aegean were all symptoms of the fact that money had inextricably commingled Persian and Greek affairs. Those affairs needed ordering, and Alexander proposed to order them.

Arrived in Asia unopposed, he went to Troy, now only a village, and entered the temple of Athena, where he dedicated his own arms and took in their place armor and weapons which the Achaeans had dedicated when the then great city of Priam had fallen eight long centuries before. Then he offered sacrifice and held games on the plain where Achilles had slain Hector. Alexander laid a wreath on Achilles' tomb, and his dearest friend Hephestion laid one on the tomb of Patroclus, beloved companion of Achilles. Then he declared Troy free, restored its democracy, and abolished the tribute exacted by Persia.

At the small Granicus River Alexander met a Persian army, including cavalry and several thousand Greek mercenaries. His second in command, Parmenion, a veteran general of Philip's army, urged him to wait till morning to attack, but Alexander judged otherwise. He fought his way across the Granicus, while the Persian leaders concentrated their tactics on killing Alexander. And, indeed, at one point Spithridates, governor of Lydia, nearly cut him down, but Clitus the Black, who commanded Alexander's cavalry guard, saved him. The Persians broke; but Alexander made little effort to pursue them. He was too busy massacring the Greek mercenaries in the Persian forces. Of those left alive, he captured some 2,000, and sent them in chains to Macedonia to forced labor "because they had violated Greek public opinion by fighting with Orientals against Greeks."[509] He then sent 300 captured suits of armor to Athens as an offering to Athena, whose temple Xerxes had once burned, and inscribed them:

"Alexander, son of Philip and the Greeks, save Lacedaemonians, these spoils from the Persians in Asia."[510]

He announced that he had come to free the Greek cities, both from the tribute levied by Persia and from the oligarchies through which Persia controlled Greek cities. A wave of democratic revolutions swept Greece-in-Asia. Memnon, who still held the Aegean for Persia, would have liked to reply in kind and to raise a democratic revolution in Mainland Greece, where Alexander's regent also governed through oligarchies. But the League of Corinth dared not move. Alexander held too many hostages: Allied army contingents, individual mercenaries, the 2,000 Greek prisoners he had captured on the Granicus. Meanwhile Memnon's Ionian crews were deserting with their ships: the oarsmen came from the poorer families; now they went home to join other democrats in their liberated cities. So democratic freedom spread. At Ephesus Alexander had to protect the oligarchs for fear of an indiscriminate slaughter.

At Miletus, a Persian garrison backed by a Persian fleet threatened to block Alexander's southward march. Parmenion urged him to order his own small fleet into action, since the Persian fleet which opposed him was even smaller. Alexander refused: he would conquer the Persian fleet on land. Miletus fell; and, when 300 mercenaries escaped to an island ready for a last-ditch stand, he bought their services for his own army. Then, short of funds for his fleet, he dismissed all his ships except the twenty that Athens had furnished. He besieged and took Halicarnassus, restored Ada, the deposed queen of Caria, allowed her to adopt him as her son, and left an army of 3,200 mercenaries to finish reducing her enemies. He himself spent the winter of 334-333 quelling the hill tribes of Lycia and Pisidia. He also conquered Pamphylia.

In the spring he went to Gordium. There in the acropolis stood a chariot, set up long ago by King Midas of Phrygia as a thank-offering to Zeus. The yoke of this chariot was fastened to the tongue by a rope made of bark from the cornel tree. The two ends of the rope were concealed in the knot and there was a local tradition that whoever could untie that knot would become lord of Asia. Aristobulus, one of Alexander's Greek technicians, reported later that Alexander merely drew out a wooden pin driven through the tongue of the chariot and the knot then fell apart, but a legend would grow that he tried and failed to untie the knot and that he thereupon drew his sword, cut through the knot, and exclaimed: "I have loosed it";

also that thunder and lightning that night seemed to certify that the prophecy had been fulfilled and that Alexander would indeed rule Asia. The cutting of the Gordian knot would become a symbol, along with Alexander's reported effort to consult the Delphic oracle before he ever came to Asia. At Delphi he had wanted to know, like Xenophon before him, whether his mission in Asia would prove successful. But the priestess would not enter the temple; he had reached Delphi on one of the inauspicious days. Then, according to the tale, Alexander tried to drag her into the temple; whereupon the priestess cried out, "Thou art invincible, my son!" Alexander took the complaint for a prophecy, decided he had had his oracle, and departed. But at least up to his visit to Gordium he had untied more political knots in Asia than he had cut with the sword. He had subverted Persian power and its subservient tyrants and oligarchies with his declaration that he was liberating Greece-in-Asia. Up to his visit to Gordium, the impatience the Delphi story imputed to him had not been one of his vices, although Parmenion, the general he had inherited from Philip, might think it was.

From Gordium Alexander marched east to Ancyra and then south to the mountain pass known as the Cilician Gates. By reaching the pass before he was expected by the enemy, he got through without the loss of a man. He entered Tarsus, which the Persians had just evacuated. There he fell ill of a fever. His Greek friend and physician, Philip, prescribed a purge. While Philip was preparing the draught, a note arrived from Parmenion. Alexander read it, took the cup from Philip, handed him the note, and while Alexander drank the prescribed draught, Philip read, "Beware Philip! I learn that Dareius has bribed him to murder you."[511]

At the mystery celebrations in Eleusis, there were things recited, things shown, things done. All three kinds of things were counted on to convey truth. The scene with the Greek doctor took its place alongside the arms Alexander had dedicated at Troy, the Greeks he had sent in chains to Macedonia for helping Persians against Greece, the Persian panoplies sent to Athens, the cutting of the Gordian knot, as things done, things done to convey meaning, symbolic actions that spoke louder than words, especially to soldiers and to masses of frightened civilians.

From Tarsus, after his recovery, Alexander moved southeastward down the Syrian coast. Then he learned that Darius was in his rear with an army. He addressed his officers. These were not provincial governors, he

said, that they would now fight, but the Great King himself. This would
be the decisive battle. He addressed individual officers by name and recalled individual deeds of heroism they had already performed. He spoke
of Xenophon and his famous march through the mountains to the Black
Sea. The officers cheered. After a night's sleep, they moved toward Darius.
In the afternoon, on a November day of 333, near Issus, the two armies
clashed. Despite the vast military potential of his empire, Darius at Issus
commanded about the same number[512] of troops as Alexander, mostly
Persian cavalry and a heavy infantry of Greek mercenaries. Alexander
fought on his own right wing where he had massed his cavalry, and it
was a cavalry charge that crumpled the Persian lines. Darius fled; but his
Greek mercenaries gave the Macedonians a rough fight, and when the
battle was lost they managed to retire in good order to Tripolis, where
they took ship for service in Egypt.

The battle of Issus brought Alexander both triumph and challenge. In
theory, he could have pacified the mountainous interior of Asia Minor
and have striven for the frontier which Isocrates of Athens had urged on
Philip: a line from Cilicia, where Alexander now was, north to the Greek
city of Sinope on the Black Sea. But such a frontier would have meant
little from a military point of view. Darius had indeed been badly beaten.
He had lost prestige; he had lost a valuable contingent of Greek mercenaries; he had even lost his mother, wife, and two daughters, who were
captured when he had fled. He had also lost a considerable treasure, stored
as war chest at Damascus. This, Parmenion and his Thessalian cavalry had
promptly seized; and by now Alexander badly needed it. But Darius had
not lost his predominance at sea, and Alexander therefore stuck to his
plan of conquering the Great King's remaining Mediterranean seacoast.
He would thereby leave the enemy's fleet without bases, and he would
cut off Persian subsidies to Sparta and other troublemakers in Greece.
He knew that Phoenicia and Egypt were already restless. Darius would
doubtless raise a fresh army: he would have to be dealt with later.

Alexander headed south toward Phoenicia. Marathus opened its gates,
and at Marathus a letter arrived from Darius. It gently took exception to
the aggressions of Philip and Alexander and justified the writer's own
acts. The battle of Issus "had gone as some god had willed it."[513] As king
to king, he begged Alexander to restore his mother, wife, and two daughters; and on his side he offered friendship and alliance. Alexander answered:

Your ancestors invaded Macedonia and the rest of Greece and did us much harm, though we had done none to them; I have been duly appointed Commander-in-Chief of the Greeks, and invaded Asia desiring to take vengeance on Persia; but it was you who began the mischief. You assisted Perinthus, which wronged my father; and Ochus sent a force into Thrace, which is under our sovereignty. My father was murdered by conspirators, whom you instructed, as you yourselves boasted in your letters, before all the world; you assassinated Arses with the help of Bagoas, and seized the throne unjustly and, according to Persian law, illegally, doing grievous wrong to Persians; you sent improper letters to the Greeks about me, urging them to declare war upon me. You despatched sums of money to the Lacedaemonians and certain other Greeks, and when no other city received these, save only the Lacedaemonians, and when your envoys corrupted my friends and sought to destroy the peace I had made in Greece, I took up arms against you; but it was you who started the quarrel. And whereas I conquered in battle first your generals and satraps, and now yourself and your own force, and hold the country—by the gift of heaven—I hold myself responsible for all of your troops who did not die in the field but took refuge with me; indeed they are with me of their own free will and of their will serve in my army. Regard me then as Lord of all Asia and come to me. If you fear lest by coming you may receive some ungracious treatment at my hands, send some of your friends to receive proper pledges. When you come to me, request and receive your mother, wife, and children, and what you will. You shall have whatsoever you persuade me to give. And in future when you send, send to me as Supreme Lord of Asia, and do not direct what you require as on equal terms, but tell me, as lord of all your possessions, if you have need of aught; otherwise I shall take steps concerning you as a misdemeanant. If you claim your kingdom, stand your ground and fight for it and flee not, since I will pursue you whithersoever you go.[514]

When did he decide that he was Supreme Lord of Asia? And how far did his Asia extend? Events had decided the first question, events and peoples and terrain. The second question no man could yet decide. But the letter was based on a role that Alexander had accepted: he was functioning in Asia as its sovereign, and more completely than Darius ever had done. He was not merely marauding. He was cutting as few Gordian knots as possible. He was organizing and administering. He was liberating Ionian cities from tribute, although he was also accepting contributions, officially voluntary, from those cities to help him complete his task. He was trying to do justice and protect law. He was treating Darius' captured family with an honor worthy of the family of a deposed king. That is, he was respecting the crown, but treating Darius himself as his own subject. On the day after the battle of Issus, according to one tradition,[515] he and Hephestion went alone to Darius' pavilion to show deference to the captive queen mother. They went dressed and armed alike, and the queen mother prostrated herself before Hephestion, since he appeared the taller. When she learned her mistake, she was confused, but Alexander denied that she was mistaken, on the grounds that Hephestion also was an Alexander. The remark was not merely a graceful way of reassuring an anxious captive; it was the illuminating pun of a man who was feeling for his role in history, almost feeling for his identity. Both he and Hephestion were Alexanders; the name meant a defender of men. Both he and Hephestion wanted to defend men; that was why they were fighting in Asia; that was why Alexander must be Lord of Asia.

Where Persia's provincial governors exercised the right of coinage, Alexander usually reserved that right to himself. There would be a common coinage, even though the Greek cities were allowed to coin too. He had won control of scarcely half of Asia Minor, but what he held was the valuable half, especially the Mediterranean coast and the great highways. Of the other half, much had never been governed by Persia either.

The Phoenician ports of Byblus and Sidon surrendered without fighting. Tyre, feeling secure on its rock island a half mile off the coast, played for time. Alexander asked leave to enter the city and sacrifice to the god Melkart, whom he identified with his ancestor, Heracles. Alexander assembled his officers and spoke:

> My friends and allies, so long as Persia is supreme at sea I cannot see how we can march in safety to Egypt. Nor, again, is it safe to pursue Dareius, leaving in our rear the city of Tyre, of doubtful allegiance, and Egypt and Cyprus still in Persia's hands, especially in view of the state of Greek affairs. There is a fear lest the Persians, again seizing the coast places, when we have gone in full force toward Babylon and Dareius, should with a larger army transfer the war into Greece, where the Lacedaemonians are at the moment fighting us; and Athens is kept in its place for the present by fear rather than goodwill towards us. But with Tyre once destroyed, Phoenicia could all be held, and the best and strongest part of the Persian navy, the Phoenician element, would most probably

come over to us. For neither the rowers nor the marines of Phoenicia will have the courage, if their cities are in our hands, to sail the sea and run its dangers for the sake of others. After this Cyprus, moreover, will either come readily to our side or be captured easily by a naval raid. Then if we hold the sea with our Macedonian ships, and the Phoenician navy too, and with Cyprus ours, we should firmly hold the sea-power, and in virtue thereof our expedition to Egypt would be easy. Then, when we have possession of Egypt, we shall have no cause for uneasiness for Greece and our own home, and we shall make the expedition to Babylon, with security at home, and with our enhanced prestige, with the whole sea cut off from Persia and all the country this side of Euphrates.[516]

The siege of Tyre began. Alexander built a causeway from the mainland to the island, and his engineers rolled out wooden siege towers to attack the massive city walls. The Tyrians ran a fireship against the causeway, and managed to burn Alexander's siege towers. Then Alexander succeeded in getting ships from Sidon; for, hearing the news of his successes in Phoenicia, the Persian fleet was disintegrating. In all he collected 220 ships and seized control of the sea around Tyre. A combined sea and land assault breached the great walls. In July, 332, after holding out for seven months, Tyre fell. During the siege, the Tyrians had captured men from one of Alexander's ships and had murdered them high on their wall in the sight of all: the victorious Macedonians now took vengeance. Some 8,000 Tyrians were slaughtered. Thousands of others were sold into slavery. And Alexander sacrificed to Melkart-Heracles and dedicated in his temple the siege engine that had finally breached the wall.

Meanwhile, he had received a second message from Darius. This time Darius offered 10,000 talents for his mother, wife, and two daughters. He offered to cede to Alexander all his provinces between the Euphrates and the sea. He offered a daughter in marriage, royal friendship, and alliance. These terms Alexander read to his staff. "If I were Alexander," said Parmenion, "I would accept these terms." "And so indeed would I," replied the young king, "were I Parmenion."[517] Being Alexander, he wrote Darius that he needed no money from Darius, nor to receive a part of his empire in place of the whole, since both the king's treasures and the king's country were already his. If he chose to marry a daughter of Darius, he would marry her with or without permission. If Darius wanted friendship, he must come to Alexander to ask it. Darius prepared to fight again.

From Tyre Alexander moved through Palestine toward Egypt. Palestine submitted, except for the strongly fortified city of Gaza, the last city before he would reach the desert that separated him from Egypt. Gaza was held by the eunuch Batis, with a strong force of Arab mercenaries. The besieged city fought hard, and Alexander himself was wounded in the shoulder by a catapult. But the siege engines that took Tyre now arrived. The walls of Gaza were battered above ground and sapped below ground, and on the fourth assault the Macedonians poured in. The Arabs fought on desperately till all were killed; the women and children were sold into slavery; and Gaza was repopulated with local tribesmen and refortified.

In late November, 332, Alexander crossed the desert in seven days to the Delta city of Pelusium, and there he found his fleet awaiting him. The Persian provincial governor of Egypt, Mazaces, had no military force capable of saving Egypt and so he surrendered the country to him. Alexander sent his fleet upriver to Memphis while he and his army followed the right bank up to Heliopolis. There he crossed over to Memphis and sacrificed to Apis the bull god and to the other gods of Egypt. It was the slaying of the sacred Apis by the half-mad Cambyses that had ushered in Persia's conquest and subjection of Egypt. Alexander's sacrifice to Apis ushered it out. He was now the new Pharaoh of Egypt.

Alexander next visited the northwestern corner of the Delta and founded there a city to serve as a strategic center of shipping and commerce, and he called his new city Alexandria. Then, taking a small force, he followed the coast of Libya westward till he was north of the Oasis of Ammon; for, as Pharaoh, he was officially the son of this Egyptian god. At the oasis was an oracle, which ranked in the Greek world with the oracle of Delphi and with the ancient oracle of Dodona in Olympias's native Epirus. For the Greeks identified Ammon with Zeus himself, who spoke to men at Dodona in the rustling of the leaves of oak trees and whose son Apollo spoke for him at Delphi. Pindar had sung of Libya's cities "fostered of men near the foundations of Zeus Ammon."[518] Herodotus had written that "Amun is the Egyptian name for Zeus,"[519] and had spoken of "the Ammonians, who follow the worship of the Zeus of Thebes."[520]

Through a sandy, waterless waste Alexander and his force marched southward; and, when an unexpected rain fell, they could only guess it was some god who saved them. Among the drifting dunes the guides lost their way, and again they were saved, as if by gods. Ptolemy, a general, later reported that two serpents led them, even talking serpents; but Aristobulus, the technician, said it was two crows who guided them to the divine oasis. Here they found olives and palms and garden trees, nourished by heavy dew. The priest greeted Alexander, some said, as son of Ammon, which Alexander had to be, since only Ammon's son could be Pharaoh. Others claimed the priest called him explicitly son of Zeus.[521] Still others insisted the priest had tried to address him in Greek, had mispronounced the word for son, and had merely seemed to say, O son of Zeus.[522]

In any case, Alexander spoke alone with the oracle and reported after his consultation that he had received the answer his soul required, a report that settled nothing. Did the priest tell him he was the son both of Zeus Ammon and of Philip the Thirteenth God? That would have been good Egyptian theology but might seem too ingenious to the Greek world, a world accustomed to gods who lay, or were said by the ancient poets to lie, with mortal women. The men of Tyre might not boggle at Egyptian theology, and Alexander in a letter to the Tyrians called himself "son of Ammon, child of King Philip."[523] To his mother he wrote that he "received certain secret responses, which he would tell to her, and to her alone, on his return."[524] A philosopher in Egypt named Psammon told him that "all mankind are under the kingship of God, since in every case that which gets the mastery and rules is divine."[525] But this could have been mere flattery to an absolute monarch. Alexander himself put it differently when he said that "although God was indeed a common father of all mankind, still, He made peculiarly His own the noblest and best of them."[526] Was he, then, son of Ammon, or of Zeus, only in the sense that all men were his sons, even though he, Alexander, resembled Zeus more than the others because, like Zeus, and by his permission, he ruled? At Ephesus the famous Greek painter, Apelles, had done his portrait and had shown him as wielder of the thunderbolt. Like his divine father? As he pondered certain secret responses, Ephesus was scarce two years behind him. Since then, he had hung up his arms at Troy and had honored with sacrifices and games his ancestor, Achilles, grandson of Zeus. He had broken the army of the King of Kings at Issus and had himself been crowned Pharaoh of Egypt, son of Ammon.

Alexander had a disciplined mind, a mind that analyzed military and political problems and directed him in his choice of means. But he had none of the Athenians' sophisticated skepticism. He was a Macedonian, with the ardor of an earlier generation of Athenians; son of a wild and passionate queen who was addicted to mystery religions. He understood that man's nature itself was a mystery and that there were some things man could communicate only by things recited, things shown, things done. A man did deeds in battle himself that made other men do deeds. He cut knots. A man sacrificed to Melkart of Tyre, who was really his ancestor Heracles, benefactor of the Hellenes, son of Zeus by a mortal mother, himself raised to godhead after death by Zeus, who ruled all. A man must know which verse from Homer or Euripides to recite, in order to illuminate the minds of men as no amount of oratory could.

In some later traditions, Alexander knew he was son of Zeus; in others he was less sure. On her marriage night, had not a thunderbolt struck the womb of Olympias? Philip had found his wife in her bed, a serpent lying beside her: had Zeus, who had come disguised to other mortal women as a bull or as a swan, now taken a serpent's form? At the marriage feast when Philip wedded Cleopatra, Attalus, Philip's general and the bride's uncle, had called drunkenly on the guests to pray the gods for a legitimate heir to the kingdom. Alexander had hurled a cup at Attalus and cried: "But what of me, base wretch? Dost thou take me for a bastard?"[527] Then Philip, in a drunken rage, had drawn his sword against his son, had tripped and fallen. And Alexander had mocked, "Look now, men! here is one who was preparing to cross from Europe into Asia; and he is upset in trying to cross from couch to couch."[528]

That was at a banquet, and at Macedonian banquets wine flowed fast. But it was also at a banquet that the young Oedipus was told he was not the son of the king and queen of Corinth. And in Sophocles' play Oedipus had agonized, in his fashion, over the ancient and very Socratic question, "Who am I?" Perhaps, Oedipus suggested at one point in the play, he was the son of Mount Cithaeron. Alexander's relations with Philip had been often strained, and Philip had repudiated Alexander's mother. No more than any other man did Alexander know who his father was, and the drunken Attalus's insult could be true. Again in a later tradition,[529] when Alexander asked the high priest of Ammon whether any of his father's murderers had escaped him, the priest bade him be guarded in his speech, since his was not a mortal father. But even if that tale was historically true, the priest might merely have been saying in a forceful way that in the eyes of Ammon, Ammon himself was the young Pharaoh's father. And, whatever the mystery of man's nature, whatever the difference between fact and metaphor, there was every political reason for accepting and exploiting the Egyptian solution: that he was the son of Ammon. As for his Greek and Macedonian friends, he could afford ironic banter. Wounded, he could fall back on Homer and remark, "This, my friends, that flows here, is blood, and not 'Ichor, such as flows from the veins of the blessed gods.' "[530] Or, again, he could regret wistfully a mortality he was ready to admit and remark "that sleep and sexual intercourse, more than anything else, made him conscious that he was mortal."[531]

Alexander returned to Memphis; and the south wind left him unscathed although, according to Herodotus, it was this same south wind that had buried Cambyses' army of 50,000 in sand nearly two centuries before. He reorganized the government of Egypt, received envoys from various states, sent Parmenion back to Asia with orders to bridge the Euphrates, and in July, 331, he and his army crossed the Euphrates at Thapsacus, and then crossed the Tigris. Darius, meanwhile, had mustered another army, which included 40,000 cavalry and some 16,000 heavy infantry. He could no longer recruit Greek mercenaries, and he had only 2,000 left.[532] His archers had already proven they could not cope with Macedonian cavalry. His generals had therefore collected cavalry contingents from all parts of his shrinking empire and had revived the use of the scythed chariots that Xenophon's men had faced when Cyrus the Younger fell. Besides 200 scythed chariots, he had 15 elephants.

On September 30, 331, Alexander's army of 40,000 foot and 7,000 horse confronted the larger army of Darius near the village of Gaugamela, not far from the ruins of Nineveh and only thirty-five miles from the town of Arbela. Should he engage immediately? Most of his officers said yes, but Parmenion wanted to wait and to reconnoiter first. This time Alexander agreed with Parmenion; he reconnoitered. Then he reassembled his officers and spoke to them briefly. This battle, he declared, would be neither for Lowland Syria nor for Egypt but for the sovereignty of all Asia. Both for them and for him all Asia meant the Persian Empire, including its conquests in the Punjab, the Land of the Five Rivers, of which four were tributaries of the fifth, the Indus. Then he ordered them to mess where the army now stood and to get some rest.

That night Parmenion came to his commander's tent and urged him to attack the enemy by night and to hope for panic in the Persian ranks. Alexander replied that he would not steal a victory. His decision did more than impress his followers with his confidence. It guaranteed his own troops against the panic that fighting in darkness might easily cause on either side. But, in any case, his problem was not the purely military one of defeating Darius a third time. It was the political problem of convincing the subjects of Darius that a third defeat at Alexander's hands was no accident but accurately reflected Alexander's invincibility.

Next day the two armies maneuvered for position and Darius' Sacan contingent of 1,000 cavalry, sheathed in chain mail, struck. The fighting was hard. But the scythed chariots were successfully evaded and finally their drivers and horses were cut down. In the end a cavalry charge by Alexander and his picked corps of young Macedonian noblemen known as the Companions broke the Persian line. As at Issus, Darius fled, this time toward Media, while his mercenary Greeks managed to delay pursuit. On the left, Parmenion had been outgeneraled, and Parthian and Indian horse had split the Macedonian phalanx in two. But Parmenion recovered; news of Darius' flight demoralized the Persian army; and it too fled. Alexander pursued it till dark, cutting it to pieces. Then he and his men rested till midnight, when they chased it again as far as Arbela. Afterward, when his army was well rested, he marched against Babylon.

The Persian governor of Babylonia, Mazaeus, opened the bronze gates of Babylon and received him with honor. Thereupon, Alexander confirmed Mazaeus as governor of Babylonia, although he placed the military power of the province in the hands of a Macedonian general. This was the first time he had left a Persian governor in charge even of civil affairs. He sent one of his officers to Phoenicia to hold his sea communications open with Europe and, if necessary, to help Antipater, his regent in Europe, against Sparta. For King Agis of Sparta had finally declared open war on Macedonia. Sparta had never joined the League of Corinth, which Philip had founded and which Alexander now officially headed. Sparta had not helped Athens and Thebes when Philip and Alexander crushed them at Chaeronea. Now, too late, she attacked. Near Megalopolis Antipater's Macedonians and his Greek Allies defeated King Agis. Agis was killed in battle, and Sparta was forced to join the League of Corinth.

Alexander stayed for more than a month in Babylon. In Egypt he had exploited the blasphemous behavior of its Persian conqueror, Cambyses;

now in Babylon he exploited the blasphemies of Xerxes, who had destroyed many of Babylon's temples, including the temple of its greatest god, Marduk. Alexander ordered all the temples rebuilt and, by sacrificing to Marduk, made himself Marduk's vicar, the rightful ruler of Babylonia. He now held approximately the territory which Cyrus the Great and his son Cambyses had conquered, either in the west or in the south. He controlled Greece-in-Asia, the whole Fertile Crescent from the Persian Gulf to Palestine, as well as the rich kingdom of Egypt. But, as he worked that month in Babylon, the whole Iranian plateau, the whole of modern Iran and Afghanistan, was nominally in the hands of Darius. Somewhere in those towering mountains was Darius himself. There, too, and relatively near, was Susa, the capital of the Persian Empire and Babylon's only rival as leading city. For many decades Greek envoys and Greek captives had 'gone up' to Susa, following the royal road from Sardis near the Aegean. Also, not far beyond Susa in the home province of the Persian dynasty, stood Parsa and Pasargadae. It was from these mountain fastnesses that decade after decade had poured forth the archers and horsemen who seized the Fertile Crescent, who conquered Egypt, and assaulted Mainland Greece.

In a twenty-day march, Alexander reached Susa. In its treasury were 50,000 talents, which he seized. Reinforcements reached him from Macedonia, and he sent his regent, Antipater, 3,000 talents. At Susa he found also the bronze group of Harmodius and Aristogiton, the Athenian tyrannicides who slew Hipparchus, son of Pisistratus. Xerxes had seized these bronzes when he occupied Athens, and now Alexander returned them to Athens. Alexander took over the royal military academy which trained the sons of Persian nobles to lead the Great King's armies. These young nobles thereby became his hostages for the behavior of their fathers, and at the same time Darius' chief source of future officers was cut off.

Then Alexander struck at Parsa, which the Greeks renamed Persepolis, so swiftly that its garrison had no time to remove its royal treasure of 120,000 talents. And at nearby Pasargadae, where Cyrus the Great lay buried, he seized 6,000 more. Persepolis stood on a high plain, and there on artificial terraces at the foot of a mountain was ranged a group of palaces. These were reached by a stairway, wide enough for ten horsemen to ride up it abreast. Darius I, whose fleet had been lost at Mount Athos, had leveled these rock terraces and had constructed a palace and an audience hall whose roof was supported by a hundred columns. Xerxes had completed the group, and here the Macedonians gazed at his lofty colonnaded porch, guarded by colossal winged bulls of the sort a simpler generation of Persians had first seen in Assyria. The capitals of his columns were carved in the shape of crouching bulls. These magnificent palaces, symbols of Persian pride and oppression, Alexander decided to burn. In vain Parmenion argued that this property was now Alexander's and that burning the royal palaces would convince Asians that he had come to pass through in triumph, not to rule. Alexander was determined to take vengeance for the wrongs the dynasty had done Greece, wrecking Athens, burning temples. And he had every reason to believe that his act of vandalism would impress Babylon, whose great temple, E-sagila, Xerxes had burned, and the Egyptians, whose religious beliefs Cambyses had flouted. Later, of course, the Greeks would tell how Thaïs, an Athenian mistress of one of his generals, Ptolemy, had incited Alexander at a drunken orgy to set the torch to the Great King's splendor. In any case, for days the Macedonian army pillaged the town below the palace. Persepolis was laid low, and it was here at Persepolis that Alexander first got word that Antipater had defeated Sparta.

In the summer of 330 he marched to Ecbatana, in Media. Ecbatana was the summer capital of the kings of Persia, and Herodotus had written[533] of the Median king's stronghold, crowning a hill, coated with silver and gold. In this citadel Alexander stored the gold and silver ingots from the various treasuries of Darius, and ordered Harpalus, his imperial treasurer, to mint them into money for his empire. He left Parmenion to protect his treasury at Ecbatana and to take charge of communications with the imperial army. The terrible vengeance Alexander had taken on Persepolis symbolized the end of the panhellenic crusade against Persia. Antipater had Mainland Greece under control, and Alexander's Greek soldiers were therefore no longer needed as hostages for the good behavior of the states they had come from. So he paid off all his Greeks, including the Thessalians, gave them a handsome bonus, and sent them home, except for those soldiers who might prefer to engage individually as mercenaries.

Alexander's role and function now shifted, as the inexorable result of his own victories. His hero, Achilles, had gone to Asia to avenge at Troy the theft of an Argive queen. Alexander had led his Greeks and Macedonians to Asia, ostensibly to avenge Persia's attacks on Mainland Greece. But if his panhellenic war of vengeance had now ended, it had ended not without irony. At Salamis and at Plataea, the Hellenes had fought in order that their small, free city-states should not be ruled by the Great King; and now the Great King ruled them, though he had been born in Macedonia, not in Susa or Persepolis. His garrisons occupied Greece; and though formally Athens and Sparta and the other states of Greece were his allies and though they paid no tribute, no intelligent Greek could doubt who controlled Mainland Greece.

But Alexander's own fate did not lack irony either. He had come to conquer Asia, and now he was enmeshed in the affairs of a disintegrating empire. He was learning the full force of Aristotle's teaching[534] that the purpose of war is peace, as the purpose of business is leisure, and as the training of the body is for the sake of the soul. What would be the conditions of a just and durable peace? When Darius, after his defeat near Issus, had tried to negotiate, Alexander had demanded that Darius recognize him as Lord of Asia, and he had held to that position at Tyre. Since that time, he had annexed everything of consequence that Darius ruled, up to the Iranian plateau, and had even occupied the provinces of Persis and Media. But Darius was somewhere to the northwest, still alive, still undeposed. Peace could not be organized under two warring heads. The victories Alexander had won had left many problems unsolved. The sword could not solve them: it could only decide who was responsible for solving them. One of these problems, even under a King of Kings, was the consent of the governed, if the empire was ever to be more than occupied territory. When Alexander confirmed the Persian Mazaeus in his governorship of Babylonia, he was already involved in the problem of consent.

Aristotle envisaged three types of just war. Men might justly prepare for war, not to

> enslave those who do not deserve slavery, but in order that first they may themselves avoid becoming enslaved to others; then so that they may seek suzerainty for the benefit of the subject people, but not for the sake of world-wide despotism; and thirdly to hold despotic power over those who deserve to be slaves.[535]

Assuming Alexander agreed with this view, he could justify his war. First, he was attempting to end Persia's secular efforts to enslave Hellas. Secondly, he might hope to benefit the subject peoples who were being badly ruled by a decadent and exploitative Perisan dynasty. Thirdly, he might subject to his will, as one would subject animals, the hill tribes, who were both barbarous and dangerous. But problems could still remain. Both Aristotle and Plato thought that the ideal polis should be small, but no Greek polis yet, not Athens, not Sparta, not Thebes, had devised a constitution for a new human community that had slowly been emerging and that no city-state could contain. The small polis of the philosophers' dreams seemed doomed by history to collide fatally with its neighbor or to be pulled apart by revolution. The affairs of Hellas, of Macedonia, and of Persia were hopelessly entangled. If polis meant a human community of gods and men, then commerce and money and ideas had created a kind of polis out of the whole known civilized world, a polis out of the cosmos, a cosmopolis. Not even Philip's dream was large enough, his polis composed of Macedonia and Hellas, in which Macedonia would contribute a ruler, a disciplined army, money, adequate land, and peace within this new, enlarged polis, while Hellas, and especially Athens, would contribute the ideas, the civilization.

No, Philip's dream was too small. It was clear that the new cosmopolis included not only Greece-in-Asia but Egypt, with a far older culture than that of Hellas, and ancient Babylonia, and Persians like Mazaeus whom Alexander was learning to respect. The real problem was to find the frontiers of cosmopolis. They must be militarily defensible. So far as possible, they must include all civilized peoples, and perhaps some that were just now becoming civilized. They must exclude, so far as possible, all those barbarians who in Aristotle's words deserved to be slaves. It was this political problem that Alexander faced, high on the plateau of Media, among strange peoples, who wore strange costumes and spoke strange tongues. Even had he wanted to rule all these peoples despotically, by terror, he could not hope to do it. He had used force to secure their momentary obedience; to make that obedience permanent, he must give law, he must guarantee justice, he must arouse loyalty. To do these things, he must first destroy Darius; Darius must be viewed as a pretender to the throne he had forfeited. And Alexander must shift his own role, at least in Asia, from European conqueror to Asian King of Kings. He appointed Persian governors for Media and for Media Paraetacene and prepared to track down Darius.

In midsummer of 330 he heard that Darius was collecting reinforcements and withdrawing toward Bactria, a province in the northeastern portion of what is now Afghanistan. Alexander moved by forced marches eastward, with the desert of Parthia on his right and the lofty Elburz Range on his left. Word came that two of Darius' provincial governors had deposed him. The next news stated that one of the governors, Bessus of Bactria, had been acclaimed king by his Bactrians and by most of the followers of Darius. Would the eastern provinces, provinces noted for their tough fighters, now rise against Alexander? With a detachment of horse Alexander speeded his pursuit. At last, near the site of modern Shahrud, they came on Darius. One of his provincial governors and the commander of the cavalry with Darius had wounded him and had fled. Before Alexander rode up, Darius had died. Alexander covered the dead king's body with a purple cloak and sent it to Persepolis to the royal tomb.

Darius had occupied, if only briefly and by dubious means, Alexander's own imperial throne, and royalty was to be respected. The enemy was not the corpse of Darius, whom Alexander had overthrown in battle, but Bessus, governor of Bactria, who had helped betray his king and who now sought to seize the crown. Those Persian nobles who had remained loyal to Darius, Alexander now honored. When the Greek mercenaries of Darius surrendered, he released all those who were in Persian service before the conclusion of the alliance between Macedonia and the League of Corinth. The others he ordered to join his own forces at the same rate of pay.

Word came that Bessus was wearing the royal tiara, had collected an army of Bactrians and of Persians who had fled to Bactria, and was trying to raise the Scythians. The province of Areia was up, and the Areians were marching to the support of Bessus. Alexander quelled Areia and founded another Alexandria on the site of modern Herat. This was a land of fortresses and villages and he wanted cities. He appointed a Persian to govern Areia. Then he headed south to the royal residence of Phrada, not far short of the Helmund River.

Here in the east, while Bessus mustered an army against him, conspiracy flared within his own general staff. He learned that Philotas, the one remaining son of Parmenion and commander of the Companions, had conspired against him. Once before, in Egypt, Philotas had been accused of conspiracy, but Alexander had refused to believe him disloyal. Philotas was now tried by court-martial, was judged guilty, and was shot down by javelins, along with several fellow conspirators. The traitor's father, Parmenion, remained a problem. Had he shared in his son's conspiracy? Whether he had or not, would he seek revenge? Parmenion had been Philip's right-hand man; Alexander had inherited him along with Philip's army. Alexander had rarely followed Parmenion's advice, and Alexander had consistently been proven right. Parmenion had all but failed him at Gaugamela, the final, crucial battle with Darius. Parmenion's enemies were suggesting that he had not wanted Alexander to win, and Alexander had left him at Ecbatana, far to the rear, in charge of communications. But Parmenion was popular both with the Macedonian soldiers and the Greek mercenaries of Alexander. Parmenion symbolized Macedonian military conquest as distinguished from the political problems of pacifying Asia which now confronted a King of Kings.

Alexander's title to the Persian throne was clouded by the claim of Bessus. Bessus was of the blood royal, was in the field with an army, and held the wild northeast provinces. In short, although Alexander had now overrun most of the Empire, the succession was still in doubt. The Macedonian way and the Persian way of handling this problem had been illustrated when Alexander and Darius mounted their thrones in 336. The two ways were identical and traditional: the way was murder, murder of claimants, of conspirators, and of the kinsmen of claimants and conspirators. Alexander simultaneously faced a powerful claimant to his Persian throne and a popular father of a conspirator. Therefore he sent word to three of his generals in Media to put Parmenion to death. The power Philotas had held as commander of the Companions' cavalry Alexander now decided to entrust to no man. He divided the cavalry in two sections and put one section in the hands of Hephestion, the friend he loved most, and one in the hands of Clitus the Black, the boyhood friend who had saved his life at the battle of the Granicus. Clitus' command included the royal horse-guard.

At Phrada, Alexander founded yet another Alexandria. He marched south to the Helmund River through the country of the Ariaspian tribesmen, who were also called the Benefactors, because about two centuries earlier they had helped Cyrus in his campaign against the Scythians. Alexander, who now held Cyrus' throne, did not subjugate the Benefactors, both because of their services to the crown and because of "his own observation that they were not governed like the other tribesmen of these parts, but also claimed to practise justice, like the best of the Greeks."[536] He reduced the southeastern provinces of the Persian Empire, Drangiana, Gedrosia, and Arachosia, fighting in mountain snows on short provisions. But now Areia, with the help of troops sent by Bessus, blazed into revolt; Alexander sent back forces, which suppressed this rebellion, while he himself marched up the valley of the Helmund into Bactria, founding another Alexandria on the way.

Then, in the spring of 329, Alexander crossed the snow-covered Hindu Kush, which his army called Mount Caucasus and which really was part of the vast broken range that swept from the Caucasus Mountains to the Himalayas. Like Xenophon's men in other Asian mountains less far from home, they suffered from cold and snow blindness. On the far side of the mountains in Bactria, they found that Bessus had ravaged the country to impede their march; Bessus and his army then crossed the Oxus River into the province of Sogdiana and burned their boats behind them. Alexander's men also crossed the Oxus, lying flat on skins stuffed with rushes.

When two Sogdian nobles revolted from Bessus and notified Alexander that they had arrested Bessus and were ready to give him up, Alexander sent a detachment under Ptolemy to fetch the pretender to the throne. Bessus was brought to Alexander naked, bound, wearing a wooden collar, and was stationed by the roadside while the army of Alexander marched past. When Alexander himself reached Bessus, he "asked him why he had first seized Dareius, who had been his king, his relative, and his benefactor, then led him about in chains, and then murdered him."[537] Bessus pleaded that he was only one of many who had done these things. Alexander ordered him scourged; during the scourging the herald was to proclaim the crimes Alexander had just reproached Bessus with. Then Bessus was sent to Bactra to await final judgment. Alexander, King of Kings, had done provisional justice to a rebel against Darius, King of Kings, now honorably interred among his royal predecessors.

Alexander next took possession of the royal summer palace at Maracanda, modern Samarkand, and reached the Jaxartes River, the northeastern frontier of Darius' empire. There he summoned the great nobles of Sogdiana to meet with him. Instead, the Sogdians rose in revolt and massacred five garrisons he had left behind him. In the space of two days Alexander and his army put down the Sogdians with hideous slaughter. Then he marched against Cyropolis, the City of Cyrus, razed it, and built his own frontier fortress on the south bank of the Jaxartes River, to protect Cosmopolis from the wild Scythians on the other side. This new city he called Alexandria the Farthest, and he peopled it with tough veterans, both Greek mercenaries and Macedonians. Now his soldiers prepared to cross the river on stuffed hides, as they had earlier crossed the Oxus. He frightened the Scythians who patrolled the farther bank with an attack by catapults, moved his men across the river, outgeneraled the enemy, but was unable to pursue them far. He had come down with dysentery and was carried back into camp. The pursuit had taken place in great heat, the army had suffered from thirst, and he himself had drunk foul water. The pursuit had carried him north almost as far as the site of modern Tashkent.

News came that Spitamenes, one of the two nobles who had surrendered Bessus to Alexander and one of the great nobles of Sogdiana who had revolted and had besieged Maracanda, had ambushed some of Alexander's forces and all but annihilated them. By forced marches Alexander reached Maracanda in four days, but Spitamenes had heard he was on the way and had fled.

The army had gone through two years of savage fighting; Alexander therefore led it back to winter quarters at Bactra, even though Spitamenes was safe at Bokhara, unpunished for his recent ambush of Alexander's men. During that winter of 329-328 at Bactra, Alexander was busy receiving reinforcements from Europe and mercenaries from Greece-in-Asia, treating with his neighbors beyond his new northern frontier, planning the reduction of Sogdiana. Bessus was tried for treason and condemned. His punishment was again Persian: his ears and nose were cut off and he was sent back to Ecbatana to be executed. An ally from south of the Aral Sea offered to show Alexander a northern route to the Black Sea, but Alexander was determined, as soon as Spitamenes had been put down and Sogdiana pacified, to move into India. For in India the Persians had once held, and later lost, a province.

In the spring of 328, Alexander moved across the Bosphorus again, conquered Spitamenes in a hard summer campaign, and tied down the province of Sogdiana with a network of fortified posts.

That same summer at Maracanda both hybris and catastrophe entered Alexander's life. Unlike his father Philip, he was not inordinately given

416

either to women or to wine. During six years of campaigning in Asia, when he could have possessed any woman he saw, including the daughters of Darius, during six years at the head of an army in which the Macedonians at least could generally be counted on to drink hard and in which thousands of soldiers were followed by their concubines, his own evident continence astonished those who knew him, and his habit of lingering long over his wine rather than getting drunk was a matter of common gossip. But the strain of those six years was taking its toll, even in a man still under twenty-eight. Macedonian and Greek warfare alike demanded that he plan his battles, infuse his men with courage by speech, and fight with the best of them when they closed with the enemy. He knew fatigue and thirst, and if his men both feared and adored him, if he exerted on them that indefinable magnetic charm Xenophon noted in the great military leader, it was partly because he so clearly asked more of himself than of others. During those six years he had known illness and he had known wounds. He had even known the deepest wounds of all, betrayal by those he trusted.

But in addition to mapping his strategy and fighting in the melee of battle as his ancestor Achilles had fought, he was conducting political warfare, receiving embassies, planning cities with his architects, cities that would create civilizing commerce, cities that would serve as forts to protect Cosmopolis. Worse still, he was struggling with his most difficult problem of all: Who am I? Son of Philip, son of Ammon, or son of both, however that might be? He was certainly king of Macedonia, king in an almost Homeric sense, among fighting nobles who demanded that respect be mutual. He was simultaneously Pharaoh of Egypt, and his Egyptian coins showed a Heracles with the features of his divine descendant, Alexander. Coins later pictured Alexander with the ram's horns of Ammon showing through his locks of hair. His mint at Babylon commonly issued coins which bore the initial M for Metropolis: was not Babylon the mother-city, in size, in economic power, and in strategic location for commerce, of his entire Cosmopolis? But about 324 an issue from the Babylonian mint would sum up his political problem. It would show him as a god, wearing a Greek breastplate and sword, a Macedonian cloak, a half-Greek and half-Persian helmet, and carrying in his right hand the thunderbolt of his father, Zeus. He was king of ancient Babylonia and the chief servant of Baal-Marduk; here now in distant Bactra he wore the tiara of the Great King, a Great King who controlled Hellas because he had launched a war of vengeance against an empire, now his own, which had in turn once dared threaten the freedom of Hellas; a Great King who had decided somewhere along his route to be Lord of Asia, meaning the Asia which Darius had tried to rule. And now he, Asia's conqueror, was trapped by Asia. To prevent his conquest from fading out of memory as a raid by marauding Macedonians, he had found himself discharging the function of Great King, doing the *ergon*, the work, of Asia's king, appointing Persians to rule provinces, absorbing Persian forces into his Macedonian army. He unquestionably wanted as a fighting man the glory, the earned fame for excellence, for which Achilles strove on the Trojan plain, the earned fame hymned in Pindar's odes. But he was a statesman, too. He knew that in many real senses Hellas and Macedonia and Egypt and Babylonia and the peoples of the Iranian plateau were a community; but his Macedonians did not know it and they had begun to sense that the young king they had followed through so many hardships was somehow eluding them. They began to feel they had been merely used by Alexander.

And then, one night in Maracanda, Alexander and his friends drank in the true Macedonian fashion. They had many things to forget, the massacres of natives, the things men had always done in war. Alexander and many others present were clearly drunk. The talk turned to the Homeric heroes, Castor and Pollux, brothers of Helen of Troy, and it turned also to the question of whether the brothers were indeed sons of Tyndareus or sons of Zeus himself, as Heracles was. There were flatterers present who urged that the deeds of Alexander were greater even than those of Heracles. Then Clitus the Black, who was in his cups, and who had for long disliked Alexander's apparent transformation from Macedonian soldier-king to Asian despot, grew angry that the deeds of the heroes of old, now divine beings, should be belittled. It was not Alexander alone, he cried, who had done these things, but the Macedonians. Alexander turned to two of his Greek guests: "Do not the Greeks appear to you to walk about among Macedonians like demi-gods among wild beasts?"[538] When someone present spoke slightingly of Macedonian Philip, Clitus praised Philip's achievements in comparison with those of Alexander. He reminded Alexander of the day, six strenuous years before, when they had fought their first Asian battle beside the Granicus, and when he, Clitus, had saved the king's life. He raised his right hand proudly: "This very hand, Alexander, saved you then!"[539] But Alexander happened to share more with Achilles than courage and the love of fame: he shared his kindling wrath, a wrath he had learned generally to control. Tonight wine had stolen his self-control; like Philip at another banquet, he leapt up to strike Clitus. His friends restrained him, and he called for his bodyguard. But the bodyguard discreetly refrained from intervening in the brawl. And so, he shouted, he had come to the same pass as Darius, when Bessus had held him prisoner: he was king in name only. He snatched a spear from a guard. Ptolemy managed to get the drunken Clitus out of the banquet hall. But Clitus broke loose; and when he heard Alexander calling out "Clitus!" he entered by another door, crying: "Behold, here is Clitus, Alexander!"[540] and Alexander launched the spear into his body.

The murder sobered Alexander. Some reports asserted that he immediately tried to kill himself. In any event, he took to his bed and lay for three days without food, crying out the names of Clitus and of Clitus' sister, Lanice, who had nursed Alexander as a baby, and calling himself the slayer of his friends. It was later said that Anaxarchus the Sophist, when he found Alexander moaning in grief, laughed at him and insisted that, just as whatever Zeus did was just, so whatever a great king did should be held just, both by himself and by others. It was also reported that Alexander was somewhat consoled by this argument.

But neither the wine that caused the brawl, nor the murder, nor the repentance, nor the consolation was the basic problem. The basic problem remained: Who was Alexander; where was Cosmopolis; and what was Alexander's relation to Cosmopolis? Aristotle's nephew Callisthenes, the court historian, had sent back to Greece his account of the conquest of Asia, so far as it had gone, and Callisthenes' history made it clear who Alexander was: he was the son of Zeus; Apollo's oracle at Didyma, near Miletus, had said so; the priest of Ammon in the oasis in the Libyan desert had said so. These stories fitted in neatly with the gossip that Philip had doubted whether Alexander was his own son; they fitted also with Olympias's claims[541] that she had borne a son to a god. Everybody knew that the Macedonian dynasty descended from Heracles, and Heracles was certainly a son of Zeus. If Zeus had fathered Heracles, he could certainly have fathered Alexander. But the problem was more complicated even than his unknown paternity. Heracles had later been raised by Zeus to

419

godhood. So had Castor and Pollux. Did Zeus intend to do the same thing for Alexander?

Some of the Greek sophists, like Anaxarchus, who were present at Alexander's court when he was at Bactra, and some of the Persians and Medes at court, agreed with Alexander that the question of his possible divinity should be raised over the wine at a coming banquet. There Anaxarchus opened the discussion. He argued that clearly Alexander would be honored as a god after his death. Why not now? And Macedonians ought to prefer him as a god to Heracles, who was but an Argive, or to Dionysus, who was but a Theban. Others agreed and urged that those present prostrate themselves here and now before Alexander. Actually, the subjects of the King of Kings had always prostrated themselves before their monarch, without thereby implying that he was divine. But Macedonians had no such ceremonial, and the proposal of prostration this evening left those Macedonians who were present glumly silent. It was not they but Callisthenes who spoke. He argued that only gods should be accorded the honor of prostration. Then, surprisingly, in view of what he had written in his history, he pointed out that he was advising, not

> some Cambyses or Xerxes, but a son of Philip, by race a descendant of Heracles and of Aeacus, whose forefathers came from Argos to Macedonia, and long held sway there, not as tyrants but as constitutional monarchs of Macedonia. But not even to Heracles himself were divine honours paid by the Greeks while he yet lived; nay, even after his death they were not paid before an oracle was given by the god of Delphi that Heracles was to be honoured as a god. If, however, we must think in foreign fashion, since our discussion takes place in a foreign country, yet even so I beg you, Alexander, to remember Greece, for whose sake all your expedition took place, to add Asia to Greece. Moreover, consider this also, on your return to Greece will it be Greeks, the most free of all mankind, whom you will compel to bow down before you, or will you perhaps exempt the Greeks, and shackle the Macedonians with this shame? or will you draw a line thus in the matter of honours for all the world, that by Greeks and Macedonians you shall be honoured as a man, but by foreigners only in this foreign fashion? But if it is said of Cyrus son of Cambyses that Cyrus was the first of men to receive this homage of bowing to the ground, and that therefore this humiliation became traditional with Persians and Medes, yet you must remember that this very Cyrus was brought to a better mind by Scythians, a poor but free people;

Dareius too by other Scythians, Xerxes by Athenians and Lacedae-monians, and Artaxerxes by Clearchus and Xenophon and their Ten Thousand, and Dareius now by Alexander, as yet unworshipped by pros-trations.[542]

Alexander was angered, but the Macedonians were clearly pleased. Alexander curtly ordered them not to adopt the custom of prostration. There was silence. But, then, led by their eldest, the Persians rose one by one and prostrated themselves before their king. Even Hephestion, Alexander's dearest friend, and one or two other Macedonians joined in. But Callisthenes had touched a nerve: Who lived in Cosmopolis, and what was their relation to Alexander to be? To the Macedonians Cosmopolis did not exist; only Macedonia existed, and the foreign provinces which the Macedonians had conquered with the sword under the able leadership of Philip's son, whom they dearly loved. To the Persians Cosmopolis offered something like equality with their conquerors, something like law and justice under their traditional monarchy, in which the reigning monarch was indeed a European but a European who had increasingly accepted the costume and the customs of Persia.

Not long after the murder of Clitus, another conspiracy was discovered, this time of the Royal Pages, young Macedonian nobles who attended the king. One of them, Hermolaus, offended Alexander while hunting, and Alexander's very Macedonian punishment was to have Hermolaus whipped and his horse taken from him. Hermolaus was furious, and persuaded other pages who were friends of his to conspire with him to assassinate Alexander. When the conspiracy was discovered, the conspirators were executed. But Hermolaus, the ringleader, happened to be a pupil of Callisthenes, who had dared instruct the king on the difference between gods and men. The pages claimed that they had been urged on by Callisthenes. Callisthenes was therefore accused and convicted, although later accounts differed as to whether he died of illness while a prisoner or whether he was first tortured and then hanged. Some men claimed that Hermolaus at his trial declared that no freeborn man could endure the arrogance, the hybris, of Alexander; that Philotas had been unjustly put to death; and that Parmenion's execution was even more unlawful. They said Hermolaus spoke too of the murder of Clitus, of Alexander's adoption of the Persian costume, of his heavy drinking, of his continued preference for prostration. The plot of the Royal Pages increased the strain between

Alexander and his Macedonians, between the expanded polis that Philip had bequeathed his son, if indeed he was his son, and the vaster Cosmopolis that Alexander was determined to construct and rule.

In the same year as the Pages' conspiracy, 327, Alexander besieged the Sogdian Rock, a high hill with sheer cliffs, which was considered impregnable. A number of Sogdians had taken refuge on the Rock, and Oxyartes, one of the Sogdian feudatories who had revolted from Alexander, had secretly sent his wife and daughters there. Alexander offered large money prizes to those who would scale the sheerest cliff, so sheer it had been left wholly unguarded. Some 300 tried it, with iron pegs and flaxen ropes; some 30 of those fell to their death and the bodies were forever lost in the snow; the rest seized the summit of the crag and signaled their arrival. The Sogdians panicked and surrendered. Among the captives was Oxyartes' daughter, Roxana. It was later reported that it was because Alexander fell in love with her that he married her. Whether that report was true or false, the marriage had important political implications for the ferocious war in Sogdiana and Alexander's ability at last to end it.

After this, he reorganized his army and prepared to march down the narrow valley of the Cophen River, the modern Kabul, to the Khyber Pass and into 'India.' That meant the Punjab province in modern Pakistan and whatever else the kings of Persia had once held. Alexander had left most of his mercenaries in the various cities he had founded. But Antipater, having defeated Sparta, was now able to send him some seasoned troops under the command of Clitus the White. The sons of a few great Persian nobles were included in the Royal Squadron once commanded by Clitus the Black, which Alexander himself had, since the murder of Clitus, commanded. He sent home much of his European cavalry and recruited some of the excellent cavalry he had just defeated in the eastern provinces. He entered India with a smaller army than the one he had brought across the Hellespont seven years earlier; not more than 30,000 at most. But there trailed behind his fighting force a moving polis of concubines, children, technicians, writers, traders, and auxiliary services.

Alexander believed that India was a peninsula jutting eastward from the Iranian Plateau and that beyond it flowed the Ocean Stream. He did not know whether the Indus was the upper Nile or whether it flowed into Ocean and never came near Egypt. To help him explore, he had brought out from Egypt and Phoenicia both shipwrights and sailors. For he was interested not only in completing the conquest of anything that had belonged to Persia; he wanted also to find the defensible frontiers of Cosmopolis, frontiers which might prove in the east to be Ocean. He did not know how far the steppes extended in the north; he himself had been turned back by sickness when he was still short of the area of modern Tashkent. But a case could be made anyhow for the Jaxartes as his northern frontier and for the exclusion of the Scythian nomads from Cosmopolis. Buddha had lived and died, but Alexander knew nothing of Buddha's India; Confucius had lived and died, but Alexander knew nothing of China.[543] His Cosmos, his world, could not include them. He was not even familiar with Herodotus' claim that Darius I had sent ships under a Greek named Scylax down the Indus and around Arabia to the Red Sea.[544]

Alexander sent Hephestion and Perdiccas with the baggage and part of the army down the Kabul River. With them went an Indian ally, Taxiles, who had come to seek Alexander's aid against his aggressive Indian neighbor Porus. Alexander bore northward of the Kabul valley to protect Hephestion and Perdiccas from attack by tribesmen on the left flank. This supporting movement led to very hard fighting, in strange and wild country. He spared a town named Nysa, because its chief magistrate convinced him that, when the god Dionysus had conquered the Indians and was returning toward the Greek Sea, with his discharged soldiers following him as Bacchic revelers, he had founded Nysa; and the magistrate showed the Macedonians the god's beloved ivy growing and assured Alexander it grew nowhere else in India. Alexander hoped this information would fill his soldiers with longing to follow him beyond the limits of Dionysus's conquest. His homesick soldiers crowned themselves with the ivy and sang hymns to the god, and Alexander himself sacrificed to Dionysus. Later, the tale was also told that they found a cave in which, undoubtedly, Prometheus had been chained when the eagle of Zeus fed daily on his liver, till Heracles delivered him. Moreover, the army saw cattle branded with the image of a club, additional evidence that Heracles, who always bore a club, had reached India before them. In any case, some of the cattle they made off with were so handsome that Alexander sent breeding stock back to Macedonia. They also assaulted the impregnable rock they called Aornus, which Heracles, or some Indian god they identified with Heracles, had failed to capture. The descendant of Heracles took the rock.

Alexander joined up with Hephestion and Perdiccas at the Indus, which Hephestion had bridged; and marched to Taxila, the city of their ally. Here for the first time they saw a great Indian city, famous alike for its commerce and its learning. Here the Brahmans, who had long ago come out of the northwest mountains like the later Persians and now the Macedonians, taught their doctrines. Alexander's men held athletic contests and cavalry games. His ally Taxiles furnished him 700 horse, and they all set out for the next river, the boundary of Porus' kingdom. This river was the Jhelum, known to them as the Hydaspes. There they found Porus on the farther bank awaiting them, with his cavalry and his 200 war elephants. After a desperate battle, Alexander finally broke his opponent's army, and Porus surrendered. When Alexander asked Porus how he wished to be treated, he answered, "Treat me, Alexander, like a king."[545] Alexander made him his ally and treated him with the same grave courtesy he had shown the royal family of Persia.

Where Alexander's camp had stood, near the battlefield, he founded a city, Alexandria Nicaea, or Alexandria Victorious. The horse which Philip had given him when a boy because he alone had had the combined courage and intelligence to break him in, the horse he had used throughout his conquest of the Persian Empire, died on the battlefield itself, not of any wound but of old age and exhaustion. His name was Bucephalus, so there Alexander founded Alexandria Bucephala. For Porus' benefit he subdued some nearby tribes. Then, in early July, 326, though the monsoon rains were on and the Chenab in flood, he crossed that river and the Ravi too, and after desperate fighting, stormed and took Sangala. Next, he continued southwest to the Beas, the last of the Five Rivers which were tributary to the lower Indus.

But here at the Beas the army began to grumble. The monsoon rains and humid heat of July had taken their toll. Alexander had already marched some 11,185 miles since leaving Amphipolis. The fighting at Sangala had been costly, and rumor had it that across the river dwelt people kin to the fighters the army had just been up against, and that these people had more and better war elephants. But it was more than that. Alexander summoned his chief officers and addressed them:

> I observe that you, Macedonians and allied forces, are not following me into dangers any longer with your old spirit. I have summoned you

together, either to persuade you and go forward, or to be persuaded by you and turn back.[546]

Had they not, he asked, won rich reward for their labors to date? He named off the provinces of the vast empire they had conquered. Were they afraid of the tribesmen of India? He described the weakness of these tribesmen, not too accurately. Did his officers want to know how much farther they must go? He insisted they had almost reached the Ganges River and the eastern sea already. This sea connected with the Caspian and with the Indian Gulf, which in turn connected with the Persian Gulf. From there the fleet could sail round to Libya, clear to the Pillars of Heracles, and the Mediterranean coast from Egypt to the Pillars could be theirs, as well as the whole of Asia, boundaries God himself had set for the whole earth. However, if the natives beyond this Beas River were left unsubdued, most likely their new and unconsolidated empire would collapse and all their labor to date would then be wasted. "But," he continued,

do you abide constant, Macedonians and allies. It is those who endure toil and who dare dangers that achieve glorious deeds; and it is a lovely thing to live with courage, and to die, leaving behind an everlasting renown.[547]

Did they not know that "our forefather," meaning his ancestor Heracles, would never have won fame by staying at home in Tiryns or Argos, nor even have been made a god? Dionysus, too, faced dangers. The Macedonians had now won the rock of Aornus, which Heracles had tried in vain to win, and passed beyond Dionysus' city of Nysa.

If then while you were bearing labours and bearing dangers I had led you, myself, your leader, without labours and without dangers, you would not unnaturally have become weary in your hearts; when you alone had all the labours, and were procuring the prizes thereof for others; but it is not so; our labours are shared in common; we bear an equal part in dangers; the prizes are open to all. For the land is yours; it is you who are its viceroys; the greater part of the treasure comes to you, and when we master all Asia, then—by Heaven!—I will not merely satisfy you, but will surpass the utmost hope of good things for each of you, I will send home all who desire to go home or will myself lead them back; those who stay, I shall make to be envied by those who go back.[548]

He had finished. For a long time, his officers were silent. He invited them, if they disagreed, to say so. But the silence continued. Then Coenus, son-in-law of Parmenion, spoke:

> Seeing that you, sir, do not yourself desire to command the Macedonians tyrannically, but expressly state that you will lead them on only by gaining their approval, and failing this you will not compel them, I shall not speak these words on behalf of us here present, who, being held in honour beyond the rest, have, most of us, already received the prizes of our labours, and in virtue of our authority, because we have power, are in all things heartily ready beyond others to forward your interests; rather I shall speak for most of the army.[549]

Carefully, respectfully, he pointed out how few of the original army were left; how some had been settled in the newly founded cities, many of them unwillingly; how some had been left behind, wounded; how of all Alexander's original host, only a small fraction remained, and these weakened in body and weary of spirit. "But do not be a leader of unwilling troops."[550] Coenus urged Alexander to postpone his Indian campaign eastward until another time, with another army. And he urged on his king the self-restraint that warded off hybris and catastrophe.

Some of the bystanders applauded, some wept; but Alexander was angry. He dismissed them. Next day he called them in again. He would, he announced, compel no Macedonian to go with him against his will. He had other subjects who would follow him. The Macedonians could go home and could tell their friends they had left their king to face his foes without them. Then, like another Achilles, he withdrew to his tent and waited for them to change their minds. He waited for three days, seeing no one. Outside, there was sullen, obstinate silence. Then he prepared to go without them, and sacrificed before crossing the Beas; but at the sacrifices the auspices proved unfavorable. He conferred with his intimates. Then he publicly proclaimed that he was turning back.

The army shouted for joy; many soldiers wept. They crowded to the royal tent and invoked blessings on their king. He set up twelve huge altars to the twelve great gods of Olympus, sacrificed upon them, and held athletic contests and cavalry exercises. Everything east of the Jhelum he formally assigned to his former enemy, Porus, to rule. He would never find his eastern frontier, nor a coast of Ocean for his Greeks to colonize.

But the army had only partly won the contest of wills, for he was determined not to go back the way he had come: he would explore the Jhelum downstream. He completed the building of his fleet, a fleet of between 800 and 1,000 ships. Nearchus the Cretan would command it. Alexander had seen crocodiles in the Indus and nowhere else except in the Nile; what looked like Egyptian beans grew near the Indus. He wrote his mother he thought he had discovered the sources of the Nile, but the Indians insisted the Indus flowed through two mouths into the Great Sea, so he corrected his letter to Olympias.

At dawn of a November day in 326 he embarked; he poured a libation into the Jhelum and libations to his ancestor Heracles and other gods; the bugle sounded, and the ships started in order downstream, with the boatswains calling the stroke to their crews, and with the chanteys the crews sang reverberating from the high banks. The natives, astonished by their first view of horse transports, came running to the banks and followed along, singing their wild, strange songs. Most of his army followed along the two banks too, infantry, cavalry, and some 200 elephants which he had acquired. On the way down he stopped to conquer the Mallians, who were reportedly preparing to resist him. Crossing a desert to a walled city of theirs, he surprised many of them unarmed outside the walls: he killed thousands of them.

Some of the Mallians had taken refuge in a city of the Brahmans: the city was taken and some 5,000 Indians were slaughtered. The remaining Mallians made their last stand in another of their walled cities, their greatest. Convinced that some of his own men were hanging back from scaling the walls, Alexander seized a ladder and climbed the wall himself. Peucestas, the royal shield-bearer, followed, carrying the sacred shield of Athena which Alexander had brought from Troy and which always protected the king in battle. Others tried to follow, but the ladder broke. Alexander was now a target for arrows. He leapt down inside the city, while Peucestas and two others followed. There they fought alone; one was killed, and Alexander was wounded almost mortally by an arrow. Just then the Macedonians broke in. Some of them carried off the king, on his shield. The others slaughtered the Mallians inside, man, woman, and child.

The Mallian campaign was one of the most savage Alexander had ever fought, whether because many of the Mallians preferred death to surrender, or because Alexander's men were frightened by signs of a general uprising, or because they were eager to get home and therefore quick to punish brutally the least resistance. When news spread that Alexander had fallen, his army feared they would be trapped amidst these uncharted rivers, swamps, and deserts, and be wiped out. The men suspected that those Indian peoples who had not yet attacked were held in check only by their fear of Alexander. To reassure the army, the wounded king was brought past them in his boat. The awning was removed. He raised an arm, and the army shouted, and some of his men wept for joy. The ship stopped and a litter was brought. But he demanded a horse; the men clapped wildly and the banks echoed the sound. He rode nearly to his tent, dismounted, and walked. Then the army went wild with relief and joy.

Alexander continued his southward march, subduing tribesmen, executing Brahmans who had incited revolts, receiving embassies, founding cities. When he reached Pattala, where the Indus divided, he began to build a great harbor with docks and then explored the western outlet to the sea. There his navy, unaccustomed to tides, was alarmed by a sudden tidal bore that rushed upstream and even destroyed some of the ships. At last, in July, 325, he sailed out into the Indian Ocean, where he sacrificed bulls to Posidon, god of the sea. He explored the eastern outlet and built another harbor and dockyards. Then he prepared to dispatch Nearchus and his fleet westward along the coast toward Mesopotamia while he himself led his army along beside it to dig wells and establish depots of food for the navy. When the southwest monsoons should stop blowing in October, Nearchus would start. But local tribesmen were threatening, and Nearchus started in September.

The land march through the Gedrosian desert proved deadly, with attacks by tribesmen, with provisions running short, with his guides losing their way. So great was the heat that the men could march only at night. They were reduced to eating their baggage animals and to burning their carts for firewood. The sick and the exhausted followed the army as long as they could, then sank into the sand like men who drowned at sea. The stragglers died. The horses and mules sank into the sand dunes, stumbled, and fell. Sometimes in the desert there were myrrh trees, and the Phoenician traders with the army collected the valuable gum and loaded it onto their mules. Sometimes the spikenard grew so plentifully that, when the marching army trod it underfoot, the perfume filled the desert air. What looked like giant thistles grew on stalks so high and so strong that the spikes dragged horsemen from their horses, and the stalks yielded juice that tasted sharper than the juice of figs in spring at home. When they finally found provisions, Alexander tried to send some to the desert coast for the navy; but the men charged with carrying them, in their hunger pillaged them. The wadis, or arroyos, either lacked water altogether or fresheted in the night from sudden rains upcountry and swept away animals and tents and even weapons. Water was often so scarce that once when some was found it barely filled a helmet; it was offered to Alexander. He thanked those who brought it but, unwilling to drink while his men thirsted, he poured it out into the sand. And the gesture heartened his suffering men. At last, after more than sixty days, they reached the Anamis River, where Craterus joined them after a more northerly march through the Mulla Pass, bringing the bulk of the baggage, the siege train, the sick and wounded, the elephants, and an army escort. Here at the river Alexander founded another Alexandria, and his army rested while he anxiously awaited news of the fleet.

The fleet had its own hardships. They carried provisions for ten days and water for five. Sometimes the barren coast yielded fish, which the natives dried and ground into meal, sometimes it yielded wild dates, sometimes nothing. The fleet had its own adventures too. They discovered the island of a mermaid, who changed sailors into fish. They met a number of whales, which spouted water into the air, and the sailors were so startled that they dropped their oars. Nearchus encouraged his men and ordered them to turn their ships' prows toward the monsters, then raise their battle cry and charge them. The bugles blared, the men shouted and splashed their oars, and at the last, dangerous moment the whales dived. They discovered stone-age tribes with wooden spears who lived on raw fish, on flocks of sheep which had only fish to eat, and on bread made from fish meal. After a grueling voyage of eighty days they reached the Anamis River, ragged, shaggy-haired, and weak, but with the loss of only four ships; and there they made contact with Alexander and the army. Army and navy feasted and held athletic contests. From India to the Arabian Gulf the coast of Asia had been methodically explored.

Alexander returned to the province of Persia and found his empire in considerable disorder. Some of the provincial governors had enrolled mercenaries and had become in effect rulers of sovereign states. Some were guilty of extortion and other oppression. In Media and Carmania pretenders to Alexander's throne had appeared. As symbol of the disintegration of empire, the tomb of Cyrus the Great had been broken open and robbed. The inscription over the door still cried out, "Mortal! I am Cyrus, son of Cambyses, who founded the Persian empire, and was Lord of Asia. Grudge me not, then, my monument."[551] Alexander repaired the tomb and tried to repair the empire.

But there were other omens of the mortality of men and of empires. In India he had come on a group of Indian wise men standing in a meadow, where they were accustomed to hold their disputations. When they saw Alexander and his army, they said nothing but stamped the ground with their feet. When Alexander's interpreter asked what this action meant, they replied,

> O King Alexander, each man possesses just so much of the earth as this on which we stand; and you being a man like other men, save that you are full of activity and relentless, are roaming over all this earth far from your home, troubled yourself, and troubling others. But not so long hence you will die, and will possess just so much of the earth as suffices for your burial.[552]

At Taxila, in India, he saw wise men who went naked; he admired their endurance and wanted to persuade one of them to join him. In a later tradition, their leader rejected the proposal: he himself, the Indian declared, was just as much the son of Zeus as Alexander was. He needed nothing from Alexander, since he was already content with what he had. He noted that those who were wandering over land and sea were no better off for it all, and were still doomed to wander. But one of their number did agree to go, covered with the reproaches of his fellow philosophers for serving some other master than God. The renegade was called Calanus.

In the province of Persia, Calanus fell ill for the first time in his life. But he declined medical care, decided he was ready to die, and requested that a pyre be built. In vain Alexander argued with him. So a military procession marched to the pyre, with Calanus borne on a litter. He was crowned with garlands in the Indian fashion and was singing Indian hymns to the gods of India. He mounted the pyre and distributed to his friends the precious gifts that had been placed on it. He said farewell to

Alexander's generals; but to Alexander he said merely that he would see him again at Babylon. The pyre was lighted; Calanus never flinched; and while the trumpets sounded and the army raised the battle cry and the elephants trumpeted, Alexander watched in sorrow as Calanus died.

But he himself was still alive, and the responsibilities he bore were heavier than those of any other man in his Cosmopolis. He was only thirty-two. But he was exhausted. He had been on campaign in Asia for ten hard years. He had suffered illness at Tarsus; had been wounded at Issus; had been wounded severely at the siege of Gaza. He had lost part of his tibia, fighting the Scythians near the Jaxartes; had been struck in the neck by a stone at Cyropolis; had suffered a debilitating attack of dysentery north of the Jaxartes, again fighting the Scythians. He had been wounded fighting the Aspasians in India, and the arrow planted in his breast when he stormed the city of the Brahmans had nearly proved fatal. He had driven himself mercilessly in the mountain snows of the Hindu Kush and again in the terrible march through the burning desert sands of Gedrosia. But above all, like Odysseus, he was a man of many sorrows and he was still looking for his Ithaca: some way to persuade his generation to cease their petty strife and enter his Cosmopolis.

So now at Susa, with his faithless provincial governors executed and replaced, with the desecrated tomb of his empire's founder repaired or under repair, he tried to weld the disparate elements of that empire. He persuaded eighty of his officers to marry girls of the native aristocracy. He himself, though he never accepted the idea of a king's harem, did take a second wife, one of Darius' two daughters, Barsine,[553] and Hephestion, now the second man of the empire, married the other. But the mass wedding went further: some 10,000 soldiers married their native concubines, to all of whom the king gave dowries. He then undertook to pay the debts of all his men.

In addition to his attempt to fuse the cultures of Cosmopolis by mass marriage, he enlisted in his army 30,000 native youths who had been given Macedonian military training and now wore Macedonian dress. He himself wore Persian dress. So did Peucestas, who had also learned to speak Persian and governed the province of Persia. But if Alexander sought to make his Cosmopolis something which Persians as well as Macedonians could feel loyal toward, yet it was the Athens of Aristotle and the Lyceum, of the Parthenon he had seen and the tragedies of Euripides he had read, and no polis in Asia, not even mighty Babylon, that represented in his mind civilization. Athens, for him, was the kind of society in which all of man's powers, moral, intellectual, and physical, could be most nearly actualized. In Aristotle's terms, it was a polis in which men could acquire the moral and intellectual virtues and thereby happiness, and in which some men through contemplation might briefly achieve a happiness that God knows eternally. Yet, try as Alexander might, Greece remained sullen. He had felt it necessary to destroy Thebes and to defeat Sparta, but he had wistfully cherished Athens; and, in form at least, though only in form, he was the Hegemon, the freely chosen leader, of the Hellenes of Mainland Greece.

The Mainland Greeks resented the peace between their cities which Alexander's deputy, Antipater, imposed. The oligarchies he supported had exiled thousands of democrats now adrift in Greece, some of them ready to serve anybody in need of mercenaries. But Greece could no longer endanger his rear while his hands were tied in Asia. He wanted to reconcile the Hellenes, polis with polis, oligarch with democrat. If he broke his sworn covenant with the League of Corinth, if in effect he annexed Greece instead of preserving appearances, he could order the cities to amnesty their exiled democrats. Instead he chose a more complicated method, a proclamation at the Olympic Games of 324: to restore all exiles and have someone propose his own deification. Obeying a god would not, formally at least, be the same thing as bowing to Macedonian power.

Thousands of hopeful exiles crowded Olympia and awaited the word of Alexander in Asia. All the cities sent envoys, and Athens sent Demosthenes. Nicanor, son-in-law of Aristotle, served as Alexander's messenger, and the royal message in effect ordered the cities to recall their political refugees. Nicanor also suggested that the cities accord divine honors to Alexander. There was grumbling, but educated Greeks no longer felt as strongly about the Olympic deities as Callisthenes had implied when he rejected the ceremony of prostration before the King. According to later tradition Sparta's decree on the subject preserved her reputation for laconism: "Since Alexander wants to be god, let him be god."[554] The Athenian orator, Demades, who had always served Macedon, was fined for proposing that Athens also accept Nicanor's suggestion. As for Macedon's bitter enemy, Demosthenes, he "conceded in the Assembly that

Alexander might be the son of Zeus and Poseidon too, if he wished."[555] Most cities sent envoys to Babylon, with instructions to treat Alexander as a god but to try to evade the order to recall the exiles.

Soon afterwards, Alexander joined his fleet on the Eulaeus River, sailed down to the Persian Gulf, and up the Tigris, clearing it of the weirs which the Persians had installed to block enemy ships. At Opis on the Tigris he summoned his Macedonian forces, told them he was sending home to Macedonia those whom age or service wounds had weakened, and promised them a generous bonus. Instead of being pleased, the whole army read his decision in the context of his new Persian soldiers, of his introduction of foreign cavalry into the ranks of the proud Companions, and of his own frequent use of Persian dress. They again concluded that they had been used and were now being discarded. They demanded that all of them, and not merely the incapacitated, be sent home and that Alexander carry on the war himself with the help of his father.

Alexander's old Achillean wrath flamed. It might well have flamed even if the unspeakable horrors of the Indian campaign and the misconduct of his provincial governors and the burden of administration had not made him more irritable. But, in addition, there was the gnawing problem of Cosmopolis, of the strain between conquerors and conquered, of his own tangled relationship with many peoples of many and varied customs, and even of the unresolved question, Who am I? The phrase "with the help of his father" was too obvious an allusion to miss, and too obvious to forgive for a king grown accustomed to the sort of respect his Asian and Egyptian subjects must perforce yield, even had there been no theological doubts in his own mind, even if the whole matter of divinity had been merely a coldly calculated political hoax.

In any case, he leapt from the platform from which he had been speaking, pointed out thirteen ringleaders to his officers, and ordered them executed. A dead silence followed. Then he remounted the platform and spoke:[556]

> I now propose to speak, Macedonians, not with a view to checking your homeward impulse; so far as I am concerned, you may go where you will; but that you may know, if you do so go away, how you have behaved to us, and how we have behaved to you. First then I shall begin my speech with my father Philip, as is right and proper. For Philip found you vagabonds and helpless, most of you clothed with sheepskins, pasturing a few

sheep on the mountain sides, and fighting for these, with ill success, against Illyrians and Triballians, and the Thracians on your borders; Philip gave you cloaks to wear, in place of sheepskins, brought you down from the hills to the plains, made you doughty opponents of your neighbouring enemies, so that you trusted now not so much to the natural strength of your villages as to your own courage. Nay, he made you dwellers of cities, and civilized you with good laws and customs. Then of those very tribes to whom you submitted, and by whom you and your goods were harried, he made you masters, no longer slaves and subjects; and he added most of Thrace to Macedonia, and seizing the most convenient coast towns, opened up commerce to your country, and enabled you to work your mines in peace. Then he made you overlords of the Thessalians, before whom you had long died of terror, and humbling the Phocians, made the highroad into Greece broad and easy for you, whereas it had been narrow and difficult. Athens and Thebes, always watching their chance to destroy Macedon, he so completely humbled—ourselves by this time sharing these his labours—that instead of our paying tribute to Athens and obeying Thebes, they had to win from us in turn their right to exist. Then he passed into the Peloponnese, and put all in due order there; and now being declared overlord of all the rest of Greece for the expedition against Persia, he won this new prestige not so much for himself as for all the Macedonian people.

All these noble deeds of my father towards you are great indeed, if looked at by themselves, and yet small, if compared with ours. I inherited from my father a few gold and silver cups, and not so much as sixty talents in his treasure; and of debts owed by Philip as much as five hundred talents, and yet having myself borrowed over and above these another eight hundred, I set forth from that country which hardly maintained you in comfort and at once opened to you the strait of the Hellespont, though the Persians were then masters of the sea; then, crushing with my cavalry Dareius' satraps, I added to your empire all Ionia, all Aeolia, Upper and Lower Phrygia, and Lydia; Miletus I took by seige; all else I took by surrender and gave to you to reap the fruits thereof. All good things from Egypt and Cyrene, which I took without striking a blow, come to you; Coele-Syria, and Palestine and Mesopotamia are your own possessions; Babylon is yours, Bactria, and Susa; the wealth of Lydia, the treasures of Persia, the good things of India, the outer ocean, all are yours; you are satraps, you guards, you captains. So what is left for myself from all these toils save the purple and this diadem? I have taken nothing to myself, nor can anyone show treasures of mine, save these possessions

434

of yours, or what is being safeguarded for you. For there is nothing as concerns myself for which I should reserve them, since I eat the same food that you eat, and have such sleep as you have—and yet I hardly think that I do eat the same food as some of you, who live delicately; I know, moreover, that I wake before you, that you may sleep quietly in your beds.

Yet you may feel that while you were enduring the toils and distresses, I have acquired all this without toil and without distress. But who of you is conscious of having endured more toil for me than I for him? Or see here, let any who carries wounds strip himself and show them; I too will show mine. For I have no part of my body, in front at least, that is left without scars; there is no weapon, used at close quarters, or hurled from afar, of which I do not carry the mark. Nay, I have been wounded by the sword, hand to hand; I have been shot with arrows, I have been struck from a catapult, smitten many a time with stones and clubs, for you, for your glory, for your wealth; I lead you conquerors through every land, every sea, every river, mountain, plain. I married as you married; the children of many of you will be blood-relations of my children. Moreover, if any had debts, I, being no busybody to enquire how they were made, when you were winning so much pay, and acquiring so much plunder, whenever there was plunder after a siege—I have cancelled them all. And further, golden coronals are reminders to the most part of you, both of your bravery and of my high regard—reminders that will never perish. Whosoever has died, his death has been glorious; and splendid has been his burial. To most of them there stand at home brazen statues; their parents are held in esteem, and have been freed from all services and taxes. For while I have led you, not one of you has fallen in flight.

And now I had in mind to send away those of you who are no longer equal to campaigning, to be the envy of all at home; but since you all wish to go home, depart, all of you; and when you reach home, tell them there that this your King, Alexander, victor over Persians, Medes, Bactrians, Sacaeans, conquerer of Uxians, Arachotians, Drangae, master of Parthyaea, Chorasmia, Hyrcania to the Caspian Sea; who crossed the Caucasus beyond the Caspian gates, who crossed the rivers Oxus and Tanais, yes, and the Indus too, that none but Dionysus had crossed, the Hydaspes, Acesines, Hydraotes; and who would further have crossed the Hyphasis, had not you shrunk back; who broke into the Indian Ocean by both mouths of the Indus; who traversed the Gadrosian desert—where none other had passed with an armed force; who in the line of march captured Carmania and the country of the Oreitans; whom, when his fleet had sailed from India to the Persian Sea, you led back again to Susa—tell them, I say, that you deserted him, that you took yourselves off, leaving him to the care of the wild tribes you had conquered. This, when you declare it, will be, no doubt, glorious among men, and pious in the sight of heaven. Begone![557]

He leapt from the platform again and passed swiftly into the royal headquarters. The Macedonians, who had been deeply moved by his speech, simply stood there silent, without purpose, like bereaved children. Neither that day nor the next was he seen. On the third day he summoned picked men among the Persians and began commissioning them. As news that one famous unit after another was passing into Persian hands, the Macedonians broke down. They ran to his quarters, threw their arms in submission before his door, and begged to be let into the presence of the man they had followed through such untold horrors, the man whose incredible triumphs they had also shared, the man they had come so deeply to adore. They wept. Alexander came out. When he saw them humble and loving, he melted; he, too, shed tears. Callines, a famous officer in the superb Companions' cavalry, said:

> This, O King, is what grieves the Macedonians, that you have made Persians your kinsmen and Persians are called 'Alexander's kinsmen,' and they are permitted to kiss you; but no Macedonian has tasted this privilege.[558]

And the King said quickly,

> But all of you I regard as my kinsmen, and so from henceforth I call you.[559]

All who desired to were allowed to kiss him. And they marched off to their camp, singing the victory paean.

The reconciliation that caused that paean of victory grew, at least in symbol, into a wider reconciliation and another song of victory over conflict. For Alexander gave a feast, to which he invited not only his Macedonians but the Persians and men from many other nations of those he now ruled. Some 9,000 guests sat at Alexander's cosmopolitan feast and prepared to break bread together. Greek seers and Persian magi alike officiated. When the hour for wine came, Alexander and those at his table poured the same libations to the gods with wine from the same great bowl; and the whole throng joined them, each group making libation with wine from its own bowl. And they all drank, all in each group from its own common bowl; and they all sang together one paean. Three centuries afterwards it would be related in Greece that Alexander "believed that he came as a heaven-sent governor to all, and as a mediator for the whole world"[560]; that

> those whom he could not persuade to unite with him, he conquered by force of arms, and he brought together into one body all men everywhere, uniting and mixing in one great loving-cup, as it were, men's lives, their characters, their marriages, their very habits of life. He bade them all consider as their fatherland the whole inhabited earth, as their stronghold and protection his camp, as akin to them all good men, and as foreigners only the wicked; they should not distinguish between Grecian and foreigner by Grecian cloak and targe, or scimitar and jacket; but the distinguishing mark of the Grecian should be seen in virtue, and that of the foreigner in iniquity; clothing and food, marriage and manner of life they should regard as common to all, being blended into one by ties of blood and children.[561]

How close to that later report did his words really come? At least he prayed for all sorts of blessings, including *Homonoia* and *Koinonia*, Harmony and Fellowship, in the empire, between Macedonian and Persian. In Alexander's own mind, what did Opis mean? A sacramental initiation into the Cosmopolis he had brought to birth? A quick, shrewd effort to convert his personal reconciliation with the Macedonians into one that would include the Persians and permit one ruler to rule two such different races?

But what, in Homer's mind, had the *Iliad* meant? That the war in which the warrior Achilles found release, work to do, a chance to excell, and fame, was desirable? Or that Ares, god of war, was justly the most hated god on Olympus? Alexander kept the *Iliad* under his pillow while on campaign; and if Homer had not taught him the complexity of that question, he could have learned it from the glories and miseries of his own war, from the field where Achilles had fought to the blood which his men, and he himself, had mixed with the monsoon rains of India. Now he wanted peace, the consent of the governed, and the friendship between the governed which Aristotle knew every polis must have and which Alexander as statesman knew Cosmopolis must therefore have. But Alexander had always shown the ability to use the symbol: whatever he said at Opis, it was not a lecture on political philosophy. It was things recited, things shown, things done.

Meanwhile, he needed the wisdom of Solon and of Lycurgus, too, if he was to bring the genuine peace his victories in war had made him responsible for. A mammoth task of organization faced him. Olympias plagued him with letters, complaining that his regent in Europe, Antipater, was arrogant; and Antipater's constant cry was that the queen mother was high-tempered and interfering. Alexander remarked that Antipater could never understand that one tear of Olympias would outweigh all Antipater's dispatches; and on another occasion, that his mother was exacting a heavy price from him for her nine months' housing of him. He ordered Antipater to join him in Asia with fresh Macedonian troops and sent back the invalided Craterus to take his place. Craterus conducted with him some 10,000 Macedonian veterans, now reconciled with their king and more than willing to go home.

And then, in the autumn of 324, Hephestion, who had been to Alexander what Patroclus had been to Achilles, fell ill at Ecbatana and in seven days was dead. Alexander was wild with grief. For three days he tasted no morsel of food. He would have agreed with Pericles that heroes have the whole earth for their tomb;[562] nevertheless, the body of Hephestion was burned on an immense pyre at Babylon, and 3,000 contestants took part in the funeral games. Alexander assuaged his grief by a winter campaign against the Cossaeans, a hill tribe between Ecbatana and Babylon who lived on brigandage and whom the Persians had failed to bring to heel. The Cossaeans were destroyed.

In the spring Alexander returned to Babylon, where he received envoys from the Libyans; and from Italy, Bruttian, Lucanian, and Etruscan envoys. He ordered an expedition to explore the Caspian Sea. To encourage commerce, he founded another Alexandria at the mouth of the Tigris. He laid plans to plant a colony of Phoenician seafarers on the east coast of the Persian Gulf and began at Babylon a harbor and dockyards for merchantmen: he wanted commerce with India. He planned to lead a joint military and naval expedition to find a route around Arabia to Egypt: he wanted a commercial sea route between Babylon and Egypt. While the fleet was being prepared, he improved the irrigation system of Mesopotamia.

Alexander was still not quite thirty-three. He still radiated the youth, strength, health, and beauty of person that made him seem to those around him so much more alive, more awake, than other men. He would have agreed with Heraclitus that all those who are awake have one ordered universe common to all, whereas in sleep each man turns away from that common world to a private world of his own.[563] Was not Alexander, being among those few who were awake, trying in agony to point out to those who slept, the common universe, the Cosmopolis that was adumbrated around them? Much of his courtesy, his politeness, to others was the politeness of the *polites*, the citizen, of that new and opening world. Aristotle, who saw the difference between the educated man and the uneducated man as the difference between the man awake and the man asleep, could have asked with justifiable pride why on earth his famous pupil should not be wide awake. But it was the pupil, and not the master, who was dealing with the opposite of the *polites*, or citizen; and in Greek that opposite was called *idiotes*. In the context of emergent Cosmopolis, Demosthenes' patriotic tirades were more idiotic than polite. For city-state patriotism had become the private world of idiocy.

Alexander had already proven himself a consummate general, and part of that proof lay not only in what he did with an army to win victory but in what he did as a statesman after victory with those who had submitted. He thought of himself as a Hellene, creating a Hellenized new world, but to many Athenians besides Demosthenes he was an outsider. It would have been hard for any cultivated Athenian in the disillusioned, commercialized Athens of the late fourth century to see himself as Achilles and to feel Achilles acting in himself. Perhaps it would have been hard for him to feel the kind of wonder Odysseus felt when faced with a strange sea and a half-descried coast. Or to feel the urgency of a Solon longing to bring law in place of violence. Alexander did not feel himself a member of Hesiod's race of iron but of an earlier race of heroes. The Mainland Greeks could call him tyrant as they liked: he had at least freed Greece-in-Asia from its Persian master. And no disciple of Aristotle was likely to desire human freedom in the sentimental terms of a Demosthenes. He showed the awareness of Aeschylus, and of Aristotle, that only Zeus was free and that in the last analysis man won freedom only by imitating

439

God, or at least God's act of understanding. He wanted all that polis meant to Pericles, but he knew it could no longer be found in a city-state: he wanted the polis to be a school that civilized and ennobled its members. He was a questioner, like Socrates, but as a king, he was doomed to employ not only wisdom, but force. He hated the obstinate, blind, bestial strife which destroyed polis, the kind of strife that the Peloponnesian War became, that the revolution in Corcyra became, with results fatal for Hellas. He was punctilious in his observances of Greek official religion, as Xenophon had known that warfare made men be; but he knew of religious problems which Xenophon never dreamt of. He could be as cunning, as harsh, as politic as Philip; but one of his many other fathers, Aristotle, had inspired him with a moral nobility, a capacity for disinterested inquiry, and a kind of grace of spirit that Philip did not exhibit.

Above all, Alexander's sureness in performing the symbolic act had turned him into myth long before that hot June in Babylon when he planned to explore, perhaps to annex, the coasts of fabled Arabia. His acts generated meanings, meanings capable of breeding further meanings; and he supplemented his acts, as Odysseus had supplemented his, with dreams, signs, tokens, wingèd words, and prayers, to conquer and grasp and comprehend a world which the sword alone could never wholly conquer, nor the most royal scepter hold. His acts generated meanings as surely as did the acts of any hero in Greek tragedy, whether Orestes or Oedipus, until it became hard to disentangle the historic truth about him from the truth Aristotle had considered more philosophic than history: poetic truth.

Nevertheless, he had thus far failed to weld his empire into one. Labor as he might to pacify, to reconcile, to mediate between men, Cosmopolis throbbed with repressed violence. If he dreamed of all men as brothers under their common father Zeus, with himself as son of Zeus in some special sense, charged to make the will of Zeus the will also of men, yet he was a savior with a sword, and, at least in the myth his actions had created, the knot at Gordium had been cut, not untied. True, he had become Lord of Asia; but in what sense Lord? A Lord who brought what appeared, indeed, when the libations were being poured at Opis, like Harmony and Fellowship throughout Cosmopolis. But a Lord who, battle by battle, found himself not only breaking judiciously Darius' resistance at Issus but murdering Black Clitus in drunken rage, murdering

Parmenion with the swords of others, massacring natives in his northeast provinces, and massacring even more savagely in India, so that part of the myth he had already created before this year of 323 was that of blood and agonizing death, of depopulation, of drunken orgy and barbarous vandalism, of an insane striving for world conquest, and above all of the paranoiac, sacrilegious hybris of a man determined to be God. Did part of the tenseness, the irritability, which he had given vent to in these later years, come from the horrified discovery that, though he had indeed forced open Asia's door to the more rapid expansion of Greek commerce in commodities and ideas, yet his dream of a Cosmopolis worthy to be the polis of Zeus was an empty dream? That his attack on Persia had not even exorcised the violence that had so degraded Hellas, as Isocrates had perhaps hoped his father Philip might have exorcised it? That to reconcile men would require something other than a sword or even something opposite to it? And that now all one could do was shed more blood, this time in Arabia?

Around the beginning of June, Alexander and his friends sacrificed, partly in thanksgiving for many blessings already received and partly because his seers were troubled by curious omens of misfortune. Then they feasted and drank late into the night. He started to retire but a trusted Companion named Medius persuaded him to come with him for a smaller, final party. The royal diaries reported that he drank merrily with Medius, bathed and slept, dined with him and again drank late, then again bathed. Then he slept where he was because he felt unwell. He was running a fever. But he continued to confer with his officers about the Arabian expedition, which was due to leave in four days' time. It was hot. They took him across the wide Euphrates in a boat to a garden, and there he bathed and again rested. Next day he lay in his room, talking to Medius, and planned to meet his officers the following morning. Though he ran a high fever the whole night, he nevertheless kept his morning appointment with his admiral, Nearchus, and the others and gave directions for the great expedition. The fever continued, but next day the conferring continued too. By night he was very ill; yet on the day after that he was still planning with his officers. But the following day, he ordered his officers to wait in the court. He was brought back across the river to the palace. When the officers followed and were ushered in, he knew them but he could no longer speak.

441

For two nights and two days more the fever raged. The royal diaries reported that his soldiers begged to be admitted to see him. They filed past. He could not speak, but his eyes showed he knew them. In the temple of Sarapis, an Egyptian god who often gave medical advice, some of the king's friends kept vigil. They asked the god whether the king should be brought to the temple too, for prayer and healing. The oracle replied that it would be better for Alexander if he remained where he was. Meanwhile, neither in his recent conferences nor earlier had he dealt with the problem of succession in case of his death. Roxana was now with child. Was he counting on a son? On his own health, which always after illness had returned? On his own extraordinary good fortune in battle, that could be counted on in Arabia as elsewhere? According to some reports his Companions, before the fever had stolen his power of speech, asked him to whom he left his empire, and he replied, "to the strongest."[564] Others said that he, who had so lately ordered the magnificent athletic contests at the funeral of Hephestion, added that he foresaw a great funeral contest on his own death. Did he speak in despair? In weariness? In grim irony?

CHRONOLOGICAL SUMMARY

Circa 2000-1700	Achaean invasion of Mainland Greece.
c. 1700	Destruction of Minoan palaces at Crete.
c. 1600-1500	Crete the entrepôt for Egypt and the Aegean.
c. 1600-1100	Mycenaean Age in Mainland Greece.
c. 1400	Collapse of Minoan power.
c. 1200-1180	Trojan War.
c. 1150	Dorian invasion; coming of iron; beginning of Dark Age; development of Phoenician trade; migrations from Mainland Greece to Asia Minor.
c. 900-800(?)	Construction of Greek alphabet in Ionia. Composition of the *Iliad*. Introduction of cavalry to Greece.
c. 800-700(?)	Hesiod. Composition of the *Odyssey*.
c. 800-600	Growth of city-state. Development from monarchy to aristocracy to, sometimes, tyranny. Greek colonization.
c. 800-500	Ionian school of lyric poetry.
776	First Olympic Festival.
c. 740-720	Spartan conquest of Messenia.
701	Phoenicia conquered by Assyria.
c. 700-600	Development of coinage. Tyrtaeus.
c. 700-500	Ionian school of philosophy.

c. 700	First hoplites.
c. 640	Second Messenian War.
c. 632	Cylon tries to seize Acropolis.
621	Dracon's legal reforms at Athens.
c. 600	Phocaeans found or take over Marseilles; tap Rhone River route to northern Europe.
c. 594	Solon archon of Athens.
c. 585-546	Thales *floruit*.
574	Phoenicia taken over by Chaldea.
c. 570	Athenian conquest of Salamis.
c. 561	Pisistratus becomes tyrant of Athens.
c. 560-546	Ionia a protectorate of Croesus of Lydia.
c. 555-552(?)	First exile of Pisistratus.
c. 552	Pisistratus's restoration and second exile. Cyrus the Great of Persia conquers Medes.
546	Cyrus conquers Lydia.
c. 539	Cyrus takes Babylon.
529	Death of Cyrus.
c. 527	Death of Pisistratus. Hippias and Hipparchus succeed him at Athens.
525	Cambyses of Persia annexes Egypt.
514	Hipparchus assassinated.
512	Darius of Persia conquers Thrace to Danube.
510	Spartan army liberates Athens from Hippias.
508-507	Sparta fails to restore aristocracy at Athens. Clisthenes destroys political power of tribes.
506	Attica repels attack by Peloponnesians, Boeotians, and Chalcidians. Plants outsettlers.
c. 505-366	Peloponnesian League.
499	Ionia revolts from Persian Empire.
498-438	Pindar *floruit*.

444

c. 498	Athens at war with Aegina. Ionians, Athenians, Eretrians take Sardis and are then defeated.
494, SUMMER	Persia's fleet defeats Ionia's at Lade. Miletus razed.
493, SUMMER	Collapse of Ionian Revolt.
492	Darius leads first Persian expedition against Mainland Greece.
490, SPRING	Darius leads second Persian expedition against Mainland Greece.
490, SEPTEMBER(?)	Battle of Marathon.
489	Miltiades defeated at Paros. Prosecuted at Athens.
485	Athens ostracizes Xanthippus.
484	Aeschylus's first victory in dramatic competition.
483-482	Athens ostracizes Aristides. Themistocles turns Athens to the sea.
481-461	Panhellenic league against Persia.
480	Xerxes leads third Persian expedition against Mainland Greece. Athens recalls Xanthippus and Aristides under general amnesty. Sicilians defeat Carthaginians at Himera.
480, AUGUST(?)	Battles of Thermopylae and Artemisium.
480, SEPTEMBER(?)	Battle of Salamis.
479, JUNE	Mardonius invades Attica.
479, AUGUST 27(?)	Battles of Plataea and Mycale.
c. 479-478	Xanthippus besieges Sestos.
478-476	Rebuilding of walls of Athens.
476	Foundation of League of Delos.
475	Cimon takes Eion, near Amphipolis.
473-472	Democratic revolts in Peloponnese.
472	Production of Aeschylus's *Persians*, with Pericles as choregus.

445

472	Themistocles ostracized in clash with Cimon.
470-469	Naxos revolts from League of Delos; is reduced by Athens.
468	Aeschylus defeated by Sophocles in dramatic competition.
c. 468	Cimon destroys Persia's fleet at Eurymedon.
464	Death of Xerxes. Accession of Artaxerxes. Themistocles at Persian court.
464, SUMMER	Spartan earthquake. Helot rebellion.
c. 462	Themistocles dies in exile.
462-461	Laws passed depriving Areopagus of power to oversee Athenian constitution.
c. 461-456	Construction of Long Walls from Athens to Piraeus.
461	Cimon ostracized. Ephialtes assassinated. Pericles heads democratic party at Athens.
459	Athens aids Egypt's revolt against Persia.
458	Production of Aeschylus's *Oresteia*.
457	Spartan alliance defeats Athenians at Tanagra. Athens gains control of Boeotia and Phocis at Oenophyta. Cimon recalled from exile.
455	Production of Euripides' first tragedy.
454	Failure of Athens' expedition to Egypt. Treasury of League of Delos moved to Athens.
451-446	Five-year truce between Athens and Sparta.
450-449	Death of Cimon on campaign.
449-448	Peace of Callias between Athens and Persia begins.
c. 448	Pericles tries to convene Panhellenic Congress.
447	Athens loses Boeotia at Coronea, and finally control of central Greece.
447-432	Building of Parthenon.
446-445	Thirty Years' Peace between Athens and Sparta begins.

446	Athens subjects Euboea. Megara revolts.
c. 446	Herodotus reads his *History* at Athens.
c. 444	Athens ostracizes Damon, Pericles' friend.
443	Pericles founds Thurii.
440-439	Revolt and reduction of Samos and Byzantium. Pericles' first funeral oration.
438	Phidias's statue of Athena set up in Parthenon.
435	Sea fight between Corinth and Corcyra over Epidamnus.
434	Athens forbids Allies to coin money.
433	Athens renews treaties with Leontini and Rhegium. Alliance between Megara and Corinth. Athenians assist Corcyra against Corinth. Revolt of Potidaea from League of Delos.
432	Prosecution at Athens of Anaxagoras, Pericles' friend. Athens closes markets to Megara.
431-421	Peloponnesian War.
431	Athens expels Aeginetans and resettles island.
c. 431	Athens exiles Phidias.
430	Phormio fights Peloponnesians in Gulf of Corinth. Pericles' second funeral oration (March).
c. 429-422	Cleon foremost political leader at Athens.
429, AUTUMN	Death of Pericles.
428-427	Revolt of Mitylene.
427-425	Corcyrean revolution.
427	Surrender of Plataea. Production of Aristophanes' first comedy, the *Banqueters*.
426	Demosthenes invades Aetolia.
425	Athenians capture Pylos.
424	Athenians capture Cythera and Nisaea. Defeated at Delium. Brasidas leads Spartan expedition to Thrace; takes Amphipolis.

447

	Congress of Gela, in Sicily. Thucydides, the historian, exiled by Athens.
c. 424	2,000 freed Helots disappear in Sparta.
423	Athens makes one-year truce with Sparta. Production of Aristophanes' *Clouds*.
422	Cleon and Brasidas killed at Amphipolis.
421	Peace of Nicias between Athens and Peloponnese. Production of Aristophanes' *Peace*. Athens quells revolt of Scione in Chalcidice.
421-420	Defensive alliance between Athens and Sparta.
420	Alcibiades effects anti-Spartan alliance in Peloponnese.
418, AUGUST	Anti-Spartan alliance defeated at Mantinea. Argos makes treaty with Sparta.
416	Athenians massacre Melians.
415, C. JUNE 7	Desecration of Herms at Athens.
415, C. MIDSUMMER	Athens launches expedition to Sicily.
415, C. AUTUMN	Alcibiades ordered home for trial; escapes to Sparta; sentenced to death at Athens, *in absentia*.
414	Sparta intervenes in Sicily. Production of Aristophanes' *Birds*.
413	Sparta takes Decelea. Second Athenian expedition to Sicily. Massacre at Mycalessus by Thracian mercenaries. Athenian disaster in Sicily. Execution of Nicias and Demosthenes.
412	Athenian allies revolt.
411, JANUARY-FEBRUARY	Production of Aristophanes' *Lysistrata*.
411, JUNE	Council of 400 at Athens. 'Polis' at Samos elects Alcibiades general.
411, SEPTEMBER	Revolt of Euboea. Fall of Council of 400.
411, AUTUMN	Moderate constitution set up at Athens.

410	Athenians defeat Peloponnesian fleet at Cyzicus. Restoration of democracy at Athens.
409	Athenians lose Pylos and Nisaea.
407, SUMMER	Alcibiades, elected general by Athenian Assembly, returns to Athens.
407	Alcibiades' fleet trapped at Notion. Alcibiades flees to Hellespont. Conon trapped at Mitylene. Erectheum completed.
c. 406-367	Dionysius I tyrant at Syracuse.
406	Defeat of Peloponnesians at Arginusae. Trial of Athenian generals.
c. 406	Death of Euripides at Macedonian court.
405	Athenian disaster at Aegospotami. Production of Aristophanes' Frogs.
404	Fall of Athens' Long Walls. Thirty Tyrants installed at Athens. Death of Alcibiades and Theramenes.
403	Fall of Thirty Tyrants. General amnesty at Athens.
401, MARCH 6	Xenophon and the Ten Thousand begin their March Up Country.
401, SEPTEMBER	Cyrus slain at Cunaxa.
399, FEBRUARY	Trial of Socrates.
399, MARCH	End of Anabasis. Xenophon exiled by Athens.
394	Xenophon fights under Agesilaus against Athens at battle of Coronea.
c. 392	Isocrates founds school at Athens.
387	Celts seize Rome. Plato's first visit to Syracuse.
c. 387	Plato founds Academy at Athens.
386	Peace of Antalcidas, or King's Peace. Thessaly united under Jason of Pherae.
378-377	Second Athenian Confederacy.
371, JULY	Epaminondas defeats Spartans at Leuctra.

370-369	First and second Boeotian invasions of Peloponnese.
369-368	Pelopidas of Thebes invades Thessaly.
367	Dionysius I wins first dramatic prize at Athens. Dies. Succeeded by Dionysius II. Plato's second visit to Sicily.
c 367	Philip of Macedonia taken to Thebes as hostage. Athens terminates Xenophon's exile.
c 366	Third Boeotian expedition to Peloponnese. Aristotle enters Plato's Academy.
365-359	Perdiccas III active in Macedonia.
365	Xenophon returns to Athens.
362	Epaminondas defeats Sparta at Mantinea and dies in battle.
361	Plato's third visit to Syracuse.
359	Philip becomes regent, then king, of Macedonia.
357	Philip tricks Athens at Amphipolis. Dion takes over Syracuse.
356-346	The Sacred War.
356	Athenians driven from Chalcidice. Philip conquers Potidaea, Pydna, and defeats Illyrians.
354	Philomelus of Phocis commits suicide; Onomarchus takes over. Murder of Dion of Syracuse. Demosthenes' first oration in Athenian Assembly.
c. 354	Death of Xenophon.
353	Philip takes Methone.
352	Philip puts Thessaly in order. Marches to Thermopylae.
351	Demosthenes' *First Philippic.*
348-347	Philip takes Olynthus. Coins golden philips. Death of Plato.
c. 347	Aristotle leaves Plato's Academy for Assus.

346	Philip elected president of Amphictyony after ending Sacred War. Isocrates' *Address to Philip*.
343-342	Aristotle goes to Macedonian court as tutor to Philip's son, Alexander.
341	Philip dethrones Cersobleptes of Thrace, invades Chersonese, attacks Byzantium.
338, AUGUST(?)	Philip wins control of Greece at Chaeronea.
337	Philip establishes League of Corinth.
336	Philip assassinated at Aegae. Succeeded by Alexander. Accession of Darius III to Persian throne.
335	Alexander razes Thebes.
c. 335	Aristotle founds Lyceum at Athens.
334, SPRING	Alexander opens campaign in Asia. Battle of the Granicus.
333	Alexander at Gordium.
333, NOVEMBER	Battle of Issus.
332, JANUARY-JULY	Siege of Tyre.
332, WINTER	Alexander becomes Pharaoh of Egypt.
331, WINTER	Alexander founds Alexandria in Egypt and visits Ammon.
331, AUTUMN	Battle of Gaugamela (October 1). Babylon surrenders to Alexander. Sparta defeated at Megalopolis.
330	Alexander takes Persepolis. Death of Darius III. Philotas and Parmenion executed.
329	Bessus of Bactria betrayed to Alexander.
328, SUMMER	Alexander murders Clitus.
327	Pages' conspiracy. Alexander marries Roxana. Start of Indian expedition (summer).
326	Alexander crosses the Indus. Battle of the Hydaspes, or Jhelum, River. Army balks at Beas River (July). Sails down Jhelum (November).

325, JULY	Alexander enters Indian Ocean.
324	Restoration of Greek exiles proclaimed (July-August). Alexander marries Darius' daughter, Barsine. Alexander at Opis. Death of Hephestion (autumn).
323	Alexander dies at Babylon. Aristotle charged with impiety; flees to Euboea.
322	Death of Aristotle.

BIBLIOGRAPHICAL NOTE

THE READER of the foregoing pages may wish to know more about the events of Greek history than this book has told him. He may therefore wish me to supply him with some sort of reading list. Of the hundreds of books by modern scholars which I read in preparation for writing this history, and of the hundreds of others I had to consult, there are indeed some that I am tempted to urge on anybody who has been my traveling companion thus far. But which books I would recommend to any given reader would depend on the special interests this history might have awakened in him.

If the many omissions in my narrative leave the reader hungry for more historical detail, I would recommend that he try one of four general histories of Greece written by modern historians. Perhaps the best known in this country is J. B. Bury: A *History of Greece* (2d ed., London, 1913). But in several ways this work has been recently superseded by N. G. L. Hammond: A *History of Greece* (Oxford, 1959). Hammond's text is enlivened and illuminated by a happy use of quotation.

Those who read French will find a more readable account than either in Gustave Glotz: *Histoire Grecque* (with the collaboration of Robert Cohen; 4 vols., Paris, 1925-38). Glotz exhibits the capacity for synthesis so frequently found in French historians. But if the reader chooses Glotz, he will confront several difficulties. First, volumes III and IV are out of print and exceedingly difficult to find. Secondly, although, unlike Bury and Hammond, Glotz gives an extensive bibliography for each chapter, the titles in these bibliographies are listed with comments addressed rather to the scholar than to the general reader. Thirdly, although Glotz is equipped with that indispensable tool, historical imagination, his inferences seem to me sometimes bolder than the evidence he cites can justify. Despite this word of caution I heartily recommend Glotz's history for a general view of the subject.

Above all three of these works, in terms of total intellectual achievement, I would rate George Grote's *A History of Greece* (12 vols., London, 1846-56). It was written before a century of historical and archaeological labor had further clarified many problems. It was written before Schliemann had unearthed Troy and Mycenae, before Evans had uncovered Knossos. It was written by an English Radical, whose view of the world now seems fatally limited, and this limitation becomes especially apparent in his treatment, for example, of Demosthenes and Philip. But his history has greatness, and it is an intellectual scandal that it should now be out of print. Fortunately, many good public libraries still possess Grote's work.

These general histories are the only works by moderns that I shall list here. What I really recommend to my reader is to read or re-read the Greeks themselves, and this for two reasons. First, nobody today could construct a history of Hellenic culture without the aid of the thousands of scholars, whether in ancient Alexandria or in our own modern world, who have labored with the pen and with the spade to render the documents available and ready for use. But too often we know what the Greeks said chiefly by knowing what our modern scholars say they said. Only a first-hand knowledge of the text brings the commentary into perspective. Secondly, it is not possible to narrate or even understand the history of a culture without immersion in that culture. The precise date of a battle cannot matter much if we have no insight into what led men to fight it.

I was not led to write *The Will of Zeus* by what modern historians have written, much as I owe to them, but by a direct and sometimes shattering encounter with the Greeks themselves. And even then I would not have written but for the hope that I could help bring about direct encounter or re-encounter between the Greeks and my reader, an encounter that would necessarily differ in many ways from my own.

I therefore urge the reader of this Bibliographical Note to turn next to the Greeks themselves. If he has already read them, he will already know they bear many readings. I make bold to urge that he read them as Socrates consulted the god at Delphi and not as Xenophon consulted him—that is, that he listen and reflect rather than try to discover the answers to specific questions he has already formulated, on the assumption that we moderns already know all the good questions. Ideally, of course, he should read them in the original Greek. However, the past few decades have fortunately witnessed the translation of many Greek works, and in many of these translations the intellectual light shines through with unmistakable brilliance. No snobbish talk about originals versus translations should deter the modern reader who cannot read Greek. If he wants still richer rewards, he can reflect that many men, from the Romans to ourselves, have learned Greek, even late in life.

The Greek authors listed below appear in the Loeb Classical Library, now published in this country by the Harvard University Press. It is their works on which I have drawn most heavily for this history. For the reader who knows even a little Greek, or will take the time to learn a little, the Loeb Classics offer the advantage of a double text: Greek on the left-hand page and an English translation on the right. The Loeb translations were made by many scholars and, as one might expect, are in varying degree successful. All or most of the extant works of the following authors are available in Loeb:

Aeschylus	Homer
Aristophanes	Isocrates
Aristotle	Pindar
Arrian	Plato
Demosthenes	Plutarch
Euripides	Sophocles
Herodotus	Thucydides
Hesiod	Xenophon

I have also drawn on the following collections of poems in Loeb:

The Greek Anthology
Greek Elegy and Iambus
Lyra Graeca

A convenient collection of the fragments which survive from the writings of the pre-Socratic philosophers can be found in Kathleen Freeman's *Ancilla to the Pre-Socratic Philosophers* (Oxford, 1948). These fragments appear in English, keyed in with the Greek texts published in *Die Fragmente der Vorsokratiker*, edited by Hermann Diels (3 vols., Berlin, 1951-52).

Finally, I should like to call attention to certain other translations, some of them old favorites, some of them quoted in this history, some of them available also in paperback editions. Each of these translations has in some way or ways achieved great success in a difficult art:

Of Aeschylus, Euripides, and Sophocles—
The Complete Greek Tragedies, edited by David Grene and Richmond Lattimore, 4 vols., Chicago, 1959.
Of Aristophanes—
The Complete Greek Drama, edited by Whitney J. Oates and Eugene O'Neill, Jr., New York, 1938. Vol. II.
Herodotus: *The Persian Wars*, translated by George Rawlinson, New York (Modern Library), 1942.
Hesiod: *Works and Days, Theogony, The Shield of Herakles*, translated by Richmond Lattimore, Ann Arbor, Mich., 1959.

Homer: *The Iliad*, translated by Richmond Lattimore, Chicago, 1951.

Homer: *The Odyssey*, translated by T. E. Shaw, *i.e.*, T. E. Lawrence, New York, 1932.

Pindar: *Pythian Odes*, translated by H. T. Wade-Gery and C. M. Bowra, London, 1928.

Plato: *The Dialogues of Plato*, translated by Benjamin Jowett, 2 vols., New York, 1937.

Thucydides: *The Peloponnesian War*, translated by Thomas Hobbes, edited by David Grene, 2 vols., Ann Arbor, Mich., 1959.

Xenophon: *Anabasis: The March Up Country*, translated by W. H. D. Rouse, Ann Arbor, Mich., 1958.

And now, if you, my reader, choose to embark, or re-embark, on these Greek seas, may you, like Odysseus, see the cities and learn the minds of many men before you find home.

S. B.

NOTES

Books not fully identified in the Notes will be found so identified in the Bibliographical Note, p. 453.

CHAPTER ONE

1. If indeed the same poet wrote both poems. But was either the *Iliad* or the *Odyssey* the work of one man? The Homeric question is still a matter of vigorous debate.
2. Homer: *Iliad* I, 5. Loeb.
3. Ibid., XII, 5 ff.
4. A. Jardé in *The Formation of the Greek People*, New York, 1926, p. 28, gives this list, except for the lynx and the roe; but he implies that the lion, leopard, and panther were not found south of Macedonia in classical times. Yet see Herodotus VII, 125-26, on the lion. And all three species may well have ranged in Greece in 2000 B.C., when the Achaeans were probably arriving there. The δορκάς, or roe, was hunted in the Peloponnese in the fourth century, according to Xenophon: *Anabasis* V, iii, 10 (translated in Loeb as gazelle, but as roe in Liddell and Scott: *Greek-English Dictionary*, 8th ed.). Xenophon (*Scripta Minora*, On Hunting XI, 1, Loeb) claims that "lions, leopards, lynxes, panthers, and bears" were found in his day, not only in Thrace and in Asia Minor, but on Mount Pindus, the mountain range separating Thessaly from Epirus.
5. A. Jardé: *The Formation of the Greek People*, New York, 1926, p. 48.
6. Or destroyed by earthquake. This is a moot point among modern historians of Minoan civilization.
7. Homer: *Odyssey* I, 57-59. Loeb.
8. Ibid., V, 462-63.
9. Ibid., XVII, 326-27.
10. Ibid., XIX, 409.
11. Ibid., VII, 307.
12. Ibid., XIX, 118.
13. Ibid., IX, 316-17.

14. Ibid., IX, 502-5.
15. Ibid., VIII, 147-48.
16. Ibid., XXIV, 36-94.
17. Ibid., I, 302.
18. Ibid., XXIV, 196-98.
19. Ibid., XXIV, 433-35.
20. Ibid., III, 236-38.
21. Ibid., I, 205.
22. Ibid., IX, 19-20.
23. Ibid., XIX, 395-96.
24. Ibid., X, 305.
25. Ibid., II, 117-18.
26. Ibid., IX, 174-76.
27. Ibid., IX, 229.
28. Ibid., XII, 49-52.
29. Ibid., XII, 191.
30. Ibid., XII, 249-50.
31. Ibid., XII, 258-59.
32. Ibid., X, 436-37.
33. Ibid., IX, 112-15.
34. Ibid., IX, 276.
35. Ibid., I, 65-7.
36. Ibid., XIII, 293-95.
37. Ibid., XIII, 332.
38. Ibid., XIII, 299.
39. Ibid., XIII, 310.
40. Ibid., III, 48.
41. Ibid., XVI, 160-61.
42. Ibid., XVI, 178-79.
43. Ibid., XVI, 187-89.
44. Ibid., I, 320-21.
45. Ibid., I, 324.
46. Ibid., III, 23.
47. Ibid., III, 26-7.
48. Ibid., XIX, 560-61.
49. Ibid., XIX, 29; XVII, 57.
50. Ibid., XVIII, 130-31.

CHAPTER TWO

51. The Greeks of the Dark Ages, roughly the eleventh, tenth, and ninth centuries before Christ, had less historical understanding of what Minoan Crete had been, of what Mycenae had signified, than contemporary archaeologists have now acquired by 'digs' and by toilsome study of the forgotten writing of Minos' commercial empire. And the Greeks of Thucydides' day knew little more of Minoan Crete and Mycenae than their ancestors of the Dark Ages had known.

52. Margaret Wason: *Class Struggles in Ancient Greece*, London, 1947, pp. 19-31. Even if Wason underestimates the military importance of iron,

there is still a chance that it was not iron weapons but iron fighting men that the Achaean-Pelasgian society could not beat back.

53. That is, to the style which modern archaeologists call "Orientalizing."

54. The origins of the earlier Greek alphabets are matters of dispute.

55. On the moot question as to how Homer's *Iliad* and *Odyssey* were transmitted to modern times, see Cedric Whitman's discussion in *Homer and the Heroic Tradition*, Cambridge, Mass., 1957, particularly chap. 4.

56. A glance at a map of the Mediterranean will suffice to confirm this judgment.

57. The saddle would not be used for several centuries yet, although in the fourth century Xenophon would report the use of a pad.

58. Homer: *Iliad* I, 159. Loeb.

59. *Greek Elegy and Iambus* II, p. 99, Archilochus 2. Loeb.

60. Ἐκεχειρία. Glotz: *Histoire Grecque*, vol. I, p. 515. Justice often expressed itself in legal forms that we today associate with those other Middle Ages, our own, in Western Europe, centuries after the Greek polis had flourished and had perished.

61. The Romans would translate this phrase into Magna Graecia.

62. The simile is Plato's. *Phaedo*, 109B. Loeb.

63. The chronology of early coining by city-states is a vexed question. See Charles Seltman: *Greek Coins*, 2d ed., London, 1955, pp. 13-44.

64. I use here the date given by H. L. Lorimer in *Homer and the Monuments*, London, 1950. See chap. 5.

65. Probably, but not certainly. We first encounter the term in Archilochus of Paros, who applies it to the Lydian king, Gyges, a usurper.

66. Some modern scholars have doubted whether the *Theogony* was the work of Hesiod.

67. Poets presumably have as much right to tell their readers how to farm as scientists have. Naturally they sing when they do it.

68. Hesiod: *Theogony*, 737. Loeb.

69. Ibid., 440.

70. Ibid., 117.

71. Hesiod: *Works and Days*, 91. Loeb.

72. Ibid., 112-13.

73. Ibid., 152.

74. Ibid., 174-78. If the modern reader is tempted to reply that every generation believes that things are going to ruin, he might perhaps remember that sometimes it is true. The Minoan culture really had gone to ruin; and its Mainland derivative, the Mycenaean culture, had later gone there too.

75. In the fifth century the historian Herodotus guessed (Herodotus II, 53) that Homer and Hesiod lived not earlier than the ninth century. Modern historians cannot agree on the dates for either Homer or Hesiod. See, for example, Richmond Lattimore, pp. 12-13 of the Introduction to his translation of Hesiod, as against H. G. Evelyn-White in the Introduction to his translation of Hesiod in the Loeb edition.

76. Hesiod: *Theogony*, 220-22. Loeb.

77. Hesiod: *Works and Days*, 252-55. Loeb.

78. Ibid., 222-24.

79. Ibid., 6.
80. Ibid., 276-80.
81. Ibid., 289-90.
82. Ibid., 303-4.
83. Ibid., 320.
84. Ibid., 382.
85. Ibid., 397-98.
86. Ibid., 11-26.
87. Hesiod: *Theogony*, 224-25. Loeb.
88. Ibid., 226-30.
89. Or some disciple who put the words of the poem in Hesiod's mouth.
90. Hesiod: *Theogony*, 22-34. Loeb.
91. The reader will note that I have nowhere explained or assumed that the Greek gods were figments of the Greek imagination. I have refrained from doing so, partly because so many modern historians have done it at length, and partly because none of them has offered evidence that the gods did not exist. We cannot here fall back on the statistical method, since we do not know whether the Greeks who reported seeing a god have been as yet outnumbered by moderns who have asserted there were no gods to see. In any case the gods were often clothed in mist. I have decided to report in this volume what the Greeks reported, and I still seek evidence that they lied or were mistaken.

CHAPTER THREE

92. *Homeric Hymns* III, To Delian Apollo, 147-55. Loeb. The hymn to the Delian Apollo was probably sung as early as the eighth century.
93. *Greek Elegy and Iambus* II, p. 101, Archilochus 6. Loeb. The Saians were a people of Thrace.
94. Ibid., II, p. 175, Archilochus 118. F. L. Lucas, in *Greek Poetry for Everyman*, Boston, 1956, p. 234, translates this epigram: "Many a trick the wise fox knows;/ But the hedgehog has one, worth a lot of those."
95. Alcaeus, Fragment 12, in C. M. Bowra: *Greek Lyric Poetry*, Oxford, 1936, p. 161.
96. Ibid., Alcaeus, Fragment 93, p. 151.
97. *Lyra Graeca* II, p. 181, Anacreon 84. Loeb.
98. Ibid., I, p. 187, Sappho 2.
99. Ibid., I, p. 263, Sappho 111.
100. *Greek Elegy and Iambus* I, p. 201, Xenophanes 11. Loeb.
101. Ibid., I, p. 211, Xenophanes 32.
102. Ibid., I, p. 201, Xenophanes 15.
103. Ibid., I, p. 203, Xenophanes 16.
104. Ibid., I, p. 207, Xenophanes 23.
105. Ibid., I, p. 67, Tyrtaeus 6.
106. Tradition could later point to similarities between the Cretan and Spartan constitutions as evidence that Lycurgus did go to Crete. See K. M. T. Chrimes: *Ancient Sparta*, Manchester, 1949.
107. Herodotus I, 65. Loeb.
108. Presumably. But modern historians know little of the Dorian invasion.
109. Otto Kern, ed.: *Orphicorum Fragmenta*, Berlin, 1922, p. 65.

110. This custom of Sparta's often stirs the incredulity of modern historians. Yet it is perfectly consonant with other Spartan customs that modern historians cheerfully accept.

111. Homer: *Iliad* VI, 208. Lang, Leaf, and Myers translation, New York (Modern Library), 1935.

112. *Greek Elegy and Iambus*, I, pp. 69, 71, Tyrtaeus 10, lines 1-2, 27-32. Loeb.

113. Xenophon: *Scripta Minora*, Constitution of the Lacedaemonians IV, 2. Loeb.

114. Xenophon: *Scripta Minora*, Constitution of the Lacedaemonians XI, 3, states that the color made the tunic bear "least resemblance to women's clothing." But Plutarch in his *Moralia* III, Ancient Customs of the Spartans, 238F, says it was the color that least showed blood.

115. This synoecism was traditionally ascribed to Theseus.

116. The areas are from A. Jardé: *The Formation of the Greek People*, New York, 1926, p. 145.

117. It has sometimes been suggested that it must have been the landlord, not the tenant, who received one-sixth, since no peasant could have lived on so small a portion of his crop. But would a landlord, in a country where arable land was as scarce as it was in Greece, give up five-sixths of a crop for the factor of labor alone? In Iran today a tenant may receive anywhere from one-tenth to nine-tenths, but this depends on the province the land is in, and even more on who provides the seed, the draft animals, the tools, the manure, the irrigation water; on how much labor the particular crop requires; and finally on how scarce farm labor is. See Ann K. S. Lambton: *Landlord and Peasant in Persia*, London, 1953.

118. *Greek Elegy and Iambus* I, p. 143, Solon 28a. Loeb.

119. Ibid., I, p. 121, Solon 4, line 33.

120. The term elegy was a purely metrical term.

121. *Greek Elegy and Iambus* I, p. 151, Solon 36, lines 10-12. Loeb.

122. Ibid., I, p. 151, Solon 36, line 16.

123. Ibid., I, pp. 149, 151, Solon 36, lines 3-7.

124. H. T. Wade-Gery: *Essays in Greek History*, Oxford, 1958, p. 13.

125. *Greek Elegy and Iambus* I, p. 105, quoting from Suidas' Lexicon, on Solon. Loeb. Author's translation of μηδὲν ἄγαν.

CHAPTER FOUR

126. Αἰσυμνήτης, judge, umpire—a not uncommon Greek device.

127. Known in modern histories of Greek art as the archaic smile.

128. The 6,000 may have represented the necessary quorum out of which a majority sufficed to ostracize. On this point authorities differ.

129. Herodotus I, 53. Loeb.

130. Ibid., I, 90.

131. Ibid., I, 91.

132. Glotz, in his *Histoire Grecque*, vol. II, p. 18, believes he got as far as the Volga.

133. Ibid., vol. II, pp. 19-20. But Hammond (A *History of Greece*, p. 178) thinks Ionia's grievances were less economic than political.

134. Herodotus VI, 44. Loeb.

135. Aeschylus: *Agamemnon*, 659-60. Grene-Lattimore. Of the Achaeans, wrecked when returning from triumph over Troy.

136. Glotz's estimate. *Histoire Grecque*, vol. II, p. 33.

137. Herodotus VI, 100. Loeb. Glotz (*Histoire Grecque*, vol. II, p. 34) says 2,000, but does not defend his correction of Herodotus.

138. Herodotus (VI, 106, Loeb) says "the day after he left Athens."

139. Herodotus (VI, 112, Loeb) says they "charged at a run [δρόμῳ ἵεντο]." Some modern historians object that the Greeks could not run a mile with weapons and armor weighing around sixty pounds and still have strength for a hand-to-hand combat. Also that the long run would disorder their line, a line they traditionally counted on presenting unbroken, shield to shield.

But the Greek line might have been even further disordered if it had advanced at a walk under a shower of Persian arrows, when the Greeks themselves were without archers. The Greek strategy was to close quickly with the Persians. As to the objection that they would arrive too exhausted for hand-to-hand combat, the assertion is risky in view of the hard exercise and frugal fare to which the Greeks were accustomed from childhood upward. But actually δρόμῳ is often translated from Greek military histories as "at the double," or at a dogtrot.

It has been objected that the range of Persian bowshot was far under a mile and that there was hence no point in running until the Greeks came within range. But there is strong reason to suppose that the Greeks had other motives for a quick advance than to diminish the period of time during which Persian weapons could kill Greeks but Greek weapons could not kill Persians. It was to the advantage of the Greeks to catch the Persians at the vulnerable moment of embarkation and to catch those who expected to march south by land when these were ready to march but had not had time to get clear. Once the Greeks were detected advancing, it was to their advantage on both these scores to strike quickly.

140. Later Greek historians differ widely on the number in the Persian camp. Glotz (*Histoire Grecque*, vol. II, pp. 37-8) holds that, fearing reinforcements from Sparta, the Persians had begun re-embarking in order to sail around Sunium and attack the city of Athens. He suggests that the Persian army which fought the Greeks outnumbered the Greeks by "at least two to one."

141. Pausanias: *Description of Greece* I, xxxii, 5. Loeb.

142. Glotz reasonably follows Diodorus Siculus on the question of an alliance (*Histoire Grecque*, vol. II, p. 45, note 13).

143. Or, more precisely, nearby Mycenae.

144. The metaphor is that of Aeschylus in the *Persians*, line 72. Grene-Lattimore.

145. Glotz's estimates (*Histoire Grecque*, vol. II, pp. 49-50). Hammond (*A History of Greece*, p. 228) estimates the number "in the region of 500,000." A few decades after the invasion, Herodotus believed that the combined land and sea forces of Xerxes, including the recruits he picked up in Europe, ran to 2,641,610. He guessed that this fighting force was supported by an equal number of service troops and he therefore brought the grand total by the date of Thermopylae to 5,283,220. To this grand total he added uncounted "cook-

ing women, and concubines, and eunuchs" (Herodotus VII, 185-87, Loeb).
Modern historians disagree widely on the size of Xerxes' forces. It is hard to
imagine supplying such forces as Herodotus calculates, given the means of
transport then available. For this and other reasons, recent historians at least
agree that he grossly exaggerated the size of the invading forces.

146. Herodotus VII, 101. Loeb.
147. Ibid., VII, 102.
148. Ibid., VII, 104.
149. Glotz: *Histoire Grecque*, vol. II, p. 57.
150. Glotz's estimate. Ibid., vol. II, p. 60.
151. Herodotus VII, 56, 203. Loeb.
152. Ibid., VII, 140.
153. Ibid., VII, 141.
154. Pindar: *Pythian Odes* VIII, 95-7. Loeb. Author's translation.
155. Aeschylus: *Agamemnon*, 653. Grene-Lattimore.
156. Aeschylus: *Persians*, 88. Grene-Lattimore.
157. Herodotus VII, 209. Loeb.
158. Epialtes. I have followed the spelling in both Greek text and English
translation of the Loeb Classics: Herodotus VII, 213, 214, 215, 218. Both
Hammond (*A History of Greece*) and Glotz (*Histoire Grecque*) spell the
name as Ephialtes.
159. *Lyra Graeca* II, p. 353, Simonides 118. Loeb.
160. Ibid., II, p. 353, Simonides 119, with author's substitution of "obedient" for "in obedience."
161. Herodotus VIII, 22. Loeb.
162. Herodotus (VIII, 37, 39, Loeb) reports that the rocks could still be
seen in his day. Ingenious moderns have avoided the miraculous by pointing
out that after the war, when the Delphic oracle was under criticism for medizing and serving Xerxes' cause, the Delphians were anxious to prove that they
had not been spared by Xerxes but saved by a god and that they invented the
story of the rocks. But the modern reader can accept the rocks without the
embarrassment of accepting divine intervention. The rocks could have fallen,
as countless similar rocks have fallen. Herodotus reports what witnesses inferred
was divine intervention. Hammond (*A History of Greece*, p. 237) guesses
that the Persian army had orders to spare the temple; reports that the rocks
fell; and implies that both the Greeks and Persians believed the gods had
intervened.
163. Aeschylus: *Prometheus Bound*, 993-94. Grene-Lattimore.
164. Herodotus VIII, 84. Loeb.
165. Aeschylus: *Persians*, 402-5. Loeb. Author's translation.
166. Ibid., 421-28. Grene-Lattimore.
167. Aeschylus: *Persians*, 275-77. Grene-Lattimore.
168. Glotz: *Histoire Grecque*, vol. II, p. 77. But J. A. R. Munro, in the
Cambridge Ancient History, vol. IV, p. 313, gives September 23.
169. Aeschylus: *Persians*, 238. Loeb.
170. Herodotus (VIII, 113, Loeb) says Mardonius got 300,000 men, a figure
scarcely acceptable if we take the estimate for the total army given by either
Glotz or Hammond. See note 145.

171. Herodotus VIII, 114. Loeb.

172. Ibid.

173. Known to modern historians as Alexander I. Alexander the Great (356-323) is known as Alexander III.

174. Herodotus VIII, 143. Modern Library, 1942.

175. Herodotus (IX, 32, Loeb) guesses that, in addition to his 300,000 picked Asian troops, including cavalry, Mardonius commanded around 50,000 Greek infantry, not to mention Greek cavalry. He estimates (IX, 28-30) that Pausanias commanded 110,000 infantry, of whom only 28,000 were heavy-armed, but his calculations present difficulties. In any case historians consider his estimates for both Mardonius's army and that of Pausanias far too high. I have followed for both armies the estimates of Glotz: *Histoire Grecque*, vol. II, p. 86.

176. Herodotus IX, 39, 49. Loeb.

177. Aeschylus: *Persians*, 816-18. Grene-Lattimore.

178. Ἑρμηχθονίῳ.

179. Plutarch: *Lives* II, Aristides xxi, 5. Loeb.

180. Luigi Pareti, in his *Studi Siciliani ed Italioti*, Florence, 1914, pp. 141, 161, estimates Hamilcar's forces at 35,000-40,000 infantry.

181. Herodotus IX, 98. Loeb. But I have followed George Rawlinson's (Modern Library, 1942) translation of σύνθημα as "watchword," and I have inserted a comma after "him that hears me not" to clarify the sentence.

182. Herodotus (IX, 100, Loeb) would seem to have used *phēmē* in its original and primary sense. His translators tend to prefer its secondary sense of a mere rumor, the kind all armies abound in, and the kind some commanders purposely start.

183. See Herodotus IX, 101. Loeb.

184. Aeschylus: *Persians*, 736. Grene-Lattimore.

CHAPTER FIVE

185. Plutarch: *Lives* II, Themistocles x, 6. Loeb.

186. Scholars have guessed that *barbaros* was an onomatopoetic word intended to describe a man who could not speak Greek and could only cry *bar-bar* and utter other unintelligible sounds.

187. Homer: *Iliad* XVIII, 309. Loeb. I have followed the rendering given in Simone Weil's article, "The Iliad, or the Poem of Force," *Politics*, November, 1945.

188. Herodotus VIII, 79. Loeb.

189. Plutarch: *Lives* II, Themistocles xix, 2. Loeb.

190. Ibid., Themistocles xix, 3-4.

191. Karl Müller, ed.: *Fragmenta Historicorum Graecorum*, Paris, 1848-74, vol. III, p. 15: Nymphidis Heracleotae.

192. Thucydides I, cxxxii, 2. Loeb.

193. Plutarch: *Lives* II, Cimon xvi, 8. Loeb.

194. Thucydides I, ci, 2. Loeb.

195. Plutarch: *Lives* III, Pericles ix, 4. Loeb.

196. Glotz: *Histoire Grecque*, vol. II, pp. 224-28. These figures are for 431 and are all highly conjectural. No really dependable figures are available.

197. Herodotus, I, 1. Loeb.

198. Of these only seven tragedies survive in more than fragmentary form.

199. It is the only complete trilogy that has been transmitted to modern times. The *Proteus* has not survived.

200. Athenaeus: *Deipnosophists* VIII, 347e. Loeb.

201. In Greek the Furies are *Erinyes* and the Gracious Goddesses are *Eumenides*.

202. See Roy C. Flickinger: *The Greek Theater and Its Drama*, Chicago, 1922, p. 272, for the somewhat conjectural details on how the judges for dramatic contests were elected.

203. Only seven of his tragedies and one satyr play are still extant.

204. Aristotle (*Athenian Constitution* XXIII, 4 – XXIV, 2, Loeb) cannot be adduced to prove that Aristides planned the Athenian Empire and would have agreed with Pericles.

205. Plutarch: *Lives* III, Pericles xxxi, 5. Loeb. Like Léon Homo (*Périclès*, Paris, 1954, p. 281), I have followed Plutarch. Some authorities claim Phidias was exiled.

206. Herodotus VII, 104. Loeb.

207. Plutarch: *Lives* III, Pericles, viii, 6. Loeb.

208. Thucydides II, xxxvii, 1-3. Loeb. Luckily, his words were recorded, conceivably verbatim, by an Athenian of genius, Thucydides—not that other Thucydides, Cimon's son-in-law, who had tried to carry on the conservative opposition to Pericles and who had been ostracized for his pains.

209. Ibid., II, xxxviii, 2.

210. Ibid., II, xxxix, 1.

211. Ibid., II, xl, 1-3.

212. Ibid., II, xli, 1.

213. Ibid., II, xlïv, 2.

214. Ibid., II, lx, 3-4.

215. Ibid., II, lxiii, 1-3.

216. Ibid., I, cxxii, 3.

CHAPTER SIX

217. The obvious solution, in the view of many modern historians, would have been some sort of common government, operated by elected representatives of all Hellas. Or, since this appeared impossible, the Athenian Empire could have been reorganized, the subjects of Athens could have been given the same rights as Athenians, and the Empire could have refrained from conquest and hoped that Hellenic states outside its borders would voluntarily choose to join it. Clisthenes, who restored and reformed the constitution of Solon, after the overthrow of the Pisistratid tyranny, had provided for a council whose members were elected by his new, artificial tribes. The Boeotian Confederacy, established in 447, was a federation of city-states with a kind of representative government. It was ruled by a common council if not by the Boeotarchs they chose. There were signs of federation in Thessaly. But, in general, these efforts toward federal union were made by oligarchs. The democrats showed a marked distrust for them and preferred primary assemblies, attended, at least in theory, by every free, adult, male citizen, regardless of

birth or wealth. See J. A. O. Larsen: *Representative Government in Greek and Roman History*, Berkeley, 1955.

218. Thucydides III, lxxxii, 2. Loeb.
219. Ibid., III, xxxvii, 3.
220. Ibid., III, xxxviii, 4.
221. Ibid., III, xl, 4.
222. Ibid., III, xliii, 3.
223. Ibid., III, xlvii, 1-4.
224. Ibid., III, lxxxi, 2-5.
225. Ibid., III, lxxxii, 1-2.
226. Ibid., III, lxxxii, 4.
227. Ibid., III, lxxxii, 8.
228. Ibid., III, lxxxiii, 1-4.
229. Ibid., III, lxxxiv, 2-3.
230. *Greek Elegy and Iambus* I, p. 67, Tyrtaeus 6. Loeb.
231. There are difficulties in Thucydides' assumption that both entrances were narrow. See George B. Grundy: "Investigation of the Topography of the Region of Sphacteria and Pylos," *Journal of Hellenic Studies*, vol. XVI, pp. 1-54.
232. Thucydides IV, xxxviii, 3. Loeb.
233. Herodotus VII, 104. Loeb.
234. Thucydides IV, xl, 2. Loeb.
235. Ibid., IV, xlvii, 3 – xlviii, 6.
236. Ibid., IV, lxxxvii, 2-6.
237. Plutarch: *Lives* III, Nicias ix, 7. Loeb.
238. Thucydides I, xxii, 4. Translated by Richard Crawley, Everyman's Library, 1910.
239. Cornford (F. M. Cornford: *Thucydides Mythistoricus*, London, 1907) suggests that Thucydides intended merely to report what was actually done and said, that he was unconsciously drawn into the pattern of Aeschylean tragedy, and that hence he was led to seek cause in personal motive rather than in economic conditions, for example. But though Cornford's study of Thucydides is most illuminating, I dissent from his analysis on two counts. First, I see no evidence for the statement that Thucydides' acceptance of the tragic pattern was unconscious. The author of a Greek tragedy was imitating life—not just any human life, it is true, but the life of a certain kind of person. Thucydides could have readily guessed, when the war began, that Athens was about to achieve tragedy and that for this reason coming events would be significant, hence worth recounting. Secondly, although the myth of economic determinism was not the myth he used, he was acutely aware of material causes. I invite the reader to read Thucydides with pencil in hand and to mark every passage with economic implications: if he does, he will badly deface his text. But where we moderns often make economic and sociological abstractions the only real agents in history, Thucydides focused mainly on human agents. See Cornford, especially chaps. 5 and 8.
240. Thucydides I, xxii, 1. Loeb.
241. Only eighteen of his tragedies and one satyr play survive.
242. Euripides: *Trojan Women*, 1156-1206. Grene-Lattimore.

243. The famous device of the *deus ex machina*, which some critics accused Euripides of overworking, as his only remaining means of saving himself from a poor plot.

244. Euripides: *Heracles*, 1263-65. Grene-Lattimore.

245. Ibid., 1341-46.

246. *The Banqueters*. Not extant. Aristophanes composed some forty comedies, of which eleven have survived.

247. No play by Eupolis or Cratinus is extant.

248. Unfortunately, most translators have not dared to translate Aristophanes without shamefully whitewashing the text. An honorable exception may be found in *The Complete Greek Drama*, two volumes edited by Whitney J. Oates and Eugene O'Neill, Jr. It is interesting that in this edition, except for the *Frogs*, an almost decorous play translated by Gilbert Murray, the extant comedies of Aristophanes have been most joyously rendered, and signed— "Translator Anonymous."

249. Aristophanes presumably knew about Thalia, since presumably he knew his Hesiod. But it was not until late Roman times, nearly a millennium after Aristophanes' death, that men discovered which Muse inspired comedy.

250. Aristophanes: *Peace*, 174-76. Oates-O'Neill.

251. Ibid., 211-19.

252. Ibid., 270.

253. Ibid., 819-23.

254. Thucydides V, lxxxix. Loeb.

255. Ibid., V, xc-cv, 3.

256. Hesiod: *Works and Days*, 276-80. Loeb.

257. *Lyra Graeca* III, p. 241, Euripides 1. Loeb. Fourth in the chariot race, not third, according to Alcibiades himself in Thucydides VI, xvi, 2. Loeb.

258. Aristophanes: *Frogs*, 1425. Oates-O'Neill.

259. Ibid., 1431-32.

260. Thucydides VI, viii, 2. Loeb.

261. Ibid., VI, xii, 2 – xiii.

262. Ibid., VI, xvi, 1-3.

263. Ibid., VI, xvi, 6 – xvii, 1.

264. Ibid., VI, xviii, 3, 4, 7.

265. Ibid., VI, xxx, 1 – xxxii, 2.

266. Ibid., VI, xc, 2-4.

267. Ibid., VI, xcii, 1-5.

268. Ibid., VII, lxxv, 1-7.

269. Ibid., VII, lxxxiv, 3-5.

270. Ibid., VII, lxxxvi, 5.

271. Ibid., V, cv, 2.

272. Ibid., VII, lxxxvii, 5-6.

273. Ibid., VIII, xlvii, 2.

274. Ibid., VIII, lxxxi, 3.

275. Xenophon: *Hellenica* I, i, 23-4. Loeb.

276. Ibid., I, iv, 20. As *hegemon autokrator*.

277. Ibid., II, ii, 3-4.

278. Ibid., II, ii, 21-3.

279. The various stories here given are all to be found in Plutarch: *Lives* IV, Alcibiades xxxvii, 4, xxxviii, and xxxix. Loeb.

280. Euripides: *Medea*, 828-30. Author's translation.

CHAPTER SEVEN

281. *Lyra Graeca* II, p. 336, Simonides 95. Loeb. Author's translation.

282. Plato: *Apology*, 21B. Jowett.

283. Ibid., 21C.

284. Ibid.

285. Ibid., 21D.

286. Ibid., 22A.

287. Ibid., 22B.

288. When the definite article preceding *elenchos* is neuter, the word means disgrace; when the article is masculine, the word means refutation.

289. Plato: *Apology*, 23B. Jowett.

290. Xenophon: *Memorabilia* I, vi, 2. Loeb.

291. Ibid., I, vi, 10.

292. Ibid., I, ii, 36.

293. Plato: *Charmides*, 166D. Jowett.

294. Plato: *Gorgias*, 509A. Jowett.

295. This was the reason Socrates himself gave. But there is irony in his word teach. In Socrates' view, dialectic was a far more powerful device for teaching than any lecture could be, provided that teach meant to help another human mind awaken, move, and work, and did not mean merely to transmit information or unproven opinion. But Socrates may also have feared that taking fees would corrupt the teaching function by substituting profit for truth as the teacher's goal.

The great British historian, George Grote (*History of Greece*, vol. VIII, p. 491), defends the sophists against the imputations in Plato's dialogues that they were intellectually corrupt. Grote discards the word sophist because of its invidious post-Platonic meanings and suggests that they be called "Professors or Public Teachers." Whether likening them to professors would clear sophists of intellectual corruption in Socrates' eyes would be a question worth exploring.

296. Plato: *Meno*, 86B-C. Jowett.

297. Ibid., 98B.

298. Plato: *Theaetetus*, 148-151E. Jowett. Although this conversation occurs in one of Plato's later dialogues, which are assumed to reflect his own thought far more than the thought of Socrates, it is thoroughly in character. Socrates' view of himself as an intellectual midwife was common knowledge.

299. Plato: *Protagoras*, 314E-315B. Jowett.

300. The scene gives a richer meaning to the phrase many teachers use: "Do you follow me?" Perhaps Socrates has such peripatetic questions in mind when, in Plato's *Cratylus*, he teases Cratylus and Hermogenes with his rapid-fire parody of the etymologists' speculations: "Pray observe how I gallop when I get on smooth ground." And "if I am not careful, before tomorrow's dawn I shall be wiser than I ought to be." (414B, 399A, Jowett.)

301. Plato: *Protagoras*, 329A-B. Jowett.

302. Ibid., 334C-335C.

303. Ibid., 338C-E.
304. Ibid., 347B-349A.
305. Ibid., 361D-362A.
306. Since Socrates' goal was the direct encounter of two minds, amicably wrestling together to find more truth, courtesy was the most probable means within his power of helping his opponent shift from the blindness and willfulness of self-interested eristic to the possible insights of disinterested dialectic. Socratic courtesy reminds one of Jesus of Nazareth's admonition that, when one man strikes another, the victim should offer him the other cheek to strike, thereby supplying the necessary condition for a direct encounter of two souls in mutual love, where striking back would supply the condition for the collison of two bodies in mutual hate. Mohandas K. Gandhi understood the admonition of Jesus, an admonition extremely unpopular in Western Christendom. Gandhi therefore advised that, in facing an opponent, one should always ascribe to him the highest motives capable of explaining his actions. He perhaps noted the tendency of Christians, with the aid of not too profound Marxians and Freudians, always to ascribe the lowest motives capable of explaining the actions of one's opponent. Obviously this formula offers great advantages to the self-righteous and saves energy. Similarly, it takes less energy in an argument to denounce an opponent for talking nonsense than to assume that what he says is true and to get his further help in understanding it. But the more courteous, and unusual, procedure at least permits the direct encounter of minds. Unfortunately, this sort of intellectual courtesy requires close listening. This requirement Socrates had learned to meet.
307. Aristophanes: *Clouds*, 228-34. Oates-O'Neill.
308. Ibid., 94.
309. Ibid., 365.
310. Ibid., 1476-77.
311. Ibid., 1506-9.
312. See A. E. Taylor: *Socrates*, London, 1953, pp. 55-93, for this deduction. When I first read this book, I rejected Taylor's inference, much as I had always admired his scholarship. On longer reflection, I was driven to accept his reconstruction of the events of Socrates' youth as highly probable.
313. A party portrayed in Plato's *Symposium*. Plato himself was not present. In that year, 415, he was only twelve or thirteen. Plato has Apollodorus recount to a companion the events and especially the conversation that occurred at the banquet. He in turn got the story from Aristodemus, and years later he got confirmation of some parts of it from Socrates himself. The speeches in the *Symposium* are therefore as unauthentic as some of those in Thucydides and should not be used as courtroom transcripts. Whether they represent essentially what was said poses a subtler problem.
314. Plato: *Symposium*, 202E. Jowett.
315. Ibid., 212D-213A.
316. Ibid., 214A.
317. Ibid., 214E-217A.
318. Ibid., 219E-222A.
319. Ibid., 223C-D.
320. Freeman: *Ancilla to the Pre-Socratic Philosophers*, Heracleitus 89.

321. *Lyra Graeca* II, p. 336, Simonides 95. Loeb. Author's translation.

322. A. E. Taylor, in his *Plato: The Man and His Work*, New York, 1936, pp. 263-64, guesses that the conversation Plato imagined as the *Republic* should be placed about 421. Paul Shorey, in the Introduction to his translation of the *Republic* in the Loeb edition, estimates that Plato wrote it between 380 and 370. Plato does not claim that he himself was present at the conversation the *Republic* purportedly records. The *Republic* comes no closer to history, therefore, than the *Symposium*, Plato's version of Socrates' account, rendered several decades earlier, of a long and intricate discussion that had occurred the night before. The *Apology*, on the other hand, purports to give Socrates' personal defense in a court of law, a defense which he and hundreds of persons, many of whom would still be alive when Plato wrote, had personally heard Socrates deliver. Thucydides, the historian, did indeed report both those speeches which he had heard and other speeches admittedly composed to fit a given occasion. But in the case of either category, Thucydides' basic purpose was the historian's purpose of recording as accurately as he could what some speaker had actually said. The basic purpose of Plato's dialogues, on the other hand, was to present philosophic dialectic of the sort his beloved Socrates engaged in. Viewed as historical document, the conversation presented in the *Republic* is therefore more like one of Sophocles' tragedies or Aristophanes' comedies than like any speech quoted by Thucydides, since at any given moment a speech in the dialogues may have even more bearing on Plato's thinking in the fourth century than on Socrates' thinking in the fifth. If a tape-recorder could have been used in Cephalus's home in Piraeus to record the conversation that took place there, the result would have been more factual, as we say nowadays, than Plato's recreation of such a conversation in his book the *Republic*. Whether it would have been a more truthful account would depend on the use to which a given historian put it. For the purposes of the present volume, it is perhaps no loss if Plato's mind is allowed to participate in the dialectic. 'The Platonic Socrates,' especially of the earlier dialogues, may be the most real, the most historical Socrates. We know Socrates by what his mind provoked Plato to write, not by what his voice might have caused a tape-recorder to record, if Hellas had produced tape-recorders instead of producing Plato.

323. Plato: *Republic* I, 336B-338D. Jowett.

324. Ibid., I, 341A-C.

325. Ibid., I, 342D-343C.

326. Ibid., I, 344C-345C.

327. Ibid., I, 350C-E.

328. Ibid., I, 354A-C.

329. Ibid., II, 369D.

330. Ibid., II, 372D-373E.

331. Does the "unlimited accumulation of wealth" fairly translate the contemporary American's 'ever rising standard of living'? Or does the American phrase intend that only the standard of the needy shall rise?

332. Aeschylus: *Eumenides*, 19. Grene-Lattimore.

333. Plato: *Republic* VI, 511B-C. Jowett.

334. Ibid., VII, 514A-519D.

335. Ibid., IV, 422E-423A.
336. Ibid., VIII, 562E-563E. Socrates was not concerned to offer a cyclic theory of history according to which every society followed the evolution: aristocracy to oligarchy to democracy to tyranny; or, otherwise stated, rule by the wise to rule by the brave to rule by the rich to rule by those who prize liberty and pleasure to rule by a tyrant. He and Glaucon both must have known that in historical fact the usual function of the Hellenic tyrant, whether Pisistratus of Athens or another, was to effect by force the transition from a timocracy of nobles turning into an oligarchy of the rich to an oligarchy tempered with democracy.
337. Ibid., IX, 591E-592B.
338. Ibid., VI, 499D, 502C.
339. Xenophon: *Hellenica* II, iii, 13. Loeb.
340. Ibid., II, iii, 56. Author's translation of τῷ καλῷ.
341. Ibid.
342. Ibid., II, iv, 20-22.
343. Scholiast Aeschines I, 39, 5. Edited by Wilhelm Dindorf, Oxon., 1852. μνῆμα τόδ᾽ ἐστ᾽ ἀνδρῶν ἀγαθῶν, οἳ κατάρατον δῆμον᾽ Ἀθηναιών ὀλίγον χρόνον ὕβριος ἔσχον. Author's translation.
344. Xenophon: *Hellenica* II, iv, 40-2. Loeb.
345. Xenophon: *Apology*, 29. Loeb.
346. Or the poet's son. There is some doubt as to which.
347. Plato: *Apology*, 23E. Jowett.
348. Xenophon: *Memorabilia* I, i, 1. Loeb.
349. Plato: *Apology* 30A-C. Jowett.
350. Ibid., 30D-31A.
351. Ibid., 34E.
352. Ibid., 35C.
353. Ibid., 35D.
354. Ibid., 36B-D.
355. Ibid., 38A.
356. Ibid., 38B-C.
357. Ibid., 39A-B.
358. Ibid., 40A.
359. Ibid., 41C-42.
360. Plato: *Phaedo*, 114D-118. Jowett.

CHAPTER EIGHT

361. Xenophon: *Anabasis* I, i, 11. Rouse.
362. Ibid., III, i, 4-7.
363. Ibid., III, i, 10.
364. Modern historians commonly reject Xenophon's figures in *Anabasis* I, vii, 10-11. We have no other, more trustworthy source. See Glotz: *Histoire Grecque*, vol. III, pp. 37-9.
365. Xenophon: *Anabasis* III, i, 3. Rouse.
366. Ibid., III, i, 4. Loeb.
367. Ibid., III, i, 11-13. Rouse.
368. Ibid., III, i, 23-5.

369. Ibid., III, ii, 7.
370. Ibid., III, ii, 9.
371. Ibid., III, ii, 25-7.
372. Ibid., III, ii, 32.
373. Ibid., IV, v, 12-14.
374. Ibid., IV, v, 26-7.
375. Ibid., IV, v, 31-2.
376. Ibid., IV, vii, 21-6.
377. Ibid., IV, viii, 14.
378. Ibid., IV, viii, 16.
379. Translation disputed.
380. Xenophon: *Anabasis* IV, viii, 25-8. Rouse.
381. Ibid., V, i, 2-4.
382. Ibid., V, iv, 32-4.
383. Ibid., V, vi, 15-6.
384. Ibid., VI, iv, 3-8.
385. Ibid., VII, i, 33-7.
386. The exile is certain. The date is not. Neither is the charge. I have followed Edouard Delebecque: *Essai sur la vie de Xénophon*, Paris, 1957, on both points, and on much else. Many of the dates of Xenophon's life and some of the events as well are only informed guesses.
387. Aristophanes: *Plutus*, 181-85. Loeb. Author's translation.
388. Xenophon: *Hellenica* V, i, 31. Loeb. The King's announcement is called by modern historians either The King's Peace or the Peace of Antalcidas, Antalcidas being the Spartan general who negotiated the settlement.
389. Plutarch: *Lives* VII, Artaxerxes xxii, 2. Loeb.
390. Edouard Delebecque, in his *Essai sur la vie de Xénophon*, Paris, 1957, pp. 507-9, has made informed guesses at the dates of Xenophon's works. Though not citing those precise dates, I have followed his sequence.
391. Aristotle: *Politics* V, vii, 19. Loeb.
392. See Pierre Lavedan: *Dictionnaire illustré de la mythologie et des antiquités Grecques et Romaines*, 3d ed., Paris, 1954, article on "Exposition des enfants," p. 411.
393. Aristotle: *Politics* II, vi, 11. Loeb.
394. Demosthenes: *Private Orations*, Against Aphobus I, 9. Loeb.
395. H. W. Parke: *Greek Mercenary Soldiers*, Oxford, 1933, pp. 20-1.
396. Historians of art have sometimes written as if the earlier sculptors lacked the eye to see these differences or perhaps the skill to render them. Does it require more credulity to believe that the differences simply did not interest them?
397. In July, 356, according to Glotz: *Histoire Grecque*, vol. III, pp. 232-33. D. G. Hogarth, in *Philip and Alexander of Macedon*, New York, 1897, places the birth of Alexander in October.
398. Plutarch: Apothegms . . . of Kings and Great Commanders, Philip. In *Plutarch's Complete Works*, Thomas Crowell & Co., New York, 1909, vol. I, p. 26.
399. Diodorus Siculus XVI, 35, 1. Loeb.
400. Xenophon: *Scripta Minora*, The Cavalry Commander IX, 8-9. Loeb.

401. Demosthenes: *Philippics* I, 10-12. Loeb.
402. Demosthenes: *De Corona*, 235-37. Loeb.
403. Demosthenes: *Philippics* I, 12. Loeb.
404. Not, at least, in any of his surviving orations. This evidence is admittedly negative.
405. See Plato: *Gorgias*, especially line 465.
406. Plutarch: *Lives* VIII, Phocion v, 4. Loeb.
407. Isocrates: *Antidosis*, 253-57. Loeb.
408. Ibid., 302.
409. Ibid., 305.
410. Ibid., 308. Author's translation.
411. Isocrates: *Panegyricus*, 50. Loeb.
412. Isocrates: *Address to Philip*, 15-6. Loeb.
413. Ibid., 120-21.
414. Ibid., 149.
415. Ibid., 154.
416. The numbers are uncertain. I have followed Glotz: *Histoire Grecque*, vol. III, p. 359.
417. Plutarch: *Lives* VII, Demosthenes xx, 3. Loeb. Transliterated from the Greek: "*Dēmosthénēs/ Dēmosthénous/ Paianieùs/ tád' eîpen.*"
418. Homer: *Iliad* XVIII, 309. Loeb. I have followed the rendering given in Simone Weil's article, "The Iliad, or the Poem of Force," *Politics*, November, 1945.
419. Isocrates: *Letter to Philip* II, 2-3. Loeb.
420. Pausanias: *Description of Greece* VIII, vii, 6. Loeb.
421. Diodorus Siculus XVI, 92. Translated by G. Booth, London, 1814.

CHAPTER NINE

422. Plato: *Epistle* VII, 324E. Loeb.
423. Diodorus Siculus, Fragment 222, in H. W. Parke: *The Delphic Oracle*, 2 vols., Oxford, 1956, vol. II.
424. Plato: *Epistle* VII, 326A-B. Loeb.
425. Freeman: *Ancilla to the Pre-Socratic Philosophers*, Democritus 117.
426. Ibid., Democritus 247.
427. Ibid., Democritus 267.
428. Ibid., Metrodorus 2.
429. Ibid., Metrodorus 1.
430. Ibid., Critias 25.
431. Ibid., Antiphon 44.
432. Plato: *Republic* VI, 499B-C. Jowett.
433. Plato: *Epistle* VII, 328A. Loeb.
434. Ibid., 328C.
435. Ibid., 329B. Zeus Xenios was Zeus considered as the god of hospitality, who would govern Plato's relations with Dion and other hosts of his at Syracuse.
436. Plutarch: *Lives* VI, Dion ix, 5. Loeb.
437. I have followed A. E. Taylor's conjectural dating of the various

dialogues. See his *Plato: The Man and His Work*, New York, 1936, especially p. 21.

438. Pindar: *Pythian Odes* VIII, 94-8. Loeb. Author's translation.

439. Plato: *Epistle* VII, 341C-D. Loeb.

440. Plato: *Timaeus*, 41C. Jowett.

441. Ibid., 44C.

442. Those readers who are disturbed by Plato's image of the universe as "a living creature truly endowed with soul and intelligence" might be interested by a hauntingly similar account by a distinguished twentieth-century scientist, Pierre Teilhard de Chardin: *The Phenomenon of Man*, Introduction by Sir Julian Huxley, New York, 1960. The Platonic creation myth in the *Timaeus* should be much more intelligible to a modern scientist than to scientists of a century ago.

443. Plato: *Timaeus*, 75E. Jowett.

444. Plato: *Epistle* VIII, 352E-353A. Loeb.

445. Plato: *Timaeus*, 92C. Jowett.

446. *Lyra Graeca* I, p. 115, Alcman 124. Loeb.

447. Plato: *Timaeus*, 41E-42A. Jowett.

448. Freeman: *Ancilla to the Pre-Socratic Philosophers*, Alcmaeon of Crotona 2.

449. Plato: *Laws* I, 641E. Jowett.

450. Ibid., IV, 716C.

451. Ibid., IV, 714A.

452. *Greek Anthology* II, Bk. VII, 256. Loeb. Of the people of Eretria, whom Darius I had deported to the high plateau of Media, beyond even the furthest eastward march of Xenophon and his retreating polis of Greek mercenaries.

453. Ibid., II, Bk. VII, 265.

454. Ibid., I, Bk. V, 79.

455. Ibid., II, Bk. VII, 669.

456. Ibid., III, Bk. IX, 506.

457. Hesiod: *Theogony*, 27. Loeb.

458. Plato: *Epistle* VII, 326B-C. Loeb.

459. *Greek Elegy and Iambus* I, p. 143, Solon 28a. Loeb.

460. Plato: *Laws* IV, 718B. Jowett.

461. A. E. Taylor: *Plato: The Man and His Work*, New York, 1936, p. 437.

462. Plato: *Epistle* VIII, 354C. Loeb.

463. Aeschylus: *Prometheus Bound*, 50. Loeb. Author's translation.

464. Plato: *Epistle* VIII, 354E-355A. Loeb.

465. Plutarch: *Lives* II, Aristides xxi, 5. Loeb.

466. Plato: *Laws* I, 641C. Jowett.

467. Xenophon: *Hellenica* II, ii, 23. Loeb.

468. *Lyra Graeca* II, p. 336, Simonides 95. Loeb.

469. Diogenes Laertius: *Lives* III, Plato, 5-6. Loeb.

470. Plato: *Laws* VII, 816D-E. Jowett.

471. Ibid., VII, 817B.

472. *Greek Elegy and Iambus* II, p. 11, Plato 18. Loeb.

473. Diogenes Laertius: *Lives* III, Plato, 5. Loeb.
474. Ibid., Plato, 8.
475. Aeschylus: *Agamemnon,* 1426. Grene-Lattimore.
476. Plutarch: *Lives* IX, Caius Marius xlvi, 1-2. Loeb.
477. The discussion of Aristotle's works which follows is necessarily based on what survives. But what survives appears to be sometimes lectures strung together by later editors and sometimes not much more than notes for the lecturer—though hardly, as some have asserted, merely notes by pupils who had heard lectures. Aristotle was said to have published some finished literary productions, but these are not extant. His case is precisely the opposite of Plato's. In Plato's case the lecture notes, if he spoke from notes, perished; and the finished literary productions, the Dialogues, survived.
478. Aristotle: *Metaphysics* I, i, 1. Loeb. Author's translation.
479. Aristotle's *First Philosophy* acquired the name of the *Metaphysics* through an editorial accident. Some three centuries after his death, a scholar who listed his numerous works placed his *First Philosophy* after (*meta*) his *Physics*.
480. Aristotle: *Politics* I, i, 9. Loeb.
481. Pindar: *Isthmian Odes* V, 14-20. Loeb.
482. Pindar: *Pythian Odes* III, 109-10. Loeb. Author's translation. The Greek word is *athanaton*—immortal life.
483. Aristotle: *Nicomachaean Ethics* X, vii, 8. Loeb.
484. Aristotle: *Politics* III, iv, 7. Loeb.
485. Compare for example his grave refutation, in *Politics* II, i-ii, of Socrates' gay and witty assaults on private property (Plato: *Republic* V).
486. Aristotle: *Politics* VII, vi, 1. Loeb.
487. Ibid., I, ii, 3.
488. Ibid., I, ii, 4-5.
489. Ibid., I, ii, 7-8.
490. Ibid., I, ii, 12.
491. Ibid.
492. Ibid., I, ii, 13-15.
493. Diogenes Laertius: *Lives* V, Aristotle, 19. Loeb.
494. Freeman: *Ancilla to the Pre-Socratic Philosophers,* Heracleitus 89.
495. Aristotle: *Politics* I, iii, 9. Loeb.
496. Aristotle: *Nicomachaean Ethics* VIII, xiv, 3. Loeb.
497. Aristotle: *Politics* I, iii, 23. Loeb. The Greek word for offspring, interest, is *tokos.*
498. Ibid., I, iv, 6.
499. Ibid., I, iv, 5-6.
500. Ibid., VII, vi, 1.
501. Aristotle: *Poetics* VI, 2-3. Loeb.
502. Plato: *Republic* II, 372D. Jowett.
503. Plato: *Republic* II, 372E. Loeb: *phlegmainousan.*
504. Aristotle: *Poetics* IX, 3. Loeb.
505. Ammonius Hermeiou: *Vita Aristoteles,* Leiden, 1621, 68: Literally, "*Non concedam Atheniensibus bis peccare in Philosophiam.*"

CHAPTER TEN

506. Plutarch: *Lives* VII, Alexander viii, 3. Loeb.

507. Demosthenes' actual words (Plutarch: *Lives* VII, Demosthenes xxiii, 2, Loeb) are *pais* and *Margites*.

508. Aristotle: *Metaphysics* I, i, 1. Loeb.

509. Arrian I, 16, 6. Loeb.

510. Ibid., I, 16, 7.

511. Ibid., II, 4, 9.

512. W. W. Tarn (*Alexander the Great*, 2 vols., Cambridge, 1948, vol. I, p. 26) estimates Alexander's army at 25,000-29,000, but modern estimates of both armies differ widely.

513. Arrian II, 14, 3. Loeb.

514. Ibid., II, 14, 4-9.

515. Ibid., II, 12, 6-7.

516. Ibid., II, 17.

517. Plutarch: *Lives* VII, Alexander xxix, 4. Loeb.

518. Pindar: *Pythian Odes* IV, 15. Loeb.

519. Herodotus II, 42. Loeb.

520. Ibid., IV, 181. Amon-Re, great god of Thebes in Egypt, was called Ammon at his desert shrine.

521. Thus Callisthenes, Aristotle's nephew and the official historian of Alexander's expeditionary force. Callisthenes may have been present when the priest of Ammon greeted Alexander. In any case he later wrote that the priest called Alexander son of Zeus. On this whole matter, see W. W. Tarn: *Alexander the Great*, 2 vols., Cambridge, 1948, vol. II, Appendix 22.

522. Plutarch: *Lives* VII, Alexander xxvii, 5. Loeb.

523. Pseudo-Callisthenes: *The Life of Alexander of Macedon*. Translated and edited by E. H. Haight, New York, 1955, I, 35, 5.

524. Plutarch: *Lives* VII, Alexander xxvii, 5. Loeb.

525. Ibid., Alexander xxvii, 6.

526. Ibid.

527. Ibid., Alexander ix, 4.

528. Ibid., Alexander ix, 5.

529. Ibid., Alexander xxvii, 3-4.

530. Ibid., Alexander xxviii, 2. Also Homer: *Iliad* V, 340. Loeb.

531. Plutarch: *Lives* VII, Alexander xxii, 3. Loeb.

532. Hammond (*A History of Greece*, p. 615) says "perhaps 6,000."

533. Herodotus I, 98. Loeb.

534. Aristotle: *Politics* VII, xiii, 8. Loeb.

535. Ibid., VII, xiii, 14.

536. Arrian III, 27, 5. Loeb.

537. Ibid., III, 30, 4.

538. Plutarch: *Lives* VII, Alexander li, 2. Loeb.

539. Arrian IV, 8, 7. Loeb.

540. Ibid., IV, 8, 9.

541. Ibid., IV, 10, 2.

542. Ibid., IV, 11, 6-9.

543. These statements are based on purely negative evidence.

544. Herodotus IV, 44. Loeb.
545. Arrian V, 19, 2. Loeb.
546. Ibid., V, 25, 3.
547. Ibid., V, 26, 4.
548. Ibid., V, 26, 7-8.
549. Ibid., V, 27, 2.
550. Ibid., V, 27, 7.
551. Ibid., VI, 29, 8.
552. Ibid., VII, 1, 6.
553. Arrian gives her name as Barsine. Other historians called her Stateira and claimed that a Barsine had been Alexander's mistress since early in his Asian campaign.
554. C. Aelianus: *Varia Historia*, Leipzig, 1780, II, 19.
555. *Minor Attic Orators* II, Hyperides: Against Demosthenes, Fragment vii, col. 31. Loeb.
556. Flavius Arrianus, who quotes this speech, wrote his account of Alexander's conquests some five centuries after they occurred. His chief sources were Ptolemy, one of Alexander's generals, and Aristobulus, a Greek technician, both of whom served in Alexander's army and both of whom left histories of the campaign. Arrian does not specify his source for this speech and we have no guarantee that his version is verbatim. Neither are we in a position to impugn Arrian's version.
557. Arrian VII, 9-10. Loeb.
558. Ibid., VII, 11, 6.
559. Ibid., VII, 11, 7.
560. Plutarch: *Moralia* IV, On the Fortune of Alexander, 329C. Loeb.
561. Ibid., On the Fortune of Alexander, 329C-D.
562. Thucydides II, xliii, 3. Translated by Richard Crawley, Everyman's Library, 1910.
563. The Heraclitus fragment (89) follows: ὁ Ἡ. φησί τοῖς ἐγρηγορόσιν ἕνα καὶ κοινὸν κόσμον εἶναι, τῶν δὲ κοιμωμένων ἕκαστον εἰς ἴδιον ἀποστρέφεσθαι. Diels: *Die Fragmente der Vorsokratiker*. Translated in Freeman: *Ancilla to the Pre-Socratic Philosophers*.
564. Arrian VII, 26, 3. Loeb. Author's translation.

INDEX

Abdera, 82
Abydos, 92, 120
Academy, Plato's, 340, 342, 358-64, 366, 372, 374-76, 378
Acanthus, 86, 186
Acarnanians, 178
Achaea, 107
Achaeans, 4-19, 32-34, 49, 61, 124, 327, 347, 397
Acharnae, 159
Achilles, 4-10, 16-19, 22, 24-25, 34, 44, 59, 61, 64, 70, 100, 134, 143, 192, 332, 390, 393, 397, 405, 410, 417-19, 426, 437-39
Acropolis, 33, 66, 72, 74, 91, 99, 107, 109, 131, 146-47, 149-50, 155, 164-65, 227
Acte, 86, 93
Ada, 398
Aegae, 327, 351
Aegaleos, 109
Aegean Islands, 87, 96, 118
Aegean Sea, 5, 12, 30-32, 131, 133
Aegina, 14, 65, 79, 97-98, 107-9, 111, 114, 117, 121, 137, 140, 143
Aeginetans, 107-9, 185
Aegospotami, 122
    battle of, 227-28
Aeolians, 49, 51-52, 82
Aeolis, 49
Aeschines, 346
Aeschylus, 5, 90, 190-92, 194-95, 323-24, 439
    Agamemnon, 149-50, 339, 374
    Eumenides, 149-51
    Libation Bearers, 149-50
    Oresteia, 149-52, 158, 168, 236, 344

Aeschylus (continued)
    Persians, 109-10, 115, 134, 149
    Prometheus Bound, 371
    Proteus, 149
    translations, 455
Aetolians, 178, 180, 182
Afghanistan, 82, 409, 413
Africa, North, 36, 37
Agamemnon, 5-7, 9-10, 16, 19, 26, 34, 149, 151, 190, 348
Agariste, 121
Agathon, 253-54, 259, 327
Agesilaus, 314-16, 318-19, 326
Agis, 214, 221-22, 224-25, 226, 228-29, 408
Agrianians, 395
Ajax and Teucer, 108
Alalia, 82
Albania, 38
Alcaeus, poet, 51-52
    quoted, 51
Alcander, 58
Alcibiades, 157, 199-201, 205-14, 221-32, 248-49, 251, 253-59, 273, 284-85, 288, 320, 352-53
    on Socrates, 255-58
    speech on Sicilian expedition, 206-8
    speech to Spartans, 212-13
Alcmaeon of Crotona, quoted, 364
Alcman, poet, 59
    quoted, 364
Alcmeonids, 66, 77, 130, 199
Aleuadae, 92, 98
Alexander (Paris), 5-6, 55
Alexander I, 112, 134, 327-28
Alexander III, the Great, 333, 347-48, 351, 375, 393-442, 464

479

Alexander III, the Great (*continued*)
  deification of, 351, 405-7, 418-20,
    432-33
  empire, 409
  speech at the Beas, 424-25
  speech at Opis, 433-36
Alexandria (Anamis), 429
Alexandria (Bactria), 415
Alexandria (Egypt), 404
Alexandria (Farthest), 416
Alexandria (Herat), 413
Alexandria (Phrada), 414
Alexandria (Tigris), 438
Alexandria Bucephala, 424
Alexandria Nicaea, 424
Alexandropolis, 394
Alphabet, 30
Amazons, battle of, 158
Amber, 30, 356
Ambracia, 114, 349
Ambraciots, 180
Amisus, 143
Ammon, 404-7, 417, 419, 476
Amon-Re, 476
Amphictyonic League, 105, 333, 335,
    346-47
Amphictyonic War, 333-36
Amphimedon, 19
Amphipolis, 186-90, 198, 328, 330-31,
    375, 424
  battle of, 234
Amphissa, 347
Amyclae, 31
Amyntas III, 328, 375
Anabasis, Xenophon's, 299-312, 317
Anacreon, poet, 52, 75
Anactorium, 114
Anamis River, 429
Anaxagoras, 155, 157
Anaxarchus, 419-20
Anaxibius, 308, 310-11
Anaximander, 53
Anaximenes, 53, 251
Anchor, 31
Ancona, 356
Ancyra, 399
Andros, 143, 226, 375
Antalcidas, Peace of, 472
Antimoerus, 245
Antiochus, captain, 226
Antipater, 348, 391, 408-10, 422, 432,
    438
Antiphon, sophist, 356, 367
  quoted, 355

Anytus, 287-89
Aornus, 423, 425
Apelles, painter, 405
Aphrodite, 52-53, 325
Apis, 404
Apollo, 16, 56-57, 80-81, 87, 91, 98-99,
    100-101, 104, 106-7, 110-11, 116,
    119, 129, 150, 154, 175, 236, 241,
    259, 270, 300, 309, 331, 333-36,
    339, 346-47, 365
Apollo Lyceius, 376
Apollodorus, 292, 296
Arabia, 438, 440-41
Arabians, 82, 95-96, 404
Arachosia, 415
Aral Sea, 416
Arbela, battle of, 407-8
Arcadia, 132, 189
Arcadians, 303
Archelaus, 192, 282, 327-28
Archidamus, 343
Archilochus, poet, 51
  quoted, 34, 51, 460
Archons, 65, 122, 124, 141-42
Archytas, 356
Areia, 413
Areians, 95
Areopagus, 68, 124, 133, 135-36, 151
Ares, 17, 125, 437
Argilus, 187
Arginusae, battle of, 227, 231, 289
Argonauts, 27, 307
Argolid, 13-15
Argos, 34, 64, 85, 92, 113, 132, 136,
    140, 150, 200-1, 209, 215, 312,
    327, 346
Argos (hound), 17
Ariadne, 14
Ariaspians, 414
Aristagoras, 83
Aristides, 108-10, 114, 121, 126-29, 131,
    133, 137, 156-57, 189, 235, 244,
    465
Aristobulus, 398, 405
Aristocracy, 33-35, 41-42, 45-46, 70, 74,
    77, 99-100, 123-25, 130, 134-36,
    142-43, 319-21, 353-54, 383
  in Athens, 65-66, 79
  in Sparta, 55-58, 61-62
  Socratic, 269, 279, 369-70
Aristodemus, 259
Ariston, 353
Aristophanes, 195-99, 250-53, 259, 323,
    373

Aristophanes (continued)
 on Alcibiades, 205, 211
 Acharnians, 196-98
 Banqueters, 467
 Birds, 282, 345
 Clouds, 250-53, 352-53
 Ecclesiazusae, 282
 Frogs, 205, 467
 Lysistrata, 282
 Peace, 196-98
 Wealth, 313
Aristotle, 374-92, 394, 396, 432, 437,
 439-40, 475
 four causes, 379-80
 Metaphysics, 375, 377-78, 391, 475
 Nicomachean Ethics, 378-80, 382-88
 Organon, 377, 387-88
 Physics, 379-80
 Poetics, 388, 390-91
 Politics, 320, 378-80, 382-88, 411
 Rhetoric, 388
Armenia, 305
Arms and armaments, see Warfare
Arrian, as a historian, 477
 quoted, 401-3, 420-21, 424-26, 430,
 433-36
Arses, 401
Artabanus, 94
Artabazus, 115-16
Artaxerxes I, 132, 139
Artaxerxes II, 299, 301, 314-15
Artemis, 133, 309
Artemisium, 101-2, 105-6, 109
 battle of, 106
Asclepius, 296, 375
Ascra, 45
Asia Minor, 12, 13, 15, 16, 32, 39, 48-
 54, 81-84, 86
Aspasia, 156-57, 164
Assembly, in Athens, 65, 68-69, 78
 in Sparta, 57-58
Assinarus River, 220
Assus, 375
Assyrians, 29, 33, 49, 80, 95, 410
Astacus, 143
Astyages, 80
Atarneus, 375
Athena, 17, 19-21, 23-25, 59, 74, 99,
 107, 128, 131-32, 141, 146-47, 150-
 51, 157, 164, 168, 286, 397, 427
 Polias, 127
Athenaeus, quoted, 150
Athenian Empire, 139, 145, 166-67, 172-
 73, 222, 230, 285, 316, 339, 465-66

Athos, Mount, 86-87, 91-93, 102, 119,
 159
Atlantic, 29
Atlantis, 370, 382
Attalus, 351, 406
Attica, 11, 13, 15-16, 49, 64-65, 67, 77,
 79, 82, 87-88, 99, 106-7, 109-10, 113,
 139-40, 163, 174, 179-80, 214, 225
Autolycus, 21
Axios River, 93

Baal-Marduk, 417
Babylon, 82, 408-10, 431, 433, 438, 440
Babylonia, 49, 80-82, 411-12
Bactra, 416-17, 420
Bactria, 413, 415
Bactrians, 95, 111
Baghdad, 301
Bagoas, 401
Balkans, 11
Barbarians, 37, 123, 125, 343-45, 355,
 384, 464
Barsine, 431, 477
Basileia, 282
Batis, 404
Beas River, 424-25
Beer, 306
Beirut, 29
Bendis, 260, 266
Benefactors (tribe), 414-15
Bessus, 413-16
Bias of Priene, 82
Bireme, 31
Black Sea, 27, 35, 38, 40, 50, 74, 76,
 83-86, 93, 100, 119, 128, 133, 139,
 187, 225, 307, 309-10, 336
Boeotia, 15, 45, 92, 98, 107, 113, 118,
 137-39, 178, 190, 214-15, 329-30,
 347, 395
Boeotians, 159, 185
Boeotian League, 79, 88, 116, 465-66
Bokhara, 416
Boreas, 87, 90, 102
Bosphorus, 38, 83, 133, 139, 225, 310
Brahmans, 424, 427-28
Brasidas, 181, 185-88, 190, 198, 283
 speech at Acanthus, 186
Brea, Thrace, 143
Briseis, 6-7
Bronze, 12, 29, 33
Bruttians, 438
Bucephalus, 424
Buddha, 423
Bury, J. B., historian, 453

Byblus, 29, 402
Byzantium, 38, 83-84, 128, 131, 145, 310-11, 321, 346

Cadiz, 29
Calabria, 37
Calanus, 430-31
Callias, 130, 139-40, 245, 247, 249
  Peace of, 139
Callicles, 240-41
Callicrates, 146
Callicratidas, 227
Callimachus, 89, 90
Callines, 436
Callipus, 361
Callisthenes of Olynthus, 396, 419-21, 432
Calpe's Haven, 310, 345
Calypso, 17, 20, 38
Cambyses, 82-83, 404, 407-10
Caria, 84, 133, 398
Carians, 96, 106, 145
Carmania, 430
Carthage, 29, 85, 117, 140, 210, 356, 361
Carthaginians, 49
Caryatids, 51, 324
Carystus, 87, 133
Caspian Sea, 11, 438
Caspians, 95
Cassandra, 236, 339
Castor and Pollux, 418, 420
Catana, 211, 219-20
Caucasus, 50, 82, 416
Celts, 356-57
Ceos, 75
Cephalus, 260
Cephissus, 13
Ceramic Gulf, 225
Cerasus, 309
Cersobleptes, 336, 346
Chaerephon, 235-37, 252
Chaeronea, battle of, 346-48, 394
Chalcedon, 38
Chalcidian League, 328
Chalcidice, 86, 114, 159, 185, 187, 206, 326, 332, 345
Chalcis (Euboea), 14, 42, 65, 79, 84, 87, 326, 349, 375
Chalybeans, 306
Chalybes, 50
Charicles, 240
Charmides, 240, 245, 288, 353
Chenab River, 424

Chersonese, Thracian, 89, 120, 143, 345
Chilon, 62
Chios, 129, 172, 221, 225
Chirisophus, 308
Chiron, 381
Choerilus, poet, 327
Cilicia, 300, 400
Cilician Gates, 399
Cilicians, 84, 96, 106
Cimon, 130-31, 133-39, 141-42, 154, 157, 318, 320
Circe, 20-22, 38
Cissians, 95, 103
Cithaeron, Mount, 406
Citizenship (Athens), 77-79, 142-43, 146, 157, 167
City-state, see Polis
Clazomenae, 155, 314
Clearchus, 300-302, 305
Cleomenes, 83-84, 103
Cleon, 171-74, 179, 181-83, 187-89, 198, 208, 285, 322
  speech on Mytilene, 172-73
Cleopatra, daughter of Philip, 351
Cleopatra, wife of Philip, 351, 394, 406
Cleruchs, 79-80, 131, 139, 143, 146, 156, 174, 204, 316
Clinias, 157, 199
Clisthenes (Athens), 77-78, 121, 130, 142, 199, 465
  constitution of, 77-78, 85, 145
Clisthenes (Sicyon), 76
Clitus the Black, 397, 414, 418-19, 422
Clitus the White, 422
Clytemnestra, 150
Coenus, 426
Coinage, 40-41, 144-45, 331-32, 335, 369, 384, 402, 417, 459
Coiratadas, 311
Colchians, 307
Colchis, 50
Colonization, 32, 35-40, 50, 66, 79, 81
Colonus, 152, 223
Colophon, 53
Comedy, 195-98, 323-24, 372-73
Companions, Macedonian, 408, 413-14, 433, 436, 441-42
Confucius, 423
Conon, 227
Constantinople, 38
Copaïs, Lake, 15
Cophen River, 422
Copper, 29

Corcyra, 132, 159, 209, 225, 285, 373
revolution at, 175-80, 183-84
Corfu, 175
Corinth, 13, 27-28, 53, 55, 59, 65, 67, 76, 85, 108, 114, 116, 118, 137-39, 158-59, 168, 175, 190, 205, 211, 215-16, 229, 284, 312, 318, 326, 347, 361
Gulf of, 107
Isthmus of, 59, 93, 97-98, 101-2, 107-8, 113, 127, 139, 179
League of, 349-50, 395, 398, 408, 413, 432
speech of Corinthians, 164
Cornford, F. M., on Thucydides, 466
Cornwall, 29
Coronea, battle of, 99, 139, 157, 317-18
Corsica, 82, 85, 117, 304, 345
Cosmopolis (Alexander), 412, 416-17, 419, 421-23, 431, 433, 437, 439-41
Cossaeans, 438
Cotton, 95
Council, 33
in Athens, 45
in Sparta, 56-57
Council of Four Hundred, 68, 223-25
Courts, at Athens, 69, 142, 144, 159, 165, 288
Craterus, 429, 438
Cratinus, 158, 195
Crenides, 331
Creon, 154
Cretans, 308, 395
Crete, 12-15, 360, 364-65, 460
Critias, 230, 283-86, 288, 352-56
Crito, 292-96
Critobulus, 292
Crocodiles, 427
Croesus, 50, 54, 80-82, 98, 148, 153, 236, 241, 300, 334
Cronus, 365
Croton, 107
Cumae, 38-39
Cunaxa, battle of, 301, 307, 309, 343
Cybele, 69, 84, 147
Cyclades, 13
Cyclopes, 18, 21-23, 28, 133
Cyllene, 211
Cylon, 66
Cyme, 45
Cynegirus, 90
Cynossema, battle of, 231, 284-85
Cynosura, 88

Cyprus, 15, 39, 59, 71, 84, 96, 128, 139, 314, 402-3
Cyrenaica, 13
Cyrene, 59, 138, 321
Cyropolis, 415-16
Cyrus the Great, 80-83, 91, 95, 148, 236, 409, 414, 420
tomb of, 430
Cyrus, the younger, 226-27, 299-301, 304, 310-11
Cythera, 184, 201
Cyzicus, 321
battle of, 225, 231, 283

Daimōn, 25, 236, 259, 266, 374
Damascus, 400
Damocles, sword of, 360
Damon, 154-55, 157
Danube River, 11, 83, 93, 395
Dardanelles, 38
Darius I, 82-87, 91-92, 97, 119, 409-10, 412-13
Darius III, 394-95, 397, 399-403, 407-15
Dark Age of Greece, 3, 5, 16, 32, 38, 48, 127, 458
Decarchies, 283
Decelea, 212-16, 221-22, 224-25, 285
Delium, battle of, 185, 200, 234, 258
Delos, 87, 111, 117, 129-30, 136, 138, 293
League of, 129-31, 133-38, 140-41, 144-45, 156
Delphi, 14, 80, 116, 128, 150, 333, 335, 463
games at, 35
Delphians, 106-7
Delphic Oracle, 56, 58, 80-81, 98-101, 104, 112, 153-54, 175, 180-81, 189, 236, 252, 270, 300, 333-35, 350-51, 353-54, 399, 404, 420, 463
quoted, 56, 81, 91, 98-99
Demades, 348, 432
Demaratus, 83-84, 92, 96-97, 103, 158, 183
Demes, in Athens, 77-78
Demeter, 76; see Earth goddess
Demiurge, 362
Democracy, 85, 86, 161, 167, 383, 471
at Athens, 77-79, 230-32
Alcibiades on, 211-12
Socrates on, 279-80
Democrats, 100, 123-24, 132, 134-35, 138, 141, 145, 169, 171-72, 175-78,

183-84, 191, 208, 223-24, 228, 398, 432, 465
Democritus of Abdera, 354, 356
Demosthenes, general, 178-83, 187, 214-20
Demosthenes, orator, 321-22, 337-42, 345-48, 364, 373-74, 389, 394-96, 432-33, 439
  De Corona, 338
  Philippics, 337-38
Deus ex machina, 194, 467
Dialectic, Socratic, 237-44, 246-50, 259-60, 267, 359, 376-77, 468-69
Didyma, oracle at, 419
Diké, 58, 65; *see also* Justice
Diodotus, 173-74, 179
Diolkos, 59, 93
Dion, games at, 328
Dion, of Syracuse, 356, 358-61
Dionysiac festivals, 75-76, 196
Dionysius I, 343, 356-58
Dionysius II, 357-60, 366
Dionysus, 76, 149-50, 191, 205, 420, 423, 425
  Theater of, 151, 165, 195
Diotima, 254
Dnieper River, 93
Dniester River, 93
Dodona, oracle at, 80, 404
Don River, 93
Dorians, 16, 27, 32, 44, 48-49, 55, 61, 64-65, 96, 205, 207, 253, 327, 391
Doris, 16, 49
Doriscus, 94-95, 131, 183
Dracon, 66-67, 74
Dracontios, 307-8
Draft animals, 31-32
  harness, 31-32
  horseshoes, 32
Drama, 76, 145, 149-50, 465; *see also* Comedy *and* Tragedy
  Aristotle on, 390-91
Drangiana, 415
Durazzo, 175
Dustyfoot, 34, 42-43, 68, 76, 79; *see also* Thetes
Dwellers-round-about, 57, 60-61, 67, 134, 312

Earth goddess, 69, 84, 147; *see also* Demeter
Ecbatana, 368, 410, 414, 416, 438
Echecrates, 293, 296

Echetlus, 91
Education, Aristotle on, 387
  in Athens, 122-23, 161-62
  Isocratean, 340-42
  Platonic, 269-71, 277-78, 358-59, 371
  Spartan, 62-63
Egypt, 13, 15, 39, 50, 56, 71, 82-83, 91, 148, 400-407, 412, 422-23, 438
  Athens in, 137-38, 140
Egyptians, 84, 92-96, 128, 409-10
Eion, 131, 187
Elatea, 347
Elburz Mountains, 413
Elea, 53
Eleatic school, 155
Electrum, 40
Elenchos, 237-39, 468
Eleusis, 31, 76, 151, 284, 399
  mysteries, 208, 210, 226, 399
Eleutheria, festival of, 116
Elis, 31, 132, 190, 200, 318, 346
Empedocles, 144, 362
Epaminondas, 316, 326, 329-30, 357
Ephesus, 54, 132, 226, 321, 405
Ephialtes, 134-36, 141, 151
Ephors, 57, 61, 62
Epialtes, 103-4, 463
Epidamnus, 175
Epidaurus, 34
Epipolae, 211
Epirus, 16, 38, 49, 346
Er, myth of, 281-82
Erechtheum, 164, 324
Erechtheus, 147
Eretria, 42, 84-87, 92, 111, 114, 119, 143
Eretrians, 175, 368, 474
Ergon, 46, 418
Erinyes, 465; *see also* Eumenides
Eris, 46, 57, 63, 67-69, 77-78, 91, 126, 168-69, 239-40, 250, 332
Eristic, 239-40, 250, 350, 382, 469
Eros, 253-54
Eryximachus, 253
E-sagila, 410
Ethiopians, 95
Etruria, 140, 143, 356
Etruscans, 39, 49, 85, 438
Euboea, 40, 79, 84, 87, 101-2, 105-6, 131, 133, 139, 160, 214, 224-25, 285
Eubulus, 337
Eucles, 187, 190
Euclides, 353

Eucrates, 171
Eulaeus River, 433
Eumaeus, 25
Eumenides, 151, 465; see also Erinyes
Eunomia, 58-59, 67-68, 70, 78, 168
Eupatrids, 65, 68, 199; see also Aristocracy
Euphrates River, 403, 407, 441
Eupolis, 195
Euripides, 5, 192-99, 282-83, 323, 327-28, 394
  on Alcibiades, 205
  Archelaus, 328
  on Athens, 231
  Bacchae, 282, 328
  Heracles, 194-95
  Medea, 307
  translations, 455
  Trojan Women, 193-94
Euripus, 105
Euryclea, 17
Eurymedon, admiral, 176, 185, 214, 216-17
Eurymedon, battle of, 133
Eurypon, 55
Euxine, see Black Sea

Fertile Crescent, 82
Five-hundred-Bushelers, 68
Five Thousand, the, at Athens, 223-25
Four Hundred, the, at Athens, 223-25
France, colonies in, 37-39
Furies, 150-51; see also Erinyes

Gandhi, 469
Ganges River, 425
Gaugamela, battle of, 407-8, 414
Gaul, 85
Gaza, 404
Gedrosia, 415
Gedrosian desert, 428-29
Gela, 185
Gelo, 117
Gerousia, 56-57
Getae, 395
Gibraltar, Strait of, 36
Glaucon, 260, 262, 267-69, 273-82, 298, 390
Glotz, Gustave, historian, 453
Gods, 7-8, 17, 24-25, 47, 53-54, 69, 75-76, 98, 191, 194-95, 203-4, 303, 334-35, 364-65, 382-83, 405-6, 439-41, 460

Gods (continued)
  Aristotle on, 378, 380-81, 391
  in Herodotus, 148
  Olympic, 28, 47
  Plato on, 362-63, 371
  and the polis, 297
  Xenophanes on, 53-54
Golden Fleece, 27
Gordian Knot, 398-99, 440
Gorgias, 174, 283, 339-40
Gournia, 15
Granicus, battle of, 397-98, 414, 418
Great Hellas, 38; see also Western Greece
Great Mother, 69
Greece, fauna, 11, 457
  flora, 11
  geography, 11-12, 28
  roads, 31
Greeks, Aristotle on, 384, 389; see also Hellenes
Grote, George, historian, 454
  on sophists, 468
Gylippus, 213-20
Gymnias, 306
Gymnosophists, 56, 430

Hades, House of, 4, 9, 10, 19-20, 26, 59, 292
Hadria, 356
Halicarnassus, 398
Hamilcar, 117, 464
Hammond, N. G. L., historian, 453
Harmodius and Aristogeiton, 123, 409
Harpalus, 94, 410
Hectemor, 67
Hector, 10, 16, 193, 397
Hecuba, 193
Helen of Troy, 5, 6, 55, 222, 418
Helicon, Mount, 45-47, 122, 369
Heliopolis, 404
Hellenes, 5, 15, 39; see also Greeks
Hellespont, 5, 11, 38, 76, 82, 84-86, 92-94, 98, 111-12, 115-20, 128, 187, 221-22, 225-27, 230, 311, 350, 395-96
  bridges at, 92-94, 111, 120, 122, 132
Helmund River, 414-15
Helots, 57, 60-62, 64, 102, 114, 128, 134-35, 143, 180, 182-86, 215, 312
Hephaesteum, 164-65
Hephaestus, 164
Hephestion, 397, 402, 414, 421, 423-24, 431, 438, 442

Hera, 115, 176, 362
Heracles, 20, 88, 189, 307, 327, 344, 393, 402-3, 406, 417-20, 423, 425, 427
Heraclitus, 54, 477
quoted, 439
Hermeias, 375, 391
Hermes, 21, 116, 197-99
Hermione, 114
Hermocrates, 185, 211, 215, 218, 370, 421
Hermolaus, 421-22
Herms, mutilation of, 208-210, 334, 352
Herodotus, 5, 96-97, 114, 144, 148-49, 165, 190-92, 327, 404, 407, 410, 423
quoted, 96-99, 112, 118, 148, 158, 183
translations, 455
Heroes, 7-9, 16-17, 19, 21-22, 24, 44
Hesiod, 43-47, 53, 68-71, 122, 126, 160, 170, 204, 239, 362
date, 459
quoted, 44-47, 368-69
Theogony, 43, 46, 459
translations, 455
Works and Days, 43-47
Hiero, 357
Himera, 117, 214
Hindu Kush, 415
Hipparchus, 52, 76; see also Pisistratids
Hippeis, 68; see also Knights
Hippias, sophist, 245, 248
Hippias (tyrant), 76-77, 79, 84-85, 87-88, 90, 123; see also Pisistratids
Hippocrates, son of Apollodorus, 245
Hippodamus, 127, 144
Historia, 148
History, Aristotle on, 391
cyclic theory, 471
and legends, 27-28
myths as, 4-5
Thucydides on, 190
Hittites, 32
Homer, 4, 5, 30, 32, 47, 56, 70, 122, 148, 150, 254, 348, 394, 437, 458-59
date, 459
Iliad, 2, 5-10, 16, 18, 24, 27, 30, 35, 43, 148, 150, 437, 456
Odyssey, 4, 5, 16-27, 35, 456
quoted, 2, 4, 5, 8, 18, 19-26, 30, 32, 47, 125, 249, 348, 407
translations, 456

Homeric Cycle, 27, 150
Homeric Hymn to Apollo, 49, 460
Hoplite, 42; see also Warfare
Hot Gates, see Thermopylae
Hybris, 93-95, 190, 230, 240, 315, 318, 381-82, 416-19, 421, 441
Hydaspes River, 424
Hyperbolus, 171, 201
Hyrcanians, 95

Ibycus, poet, 52
Ichor, 8, 407
Ictinus, 146
Ida, Mount, 364
Illyria, 38, 175
Illyrians, 327-30, 333, 356, 395
Imbros, 143, 315
Immortals (Persians), 94, 103-5, 111
India, 56, 416, 422-23, 427-28, 430
Indian Ocean, 428
Indians, 95-96, 111, 408
Indus River, 407, 422-24, 427-28
Infanticide, 320
Iolkos, 14
Ionia, 30, 32, 49, 56, 91, 129, 221-22, 226, 401
Ionian Revolt, 83-84, 86, 107-8, 112, 117, 119
Ionians, 30, 32, 49-52, 82-84, 94, 96, 106, 109-11, 119, 122
philosophers, 53-54
poets, 51-53
Iphicrates, 313-14, 328, 330, 332
Iran, 409
Irony, Socratic, 241-42, 246, 248, 250, 288-90
Isaeus, 337
Isegoria, 124
Isocrates, 340-45, 348-49, 357-58, 364, 382, 385, 395, 400, 441
Address to Philip, 343-44
Antidosis, 340-42
Letter to Philip, 348-49
Panegyric, 342-44
on rhetoric, 340-41
Isonomia, 124
Issus, battle of, 400, 402
Isthmian Games, 35, 100
Italiots, 85
Italy, 36-38, 53, 175, 212
Ithaca, 4, 16-20, 22-24
Ithome, Mount, 134-36, 316

Jason, 27, 317

Jason of Pherae, 316
Jaxartes River, 82, 415-16, 423
Jhelum River, 424, 426-27
Jocasta, 153, 239
Justice, 42, 45, 46, 459; see also Diké
  Aristotle on, 380
  Socrates on, 262-67, 269, 281

Kabul River, 422-23
Keftiu, 15
Khyber Pass, 422
Kings, 33
  in Athens, 65
  in Homer, 8, 18
  in the polis, 43
  in Sparta, 55-57
Knights, 33; see also Hippeis
Knossos, 13-15, 364, 457
Krissa, 14
Krypteia, 61
Kurds, 305

Lacedaemon, see Sparta, Spartans
Laconia, 55, 65, 170, 184, 316, 329,
  349; see also Sparta
Laconisms, 63, 70, 105, 349
Lade, battle of, 84
Laertes, 21
Lamachus, 206, 211, 213
Lampsacus, 157, 227
Lanice, 419
Larissa, 92, 98
Latium, 356
Laurium, 97, 110, 189, 212, 214, 319
Law, 27, 33-34, 41-42, 46-47, 66-67, 69,
  74, 82, 123-25, 142, 151-52, 158-59,
  161-62, 165-68, 365, 367, 370-72
  aristocrats and, 100
  Aristotle on, 383
  of Athens, 78, 144
  of Crete, 56
  Dracon's, 66-67, 74
  Plato on, 369-72
  Spartan, 58-59, 62, 97
Lechaeum, 314
Lecythus, 187
Lemnos, 80, 143, 315
Leon of Salamis, 283-84, 290, 353
Leon of Thurii, 308
Leonidas, 102-5, 116, 128, 315
Leontini, 174-75, 205-6
Lepreum, 114
Lesbos, 51-53, 129, 171-74
Leucas, 114

Leuctra, battle of, 316, 318, 320, 329,
  357
Leutychides, 128
Libya, 36, 39, 117, 148
Libyans, 95, 438
Liguria, 117
Locri, 362
Locrians, 103, 137
Locris, 101
  Opuntian, 137, 139
  Ozolian, 137
Lucanians, 438
Lyceum, 259, 376
Lycia, 398
Lycians, 96, 133
Lycios, 306
Lycurgus, 55-64, 67, 70, 80, 254, 269,
  312, 365, 369, 371, 460
Lydia, 40, 43, 50-54, 59, 80, 82, 96
Lysander, 226-230, 283, 286, 312, 320
Lysias, 357
Lysicles, 171
Lysimachus, 235

Macedonia, 49, 86, 93, 98, 111, 185,
  192, 326-27, 331-32, 349-50, 385,
  408
  population of, 331
Macedonians, 347-48, 418, 420-22, 425-
  26, 436-37
Macronians, 307
Magnesia (Thessaly), 102, 282
Magnesia (on Meander River), 132
Malaic Gulf, 101
Malea, Cape, 59
Malis, 101, 103
Mallia, 13
Mallians, 427-28
Mantinea, 117, 132, 200-201, 207, 209
  battle of, 316, 318
Maracanda, 415-16, 418
Marathon, 74, 88-91, 108, 119, 121,
  149, 304, 370
Marathus, 400
Mardonius, 85-87, 111-19
Marduk, 409
Marmora, Sea of, 36; see also Propontis
Marseilles, 29-30, 39, 321
Marsyas, 255-56
Marsvas, Sicilian, 360
Massilia, 29-30, 39, 321
Mazaces, 404
Mazaeus, 408, 411-12
Meander River, 49, 132

Medea, 27, 307
Medes, 95-96, 103, 111, 128
Media, 80-81, 92, 408, 410-12, 430
  Paraetacene, 412
Medius, 441
Medusa, 27
Megacles, 73, 121, 130, 134
Megalopolis, 346, 408
Megara, 66-67, 79, 108, 113-14, 137,
  139-40, 159, 168, 181, 185, 190,
  225, 284, 353
Megistias, 104
Meletus, 288, 291
Melians, 263, 371; see also Melos
Melkart, 402-3, 406
Melos, 16, 201, 204-5, 210, 215, 221,
  228
  dialogue of, 201-4
Memnon, 397-98
Memphis, 404, 407
Menelaus, 5, 55
Meno, 241-42; see also Menon
Menon, 301; see also Meno
Mercenaries, 313-15, 322-23, 328, 332-
  33, 337, 346, 357
Mesopotamia, 148
Messene, 176, 316
Messenia, 55, 64-65, 134, 143, 178-80,
  183, 316, 346
  revolt of, 134-35
Messenian Wars, 55, 59
Messina, 38, 175, 356
Methone, 333
Methymna, 171, 174
Metics, at Athens, 77-78, 125, 142-43,
  280, 284, 286
Metrodorus of Chios, 354
Micon, 146
Midas, 398
Milesians, 118-19
Miletus, 5, 13, 40, 49-50, 53, 59, 65,
  82-85, 144-45, 398
Military, see Warfare
Miltiades, 89-90, 120-21, 125, 130, 142
Mimnermus, 122
Mindarus, 225
Minoan culture, 13-14, 16, 27, 30, 38,
  44
Minoan Empire, 32
Minos, 14, 27, 48, 56, 364
Minotaur, 14, 27
Mitylene, see Mytilene
Mnesicles, 146
Molossians, 132

Moly, 21
Money, Aristotle on, 388-89
  in Athens, 67
  effect on the polis, 40-42, 57-58, 124,
    130, 133, 142, 312-15, 319-20, 322-
    23
  effect on warfare, 313-15
  Persian use of, 397, 401
  Philip and, 331-32
  in Sparta, 57
Money economy and agriculture, 41, 321
Monopoly, Aristotle on, 388-89
Mulla Pass, 429
Munychia, battle of, 285-86, 353
Murex dye, 28-29
Muses, 4, 46-47, 122-23, 328, 368-69,
  467
Mycale, battle of, 117-19, 122, 128
Mycalessus, massacre at, 215
Mycenae, 13-15, 27-28, 114, 150
Mycenaean culture, 14, 16, 38, 44, 49
Myrsilus, 51
Myths, as history, 4-5, 59
  Platonic, 270, 281, 366, 370
Mytilene, 171-74, 179, 204-5, 227, 231,
  263, 275
  battle of, 231
  revolt of, 172-74

Naples, 38-39
Naupactus, 137, 140, 178, 180
Navigation, 30-31
Naxos, Island of, 87, 129, 133, 136, 143
Naxos (Sicily), 211
Neapolis, 39; see also Naples
Nearchus, 427-29, 441
Nebuchadnezzar, 29
Nemea, games at, 35, 100
Neoptolemus, 351
Nestor, 24-25
Nestus River, 333
Nicanor, 432
Nicias, 178, 182, 184, 187-89, 196, 199-
  201, 205-8, 211, 213-18, 220, 285,
  334-35
  Peace of, 188-91, 195, 199-200, 263
  speech of, 206
Nicostratus, 176
Nile, 82, 422, 427
Nineveh, 29, 305, 407
Nisaea, 59, 137, 185, 225
Notion, battle of, 231
Nysa, 423, 425

Ochus, 401
Odeon, 234
Odessa, 36
Odeum, 165
Odrysians, 395
Odysseus, 4, 5, 16-26, 34, 38, 70-71, 97, 132, 143, 439-40, 456
Oedipus, 27, 190, 406
Olbia, 35, 321
Oligarchs, 80, 85, 92, 116, 132, 138-39, 144-45, 169, 171, 175-78, 180, 183-84, 191, 201, 210, 223-24, 228, 283, 285, 287, 312, 315, 320, 366, 371, 398, 432, 465
Oligarchy, 279, 370, 383
Olive, 13, 37, 41
Olpae, 178, 180
Olympia, 31, 35, 146, 317-18
Olympias, 333, 346, 350-51, 393-94, 406, 419, 427, 438
Olympic Games, 35, 39, 59-60, 100, 102, 116, 126, 171, 205-7, 327-28, 332-33, 357, 432
Olympus, Mount, 7-9, 20, 69, 98, 122, 328
Omens, 217, 302, 305
Onomacritus, 92
Onomarchus, 333, 335-36, 345
Opis, 437-38, 440
Opora, 198
Oracles, 80-82, 92, 204, 259, 334-35, 403-4, 419, 422; see also Delphic Oracle
    in Thucydides, 191
Orchomenos, 14, 114
Orestes, 19, 150-51
Oreus, 143, 224
Oropus, 214
Ossa, Mount, 98
Ostracism, 78, 108, 121, 132-34, 136-37, 141, 201, 326, 461
Overseers, 57, 61, 62
Oxus River, 415-16
Oxyartes, 422

Paches, 171, 172, 174
Pactyes, 95
Paeonians, 329, 333, 395
Pagae, 59
Pagasae, Gulf of, 14, 102, 105, 335
Pages' conspiracy, 421-22
Pakistan, 422
Palaikastro, 15
Pale, 114

Palermo, 29, 117
Palestine, 404
Pamir Mountains, 82
Pammenes, 329
Pamphylia, 133, 398
Pamphylians, 96
Pan, at Marathon, 88, 90-91
Panathenaic Festivals, 75, 147-48
Pangaeus, Mount, 187, 330-33, 396
Panhellenic Congress, 144
Panhellenic League, 97, 116, 128-29, 136
Panionian League, 5, 50, 82
Panormus, 29, 117
Paralus, 228, 245
Paris, see Alexander (Paris)
Parmenion, 333, 397-400, 403, 407-8, 410, 413-14
Parnassus, Mount, 107
Paros, 121, 130
Parsa, 409
Parthenon, 146, 157-58, 164, 324, 335
Parthia, 413
Parthians, 95, 408
Pasargadae, 409
Patroclus, 9-10, 16, 105, 397, 428
Pausanias (in Plato's Symposium), 253
Pausanias, Spartan king, 114-16, 128-29, 131-32, 188
Pausanias, the younger, 228, 286
Pelasgians, 11-12, 15-16, 49
Pella, 327-28, 346, 351, 375
Pelopidas, 315, 326, 328-29
Peloponnese, 16, 163, 170, 178-80, 205, 207
Peloponnesian Alliance, 129, 201
Peloponnesian League, 140-41, 144, 160, 168
Peloponnesian War, 159-65, 168-89, 193, 195, 199-232, 313
Peloponnesians, 105, 108, 119-20, 126, 164
Pelusium, 404
Penelope, 17-19, 21, 25-26
Penteconter, 31
Pentelicus, Mount, 90
Perdiccas II, 185, 187-88, 327
Perdiccas III, 327-30
Perdiccas, Macedonian officer, 423-24
Pergamos, 311-12
Periander, 76
Pericles, 121-25, 127, 129, 130-38, 142-46, 149, 151-70, 172, 178-79, 185, 189-91, 199, 237-38, 246, 285, 313, 320, 353, 438

Pericles (*continued*)
 funeral oration, 160-63
 speech in 429 B.C., 163-64
Pericles, son of Pericles, 227
Perictione, 353
Perinthus, 401
Perioeci, *see* Dwellers-round-about
Peripatetics, 376
Persepolis, 409-10, 413
Perses, 45-46
Perseus, 27, 393
Persia, 80, 429
Persian Empire, 82-87, 91, 94-96, 112, 115, 139, 343-44, 396-99, 407, 409-11
Persian Wars, 80-120, 146
Persians, 88-90, 94-96, 115-20, 122, 125-26, 131-33, 137-39, 145, 148, 221-25, 300-305, 311-16, 331, 342, 350, 357, 411, 436-37
Persis, 411
Peucestas, 427, 431
Phaeacians, 17-19, 21
Phaedo, 293
Phaedrus, 253
Phaenarete, 235, 242
Phaestos, 13
Phalaecus, 345-46
Phalanx, 42, 316, 329, 408
Phalerum, 90, 99, 110, 138, 140
Pharnabazus, 221-22, 225, 230
Phaselis, 139
Phasis, 35
Phēmē, 118, 464
Pherae, 335-36
Phidias, 146, 155, 157-58, 465
Phidippides, 88, 91
Phidippides (*Clouds*), 251-52, 352
Philip II of Macedon, 326, 328-33, 335-38, 343-51, 357, 375, 382-83, 389, 393-95, 406, 414, 417-19
 and the polis, 412
Philip (physician), 399
Philippi, 331
Philippides, 245
Philips, golden, 331-32
Philocles, 227-28
Philomelus, 333
Philotas, 413-14, 421
Phliasians, 114
Phlius, 114
Phocaeans, 29-30, 82, 304, 345
Phocians, 101, 103-5, 345
Phocion, 339-41

Phocis, 13, 85, 137, 139, 178, 333, 335-36, 346-47, 395
Phoenicia, 400, 402, 408, 423
Phoenicians, 28-30, 49, 83-84, 92-94, 96, 109-11, 117, 133, 139, 167, 428, 438
Phormio, 170-71
Phrada, 413, 414
Phrygia, 49-50, 230, 312
Phrynichus, 85
Pieria, 328
Pindar, 100, 126, 161, 327, 395, 404, 418
 quoted, 100, 361, 381
 translation, 456
Piracy, 15, 16, 31, 33, 36, 38, 131, 133, 321
Piraeus, 70, 99, 124, 126-28, 130, 137-38, 140, 156, 159-60, 163, 165, 224-25, 228, 234, 284-86
Pisidia, 299-300, 398
Pisistratids, 76, 88, 91, 92; *see also* Hippias *and* Hipparchus
Pisistratus, 71-77, 88-89, 123, 147, 149, 167, 370, 409
Plague, 163-64, 169, 174, 179, 208
Plataea, 79, 107, 115, 118-19, 128, 135, 347, 371
 battle of, 113-16, 125
Plataeans, 88-91, 169, 174
Plato, 288, 292, 329, 353-56, 358-78
 Apology, 235-38, 288-93, 317, 470
 Censorship, 367-68
 Charmides, 240
 Cratylus, 468
 Critias, 370
 Crito, 293
 dialogues, 361-62, 376
 Epistles, 354, 359-62, 369-70
 Gorgias, 240-41
 Laws, 364-72, 378-79, 383
 Meno, 241-42
 Phaedo, 293-96
 poems, 368
 Protagoras, 245-50
 Republic, 260-82, 354, 358, 361-62, 364-69, 378-79, 390, 470
 Symposium, 253-59, 318-19, 368, 469
 Theaetetus, 242-45
 Timaeus, 362-63, 365, 378, 474
 translations, 456
Plemmyrium, 215
Plistoanax, 188-89

Plutarch, quoted, 126, 135, 160, 315, 333, 348, 371, 374, 406-7, 437
Polemarch, 65, 89
Polemarchus, 260
Polis, 32-37, 42, 124-26, 142-43, 153, 155, 158-60, 165, 167-69, 191, 195, 199, 224-26, 260, 297, 372; see also Cosmopolis
  Alexander and, 412, 439-40
  Aristotle and, 382-84, 387, 389-90
  army as, 303-5, 308
  Clisthenes and, 77-79
  Democritus on, 354
  early Athenian, 64-68
  and education, 373, 387
  extension of, 350
  fourth-century, 319-23
  ideal, search for, 345
  kinship in, 35
  money economy and, see under Money
  Plato on, 364-66
  Socrates and, 235-36, 267-70, 278-83, 291
  Solon and, 68-71
  Spartan, 55-57, 61, 63
  Thucydides on, 175-78
Polycrates of Samos, 52-53
Polydamas, 262
Polydectes, 55
Polygnotus, 146, 327
Polyphemus, 18, 21-23
Pontus, see Black Sea
Porus, 423-24, 426
Posidon, 10-11, 16-18, 20, 23, 26, 91, 102, 128, 146, 194, 353, 428, 433
Posidonia, 369
Potidaea, 114, 159, 163, 169, 200, 233-34
  revolt of, 175
  Socrates at, 257-59
Pottery, 28, 30, 37, 75, 78, 321
Praxiteles, 325-26
Pre-Socratics, 455
Priam, 5, 10, 16
Priene, 82
Prodicus, 244, 245
Prometheus, 423
Propontis, 38, 84-88; see also Marmora, Sea of
Propylaea, 146
Protagoras, 144, 245-50, 319, 339, 354, 356, 365
Proxenus, 200, 299-300, 302-3
Psammon, 405

Pseira, 15
Psyttaleia, 110
Ptolemy, general, 410, 415, 419
Ptolemy, Macedonian usurper, 328
Punjab, 407, 422
Pydna, 132, 330-31
Pylos, 24-25, 180-82, 184-89, 197-98, 225
Pythagoras, 53
Pythagoreans, 53, 356, 362, 364
Pythia, priestess, 81, 334, 399
Pythian Games, 100

Ravi River, 424
Red Sea, 423
Reggio di Calabria, 38
Rhegium, 38, 52, 175
Rhetras, 56, 58, 184
Rhodes, 13, 15, 16, 59
Rhodians, 305
Rhone River, 30
Rome, 356
Roxana, 422, 442
Russia, 36-37

Sacans, 90, 95-96, 111, 408
Sacred Band, Theban, 329, 347, 394
Sagartians, 96
Sagunto, 35
Salaethus, 171
Salaminia, 211
Salamis, 79, 99, 101, 106-11, 113, 117, 119, 121-27, 130, 133-34, 149, 152, 223-24, 284
  battle of, 109-111
Salamis (Cyprus), 139
Samarkand, 82, 415
Samos, 40, 52-53, 59, 111, 117-18, 121-22, 129, 136, 138, 144-45, 222-26, 348
  revolt of, 144-45, 152, 159-61
  revolution in, 222-23
Samothrace, 394
Sangala, 424
Sappho, 52-53
  quoted, 53
Sarangas, 95
Sarapis, oracle of, 442
Sardinia, 82, 85, 117
Sardis, 59, 107, 225, 300-301, 311, 409
  sack of, 84, 86-87
Scilly Isles, 29
Scione, 187, 204
Scopas, 325-26

Sculpture, 50-51, 74-75, 146-47, 325-26
Scylax, 423
Scylla and Charybdis, 20, 22
Scyros, 131, 315
Scythas, 92
Scythians, 83, 95, 346, 413-14, 416, 420-21, 423
Segesta, 205-7, 210
Selinus, 205-6, 210
Senate, in Sparta, 56-57
Sennacherib, 29
Serfs, 16, 67; see also Helots
Sestos, 120, 122, 125, 128, 141, 227
Seuthes, 311, 313
Seven Sages, 70-71, 82, 389
Shahrud, 413
Ships, 19, 31, 216; see also under Warfare, armaments, tactics
Sicilian expedition, 208-21
Sicilians, 356-59
Sicily, 15, 29, 36, 38, 85-86, 117, 140, 175, 179, 185, 205-7, 211-21, 226
Sicyon, 34, 76, 114, 118, 215
Sidon, 29, 83, 96, 117, 402-3
Silenus, 255-56
Simmias, 293
Simonides, 75, 158, 248
  quoted, 105, 158, 235, 260, 372
Sinope, 309, 400
Sirens, 22, 38
Siris, 108
Slavery, Aristotle on, 385-87, 411
  for debt, 41, 67-68
  Socrates on, 280
Slaves, 116, 124-25, 142-43, 175, 215, 286, 315, 320, 367
  in trade, 30, 36
Socrates, 199-200, 227, 233-85, 287-300, 317-19, 335, 338, 340-42, 352-56, 364-72, 374, 380, 390, 440, 469-71
  Alcibiades on, 255-58
  death of, 294-97
  on the polis, 345
  on rhetoric, 339
  trial of, 287-93
  Xenophon on, 317, 319
Sogdian Rock, 422
Sogdians, 415-16
Solon, 68-74, 77-78, 80, 122, 125, 130, 136, 154-55, 254, 287, 353, 439
  constitution of, 68-69, 71, 74
  quoted, 69, 71, 137, 370, 388

Sophists, 154, 165, 234-35, 239, 241, 244-45, 249-52, 288-89, 352-53, 468
Sophocles, 5, 151-54, 190-92, 195, 323
  Oedipus the King, 153-54, 236, 239, 390, 406
  translations, 455
Spain, 35, 85, 117
Sparta and Spartans, 5, 31, 55-57, 64, 67, 70, 79, 82-85, 88, 91-92, 97-98, 102-5, 111-18, 125, 127-44, 156, 158-60, 163-65, 168, 170-71, 175-76, 179-89, 199-201, 211-13, 216, 221-25, 283-87, 300, 310-20, 329-30, 333, 336, 342, 349, 356-57, 370, 400, 408, 410, 422, 432
  character of, 96-97
  population, 320
Spartiates, 57, 60-61, 64, 70
Speusippus, 375-76
Sphacteria, 180-83, 187, 190, 199-201, 211, 313
Spitamenes, 416
Spithridates, 397
Stagira, 375
Stateira, 477
Stratocles, 347
Strepsiades, 251-52
Strymon River, 93, 186-87, 330, 333
Styreia, 114
Sunium, Cape, 89, 90
Susa, 82-83, 87, 111, 123, 139, 149, 230, 409, 431
Sybaris, 39, 144
Sybarite, 39, 369
Syracuse, 114-16, 174, 179, 185, 205-7, 210-13, 220-21, 321, 356-58, 360-61, 367, 369
Syria, 148, 301

Taenarum, Cape, 59
Tanagra, battle of, 137
Taochians, 306
Taranto, Gulf of, 39
Tarentum, 38, 214, 356
Tarshish, 29
Tarsus, 301, 399
Tashkent, 416, 423
Taxila, 424, 430
Taxiles, 423-24
Tegea, 114-16, 132
Teilhard de Chardin, Pierre, on living universe, 474
Telemachus, 20-21, 24-25
Temenids, 327

Tempe, Vale of, 98, 101
Teos, 52, 82
Thaïs, 410
Thales, 53, 82, 388-89
Thalia, 196, 467
Thapsacus, 301, 407
  Bay of, 213-16
Thasos, 86, 146
  revolt of, 134-35
Theaetetus, 242-45
Theagenes, 66
Thebes, 14, 27, 79, 88, 98, 102, 105,
  113, 115-16, 118, 127, 137-38, 153,
  169, 229, 284, 312, 315-19, 328-
  30, 333, 336, 342, 346-49, 357, 408
  destruction of, 395
Theches, Mount, 306
Themis, 58, 65
Themistocles, 97, 99, 101, 105-12, 117,
  125-27, 130-33, 136-39, 142, 157,
  159, 162, 178, 224, 230
Theognis, 122
Theophrastus, 392
Theoria, 198
Thera, 201
Theramenes, 225, 229, 283-85, 287, 383
Thermaic Gulf, 326, 333
Thermopylae, 101-3, 106, 119, 121, 135,
  183, 336, 345-46
Thersites, 34, 348
Theseus, 14, 27, 91, 131, 195, 461
Thespiae, 107
Thespians, 104
Thesprotia, 80
Thessalian League, 335-36, 346, 465
Thessaly and Thessalians, 5, 11, 14-15,
  33-34, 85, 92, 97-98, 101, 111, 128,
  136, 138, 185, 188, 192, 316, 329,
  331, 335-36, 410
Thetes, 68-69, 133, 141-42; *see also*
  Dustyfoot
Thetis, 8
Thibron, 311
Thirty Tyrants, the, 229-30, 283-84, 286,
  288, 290, 353-54
Thirty Years' Peace, 140-41, 159, 181,
  189
Thorikos, 14
Thrace and Thracians, 37, 52, 76, 82-83,
  85, 87, 96, 100, 111, 130-31, 134,
  169, 187-88, 190, 311, 327, 329, 333,
  336, 346, 394-95
Thrasybulus, 225, 284-88, 352
Thrasymachus, 260-66, 354, 356

Three Hundred, the, at Thermopylae, 63,
  101-3, 158
Thucydides, historian, 5, 14, 142, 163,
  187, 198-99, 316-18, 341, 373, 466
  on civil war, 176-78
  economic interpretation, 466
  on history, 190
  on revolution, 183-84
  on Sicilian expedition, 209-10, 218-
  19, 220-21
  and tragedy, 191-92
  translations, 456
  quoted, 2, 128, 163-64, 172-74, 183-84
Thucydides, statesman, 141
Thurii, 144, 211, 215, 304
Thyrea, 185
Tigris River, 84, 301, 407, 433
Timaeus, 362-64, 370
Timaia, Queen, 222
Timocracy, 279, 320, 369-70
Timoleon, 361
Timotheus, 327
Tin, 12, 29, 30
Tiresias, 26, 153
Tiribazus, 305
Tiryns, 13-15, 27-28, 114
Tissaphernes, 221-26, 231, 301-2, 305,
  311
Torone, 187
Tragedy, 5, 149-54, 190-99, 297, 323,
  390-91, 440
  Aristotle on, 390-91
  and dialectic, 239-40
  Plato and, 372-73
  Thucydides and, 466
Trapezus, 307-8
Triballians, 395
Tripolis, 400
Troezen, 107, 114, 118, 121
Trojan War, 5-11
Troy, 4-10, 16, 24, 134, 193, 311, 397
Trygaeus, 196-98
Tunis, 29, 36
Tylissos, 13
Tyndareus, 418
Tyrants, 43, 67, 71-72, 74, 76, 79-80, 123,
  172, 252, 319, 323, 358-60, 370,
  383, 459, 471
  Socrates on, 280
Tyre, 29, 83, 117, 402-5, 411
Tyrian purple, 28-29
Tyrtaeus, 63
  quoted, 55, 61, 180

Utica, 29

Vine, 13, 37

Wage-earners, see Thetes
War, 169, 171, 215-16
  Aristotle on, 411
  Euripides on, 192-94
  of factions, 176-78
  mercenary, 313-15
  Socrates on, 268-69
Warfare, armaments, tactics, 179, 313-
  14, 316, 322, 330, 336; see also
  Mercenaries
  of Alexander, 396, 476
  archery, 182-84, 305
  Athenian, 141, 170
  bronze weapons, 12, 16
  cavalry, 33, 304-5
  chariots, 33, 407-8
  Corinthian naval armaments, 216
  Iphicratean, 313-14
  iron weapons, 16, 458-59
  Macedonian, 329, 332
  of Mardonius, 463-64
  money and, 313-15
  naval, 217-18
  sarissa, 327, 332
  of Xerxes, 94-6, 462-63
Wason, M., on weapons, 458-59
Weapons, see Warfare
Well-fathered, see Aristocrats
Western Greece, 39, 85-86
Women, Aristotle on, 386
  in Athens, 77-78, 124-25, 157
  in democracy, 280
  in Plato's polis, 270
  in Sparta, 63
Words and coins, 40, 144, 154, 177,
  331-32, 335, 369, 388, 402, 417
Writing, 14-16, 28, 30, 40, 66, 67

Xanthippus, father of Pericles, 121-22,
  124-25, 128, 131, 134

Xanthippus, son of Pericles, 245
Xenocrates, 375-76
Xenophanes, 155
  quoted, 53-54
Xenophon, 290, 301-13, 316-20, 332,
  340, 342-45, 400, 417, 440
  on Aegospotami, 228
  Anabasis, 299-312, 317, 342, 456
  Apology, 317
  Cavalry Commander, 319, 335
  Cyropaedia, 318, 326
  dates of works, 472
  Hellenica, 284-87, 316-18, 319, 371
  Memorabilia, 238, 240, 298, 317, 319
  On Horsemanship, 317, 319
  Republic of the Lacedaemonians, 317
  Symposium, 318-19
  Ways and Means, 319
Xerxes, 91-112, 115-17, 122-23, 127, 129,
  132, 134, 148-49, 158-59, 183, 191-
  92, 223, 304, 409-10
  army of, 94-96, 462-63
  navy of, 96-97
  and oracles, 334

Zab River, 301
Zakro, 15
Zancle, 92
Zeno, Eleatic, 155
Zeugitai, 68, 142
Zeus, 4, 8-10, 17, 20, 23, 26, 45-47, 59,
  69, 80, 99-101, 122, 125, 146, 189,
  191, 194, 196-97, 199, 204, 221,
  251, 253, 328, 352, 356, 362, 364-
  65, 371, 381, 393, 404-6, 417-19,
  430, 433, 439-41
  and justice, 45-46
  Liberator, 116, 166, 192
  Olympian, 74
  Savior, 303, 305, 307
  of Thebes, 404
  in tragedy, 154
  Xenios, 359, 473
Zeuxis, 327

494